Comparative Economic Systems

David Kennett | H. Stephen Gardner

AF855035

CENGAGE Learning®

Australia • Brazil • Japan • Korea • Mexico • Singapore • Spain • United Kingdom • United States

CENGAGE Learning

Comparative Economic Systems

Senior Project Development Manager:
Linda deStefano

Market Development Manager:
Heather Kramer

Senior Production/
Manufacturing Manager:
Donna M. Brown

Production Editorial Manager:
Kim Fry

Sr. Rights Acquisition Account Manager:
Todd Osborne

Printed in the United States of America

A New View of Comparative Economics, 2nd Edition
David Kennett

Comparative Economic Systems, by Gardner, 2nd Edition
H. Stephen Gardner

ISBN-13: 978-1-285-91771-9

ISBN-10: 1-285-91771-5

Cengage Learning
5191 Natorp Boulevard
Mason, Ohio 45040
USA

Cengage Learning is a leading provider of customized learning solutions with office locations around the globe, including Singapore, the United Kingdom, Australia, Mexico, Brazil, and Japan. Locate your local office at: **international.cengage.com/region.**
Cengage Learning products are represented in Canada by Nelson Education, Ltd.
For your lifelong learning solutions, visit **www.cengage.com /custom.**
Visit our corporate website at **www.cengage.com.**

Brief Contents

A New View of Comparative Economics by Kennett

Comparative Economic Systems by H. Stephen Gardner

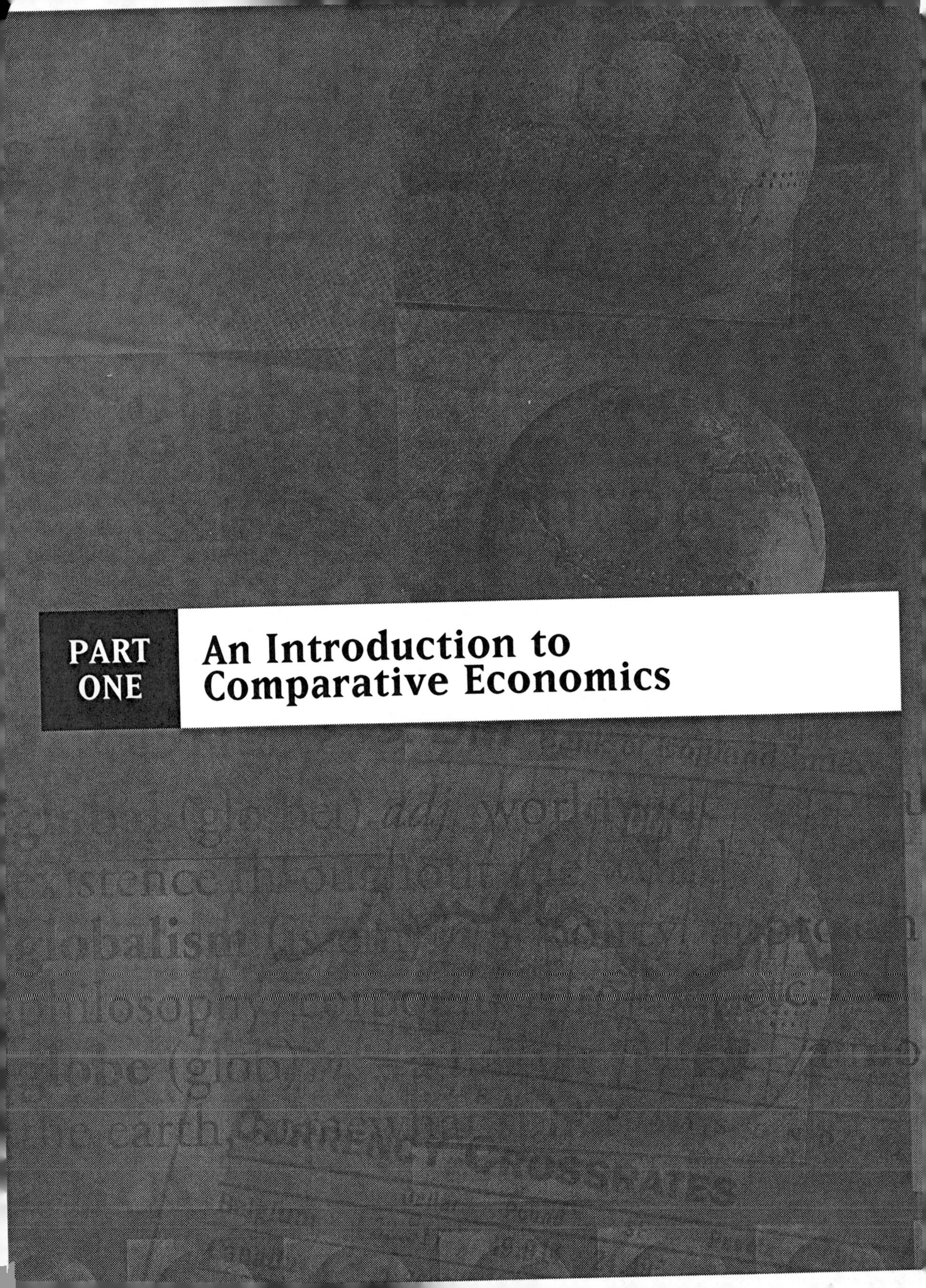

PART ONE
An Introduction to Comparative Economics

Chapter 1: Types of Economic Systems

Chapter 2: The Roots of Economic Systems

1

TYPES OF ECONOMIC SYSTEMS

INTRODUCTION

About 15 years ago the study of comparative economics underwent a series of dramatic changes. The principal reason was the collapse of the Soviet **centrally planned economic system** in the late 1980s. Soviet central planning served for many years as the clear polar alternative to the variety of capitalist systems that exist in the West. At the same time that reform swept the Soviet Union, the various offsprings of the Soviet system also experienced large-scale reform from within or change brought about by external forces. In China, economic restructuring and liberalization, although largely without the political counterpart so visible in the Russian experience, transformed its economy into one of the fastest changing and most rapidly growing on earth. Yugoslavia, the most frequently studied model of collectively owned, **worker-managed socialism**, broke apart and much of its economy still lies in ruins. Even Cuba, the bastion of socialism in the Western Hemisphere, deprived of support and subsidy from the Soviet Union, ruefully contemplates change.

In one sense market capitalism emerged the victor in this war of competing economic ideologies that was waged for much of the twentieth century. Whether this shift will be a permanent state of the world, an irreversible and linear evolution in economic and political arrangements, or merely a short-lived development is too soon to judge. A drift of popular sentiment back toward the former Communists played a feature role in recent elections in Eastern Europe and the former Soviet bloc, suggesting that it may be premature to assume that central planning is buried forever. Moreover, at the same time that economies based on centralized planning were faltering and forced toward reform, new variants of the capitalist model were emerging, especially in East Asia, as alternatives to the western model. Japan long ago joined the ranks of the "developed nations," and its success in terms of growth and world trade sparked great interest in its institutions, its economic culture, and its policies. These features of the Japanese economy are significantly different from the capitalist economies of Europe and North America.

Interest in **Pacific-Rim capitalism** found reinforcement in the emergence of the new **Asian Tigers**. Nations that only a decade before were universally regarded as "developing" made a leap into late industrial development. The economies of South Korea, Taiwan, Singapore, and Thailand seemed to exemplify a vision of rapid and sustained growth, at least until the Asian financial crisis of 1997. Western nations looked to learn lessons from their success. Scrutiny of their systems of economic organization increased accordingly, and investigation of the root causes of their present difficulties will doubtless provide further insights into the operation of alternative systems.

Even the core of Western Europe experienced substantial change. Sweden, for example, was for the entirety of the postwar period the nation whose economic system best exemplified the concept of **social democracy** and the **welfare state**. However, faced with slow growth and a deteriorating trade position, the Swedish system underwent considerable change in recent years, moving away from the extreme of egalitarian social democracy toward a less interventionist form of capitalism. At the same time, the evolution of the original six-member European Common Market into the 15-member **European Union** is a development of the greatest importance. The melding together of the various economies of Western Europe, which were until recently quite disparate institutions and traditions, is in itself a bold step. The replacement in 2002 of the national currencies of 12 of the member countries of the European Union with the "Euro," and the necessary constraints on national fiscal and monetary freedom, required substantial institutional change. Moreover, the proposed expansion of the European Union to include current economies in transition, which 15 years ago were fully centrally planned, is a major challenge. The strong interventionist spirit of the European Union, itself a product of the traditionally active role of government in the continental member states, will reinforce the contrast between the American (or Anglo-Saxon) concept of the relationship of government and business and the continental European concept, sometimes called the **Rhine model**.

These changes, far from making the study of comparative economics redundant, provide us with a new and incisive way of looking at how economies are organized and how they function. The process of transition in Eastern Europe, to take one example, forced us to compare the institutions of capitalism and socialism in a new and fundamental way. The dramatic and almost uniformly experienced collapse of output in the economies of the former Soviet bloc and the unexpectedly slow pace of recovery necessitate a careful evaluation of the differences in institutions, culture, history, and policy that made this transition more painful than predicted. These issues are the substance of comparative economics.

WHAT IS AN ECONOMIC SYSTEM?

In every society, whatever its structure, size, wealth, or level of development, certain economic decisions must be made. The most important of these decisions may be reduced to three types:

> First, it must be decided *what* goods and services are to be produced and in what quantities. This determination is generally referred to as the **production decision**, often represented in stylized form as the familiar "guns versus butter" choice. Such a two-dimensional representation simplifies society's choices and obscures the fact that decisions must be made among a huge array of goods. Nevertheless, the choice of the mix of goods that are to be produced must be faced and made in some way.

Second, a decision must be made about *how* these goods will be produced. The combination of factors of production (generally speaking labor, land, and capital—though all of these are not homogenous) that will be used and the organizations through which production will be achieved are the elements in the **choice of technique** decision.

The third set of choices relates to *who* will receive the benefit of this production, called the **distributional decision**. In all three of these broad types of decision is a temporal dimension. If we can, through saving and investment and through the choice of how rapidly we deplete or exhaust our scarce resources, alter the time pattern of consumption, then we make the choice of whether to consume now or later, and implicitly whether to benefit the current population or their descendants.

The mechanism by which these decisions are made within any economy is referred to as the economic system. The study of how such systems differ between economies and how differences in systems determine economic outcomes, comprises the field of study of comparative economic systems.

The concept of a **system** comes, albeit rather loosely, from the physical sciences. In those disciplines, a system is thought of as a collection of objects essentially closed to outside forces, within which the behavior of the objects is subject to physical laws. An economic system consists of analogies to the same essential ingredients. On the one hand are the objects (in this case economic institutions) and on the other hand are the "laws" (which in economic analysis include not only formal laws but also rules, procedures, and customs) that govern the interaction of these institutions.

Although they are broadly analogous, important differences separate the physical sciences from what we observe in economies. First, the institutions within an economic system do not always merely respond passively to the forces acting on them. Many institutions, which are organizations of human beings, are not merely inert, but seek to further specific objectives. In addition, these objectives may change over time. Second, while the laws that govern physical behavior are immutable, the "laws" that govern interactions within economies are by and large observed regularities and subject to change as culture and customs evolve.

ECONOMIC INSTITUTIONS

The kinds of institutions that characterize a modern industrial economy, whether that of the United States or any other developed market economy, will be familiar to most students from their courses in introductory economics, but some review is useful to set the stage. All economies do not, of course, possess identical sets of institutions. Different histories, cultures, ideologies, and priorities lead to different institutional forms and to differences in the way these institutions interact.

Households

The most fundamental components of almost any economic system are **households**. On the one hand, households are the suppliers of labor, and on the other, they are the ultimate consumers of the bulk of the goods and services produced in the economy. In most systems (the exceptions being primarily socialist economies), households are also responsible for the supply of capital and land to the productive sector. The household in some form is common to practically all economies, developed, less developed, and socialist, though the size, composition, makeup, and decision-making responsibilities differ substantially, even within industrial economies.

Households must be regarded as having objectives or goals, even if only in the loosest sense. Mainstream economists generally consider that the household is a "utility maximizing" institution, and they make assumptions about what factors enter into its utility function. We should note that utility maximization cannot be equated with a desire to maximize income or even material well-being, although today we seem to share a general belief that more material output is better than less. Other objectives, such as a desire for prestige, gaining satisfaction from leisure, patriotism, or a preference for an equitable distribution of income, may form important arguments in a household's utility function. Moreover, the nature of the utility function will vary from society to society, bearing the stamp of history, culture, and ideology.

Government

Common to all economies, except the most primitive ones (or theoretical conceptions of anarchy), is some form of government. In a modern industrialized economy, the government is complex and its authority far-reaching. All contemporary governments are, to some extent, involved in the establishment and protection of economic and individual rights, the regulation of business and industry, the provision of goods and services, and the redistribution of income. Because the government embodies a powerful set of agencies, and because it can make and change the rules by which the economy operates through legislation, it ranks, even in quite conservative societies, as one of the important institutions for answering the fundamental economic questions—*what, how,* and *for whom?*—that were introduced earlier. Clearly, the means by which a government derives its power, and the degree of control that it exercises over the behavior of its citizens and the other institutions that constitute the economy, varies greatly from country to country.

The goals, or objectives, that governments choose to pursue may also vary a great deal. When we speak of goals we are generally talking of something quite broad. For example, goals may be such vague objectives as "an accelerated rate of growth of output," "a more even distribution of income," "an increase in expected longevity," and so forth. A shift in these goals or in the strategy of their pursuit can take two forms: either a thorough-going reform of the system itself (as we are witnessing in Eastern Europe and the former Soviet Union), or the application of different **policies** operating within an existing system. The boundary between systemic reform and a radical policy initiative is necessarily a gray area. For example, many countries embark on extensive privatization by selling large parts of publicly owned (or "nationalized") industry to the private sector. Clearly when such an event takes place on the scale of the mass privatization that occurred in Russia, it constitutes systemic change. The sale of some public corporations within the context of the French economy is a different matter, however. Even the most radical "western" privatization as that of Margaret Thatcher in Britain in the period of (roughly) 1981 to 1989 is generally regarded more as a shift of policy within the mixed capitalist system than as a systemic change.

Policies may be defined as the actions that a government takes within an existing system in pursuit of its objectives. Examples of policies are the establishment of a fiscal deficit in an attempt to stimulate growth in national income, the use of taxes and expenditures to redistribute economic well-being from one group to another, the commitment of government to provide investment funds for industry, the creation of a national health service, and so forth. Such policies are facilitated by the use of **instruments** like the income tax, the money supply, government expenditure, or the structure of tariffs. Changes in these instruments are usually called **measures**. Thus a government of a mixed capitalist economy (system) might decide to reduce (measure) the income tax (instrument) to create a fiscal deficit (policy) to reduce unemployment (objective).

In the real world, things are necessarily more complex than depicted here, and more incisive analysis can help us understand how a system operates. For example, it is generally an oversimplification to view the government as a monolithic entity with a single objective. All governments consist of different ministries and agencies, each with different powers and functions. In all likelihood the agencies of government also have different objectives, because agencies cater to different constituencies. They are likely to be "captured" by those interests and serve them rather than some larger conception of the public good. For example, one arm of government might be responsible for furthering industrial growth, while another might have responsibility for the environment. Occasions likely arise in which the interests of these agencies are in conflict, and the outcome itself is a matter of political interaction.

Enterprises

The third broad group of institutions is composed of economic enterprises that produce goods and services. These enterprises may be owned privately, cooperatively (by a small group, usually consisting of the workforce), or socially (by society as a whole, through the agency of some level of government). Even within a market economy, enterprises may take on a wide range of institutional forms that affect their nature and performance. For example, they may be "incorporated," a form that carries with it the important characteristic of limited liability and particular tax treatment. In turn, privately owned corporations fall into two groups. They may be "public" in that their shares are traded freely, generally on a stock exchange, or "privately held," whereby ownership is limited to a small group of individuals and shares are not available for purchase or sale beyond that group. Other forms of enterprise in a market economy are partnerships or wholly owned proprietorships.

Economic enterprises, like households, pursue objectives. Economists commonly assume that in a free enterprise economy, privately owned firms are profit maximizers, at least in the long run. However, a growing body of research on the actual behavior of firms and managers within firms suggests that this view may be too simplistic. Conflicting goals, such as maximizing market share, rapid sales growth, employment maximization, or management's well-being, may all play a role, at least in the short term.

Moreover, even if profit maximization is the clear and overt objective, all firms that are more complex than a single proprietorship with no employees are beset with **principal/agent problems**. These problems arise because of the difficulty of getting workers, or management for that matter (the *agents*), to act in the way that best serves the interests of the owners (the *principals*). Thus, although the ultimate owner of the firm (the *shareholders*) might favor profit maximization, the management and the workers pursue their own goals (leisure, prestige, income, etc.), which might well be in conflict with shareholder objectives.

Labor Organizations

A fourth important set of institutions is composed of labor organizations, which may exert substantial influence on employment, workplace technique, and compensation. By uniting and solidifying the interests of individual workers and asserting a degree of monopoly power in labor negotiations, labor unions can affect decision making in the economy. Moreover, across economies unionization takes on different forms, and these distinctions result in various methods of political expression. One clear distinction is between **company unions** (common in Japan) and the **craft** or **occupational unions** (the norm in several European economies). In most of continental Europe it is generally accepted that organized labor plays an important role at the governmental level. In some countries (e.g., Sweden), the labor unions are actors in national negotiations to determine wages. In others (i.e., France) the unions have an official status in setting the objectives and priorities of governmental policy and were prominent actors in formulating the "National Plans" that were the centerpieces of French policy making for 50 years.

In the socialist, centrally planned economies, labor unions were largely powerless. The ideology of socialism asserted that, because the means of production were owned by the people, workers did not need to organize to protect their interests. Free labor organizations were therefore frequently repressed and only unions licensed by the state or party were allowed. Almost paradoxically the collapse of the "Workers' State" in Poland was brought about largely by the growth of Solidarity, the "alternative" labor union that opposed the state.

Nongovernmental Organizations

Recognition by economists and political scientists of the importance of a fifth set of institutions that play important roles in modern economies continues to grow. These **nongovernmental organizations (NGOs)** attracted considerable attention in recent years. The NGO sector is composed of organizations that are not only nongovernmental, but also operate on a not-for-profit basis, distinguishing them from firms in a capitalist economy. Broadly speaking, NGOs fall into three groups: organizations that exist to provide services to particular groups (e.g., the United Way in the United States or various developmental and health agencies that operate in the developing world), organizations that serve as centers of common interest (hobby groups and church organizations), and lobbying groups organized to influence government behavior (e.g., the AARP).[1]

Service-providing NGOs may fulfill some of the functions that are also performed by government, particularly in the fields of education, poverty relief, and health care. Given the determination to reduce the size of the governmental sector, which seems to be common to all developed market economies, the role of NGOs may be expected to expand in the years ahead. Most people would regard this increase in voluntarism to be beneficial to welfare; an NGO can replace some of the functions of government without needing to raise taxes or encountering the excess burdens that accompany taxing and spending. However, NGOs are organized to serve mainly the interests of particular groups and cannot be relied on to preserve the interests and well-being of those not in the group, and they frequently do burden the public purse because of the tax-exempt privileges extended to donors.

Markets

A final set of institutions that are significant in almost any economy is made up of the markets within which these institutions interact. In broad terms, these include goods markets, labor markets, financial markets, stock markets, and commodity markets. However, any "market" economy is characterized by many thousands of markets. Markets are organized in different ways in different economies, and the study of how they differ is one important feature of comparative economics. The depth, complexity, and richness of markets are important factors in determining economic outcomes. So too is the reliability, transparency, and probity of the markets. Market structure can only work well when participants are well-informed. Corruption, confusion, and fraud obviously have a deleterious impact on market performance, and can drive away investment and therefore growth and performance.

RULES

The preceding list is far from an exhaustive inventory of the institutions found in a modern economy. It does, however, provide us with an idea of their range and variety. These institutions interact with each other in addressing the production, distribution, and choice of technique decisions. Let us now turn to the rules that govern these interactions. It is important to note from the outset that the rules that govern any society are complex and hybrid. They consist of both *formal rules*, which are embodied and codified as **laws** and **regulations**, and *informal customs*, or **practices** and **beliefs** that influence behavior. At first glance it might seem that laws should be the more important, but the force of custom and tradition is decisive in

[1]AARP, formerly known as the American Association of Retired Persons, is a powerful organization that lobbies on behalf of senior citizens in the United States.

many issues. Moreover, custom, culture, and tradition determine not only the nature of the rules by which institutions interact; they also shape the nature of the institutions themselves.

The Legal Framework

All institutions within a society must operate under the rule of law. Laws are, by definition, those rules made by some level of government[2] and rely on the power of the government, which we may think of as having a monopoly on force in most societies, to ensure that they are obeyed. In a modern economy, the scope of the legal system is broad. As well as constituting a criminal code, laws also determine a variety of factors that are vital for the functioning of the economy. They include such things as the establishment and enforcement of contracts, the nature of property and property rights, the obligations of firms and individuals under the tax system, environmental regulations, health codes, the minimum age of workers, (in some societies) the minimum wage that must be paid to workers, what firms must disclose to their stockholders and potential owners, and how firms and individuals may enter bankruptcy.

Such laws help to determine both the character and the behavior of economic institutions. For example, the structure of the U.S. financial system was shaped by a series of federal and state regulations that limit the activities of commercial banks, investment banks, brokerage houses, and other institutions. These regulations mean that the organization and functioning of U.S. banking will be different from that in, for example, Germany, where different laws apply. Germany has never had an equivalent to the **Glass-Steagall Act**, which mandated the formal separation of the activities of investment and commercial banks.[3] Consequently, in Germany **universal banks** (sometimes referred to as U-banks), which perform a wide range of functions, are the norm, and the relationship between the financial and productive sectors is quite different from the one in the United States. Laws concerning the incorporation of firms and the liabilities of partnerships dictate the type of enterprises that may exist and the extent of their activity.

Laws mean little unless they are enforced. We can be quite deceived about the nature of a society or an economy if we only look at the laws as they are on the books and not at how they are actually administered. Later in this book we will discuss the nature of **legality** within society. Legality requires not only a comprehensive set of mutually consistent laws, but also the expectation that those laws will be generally and impartially enforced.

---

[2]Some clarification of the idea of making laws might be in order here. Laws are often made by active legislative initiative, but in many societies they evolve through precedent and may be codified after the fact or remain in force without any real form of codification. The most familiar example to most readers is the evolution of English Common Law.

[3]The Gramm-Leach-Bliley Financial Services Modernization Act of 1999 relaxes some of the Glass-Steagall separation of function and allows banks and securities firms to affiliate through a holding company structure.

Rules Within Organizations

The behavior of economic institutions is not determined by the laws and their enforcement alone. Indeed, institutions must operate within an externally imposed legal framework, but they also follow self-imposed rules that limit their behavior. These internal rules are present in government departments, stock markets, corporations, charities, or labor unions. Organizational rules are generally written and codified and must be subsidiary to the laws of society, at least as far as those laws are enforced. They pervasively influence the organization of economic activity.

Procedures

On a less formal level than that of rules, the day-to-day running of all organizations tends to be governed through procedures, which present less formal force than laws or the regulations by which organizations define themselves. It is tempting to presume that because they are less formal than laws or regulations, such procedures might be more easily changed; in reality they are perhaps more enduring. Some examples may be employment practices, systems of promotion, or the way that price or quality information is sought in purchasing.

Custom, Culture, and Tradition

The force of custom also determines the nature of economic outcomes and the behavior of economic actors within an economic system. Different societies do things in different ways and demonstrate particular beliefs and prejudices, which may be just as powerful in their effect as formal regulations or even procedures. These customs can influence a wide range of economic variables. For example, in some societies custom discourages girls from receiving anything above the most rudimentary education, a fact that greatly changes the supply of labor, productivity, and, in turn, per-head incomes. Some societies are, by custom, high consuming, while others show deep-seated tendencies toward saving and accumulation.

Such factors are frequently neglected but they can decisively influence the direction and performance of an economy. In a recent book, Francis Fukuyama made the case for the vital role of social institutions and cultural values in determining economic outcomes.[4] He argued that a distinction can be drawn between "high-trust" societies (among them Japan, Germany, and the United States), which developed the flexible civic institutions that a modern economy demands in greater abundance, and "low-trust" (or "familistic") nations such as China, France, and Italy. The presence of these institutions reduces the costs of economic interchange, which greatly facilitates commerce and leads to more rapid growth. It is, on the face of it, an interesting argument, although Fukuyama's premises may be questioned. For example, why is the United States (the most lawyer-ridden and

---

[4]Francis Fukuyama, *Trust: The Social Virtues and the Creation of Prosperity* (New York: Free Press, 1995). See also the review in *The Economist*, September 2, 1995.

litigious society in the world) classed with Japan (which is the developed economy with the fewest lawyers) as "trusting societies"?

ECONOMIC RESOURCES

Economies differ not only in their institutions and the rules that govern the interaction of those institutions but also in the endowments of wealth that they possess. Each economy possesses at any point in time a stock of capital and resources, which is in part the result of the geography, geology, and climate of the country and in part the consequence of the cumulative impact of actions taken by individuals, productive enterprises, and governments in the past. These actions consist of the myriad savings, consumption, and investment decisions that determine the stock of human and physical, human-made capital inherited from previous generations. Although this wealth exists in many forms, it is convenient and useful for our current purpose to group it into three broad types.

Natural Assets

The most fundamental part of the wealth base consists of the **natural resources** of the economy, consisting primarily of minerals (coal, oil, natural gas, ores) located within the ground of a nation's economy, and the naturally occurring vegetation, like forests, found on it. Also included in an inventory of natural resources should be water resources and certain topographical features that facilitate communication (harbors, navigable rivers, and the like). In addition, we can consider the weather and such naturally occurring features that might, for example, attract tourism.

Closely linked to the wealth that comes from natural resources is the stock of productive agricultural land. The value of this asset to the economy is determined by both the generosity of nature and the incidence of human-made improvements on it that create or enhance productivity. These improvements include infrastructural developments (like irrigation in the American West or the terracing of rice paddies in Asia). Agricultural land is in fact a combination of nature and human-made resources, although some of the improvements (clearing forests, canalizing rivers) are so ancient as to defy any normal scheme of asset valuation that would dissociate the improvement from the value of the natural resource itself.

Produced Assets

Economists, in their analyses, tend to focus a lot of attention on an economy's stock of produced assets, the extant accretion of human-made capital created in previous periods.[5] The most easily envisaged examples of this stock are the machines, the factories, and the inventories of finished goods and goods-in-process

[5]Marx in fact referred to capital as "dead labor."

in **industrial capital**. That form of capital, however, is only part of the picture. We must also take notice of the social capital embodied in roads, bridges, dams, schools, universities and the like.

Human Capital

On a global level, the most important wealth resource is embodied as **human capital** in the skills and education of individuals. A recent World Bank Study found that almost two-thirds of the value of accumulated wealth in the world lies in human capital. The importance of human capital is most obvious in the highly developed industrial nations. Japan's land and natural resources are of trivial consequence compared to the value of its human capital, which is overwhelmingly the reason it ranks third in the world in resource wealth on a per-head basis. The same is true of Germany. Similarly, Singapore, an island state with few natural resources (though its location gives the land value), is wealthy because of a highly educated and enterprising population.

HOW WEALTH VARIES AMONG NATIONS

Several recent attempts to quantify the international distribution of these resources looked at the stock of wealth available to an economy, and compared the relative endowments of different economies, as well as the changes over time. The World Bank's Environmentally Sustainable Development Project embarked on the bold step of quantifying the wealth in each of 192 nations.[6]

The explicit recognition that a country's wealth is the combination of various forms of capital—produced, natural, and human resources—led to new thinking about what constitutes wealth and how it might be measured. The figures that the World Bank came up with were necessarily somewhat rough, and debate is inevitable as to the accuracy and appropriateness of some of the estimation procedures. However, the results are fascinating and instructive.

In the World Bank analysis, produced assets (fixed capital and infrastructure) were estimated using a perpetual inventory method, using flow data on depreciation and investment to estimate the current stock of capital. The value of natural resources was estimated by classifying the land into cropland, grassland, forests, and other uses, valuing each as a multiple of per-head income in the country where it is located. (This method means that an acre of cropland in Latin America represents less "wealth" than an acre in, say, the Netherlands purely because of location.) Adjustments were made for subsoil assets and standing timber.

In this analysis, human resources were valued as the residual, after allowing for the effect of natural resources and produced capital. Such a measure therefore

[6]See *Expanding the Measure of Wealth: Indicators of Environmentally Sustainable Development* (Washington, DC: World Bank, 1997); and *Monitoring Environmental Progress: A Report on Work in Progress* (Washington, DC: World Bank, 1995).

includes not only the human capital embodied in individuals by virtue of the education, experience, and training, but also the economic value of the social institutions. Also included in this residual effect would be any cultural factors that might make that society more productive than another. Significantly for the issue at hand, the measure of human capital is conflated with the efficiency of the economic system. Notwithstanding these problems, the results of the study give considerable food for thought. Figures for some selected nations are provided in Table 1.1.

1. As a global average, almost two-thirds, 64 percent, of total wealth is embodied in human resources composed of individual human capital and social institutions.
2. The wealthiest nation on a per-head basis is Australia, which possesses large natural wealth distributed among a small, but highly educated population.
3. Most of the top 25 nations in terms of aggregate wealth have natural assets comprising less than 10 percent (and most of these less than 5 percent) of total wealth, further suggesting that accrued human capital rather than initial resource endowment is the key to prosperity.
4. The variation in per-head wealth between nations is even more pronounced than the variation in per-head income. Australia, at the top, is rated as having about 500 times the wealth of Ethiopia, the bottom country.

TABLE 1.1

Estimates of the Wealth of Nations, Dollars per Head: Selected Nations, 1995

Rank for Total Wealth	Country	Total Wealth	Human Capital	Produced Capital	Natural Resources
1	Australia	835,000	175,350	58,450	592,850
11	United States	421,000	248,390	67,360	105,250
21	United Kingdom	324,000	268,920	45,360	9,720
22	Singapore	306,000	260,100	45,900	0
31	Saudi Arabia	184,000	51,520	33,120	101,200
39	Greece	142,000	106,500	19,880	15,620
54	Russia	98,000	14,700	14,700	68,600
61	Mexico	74,000	54,020	8,140	11,840
71	Estonia	55,000	39,050	7,700	7,700
87	Iran	38,000	12,920	14,060	11,020
96	Turkey	34,000	24,480	5,100	4,420
117	Romania	17,000	11,900	2,890	2,210
161	China	6,600	5,082	990	528
175	Kenya	3,800	2,128	1,216	456
181	Rwanda	2,900	2,030	638	261
192	Ethiopia	1,400	560	294	546
	World Average	86,000	55,040	13,760	17,200

SOURCE: World Bank, *Sustainability and the Wealth of Nations*, 1995.

THE DETERMINATION OF ECONOMIC OUTCOMES

By economic outcomes we mean measurable consequences such as per-head income, the distribution of income, employment, inflation, and even demographic factors such as life expectancy. These outcomes are the result of the interaction between the available resources, the institutions, and the rules that govern the system. These relationships might be easy to envisage in terms of a functional statement, rather like a production function.

$$O_i = F_i(NR_i, PA_i, HC_i)$$

where O represents the economic outcomes, NR the natural resources, PA the stock of produced assets, and HC human capital and the subscripts represent each country. Although in structure it is like a production function,[7] what differs is that the economic systems of all of the observations under review (the economies) are different. Thus, the F_i are different for all economies and depend upon the institutions and even the goals of the systems. In part, comparative economics is concerned with how the goals of different economies vary, and how the systems of different economies contrast, such that wealth endowments result in different outcomes. Our problem, in fact, is why some societies use their factors of production more efficiently. The economist Mancur Olsen once wrote that we would like to know why some economies are wasteful in converting inputs to outputs, in his words inefficiently "leave five dollar bills on the sidewalk," while other systems are much more adept at picking up such windfalls and using their resources productively.

SOME FUNDAMENTALS OF ECONOMIC SYSTEMS

Even a cursory glance at the world shows us that economic systems are complex and hybrid, embodying a range of features. However, we may use some fundamental approaches to distinguish between different systems. Economic systems differ from each other along three important dimensions: the extent of individual rights (particularly as they pertain to property), the means of coordination of economic activity, and the incentive systems that influence the response of individuals.

The Nature and Extent of Individual Rights

All systems of government put some constraints on the rights of individuals in economic matters, although the range and force of restraint differ dramatically. The extent of the rights that the government allows, either actively or passively, to remain with the individual, coupled with the degree to which the state effectively protects and guarantees those rights against the incursions of other individuals

[7]Indeed, some economists in the World Bank look forward to the arrival of a general production function that will be able to tell us the relationship between inputs and outputs.

(and possible incursions by the state itself), is of great importance in determining the shape and functioning of the economic system.

Property Ownership and Property Rights The character of a society is determined largely by the extent of rights and freedoms that are allowed to individuals within it. From the point of view of studying the functioning of an economic system, one of the most significant of these rights is the right to own property. In practical terms almost every society, even the most collectively or socialistically organized, allows individuals the right to own some personal property, possibly limited only to food for consumption, clothing, and furniture. From an economic perspective, the most important issue is whether individuals (or groups of individuals) are allowed to own "the means of production"—the enterprises, organizations, tools, and inventories used to make goods and services.

The existence of private ownership of the means of production has been the basis for distinguishing between the two great "isms" that dominated the study of comparative economic systems in the last century. **Socialism** is a system in which the means of production are owned collectively, generally by the state. **Capitalism**, often taken as synonymous with "free enterprise," is predicated on the means of production being owned by individuals or freely associated groups of individuals.

However, on closer inspection *ownership* is not the simple matter that it might initially seem to be. What is commonly called ownership actually involves a series of potentially separable qualities or **property rights**. Of these, three are particularly important. The first is the right *to use* a good or resource in the way that the "owner" of the property sees fit. In some discussions, especially those pertaining to the debate on the efficacy of privatization, also known as the **control right**.[8] The second is the right *to receive income* or other benefits generated by the use of the property, also known as the **cash-flow right**. The last is the right *to exchange or sell* property at a price deemed appropriate by the seller—the **disposal right**. If these rights are together vested in individuals, they constitute the "right to engage in economic activity," because they confer the right to establish or acquire businesses, the right to manufacture goods, and the right to buy and sell goods.[9]

However, it is important to note that even in societies regarded as "free enterprise" or "capitalist" these rights are seldom unrestricted. For example, zoning restrictions and environmental regulations frequently constrain the nominal owner's use of property. Such regulations take away some of the property rights of the owner and confer them upon others. An individual's right to use her property as she sees fit might be balanced by the property rights of others, who have rights to clean air, light, or unpolluted water. Licensing prevents the entry into some

---

[8]See, for example, Maxim Boycko, Andrei Shleifer, and Robert Vishny, *Privatizing Russia* (Cambridge, MA: MIT Press, 1995).

[9]This right to engage in economic activity was one of the fundamental rights demanded by Gregory Yavlinsky and Stanislav Shatalin, in the somewhat overly optimistic "five hundred day plan," and defined in many ways the emergence of Russia from a socialist to a market economy.

industries, while other industries may be restricted as a governmental or private monopoly. Most economies include systems of taxation that tax away some part of both corporate and personal income, an infringement of an individual's unrestricted right to income from property.

With respect to disposal rights, many societies with market-oriented economies choose at times to prevent owners from selling property, goods, or services to whomever and at prices that they see fit. Such restrictions might be short term and quite limited. In the United States, for example, laws can be used to control prices in order to prevent "profiteering" after a natural disaster. However, some controls may be of longer duration. Recent history produced examples of both general restrictions on price changes with a view to fighting inflation, which occurred under the Nixon administration, and on specific goods (e.g., gasoline, during the oil crises of the 1970s). Rent control is a familiar feature in many western economies, and all market economies regulate the pricing behavior of privately owned utility companies to counterbalance monopoly power.

Across societies there is a spectrum of such restrictions on individual economic freedom. At one polar extreme are countries (fewer since the demise of the Soviet Union) that adopted socialist economic systems and in which the economic rights of individuals are reduced to a minimum. For example, in the Soviet Union before its dissolution and the subsequent economic liberalization in the successor states, virtually all of the means of production were owned by the state. As late as the 1980s it was estimated that 97 percent of total economic output in the Soviet Union, as well as East Germany and Czechoslovakia, was in the control of the state. This was not the result of the state outcompeting private enterprise, but rather the consequence of the denial of the right of individuals to own productive resources and to establish enterprises. At the other extreme are the highly laissez-faire states, for example Hong Kong (before 1997 while it was under British rule), in which governmental restrictions on enterprise and the labor force were minimal.

Despite the fact that under such socialist systems practically all property rights were formally vested in the state, a *de facto* complex of property rights of individuals was established by practice and custom. Even in the most completely centrally planned systems, the managers of enterprises and the political leadership, in practical terms, exercised a kind of ownership in the fruits of the enterprise. They held both some control rights (although most were held by the planners) and some cash-flow rights, because they could skim some income from the enterprises. It was well established that the *apparatchiks* in the Soviet Union had access to goods and privileges by virtue of their positions in the enterprises[10] and this access resulted in important consequences when the process of denationalizing, or privatizing, these economies occurred.

---

[10]The property rights of the bureaucrats and enterprise managers constituted a recurrent barrier to the reform of centrally planned systems. As we will see when we look at the issues of transition, the success of any liberalization agenda is contingent on the ability to ensure the participation of key players in the bureaucracy and enterprise management. They must be induced to give up the property rights and income that they held in the *status quo ante*. See, for example, Jan Winiecki, "Why Economic Reforms Fail in Soviet Type Systems: A Property Rights Approach," *Economic Inquiry* 28, no. 2 (April 1990), p. 195.

Freedom of Mobility and Employment Although property rights constitute an important dimension of the economic system, they are not the only set of rights that play a decisive role. Another set of rights relates to an individual's freedom to work and his or her choice of occupation and location. The ability to enter a profession or establish a business is an important right, the denial of which can crucially shape the nature of enterprise and economic activity.

Extent of Government Ownership A crude measure of economic freedom can be provided by the extent of government ownership of industry, services, and infrastructure. This measure varies greatly from country to country. Even within "free market" economies, governments control varying amounts of industry. Figure 1.1 shows the value added produced in the government sector in selected economies for the time period 1985–1990. It shows a considerable range. In the United States only 1.1 percent of total value occurred in the public productive sector, which is limited to a modest share of transportation (Amtrak), the U.S. Postal Service, and some utilities. Europe follows a stronger tradition of government production. In Britain, at that time undergoing the "Thatcher reforms," the share was 6.7 percent. Across the channel the French public sector, expanded by the Socialist Mitterand government, nationalized several major corporations in the early 1980s and stood at 11.2 percent. In general, less-developed countries are likely to have a larger government sector because the government promotes industry in an attempt to accelerate development. In oil-rich Venezuela, government-owned enterprise produces almost a quarter of total output, and in Zambia the comparable figure is almost one-third. It is important to recall that in centrally planned

FIGURE 1.1

Share of Total Value Added Produced in State-Owned Enterprise, 1985–1990, in Selected Countries

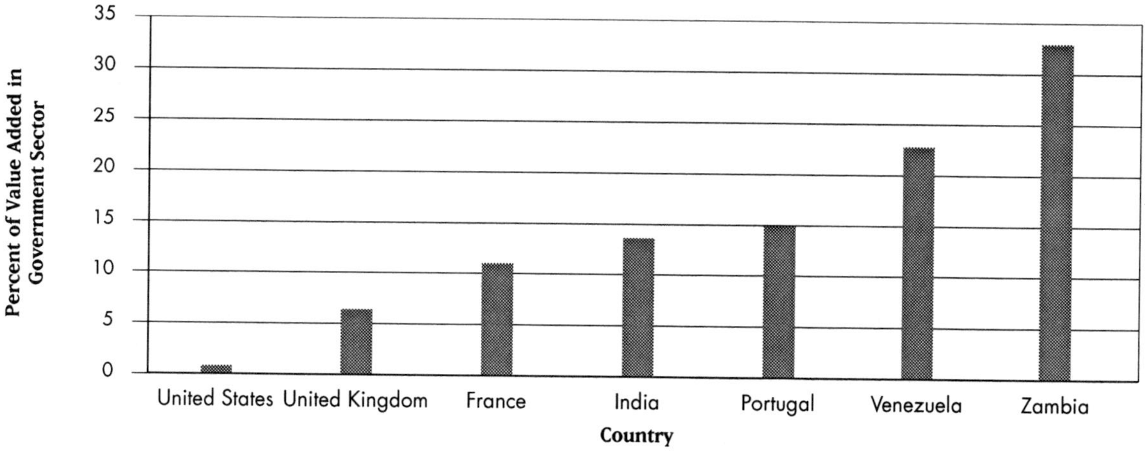

SOURCE: World Bank Development Report.

economies this figure would been close to 100 percent. These differences between countries apply not only to government production. The range of services that public authorities provide varies substantially. In some countries the government is a major supplier of health care, transportation, and financial services that are in other countries the province of private operation.

A better index of the role of government would be a measure the degree of government interference in the economy, because government regulation of private industry can be a substitute for public ownership. Privatization, the transference of assets from the government to the private sector, is often accompanied by an increase in regulation. Consequently countries with a high degree of private economic activity may be among the most heavily regulated. However, though such an index would be informative, the extent of government interference is hard to quantify.

Command Versus the Market

Another dimension by which we may compare the structure of economic systems is the degree of reliance on planning, on the one hand, or the market, on the other, as means of coordinating economic activity. Under planning, the government determines, or at least seeks to influence, the answers to those important economic questions of *what, how,* and *for whom* discussed earlier. Under a market system, in contrast, the action of individuals, acting through the institutions that they comprise, each pursuing their own objectives, leads to the set of outcomes. This process was called **the invisible hand** by **Adam Smith**, the great Scottish philosopher and economist, in his seminal book *An Inquiry into the Nature and Causes of the Wealth of Nations.*

Command Planning Planning can, of course, vary considerably in its scope and comprehensiveness. At one extreme we see the kind of economic organization established in the former Soviet Union, in which the government controlled almost all economic activity, and nearly all production occurred within enterprises owned and controlled by the government. In that system, detailed plans guided the flow of all resources, materials, and finished goods. Moreover, when those plans were finalized they were endowed with the force of law, and the economic actors on the production side were required to follow the procedures laid down, and achieve the targets prescribed, under threat of legal sanction. For obvious reasons this compulsive, top-down planning is called command planning. However, gentler variants occur as well.

Indicative Planning A different form of planning was pursued in several Western European nations (particularly France) and in Japan. In those countries the government relied primarily on the voluntary and uncoerced response of the private sector to a set of guidelines produced as a result of discussions between government, industry, and in some cases labor or other groups. The objective of the planning exercise was largely to establish a common information base and a consensus on the broad direction of the economy. The expertise of the government in marshaling statistics and producing forecasts was important, and it was the government that provided the forum and formalized the outcome. On the whole, this form of planning sought to coordinate, unify, and identify "bottlenecks" and to initiate remedial action. The powers of the government may be used to favor particular outcomes, but the scope of direct intervention was circumscribed (frequently limited to some intervention in credit markets) and scant scope for coercion was allowed. Because the main purpose of this planning was to lay out the likely course of the economy, this form is called **indicative planning**, and it was designed to function in parallel with, rather than to the exclusion of, the market. Indicative planning was quite widely used in the 1950s and 1960s but subsequently declined. In part this decline is the result of increased globalization, which makes predicting and coordinating performance within one country a more difficult task. This trend is unlikely to be reversed. Another reason for decline, however, is the widely held belief in the superiority of the market, which may well be called into question in the future.

Choice and the Market System One of the most important aspects of the market system lies in the limitation of coercion. The overall outcome of the economy must be determined primarily by the voluntary actions of individuals, and therefore the absence of bureaucratic constraints and the consequent maximization of the role of choice are essential features. As we will see in later chapters, the market cannot always be relied on to lead the economy to an optimal use of resources, nor are the distributional aspects of a market system always universally approved of. In particular, the market may lead to a pattern of income and access to basic consumer goods that might be considered unacceptable by some societies. The final distribution of income in a market and welfare are contingent on the initial distribution of wealth, position, and ability. In a variety of well-known instances of market failure, government intervention may plausibly lead to higher levels of social satisfaction. These issues will be more fully discussed in Chapter 4.

Centralization Versus Decentralization

Another way to classify economies is by looking at the centralization of the decision-making system. Again, we may take the example of Soviet-style planning, in which a single plan governing the use of all resources and the production of output was prepared, codified, and formalized as law. At the opposite pole we can conceive of nearly pure market systems in which all of the important decisions are taken by individuals or private institutions and the function of government is largely to provide a framework and stability within which markets can operate. Between these two poles is a continuum of decentralization of power; where a particular economy lies on this continuum is a useful way to gain insight into how its system operates.

Later when the difficulties of centralized planning are more fully examined, we will see that one of the major problems in the implementation and maintenance of a centralized planning system is the quantity of information that must be gathered and accurately reported to the center. Only when the planners are well informed does the plan stand a chance of using resources efficiently. This is more than a mechanical problem and involves important issues of incentives. Well-documented examples describe situations in which incentives may motivate the actors at the periphery (plant managers, etc.) to gain advantage by systematically misreporting information to the center. A simple example is to overestimate the need for capital or raw materials to ensure plenty on hand to meet the output quotas that the planners assign.

Incentives: Moral, Material, and Coercive

These issues lead us into a more general discussion of incentives. In all economic systems above the level of a totally individualistic economy we encounter what economists call principal/agent problems. As the name implies, this set of problems is concerned with the difficulties of creating a structure of incentives that encourages someone appointed as the "agent" to act for a "principal" to indeed pursue the principal's interest rather than his or her own. At the simplest level, an agency problem may be represented as: "If I hire a worker, how can I ensure that he works as hard and as well for me as I would for myself?"

This problem is pertinent from a **"Robinson Crusoe" economy** to the largest corporation, and to the most complex centrally planned economy. Why should Friday work hard when Crusoe is out of sight? Why should the management of IBM act in the interest of shareholders, who are ultimately the owners, rather than in their own interests? Why should workers or management in a factory pursue the targets that the architects of a central economic plan lay down, rather than act to maximize their own welfare?

The agency problem can be addressed in three general ways. One is to use **moral persuasion** to exhort actors to maximum performance. In such a scheme the management or government (principals) expect people (the agents) to behave appropriately because it is the "right thing to do," and perhaps find some way of granting prestige to those who conspicuously do well. This kind of incentive has frequently been found to be quite effective in the short run. In crises (wars, disasters, changes of regime), people are capable of making immense and seemingly irrational sacrifices when exhorted to do so. Encouragements such as "for the fatherland," "for the glory of God," or even John F. Kennedy's "ask not what your country can do for you; ask rather what you can do for your country" all proved effective to some degree. Communist regimes, especially during their early stages, asked for and often received large sacrifices from significant sections of the population who worked "for the revolution" or "for the Party." Moral suasion can even be effective within enterprises and corporations. A high degree of identification with the company is often cited as one of the causes of Japan's success. Governments can berate firms and achieve a modification of behavior, and sometimes rhetoric will even seem effective against other countries. However, in the longer run, moral incentives tend to be relatively ineffective unless they are backed up by the prospect of material improvement or, on the other hand, by the likelihood of **coercion**.

Material incentives apply when people work and adjust the level and intensity of their work because of the rewards, including advancement and promotion, that are proffered. On the whole we tend to think of market economies relying almost exclusively on material incentives, and the consequent absence of coercion is commonly regarded as one of that system's strengths. Each actor in a pure market system enters only into economic exchanges or contracts willingly, whether it is as a consumer or a supplier of factors of production. Work represents leisure sacrificed and will be performed only when the material compensations of work outweigh the loss of utility resultant from reduced leisure. Were it generally a reality, this aspect of choice ensures that welfare is maximized under a capitalist system. In fact, not all capitalist systems are as market reliant as may be initially assumed. First, as we noted, the initial endowments of factors are crucial in determining incomes, and the need to survive acts as an element of coercion. The "whip of hunger" does serve as a coercive element in many "market" societies. Second, within the workplace, capitalism frequently resorts to coercion, through timeclocks, piece rates, supervision, and so forth. This reality may be less draconian in the developed market economies than it once was, but overt workplace coercion is common in the developing world.

We often consider planned economies to be more reliant on coercion than market systems, which is true to some extent. Obviously under a command system of central planning, entry into many economic activities is limited because in general citizens cannot establish firms or form independent professional practices. Buying articles for resale, which in market economies would be regarded as healthy and necessary arbitrage or speculation is illegal. In some command economies the government maintain a tight grip on the labor market and allows the individual little choice in occupation, location, hours worked, or many other significant aspects of employment.

However, this scenario may not always be the case. Highly structured materials balance planning can be associated with a fair degree of liberalism in labor markets. For example, in the former Soviet Union it was illegal to be unemployed, and indeed no source of support was available for those who were able-bodied and of working age if they did not work. However, the planners assumed a reciprocal responsibility to provide a job for everyone, no matter how inept the worker. Restrictions on movement and the central determination of wages made the market for labor clumsy and unresponsive, but on the whole workers responded to material incentives just as in the developed market economies. Workers performed because of piece rates, bonuses, or the prospect of advancement as well as supervision, the same as in the West. Management operated largely in its own best interest and indulged in what economists refer to as "rent-seeking behavior." Truly coercive systems of labor allocation and job performance are those that rely on slavery, serfdom, indenturement, or peonage.

Experience suggests then that the best system of labor incentives is an eclectic one. Evidence indicates that higher productivity results when workers feel less alienated from their job, the organization that employs them, and the products that they produce. This heightened sense of identification stems in part from security of job tenure if minimum performance requirements are met. It is difficult to identify with a firm if it is about to fire you. In addition, it is useful to give workers a material stake in the enterprise, either through stock ownership or bonus systems, which encourage them to be personally interested in the firm's success. Such an approach combines the moral and the material, but it also includes a coercive element: the pressure of interested coworkers is frequently an excellent source of peer supervision.

MEASURING THE DIFFERENCES IN ECONOMIC SYSTEMS

The changes that swept through Eastern Europe and other planned economies in recent years eroded the clear contrast between the centrally planned and free market economies. These developments reinforced the recognition that the degree of economic freedom in various economies must be viewed as a continuum rather than as polar extremes. In turn, this change motivated attempts to measure the economic restrictions imposed in various economic systems and to compound the many dimensions of these restrictions into a single index. Such attempts must always be open to the criticisms that the methodology adopted, the grading methods, and the means of aggregation into an index are all highly subjective and therefore prone to manipulation.

Nevertheless, the results can be interesting and revealing if viewed with caution. Here, we consider two aggregate indices, both of which really seek to measure the degree of economic freedom and the extent to which economic and political institutions support economic growth and integration into the global economic system.

Economic Freedom

Table 1.2 shows the indices of **economic freedom** for 2002 prepared by the Heritage Foundation, a conservative U.S.–based organization. The index is computed by assessing the performance of the economy on each of 10 dimensions scoring on a 5-point scale, with 1 being "free" and 5 being "restricted." The 10 dimensions are as follows:

1. Trade policy
2. Taxation policy
3. Government consumption of output
4. Monetary policy
5. Capital flows and foreign investment
6. Banking policy
7. Wage and price controls
8. Property rights
9. Regulation policy
10. Presence of a black market

The relevance of most of these variables is self-evident. Low levels of tariffs and taxes, limited government consumption, an absence of price controls, a few restrictions on incoming foreign investment, and limited regulation in both banking and goods markets are all generally considered indicative of high degrees of economic freedom. A restrictive monetary policy is considered favorable in terms of economic freedom because money growth may produce inflation, which by acting as a hidden tax lets the government grab resources through the back door. Well-defined and well-enforced property rights are seen as essential to free enterprise, while the absence of a black market—which prospers when socially beneficial activity is prohibited—is another indicator of freedom to pursue market activity.

Most people would agree that the majority of these factors are correlated with economic freedom, but some of the particulars leave room for dispute. For example, the regulation of business might reduce the freedom of the capitalist, but it might enhance the freedom of the consumer if it is directed at limiting market failure resulting from limited information and externalities. A capitalist's freedom

TABLE 1.2

Heritage Foundation Indices of Economic Freedom

Rank	Country	Score	Rank	Country	Score	Rank	Country	Score	Rank	Country	Score
1	Hong Kong	1.35	38	Latvia	2.5	79	Algeria	3.1	118	Azerbaijan	3.5
2	Singapore	1.55	41	Uruguay	2.55	79	Brazil	3.1	118	Malawi	3.5
3	New Zealand	1.7	42	Cambodia	2.6	79	Djibouti	3.1	118	Niger	3.5
4	Estonia	1.8	43	Costa Rica	2.65	79	Gambia	3.1	121	China	3.55
4	Ireland	1.8	43	Israel	2.65	79	Madagascar	3.1	121	Egypt	3.55
4	Luxembourg	1.8	45	Armenia	2.7	79	Malaysia	3.1	121	Ethiopia	3.55
4	Netherlands	1.8	45	Belize	2.7	79	Paraguay	3.1	121	India	3.55
4	United States	1.8	45	Bolivia	2.7	79	Slovenia	3.1	125	Chad	3.6
9	Australia	1.85	45	France	2.7	79	Swaziland	3.1	125	Kazakhstan	3.6
9	Chile	1.85	45	Jordan	2.7	88	Benin	3.15	125	Kyrgyz Republic	3.6
9	United Kingdom	1.85	45	Malta	2.7	88	Cape Verde	3.15	125	Nigeria	3.6
12	Denmark	1.9	45	Panama	2.7	88	Honduras	3.15	125	Togo	3.6
12	Switzerland	1.9	45	Poland	2.7	88	Lebanon	3.15	130	Venezuela	3.65
14	Finland	1.95	53	Kuwait	2.75	88	Nicaragua	3.15	131	Bangladesh	3.7
15	Bahrain	2	53	Peru	2.75	93	Burkina Faso	3.2	131	Romania	3.7
15	Canada	2	55	Greece	2.8	93	Guyana	3.2	131	Russia	3.7
17	Bahamas	2.05	55	Guatemala	2.8	93	Kenya	3.2	134	Congo	3.75
17	El Salvador	2.05	55	Sri Lanka	2.8	93	Senegal	3.2	134	Yemen	3.75
17	Sweden	2.05	58	Colombia	2.85	97	Cameroon	3.25	136	Haiti	3.8
20	Austria	2.1	58	Tunisia	2.85	97	Gabon	3.25	137	Tajikistan	3.85
20	Belgium	2.1	60	Botswana	2.9	97	Macedonia	3.25	137	Ukraine	3.85
20	Germany	2.1	60	Ivory Coast	2.9	97	Zambia	3.25	137	Vietnam	3.85
23	Cyprus	2.15	60	Jamaica	2.9	101	Albania	3.3	140	Bosnia and Herzegovina	3.9
23	Iceland	2.15	60	Mali	2.9	101	Guinea	3.3	140	Equatorial Guinea	3.9
23	United Arab Em.	2.15	60	Mexico	2.9	101	Mauritania	3.3	142	Guinea-Bissau	3.95
26	Barbados	2.3	60	Mongolia	2.9	101	Pakistan	3.3	142	Suriname	3.95
26	Portugal	2.3	60	Namibia	2.9	105	Indonesia	3.35	144	Yugoslavia	4.05
26	Spain	2.3	60	Oman	2.9	105	Moldova	3.35	145	Myanmar (Burma)	4.1
29	Italy	2.35	60	Slovak Republic	2.9	105	Turkey	3.35	145	Syria	4.1
29	Lithuania	2.35	60	South Africa	2.9	108	Bulgaria	3.4	147	Zimbabwe	4.3
29	Taiwan	2.35	70	Philippines	2.95	108	Croatia	3.4	148	Belarus	4.35
32	Czech Republic	2.4	70	Qatar	2.95	108	Fiji	3.4	148	Uzbekistan	4.35
32	Hungary	2.4	72	Dominican Republic	3	108	Georgia	3.4	150	Turkmenistan	4.4
32	Thailand	2.4	72	Mauritius	3	108	Ghana	3.4	151	Iran	4.55
35	Japan	2.45	72	Saudi Arabia	3	108	Lesotho	3.4	151	Laos	4.55
35	Norway	2.45	72	Uganda	3	108	Nepal	3.4	153	Cuba	4.75
35	Trinidad and Tobago	2.45	76	Central African Rep.	3.05	108	Rwanda	3.4	153	Libya	4.75
38	Argentina	2.5	76	Morocco	3.05	108	Tanzania	3.4	155	Iraq	5
38	South Korea	2.5	76	Mozambique	3.05	117	Ecuador	3.45	155	North Korea	5

SOURCE: The Heritage Foundation: Index of Economic Freedom 2002, http://www.heritage.org/research/features/index.

to pollute might at some point collide with a citizen's freedom to breathe, and the issue of whose rights and freedoms are paramount becomes central. In addition, simply averaging the scores on these many dimensions to arrive at the "final score" is a questionable practice. It is possible to argue that, for example, a highly government-controlled banking structure is a bigger curb on domestic enterprise than high levels of import tariffs.

Bearing this important reservation in mind, some of the implications of the table prove quite interesting. The six "freest" nations are all small, with an average population of less than 4 million. Hong Kong is a particular puzzle. It became a special administrative region (SAR) of the People's Republic of China (PRC) on July 1, 1997. Four years later, the Heritage Foundation finds that it remains the world's freest economy, although the PRC that now embraces it ranks 122 out of 125. On the whole, it is difficult to draw lessons for the design and conduct of an economic system from the experience of such small states, no matter how rapid their recent growth experience. It is simply not realistic to assume that Russia or India will undergo sustained growth by adopting the same policies as Hong Kong or Singapore.

Economic Competitiveness

Even more ambitious than the attempt to measure economic freedom are the efforts to quantify the **economic competitiveness** of the world's economies. At least two international organizations produce such indices on an annual basis: the World Economic Forum (WEF) and the Institute for International Management Development (IMD) in Lausanne.[11] Table 1.3 is the WEF ranking of nations in terms of a growth competitiveness index (GCI), which aims to measure "the capacity of the national economy to achieve growth over the medium term, controlling for the current level of development."[12]

The GCI evolved from relatively simple beginnings in 1997 and has been refined by Jeffrey Sachs and John W. McArthur.[13] Its objective now is to provide a good predictor of economic growth and competitiveness in the medium term after allowing for the "catchup" potential of less-developed economies—ones that lie somewhat behind the growth frontier. The GCI is a composite of three subindices. The first attempts to quantify an economy's capacity to innovate and to absorb technology transfer. It is the product of 19 pieces of information, some of it hard statistical information and some survey data. The second subindex concerns the quality of public institutions, focusing on the legal environment and corruption. The final component is concerned with the macroeconomic environment.

---

[11]The IMD ranking for its *2002 World Competitiveness Yearbook* is available at http://www02.imd.ch/wcy/ranking/. The United States places first, followed by Finland, Luxembourg, and the Netherlands.
[12]Peter Cornelius, Jennifer Blank, and Fiona Paul, "The Growth Competitiveness Index: Recent Economic Developments and the Prospects for a Sustained Recovery," Chapter 1.1 of *Global Competitiveness Report 2002–2003* (New York: Oxford University Press, 2002), p. 8, available at http://www.weforum.org.
[13]See J. W. McArthur, and J. D. Sachs, "The Growth Competitiveness Index: Measuring Technological Advancement and the Stages of Development," in *The Global Competitiveness Report 2001–2002* (New York: Oxford University Press, 2002).

■ TABLE 1.3

WEF 2002 Growth Competitiveness Index Rankings and 2001 Comparisons

2002 GCI Rank	Country	2002 GCI Score	2001 GCI Rank	2002 GCI Rank	Country	2002 GCI Score	2001 GCI Rank
1	United States	5.93	2	41	Botswana	4.22	*
2	Finland	5.74	1	42	Uruguay	4.19	46
3	Taiwan	5.5	7	43	Costa Rica	4.19	35
4	Singapore	5.42	4	44	Latvia	4.14	47
5	Sweden	5.4	9	45	Mexico	4.11	42
6	Switzerland	5.36	15	46	Brazil	4.09	44
7	Australia	5.36	5	47	Jordan	4.07	45
8	Canada	5.27	3	48	India	4.03	57
9	Norway	5.24	6	49	Slovakia	4.02	40
10	Denmark	5.23	14	50	Panama	4	53
11	United Kingdom	5.17	12	51	Poland	3.98	41
12	Iceland	5.16	16	52	Dominican Republic	3.96	50
13	Japan	5.08	21	53	Namibia	3.93	*
14	Germany	5.06	17	54	Peru	3.87	55
15	Netherlands	5.03	8	55	Morocco	3.86	*
16	New Zealand	5.03	10	56	Colombia	3.86	65
17	Hong Kong	4.93	13	57	El Salvador	3.85	58
18	Austria	4.93	18	58	Croatia	3.8	*
19	Israel	4.93	24	59	Sri Lanka	3.8	61
20	Chile	4.89	27	60	Jamaica	3.76	52
21	Korea	4.89	23	61	Philippines	3.7	48
22	Spain	4.88	22	62	Bulgaria	3.68	59
23	Portugal	4.87	25	63	Argentina	3.66	49
24	Ireland	4.86	11	64	Russia	3.64	63
25	Belgium	4.81	19	65	Vietnam	3.63	60
26	Estonia	4.73	29	66	Romania	3.59	56
27	Malaysia	4.7	30	67	Indonesia	3.36	64
28	Slovenia	4.64	31	68	Venezuela	3.35	62
29	Hungary	4.63	28	69	Turkey	3.31	54
30	France	4.62	20	70	Guatemala	3.2	66
31	Thailand	4.52	33	71	Nigeria	3.17	74
32	South Africa	4.47	34	72	Paraguay	3.14	72
33	China	4.37	39	73	Ecuador	3.13	68
34	Tunisia	4.35	*	74	Bangladesh	3.12	71
35	Mauritius	4.34	32	75	Nicaragua	2.99	73
36	Lithuania	4.33	43	76	Honduras	2.98	70
37	Trinidad	4.32	38	77	Ukraine	0.97	69
38	Greece	4.32	36	78	Bolivia	2.96	67
39	Italy	4.31	26	79	Zimbabwe	2.8	75
40	Czech Republic	4.26	37	80	Haiti	2.47	*

* Not ranked in 2001.
SOURCE: World Economic Forum, *Global Competitiveness Report 2002–2003*.

The WEF continues to revise the methodology and content of the GCI in the attempt to make it a more accurate predictor. It now places more emphasis on the "fundamental drivers of growth"—technology and innovation—while keeping an eye on the quality of public institutions and the macroeconomic environment.

Top honors go to the United States, largely on its technological and innovative muscle. The U.S. institutional framework, however, is not thought of as strong.[14] A close overall second is Finland (the 2001 leader), although it places only twelfth in the Heritage Foundation list. As a group the Nordic countries fare well. The other three (Sweden, Norway, and Denmark) all place in the top 10. A close correlation is also evident between the WEF rankings and membership in the OECD, the association of 30 developed countries sometimes called "the rich nation club." Eight of the top 10, and 23 out of the top 30 on the GCI rankings are OECD members. (Luxembourg, an OECD member, is not ranked by the WEF but certainly would merit a high rank.) These rankings could represent a cultural bias in the assessment of institutional strength, but the OECD group of countries enjoys powerful economic advantages in technology and finance that position them well for future growth. EU countries are strongly placed too; of its 15 current members, only Italy and Greece are out of the top 30.

The WEF views Latin America as still in urgent need of reform. Only Chile figures in the top 20, with Mexico (45), Brazil (46), and Argentina (63), still facing daunting economic challenges. Nor does the WEF provide an optimistic prognosis for the transition economies. The best-placed ex-Soviet country is Estonia (26), but Russia is well down the list at 64 and the Ukraine comes in a disturbing fourth from last. The medium-term outlook for China (33) is judged to be rather mediocre despite its recent impressive growth record, and the prospects for Indonesia—another growth star of the early and mid-1990s—are poor. These economies are "competitive" at the moment only in their ability to exploit relatively cheap labor; they have not established an institutional basis—an economic and political system—that will lead to sustained growth. Further reform and institutional change are indicated.

The Extent of Corruption

One important determinant of the actual character of economic systems was neglected in the economic literature until recently. **Corruption** can mean that actors in the economy experience a real system that differs from the nominally defined system. "Whenever it is pervasive, corruption can deter investment, impede economic development, and undermine political legitimacy."[15] The presence of corruption in an economy can deter economic growth in two ways. First, it acts like a tax, increasing the cost of doing business and transferring income from "legitimate" participants to illegitimate ones. This might not always be the case. For example, tax officials might agree to turn a blind eye to a tax liability in return for a "cut" of the tax savings. Thus the costs for the individual firm might be reduced, because the effective rate of tax is lower than the nominal rate. However, this "selective oversight" in

[14]The United States is ranked 17, behind all of northwest Europe on the quality of its public institutions.

[15]Kimberly Ann Elliot, *Corruption and the Global Economy* (Washington DC: Institute for International Economics, 1997), p. vii.

turn is bound to lead to further inefficiency because the tax rate becomes discriminatory, favoring corrupt firms and channeling resources into the corrupt sector.

Second, corruption increases the level of uncertainty for investors because it puts the firm in a situation in which substantial consequences might result were the letter and spirit of the law to be enforced. Furthermore, the existence and tolerance of corruption opens the door for what economists now term "rent-seeking behavior." This situation occurs when resources are expended in the creation of regulations the sole point of which is to invite the payment of bribes.

Table 1.4 shows the consolidated results of several surveys, largely of foreign businesspeople experienced in dealing with national bureaucracies. Thus, the data describe perceptions of corruption in various nations, rather than actual corrup-

TABLE 1.4

Perceptions of Corruption Index, Selected Countries, 2001

Rank	Country	Score	Standard Deviation	Rank	Country	Score	Standard Deviation
1	Finland	9.9	0.6	28	Estonia	5.6	0.3
2	Denmark	9.5	0.7	29	Italy	5.5	1
3	New Zealand	9.4	0.6	30	Hungary	5.3	0.8
4	Iceland	9.2	1.1	31	Slovenia	5.2	1
5	Singapore	9.2	0.5	32	Uruguay	5.1	0.7
6	Sweden	9	0.5	33	Malaysia	5	0.7
7	Canada	8.9	0.5	34	Jordan	4.9	0.8
8	Netherlands	8.8	0.3	35	Lithuania	4.8	1.5
9	Luxembourg	8.7	0.5	36	South Africa	4.8	0.7
10	Norway	8.6	0.8	37	Costa Rica	4.5	0.7
11	Australia	8.5	0.9	38	Mauritius	4.5	0.7
12	Switzerland	8.4	0.5	39	Greece	4.2	0.6
13	United Kingdom	8.3	0.5	40	South Korea	4.2	0.7
14	Hong Kong	7.9	0.5	41	Peru	4.1	1.1
15	Austria	7.8	0.5	42	Poland	4.1	0.9
16	Israel	7.6	0.3	43	Brazil	4	0.3
17	United States	7.6	0.7	44	Bulgaria	3.9	0.6
18	Chile	7.5	0.6	45	Colombia	3.8	0.6
19	Ireland	7.5	0.3	46	Mexico	3.7	0.6
20	Germany	7.4	0.8	47	Slovak Republic	3.7	0.9
21	Japan	7.1	0.9	48	El Salvador	3.6	0.9
22	Spain	7	0.7	49	Turkey	3.6	0.8
23	France	6.7	0.8	50	Argentina	3.5	0.6
24	Belgium	6.6	0.7	51	China	3.5	0.4
25	Portugal	6.3	0.8	52	Zimbabwe	2.9	1.1
26	Botswana	6	0.5	53	India	2.7	0.5
27	Taiwan	5.9	1	54	Bolivia	2	0.6

NOTE: Only countries for which four or more surveys were extant are included.
SOURCE: Transparency International, Corruption Perceptions Index 2001, available from http://www.transparency.org/cpi/2001/cpi2001.html.

tion, and therefore considerable cultural bias is likely. The scores are standardized. A score of 10 indicates "totally clean" implying an incorruptible bureaucracy and enforcement of the letter of the law. A zero, on the other hand, indicates a totally corrupt country, with bribes to officials at all levels as the normal way of doing business. Because the data are responses to questions about perceptions, a high degree of variability results from each respondent's experience. The column labeled "Standard Deviation" indicates the statistical variance of the results, and is, therefore, an index on the level of agreement among the various sources.

Incorruptibility on this basis seems to be favored by cold climates. Finland appears at the top of the list, again, with its Baltic partners close behind. Singapore is the only non-European nation to appear in the top 10. In general this index shows a fairly close compliance to the WEF measures of competitiveness in Table 1.3. Generally speaking, Western European countries score well, which tends to confirm the existence of a certain amount of cultural bias. Note that among these nations the standard deviation is low, implying that the various surveys generally agreed on the status of these countries. Some exceptions occur among the European Union (EU) countries. The most obvious is Italy, which ranks at 29 with a score of only 5.5. Also interesting is the position of the group of countries that the World Bank calls the high-performing Asian economies (HPAEs). Although many studies stress the importance of an "insulated bureaucracy," able to respond without undue influence of business, this study finds a high perception of corruption in these countries. The best performer, after Singapore, is Japan, with a rank of 21.

OTHER MEANS OF CLASSIFICATION

As well as being classified by their structure, or some measure of competitiveness or freedom, economies may also be classified by the outcomes that the confluence of their history, endowments, and economic systems produces. We frequently speak of economies as being rich or poor, of having egalitarian or discriminatory income patterns, of achieving levels of human capital development, or of being environmentally sound with sustainable economies rather than tending to deplete resources. This approach is in some ways less analytically sound than examining the system, because it neglects the level of development and focuses on the immediate and obvious rather than the structural, but these comparisons are commonly made.

Levels of Income

One of the most obvious and frequently made comparisons of different nations is made by looking at income levels. Table 1.5 shows the division of most of the world's economies by level of recorded gross national product adjusted to dollars using 1993 exchange rates. An immediately apparent feature is that the global distribution of income is highly skewed. A few countries, representing less than 15 percent of the world's population, show high income levels and account for about 77 percent of the total of the world's gross product. At the other end of the scale, 56 percent of the global population lives in relative poverty and accounts for less than 5 percent of the world's gross product.

TABLE 1.5

Distribution of World Economies by Income per Head, 2000

Income Level of Economy	Population (Millions)	Per-Head PPP GNI (2000)	Percent of Total Population	Percent of Total GNI
Low	2,459	$1,990	40.62	10.99
Lower Middle	2,046	$4,580	33.80	21.06
Upper Middle	647	$9,170	10.69	13.32
High	903	$27,450	14.92	55.68
Total	6,054	$7,350	100.0	100.0

SOURCE: The World Bank Development Report 2001/2002.

The group of the 27 countries that are richest in terms of national income per head is by and large the same as the group usually identified as "developed market economies."[16] Only two oil-rich Gulf nations fail to meet that criterion. The membership of this group is also close to rankings of the Organization for Economic Cooperation and Development (OECD), the association composed of 30 of the world's most developed economies. Only six OECD members fail to qualify for the World Bank's higher-income economy classification.[17]

Recent Economic Performance

Another way in which we commonly classify economies is by their recent economic performance. Some possible comparisons, though by no means all, are shown in Table 1.6. Ranking economies by the rate of growth of GDP is quite common. On this basis, of the countries shown, South Korea was the star performer in the 1990s, though as we shall see, it ran into serious problems at the end of the century. Russia, which saw an annual average contraction of 7 percent as it undertook the early stages of transition, was the loser. Similarly, we can look at economies in terms of their negative features—high rates of unemployment or high rates of inflation. Russia also fared badly when we look at the inflation rate. In terms of the rate of unemployment, Japan did best, despite its relatively low rate of GDP growth.

It is common to think of those economies that export more than they import as being successful, although such a "neomercantilist" view of the world is open to

[16]The richest countries in terms of income converted to dollars at international exchange rates, in ascending order, are Slovenia, Greece, Spain, New Zealand, Israel, United Arab Emirates, Ireland, Canada, Italy, Australia, United Kingdom, Hong Kong, Finland, Netherlands, France, Belgium, Sweden, Germany, Austria, Iceland, United States, Singapore, Japan, Denmark, Norway, Switzerland, and Luxembourg. Even within this group considerable variance occurs. Swiss per-head GNP at more than $40,000 is four times greater than that of Slovenia.

[17]The six are the Czech Republic, Hungary, South Korea, Mexico, Poland, and Turkey.

question.[18] A positive balance on current account produces a similarly sized deficit on capital account and means that such an economy is building up its portfolio of assets abroad. However, another way of looking at this situation is that investment opportunities abroad seem more attractive than those at home. Japan managed to run a substantial current account surplus and is a heavy investor in other economies around the world. The United States and, as Table 1.6 shows, the Czech Republic run deficits on current account and are therefore net capital importers. Even though the negative current account balance looks to be a weakness of the U.S. economy it can be seen as a feature of the confidence that the rest of the world places in it, and their willingness to invest there. A good case can be made for the relative strength of the U.S. economy in the 1990s compared with the Japanese despite the latter's positive current account and trade balance.

The Structure of Output

We can also distinguish between economies by looking at the ways in which value is added in the economy. Some economies are relatively heavily agricultural in nature, while in others, manufacturing activity predominates. In other economies (generally but not exclusively highly developed market economies), the service sector provides the greatest amount of employment and value added. Although we can note some clear exceptions, we generally observe a transition that occurs in

■ TABLE 1.6

Economic Indicators for Selected Economies

	United States	Japan	France	Sweden	Czech Republic	Russia	South Korea
Growth of GDP, 1990–98	2.2	1.3	1.5	1.2	–0.2	–7.0	6.2
Inflation, annual rate, 1990–98	2.2	0.4	1.7	2.3	17.1	235.3	5.1
Unemployment, 1990–98	5.4	3.3	10.4	4.8	6.2	12.0	3.3
Current account balance (as % of GDP, 2001)	–4.4	2.5	1.9	2.5	–4.8	1.8	2.4

SOURCE: *World Development Report* 2001, *International Financial Statistics*, September 2002; OECD Economic Outlook, June 2001.

[18]Mercantilism was a economic doctrine favored in the sixteenth century, which held that a positive balance of trade was a policy objective to be pursued, in part because it led to an inflow of precious metals. Neomercantilism is the pursuit of a positive balance of trade and a corresponding accretion of net overseas assets.

parallel with the general level of development, with the least developed societies being more agriculturally based.

Table 1.7 shows, for example, India's high proportion of agricultural output and relatively small manufacturing sector. As per-head incomes rise and the level of development increases, we see first a movement toward manufacturing and industry, and ultimately toward services. This general association of development with falling agriculture and rising services is true both in cross-sectional and historical analyses. An oddity here is that the distinction of having the greatest share of GDP in the agricultural sector actually falls to a European nation, Albania, in which 63 percent of its GDP originates. Although significantly underdeveloped by European standards, Albania is in fact quite highly developed relative to Africa and much of Asia. Its showing here is due to the total collapse of its industrial sector during the 1980s and 1990s, following the downfall of its hard-line socialist regime. Taking a seemingly huge step backwards in terms of development, the share of industry in GDP fell from 45 percent in 1980 to just 18 percent in 1998.

The Distribution of Income

Another way of comparing the economic systems of societies is by looking at how they answer the distributive question, "for whom?" Table 1.8 gives some summary data on the distribution of income in selected countries. The countries are ranked in ascending order of incomes, and the share of income for each quintile of the population is given. In general a discernible tendency for a more even distribution of income can be noted as income rises. Thus it is in the highly developed and rich market economies that we see the most even distribution of income, and within

TABLE 1.7

The Structure of Output in Selected Economies, 2001 (% of GDP originating in each sector)

	Agriculture	Extractive Industry	Manufacturing	Services	Income Per Head (in $, current exchange rates)
Albania	63	18	na	19	810
Benin	39	6	8	47	380
India	28	9	16	46	430
China	17	26	24	33	750
Brazil	9	6	23	62	4,570
Korea	5	12	32	51	7,970
United Kingdom	2	10	21	67	21,400
France	2	7	19	72	24,940
Japan	2	13	24	61	32,380

SOURCE: The World Bank.

■ TABLE 1.8

Distribution of Economic Well-Being (% of GDP per quintile)

	Quintile					PPP*
Country	**First**	**Second**	**Third**	**Fourth**	**Fifth**	**GNP/Head**
India	8.1	11.6	15	19.3	46.1	$1,700
China	5.9	10.2	15.1	22.2	46.6	$3,220
Guatemala	2.1	5.8	10.5	18.6	63	$4,070
Russia	4.4	8.6	13.3	20.1	53.7	$3,950
Brazil	2.5	5.5	10	18.3	63.8	$6,160
Korea	7.5	12.9	17.4	22.9	39.3	$12,270
United Kingdom	6.6	11.5	16.3	22.7	43	$20,640
Netherlands	7.3	12.7	17.2	22.8	40.1	$21,620
Germany	8.2	13.2	17.5	22.7	38.5	$20,810
Sweden	9.6	14.5	18.1	23.2	34.5	$19,480
United States	5.2	10.5	15.6	22.4	46.4	$29,340
Japan	10.6	14.2	17.6	22	35.7	$23,180
Switzerland	6.9	12.7	17.3	22.9	40.3	$26,620

*PPP = Purchasing Power Parity
SOURCE: 2000 World Development Indicators, Table 2.8. Available at World Bank: Washington, DC, 2000.

that group in the welfare state societies of Western Europe—Sweden, the Netherlands, and Germany. Japan's fairly even distribution comes as a result of low unemployment rates.

The most inegalitarian nation shown in Table 1.8 is Brazil, where the richest 20 percent of society account for 63.8 percent of the income, while the poorest 20 percent only receive 2.1 percent of the product. Thus the average "rich individual" in the top 20 percent of society is more than 30 times better off than the average "poor" person. The situation is similar in Guatemala, although per-head incomes are only at 50 percent of Brazil's level. The People's Republic of China, despite its communist heritage, shows a distribution similar to India. The distribution in Russia, after 50 years of socialism, is less egalitarian than "capitalist" South Korea, and every sign concerning the impact of transition and privatization in the Russian economy indicates that the distribution is becoming more skewed. The countries of Western Europe are quite egalitarian in terms of income, and their comprehensive health and education systems, which are not reflected in these income data, tend to reinforce social equality.

The United Kingdom once saw a more uniform income distribution, but it experienced a sharp move away from the all-embracing welfare state, an ideological shift that we now refer to as "Thatcherism." A series of economic changes privatized most of state-owned industry, reduced the progressivity of the tax system, and reduced the coverage of the social safety net. The income profile of the United

Kingdom now more closely resembles that of the United States than the European social democracies. One of the more surprising features of these figures is that Hong Kong now has both a higher income per head and a more even distribution of income than the United Kingdom. However, summary figures of income distribution are incomplete descriptors of economic systems. The figures for Russia and the United Kingdom, for example, are (with the exception of income per head) quite similar.

Economists often use either diagrams or summary statistics to represent the important aspects of the distribution of income. The most frequently used graphical device is the **Lorenz Curve**, illustrated in Figure 1.2. The curve consists of a graph of the cumulative amount of wealth or income enjoyed by some cumulative breakdown of the population. Complete equality would be represented by a straight line across the diagonal of the box, and increasing degrees of inequality are expressed by the amount that the actual curve "bows away" from the diagonal. Hence the relatively egalitarian Swedish income distribution is represented by being closer to the diagonal than the more uneven distribution of income in Brazil.

FIGURE 1.2

Lorenz Curve for Brazil and Sweden

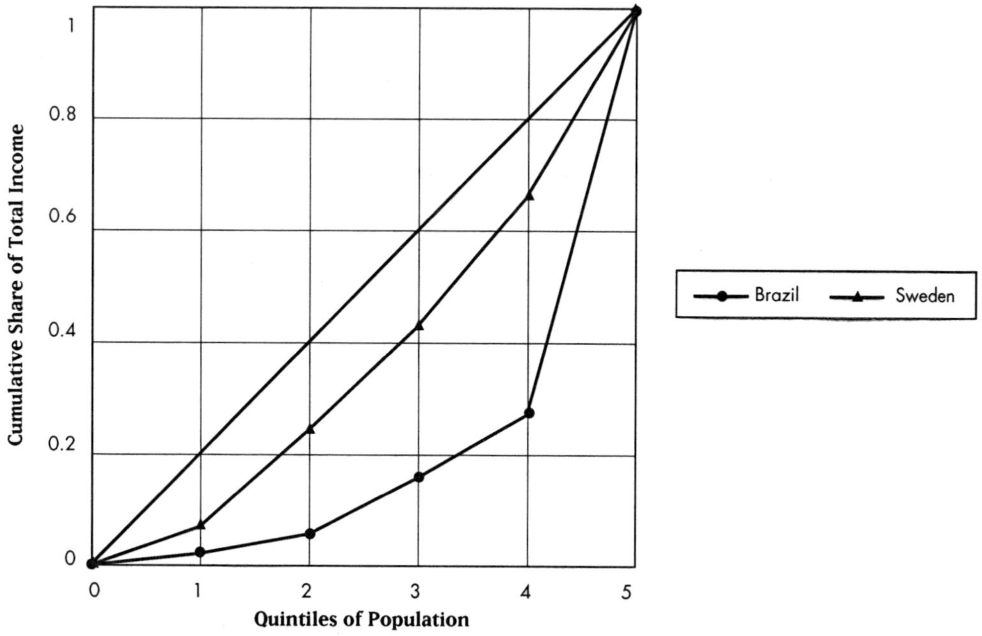

SOURCE: Data from Table 1.8.

Another way of summarizing the income distribution is by the **Gini coefficient**, which is defined by the ratio of the area between the diagonal and the Lorenz curve and the total area under the diagonal. Perfect equality would lead to the Lorenz curve and the diagonal being coincident, and hence the Gini coefficient would be zero. Complete inequality (one individual having all of the income) would lead to a Gini coefficient of 1.

ENVIRONMENTAL SUSTAINABILITY

The indices discussed to this point make no allowance for the long-term sustainability of the system, despite the fact that interest in the **environmental sustainability** of different economic systems continues to increase. The OECD, for example, recently devoted a section of its annual study reports to environmental issues and policies of its member nations. Table 1.9 shows an attempt by Yale Center for Environmental Law and Policy and Columbia University's Center for International Earth Science to establish a commonly based "environmental sustainability index" to indicate how each economic system is coping with environmental issues. The index is derived from some 67 primary variables that include the incidence of acid rain, population density, number of vehicles in a country, and the level of energy use per head. Somewhat surprisingly, Finland sits at the top of the table, again proving that economic competitiveness and respect for the environment need not be competing objectives.[19] Not all European nations perform well; the United Kingdom comes in a dismal 91. The United States, at 46, performs poorly on many indicators but is helped by a low population density, which enables it to weather the effect of environmental degradation due to overpopulation.

ARE SOME SYSTEMS BETTER THAN OTHERS?

In comparative economics it is tempting, and perhaps sometimes appropriate, to look at economies in terms of success and failure. Tables 1.2 to 1.9 provided views of different dimensions of the economic outcomes of particular systems, and show a wide variety of ways to adjudicate success. In comparing economies we must exercise the greatest care. As discussed earlier, an economy is not reducible to simple "production function" terms. The ultimate objective of human endeavor is to achieve well-being, which involves characteristics that transcend the economic. Economists tend to focus their attention on measurable concepts—like material income per head—leaving indicators of the social fabric to sociologists. Today we are increasingly aware of the costs that economic growth can impose on society and on our global environment. It does not mean an inevitable conflict between growth and social welfare, or growth and the environment. It merely emphasizes that we must look at a wide range of outcomes when we attempt to evaluate success and failure.

[19]Finland seems to be in the happy position of coming first in almost every index, including a recently released index of the freedom of the press.

■ TABLE 1.9

The Environmental Sustainability Index

Rank	Country	ESI Score	Rank	Country	ESI Score	Rank	Country	ESI Score
1	Finland	73.9	49	Belarus	52.8	96	Vietnam	45.7
2	Norway	73.0	50	Germany	52.5	97	Cambodia	45.6
3	Sweden	72.6	51	Nicaragua	51.8	98	Guinea	45.3
4	Canada	70.6	52	Papua New Guinea	51.8	99	Nepal	45.2
5	Switzerland	66.5	53	Jordan	51.7	100	Indonesia	45.1
6	Uruguay	66.0	54	Thailand	51.6	101	Burkina Faso	45.0
7	Austria	64.2	55	Sri Lanka	51.3	102	Sudan	44.7
8	Iceland	63.9	56	Kyrgyzstan	51.3	103	Gambia	44.7
9	Costa Rica	63.2	57	Bosnia & Herzegovina	51.3	104	Iran	44.5
10	Latvia	63.0	58	Cuba	51.2	105	Togo	44.3
11	Hungary	62.7	59	Mozambique	51.1	106	Lebanon	43.8
12	Croatia	62.5	60	Greece	50.9	107	Syria	43.6
13	Botswana	61.8	61	Tunisia	50.8	108	Ivory Coast	43.4
14	Slovakia	61.6	62	Turkey	50.8	109	Zaire	43.3
15	Argentina	61.5	63	Israel	50.4	110	Tajikistan	42.4
16	Australia	60.3	64	Ghana	50.2	111	Angola	42.4
17	Panama	60.0	65	Czech Republic	50.2	112	Pakistan	42.1
18	Estonia	60.0	66	Romania	50.0	113	Azerbaijan	41.8
19	New Zealand	59.9	67	Guatemala	49.6	114	Ethiopia	41.8
20	Brazil	59.6	68	Zambia	49.5	115	India	41.6
21	Bolivia	59.4	69	Malaysia	49.5	116	Burundi	41.6
22	Colombia	59.1	70	Algeria	49.4	117	Philippines	41.6
23	Slovenia	58.8	71	Bulgaria	49.3	118	Uzbekistan	41.3
24	Albania	57.9	72	Russia	49.1	119	Rwanda	40.6
25	Paraguay	57.8	73	Morocco	49.1	120	Oman	40.2
26	Namibia	57.4	74	Egypt	48.8	121	Jamaica	40.1
27	Lithuania	57.2	75	South Africa	48.7	122	Trinidad & Tobago	40.1
28	Portugal	57.1	76	El Salvador	48.7	123	Niger	39.4
29	Peru	56.5	77	Uganda	48.7	124	Libya	39.3
30	Bhutan	56.3	78	Japan	48.6	125	Belgium	39.1
31	Laos	56.2	79	Dominican Republic	48.4	126	Mauritania	38.9
32	Denmark	56.2	80	Tanzania	48.1	127	Madagascar	38.8
33	France	55.5	81	Senegal	47.6	128	Guinea-Bissau	38.8
34	Netherlands	55.4	82	Malawi	47.3	129	China	38.5
35	Chile	55.1	83	Italy	47.2	130	Liberia	37.7
36	Gabon	54.9	84	Macedonia	47.2	131	Turkmenistan	37.3
37	Armenia	54.8	85	Mali	47.1	132	Somalia	37.1
38	Ireland	54.8	86	Bangladesh	46.9	133	Nigeria	36.7
39	Moldova	54.5	87	Poland	46.7	134	Sierra Leone	36.5
40	Congo	54.3	88	Kazakhstan	46.5	135	South Korea	35.9
41	Ecuador	54.3	89	Kenya	46.3	136	Ukraine	35.0
42	Mongolia	54.2	90	Myanmar (Burma)	46.2	137	Haiti	34.8
43	Spain	54.1	91	United Kingdom	46.1	138	Saudi Arabia	34.2
44	Central African Rep.	54.1	92	Mexico	45.9	139	Iraq	33.2
45	Zimbabwe	53.2	93	Cameroon	45.9	140	North Korea	32.3
46	United States	53.2	94	Chad	45.7	141	United Arab Em.	25.7
47	Honduras	53.1	95	Benin	45.7	142	Kuwait	23.9
48	Venezuela	53.0						

SOURCE: 2002 Environmental Sustainability Index, Yale Center for Environmental Law and Policy and the Center for International Earth Science Information Network, Columbia University, February, 2002. Available at http://www.ciesin.columbia.edu/indicators/ESI/.

KEY TERMS AND CONCEPTS

Asian Tigers
beliefs
capitalism
cash-flow right
centrally planned economic system
choice of technique
coercion
company unions
control right
corruption
craft or occupational unions
disposal right
distributional decision
economic competitiveness
economic freedom
environmental sustainability
European Union
Gini coefficient
Glass-Steagall Act
households
human capital
indicative planning
industrial capital
instruments
the invisible hand
laws
legality
Lorenz Curve
material incentives
measures
moral persuasion
natural resources
nongovernmental organizations, NGOs
Pacific-Rim capitalism
policies
practices
principal/agent problems
production decision
property rights
regulations
Rhine model
"Robinson Crusoe" economy
Smith, Adam
social democracy
socialism
system
universal banks
welfare state
worker-managed socialism

QUESTIONS FOR DISCUSSION

1. Discuss the nature of national wealth. Where do you believe the greatest source of long-term increase in wealth will lie?
2. Why might a high measure of economic freedom lead to a high growth of GNP?
3. Corruption is often compared to a tax. Why?
4. Why is a more even distribution of income considered an advantage for a society? Can you think of negative aspects of an even distribution of income?

5. Why are NGOs increasing their scope of activity?
6. Why is the contemporary fixation of achieving a favorable balance of trade sometimes called *neomercantilism*?

RESOURCES

The most useful resources to accompany this chapter are those that will give the reader access to comparative data on a range of characteristics for the economies of the world.

Web Sites

Some of the most valuable resources to a researcher, because they are current, easily accessible, and by and large free, are the Web pages of the major international organizations. The most useful single link is perhaps the page of links for the United Nations system, which can be found at http://www.unsystem.org/. It provides links to the Web pages of all of the organizations of the United Nations system. These links are useful in researching the economic structure and system of a country, but the most relevant for the economist, and likely to be among the most durable links, are the major multinational organizations.

Multilateral Agencies

The International Monetary Fund (IMF) .... http://www.imf.org/
Particularly valuable at this useful site are the downloadable full-text versions of the working paper and country reports series. This site is a necessary first stop for any research project whether topical or country based. Current data and some interesting studies are available through the access to a free downloadable version of *World Economic Outlook.*

The World Bank (IBRD) .... http://www.worldbank.org/
At this useful site for research on developed and developing economies, clicking on "publications" will connect the reader with the Digital Library, an online library of full-text publications and summaries of major World Bank publications, feature articles, and abstracts from World Bank journals.

The World Trade Organization (WTO) .... http://www.wto.org/
Although not as valuable a resource as the other United Nations organizations for the study of comparative economics, it offers a good place to check on issues such as the environment, intellectual property disputes, and regional trade issues. A first-rate document dissemination facility (DDF).

The United Nations Development Programme (UNDP) .... http://www.undp.org/
This excellent Web page provides access to both the Human Development Report (HDR) and to a large number of national Human Development Reports. The HDR gives access to the Human Development Index, which is an important supplement to GDP statistics and indices of competitiveness in evaluating economic success. The nations reports are useful because they generally include background pieces and descriptions of economic structure and recent economic history. Coverage is, however, patchy—very good for Europe East and West but poor for Asia and the Pacific.

Organisation for Economic Co-Operation and Development .... http://www.oecd.org/
Unlike the preceding sites, the OECD is not a part of the United Nations system but it is probably the best site available for information on developed countries. The statistical

series are comprehensive and standardized, and the OECD Surveys include a wealth of information on economic systems, institutions, policies, and prospects.

Regional Commissions of the UN

The Regional Economic Commissions of the United Nations are responsible for monitoring and analyzing economic developments by region. They provide useful country data and analysis, much of which can be obtained from their Web sites.

Economic Commission for Africa (ECA) .... http://www.uneca.org/
This site, a good starting point for work on liberalization and reform in Africa, allows free access to the ECA's annual report, a useful library, and good links.

Economic Commission for Europe (ECE) .... http://www.unece.org/
This site is excellent for research on recent developments in both the transition economies of Eastern Europe and the member nation of the European Union. Much of the annual survey of the ECE, which covers both western and eastern Europe, is accessible from this site as well as important selected charts and tables.

Economic Commission for Latin America and the Caribbean (ECLAC)..http://www.eclac.cl/
For a good jumping off point for research on Latin America, *The Annual Survey* is available here and is a thoughtful document, with useful statistical appendices and tables.

Economic and Social Commission for Asia and the Pacific (ESCAP)..http://www.unescap.org/
The Annual Survey provides a good overview of the region, and the downloadable publications are an excellent source for country-by-country analysis of financial sector reform in the wake of the Asian financial crisis.

For studies on particular aspects of comparative economics the following Web sites of specific UN agencies with functional rather than general responsibilities are valuable:

Food and Agriculture Organization of the United Nations (FAO)..... http://www.fao.org/

International Labour Organization (ILO) ....http://www.ilo.org/

Multilateral Investment Guarantee Agency (MIGA) .... http://www.miga.org/

UN Conference on Trade and Development (UNCTAD) .... http://www.unctad.org/

UN Development Fund for Women (UNIFEM) .... http://www.unifem.org/

UN Educational, Scientific and Cultural Organization (UNESCO) ....http://www.unesco.org/

UN Environment Programme (UNEP).. http://www.unep.org/

UN Foundation .... http://www.unfoundation.org/

UN Industrial Development Organization (UNIDO)..................... http://www.unido.org/

UN Research Institute for Social Development (UNRISD)........... http://www.unrisd.org/

UN Human Settlements Programme ....http://www.unhabitat.org/

World Intellectual Property Organization (WIPO) .... http://www.wipo.int/

Other Web Sites

Columbia International Affairs Online (CIAO) .... http://www.ciaonet.org/

European Bank for Reconstruction and Development (EBRD)...... http://www.ebrd.com/

Heritage Foundation .... http://www.heritage.org/
Transparency International .... http://www.transparency.de/
World Economic Forum .... http://www.weforum.org/
Center for International Earth Science Information Network ....
....http//www.ciesin.columbia.edu/indicators/esi

Books and Articles

Brademas, J., and F. Heimann. "Tackling International Corruption." *Foreign Affairs,* September 1998, 17–23. Assessment of the consequence of corruption and the possibilities of reform to tackle it.

Elliot, Kimberley Ann. *Corruption and the Global Economy.* Washington, DC: Institute for International Economics, 1997. Collection of good readings concerning corruption. Particularly good is Paulo Mauro's "Cross Country Analysis," chapter 4. Comprehensive references and data sources.

Fukuyama, Francis. *Trust: The Social Virtues and the Creation of Prosperity.* New York: Free Press, 1995. Argues that social capital is vital for rapid economic development.

O'Driscoll, Gerald P. Jr., Kim R. Holmes, and Mary Anastasia O'Grady. *The 2002 Index of Economic Freedom.* Washington, DC: Heritage Foundation, 2002. The source of the Index of Economic Freedom.

Pearce, David W., and Jeremy J. Warford. *World without End: Economics, Environment and Sustainable Development: A Summary.* Washington, DC: World Bank, 1998.

Stapenhurst, Rick, and Sahr J. Kpundeh (eds.). *Curbing Corruption: Toward a Model for Building National Integrity.* Washington, DC: World Bank Institute Development Studies, 1999.

Tanzi, Vito. "Corruption Around the World Causes, Consequences, Scope, and Cures." Downloadable from the IMF site at http://www.imf.org/external/pubs/CAT/longres.cfm?sk52583.0.

United Nations Development Programme. *Human Development Report.* New York: Oxford University Press, 2002. A wealth of comparative data, excellent references, and each year tackles a different theme; 2002 dealt with deepening democracy. The WDR Web site can be accessed at http://www.undp.org.

World Bank. *Helping Countries Combat Corruption: The Role of the World Bank.* A downloadable synopsis is available from the World Bank site at http://www.worldbank.org/html/extdr/corruptn/coridx.htm.

World Bank. *World Development Indicators.* Washington, DC: World Bank, 1999. Useful compendium of data for developing countries.

World Bank. *World Development Report.* New York: Oxford University Press, 2002. Excellent source for all sorts of data. Excellent bibliography and each year a different theme; 2002 was concerned with the sustainable development.

Worldwatch Institute. *State of the World,* 2003. New York: W. W. Norton and Company, 2003. An annual assessment of environmental developments from an environmentalist viewpoint. Some good country data.

2

THE ROOTS OF ECONOMIC SYSTEMS

WHY AND HOW ECONOMIC INSTITUTIONS CHANGE

Economic systems are not static. A glance at history, even the history of merely the past decade, shows us that systemic change is relatively frequent. New institutions may be created and old ones terminated, and the rights of the various constituent groups and individuals of society with respect to property, economic activity, or mobility may be altered. The extent of government ownership in the productive sphere is by no means constant and varies with "privatization" (the current trend) and its converse "nationalization." Governments can change, sometimes in dramatic fashion, and new governments may bring with them an entirely new philosophical approach to the objectives of the system or the new ways of addressing those objectives. Consequently, they set about altering the web of laws and regulations that govern economic activity. Industries are taken into public ownership, or "privatized." Controls over output and prices may be tightened or relaxed.

Two questions are of great and enduring interest to students of comparative economics:

Why do economic systems change?

How do they change?

The answer to the first question is often considered to lie within two dynamics: **technological change** and **population growth**. However, neither of these is truly exogenous to the economic system and therefore cannot be regarded wholly as an external agent of change. In fact, we can see that often both the direction and pace of technology and population dynamics are influenced to a considerable degree by the nature of the economic system. For example, it can be argued that *laissez faire* capitalism rewards the kind of technical change that favors small enterprise, and therefore, as a system, it tends to foster relatively small-scale technology. Socialism, on the other hand, faces criticism both for being inimical to economic change and, where change occurred, biased to large-scale technology.

On the population side, we know that relatively less-developed societies with little provision for a social safety net tend to be characterized by high birthrates, because parents need some surviving offspring to provide care in their old age. Therefore the introduction of even modest public health measures leads to rapid population growth, at least in the short run, before societies adjust their behavior and lower the birthrate in response to changed circumstances. In subsequent sections we look at how changing technology and population are historically linked with substantial shifts in the economic system.

Evolutionary and Revolutionary Change

Studying development and change in economic systems in historical context prompts the observation that at certain points in time and space, change seems to be rapid. At other points it is much slower and even, more in line with our understanding of evolution in natural history. From this study, two schools of thought about economic change emerged. Adherents of the **evolutionary school** stress the gradual nature of change. They see shifts in an economic system as a process of gradual accommodation to the movements in technology, the resource base, and population through small continuous innovations in the institutions of the system and in the laws that govern their interaction. Problems are resolved by incremental adjustments. Societal progress is slow and, as once observed about evolution in nature, tends to "make no leaps."

In contrast to the gradualism of the evolutionist, the nineteenth-century philosopher and economist Karl Marx offered a theory of the revolutionary **laws of motion**. Marx's vision of social dynamics, like that of evolutionists, was linear. Each form of social organization gave way to a successor, in a progressive and irreversible way, but in Marx's view change tended to occur discontinuously, with periods of rapid change punctuating periods of relative constancy.

Marx's conception of the causality of social change lay in material factors. As populations grew and technology advanced, the growth of material output became constrained by the existing system of economic and social organization. These changes led to a growing tension between the societal groups that dominated the established economic system and those who would benefit from a new set of arrangements. The tension then produced antagonism, struggle, and eventually (generally after a series of crises and false starts) rapid revolutionary change. The old social order was overthrown and replaced by one better suited to maximize social output in the changed situation.

As a result of this revolution originating in material factors, the whole **superstructure** of society changed. This shift included not only political relations (who held the power and who governed) but also law, culture, custom, and even religion. The development of the social system grew out of the economic change. We can see in the thought of both the evolutionists and Marxists parallels to the theories of biological evolution propounded by Darwin. As conditions alter, the existing economic system becomes ill adapted to the maximization of output. The consequence is growing social stress. In both cases change results. In the evolutionary view it is creeping and may be tenuous, reversible, and experimental. In the other, the Marxian view, it is sweeping and total. Of course, the significant departure from biological Darwinism is that economic systems are human-made and involve therefore some human design and thought. Although natural selection occurs as the result of unplanned changes that favor the species that happen to be better suited, the change of economic system can be conscious, thoughtful, and imitative of changes that occurred elsewhere.

ECONOMIC SYSTEMS IN HISTORICAL PERSPECTIVE[1]

As a precursor to the study of the economies that exist today, it is useful to review, if only in bare outline, the procession and variety of economic systems that existed through history. In each instance we will try to outline briefly the structure of each system and to ask the following questions: What forces led these systems to change? How did that change occur? How did the change resolve the problems?

Hunter-Gatherer Societies

We begin with a look at the most primitive economic organization: the hunter-gatherer society. Our knowledge of the precise social organization of this prehistoric world is imperfect, but we can make some generalizations. We know that it was in this form of social organization that humankind existed for most of its time on earth. All successive forms of social and economic organization are crowded into the last 9,000 years or so. In fact, a few isolated hunter-gatherer societies survived until the present age.

At the heart of a hunter-gatherer system must lie the sustainability of the environment in which it exists. If the natural vegetative resources of the land are overpicked, or if the animal stocks are overhunted, then the equilibrium of such a system is threatened. Overexploitation of renewable resources arises from two roots. One lies in advancing technology; superior hunting techniques and more advanced tools and weapons take a greater toll of animal stocks and may perhaps encourage waste. The other cause lies in the growth of population. Greater numbers will place greater demands on resources. Of course, these two trends are closely related. The higher productivity associated with superior technology allows the population to enjoy living standards above subsistence, and consequently it expands. However, when overexploitation is encountered the greater difficulty of gathering food and hunting in a depleted environment causes productivity to fall. When average social productivity falls below subsistence level, the population will shrink, which in turn allows resources to replenish, generating a new cycle of potentially increased productivity. This cycle of growth and contraction of human and animal populations was the rule for many thousands of years.

Pastoral and Agrarian Societies

About 9,000 years ago, we know that some hunters began to switch to settled farming. This shift probably took the form of scratching a cultivable garden within the forest and tending edible plants. It also involved the primitive domestication of animals. Initially such enterprise provided a living only barely above subsistence, but it did enable survival in the face of increased demands on natural resources. Over time, learning from experience led to improved technique, and the develop-

[1]This section is concerned with the evolution of societies in historical perspective and can be omitted without damaging the overall flow of the text. It is recommended that any reader rejoin the discussion with "Contemporary Economic Systems" on page 57.

ment of better seed and livestock resulted in rising productivity. In turn, the growth in agricultural communities accelerated.

At this point in history, a series of social innovations could occur. First, the population engaged in agriculture generated a surplus that enabled a greater division of labor. The excess produce of the farmers could support artisans, priests, soldiers, lawyers, and doctors. In addition, the economic system and the legal framework within which it operated necessarily became more complex. A settled agricultural society requires a different set of institutions and more comprehensive laws than those needed to govern the hunter-gatherer societies. Whereas in the earlier society property was largely communal and resources open to all, in a farming society property rights become much more important. Some permanence in the tenure on the land is essential, if only between the planting season and harvest. Much longer tenure is desirable if land improvement is to be effected. Some authority competent to enforce property rights and adjudicate disputes is vital. The arrival of settled agriculture also allowed the creation of a greater social surplus than what was feasible in hunter-gatherer societies. This surplus, in turn, allowed the creation of a nobility, professional, and artisan classes that provided consumer goods and services, a religious establishment, and a permanent military.

"Oriental Despotism"

As the population of agrarian societies grew, pressure on resources increased. One of those resources, water, was essential to maintain the highly productive agriculture necessary to support the population. The social order and high productivity in agriculture depended on the preservation of the water supply for irrigation, making clear definition and enforcement of water rights imperative. In the view of Marx and others, this dependence on irrigation was the explanation of the durable, wealthy but inequitable states of Asia.[2]

In the nations of South and Eastern Asia, the organization and management of the water supply was especially important. Successful irrigation meant the difference between a highly populous and productive community and a sparsely inhabited and precarious subsistence economy. Irrigation projects were characterized by large economies of scale and required considerable, though well-rewarded, social investment. Consequently, a large public works bureaucracy emerged, with the resources and expertise to develop and maintain this water. It was precisely the great social return of these projects that accounted for what Karl Marx called **Oriental despotism** in Eastern **"hydraulic" societies**. The ruler and the associated bureaucracy were able to expropriate the greater part of the produce of society because that produce was dependent on the success of the irrigation project. The populace, aware of the importance of hydraulic organization and the great benefits provided, was powerless in the face of a bureaucracy that held a monopoly on organization and expertise as well as military power. It was forced to acquiesce to confiscatory rates of taxation.

---

[2]See especially Karl August Wittfogel, *Oriental Despotism: A Comparative Study of Total Power* (New Haven: Yale University Press, 1957), which embodies his seminal views on the relevance of water to political structure.

Classical Slave Economies

In Europe the great classical societies of Greece and Rome were less dependent on irrigation for agriculture. They relied to a much larger degree on the institution of slavery. Although the Greek city-states are frequently touted as the cradles of democracy, participation in political decision making was in fact highly circumscribed. Most residents of Greek cities had no say in their policy or destiny. The ratio of slaves to free citizen in Athens was perhaps as high as 18 to 1 at the height of its prosperity. In Rome, which was a highly centralized empire that supported a large urban population, production in agriculture was dominated by the *latifundia.* These large farms operated on a slave-labor plantation system. Slaves also formed the basic labor supply in mining, construction, and manufacturing, as well as supplying services within the household.

Although now we regard the institution as morally deplorable and therefore nonviable under any circumstances, the efficiency of slavery as an economic system depends on certain specific conditions. The objective of a slave system is to obtain labor at rates below those that would pertain under a market system of free labor. Where markets are competitive and labor is mobile, each worker is paid a wage approximate to his or her marginal productivity. Where labor is plentiful relative to land and capital, the marginal product of labor will be low and the wage will tend in the long run to move toward subsistence, the wage that ensures the survival and replication of the labor stock and no more. In such a situation slavery will not be viable because "free labor" may be had for an amount roughly equal to the subsistence wage. In contrast, slavery is likely to flourish in circumstances where labor is in short supply relative to capital and land, because then the marginal product of labor is high. Under such circumstances the potential savings in labor costs are likely to be the greatest.

However, slavery does involve costs that the employment of free labor does not, principally the cost of purchase and the cost of supervision. Purchase can be regarded as a form of capital investment. Supervisory costs consist of two components. The first involves protecting the investment from flight, theft, and illness. The second can be looked on as a form of the "agency problem" that was briefly discussed in Chapter 1. All users of labor face agency problems in getting workers to perform, to work as if they could appropriate all of the income from increased productivity. Overseers, timeclocks, and the practice of piecework all function to solve the agency problem in a free market. Under slavery these problems are more acute.

The centrality of supervision costs means that slavery is likely to be most enduring within a system characterized by a strong centralized authority, no refuge for slaves within or close to the slave society, and racial or ethnic distinction between the "free" population and slaves. When the Roman Empire was well ordered, the power of the state minimized the private costs of supervision. However, as centralized authority in Rome began to collapse under the weight of incursions by wandering tribes from the Eurasian heartland, the private costs of supervision and enforcement rose and the slave problem contributed considerably to Rome's difficulties and ultimate fall.

The Feudal System

In the aftermath of the collapse of the Western Roman Empire, Western European society became highly disordered. The institution of slavery was replaced by that of serfdom within the context of the feudal system. **Feudalism** was the dominant system of political and economic organization in Western Europe for a period of roughly 1,000 years. Although the duration of feudalism differed in different territories or regions, in broad terms we can think of it as persisting from the fall of Rome and the onset of the so-called Dark Ages of western Europe (in the fifth century) until the establishment of nation-states in about the sixteenth century. Feudalism therefore thrived in a situation where centralized control was absent, along with most of the restraints on individual behavior.

The basis of feudalism was one of hierarchical personal obligation, which, although largely determined by power, was to some extent reciprocal. In return for the provision of protection, which was necessary in such a chaotic society, individuals occupying the lower ranks of the social pyramid were required to pay rent in goods and service to those higher up. The rapaciousness of the higher-ups was curbed only by the possibility of revolt by the lower orders and the necessity of at least preserving the population and social capital for replication in the next time period. An additional constraint in some circumstances was the moderating doctrines of religion.

In feudal theory, all land was ultimately at the disposition of the monarch, but the effective title of estates was parceled out to the nobility as a reward for past services rendered and to ensure future loyalty. The upper echelons of the nobility enjoyed relatively autonomous control of their locality and its microeconomy. They in turn delegated property rights and political jurisdiction to a lower level of aristocracy, as a reward for tribute, loyalty, and service.

The nobility was to a great extent a self-appointed class that relied on power and coercion to secure its position. Herman Schwartz somewhat flippantly described them as

> [A] kind of dispersed biker gang: armor, horses, and their propensity to resort to violence elevated them above most of the rest of the population in the same way as leather and Harleys elevate movie bikers where state authority is absent.[3]

At the bottom of the social pyramid was the peasantry. In "typical" European society this class comprised about 90 percent of the rural population. Substantial variation was due to the differential productivity of the land and the peasants. Broadly speaking, higher productivity meant more superstructure (nobles, warriors, priests, etc.) could be supported. The peasantry itself was not a monolithic class; within it lay distinct gradations. The serfs (also called villeins), who constituted the most numerous group, could claim only limited property and personal rights. Serfdom as an institution differed from slavery (as, for example, in the United States) in that the serfs were regarded as part of the property of the *demesne*, or manor, and therefore could not be alienated from it by being sold in the market. Consequently the family under serfdom was a rather more stable institution than under slavery, but the lives and very existence of serfs depended on the frequently capricious and arbitrary rule of the lord. Above them in the social pyramid lay a stratum of free or

[3]See Herman Schwartz, *States Versus Markets: History, Geography, and the Development of International Political Economy* (New York: St. Martin's Press, 1994).

landed peasants, who held rights to a small plot of land, but who also owed service to the aristocrat and were just as dependent on his rule and protection.

The feudal economy was a command economy in most of its attributes, but with both centralized and decentralized aspects. At the state level, the monarch was responsible for a limited but important set of decisions, particularly over external trade, which was almost always under direct state control and usually organized as a licensed or sanctioned monopoly of the monarchs. In addition, the monarch also frequently designated the monopoly producer of certain important productive activities, or issued monopoly licenses for others to engage in them. These arrangements usually covered industries such as shipyards, ceramic factories, and armories. Resources flowed to the crown via monetary taxation, in-kind tribute of goods, and the conscription of labor for military and other service. The high frictional cost of transportation meant that most economic activity was local. Both economic hinterlands and political jurisdictions tended to be restricted to the feasible limit of a day's travel on foot or by wagon, a radius of roughly 10 miles in all directions around a central point. The manor and the village were relatively self-sufficient units in which economic activity fell largely under the direction of the lord of the manor or in many cases church authority (where the religious establishment was a major landowner).

The business of the manor and the village was largely agricultural. The basic organization of the northwest European manorial system will be familiar to most readers. The arable land of the village was commonly divided into three fields, one of which lay fallow each year. The land within the fields was divided into strips, which were allocated among the landed peasantry. Livestock was grazed on common land.

The landlords extracted their income in two ways: (1) by appropriating goods in kind, as rent, and in return for services, especially milling grain, and (2) by labor service provided as work on the aristocrat's lands. Market activity was limited, but landed peasants were able to sell the surplus produced in excess of the demands of the lord, the church, and their own subsistence, and could through purchase or barter acquire those goods (clothing, tools, etc.) that they were unable to produce themselves.

In summary, the important economic decisions were made by the commands of the monarchy and nobility: they controlled what was produced, how it was produced, and who then gleaned the benefit. In terms of incentives, the dominant mode was coercion, although elements of both moral and material incentives may be found. Some form of sharecropping was frequently practiced, giving the peasantry an incentive to maximize output in order to retain the most they could for consumption and sale in the market. Such a system did embody a material incentive, though the heavy "tax rate" tended to dull it. Great emphasis was placed by society, and especially by the church, on social order, adding an element of moral incentive. However, when all was said and done, the peasant worked for, and gave goods to, the lord of the manor because no alternative existed. The nobility's monopoly on force that could be used to coerce the peasant was also necessary to protect that same peasant from the predations of others.

Feudalism as a static economic and social system evolved following the wreck of the Roman Empire and the collapse of imperial order. Little within the system was oriented to, or supportive of, economic growth or development. The nobility were consumers rather than investors, and any economic surplus generated found its way into castles, churches, and military adventurism rather than into capital improvements to increase economic output in the long run. The uncertain status of the peasant and the absence of long-term tenure of any given piece of land under the strip system made land improvement by the peasant pointless. The authority of the monarch was limited by the power of the nobility and little impetus could come from the center.

Commercial activity as we know it today was largely incompatible with feudalism. The greatest European commercial center in the early Middle Ages was Venice, because of steps it took to separate itself from the feudal states of Western Europe, including its insular location and the maintenance of a deliberately and strategically vague allegiance to Byzantium. Within Venice, commercial activity, markets, and banking all began to thrive and to throw out seeds that eventually provided the impetus for a broader commercial revolution.

Mercantilism

Although it proved to be a durable system, lasting for about 1,000 years in parts of Western Europe, feudalism's basic economic weaknesses put it under attack from two directions. On the one hand, monarchs sought to consolidate their own power and to increase their own wealth by controlling more fully the territories nominally under their rule. On the other, the growth of market economies challenged the established system of labor servitude.

The extension of the control, and therefore the wealth, of the monarch could only be achieved by breaking the grip of the nobility on the microeconomies that existed within the state. In this respect the monarchy was assisted by change in military technology. The power of the feudal nobility to resist a centralized state derived from two sources: the fighting potential of the armored, mounted knight, and the defensive strength of the castle. The one enabled the wealthy aristocrat to be the physical superior of the unmounted fighter; the other gave the aristocrat the ability to withstand sieges and therefore to flaunt the authority of the monarchy. The arrival of gunpowder devalued both of these advantages. An aggressive monarch with a professional army and an artillery siege train was in a position to reduce any disruptive and defiant magnate. This capability cleared the way for the creation of nation-states, which established common currencies, standardized weights and measures, and uniform laws. Such states also experienced fewer internal obstacles to trade. Costly transportation still posed a problem, but much more effective division of labor was possible under a unified state. Similarly, the use of firearms became the great equalizer, because the knight became easy prey for the foot soldier.[4]

Feudalism was also under attack from within. As trade slowly revived, the potential to create wealth by arbitrage and exchange was realized and grasped by

---

[4]In Japan, feudalism lasted longer in part because firearms were prohibited, extending the *samurai* as a social class until the late nineteenth century.

a growing merchant class. Feudalism—static, consumption-oriented, and organized in geographically limited microeconomies—was antithetical to this growth of trade. Commercialism defied the existing social order by putting this wealth in the hands of commoners. When the barony attempted to confiscate the growing wealth of the merchants, those merchants turned directly to the monarch for protection. As a result, commercial activity became increasingly located in towns whose royal charters set them apart from the power of the nobility.

The growth of towns brought with it a surge in the demand for labor, and plunged the stake into the heart of feudalism—the servile system. The marginal productivity of urban employment was certainly greater than that of the serf on the manor. Town-based employers were inclined, and had an incentive, to pay workers more than laborers could receive from the rural aristocrats. Before the growth and independence of towns, a serf had no alternative to remaining on the manor, depending on a meager income and the protection of the lord. With the emergence of urban centers, flight to towns brought the prospect of freedom, independence, and a higher real standard of living. Furthermore, the *bourgeoisie*[5] were reluctant to return the serf to the manor for punishment and defied the feudal magnates. In Germany the change was expressed by the phrase *Stadtluft macht frei*—"the air of the cities makes one free." These growing towns afforded new opportunities to the peasant classes.

Competition between town and country, between capitalism and feudalism, intensified as a result of the epidemics of the "Black Death" in the fourteenth century. In many districts of Europe half of the population was lost, producing an acute shortage of labor. The surviving serfs were the beneficiaries of the competing needs of the countryside and the town. Land was so plentiful relative to labor that much of it fell out of production. The dramatic lack of rural labor caused the solidarity of the system to break down. Runaway serfs were welcomed on the land of other aristocrats and were seldom returned to their own manors. In the towns, even harder hit than the countryside by the pestilence, labor shortages pushed up wages and increased the lure to former serfs. Serfdom declined and was replaced by a much more freely operating labor market in much of Europe.[6] The simultaneous movement toward the establishment of markets and the blending of the microeconomies into a larger economic space produced the collapse of feudalism.

Mercantilism Defined The confluence of the state-building activities of the monarchy and the growing power and influence of the trading classes characterizes the system that we call "mercantile." The term **mercantilism** can be interpreted as meaning "the doctrine of merchants," which is perhaps its most literal rendering. It eventually came to mean something more complex, although loose application of the term resulted in a rather confused discussion.

Some of this confusion is due to the lack of any systematic statement of mercantilist theory by its adherents. Important arguments were laid out by pamphleteers

[5]Literally, *bourgeoisie* means "the townspeople," although it later came to have class connotations.
[6]Further east in Europe less change was seen in the institution of serfdom. In Russia the serfs were not freed until the 1860s.

usually working on behalf of a merchant lobby,[7] but they are incomplete and often conflicting. Our own understanding of mercantilism stems from the straw man created by Adam Smith in the *Wealth of Nations*, a rather coarse caricature intended to be easily demolished. In this work Smith advocated a new system better suited to the needs of an increasingly industrialized society. As a result of Smith's work, many people consider "mercantilists" as rather foolish people who failed to distinguish between real national wealth and a heap of precious metal.

What then do we mean by the term *mercantilism*? First, it involves an internal project, the creation of an integrated economic space greater than the size of the microeconomies that characterized the feudal system. In this sense the problems were quite similar to those faced in the construction of the European Union today, in that mercantilism involved the removal of fiscal and physical barriers to trade, the acceptance of a common legal code, a movement toward a common currency, and the use of a common language. Second, mercantilism is usually thought of as supporting state involvement in the development of the national economy. Thus it fell to the state to establish industries where they were lacking, especially where import substitution was possible, as well as to grant subsidies and monopolies to key industries.

Third, a positive balance of trade was desirable. In the eyes of the monarch the purpose of overseas trade was to increase national wealth, which could be directed to exert strategic influence. Even though today it might be said that the object of trade in such a system is to raise living standards by bringing plentiful cheap goods into the country and to effect a more efficient global division of labor, such a purpose was not the case under the mercantilist system. Thus a prime element was the achievement of a "favorable" **balance of trade**, or an inflow of precious metals into the country. The difference in the value between exports and imports would be settled by this inflow of precious metals, which was considered important because it could be taxed, borrowed, or otherwise acquired by the state and used to finance statecraft, conspicuous consumption, or military expenditure. This situation is the origin of the famous phrase that mercantile policy "put power [of the State] before plenty [for the individual]."

The preoccupation with the trade balance was one of the features of mercantile thought that attracted Adam Smith's derision in the *Wealth of Nations*, in which he accused mercantilists of confusing money with national wealth. Smith was at pains to explain in his seminal work that the wealth of nations lay in productive capacity, not in fallow stocks of precious metal. As a doctrine, trade fetishism was also taken to extreme by two branch "schools" of the mercantilist tree. "Bullionists" genuinely thought that the real source of a nation's wealth was the stock of precious metal within the country, rather than the productive capacity. "Cameralists" focused their attention on the fiscal position of the state, judging well-being to be measured essentially by the ability to tax and the accumulated stock of fiscal surpluses.

[7] *England's Treasure by Foreign Trade*, by Thomas Mun, a merchant, is one of the best known of these tracts. Although mainly directed at attacking legislation suggested to curb bullion export, it lays out a clear picture of the benefit of trade in national development. Available at http://socserv2.socsci.mcmaster.ca/econ/ugcm/3ll3/mun/treasure.txt.

Merchants, however, were generally not adherents of either of these extremes, and in England they lobbied against legislation advanced by bullionists that would outlaw the export of precious metals. Rather, merchants favored the positive trade balance because it acted to expand and therefore, in modern terms, "loosen" the money supply. A growing money supply led both to low interest rates and a higher rate of inflation than otherwise would prevail. Both of these factors were advantageous to mercantile interests, because traders were generally debt-financed and held a substantial inventory of goods.

The policy of promoting a positive balance of payments led in part to the aggressive acquisition of overseas possessions and colonies, which characterized the mercantile system. Incorporating into the home country, or "metropolis," territories that could produce raw materials not available at home (e.g., tropical produce) reduced the need for costly imports and for financing them with bullion. The preoccupation with trade balance also led to the widespread use of subsidies (or "bounties") for production and export. Goods that cost more to produce domestically than the prevailing price in the outside world became profitable for local producers; this practice saved bullion from foreign exchange while requiring taxation to raise the necessary subsidies.

A fourth premise of mercantilism was the establishment of a positive **balance of employment**. In simple terms, it prescribed that the labor content of exports should be greater than that of imports. Correspondingly, the most advantageous form of trade was to exchange domestically produced manufactured goods for foreign-produced raw materials, which in contemporary terms we can see as a desire to maximize value added and skilled employment in the metropolis. Such a policy would lead to a maximization of both the domestic population and the skill level embodied in that population. It led therefore to a policy of restricting, or in some cases reversing, the economic development of colonial possessions. To take an example from the British Empire, extensive legislation (the Iron Act, the Woolen Act, and the Hat Act) sought to curb development of the manufacturing industry in the American colonies in order to retain them as export markets for goods made in Britain itself. In another example, parallel policies actually led to the "undevelopment" of the possessions in India, by the destruction of textile production and the conversion of India into a producer of raw material alone.

Central to this strategy of maximizing growth within mercantilist practice were the measures that sought to control the direction of trade and the means by which trade was to be conducted. In England these measures took the form of a series of "navigation acts," but parallels are to be found in Spain, Portugal, and France. The earliest navigation acts in England determined that all trade to and from the nation should be carried in vessels of English registry; this legislation had the effect of strengthening demand for, and therefore the size and profitability of, the merchant marine. Subsequent acts ensured that all colonial imports and exports (often including those with other colonies) should be conducted through the metropolis.

It was also thought economically sensible to discourage economic development in the colonies, keeping them as suppliers of raw materials alone and not as competitors in the production of finished products. To this end, laws often prohibited the development of manufacturing industry and even certain kinds of agriculture in the colonies.[8]

Even though Adam Smith was able to attack the mercantile system to good effect, at least as far as England was concerned, many nations continue to pursue the basic ideas of mercantilism, among them late industrializing nations that successfully crossed the divide from "less developed" to "developed" status.[9] The essential ingredients introduced here (economic unification, state promotion of industry, favoring exports, discouraging imports, and an attempt to foster high value-added manufacturing) are all policies espoused by one country or another today. Indeed mercantilism seems to be a successful policy for the second best. The preeminent power of the seventeenth century was the Netherlands, which had little use for the close management of trade or state promotion of industry that lay at the heart of the mercantile system as practiced by the Spanish and the English.

The policy of establishing the Low Countries as an entrepôt of free trade was highly successful and the most competitive prices for many commodities were those on the Amsterdam market. Consumers in countries wrapped in mercantile regulations usually paid more for products and were taxed more for subsidies than where market rates pertained. However, the costs of the mercantile system fell hardest on colonial possessions that were treated as providers of raw materials and markets for the metropolis. Active policy to discourage development was the norm, but proved most injurious to the long-run economic health of colonies.

The routing of all trade with any of the colonies through the metropolis was also burdensome because it raised both the costs of exporting and the prices of imports. As a counterbalance, however, the colonies benefited from a protected market in the metropolis and from subsidies designed to encourage the production of many goods. Of the numerous attempts to estimate the economic cost of these trade acts with respect to British North America, the maximum figure arrived at was about 3 percent of annual colonial gross domestic product (GDP), a figure thought by most to be scarcely significant.

The Institutions of Commercial Capitalism

Although we can regard mercantilism as an overarching but general belief system espoused by the classes that effectively controlled society and the economy, the day-to-day economic system that prevailed between the end of feudalism and the advent of the industrial system is more descriptively called **commercial capitalism**. The title is appropriate because the dominant wealth-creating activity, at least as far as Western Europe was concerned, was commerce, and it was conducted by entrepreneurs who controlled capital and were interested in its accumulation.

---

[8] In English legislation these included the Hat Act, the Iron Act, and the Woolen Act. Spain prohibited the growth of olives and the production of wine in its American possessions.

[9] The most notable were Japan and Korea, which used regulation to good advantage while pursuing a "market friendly" approach.

This period was important in terms of institutional change because it saw the development of two innovations critical to subsequent capitalist development: the practice of incorporation of businesses and the emergence of banks as true financial intermediaries. Incorporation involves the creation of a legal entity with two essential features. First, corporations are an efficient means of commingling the funds of individuals, thereby gathering together the means for large investments. Second, the liabilities of corporations are limited by the extent of their assets. Consequently incorporation encourages risk taking, because the downside is limited, while the upside is not. Banks facilitate the pooling of saving and the lending of funds to individuals with ideas and enterprise but limited start-up capital.

Industrial Capitalism

Just as changing technology and a widening world first threatened and then destroyed the feudal order, supplanting it with mercantilism, by the end of the eighteenth century the commercial capitalist system was itself under threat. The proximate cause, in this case, was the growth of mass production and the rise of industrialized manufacturing, which was brought about by what has in the past been called the Industrial Revolution. Recent scholarship tends to dispute the idea of a short explosive burst of innovation, however, and tends to settle on a more extended and evolutionary series of innovations and institutional changes.[10] However, we can characterize the shift in productive technique as embodying four broad sorts of changes that were effected in the process of industrialization:

1. The replacement of muscle power (whether animal or human) by machine power, first water power and then steam
2. The replacement of skill and craftsmanship by the artificial and repetitive precision of the machine
3. The replacement of organic sources of raw materials by inorganic ones
4. The replacement of natural "time" by the clock (This last development was especially important for the creation of workforce discipline in the factory system.)

These developments made possible a factory system much as we know it today. In Britain, which was the first country to undergo substantial industrial urbanization, the system that developed was by and large highly competitive. Especially in the textile trades, which were the lead sector of technological change and were located largely in Northern England, the industrial structure approximated the model of competitive capitalism now embodied in textbook treatments of the theory of competitive firms. The product was close to totally homogeneous, the market included many buyers and many producers, and labor was largely undifferentiated.

[10]The debate on this issue continues to be lively, and an interested reader might want to look at Peter Temin's "Two Views of the British Industrial Revolution," *Journal of Economic History* 57, no. 1 (March 1997), pp. 63–82.

Decisions were made primarily by an entrepreneur who both managed the firm and put a substantial part of personal capital at risk. Government policy at that time was best described as "laissez faire, laissez passer."

The largest shifts in the economic regulation happened because mercantile restrictions adversely affected the long-term competitive prospects of manufacturing. At the beginning of the industrialization process, political power remained in the hands of the landholding and commercial classes, who favored comprehensive trade regulations. However, the increasing economic power of the manufacturers led, in England in 1832, to their enfranchisement, and within 15 years this growing political power resulted in sharp changes in the economic system.

The most visible of these changes was the outcome of the popular and parliamentary debate over the reform of the corn laws. The **corn laws** created tariffs that restricted the import of cereal grains into Britain leading to both higher food prices and increased returns to the owners of agricultural land. The manufacturers' interests, however, lay in minimizing costs, and higher food prices forced them to raise wages, ultimately hurting the competitiveness of British goods on international markets. After considerable pressure, the corn laws were repealed and Britain was able to freely import food and other materials. It represented in some ways recognition for the economic doctrines of David Ricardo, who rejected the idea of mercantile restrictions and presented a cogent case for the rise of the free trade movement.

The onset of British industrialization saw further changes in the role of government. Urbanization produced a plethora of problems associated with growth and the government was called on to deal with the issues of public health and pollution control (albeit in a rudimentary form). Unacceptable workplace dangers and the widespread use of child labor occasioned laws that regulated factory practices. The government also became involved in the development of human capital, in the form of education for the less privileged classes; this education increased labor productivity.

Industrialization also enabled labor to organize to an extent not previously possible. Unions began to spring up and were at first resolutely opposed by manufacturers and the government. The first union organizers were prosecuted under "combination acts" and imprisoned or deported. However, over time the legality of labor organization was confirmed and the stage was set for the emergence of mass unions representing the working class. In Britain these unions were modeled on the old craft guilds and were structured around occupations rather than around specific employers, which led to long-term consequences for the nature of collective bargaining in the British context.

The Industrial System in Continental Europe

Industrial development in continental Europe differed from that in Britain because of two factors. First, the role of government was generally greater due to different and less liberal political traditions. Second, European nations were playing catchup. Consequently, they could adopt technologies already pioneered and tested elsewhere, especially after Britain abandoned all attempts to control the export of machines and machine tools in the late 1840s. Continental industrial structures were from the start less competitive than those in Britain. Their industries, and often specific favored firms, enjoyed both more overt government support and closer relations with the banking sector than was true in Britain. It was the genesis of a political/economic system that involved much closer management of industry by government than was seen in Britain, at least prior to World War II. This close relation of government and business is in one respect a holdover from earlier mercantile practices. As one observer, Charles Tilly, put it, mercantilism appeals to the second best, or at least the latecomers, who require government support, direction, and protection against competition. This model of late industrialization that pertained to continental Europe in the late nineteenth century echoes in the policies and practices of the East Asian late industrializers in the late twentieth century.

The different role of banks on the continent was also significant. Banking had played only a small role in the creation of credit in the British Industrial Revolution. A surprisingly large amount of capital was generated through retained earnings and the granting of interfirm trade credits. Banking proved especially useful in overseas trade, and the financial sector developed in a differentiated pattern with a variety of specialized banks. On the continent, banking was much more central, largely because the average enterprise at inception was much larger than in Britain. Large firms did not grow from small start-ups but were created from whole cloth in order to take advantage of the scope of latest technology and to grasp the economies of scale required to compete with existing suppliers. Banks played a great role in providing start-up capital, and because of the size of their stake, the banks became closely associated with the management of the venture. Continental banks were not specialized but were "universal" in nature, providing loans, owning capital, granting trade credits, and being responsible for brokerage services.

Finance Capitalism and Imperialism

The close relationship between the banks and business in Europe, which was evolving in Britain and in the United States,[11] led neo-Marxian observers to see a new stage in the evolution of economic systems. Following Rudolf Hilferding, an Austrian, this system became labeled as **finance capitalism** and differed from early **industrial capitalism** in the role played by financial capital. In Hilferding's conception, which was significant to Lenin, a small coterie of bankers were capable of dominating the system. This resort to monopolization was a defensive technique employed to delay the inevitable decline in the rate of profit.

In Marxian analysis this same close group of financier/industrialists was potentially also influential on government policy. This aspect became especially important, because Marx believed that the capitalist system would face repeated crises.

[11] In the United States the most obvious example of this closeness was the takeover of the U.S. steel industry by J. P. Morgan.

The root cause of these crises was the basic tendency toward accumulation, the replacement of labor by ever-deepening capital. Capitalist societies would ultimately always be faced with problems of declining profits and insufficient demand in this system. Monopolization of production and the elimination of competition was one strategy that afforded some relief from these pressures. The other was to look abroad, outside the capitalist system. Colonies could provide both fields to invest capital at higher rates than applied at home and a source of demand for finished products. It was another way in which the fatal crisis might be postponed.

CONTEMPORARY ECONOMIC SYSTEMS

Socialism and Communism

Marx believed that capitalism would face repeated crises caused by the long-run decline in the rate of profit and ever-increasing problems of excess supply as demand failed to keep pace with production. These economic problems would be played out against a backdrop of growing worker alienation. The confluence of these forces would present the crucial limitation on capitalist production and the means by which the system would change. Like other systems before it, it would be swept away. The system that would replace it in his conception of history would be socialism, a transitional stage on the way to communism.

The word **socialism** first appeared in writings in France and Britain in the early nineteenth century. Today, this rather imprecise term covers a wide range of positions from total public ownership at one extreme to social democracy at the other. Most socialists, however, share the belief that the community as a whole should own and control the means of production, distribution, and exchange to ensure a more equitable division of a nation's wealth, either in the form of state ownership of industry or in the form of ownership by the workers themselves. In Marxian terms, the advent of socialism is characterized by a dictatorship of the proletariat and the continued existence of scarcity (which would be not be a characteristic of communism), but other conceptions also exist. Utopian socialists in Britain, for example, saw a much more limited shift in society. The economic organization they envisaged held much in common with worker-owned cooperatives.

Marx saw socialism as another stage to be passed through on the way to communism. Prior to Marx, this social and political ideology advocated that authority and property be vested in the community, each member working for the common benefit according to capacity and receiving according to needs. Numerous thinkers embraced the ideal of communism, including Plato, the early Christians, and the sixteenth-century humanist Thomas More, who saw it as expressing man's social nature to the highest degree. **Communism** was to be the final culmination of Marx's successive revolutions. In such a society, class would vanish and the state as such would largely be unnecessary. Each would contribute according to his or her ability, and each would take according to need.

Under Lenin and his successors, Soviet communism contained two main elements. The first was the leading role of the Communist Party, seen as representing the true interests of the working class. The party was to control the organs of the state, and was itself to be organized according to the principles of "democratic centralism" in which a narrow group of individuals controlled all aspects of political, economic, social, and cultural life. Thus, in effect communism became one variant of totalitarianism, with a narrow elite enjoying control. The second major element in communist doctrine was the social ownership of property and central planning of the economy.

The achievements of Soviet communism inspired revolutionary movements in many other countries, and in some developing countries, such as China, Vietnam, North Korea, and Cuba, communist parties came to power and established regimes based more or less closely on the Soviet model. In Eastern Europe, communist governments were installed under Soviet influence at the end of World War II.

However, the ideal communist state never materialized and support for communist regimes in the West fell, even among left-thinking intellectuals, as the inefficiency of the system and its lack of a democratic base became more apparent. We will study the history of the Communist experiments in Russia and in China in Chapters 21 and 23.

The Growth of the Welfare State

Although Marx was confident that the successive crises of capitalism would lead to socialist revolution in the most advanced capitalist societies, these expectations failed to materialize. Britain, the United States, and Germany, with large manufacturing workforces at the end of the nineteenth century, appeared to be the prime candidates for revolution. However, all escaped Marxist revolution. Rather than a violent shift to total public ownership and the dictatorship of the proletariat, these states instead evolved into societies that generally carry the label of **welfare state.**[12] In these nations the government assumed a much greater range of responsibilities, including responsibility for the management of the economy and the creation of what is called the social safety net. Labor got to share to a much greater degree in the increase in productivity that followed technical change, and consequently the revolutionary potential of working class discontent was diffused.

These shifts were gradual; the original impetus in Britain started before World War I, accelerated between the world wars, and culminated with a far-reaching social program immediately following World War II. This program included the creation of comprehensive social security, nationalized health care, and the assumption of public ownership of a large swath of industry. In the United States the key dates are the creation of the New Deal by the Roosevelt administration after 1933 and the Great Society program of Lyndon Johnson in the late 1960s. In this book we look at several of the welfare states and pay particular attention to

[12]*Evolution* is perhaps too mild a word for the metamorphosis in Germany, which throughout the 1920s teetered on the brink of revolution before falling to the fascists in the 1930s. After World War II, the occupying powers were highly influential in restructuring the economic system by decree. Only after this point can the German development of the welfare state be regarded as gradual evolution.

Sweden, which was especially aggressive in its pursuit of income equality since the 1930s. We also look at Britain, which was notable for its retreat from socialism in the early 1980s, in some detail.

Corporatism and Fascism

Later in this book we refer to certain economic systems as "corporatist" in nature. A corporatist society can be defined as one where interest groups, bound together by duty and obligation, triumph over the individual. The logic of **corporatism** dictates that such groups are not in conflict with each other, but seek non-confrontational relationships. In practical terms it generally means that the various institutions of both labor and capital are licensed by, and operate under, the close supervision and coordination of the state. Thus, corporatism combines the market institutions of private property and ownership of the means of production with the idea that the government is responsible for shaping and steering the actions of both labor and capital for the social good.

Corporatism has also been closely associated with the political system of **fascism**, which represented the state as being dominant in all aspects of life. The essence of fascism is that government should be the master not the servant of the people. The economic embodiment of fascism was the model of the corporate state pioneered by the Mussolini regime in interwar Italy.[13] In this system, all industries in the country were organized under state aegis into 12 "corporations," controlled by boards on which representatives of labor, business, and the Fascist Party served. In reality, they were government-sponsored trade associations, or cartels, with the responsibility for allocating output among members, fixing prices, and regulating wages. Although the objective was to promote state control of industry and rapid growth, in fact the monopolistic organization resulted in corruption and a loss of efficiency. In Germany a less-structured system gave the government a high degree of control of business and replaced free unions with the National Labor Front. Businesspeople were coerced into cooperation by the prospect of relief from the labor strife characteristic of the previous decade. In both cases the objective of the system was the triumph of collective interest over the individual, both at the level of the corporation and at the level of the state. It is, consequently, inimical to liberal capitalism because of the required trampling of individual rights and to socialists because of the nominal prevalence of private property.

Although usually associated with past dictators such as Mussolini, Peron (in Argentina), and Salazar (in Portugal), *corporatism* is a word also used to describe Sweden, where the government brings together labor unions and employers' federations to determine national wage settlements. Others used it to characterize Japan, where a triumvirate of politicians, bureaucrats, and industrialists jointly forge a national industrial policy. In its most extreme form it takes on the rather pejorative label of "Japan Inc."

---

[13]See Rondo Cameron, *A Concise Economic History of the World*, 2d ed. (Oxford: Oxford University Press, 1993), p. 363.

A recent confusion between corporatism as defined here, and the kind of political and economic system dominated by corporations in the current American sense of the word is unfortunate. A company such as General Motors is not at all the same institution as the Italian corporations organized by Mussolini. Mussolini famously remarked that "Fascism should be more correctly referred to as Corporatism," in an attempt to represent his politics as promoting the collective good and the general rights of the individual through requiring incorporation in government.[14] It is too frequently used in suggesting no distinction lies between today's corporate world and its links to government, and the political system of fascism with all its evils. Clearly many flaws can be associated with contemporary capitalism, but eliding the distinction between today's corporations and Mussolini's corporatism blocks sincere efforts to critically address them.

Economics and Islam

The apparently growing conflict between a section of the global Islamic community and the capitalist West is increasing interest in, among other things, Islamic economics. Timur Kuran tried to clarify the issues surrounding Islamic economics:

> The declared purpose of **Islamic economics** is to identify and establish an economic order that conforms to Islamic scripture and traditions. Its core positions took shape in the 1940s, and three decades later efforts to implement them were under way in dozens of countries. In Pakistan, Malaysia, and elsewhere, governments are now running centralized Islamic redistribution systems known as *zakat*. More than sixty countries have Islamic banks that claim to offer an interest-free alternative to conventional banking. Invoking religious principles, several countries, among them Pakistan and Iran, have gone so far as to outlaw every form of interest; they are forcing all banks, including foreign subsidiaries, to adopt, at least formally, ostensibly Islamic methods of deposit taking and loan making. Attempts are also under way to disseminate religious norms of price setting, bargaining, and wage determination. And for every such initiative, others are on the drawing board.[15]

Kuran is skeptical about the role that Islamic economics might play. He goes on to point out that "of all economists of the Muslim faith, only a small minority . . . identify with some variant of this new doctrine. Yet the doctrine is socially significant, if only because it advances the sprawling and headline-grabbing movement known as 'political Islam,' 'Islamic fundamentalism,' or simply 'Islamism.' "

However, its proponents argue that the practice of Islamic economics could unite the strengths of both capitalism and socialism. It is based on three fundamental precepts: (1) an opposition to the use of interest, based on an interpretation of the Qur'an; (2) the adoption of the *zakat*, a form of voluntary redistribution; and (3) the

---

[14]"The Fascist conception of life," Mussolini wrote, "stresses the importance of the State and accepts the individual only in so far as his interests coincide with the State. It is opposed to classical liberalism [which] denied the State in the name of the individual; Fascism reasserts the rights of the State as expressing the real essence of the individual."

[15]Timur Kuran, "The Genesis of Islamic Economics: A Chapter in the Politics of Muslim Identity, *Social Research* 64, no. 2 (Summer 1997).

ECONOMICS AND 9/11

It is tempting to see the events of September 11, 2001, as the result of ideological conflict between Islam and capitalism. However, it is not really a conflict of two exclusionary creeds, as was perhaps the case in the cold war rivalry between capitalism and Soviet-style communism that preoccupied the world for more than 40 years. The resentment that led to September 11 arose from clear, deep historical and religious, as well as economic, roots. Some of it can be traced to the relative decline of Islam in the last 500 years. Islamic civilization was dominant in much of the world in the sixteenth century. At that time, Moslems held power from mid-Europe to Zanzibar and from Morocco to the East Indies. The European "voyages of discovery" were actually an incursion into a vast civilization that was learned, skilled, sophisticated, and urban. The following five centuries saw progressive decline in Islamic global influence, with the twentieth century particularly catastrophic. The defeat and division of the Ottoman Empire, the extension of western political interests to ensure the reliability of the oil supply and the establishment of the state of Israel all dealt severe blows and incited anti-Western feeling.

Today the countries of the world that either have Islam as their official religion or are inhabited in the majority by Moslems are generally much worse off in terms of income per head than are the inhabitants of the developed western nations. According to the World Bank Development Report 2000/2001, average income per head in the United States is about $30,600. The average income in terms of purchasing power parity for the 28 richest countries is $23,430 per year. In contrast the average for the 291 million people living in North Africa and the Middle East is only $4,600 per year, about one-fifth of the level. Some Moslem countries are even poorer. Indonesia, Pakistan, and Bangladesh, which are the most populous of the Islamic nations, have together a population of 370 million people. Average per-head incomes are $2,439, $1,757, and $1,475, respectively. On this rough basis we can see that the average Moslem is likely to have an income of about $3,000 a year, 10 percent of the average in the U.S. income.

Moreover, poverty is reflected in other measures. Fifteen percent of children in the Middle East and North Africa are affected by malnutrition, 136 children out of every 1,000 die before the age of 5, compared with 15 in 1,000 in the high-income nations, and life expectancy is 67 years compared to 78 years in the developed West. Such relative poverty might well be a cause of anger, and might be a contributory cause of anti-American terrorism but cannot be said to be the sole cause. Other nations' relative standing in terms of income and health is even lower.

Americans and other Westerners tend to see their affluence as flowing from their own hard work and the productivity of their institutions. They tend to believe that the key to prosperity abroad lies in adopting similar ethics and structures. Nonwesterners, especially Moslems today, are much more likely to see the affluence of the West and the poverty of their own societies in terms of a zero-sum game, and consider the prosperity of the West to be the result of conquest, tribute, or unequal exchange. This argument is particularly cogent with respect to the Moslem Middle East and East Indies, so well-endowed with natural resource wealth but lacking the living standards that should follow.

filtering of all economic decisions through Islamic moral norms. The most important of these ideas in practice is the prohibition on interest. Other societies attempted to do without the use of interest but none very successfully.[16]

[16]Similar restrictions on "usury" were placed by the Roman Catholic church, which is thought to have been one of the factors that impeded economic growth in the predominantly Catholic countries of the Mediterranean. See, for example, R. H. Tawney's *Religion and the Rise of Capitalism: A Historical Study* (New York: Harcourt Brace, 1926).

The Islamic economists' solution is to rely on the sharing of risk through equity rather than a secure lender advancing investment funds to a borrower. One Islamic economist has articulated the essential principles of Islamic finance:

> [N]either the principal nor a rate of profit (tied up with the principal) can be guaranteed. The subscribers must enter into the fund with a clear understanding that the return on their subscription is tied up with the actual profit earned or loss suffered by the Fund. If the Fund earns huge profits, the return in their subscription will increase to that proportion; however, in case the Fund suffers loss, they will have to share it also, unless the loss is caused by the negligence or mismanagement, in which case the management, and not the Fund, will be liable to compensate it.[17]
>
> ... [T]he amounts so pooled together must be invested in a business acceptable to Shariah. It means that not only the channels of investment, but also the terms agreed with them must conform to the Islamic principles.[18]

Kuran argues that the prohibition of interest, so key to the theory of Islamic economics, is due to a misinterpretation of the Qur'an, which sought only to outlaw a particularly grievous practice, whereby the principle was doubled in the event of a default.[19] However, fundamentalists insist on the notion that it is immoral to earn income from capital without assuming risk. Instead of the use of loans, therefore,

PAKISTAN AND INTEREST FREE ECONOMICS

Although the use of interest is generally thought of as being against fundamentalist Islamic belief, it is generally tolerated in most countries. Recently Pakistan looked as if it were going to make a serious move toward eliminating the use of interest payments. The Federal Shariat Court (FSC) is an unusual institution charged under the Pakistani constitution with determining whether "any law or provision of law is repugnant to the injunctions of Islam." In 1999, the FSC determined that the laws and commercial code necessary to support the use of interest rates in banking were repugnant to Islam and ordered all such laws to be removed from the statute books. The government appealed to the Supreme Court of Pakistan, which upheld the decision of the FSC. The supreme court ordered that all such legislation supporting the use of interest should cease as of June 30, 2001. Fearing that this move would seriously affect the economy, the government questioned the competence of the FSC in this area and did little to facilitate removing the "obnoxious" legislation. In the aftermath of the invasion of Afghanistan the government seemed more resolved to resist the Islamic fundamentalists and nothing further occurred. We now must wait to assess the practicality of a major economy operating without the use of interest.

[17]This statement was written by Muft Taqi Usmani, an expert in the fields of Islamic law and economics and Hadith. For the past 35 years, he taught at the Darul-Uloom in Karachi, established by his father Mufti Muhammad Shafi, the late Grand Mufti of Pakistan.

[18]Islamic law.

[19]Timur Kuran, "Islamic Economics and the Islamic Sub-Economy," *Journal of Economic Perspectives* 9, no. 4 (Fall 1995), pp. 155–173.

business finance must be placed exclusively on a basis of shares or "equity" participation. Thus, the Islamic Development Bank, founded in 1974 by the Organization of the Islamic Conference to promote Qur'anic principles in the economies of member states, makes no loans but finances development projects only in return for a share of the profits, or for a "commission rate." This practice is not unknown, of course, in Western economies. Indeed, the entire venture capital industry, which financed much of the high-tech small company growth in the United States, relies on equity participation rather than loans.

However, as we will see later in this book, modern economics tends to stress the role of interest as "the price of capital," considered necessary for the efficient operation of an economy, especially in the intertemporal context. In some ways the problem for Islamic systems is parallel to that experienced by centrally planned economies, which, too, eschewed interest rates on principle. Without a market for finance, both the savings/investment decision and the choice of technique decision become more complex and prone to an inefficient outcome.

KEY TERMS AND CONCEPTS

balance of employment
balance of trade
commercial capitalism
communism
corn laws
corporatism
evolutionary school
fascism
feudalism
finance capitalism
"hydraulic" societies
industrial capitalism
Islamic economics
laws of motion
mercantilism
Oriental despotism
population growth
socialism
superstructure
technological change
welfare state

QUESTIONS FOR DISCUSSION

1. Why does technological change frequently cause changes in the economic system? Can different economic systems be compatible with a single technology?
2. Why did the system of irrigated agriculture practiced in much of South and East Asia allow the surplus to be appropriated by the state?
3. How did the revival of trade and the advent of the Black Death undermine the feudal system?
4. What economic rationale might be given for a merchant class to favor a balance of payments surplus?

5. In what ways did the repeal of the corn laws in Britain represent a victory for the manufacturing classes over the landowners?
6. In what ways did economic development on Continental Europe differ from development in Britain?
7. Distinguish between socialism and communism as economic systems. What defines a corporatist state?
8. "Fascism should be more correctly called corporatism." Should this statement be a criticism of contemporary corporate America?
9. What alternatives do Islamic economies use to handle the restriction on the use of interest rates?

RESOURCES

Web Sites

This chapter is largely concerned with economic history and the history of economic thought. A good starting point for any research into the history of economic thought is the "History of Economic Thought" Web site, which can now be found at the New School University Web site at http://cepa.newschool.edu/het/. It provides links to Web information on all major economists (living and dead), access to biographies, critiques, and economists' work that is downloadable from the Web. Two particularly useful sites in the context of this course are the following:

1. A searchable and downloadable copy of Adam Smith's *An Inquiry into the Nature and Causes of the Wealth of Nations*, available at http://www.econlib.org/library/Smith/smwn.html.
2. The Marx/Engels Internet Archive contains links to all of the Web-accessible work of Karl Marx and Friedrich Engels and other Marxists. It is available at http://www.marxists.org.

A growing number of sites provide information about Islamic economics from the point of view of its proponents. One with useful links can be found at http://www.islamic-economics.com/.

Books and Articles

Cameron, Rondo. *A Concise Economic History of the World*, 2d ed. (p. 363). Oxford: Oxford University Press, 1993.

Coleman, D. C. *Revisions in Mercantilism*. London: Methuen, 1969.

Farouqui, Mahmood (ed.). *Islamic Banking and Investment: Challenge and Opportunity*. New York: Kegan Paul, 1998.

Fei, John C. H., with Gustav Ranis (contributor). *Growth and Development from an Evolutionary Perspective*. London: Blackwell, 1997.

Hansen, Ejvind Damsgard. *European Economic History: From Mercantilism to Maastricht.* Copenhagen: Copenhagen Business School Press, 2001. Available at http://www.amazon.com/exec/obidos/tg/detail/-/8716134966/qid=1035745143/sr=1-1/ref=sr_1_1/103-0666588-0560602?v=glance.

Hodgson, Geoffrey M. *Evolution and Institutions: On Evolutionary Economics and the Evolution of Economics.* White Plains, NY: Edward Elgar, 1999.

Kuran, Timur. "Islamic Economics and the Islamic Sub-Economy." *Journal of Economic Perspectives* 9, no. 4 (Fall 1995), 155–173.

Kuran, Timur. "The Genesis of Islamic Economics: A Chapter in the Politics of Muslim Identity." *Social Research* 64, no. 2 (Summer 1997).

Nelson, Richard. *Evolutionary Theory of Economic Change.* Cambridge: Harvard University Press, 1985.

Presley, John, and John Sessions. "Islamic Economics: The Emergence of a New Paradigm." *Economic Journal* 104 (May 1994), 584–596.

Schwartz, Herman. *States Versus Markets: History, Geography, and the Development of the International Political Economy.* New York: St. Martin's Press, 1994.

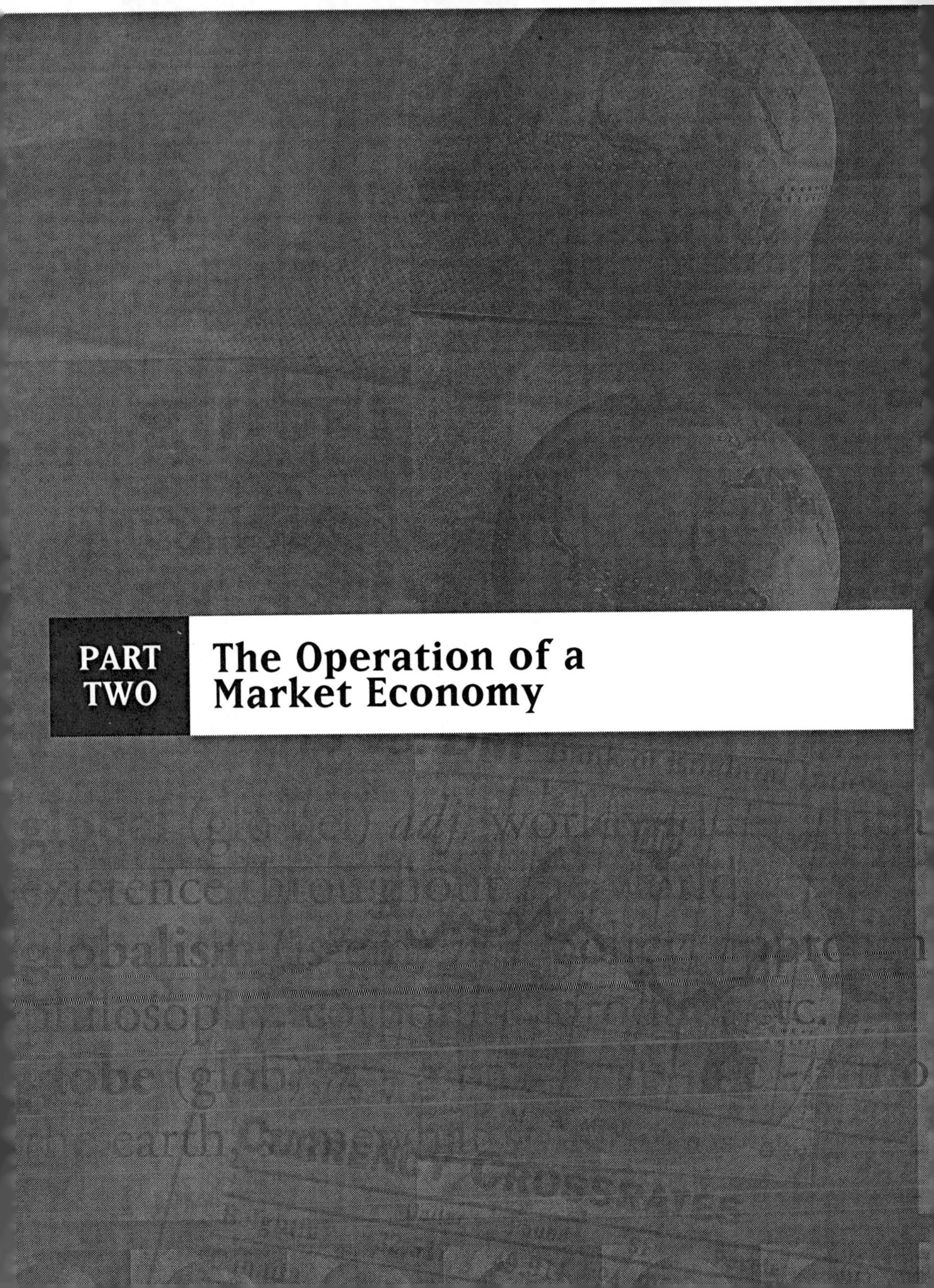

PART TWO The Operation of a Market Economy

3

HOW A MARKET SYSTEM WORKS

ADAM SMITH AND THE INVISIBLE HAND

Adam Smith's description of the operation of a private property market system in his seminal work *An Inquiry into the Nature and Causes of the Wealth of Nations*, inspires an awe of the functioning of markets, rooted in the apparent paradox of his "invisible hand" theorem.[1] In Smith's conception, individuals act only to benefit themselves, yet, given certain preconditions, such behavior results in a social optimum. Selfish individuals collectively generate a level of efficiency and economic well-being that more "rational" systems of central planning are unable to match. In this chapter, we take a closer look at the operation of market capitalism. How, exactly, does a market system work? What are its essential features? Why does it perform so well in some areas—growth, allocative efficiency, and technological innovation—and what are its shortcomings?

Much of what we know about the market system today was well understood by Smith in 1776, although the tools that we use to analyze it differ. Smith argued that the ability to exchange and barter was both fundamental and universal to humankind. It was also unique, one of the things that set humans apart from the animals. In *The Wealth of Nations* he wrote:

> [T]he propensity to truck, barter, and exchange one thing for another . . . is common to all men, and is to be found in no other race of animals, which seem to know neither this nor any other species of contracts. Nobody ever saw a dog make a fair and deliberate exchange of one bone for another with another dog. Nobody ever saw one animal by its gestures and natural cries signify to another, this is mine, that yours; I am willing to give this for that.[2]

Another of Smith's important insights dealt with the need for specialization and **division of labor** in order to maximize the social product. Rather than meet all of their own needs, individuals are better served by concentrating on what they do

---

[1]Smith (1723–1790) was an eighteenth-century Scottish political economist and philosopher who laid the foundations of our understanding of the workings of competitive economies in his 1776 book *An Inquiry into the Nature and Causes of the Wealth of Nations*.

[2]Because the versions of *The Wealth of Nations* are so numerous, citing the page number of a particular edition might not be helpful to the reader. It is probably clearer to cite the book, chapter, and rough line number. This quote is from book I, chapter 2, line 4 and following. Links to useful hypertext version are given at the end of this chapter.

best and relying on exchange in the marketplace to meet their needs and to improve their welfare. In Smith's own language, it was

> the certainty of being able to exchange all that surplus part of the produce of his own labour, which is over and above his own consumption, for such parts of the produce of other men's labour as he may have occasion for, encourages every man to apply himself to a particular occupation, and to cultivate and bring to perfection whatever talent or genius he may possess for that particular species of business. The difference of natural talents in different men is, in reality, much less than we are aware of; and the very different genius which appears to distinguish men of different professions, when grown up to maturity, is not upon many occasions so much the cause, as the effect of the division of labour.[3]

The ability to specialize and exchange, coupled with the single-minded pursuit of their own interests, leads individuals to serve the public good in a much more effective way than if they altruistically sought to benefit others. This concept is the essence of Smith's **invisible hand**, one of the most compelling and important metaphors in modern social thought. It can be seen as both paradoxical and beautiful, in that individual self-interest leads to a social optimum much more effectively than when people try to promote the general well-being. In fact, as the last two sentences of this quotation reveal, Smith harbored a deep cynicism of the motives of people who claimed to act in the public good:

> [An individual] intends only his own gain, and he is in this, as in many other cases, led by an invisible hand to promote an end which was no part of his intention. Nor is it always the worse for the society that it was no part of it. By pursuing his own interest, he frequently promotes that of the society more effectually that when he really intends to promote it. I have never known much good done by those who affected to trade for the public good. It is an affectation, indeed, not very common among merchants, and very few words need be employed in dissuading them from it.[4]

MARKETS IN A MODERN ECONOMY

Smith's insights into the operation of markets remain in many respects as valid today as in the eighteenth century when he first made them. However, in the increasing complexity of modern economies, every economy based on exchange consists of many thousands of individual markets, for example, financial markets, labor markets (which exist for many different kinds of labor), agricultural markets, markets for intermediate goods, and so on. These markets do not function in isolation but are linked so that each one interacts in some way with the others. Changes in the taste for a single good require adjustment not only in its own market but also in all other markets; the present and future prices of labor, intermediate goods price, and factors of production will all change, perhaps only to some infinitesimally small degree. Because the consequences for other markets are in many cases

[3]Book I, chapter 2, line 30 and following.
[4]Book IV, chapter 2, line 40 and following.

small, economists often look at the impact of a disturbance on a single market alone. This approach is called **partial equilibrium**. However, we must always be aware of the impacts felt in all other markets, on all goods and factors, in all places and times. The full effect leads to an adjustment to a new **general equilibrium**.

Acting together, these markets determine a price for all goods, factors, and services, and they also determine the quantities of each that will be supplied. It is instructive to consider the alternative to reliance on the market to make these decisions. If a planning authority made all these decisions, the amount of information required at the center of the economy would be huge. Planners would need to estimate the demand for products and gear the entire production process toward its satisfaction. The ability of a market system to coordinate itself in the absence of a central coordinating authority provides one of its most appealing features.

Goods Markets

To illustrate this market function, let us begin by looking at a single market for a good, depicted in Figure 3.1. The tools we will need are familiar to most students from their work in introductory and intermediate economic theory, and a thorough review of that material would be beneficial. Here we look only at some important features of competitive markets, focusing on issues of supply and demand. Dr. Johnson, Adam Smith's contemporary, acerbically observed that he could teach a parrot all that was essential about economics if he could get it to say the two words *supply* and *demand.* Although this generalization oversimplifies the issue, the important features of competitive markets can be illustrated using these concepts.

On one side of the analysis we find a **market demand curve, D**. It consists of an array of pairs of prices and quantities that reflect how much of a good the individuals who compose the market would be willing to purchase at given prices. This market demand curve is an aggregation of the demands of individuals, households, firms, and government. It is in a sense an abstraction, and valid only instantaneously, based on the assumption that the prices of all other goods, as well as

▪ FIGURE 3.1

A Simple Market Model

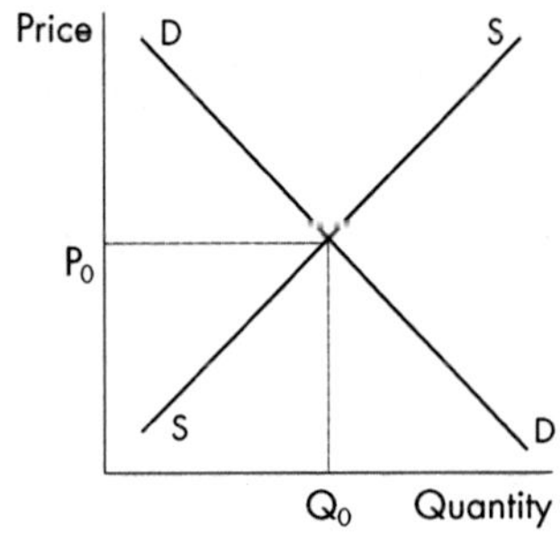

incomes and tastes, are constant. We expect and assume the demand curve to be downward sloping, which reflects the generally held principle that for all consumers the more of a good that they possess the less they will value the last, or marginal, unit of that good.

On the other hand we note the **market supply curve, S**. Like the demand curve, it indicates the collection of pairs of prices and quantities. This curve reflects how much the market participants would be prepared to sell at various prices. In the case of a good that can be newly produced (let us say agricultural products or manufactured goods), the supply curve appears as upward sloping because marginal costs of production are assumed to rise (in the medium term at least) as production increases. The intersection of the supply curve and the demand curve gives us the equilibrium price—that price at which the consumers will be able to buy all that they wish to and the sellers will be able to part with exactly what they want to sell. For a market to be competitive, many sellers and many buyers are necessary, and no one seller or buyer is important enough to affect the sale price. The price therefore moves to equilibrate the demand and the supply sides of the market, without any one individual or firm decisively influencing the outcome.

Two things should be noted here. First, neither demand nor supply curves are readily observable. The point defined by the equilibrium price and quantity pair is the only one that we actually observe on either curve.[5] Second, because of the interaction of the many thousands of markets, equilibrium in any product market is likely to be a fleeting affair. Conditions in other markets will change, creating changes in all markets as the interactive system searches, constantly, for a general equilibrium.

An important feature of markets is that, under competitive assumptions, the market price of a good will be equal to its marginal cost of production. This result follows because the equilibrium price lies on the supply curve, and the supply curve is the aggregation of the marginal cost curves of suppliers. Because the equilibrium price also lies on the demand curve, we can be sure that it will also be equal to the valuation that the marginal consumer puts on his or her last unit of purchase. Thus a competitive market ensures that goods will be produced up to, and not beyond, the point where the marginal cost of production is equal to the value that the marginal consumer places on it. If all markets were competitive, then all prices would be equal to their marginal costs. Economic theory further tells us that this outcome would be efficient in the sense that no other allocation of resources could produce more of any one good without reducing the output of another. It also appeals to some people as being equitable. Those who consume goods must pay the marginal costs of production of those goods.

A Shift in Demand What happens if the demand for a good changes as a result of some exogenous event? As a first example, consider a shift in consumer tastes favoring the good, which is represented in Figure 3.1. The higher demand is represented by a shift in the demand curve to the right—more is demanded at every

[5]Using econometric techniques we are able, under certain conditions, to estimate both curves.

price of the good. The adjustment to this disturbance can be looked at in three phases. In the short run, the supply of the good is fixed, and the supply curve S_{Short} will be perfectly inelastic, or vertical. The full response to the change in demand will be reflected by price change. The price of the good will increase sharply from P_0 to P_S reflecting the short-term scarcity. Those fortunate enough to be holding stocks of the good will be able to reap **windfall profits**. This scenario appears in Figure 3.2, where the shaded area reflects those windfall profits.

In the medium term, shown in Figure 3.3, the higher prices will encourage existing producers to increase their output, probably by hiring additional labor. Capital, which is normally regarded as invariate in the medium term, cannot be increased within this time frame. Only variable inputs (usually labor) can be changed. Therefore the supply curve S_{Medium} is upward sloping and moderately elastic (responsive to price). The additional output ($Q_M - Q_0$) is produced at higher marginal cost than the original output, because on average each worker is working with less capital than previously. The "law of diminishing returns" suggests that as variable inputs (labor) are increased against a fixed input (capital) the marginal product of labor will fall. However, the rate of return on capital will rise, because capital is now relatively scarce in this industry. The higher than average rate represents "economic profit" and will attract new capital to the industry, lowering marginal costs and establishing a new long-term equilibrium.

Economic profits, defined as returns on capital above the normal rate, are vital for the efficient functioning of a market system in responding to changes. Such profits, or their equally important counterpart, economic losses, are generated in the short term and medium term when shifts occur in supply or demand. Profits and losses, therefore, are signaling devices in a market system. The existence in some industries or product lines of rates of return on capital that are above the economy-wide average, or normal, rate of return will cause capital to flow to those sectors. This capital will, in turn, lead to increased output, moderated prices, and the eventual complete erosion of the super-normal profits. Most important, capital will flow into those industries where its productivity is greatest, leading to a more

▪ FIGURE 3.2

Adjustment to Demand Shift in the Short Run

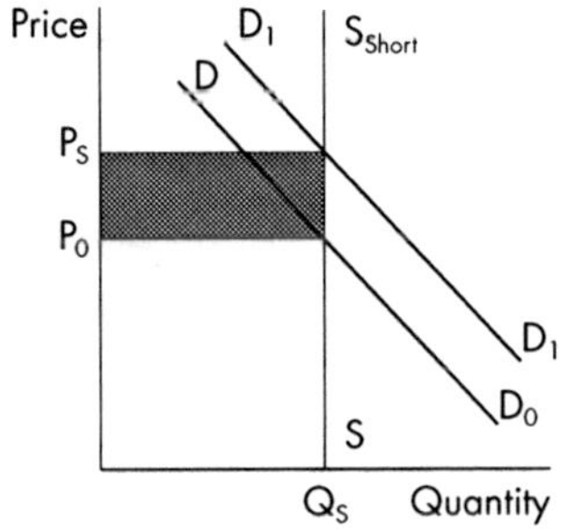

FIGURE 3.3

Adjustment to Demand Shift in the Medium Term

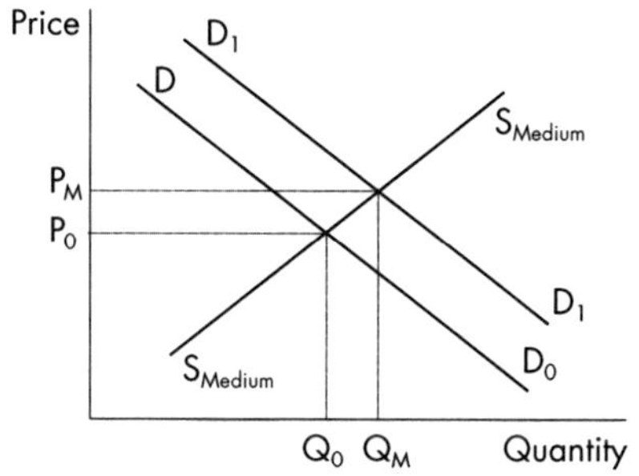

efficient allocation of resources. Figure 3.4 illustrates the consequences of this capital inflow. The long-run supply curve S_{Long} is likely to be more elastic (flatter) than its short and medium counterparts. The increase in consumer demand results in increased output and only moderately increased prices, which reflect the marginal cost of the production of the good after new investment enters the industry.

Innovation Let us consider now a second form of market disturbance. A single supplier makes an innovation in the production process that results in a lower marginal cost of production. Initially the single supplier who is the only producer to make this innovation will earn excess profits in the form of "economic rent." **Economic rent** is a return over and above the average rate of profit. This rent accrues to the supplier because of ownership of a specific factor of production; in this case the productive innovation. The rent will be earned as long as the innovator holds the monopoly of this knowledge and in all likelihood market share will

FIGURE 3.4

Adjustment to Demand Shift in the Long Run

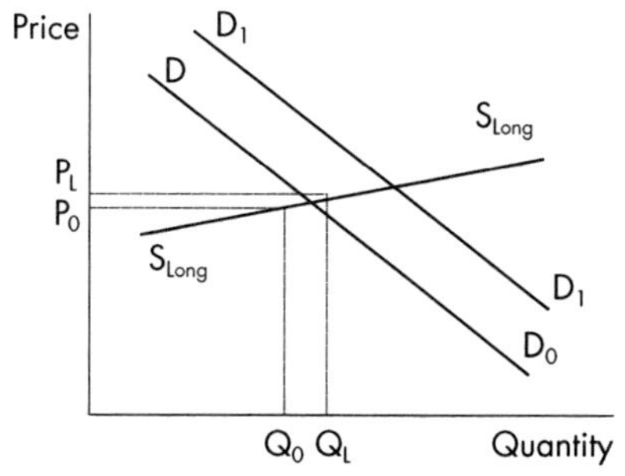

increase. In the long term, other producers must either match the cost savings that result from the innovation or go out of business.

The market encourages innovation by providing unusually high rates of return to those producers that successfully introduce a cost-saving improvement. The same process in effect requires that all producers match the innovation or improve on it, or they will lose their market share to more efficient competitors.

Other Disturbances We could show in a similar diagrammatic fashion how the market deals with other kinds of disturbances. A sudden exogenous reduction in supply (represented by a shift of the supply curve to left) will again, under conditions of constant demand, yield windfall profits to the remaining producers and provide incentives to channel new investment into the industry. A sharp exogenous increase in supply (a rightward shift in the supply curve) will result in the reverse effect. It will lower the market price and cut the rate of return in the industry below the level of the economy at large. New investment will be diverted from the industry to other uses, and when the historically committed capital is depleted by depreciation it will not be replaced until average rates of return rise to the economy-wide level.

Requirements for Market Efficiency

Perfect markets require such an exacting set of preconditions that we can, by and large, dismiss their existence in the real world. For example, perfection would require that all participants in the market know all prices for all goods and factors, both current and future. A more realistic concern centers on whether markets are reasonably allocatively efficient and handle the task of answering the essential economic questions in the fashion most prone to increase consumer welfare. Even this lesser standard requires a number of preconditions, some of which may not be met, resulting in "market failures." We mentioned some of these in passing. For example, efficient markets are characterized by many suppliers and many buyers so that there is no accretion of market power to be exploited. Efficiency also requires good information. Buyers must be aware of the prices of all substitute goods and need to know about the future movement of prices. Producers must be similarly well-informed about the prices of other potential products, as well as raw materials and factors of production.

The Role of the Entrepreneur The existence of the **entrepreneur** is vitally important for the efficient functioning of markets. The establishment of a supernormal rate of profit as a signal proves effective only insofar as someone recognizes, appreciates, and acts upon the signal. In the eighteenth-century world of Adam Smith, as well as in the nineteenth-century milieu of Alfred Marshall,[6] the

[6]Alfred Marshall (1842–1924), an Englishman, is regarded by many as the father of modern economics. Marshall's work pioneered the marginalist or neoclassical model of the functioning economy. A useful Web site for investigating the life of Marshall and for accessing many of his works is http://cepa.newschool.edu/het/profiles/marshall.htm.

ownership of capital and the management of business were by and large embodied in the same people. These entrepreneurs represented restless, potentially footloose capital, which was mobile enough to flow into industries in which profits were unusually high. One question that hangs over the analysis of contemporary markets is whether institutional change, particularly the separation of ownership from management, leads to the weakening of entrepreneurial activity, and a consequent reduction in market efficiency.

Factor Markets

So far we have discussed the functioning of markets for goods, but an efficient system also requires the market mechanisms to determine the allocation of factors of production (capital, land, and labor) between competing uses. Similar basic principles apply here as in the goods markets. In a free enterprise system individuals can offer their labor to any employer. Generally they will choose that occupation and employer who offers the highest wages or compensation package, although nonpecuniary factors like job satisfaction, working conditions, hours of work, and security of job tenure will also play a part in a worker's rational choice.

The employer in turn is free to hire as much labor as he or she chooses and will be indifferent between workers as long as they all contribute the same amount to output. It is a normal assumption of economics that, at least after a certain point, the marginal product of workers declines, the result of an important observed generality termed the *law of diminishing marginal returns.*[7] Employers will hire labor up to the point where the contribution that the marginal worker makes to revenues (termed the **marginal revenue product**) equals the wage that must be paid. If hiring proceeds beyond this point, under diminishing returns, additional workers will reduce profit. If all workers are indistinguishable in terms of their contribution, and therefore interchangeable, then the wage will be the same for all and will be equal to the revenue product of the marginal worker.

This situation embodies again both efficiency and a form of fairness. The worker is paid the contribution that he or she makes to the revenue of the enterprise. If this marginal revenue product were greater in other employment, the worker would, everything else being equal, change jobs and earn the higher wage. This migration to other employers would happen because the owner or manager of the firm in which the worker's marginal revenue product were greater would offer the worker a higher wage to leave his or her current occupation. No employer would offer more than its marginal product, but each would be prepared to pay up to that amount. The employer to whom the worker is most valuable would win out. This competitive process ensures that workers are employed in their socially highest value use, which would, in its turn, produce an efficient outcome for the economy as a whole. It can also be argued that this process is in a sense equitable, because each worker is paid the amount by which he or she increases the social product. Even though this feature of market systems appeals to some, to others it reveals a

[7]Like all economic laws, the law of diminishing marginal returns is a generalized assumption based on both reasoning and observation.

more problematic proposition and one that merits further examination in Chapter 4 when we consider whether the distribution of well-being that results in a market economy may appropriately be considered as a failure of the system.

Capital Markets

In a modern market economy the **capital market** plays a particularly central role. In the eighteenth or nineteenth century, it was often true that a single entrepreneur was both the manager of the enterprise and the owner of the capital. Today, enterprises are larger and much more use is made of financial intermediaries to provide the funds for investment. Small savers place their money in banks for which they receive interest payments, and these resources are commingled and loaned by the banks to firms. Alternatively, a firm can turn to venture capitalists for a loan (usually pledging some share of future profits) or issue instruments of debt, corporate bonds, in order to gather investment funds. A further avenue is provided by the sale of stocks or shares in the future profit stream of the enterprise.

The function of financial markets is to assess the combination of expected returns and potential risks and to allocate the capital to those ventures that offer the best combination of risk and return. In the case of a bank-financed start-up, the entrepreneur must present a business plan and collateral and the loan officer of the bank must decide whether the potential borrower is creditworthy. The bank wants to loan its limited resources to those borrowers with the highest probability of repayment. Alternatively, if the entrepreneur seeks finance by issuing stock, she or he will try to sell the shares into the stock market at an appropriate price. In this way the financial markets are the midwives for new ventures. Acting together, the individual actors will allocate society's scarce capital resources among potential users. It is important for the efficiency of the system that they act impartially, focusing solely on the hard financial facts, and remain unswayed by personal or political factors.

As well as providing means for the birth and growth of firms, the financial markets also act as undertakers, even executioners, by ensuring that existing firms whose prospects do not merit continued investment are culled from the system. By refusing to issue new loans, or by the protracted fall in the value of companies' shares, the financial markets signal to the management and ownerships of firms a judgment concerning the prospects and performance of the firm. In the short term this signal can just be a warning to mend its ways; in the longer term it is a death sentence. Michael Keren expressed this idea well:

> The capital market as well as providing for the birth of firms, also provides for their death, and for changes in their course in midlife. It plays a Darwinian role of selection. As in Darwinian natural evolution, here too the role of chance is great and the dependence on time is paramount. What succeeds today may be what failed yesterday, because yesterday was not ripe for the idea, or because it was not properly packaged.[8]

Most important, the judgment of the capital market is an impartial one. It is not the opinion of an individual, a politician, or even a "National Board of Investment"

[8]From "On the (Im)possibility of Market Socialism," *Eastern Economic Review* 19, no. 3 (1993), p. 333.

that motivates the decision in a free market economy, but the result of the interplay of many groups. The verdict is a weighted one that takes into account the informed views of a range of people. Bankers, loan officers, fund managers, and individual investors must all make the best informed decisions that they can, otherwise the capital that they own or manage will be lost. A loan officer who shows protracted and systematic bias puts at risk both job and future of the bank. A fund manager who favors pet theories that run counter to logic will see performance suffer and have less capital to manage. The dispassionate function of capital markets is one of the strengths of the market system.

As we shall see in subsequent chapters of this book, one of the drawbacks of centralized socialist planning is the pervasive influence of what is known as a **soft-budget constraint**. This phenomenon was observed long ago. In the 1930s the Austrian economist Ludwig von Mises[9] attacked the theory of socialism on the grounds that rational calculation was impossible without a clearly defined "bottom line."[10] However, the seminal work on the soft-budget constraint, and the coining of the term itself, was by an "insider," the Hungarian economist Janos Kornai[11] who observed firsthand, under central planning, the operation of an economy without capital markets. He noted that in the absence of impartiality in credit and investment funds, and with the lack of a mechanism to gauge and act on performance, an enterprise manager will feel little incentive to perform in a socially efficient way. Rather the manager can make more efficient use of time influencing those politicians and planners who determine access to credit. Instead of being confronted by a "hard" budget constraint, where the amount that they could spend or borrow relates to performance, managers operating under a soft-budget constraint have their fate determined in large part by the degree to which they are favored by their political masters.

Arbitrage and Speculation

Profits are important in a market system because they attract the attention of entrepreneurs and channel new capital into an industry. However, the quest for profit is also vital in keeping the markets themselves "orderly"—that is to say, consistent across space and time. The differential in the price of a good between any two geographical points should be no greater than the cost of transportation between those points. Orderly markets require the action of **arbitrageurs** who engage in a simultaneous transaction of buying where the price is high and selling where the price is low, earning a profit at least enough to cover the transaction and transportation costs.

The orderly nature of markets is furthered by the activity of **speculators**. Unlike arbitrageurs, speculators take a position based on the direction they anticipate

[9]Von Mises (1881–1973) was considered by Milton Friedman to have done more to spread the fundamental ideas of free markets than any other individual. The curious can start their search at http://cepa.newschool.edu/het/profiles/mises.htm.

[10]See Ludwig von Mises, *Socialism: An Economic and Sociological Analysis*, 2d ed. (New Haven: Yale University Press, 1951).

[11]See "The Soft Budget Constraint," *Kyklos* 39 (1986).

prices will move. Investing in shares traded on a stock exchange or the commodities traded on a mercantile exchange is classic speculative activity. It is a popular misconception that speculators increase the volatility of markets. Pure speculation will be profitable only if the speculator "buys low and sells high." A speculator, therefore, increases the demand for the good at the bottom of a price cycle and increases the supply when the price it at the highest. Thus speculation actually reduces the amplitude of market swings and assists in the efficient operation of markets. The exception occurs when the speculator is successful in gaining significant market power and in the extreme can become a monopolist by cornering the market.

CHARACTERISTICS OF THE MARKET SYSTEM

A competitive market system is characterized by a number of advantageous features worth briefly reviewing here:

Under a Market System Disequilibria Are Self-Correcting

Self-correction is certainly one of the most important features of a market system. Because of the flexible prices, disequilibria created by supply shocks or demand shifts invoke a coordinated and automatic response. Any disturbance in the system will set in motion a series of reactions that will adjust the entire system to take account of the changed circumstances, resulting in **self-correcting disequilibria**. Consider a rise in demand. As a first-order effect, the price of the good itself will rise, as will the factors of production and materials that go into making it. The prices of substitutes will rise too, those of complements will fall. Thousands of prices will change in thousands of markets without any central authority directing it. Under central planning the whole menu of prices would require adjustment, relying on ad hoc decisions or models to arrive at a new equilibrium.

An example of this process of adjustment was provided by the market response to the oil shocks of the 1970s. As an example it is complicated by the fact that some "free market" governments (including the United States) acted to impose price controls that prevented the market mechanism from adjusting swiftly and fully to the shock. However, what we did see was a restriction of supply, creating short-run profits and precipitating a series of further adjustments. Higher prices encouraged reduced consumption of oil and oil products. Homes became better insulated, thermostat sales increased, car engines became smaller. Industry sought new, less energy-intensive techniques. The prices of energy substitutes rose, and returns to capital and labor in those industries increased. New sources of supply were brought on line; new capital was invested in oil exploration, production, and oil field rehabilitation. Some believed it to be a potentially catastrophic blow to the global economy. By the early 1980s, however, market action absorbed and corrected those events. Government policy, whether price controls or promotion of alternative fuels, had little impact on the resolution of the crisis. In the Soviet bloc countries, energy prices did not change substantially despite the shift in world prices. Those countries continued with cheap energy, energy-intensive production techniques, and waste until the end of the 1980s, with damaging consequences for their competitiveness when they ultimately emerged into the world economy.

Markets Minimize the Need for Information Flows

For a planning agency to engineer the complex adjustment to prices, quantities, and production techniques across the board that the response to the oil shock produced, and to get the response right, it would have to be both extremely well informed and rather lucky. The market system relies on no such centralization of information. The individual actors in the system need only to know the information required for each unit to maximize its own welfare. No one individual or agency needs access to all price and cost information, and no one needs a full understanding how the whole system works. Thomas Schelling put it this way:

> The dairy farmer doesn't need to know how many people eat butter and how far away they are, how many other people raise cows, how many babies drink milk, or whether more money is spent on beer or milk. What he needs to know is the prices of different feeds, the characteristics of different cows, the different prices [for milk], the relative cost of hired labor and electrical machinery, and what his net earnings might be if he sold his cows and raised pigs instead.[12]

This economy of information is valuable. It saves the expense of collection and relay of data, and the resource cost of the bureaucracy to process it, issue directives, and monitor the fulfillment of the objectives. Perhaps most important, the market offers few opportunities to gain advantage by falsifying data or misrepresenting a situation. As we shall see when we discuss the economic consequences of the centrally planned economy in more detail in Chapter 17, the information gathered by central planners is frequently flawed because the enterprise managers in planned systems encounter incentives to provide inaccurate information to the center. In some cases they might deliberately understate their potential output, enabling them to limit their production quotas. In other cases they might overstate their need for material inputs. Gathering data is expensive, and checking the accuracy of data may be prohibitive. A system that minimizes information demands and decentralizes decision making avoids the problems of a whole system orientating itself on data that are themselves faulty.

A Market System Provides Stimulus to Innovation

Under a market system **innovators** who pioneer new, lower-cost processes or new products that appeal to consumers are rewarded in the short run by **super-normal profits**, or economic rent. It costs resources to develop new processes or goods, and

[12]Cited in Richard Lipsey, Peter Steiner, Douglas Purvis, and Paul Courant, *Economics*, 9th ed. (New York: Harper and Row, 1990), p. 423.

in a market system this investment is made in the expectation of gain through profit. Many innovative ventures fail, and the would-be innovator loses the investment, but some that greatly affect our well-being prove successful.

A planned system, on the other hand, leaves the development of new products largely to the research agencies of the state. An enterprise manager has little incentive to research new techniques or goods other than those that he or she is charged to adopt or produce by the planners. Attempts at innovation could only prove a distraction, taking the manager's attention and budgeted resources away from the prime task of meeting physical production targets.

Under a Market System Relative Prices Reflect Relative Costs

Under a competitive system, the tendency is for the price of a good to be driven toward the marginal cost of its production. At the margin of his or her consumption, therefore, the consumer must be prepared to pay the costs of the inputs and factors used in the production of the marginal unit of the good. The relative prices of goods thus reflect the relative costs of the production. This relationship is sometimes expressed in microeconomic terms as: The marginal rate of substitution in consumption is equal to the marginal rate of transformation in production. This outcome is allocatively efficient. Society directs its scarce resources toward the production of goods that demonstrate the highest values in the eyes of the consumer, maximizing social welfare. An increase in the cost of a resource will raise the cost of the good in whose production it is used. When governments intervene and determine either the quantities of goods to be produced or the prices that shall be charged for them, it is more than likely that relative prices and relative costs of production will diverge. This problem is not seen exclusively in centrally planned economies either. Western governments frequently use price controls to depress the costs of goods or services that politicians, in the name of equity, think should be cheap, generally with unfortunate results for both long-term supply and allocative efficiency.

A Market System Opposes the Concentration of Power

As we shall see when we look at the behavior of planned economies, their function requires combining political and economic power. The political masters not only control the lives of the citizenry through the legal system, but they also control their real incomes through the availability of goods and the prices charged for them. A highly competitive market structure discourages the concentration of economic power. Again, we note that the kind of capitalist market systems we actually confront allows for considerable accretion of economic power. The leaders of industry and trade unions do hold considerable power, both in the marketplace itself and through lobbying in the halls of government. In the late nineteenth century, economic power in the United States became so concentrated that it motivated the intervention of government to break up the mammoth trusts that emerged. The 1950s and 1960s saw considerable alarm over the possibility that the economic and political systems of the developed market economies were evolving into a form of corporatism, but one in which the state was subsidiary to the needs of the corporations rather than vice versa.[13] The sovereignty of the consumer is constantly under threat, but compared to the concentration of power that occurred in the Soviet Union under communism or that is still observed in China today, the consequences were modest.

Even if the leaders of an authoritarian state are well-intentioned and seek nothing but the general good of the population, the task of organization and necessary coercion are so onerous that relying on the enterprise of individuals is more likely to render a happier conclusion. This belief too was held by Adam Smith, and we conclude this chapter with another quote from his most insightful work:

> All systems either of preference or of restraint, therefore, being thus completely taken away, the obvious and simple system of natural liberty establishes itself of its own accord. Every man, as long as he does not violate the laws of justice, is left perfectly free to pursue his own interest in his own way and to bring both his industry and capital into competition with those of any other man or order of men. The sovereign is completely discharged from a duty, in the attempting to perform which he must always be exposed to innumerable delusions and for the proper performance of which no human wisdom or knowledge could ever be sufficient—the duty of superintending the industry of private people and of directing it toward the employments most suitable to the interest of the society. . . . [T]he sovereign has only three duties to attend to; three duties of great importance, indeed, but plain and intelligible to common understandings: first, the duty of protecting the society from the violence and invasion of other independent societies; secondly, the duty of protecting, as far as possible, every member of the society from the injustice or oppression of every other member of it, or the duty of establishing an exact administration of justice; and thirdly, the duty of erecting and maintaining certain public works and certain public institutions.[14]

KEY TERMS AND CONCEPTS

- arbitrageurs
- capital market
- division of labor
- economic rent
- entrepreneur
- general equilibrium
- innovators
- invisible hand
- marginal revenue product
- market demand curve
- market supply curve
- partial equilibrium
- self-correcting disequilibria
- soft-budget constraint
- speculators
- super-normal profits
- windfall profits

[13]These ideas about the concentration of economic and political power in the United States were addressed in John Kenneth Galbraith's *The New Industrial State.*

[14]Adam Smith, *An Inquiry into the Nature and Causes of the Wealth of Nations,* book IV, chapter IX.

QUESTIONS FOR DISCUSSION

1. Describe the role of profit and the role of the entrepreneur in correcting disequilibria.
2. Why are arbitrage and speculation important for the orderly operation of markets?
3. Why are market systems economical in the need for centralizing data?
4. Why is it important for relative prices to reflect relative costs of production in general?
5. What economic functions does Smith conceive of as being the preserve of the sovereign?
6. Why is the capital market both "midwife" and "undertaker"?
7. How does a competitive market system oppose the concentration of power?
8. Is the tendency of wages to reflect the marginal revenue product under competition a recipe for "fairness"?

RESOURCES

Web Sites

The History of Economic Thought..http://cepa.newschool.edu/het/
More about Smith, Marshall, and von Mises can be found at this site.

The von Mises Institute..http://www.mises.org/
The von Mises Institute is a libertarian think tank and lobby group.

The Cato Institute..http://www.cato.org/
A great deal of other libertarian information and ideas can be found at this site.

The Adam Smith Institute..http://www.adamsmith.org/
Devoted to the study of the founder of the modern Anglo-American approach to economics.

Books and Articles

Fry, Michael (ed.). *Adam Smith's Legacy: His Place in the Development of Modern Economics.* New York: Routledge, 1992.

Galbraith, John Kenneth. *The New Industrial State.* Boston: Houghton Mifflin, 1971.

Keren, Michael. "On the (Im)possibility of Market Socialism." *Eastern Economic Review* 19, no. 3 (1993), 333–344.

Kornai, Janos. *The Socialist System: The Political Economy of Communism.* Princeton: Princeton University Press, 1992.

Kornai, Janos. "The Soft Budget Constraint." *Kyklos* 39, no. 1 (1986), 3–30.

Smith, Adam. *The Wealth of Nations,* D. D. Raphael (ed.). London: Everyman's Library Series, 1991.

von Mises, Ludwig. *Economic Calculation in the Socialist Commonwealth.* Auburn, AL: Ludwig von Mises Institute, 1990.

4

MARKET FAILURE AND GOVERNMENT FAILURE

At the close of Chapter 3, we saw that Adam Smith envisaged the task of government as highly limited and beneficent only in three areas: national defense, the administration of justice, and in certain large-scale infrastructural investments that private industry would not, or could not, assume. However, a glance at any modern market economy reveals that government activity is not confined to these areas but extends into production, regulation, and redistribution. In the wealthy countries of the Organization for Economic Cooperation and Development (OECD) governments take in and spend an average of about 40 percent of gross domestic product (GDP).[1] Despite the common political rhetoric of the 1980s and 1990s on the need to downsize government, the trend, measured in terms of governments' share of GDP, seems to be inexorably upward.[2] How is such widespread interference in the market economy explained? The two main answers include (1) the correction of several well-known instances of "market failure" and (2) the redistribution of the social product toward disadvantaged, primarily economically inactive, groups.

MARKET FAILURE

One general justification for government intervention in the operation of free enterprise economy is **market failure**. Although many modern economies are characterized by highly competitive markets for some products and factors of production, the conditions necessary to establish perfect competition in all markets are seldom encountered. We briefly list the four phenomena considered to lead to serious inefficiencies here:

1. **Market power.** The possession of substantial market power by a single or small group of market participants creates conditions under which prices deviate from marginal costs, an allocatively inefficient outcome. Similarly we might encounter market power in the supply of labor through unionization,

[1] Average general government receipts comprised 38.2 percent of GDP in the OECD nations in 1996. Disbursements averaged 41 percent, creating an average general government deficit of 2.8 percent of GDP.
[2] This apparently universal and irresistible trend is labeled *Wagner's law,* after the work of the nineteenth-century German political economist Adolph Wagner.

implying that the price of labor will differ from the value of its marginal product.

2. **Lack of information.** Any inability of relevant market participants to access relevant information at reasonable cost prevents them from acting in an economically rational fashion.
3. **Public goods.** Goods that are nonrival in consumption and for which the marginal cost of supply is zero will not be produced in efficient quantities by a private market.
4. **Externalities.** Outcomes based on private costs and private benefits are inefficient when social costs and social benefits are economically significant.

Government intervention is frequently viewed as a corrective to these problems, but in recent years action by the government is criticized as more harmful than the market imperfections that occasioned it. In this chapter we first examine the rationale for such intervention and then assess to what degree government action is likely to benefit, rather than harm, the general welfare.

Sources of Market Failure: Market Power

Markets function efficiently only when no participant holds substantial market power. Such power may be found on either side of the market. However, it is power on the supply side, monopoly (a single seller) and oligopoly (a few sellers) are considered as most injurious to economic welfare and the frequent target of governmental legislative, judicial, and regulatory activity. Market power on the buying side (monopsony) is considered less harmful to public welfare and is rarely a target of regulatory activity.[3]

The Problem of Monopoly

In perfectly competitive markets, firms act as **price takers**, facing a horizontal, or infinitely elastic, demand curve. Any deviation of price from that dictated by the market will result either in a lower than normal profit rate, untenable in the long run, or a total loss of sales to lower-priced producers. Competitive pressures ensure that the market price is equal to the marginal cost of production. Whenever markets are not perfectly competitive, the demand curve that a firm faces is not horizontal but slopes downward; the firm becomes a **price setter** as it exercises some control over the prices that it charges.

Confronted by downward-sloping demand curves, profit-maximizing firms restrict production, raise prices, and, therefore, generate economic profits, returns above the "normal rate" for all industries. In the case of monopoly the existence of

[3]In fact monopsony is most likely to lie with the government, which is often the sole purchaser of defense output and which in the welfare states of many European countries is the sole purchaser of health-related goods. Little harm to the general welfare derives from this form of monopsony, which is frequently seen as a "countervailing power" to monopoly power.

barriers to entry prevents these super-normal profits from serving their important economic function, which should be to attract new entrants and capital into the industry that would, over time, return the profit rate to normal. Importantly, monopoly drives a wedge between the price that the buyer must pay and the marginal cost of production. Reduced consumption and lost consumers' surplus then create economic inefficiency as illustrated in Figure 4.1. The monopolist maximizes profit by setting output at the point where marginal cost is equal to marginal revenue. This results in a lower output than might be the case under competition Q_M as opposed to Q_C, and a higher price, P_M as opposed to P_C. The loss of welfare is denoted by the triangle labeled "Deadweight loss in consumption."

Monopoly also results in a transfer of welfare from consumers to the monopolist, as shown in Figure 4.1 by the area labeled monopoly profit. Such a transfer is not a loss to society in which both consumer and monopolist are members, but because it is often seen as inequitable and it can be at least as important as the deadweight loss in motivating government action. Correction of this form of market failure, in order to promote efficiency and protect consumers, is considered in many countries a reason for government action.

Natural Monopoly Economists traditionally distinguished between two forms of monopoly. One, usually termed **natural monopoly**, occurs because of high fixed costs and declining or constant marginal costs, which cause the long-run average cost curve to be falling across the relevant output quantities. Competition can be created only at the cost of the expensive and wasteful replication of facilities. In

■ FIGURE 4.1

Monopoly

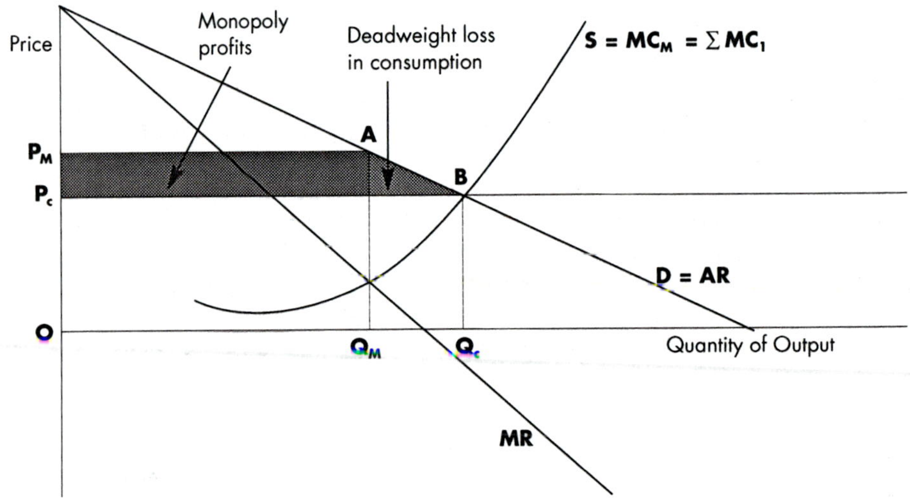

such cases monopoly is generally tolerated, but it is modified by government action, generally through the control of prices by a public agency.

Natural monopoly commonly can be found in industries in which high fixed costs result from extensive initial capital investment. Electricity supply, telephone networks, and TV cable distribution are frequently cited as typical examples of natural monopoly. The existence of natural monopoly in fact involves a dual problem. As shown in Figure 4.2, in the absence of price regulation, a profit-maximizing monopoly would fix output at Q_M and price at P_M, thus earning profits in excess of the normal rate of return and providing a rationale for government intervention to fix the price, usually through the activity of a public utility commission.

However, after the decision to regulate is made, the appropriate price remains a subject of contention. From an efficiency point of view, a case can be made for regulators to fix the price at marginal cost. In Figure 4.2, we can see that in declining average cost industries marginal cost lies below average cost for all relevant output levels. Marginal cost pricing would give a price of P_E, and would require an output of Q_E. However, at such a price, revenues would fail to cover the total costs of the enterprise. Such policy would require a subsidy (ideally in the form of a block grant) to the utility from the government to cover fixed costs. The political unattractiveness of subsidies of this kind often stimulate common "compromise" solutions in which regulatory commissions fix the price at average total cost, as shown in the diagram as P_R. This price, above the marginal cost, allows the utility to cover all fixed and variable costs including a "normal" rate of return on capital.

FIGURE 4.2

Natural Monopoly

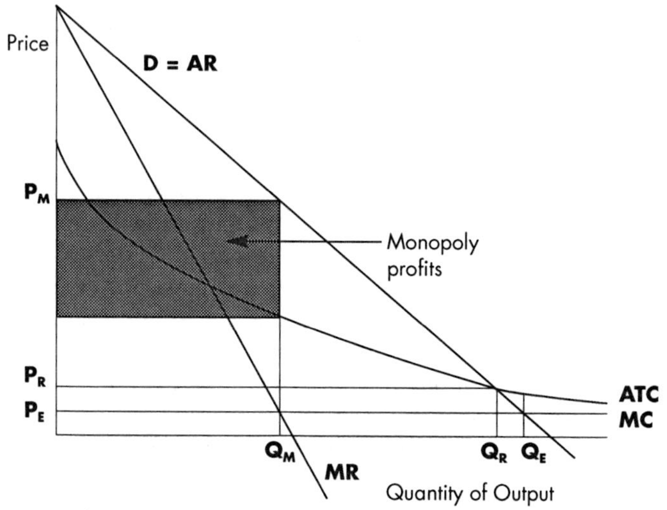

This solution avoids the "gouging" potentiality of an unregulated monopoly, but it does dilute incentives to strive for optimal efficiency. It also presents the possibility of capture of the regulatory agency by the regulatee, a topic we will return to as an example of "government failure."

Natural monopolies do not represent a fixed and unchanging set of industries but are a function of the state of technology. They are a much less significant phenomenon in the long run than in the short run, and economists now regard them as a less of an impediment to efficiently functioning markets than in the past. Changes in technology are capable of bringing about the emergence of competitors that may obviate the need for regulation, and sometimes regulation is a barrier to their emergence.

Consider, for example, long-distance telephone services. All phone traffic was once carried on fixed cables, and the construction of those networks meant great expense. It presented an opportunity to earn monopoly profits because the high cost of establishing the network made the entry of a second or third supplier unlikely. Furthermore, in most people's minds it would be socially wasteful to replicate the network. The emergence of satellite technology to replace cables profoundly affected competitive structure and eased entry, obviating the need for regulation. However, it took regulatory changes (in the United States it was the breaking up of AT&T, the telephone monopoly, and in much of Europe it meant the end of state-provided phone service) to allow the wind of competition to blow through the communications marketplace. In electricity supply, a similar change occurred, due to the realization that, although the grid of cables itself is a natural monopoly, vigorous competition is possible among the suppliers who serve users connected to the grid. Thus, rather than regulating the delivered price of electricity, most of the benefits of competition might be grasped through regulating the price of conveyance on the grid and allowing electricity suppliers to compete on a price basis.

In some cases, government's willingness to intervene in the market can lessen competition and act against the consumers' interest. For example, all transportation modes are gross substitutes and are to some degree in competition with each other. In a market context they can act as a limit on the price behavior of each other. Regulating transportation on a mode-by-mode basis, with mode-specific agencies, can tend to reduce competition in the broader industry and be counterproductive to consumer welfare.

Antitrust Policy The other form of monopoly, which can be termed *unnatural* or *artificial monopoly*, comes through the gathering of market share by a dominant enterprise that then erects barriers to entry to forestall competition. The United States counters this behavior through **antitrust policy**, regulatory and legal action designed to promote freedom of entry and to prohibit the merger (or collusion) of competitive firms that would result in harm to consumers.

All developed nations have a government agency nominally charged with the maintenance of competition, although in some countries it is more vigilant than in others. In the United States the relevant agency is the Federal Trade Commission, an arm of the Department of Justice, empowered to investigate and bring suit in defense of trade. In the United Kingdom it is the Competition Commission, formerly known as the Mergers and Monopoly Commission. Within the European Union competition policy is in the control of the Directorate General for Competition. Such agencies are charged with reviewing competitiveness on an industry basis, assessing the impact of mergers on competition, and, in cases where the evidence merits, taking legal action because of real or potential harm to the public interest.

In doing so, such agencies are looking for accretion of economic power and its impact on economic welfare. In the past much attention focused on the existence of power as measured by "concentration ratios," defined as the share of domestic market consumption represented by a given number of firms. The logic behind these ratios is that the greater the domination of the market by a small number of firms, the less likely is competition to be intense.[4] The most common index is the **four firm concentration ratio**—as calculated by the amount of total sales accounted for by the largest four firms. In the United States, using this basis, the most concentrated industries reported in the Census of Manufacturing were chewing gum and cigarettes (96 and 92, respectively). Another measure is the so-called **Herfindahl Hirschman index** (HHI, named for its originators, O. C. Herfindahl and A. O. Hirschman), which takes into account the market composition.[5]

However, recent developments led to a change of thought about how we should measure economic power or loss of welfare. First, there is skepticism of the view that either market share or concentration ratios are useful indices. Many economists today believe that what matters to keep a market functional, even if not perfect, is not how static market shares add up but the degree to which the market is **contestable**.[6] The threat of a competitor may be as effective as the existence of one in moderating excesses in pricing behavior. If few firms are in the market and **barriers to entry** are high, potential competition is certainly choked. However, even a total monopolist may be subject to restraint, and behave therefore more like a competitor, if entry into the market is easy. The issue therefore becomes not one of the size of market share at any moment in time but rather the height of the barriers to entry that determines the level of contestability.

Consider the position of Microsoft, Inc. In many areas of personal computer software, the company holds a near total monopoly. However, historically, entry into the industry has been relatively easy, and high product prices would serve to lure competitors into the industry. Consequently it is the threat, rather than the actuality, of competition that moderates Microsoft's pricing behavior. If, as was alleged

---

[4]A good discussion of these issues of entry can be found in W. Kip Viscusi, John Vernon, and Joseph Harrington, *Economics of Regulation*, 2d ed. (Cambridge: MIT Press, 1995).

[5]The HHI is calculated by summing the squares of the market share of all the firms in the market. Hence the highest value (perfect monopoly would be 100^2 or 10,000. Competition is reflected by a lower score. Ten firms each with 10 percent of the market would have an HHI of 1,000. A good discussion of these measures as well as issues of entry can be found in W. Kip Viscusi, John Vernon, and Joseph Harrington, *Economics of Regulation and Anti Trust*, 2d ed. (Cambridge: MIT Press, 1995).

[6]The original discussion on this topic can be read in William J. Baumol, John C. Panzar, and Robert Willig, *Contestable Markets and the Theory of Industry Structure* (New York: Harcourt Brace Jovanovich, 1982).

in the recent antitrust suit, Microsoft can use its market power to restrict entry, the market is no longer contestable and loss of welfare can result.

The growing integration of the world economy and generally falling barriers to international trade accelerated the decline in reliance on domestic concentration ratios as indices of market power.[7] In the past, domestic markets tended to be relatively closed to each other compared to the situation today. Tariff barriers were higher and frictional impediments to trade more significant because of high communications and transportation costs. **Trade to GDP ratios** were generally lower than they are today. Because of the comparatively closed nature of national economies, power in the domestic market represented a definite threat to the welfare of domestic consumers. Now in general the greater volume of trade, lower average tariff levels, and an increasing number of regional free trade blocs all make the structure of domestic concentration increasingly irrelevant. In such circumstances, domestic markets, although perhaps highly concentrated, may be highly contestable because of growing competition from abroad and relatively low barriers to entry to foreign firms. For example, the four firm concentration ratio for the U.S. automobile market in the late 1960s was high, with one firm, General Motors (GM), representing more than half of the market. Conventionally measured market power was high, but the surge of imports in the 1970s showed how easily contestable the market was. The Federal Trade Commission closed its ongoing investigation of GM in the mid-1970s.

In some cases the existence of this high degree of contestability of domestic markets due to potential entry of foreign firms led to the virtual abandonment of traditional antitrust policy. Many governments tolerate, encourage, or even help to create through merger **national champions** to monopolize the domestic market and control the resources to compete with foreign firms.[8] This policy is justified generally by the belief in substantial economies of scale in production or, more relevant recently, in research and development.

Labor Unions

So far we discussed only monopoly in the supply of goods and services. Labor organizations represent the attempt to monopolize a factor of production, generally with a view to restrict supply and raise its price. The consequences are usually higher wages and better benefits for workers, and a higher level of unemployment than would exist otherwise.

Governmental policy toward labor unions varies widely from country to country. It also changed a good deal over time. For example, in the first capitalist industrial society, nineteenth-century Britain, the government, elected by and

[7]On balance, trade barriers have been falling across the world due to unilateral tariff cutting and the action of the successive rounds of trade negotiations under the General Agreement on Tariffs and Trade (GATT) and now the World Trade Organization (WTO). One counter to this trend has been the increase in nontariff barriers to trade (NTBs) in recent years.

[8]French policy often leaned in this direction, especially in the 1970s and 1980s when a policy of creating publicly owned national champions in key industries was espoused.

largely beholden to property owners, took a dim view of the union movement because it sought to shift income from capital to labor. It was, therefore, criminalized through the Combination Acts,[9] and union organizers were arrested, imprisoned, and on occasion deported. After the extension of the electoral franchise to nonproperty owners in the 1880s, labor won the right to organize and formed its own political party to protect such gains. Other industrialized nations also saw violence and political upheaval in the birth of the movement.

Today most industrialized countries not only recognize unions, but also make organized labor part of the process of economic management. In Europe especially, organized labor plays a prominent role in both politics and economic management, as we will discuss more fully in the chapters on Sweden, France, and Germany. However, the decline of heavy industry and the growing surplus of labor in these economies, as indicated by historically high rates of unemployment, weakened the power of the union movement. Union power in the European economies remains greatest now in the public sector, where it shows resistance to market forces because of a clear link to electoral politics.

Late-industrializing countries are still passing through the stage of union establishment. The Japanese miracles of the 1960s through 1980s were assisted by the repression of the labor movement in the late 1950s. After decades of opposition by employers and government, Korean unions are now emerging. In countries more remote in development terms, such as Indonesia, independent unions are still banned.

LACK OF INFORMATION

Market systems work well only if consumers can access reliable information about the product that they are buying. In the case of simple commodities, reliance on the old maxim **caveat emptor** ("let the buyer beware") is probably adequate; in such cases information is relatively cheaply available and reputation is an important asset when repeat purchases are frequent. However, in the case of more complex goods or goods that are purchased infrequently, information might be difficult, or expensive to obtain.

Where information is expensive, governments frequently step in to "protect" the consumer. In some cases this is done by prescribing behavior for those who make and sell products to the public or by dictating particular product standards. Rules or laws specify what information a seller must offer to the buyer and what recourse is available to the buyer in the case of disappointment. In other industries or professions, the government may create barriers to entry by limiting access to the industry to those who demonstrate "appropriate qualifications," preventing the unqualified from offering such goods or services. Such licensing is common in a wide variety of professions from lawyers to morticians.

[9]The Combination Acts were legislated in 1800 and repealed in 1825; although unions were legal, leaders were still frequently prosecuted for specific job actions, such as strikes. See Rondo Cameron, *A Concise Economic History of the World* (New York: Oxford University Press, 1989), p. 218.

This type of regulation and licensing may provide an effective way of minimizing the consumers' need for expensive information. Consider, for example, a potential patient choosing a surgeon. In most countries only people who have attended medical school, served an internship, and passed examinations can hang up a shingle and offer surgical services. Performing surgery without such qualifications is forbidden. In contrast, fewer restrictions limit who can offer to shave people or cut hair. In more remote times, such licensing was not considered essential for surgeons, and indeed barbers performed surgery along with their shaving duties.

Why is government intervention merited in one case and not the other? The answer lies in the availability of information and the consequences of not being able to get it. When it comes to hairdressing, we feel we can rely on reputation to weed out poor performers. One bad haircut does not kill and serves in itself to tell others about performance. One poor surgery can kill, and licensing, while not eliminating the problem entirely, does, it is argued, reduce the risk to the public. The goal of protecting of the public has spawned a large regulatory industry. In the United States, the government hires inspectors to tell consumers what meat is "choice," requires product information on labels, looks for "misleading" advertising, requires approval of drugs, and so forth. Few people would argue that all of this regulation and inspection is necessary, especially in view of the fact that market remedies are available in many cases. Frequently such licensing is the result of rent-seeking behavior, a phenomenon that we will discuss in greater detail later in this chapter.

PUBLIC GOODS

The third major class of market failure is due to the existence of "public goods." The qualities of public goods may best be understood by looking first at those of private goods. Private goods and services, whose supply is left to individual rather than collective action, share two important qualities: excludability and diminishability. **Excludability** enables producers or sellers to charge a price for private goods and services because they can deny access to those who fail to pay the price. **Diminishability** implies that one person's consumption of a good or service reduces the supply available to others. It is really another way of saying that the marginal cost of consumption is greater than zero. Efficiency, therefore, requires that suppliers of private goods charge a price that is greater than zero as well. Excludability establishes a feasible mechanism by which to impose a charge.

In contrast, pure public goods are neither diminishable nor excludable. The marginal cost of additional unit of consumption is zero, and therefore economic efficiency requires a zero price. Anyway, the absence of excludability means no cost-effective way of charging for the service. The absence of excludability leads to the **free rider problem**, in which people are able to enjoy the service without payment and therefore may make no financial contribution to their "fair" share of costs. Consequently, private institutions will fail to supply, or will chronically undersupply, such goods, and only the government with its ability to coerce payment through taxation holds the potential to supply the goods at the optimal level.

Although pure public goods are theoretically important, in reality they represent a relatively small class. National defense, the system of administration of justice, and public health measures are salient examples. In none of these cases can an individual be excluded from benefit without fundamentally altering the nature of the good. In virtually all countries, these goods are provided by the government and are financed out of tax revenue. Moreover, such goods are probably essential for the existence of the modern state. It is difficult to imagine in these cases how a private substitute could be created.

The provision of lighthouses is a much-used example of public goods in the economic textbooks. Its frequency stems more from its tractability than its economic significance. Lighthouses are not as fundamental to an economy as defense or the law, but they obviously do provide economic benefits. Use of the services of lighthouses is susceptible to free ridership, and would therefore be undersupplied by private institutions,[10] which would have to rely on donations from shippers, sailors, and the general public to finance them. It requires a considerable step to assume that the government would get the level of provision right. To supply even pure public goods at an optimal level, the government must find a means of accurately estimating benefits or inducing consumers (in this case the shippers and sailors) to reveal their demand. It is quite conceivable that the government would err just as much as a private system based on subscription or contribution. In fact, the nature of politics and lobbying would probably lead to oversupply, for reasons discussed later in the chapter.

In general, socially provided goods are not "public" in the rigorous sense. In most cases they are excludable, as we can see by looking at the examples of education, health services, highways, recreation facilities, and so forth, all of which have counterparts in the private sector. In most countries, services that are clearly diminishable (for example, postal services or garbage disposal) are provided by the government as well as the private sector. To justify government supply of such potentially private goods and services, market failure is not sufficient. The actual motivations might include distributive concerns, a need to establish equitable standards, or a conviction that government is superior in efficiency terms to private enterprise in some tasks. In recent years economists focused considerable attention on public goods supply and frequently arrived at the conclusion that it is determined at least as much by the lobbying activity of interested parties as by a concern for correcting market failure.

EXTERNALITIES

The final class of market failure to be introduced here consists of imperfections created by the presence of *externalities*, external economies and diseconomies, sometimes called spillovers. These consequences to third parties (or bystanders) derive

[10]In fact, despite the clear public good qualities of lighthouses, in the nineteenth century they were provided largely by private charities or by placing a levy or surcharge on harbor fees.

from the economic activities of others. Such consequences may be either positive, contributing to the welfare of the third party, or negative. Because of the unrequited nature of externalities (we do not receive compensation for negative effects, nor do we pay for the positive ones), they do not enter into the decision process of the individuals initiating the activity. Both consumers and producers make decisions by considering private benefits and private costs. From a societal point of view, the appropriate considerations should be social benefit and social cost.

Figure 4.3 illustrates how the existence of a substantial externality (perhaps the ability of producers to emit smoke into the atmosphere without paying any pollution fee or compensation to those affected) causes a divergence between the **private marginal cost** and the **social marginal cost**. The consumer is confronted by prices based on the private, not the social marginal cost. Correspondingly, the market system with the imperfection of uncompensated externalities tends to overproduce the good, to the point Q_P in Figure 4.3, rather than the socially optimal position of Q_S.

One of the most obvious and pressing examples of externalities lies in the analysis of environmental issues. Consider a factory that emits air pollution as a by-product of manufacturing a good. In the absence of any control, the manufacturer considers only private benefit and treats the environment as a free resource, despoiling the air and reducing the welfare of others in the process.

Government regulatory activity to counter pollution can be of several kinds:

1. It can ban the polluting process entirely.
2. It can establish minimum compliance standards for the manufacturer to meet.
3. It can offer subsidies to the manufacturer to reduce pollution.
4. It can charge the manufacturer a fee per unit of pollution emitted.

■ FIGURE 4.3

Private and Social Marginal Costs and Benefits

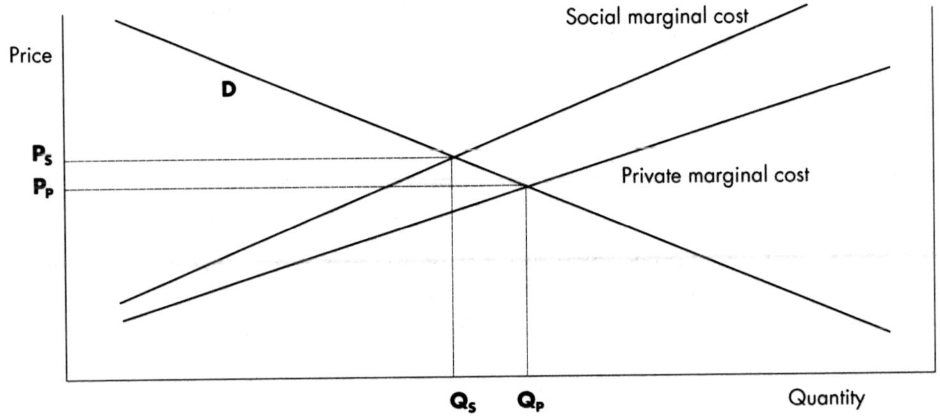

The first two remedies are generally held by economists to be allocatively inefficient. In the first case, banning the production totally will generally result in an undersupply of the polluting good; the loss of consumer welfare from the absolute nonavailability of the product may outweigh the gains of completely clean air or water. In the second case, establishing minimum standards for pollution leaves no incentive for manufacturers to press for a further reduction below the standard, even though an additional cut might be socially beneficial. The third and fourth courses of action can both lead to an economically efficient outcome. A subsidy to reduce pollution can produce the same effect as a pollution fee because either can be designed to reflect the marginal cost of the polluting activity. What is obviously different is the distributional impact of the two approaches. Policy 3 grants the right to pollute to manufacturers and bribes them to stop. Policy 4 gives the manufacturers no rights but forces them to purchase the ability to pollute from the state.

Some economists argue that the problem of externalities is solely the result of the inadequate specification of property rights. Private individuals who hold clear rights of ownership and live in countries where the legal system functions well, can pursue recourse against the despoliation of their property or loss of health through a civil suit. The threat of litigation results in negotiation and in many cases a contract that will result in a mutually acceptable, and therefore efficient, solution to "externality problems." Consider, for example, a case in which my neighbor was about to reduce my welfare by building a skyscraper that would block the sun. If my right to access to light were clear and legally guaranteed, then the neighbor could only proceed if we were able to arrive at a contract whereby my permission to build was granted on the basis of some form of compensation. Alternatively, if the neighbor clearly holds the right to use his site in any way he chooses, irrespective of third-party consequences, I might dissuade him from construction through a contract that appropriately compensated him for his lost opportunity and revenue. Either solution would be efficient although the distributional effects (who gained and who lost welfare) would be markedly different according to how the property rights were determined.

This approach to the problem of externalities is exemplified by the work of Ronald Coase.[11] His work suggests that the externality problem might be solved through the complete definition of property rights. Fully comprehensive and well-specified property rights would result in the "internalization" of externalities, and the optimal solution would be arrived at through negotiation and contract. This happy result of the Coase theorem is, however, subject to some limitations. "Internalization" leading to mutually agreeable contracts, and therefore efficiency, might be the outcome in cases where the number of participants is small, but as soon as we get to a case where either the affecting or the affected party is numerous the costs of negotiating the appropriate contract may become prohibitively high. In such cases government intervention may achieve close to equivalent results at the cost of fewer resources. Most of the discussion about externalities relates to negative effects, partly because issues as important as pollution, global warming, and

[11]Ronald Coase, "The Problem of Social Cost," *Journal of Law and Economics* 3 (October 1960), pp. 1–44.

traffic congestion play prominent roles in our lives. However, we should not discount the responsibility of governments to correct the market failure of the underprovision of positive externalities. Indeed, it can be argued that much of the benefit of public education lies in the production of external benefits stemming from educated and productive citizenry.

GOVERNMENT FAILURE

Each of the four phenomena discussed previously is real and each can cause markets to fail, leading to a less efficient outcome than would be the case if markets were perfect. Thus, there is an initial rationale to consider the use of government action to address market failure. However, it would be imprudent to conclude that government intervention in such cases will always increase welfare. Such a conclusion unwisely compares imperfect markets to a perfect government. In recent years, economists have taken a more skeptical view of the capabilities of government, recognizing that there are many sources of **government failure**, which can themselves be at least as damaging as the market failure they seek to correct.

We cannot assume that governments will always be, in Anne Krueger's phrase, "benevolent, costless social guardians."[12] It is problematic even to consider a homogenous "public" interest, because only rarely will all members of the public be affected in a symmetrical fashion; in any action, some will gain more than others. Government, even if it is motivated to increase aggregate welfare, will inevitably face the problems of determining the preferences of citizens in the absence of markets and meaningful prices. Furthermore, like the rest of us, bureaucrats and politicians are subject to complex incentives. They will, in most cases, pursue their own interest, as do employers, workers, and households. Of course, this dilemma is nothing new. It leads us back once more to Adam Smith, whose opinion of government was just as poor as his opinion of manufacturers. He wrote in *The Wealth of Nations:*

> Great nations are never impoverished by private, though they sometimes are by public, prodigality and misconduct. The whole, or almost the whole, public revenue is in most countries employed in maintaining unproductive hands. Such are the people who compose a numerous and splendid court, a great ecclesiastical establishment, great fleets and armies, who in time of peace produce nothing, and in time of war acquire nothing which can compensate the expense of maintaining them, even while the war lasts. Such people, as they themselves produce nothing, are all maintained by the produce of other men's labor.[13]

Sources of Government Failure

We turn now to look at some of the specific sources of government failure.

[12]Anne Krueger, "Economists' Changing Perceptions of Government," *Weltwirtschaftliches Archiv* 126, no. 3 (1990), p. 419.
[13]Adam Smith, *Wealth of Nations,* book II, chapter III.

Availability of Information One of the beauties of the market system lies in its economy of information: it operates in a decentralized way, with no participant needing to see "the whole picture." Government action, on the other hand, requires all relevant information to be centralized. Even if we make the contentious assumption that the objective of bureaucrats and politicians is to maximize public welfare, rational choices about what public goods to supply and in what quantity require an accurate picture of the total costs and benefits of that activity. Later in this book we discuss the experience of the socialist planned economies more fully and examine in some detail the problems and the resource costs of maintaining a reliable flow of information from periphery to center. However, the problem of gathering accurate information is not unique to centrally planned economies. In a mixed market economy, groups that benefit from the provision of a publicly supplied good find it in their interest to overstate their demand by strategically misleading behavior. Government will only outperform even an imperfect market if it has access to all appropriate information. This task, however, is at best expensive and at worst impossible when participants see an incentive to provide misleading information.

The Capture of Regulators The presence of monopoly power can reduce social welfare, and for this reason public policy to regulate monopolies often becomes a staple of government activity. The main device for the control of monopoly power generally lies with regulatory agencies established to supervise pricing and output. However, a large body of literature suggests that, over time, a regulated industry tends to "capture" the regulatory body set to oversee it. Regulators often identify more with those of the industry that they, in theory, control than with the public at large. In part this **capture of regulators** occurs because of a "revolving door" of personnel between the agency and the industry, as well as an understandable and human need to limit the frequency of adversarial behavior between the regulator and the regulated.

Regulation may also impair the long-term performance of an industry. A regulated industry generally enjoys guaranteed profit margins set by the agency. Given this guarantee, firms tend to grow cautious about innovation and often pay too little attention to cost control. The industry actually comes to enjoy the protection of the agency set to constrain it. A comfortable symbiosis develops, characterized by high costs, excess capacity, and a lack of enterprise. Prices to the consumer, often set by the regulatory agency to cover average costs, trend upward in accommodation of increasing inefficiency and waste. The actions of regulators establish a "soft-budget constraint," which alters the cost structure of the industry at the expense of consumers. Anne Krueger points out "that the real truth of the capture theory is frequently revealed when deregulation is proposed: it is more often than not, those in the regulated industry themselves who are the loudest in protest against deregulation!"

Collective Action In his important book *The Logic of Collective Action*, Mancur Olsen argues that small interest groups can organize much more easily and forcefully than large ones.[14] Small groups with intense preferences, through their **collective action**, will lobby hard for some types of expenditure, even if total costs well exceed benefits, precisely because the costs will be spread among large numbers, while the benefits are more compactly distributed. Members of beneficiary groups try to "free-ride" on the broader tax-paying population, and the consequence is that some public goods will be oversupplied. Moreover, in a process known as "log rolling," pressure groups band together to form coalitions and are thus able to receive the support of other small groups for their cause in return for reciprocal support of the other groups' schemes. The result of this process is a general oversupply of public goods.

The same lobbying phenomena carry implications elsewhere in the sphere of government action. Consider, for example, the issue of trade protection. An industry and its workers may maintain strong preferences concerning the imposition of a protective tariff and may lobby hard for it. They will frequently prevail although the impact on overall consumer welfare might be strongly negative, purely because they are easily organized and highly focused, while the "losers" are dispersed and disorganized. A good example of this phenomenon can be seen in the U.S. automotive industry during the 1980s, which was adversely affected by foreign (primarily Japanese) competition and a surging import market share. Extensive lobbying in Washington produced government sympathy, which in turn led to pressure on the Japanese to impose "voluntary export restraints," which curtailed the number of vehicles shipped into the United States (though not their value). Estimates of the cost of this action include an increase of $960 in the price of each new automobile sold in the United States and an extra burden on consumers of $160,000 per job saved.[15] Automobile company profits rose sharply, and motor executives earned record salaries, not for their leadership in production but for their persuasive lobbying. In short, the total costs of government action certainly exceeded the benefits, but a compact lobbying group for control overwhelmed a dispersed opposition and earned monopoly rents.

Rent-Seeking Behavior This example from the U.S. automotive industry introduces us to **rent-seeking behavior**, defined as *the expenditure of real resources in the attempt to appropriate a surplus in the form of rent*. In the previous example, auto company executives employed lobbyists (which represent real resources) to convince the government to restrict competition from abroad (the "voluntary" export restraints). Their efforts reduced supply and created monopoly rents, which accrue to management, capital, and labor in the motor industry.[16]

---

[14]See Mancur Olsen, *The Logic of Collective Action: Public Goods and the Theory of Groups* (Cambridge: Harvard University Press, 1971).

[15]Robert Crandall, "Import Quotas and the Automobile Industry: The Costs of Protection," *Brookings Review*, summer 1984, 8–16.

[16]Note that the Japanese motor industry shares in these rents that are extracted from the U.S. consumer. Also bear in mind that the government action produces a deadweight loss (due to reduced consumption) as well as the redistribution from consumers to the industry, which is due to increased prices.

A common form of government intervention, ostensibly motivated by a desire to protect the consumer, denies access to specific industries or professions to those not appropriately qualified. This regulation reduces the supply in such activities and enables the successful entrants to earn a monopoly rent. The possibility of this reward encourages rent-seeking behavior. The loss to society takes the form of use of real resources to secure monopoly rents as well as the dead weight loss of monopoly pricing policy. Rent seeking is frequently analyzed and discussed in the context of less-developed countries where it appears in many forms, from the ability of customs clerks to generate bribes to the allocation of large-scale import licenses. However, it is important to recognize that such behavior can be found in developed economies too.

Pork Barreling Politicians, whether democratically elected or not, are prone to use government expenditures to bolster their own position. James Buchanan was awarded the Nobel Prize in economics for work in political economy based on the premise that politicians in a democracy act to maximize the probability of their reelection.[17] Representatives of a particular district will lobby hard for specific expenditures that will benefit their own electorate. In this activity, known as **pork barreling**, projects may take the form of public expenditure on infrastructure or government facilities that benefit the locality but the cost of which is spread over the tax-paying population of the entire economy. We can also note that even though they show less sensitivity to the vagaries of public opinion, dictators or other authoritarian regimes also use the public exchequer to build coalitions of supporters.

We can find examples of politicians opportunistically using expenditures to enhance their future in many contexts. For example, in the runup to the Russian presidential elections in 1994, Boris Yeltsin acted to relax the relatively tight monetary policy of the central bank. This move ensured that joblessness and the failure of enterprises to pay wages to their workers would result in only minimal impact on electoral preference. U.S. presidential candidates may support higher levels of defense expenditure to capture votes in politically marginal areas where the local economy is highly defense dependent.

This "pork barrel" analysis presents three general implications for government activity. First, voters or groups of voters who care a great deal about a specific issue are likely to be rewarded for their concern, especially in the case of "single issue" voters. For example, in the United States it would be difficult to reduce health care expenditure for the elderly largely because this issue is so decisive for a large group of voters. Second, in countries where politicians rely on contributions to finance their election campaigns, the concerns of the check-writing rich are, *ceteris paribus*, likely to receive greater attention than those of the poor. Finally, because of log rolling, the creation of coalitions will result in a general oversupply of quasi-public goods.

---

[17]James M. Buchanan and Gordon Tullock, *The Calculus of Consent* (Ann Arbor: University of Michigan Press, 1989).

Agency Inertia Once created, bureaucracies tend to take on a life of their own, and they will seek to perpetuate their existence by finding work to do. In 1935 the Roosevelt administration founded the Rural Electrification Authority (REA) to facilitate the provision of electricity to rural farms and households. Practically all households now have power, and those who don't live a lifestyle so remote that they can be presumed to be avoiding it, its task is now finished. However, it managed to stay in business, albeit under the new name of the Rural Utilities Service, initially by providing subsidized funds to ski areas and golf courses. With the arrival of the Web, it found a new role ensuring that rural schools obtained high-speed Internet access. This **agency inertia** can occur when bureaucrats show little interest in cutting their own jobs and in some cases maintain a chokehold on the information about their own activities.

Deadweight Loss and Taxes The case for "correcting" market failure rests on imperfect markets causing a **deadweight loss**, a fall in economic welfare that accrues to no one. However, government action is not costless and must be financed in one of three ways—taxation, borrowing, or the printing of money—any of which inevitably produce an adverse effect on the operation of the market and therefore its own deadweight loss.

With the exception of lump-sum taxes, all taxes influence economic choices by changing relative prices.[18] They thereby impose an excess burden and reduce economic welfare. Taxes on income, for example, drive a "wedge" that distorts the household's choice between labor and leisure. Consumption, value-added, and excise taxes also change relative prices, distorting choice and creating deadweight losses.

Sometimes a particular tax results in a large excess burden while generating little revenue. In the late eighteenth century, for example, Britain imposed a revenue-raising tax on the improbable tax base of number of windows. The rationale behind this was that the number of windows in a dwelling provided a rough approximation of the wealth of the occupant. It also had the advantage of being a highly visible tax handle. However, in order to avoid the tax, many occupants simply bricked up windows, hence, reducing the tax base. Any change in behavior occasioned solely by the imposition of a tax is an example of deadweight loss.

Although less visible than taxes, the other means of finance for government also imply deadweight losses. An increase in government borrowing tends to raise interest rates, thereby distorting the choice between saving and consumption, and leading, to a crowding out of private-sector investment. Printing money prompts inflationary consequences that, even if anticipated, distort the choice between present and future consumption, and if unforeseen by some will cause profound distributional consequences. It is therefore important to recognize that any government expenditure must be financed by means that impose welfare losses. Any efficiency gains that can be anticipated by the establishment of regulatory agencies or the provision of public goods must be weighed against the efficiency losses that are occasioned by raising the revenue to finance them.

---

[18]Lump sum taxes are those levied on a base that is totally inelastic. An example is the **poll tax**, the base of which is population.

GOVERNMENT AND REDISTRIBUTION

Government action is not limited to regulation nor is government expenditure limited to the provision of goods and services. A large part of government spending, particularly in industrialized countries, consists of redistributive expenditures. This particular portion of the government budget grew most rapidly in recent years and will, for the reasons of interest group politics outlined earlier, be difficult to contain or curtail in the years ahead.

Redistributive expenditures can take two forms. They may be direct **transfer payments** of cash (such as old age pensions, unemployment compensation, and cash welfare benefits). Alternatively, redistribution may take an in-kind form such as the provision of subsidized housing, free education, free medicine, and so on. Although the market may provide these goods and services, those who are less well off will face limited access because they are constrained by limited budgets. These redistributional expenditures presently dominate the public finances in most of the developed market economies. In Western Europe and the United States, subsidized housing and social security payments taken together represent between 38 percent and 60 percent of total government expenditure. However, these and similar statistics tend to overstate the redistributive stance of most government policy toward lower income groups. Although many direct program expenditures are targeted toward the poor, they are by and large offset by **tax expenditures** that favor higher-income groups. Such tax expenditures take the form of tax relief for *inter alia* pension contributions, insurance premiums, mortgage payments, and property tax payments, all of which are expenditures that rise more than proportionally with income.

The justification for government's role in reshaping the distribution of income that results from market interaction must be different from that which legitimizes the "correction" of market imperfections that reduce allocative efficiency. Although the skewed income and wealth distributions that result from a market economy are frequently seen as one of its "failures," it is not apparent that efficiency suffers from this increased inequality. A somewhat tenuous case can been made that a more even income distribution can enhance social cohesion, and thus increase "social productivity," but it is by no means universally accepted.[19]

The claim for the "justness" of the distribution of income that results in a market system depends on the idea that material reward should be directly related to contribution.[20] Given the appropriate assumptions, each factor of production in a market economy may be thought of as being appropriately rewarded when it receives its marginal value product; that is, each factor is paid what it contributes at the margin. An individual or a family income is therefore the sum of the

[19]The "Swedish model," which we review in Chapter 7, emphasizes social cohesion and egalitarianism.

[20]For an interesting discussion of the justice of rewards in a market economy, see Arthur Okun, *Equity and Efficiency: The Big Trade-off* (Washington, DC: Brookings, 1975), pp. 40–50. Reprinted in part as "Rewards in a Market Economy," in Bornstein, *Comparative Economic Systems: Models and Cases*, 7th ed. (Burr Ridge, IL: Richard D. Irwin, 1994).

contributions of the factors of production that the unit owns or controls. These factors derive from six sources:

1. *Natural talent and ability.* Ability is not equally distributed at birth. Some people possess characteristics (intelligence, strength, stature) that allow them to be more productive and therefore more rewarded than others.
2. *Acquired skills.* The earning power of congenital characteristics is qualified by the skills and experience acquired during education and working life. Economists generally regard this process as the accumulation of human capital (investment in oneself) made by education and foregone earnings.
3. *Effort.* Inasmuch as effort is a determinant of productivity, it should affect earnings. Employers should hire the hard worker and pay him or her more than a time server. The ability to selectively compensate employees is conditioned on the ability of employers to pay different rates for the same job description, which is often organizationally difficult or in some cases legally prohibited.
4. *Inherited wealth.* In almost all of the countries for which good statistics are compiled, wealth is distributed less equally than income. Much of this inequity results from inheritance whereby blocs of wealth, represented by productive physical and financial assets, are passed from generation to generation. It is also important to note that human capital and inherited wealth are highly correlated. More affluent parents tend to invest more in the human capital of their offspring.
5. *Accumulated savings.* Not all physical and financial assets are inherited. One's stock of productive assets is also a function of savings and consumption decisions made over a lifetime. The more one foregoes in one time period, the greater will be the capital to be consumed in a later one.
6. *Related supply and demand considerations.* Finally, income depends a great deal on circumstances over which we can exercise little control. The value of a worker's marginal product, for example, is a function of the supply and demand, and therefore the price of the product that he or she makes. Consider a coal miner. His income would rise should the world oil supply be restricted, but it might fall were a technology for cheap solar energy devised.

Given these complex considerations (compounded by the many imperfections of both product and factor markets), it becomes difficult to sustain a belief in the unique justice of market-based distribution. Most people would accept the premise that the amount of effort (item) one puts into one's work, as well as the amount of saving and investment in one's own human capital (item), should be rewarded. These represent sacrifices that should be compensated, and should be seen to be compensated, because of favorable incentive effects.

On the other hand, strong disagreement on the ethics of inheritance still remains. In the immediate post–World War II period, especially in the European social democracies, egalitarian sentiment supported the enactment of almost confiscatory estate taxation designed to break up inherited wealth and "level the playing field" for a new generation. However, loopholes enabled those who availed themselves of forward-thinking estate planning to avoid the tax, and the incidence of estate taxation fell only on the unwary. Today, tax planners refer to the estate tax in the United States as "the voluntary tax." Republicans stigmatized it further by terming it the "death tax" and it looks as if it will disappear entirely in the United States in the next decade.

Governments not only affect the income distribution by tax and transfer, but they may also attempt to influence the structure of wages. One frequently used policy is the institution of a minimum wage. The original justification was that all jobs should pay at least "a living wage." Within the United States at least this goal clearly has not been achieved. Many critics claim that the imposition of a non-market-clearing wage resulted in high levels of unemployment, especially among young people.

Attempts are also made to address differences that may be related to income or gender. Currently in the United States and in some nations of Europe, governments face pressure to regulate the labor market through the imposition of a wage structure based on "comparable worth." In simple terms, this theory suggests that two jobs that require roughly similar effort, education, and qualifications should be paid similarly. It was used to justify setting public-sector pay scales in line with private ones as part of the Swedish system of wage settlement. It also plays a substantial role in an argument to raise the rates of pay in typically "female" occupations to eliminate the gap between male and female average wages.

Justifications for Redistributive Policy

The predominance of redistribution in government expenditures results in far-reaching effects on the economic system. It it is important to examine the rationale for government intervention to amend or correct the income distribution determined by the market. None of the following explanations is in itself dominating, but all were used in recent years to justify redistributive "tax and spend" policies.

Utilitarianism If we start from a generally held position in economics, that the more one has of a good the less it is valued at the margin, it can be argued that the intrinsic value of $1 is greater to a poor person than a rich one. Consequently, taking $1 from a rich person and giving it to a poor one would increase social well-being. **Utilitarianism** (or "the greatest happiness of the greatest number principle") makes a case for the maximization of social well-being through redistribution. It follows that an enlightened social guardian might pursue redistribution on these grounds, subject always to the caveat that the disincentive effects on total output are less than the welfare gain.[21] However, in reality such a picture of government is at variance with the views that we laid out earlier.

---

[21] Utilitarianism was a school of social philosophy founded by Jeremy Bentham (1748–1835). It provided much of the philosophical basis for nineteenth-century economic thought.

Altruism It is attractive to see the development of a wide system of social programs as the outgrowth of collective **altruism**. In such a view the welfare-promoting aspects are even greater than the utilitarian rationale. Under altruistic motivation, giving, like Portia's "quality of mercy" in Shakespeare's *Merchant of Venice*, would be twice blessed, enhancing the welfare of both givers and receivers. Again, however, this rationale falls short as an explanation for the growth of major social programs, although it might be important in private redistributive charities.

Social Contract A more contemporary view of redistribution sees it motivated by quasi-contractual relationships. In this concept of **social contract**, citizenship, or residence, endows everyone with rights to a minimum standard of living. Thus it is the right of the old, the young, the halt, the lame, and the unemployed or others who possess little to sell in the market system to be supported to some minimum level. A key question centers around where that minimum level should be located.

In early capitalist economies, the right was to subsistence alone, and no more. Support above that level was denied because it would reward indigence and, according to **vacuum theory of population**, attributed to Malthus, it would increase the number of paupers. Consequently, support for the poor whether "indoor" (that is in poorhouses) or "outdoor" using cash grants and in-kind support was minimal. The rise of the liberal welfare states and the extension of the voting franchise changed support levels. In contemporary European social democracies, the level of support is relatively high, and the income distribution that results is quite egalitarian. The income share of the richest 20 percent in Europe is generally around five times that of the poorest 20 percent, as opposed to about 8:1 in the United States. Such redistribution is criticized by supply-side economists because they feel it reduces the incentive to find work and contributes to the high level of unemployment. On the other side of the coin, financing redistributive policies require high rates of taxation, which lower the incentives to work and to save. Thus redistribution can be seen as a root cause of economic stagnation. When transfers are regarded as rights or entitlements, demographics play a powerful role in determining the structure of expenditures. Low birthrates and a sharp increase in life expectancy result in a pronounced aging of the population in industrial societies and require ever-higher levels of transfer.

The Increase of Social Productivity Redistribution is sometimes justified as contributing a positive impact on social productivity. This benefit might be achieved in two ways. By elevating social cohesion it might solidify institutions that are beneficial to growth. Moreover, redistribution can lower social problems, leading to savings on expenditures (like crime or remedial education). This line of thinking remains important in contemporary European political thought, and can be seen in the justification of redistribution in the European Union.

Social Control A fifth view sees redistribution in contemporary market economies as a tool in a struggle to maintain social peace and stability. Potentially disruptive elements of society are bought off by providing access to generous pensions and goods.

This strategy certainly relies on history. Imperial Rome secured the quiescence of the Roman unemployed through the provision of free "bread and circuses." In response to contemporary urban disturbances, industrialized countries frequently increase the number and funding of social programs oriented toward the disaffected group. Redistribution can be regarded as a substitute for expenditure on more conventional aspects of law enforcement. The level of distribution is not determined by concern for, or by rights of, groups disadvantaged by the market process but rather by the potential power of disaffected groups to create problems.

Shared Growth Economists are not unanimous about the relationship between income distribution and economic growth. Some consider egalitarianism to result in a lowering of incentives and a consequent slower growth path. Others are adamant that sharing of the proceeds of growth is essential to maintain a growth trajectory; growth that benefits only a few is likely to be unstable because it leads to a loss of social unity. Each opinion is based on some merit: both extreme egalitarianism and an extreme reliance on material incentives (which leads to an unequal distribution of income) are likely to present problems. Some commentators on the strong growth performance of East Asian economies in the 1990s note the sharing of growth as an important factor in sustaining economic expansion.

The Democratic Process In modern democracies the key to the increased share of redistributional expenditure is likely to be found in the ballot box. Earlier we discussed how politicians act so as to ensure their subsequent reelection, and providing access to redistribution is one way of influencing voter behavior. This explanation sounds especially potent when the potential group is unified and "single-issue oriented." This basic thought underlies much of the work of James Buchanan, Nobel laureate in economics.

Demand Stabilization Capitalist economies are subject to variations in the level of macroeconomic activity, and at times this variation can be ascribed to a systemic tendency toward underconsumption. Inasmuch as the less well off show a higher marginal propensity to consume than the better off, redistribution from rich to poor lowers the societal marginal propensity to save and reduces the chance of an "underconsumptionist trap." From the English liberal economist John Hobson[22] forward, and particularly in mainstream Keynesian schools of thought, some economists advocate domestic redistribution as an antidote to recession. While it is hard to see such a clear espousal of a particular macroeconomic theory by the politicians who ultimately determine redistributive policy, it is a fact that developed nations managed to steer clear of major recessions since the inception of mass redistribution programs.

---

[22]Hobson anticipated many of Keynes's views on the dangers of underconsumption, although his main agenda was to restrain overseas imperialism, which in its relentlessness to attach for foreign markets by force was an alternative remedy to redistribution for domestic stagnation.

CONCLUSION

Where does this discussion leave us in evaluating the role of government in correcting the inefficient or unacceptable features of market logic? In the light of these observations, few would assert that each and every market imperfection is a case for government intervention. The particular failures of the market must be evaluated against the cost and potential failures of government intervention before any action is initiated.

Even in those cases where market failure is so pronounced that some government intervention is merited, economists would be best employed in considering solutions that are designed to reduce the risk of government failure, rather than assuming that regulation by a government body was necessarily beneficial. The new view of government suggests that policies that provide individuals with incentives and freedom to correct market failure might be best. Experience to date offers us few examples of these kinds of policies, which might be described as **incentive-compatible** or **market augmenting policies**. Promising approaches seem to lie in the use of **quasi-markets** to assist in the provision of services currently supplied largely by the government. This approach would allow the simultaneous addressing of the equity and the efficiency issue. Such a device would be the use of vouchers provided gratis by the government to eligible families with children, but which could then be used to pay for educational services. Market-augmenting approaches used in Asian countries attempt to determine which firms should receive government support, and these efforts will be looked at again when the economies of Japan and Korea are presented in Chapters 12 and 13 of this book.

It is sufficient at this point to suggest that the direction of future research should be to identify the areas of comparative advantage for government and to examine how the logic of the market and appropriately designed incentives may be used to better the performance of government.

KEY TERMS AND CONCEPTS

agency inertia
altruism
antitrust policy
barriers to entry
capture of regulators
caveat emptor
collective action
contestable markets
deadweight loss
diminishability
excludability
externalities
four firm concentration ratio
free rider problem
government failure
Herfindahl-Hirschman Index
incentive-compatible policy
lack of information
market-augmenting policy
market failure
market power
national champions

natural monopoly
poll tax
pork barreling
price setter
price takers
private marginal cost
public goods
quasi-markets
rent-seeking behavior
social contract
social marginal cost
tax expenditures
trade to GDP ratio
transfer payments
utilitarianism
vacuum theory of population

QUESTIONS FOR DISCUSSION

1. Evaluate the arguments for and against the use of government power to curb monopolies.
2. How has the need to regulate "natural monopolies" changed in recent years?
3. Why are concentration ratios not thought of as good indices of the level of industry-wide competition? What may be a better approach?
4. How does lack of information impede the operation of a market system? How can a government act to correct this impediment?
5. Define *public goods*. Are pure public goods an important category? Give some examples. Is information a pure public good?
6. Why may government action be required to correct externality problems such as pollution? Which type of system, planned or market, would you expect to lead to most pollution?
7. Why is the government not a "benevolent, costless social guardian"?
8. Give some reasons why redistribution via both cash and in-kind payments is the fastest growing governmental activity.

RESOURCES

Web Sites

U.S. Federal Trade Commission.. http://www.ftc.gov/
This site provides useful information and downloadable papers on specific industries.

U.K. Office of Fair Trading.. http://www.oft.gov.uk/
This site gives the background, philosophy, and structure of U.K. policy against monopoly.

Books and Articles

Baumol, William J., John C. Panzar, and Robert Willig. *Contestable Markets and the Theory of Industry Structure*. New York: Harcourt Brace Jovanovich, 1982.

Brock, Gerald W. *Telecommunication Policy for the Information Age: From Monopoly to Competition.* Cambridge: Harvard University Press, 1998.

Buchanan, James M., and Richard A. Musgrave. *Public Finance and Public Choice: Two Contrasting Visions of the State.* Cambridge: MIT Press, 1999.

Buchanan, James M., and Gordon Tullock. *The Calculus of Consent.* Ann Arbor: University of Michigan Press, 1962.

Coase, Ronald. "The Problem of Social Cost." *Journal of Law and Economics* 3 (October 1960), 1–44.

Crandall, Robert. "Import Quotas and the Automobile Industry." *Brookings Review,* Summer 1984, 8–16.

Krueger, Anne. "Economists' Changing Perceptions of Government." *Weltwirtschaftliches Archiv* 126, no. 3 (1990), 419.

Musgrave, Richard A. *Public Finance in a Democratic Society: The Foundations of Taxation and Expenditure.* White Plains, NY: Edward Elgar, 2000.

Okun, Arthur. *Equity and Efficiency: The Big Trade-Off.* Washington, DC: Brookings Institution, 1975.

Olsen, Mancur. *The Logic of Collective Action: Public Goods and the Theory of Groups.* Cambridge: Harvard University Press, 1971.

Train, Kenneth E. *Optimal Regulation: The Economic Theory of Natural Monopoly.* Cambridge: MIT Press, 1991.

Viscusi, W. Kip, John Vernon, and Joseph Harrington. *Economics of Regulation and Antitrust,* 2d ed. Cambridge: MIT Press, 1995.

5

THE INSTITUTIONS OF A MODERN MARKET ECONOMY

In Chapter 1 we discussed in broad outline the types of institution that comprise any economy, and in Chapter 4 we visited the important issue of market failure and looked at some of the ways government acts to attempt to remedy market failures. In this chapter we will look in more detail at the framework of a "developed market economy," and how the established institutions operate to shape and steer the functions of the economy. We start with a discussion of the various objectives of government policy and how they fit together, and sometimes conflict, in an overall picture of government activity.

THE OBJECTIVES OF GOVERNMENT POLICY

It seems almost too obvious to state, but in a mixed market economy (like the United States, Japan, and Germany) the government is one of the most important institutions. Even in those countries that are popularly regarded as the bastions of free enterprise and capitalism, a large part of the gross domestic product (GDP) passes through the government sector, with public employment representing a considerable share of the total. The revenues of industrial giants such as General Motors, Exxon, or Microsoft are quite small compared to the receipts and expenditures of governments in developed industrial economies. The debts of banks, corporations, and households similarly pale when compared to government debt. Government regulations, civil, criminal, and administrative law control or shape almost every aspect of our lives. One way of viewing government activity is to see government as being divisible into three functions: allocation, categorization, and stabilization.[1] This functional characterization enables us to view the operation of government systematically. However, we must always bear in mind that policies implemented to achieve goals related to one function inevitably lead to "spillovers" that affect the others.

The Allocation Function

The existence of market failures, as discussed in Chapter 4, suggests the need for government intervention because the market alone either failed to supply some

[1]For a full discussion of this view of the responsibilities of government, see Richard and Peggy Musgrave, *Public Finance in Theory and Practice* (New York: McGraw-Hill, 1984).

goods altogether or supplied certain goods at allocatively inefficient quantities and prices. We also discussed the problem of government failure, which occurs when the costs of government intervention are greater than any potential social gain, or when the action of the governmental/political process frustrates the possibility of socially advantageous intervention. Nevertheless, governments of all mixed capitalist societies are involved in the production of goods and the regulation of business, with overt justification of improving the allocative efficiency of the economy. This activity is what we term the **allocation function** of government.

Government Production of Pure, Public, Quasi-Public, and Merit Goods

We established in Chapter 4 that although pure public goods are theoretically important, operationally they form a rather limited class of goods. The market could also provide most of the goods that are provided governments. A list of what is actually produced, at least in part, by some level of the government in the United States, includes national defense, passenger rail transportation, urban mass transit, law enforcement, electricity supply, education, health services, information, public health measures, research and development, water supply, postal services, and housing. We would obtain a similar list if we looked at most of the developed market economies in Europe or in Japan. As a general but not universal rule, the lower the overall level of development, the greater is the likelihood that the government assumes more extensive production responsibilities. Economic development tends to place greater reliance on private production, especially since the "transition" of the formerly planned economies. What is striking, however, is that almost all of the goods produced by governments are either also produced at the same time in the private sector or have close substitutes that are.

Some of the goods or services on the list of government production can be justified by the fact that the market would supply the goods only in suboptimal quantities and at prices that are too high. These goods generate substantial positive externalities or **spillovers** that are socially beneficial and not captured in the private market. Production by the public sector causes these goods to be supplied at a level closer to the optimum and priced more efficiently through the operation of a public subsidy, or at least priced at less than the profit-maximizing rate. Goods of this type might include information, education, electricity supply, public transportation, and water supply.[2] Finally, the government provides some goods as a form of income transfer; housing, health care, and to some degree education, fit this category.

Table 5.1 shows the structure of current government expenditure in 19 nations using standardized are Organization for Economic Cooperation and Development (OECD) classifications. The categories have been divided into "public goods" and "merit goods."[3] What characterizes the public goods is that they are supplied to the economy as a whole and there is no possibility of excluding any individuals. Merit

[2]One element that often becomes a factor in these industries is the possibility of cross-subsidization. High-cost users are charged the same rate as low-cost users, facilitating a single pricing scheme and coverage.

[3]"Merit goods" are supplied by the public sector at a level above that that would be demanded on a "fee for service basis," and involve, therefore, some interference with individual preferences.

■ TABLE 5.1

The Structure of Government Outlays by Function as a Percent of GDP

		Public Goods				Merit Goods			
Total Expenditure		Total	Defense	General Public Services	Other Functions	Total	Education	Health	Other Social Services
Australia	37.7	8.2	1.9	3.0	3.3	10.5	4.5	5.5	0.5
Austria	52.2	4.5	0.9	3.6	0.0	11.9	5.3	5.7	0.8
Canada	46.3	2.9	1.4	1.5	0.0	12.3	5.8	6.5	0.0
Czech Republic	40.8	3.9	1.6	2.3	0.0	11.1	4.4	6.1	0.5
Denmark	59.9	6.0	1.7	4.3	0.0	16.5	6.5	5.1	4.9
Finland	54.3	3.3	1.6	1.6	0.1	15.2	6.6	5.6	3.0
France	55.4	9.2	2.9	4.5	1.8	14.1	5.9	7.1	1.1
Germany	49.7	5.2	1.4	3.9	0.0	13.9	4.5	8.0	1.3
Italy	52.2	6.5	1.7	4.5	0.3	10.2	4.5	5.3	0.3
Japan	36.5	4.5	0.9	3.6	0.0	10.1	3.8	5.6	0.6
Korea	19.2	5.7	2.9	2.0	0.8	5.6	3.6	1.8	0.2
Netherlands	52.2	11.6	1.8	9.8	..	12.0	4.6	6.5	1.0
New Zealand	38.9	5.3	1.1	4.2	0.0	10.6	5.2	5.3	0.1
Norway	52.0	6.3	2.6	3.1	0.6	18.4	6.8	6.6	5.1
Portugal	49.9	8.3	2.2	2.0	4.1	10.6	5.4	4.7	0.5
Spain	45.2	9.9	1.4	1.8	6.7	10.6	4.8	5.5	0.3
Sweden	64.5	5.4	2.3	3.0	0.1	17.2	6.6	5.7	4.9
United Kingdom	43.6	5.4	3.2	1.9	0.2	11.5	4.6	5.7	1.2
United States	34.3	9.2	5.2	2.9	1.0	11.9	5.0	6.5	0.4

SOURCE: OECD 2001; Economic Survey of Czech Republic, 2001.

goods such as health and education could be provided by the private sector, but the government chooses to supply them as a redistributive or egalitarian measure. The first thing that strikes us about the data in Table 5.1 is the wide variation in the scope of government as a percentage of GDP; Korea is the lowest followed by the United States and Japan. In general, the continental European nations engage in the highest levels of government activity, reaching a peak in the Scandinavian states of Denmark and Sweden. Less variation appears between nations in terms of current expenditures, though the features of individual economies can be quite important. Some nations show especially high levels of particular social expenditures, for example health care in Germany or educational expenditures in Norway. The United States far outpaces the other OECD members in terms of defense spending.

Information as a Public Good The provision of information performs an important function of a modern government. Without good information on a wide range of topics (from the weather to the unemployment rate), the economic actors cannot make informed and therefore rational decisions. Information is not, however, a pure public good. Even though the marginal cost of providing information to additional users is low (especially in the age of television and the Web), it is quite possible to charge for information and exclude nonpayers from receiving it. A whole industry of consultants relies on the charging of a fee for "proprietary" information, at prices that reflect a monopoly rent rather than the cost of dissemination. Information may, therefore, be thought of as a *quasi-public good.*

Nevertheless, information gathering is costly, and social resources can be saved if needless duplication can be avoided. Thus a government's role in the collation and dissemination of information may be justifiable on efficiency grounds. Improved information flows allow better decisions to be made and enhance the overall efficiency of the market system.

Regulation of Products A large part of government activity is concerned with product regulation of one form or another. In the United States, for example, regulatory agencies set standards for the safety, quality, and efficacy of many products. The economic basis for regulation, in terms of improving the allocative efficiency of the economy, lies in the fact that it economizes information costs for consumers.

Regulation of Industry Moreover as we discussed in Chapter 4, governments have extensive powers to regulate prices and outputs in industry most frequently to address market failure due to monopoly.

The Distribution Function

Income Support The **distribution function** of government actually entails redistributing income. Although this activity is not new (even ancient Egypt and Rome instituted income support policies) it has grown enormously in importance in recent decades. A large part of government expenditure moves toward some form of amelioration of income distribution. In previous centuries, governments oriented their assistance toward poverty relief and intended only to raise the indigent to the subsistence level.

In the twentieth century the government assumed increased responsibility for stabilizing the economy. It also came to be held increasingly responsible for the individual as well as the aggregate consequences of joblessness. "Social security" became a common feature (and a burgeoning bureaucracy) in all developed economies during the twentieth century. Support was provided not only for the unemployed but also for the elderly, single parents, and the disabled. As a result, transfer payments required a larger share of government expenditure.

The economic consequences of this steady progress toward guaranteed income are much debated. Today the prevailing orthodox view is that redistributive payments have sharply reduced the flexibility of labor markets. Providing support for people without jobs reduces the urgency of job search, lowers incentives to find work, and encourages higher wage demands. These factors in turn lead to higher levels of unemployment. In the countries of Western Europe, where the reduction in take-home income on losing a job can be as little as 10 percent, the cost of being unemployed is correspondingly low and unemployment rates are high.

Concern over the disincentive consequences of income transfer schemes continues to grow. Measures to reduce unemployment benefits and tighten accessibility rules have been made in some developed market economies. Some evidence indicates that sharp falls in unemployment often accompany such steps. Britain provides a case in point, which following a trimming of the welfare state now experiences its lowest unemployment rate in decades. On the other hand, countries that maintain high benefit rates continue to see unemployment grow (e.g., France). Although these examples suggest a link, evidence that transfers payments actually *cause* unemployment is slight. Some income support for the jobless can be justified in terms of raising the allocative efficiency of the economy because it allows a more rational process of job search and a better resultant fit.

Redistribution In-Kind Economic theory tells us that an individual's welfare is raised by increasing his or her ability to choose. Consequently, welfare-maximizing redistribution, at least from the recipient's viewpoint, should consist of unrestricted cash grants. However, much **redistributive in-kind** activity actually takes the form of public provision of goods that might well be supplied privately, including health care, education, housing, and food. The adoption of such a system can be justified in two ways. First, it is claimed that these goods generate social externalities. Consequently, the loss of an individual recipient's welfare through constraining choice is compensated by a rise in the welfare of third parties. Second, some may argue that the recipients may be ill-informed or irrational and act against their own long-run welfare. If given free control over resources they would dispose of them in a fashion that would favor short-term gratification over long-term well-being. Hence an element of paternalism is used to justify the public provision of such goods, rather than providing cash to purchase the appropriate amount in private markets. This interference with individual preferences creates a class of goods that are referred to in the literature as **merit goods**, and they are widespread in most economies.

In recent years the state-owned industries and bureaucracies created by the public provision of these goods have come under attack because of their alleged inefficiency and inflexibility relative to the private sector. In the United States criticism focused on publicly provided education. In Britain the National Health Service fell under siege. One possible avenue of reform involves the use of **voucher systems**, which have attracted much support in recent years. Although they may result in interference with personal preferences, because of their (unlike cash) service-specific nature, they introduce consumer choice between suppliers and therefore foster competition, ideally leading to greater efficiency.

The Stabilization Function

The idea that governments should be responsible for the level of macroeconomic activity—the level of unemployment, the rate of inflation, and the rate of growth—is a relatively recent one. The argument for government's **stabilization function** comes from two sources. One was political reform that broadened the franchise and gave a louder voice to those most affected by unemployment. The second lay in the developments in macroeconomic theory and statistical collation that occurred in the twentieth century, especially in the Depression-troubled 1930s, which made government management of the economy more feasible. Emphasis on government responsibility for the macroeconomy reached its height in the 1960s when it was widely held that the principles underlying economic activity were so well-understood that the economic task of government was merely to fine-tune the economy. However, faith in the ability of government to deliver low inflation and high employment faltered in the economically turbulent 1970s. Stabilization policy apparently failed and came to have negative connotations. Confidence in the effectiveness of fiscal policy waned, and government activity came to be seen by a growing number of economists as the cause of instability rather than its antidote.

During the 1960s much of stabilization policy was framed in terms of the judicious trade-off between inflation and unemployment. Then, a new orthodoxy emerged in the 1970s suggesting that unemployment. Then, at least below a threshold "natural" level, was, after all, not something that the government could do much about. Attempts to raise employment accelerated the rate of inflation, without showing any long-term results. Slow growth became associated with government interference in demand management as public expenditure crowded out private investment. Today we find ourselves back in the middle of the road. Confidence in our ability to guarantee stability may occasionally be shaken, but postwar recessions proved to be relatively mild and most economists believe that economic policy can be effective in shaping economic outcomes for the better.

The Instruments of Stabilization In most mixed market economies governments have at their disposal two distinct sets of policy measures: fiscal (those that involve the changing of tax rates and government expenditure) and monetary (those that involve the manipulation of the money stock in the hands of the public).

Fiscal Policy To be effective, **fiscal policy** requires a well-developed and defined tax system in which tax rules are both visible and enforced. This system, in turn, presupposes a government supported by an established and competent bureaucracy. In less-developed economies, and also in the transition economies of Eastern Europe, the lack of the essential infrastructure for tax gathering limits the effectiveness of fiscal policy. Fiscal policy concerns itself not only with the changing of taxes and tax rates, but also with the role of government expenditures on macroeconomic activity. Stabilization can be effected by shifts in government expenditures (for example, by the initiation of public expenditure projects or the curtailment of unemployment insurance payments). Government expenditures, like taxes, tend to have an automatic stabilizer effect, because even in the absence of policy shifts they rise as the economy contracts.

In modern mixed market economies, tax capabilities are by and large similar. Some countries have more efficient tax systems and greater degrees of tax compliance than others, which affects economic performance. However, the larger differences lie in the kind of tax structure adopted. The United States, for example, relies heavily on income taxes, social security taxes, and corporate income taxes at the federal level.[4] State finance is predominantly based on sales taxes, supplemented by individual and business income taxes. Other economies depend more on indirect taxes at the national level. In Europe, for example, much greater reliance is on indirect taxation, largely through value-added taxes.

Monetary Policy The other broad technique of macroeconomic stabilization is the use of **monetary policy** to influence the rate of interest, the rate of inflation, and therefore the price level. Responsibility for the implementation (and in many economies the determination) of monetary policy resides with the central bank whose functioning we later discuss more fully in the context of the financial system.

THE TAX SYSTEM

What really sets the government apart from other institutions is that it holds a monopoly on the power to tax. No other institution can demand that resources be transferred to it with no specific *quid pro quo* under the threat of sanctions that include imprisonment. This unique feature makes the activity of government of prime importance and the design and functioning of the tax system a decisive feature for the operation of the economic system. Taxes are generally divided into two types: those imposed on people or firms (direct taxation) and those levied on goods (indirect taxation). The most important direct tax—measured in terms of the share of total revenue that it raises—is the personal income tax in most economies. Direct taxation also includes social security taxes, corporate taxes, expenditure taxes,[5] and some forms of wealth and estate taxation.

The degree of progressivity of direct taxation differs sharply between economies. Under a **progressive tax** the average tax rate rises as the individual's or household's base of the tax (income, expenditure, or wealth) increases. Progressivity was at one time almost universally considered a desirable characteristic in a tax system. Some people justified it on moral or ethical grounds arguing that equal sacrifice of welfare across the population required an increasing average rate of income tax because the marginal utility of money declines as income increases. To others it offered the more pragmatic virtue of constituting an "automatic stabilizer," which would limit or dampen the cyclical behavior of the macroeconomy. As the economy expanded, under a progressive tax system, tax revenues would increase at a faster rate than national income. Thus the size of the government fiscal deficit would shrink (or the size of the surplus increase), hence slowing economic growth. The reverse would hold in cyclical downturns.

---

[4]In 2000, 42.6 percent of federal revenue came from the individual income tax, 36 percent from social security taxes, and 12 percent from corporate income taxes, with the remaining 8 percent from other sources, chiefly excise taxes, as reported in the *Economic Report of the President*.

[5]Expenditure taxes are levied on an individual's or household's total aggregate consumption expenditure and should not be confused with sales taxes, which are indirect taxes imposed at the point of purchase.

In more recent years, however, the consensus favoring progressivity weakened, largely because the negative supply-side effects of high personal taxation attracted more concern. Equity and equal sacrifice are now thought of more in terms of proportionality (i.e., constant average and marginal rate taxation) rather than requiring progressivity. Consequently, the number of tax brackets declined and lower tax rates applied more generally. This change pertained especially to the taxation of capital. In many economies, so-called unearned income (interest, dividends, properties, rents, etc.) was once taxed at higher rates. Sometimes these rates were close to confiscatory—70 percent and higher. Today differential rates for earned and unearned income are largely a thing of the past. In fact, in some countries, the pendulum has swung toward the other extreme and income from capital is actually taxed at lower rates than that from labor. In the United States, changes in the treatment of capital gains resulted in some forms of capital income being taxed at a lower rate than wage or salary income. Lower marginal tax rates also provide the beneficial effect of lowering the incidence of both tax evasion and tax avoidance.[6]

Taxes can be levied on objects rather than on individuals, and this constitutes indirect taxation. Imposing taxes on things (commodities, imports, exports, houses, land, etc.) tends to be administratively easier than all but the simplest direct taxes on individuals. A glance at history tells us that states once generally relied on commodity or land taxation for public finance. In modern mixed capitalist societies, commodity taxation is still widely practiced (see Table 5.2). In the United States, local government is largely financed by taxes on real property, while some form of sales taxation predominates at the state level.

Countries in a lower state of economic development often rely on a relatively simple form of indirect taxation with highly visible "tax handles" that do not require a sophisticated enforcement mechanism (although evasion through an under-the-counter cash market is frequent). In history, several nations relied on "salt taxes," which, because the taxes fell on a good with a low price elasticity, were relatively efficient with minimal deadweight loss. However, such single commodity taxation cannot raise the volume of revenue required by a modern state. Consequently, a broader base is often sought. Unfortunately, simple turnover and gross receipts taxes, which are the easiest to administer, bring with them the drawbacks of being inefficient and distortionary, and nondistortionary indirect taxes like the value-added tax (VAT) are preferable where possible.

We have distinguished to this point between direct taxes, which are levied on the characteristics of individuals or families, and indirect taxes that fall upon objects or activities. Taxes levied on the profits of businesses, organized corporations, or public limited liability companies, are usually classed as direct, as if they fell upon an individual. Such taxes make up a significant element of the overall public finance system of developed economies, and the tax base is the profit stream of incorporated business.

---

[6]Tax evasion is the illegal concealment of tax liabilities from the authorities. Tax avoidance is the alteration of behavior to limit tax exposure; it involves a deadweight loss to society.

TABLE 5.2

The Structure of the Tax System in Selected Countries (tax structures as a percentage of total tax receipts)

	Total Tax Receipts (percentage of GDP)	Personal Income Tax	Social Security Contributions		Total Taxes on Income	Corporate Income Tax	Taxes on Goods and Services	Other Taxes
			Employees	Employers				
Australia	29.9	43.3	0	0	43.3	15.2	25.5	16
Belgium	45.9	30.7	9.7	19.2	59.6	8.5	24.9	7
Canada	37.4	37.8	5.3	8.1	51.2	10.5	24.7	13.6
Czech Republic	38.3	13.6	10.1	28.8	52.5	9.7	31	6.8
Denmark	49.8	51.6	2.4	0.7	54.7	5.6	33.2	6.5
France	45.2	17.4	8.7	25.2	51.3	5.9	26.6	16.2
Italy	42.7	25	6.3	20.5	51.8	7	27.4	13.8
Japan	28.4	18.8	15	19.6	53.4	13.3	18.8	14.5
Korea	21.1	20.1	3.3	7.7	31.1	12.2	40.5	16.2
Poland	37.9	22	0	32.3	54.3	7.5	34.4	3.8
Sweden	52	35	5.8	22.5	63.3	5.7	21.6	9.4
Turkey	28.7	27	5.7	7.3	40	5.8	35.7	18.5
United Kingdom	37.2	27.5	7.3	9.4	44.2	11	32.6	12.2
United States	28.9	40.5	10.2	12.2	62.9	9	16.2	11.9
EU Average	41.3	25.6	8.2	15.9	49.7	8.7	30.2	11.4
OECD Average	37	27	7	14.9	48.9	8.9	31.3	10.8

SOURCE: *OECD in Figures*, 2001, p. 38.

At the federal level, the United States depends almost exclusively on direct taxation. The individual income tax constitutes 45 percent of total revenue, and the social security payroll taxes contribute 38 percent. Thus taxes on personal income comprise 83 percent of total revenues. Corporate income taxes constitute about 11 percent of total revenues, and the balance of about 6 percent is made up of excise taxes, gift and estate taxes, and custom duties. At the state level there is a much greater reliance on sales taxes and property taxes, indirect taxes which amount to more than half of the revenue. The tax systems of other nations differ in terms of the balance of reliance on direct versus indirect taxation. In Europe, for example, the value-added tax, an indirect tax, contributes an important part of central government revenue.

It is clear that both the design of the tax system and the overall tax burden have important effects on economic growth and performance. Taxes are not only generally distortionary, but also are frequently structured to favor particular groups or activities. However, just as important as the overt or nominal tax structure are the efficiency and the even-handedness of tax administration. Healthy economies require honest and efficient tax administrations. Without them it is hard for a nation to prosper.

THE LEGAL SYSTEM

Any modern market economy depends on a clear and enforceable system of property rights, and the clarification and enforcement of such rights are the most important economic roles of the legal system. A complex and resource-expensive system has grown up in market economies to control these functions. Some would argue that the role and scope of the law have become too broad and the cost of the legal system too high. Nowhere does the law and the role of lawyers figure so prominently as in the United States. In most market economies the percentage of national income accounted for by the legal system remains small compared to the United States, but is generally growing.

Ownership and Property Rights

In Chapter 1 we discussed the concept of property ownership, and we saw that it is a rather more complex matter than might seem at first glance, embracing the issue of property rights, which extend beyond merely physical property. It is concerned with rights as varied as the right to clean air, the right to quiet, the right to access to sunlight, the right to earn income from an invention, and the right to broadcast over the airwaves. In the West, property rights developed incrementally and subsequently adapted and extended to take account of new complexities, both by legislation and by precedent in law. New technologies and new external circumstances continue to require that new rights be defined. For example, the issues of environmental property rights, intellectual property rights, and the right of access to radio frequencies recently leaped to prominence.

Although even the limited right of ownership and transfer of physical property will ensure the development of some forms of market relations, it does not go far in stimulating economic efficiency. Alone it will lead, in the words of Evgenii Yasin, a Russian reform economist, to a "bazaar" rather than a "market." A market system requires much more. As one of its functions, the complex legal system of western nations promotes efficiency in the use of scarce resources. Of course, this is not the sole function of the law. It must also protect individual and group rights against a variety of incursions. Moreover, although many laws and regulations have evolved to contribute to the efficient operation of a market economy, a good deal of legislation serves the interest of quite narrow groups and does little either for economic efficiency or human rights.

Freedom to Engage in Economic Activity

In order for prices of goods to even approximate resource costs, markets must be relatively competitive, and this requiring that individuals, and groups of individuals or firms, have the right to engage in whatever economic activity they perceive as offering the greatest return. In simple terms, people must have the right to choose their own professions (among them being a self-employed entrepreneur) and choose the physical locations where they pursue these professions. This is much the same as granting individuals the right to enter any business or industry that they choose and to live wherever they want. Without a guarantee of free market entry, private monopolies, with their attendant inefficiencies, would arise. Under such conditions prices would not reflect the resource costs of production and monopoly rents[7] would be appropriated, harming efficiency. A major target of Adam Smith's *Wealth of Nations* was the system of royal licensing and monopoly that restricted the action of the individual. If the state can prevent the entry of individuals into a trade or profession, then the consumer, indeed society as a whole, is the loser while the monopolist or the official that grants it monopoly powers is the winner.

Even today free entry into all economic activities is not guaranteed in overtly market systems. Many professions and trades require licenses or permits; this practice is usually defended as being efficient because customers cannot always gather all the information they need. Certifying lawyers, stockbrokers, or auto mechanics provides cheap information designed to protect the consumer, though clearly certification is no guarantee of competence or honesty. Although market radicals, such as Milton Friedman, denounce such regulation as monopolistic and therefore inefficient, such barriers are an integral part of economic life in most market systems.

The Enforcement of Contracts and Compensation

Ownership and entry will create an infrastructure in which rudimentary exchange can take place, but such a market could operate only with a short time horizon. Longer-term economic relationships are made viable by the use of contracts that bind parties to specific performance standards. Contracts are an integral part of moving from the "bazaar," where already-produced goods are exchanged, into a longer-term system of stable interrelations enabling planning and foresight. A contract specifies what both parties must do, whatever the change in external circumstance, and provides for enforcement or compensation for nonperformance.

Some long-term relationships can be established even in the absence of enforceable contracts, because the market can produce its own remedies often through reputation effects. A supplier, for example, who persistently failed to deliver, would encounter a great deal of difficulty finding future customers as knowledge of his persistent failures to perform became widespread. However, contract law removes part of the costs of gathering information from the contracting parties by providing general remedies and compensation for failure to perform and to deliver. This feature obviates the need for a socially expensive search, although it introduces costs of making and enforcing contracts. To promote economic efficiency, contract enforcement need not always require strict performance to the letter of the contract, but it may instead give the injured party compensation for the losses incurred as a result of nonperformance. Strict enforcement would be burdensome and inefficient in some cases where expected circumstances have changed and fulfilling the contract in its literal terms becomes impossible. However, the law must provide both the means for the injured party to be compensated and an appropriate system of adjudicating damages resulting from nonperformance.

---

[7]Monopoly rent is the margin above normal profit that results from the exercise of monopoly power.

Bankruptcy Law

Frequently overlooked in the discussions of infrastructure is the role of bankruptcy legislation. Capitalism is, in Schumpeter's words, a "gale of creative destruction." Company failure and the dissolution of corporations must be regarded as a normal facet of the system. The efficient operation of that system, however, is highly dependent on the predictable disposition of the assets of the firm in the event of failure. A necessary condition for orderly capital markets is a full and enforceable set of defined property rights, and bankruptcy law is one component of these rights.[8] The risks that lenders and materials suppliers assume in supplying a firm can only be assessed when there is full knowledge of the pecking order in which debtors will be arrayed should the firm go into bankruptcy. As developments in the energy giant Enron and communications titan WorldCom recently showed us, lenders are well advised to look into their claims of repayment in the event of bankruptcy even when lending to firms that look large and prosperous.

Accounting and Financial Disclosure

The law plays a vital role by requiring that firms report their financial results in a specified standard accounting system and that this information be made publicly available. The efficiency aspects of this requirement become obvious if we consider the alternative: without required and standardized disclosure, the costs of information to an individual or other firms, whether potential shareholders, suppliers, or customers, would be very high. Thus required disclosure has clear social efficiency in reducing information costs. This is of great importance in the operation of equity markets, where buying shares without access to accurate information on the financial state of the company would be undesirably risky and share prices would not reflect underlying values. It is also of great relevance to those who supply the company with raw materials and inputs and those who provide credit to firms in more direct ways. The results of inadequate standards in financial disclosure can be seen in the scandals that plagued the U.S. economy in 2002.

A Clear Definition of Governmental Responsibility

Just as a lack of clarity and stability in tax regimes is a disincentive to business activity and investment, so is any imprecision or opaqueness in the role of government. Confusion about government restriction or subsidies, or which level of government has jurisdiction, can constitute an impediment to the growth of economic activity. As the size and scope of governmental activity has grown, the codification of governmental responsibility and its limits has become more vital. For example, a worker's rational behavior in the labor market is contingent on a clear understanding of his or her rights in the social security system. These rights must therefore be clearly and comprehensively stated to avoid their arbitrary implementation. Firms need to know government's responsibilities in providing services, enforcing

[8]See J. Mitchell, "Managerial Discipline, Productivity and Bankruptcy in Capitalist and Socialist Economies," *Comparative Economic Studies* 22, no. 3 (Fall 1990).

THE CRASH OF 2002

The consequences of failure to provide clear and reliable financial disclosure became abundantly clear in the United States during the stock market downturn of 2000–2002. After the boom of the late 1990s several important companies resorted to creative accounting techniques to boost the public's perception of their revenue and profits. The accounting firms proved too complacent and were often compromised by acting both as consultants to companies as well as auditor of their books. Investors became alarmed by their inability to determine a company's true financial position. Suppliers and buyers also felt reluctant to enter into contractual relationships with firms who might be closer to bankruptcy than their published accounts seemed to show. Among the major casualties were the energy trader, Enron, and the telecommunications firms, Global Crossing and WorldCom. Drastic consequences also befell Arthur Andersen, one of the world's largest accounting firms, which seemed to be a willing tool of the companies rather than an independent arbiter of a firm's financial condition.

The U.S. government's response focused on changing the regulating framework. In the short term, chief executive officers are to be required to certify, under penalty of law, the correctness of the accounting statements. More reform is probable, including a prohibition on accounting firms acting both as consultant and auditor.

The real consequences of the crisis for the U.S. economy remain at the present difficult to fathom. The flight of investors from the market may greatly affect the way that companies raise money, and may affect investment and the growth of the U.S. economy. The reaction of foreign investors might also be particularly severe. Far from being the safe haven of capitalism, the United States began to look riskier than many other markets, especially Europe where the heavier hand of government generally practiced high accounting standards.

standards, and regulating labor before they can optimize their behavior. In developed market economies, therefore, a large body of administrative law evolved to define governmental responsibility.

One area of the world where we can see a pressing need for a clear definition of governmental responsibility is in the economies now in transition where once the state was both all-powerful and all-responsible. With no distinction between where the activities of government ended and the activities of enterprises began, the state was both the producer of almost all goods and the provider of social services. In such a situation the productive enterprises, as wholly owned agents of the state, understandably assumed a much greater responsibility toward the social welfare of their employees. Now the smooth functioning of industry and the labor market requires a clear and comprehensive definition of a government-provided social safety net.

A System of Civil Compensation

A functioning civil code provides an aid to business. Just as incorporation[9] removes the shareholders from exposure to unlimited financial loss due to failure or the infliction of harm to third parties, so a **civil compensation** code removes businesspeople

[9]A fuller discussion of the corporate form and its advantages is provided later in this chapter.

from the threat of criminal proceedings in all but the most blatantly negligent incidents. It might be argued that chief executive officers would be even more careful about the behavior of their corporations and underlings if they were liable to a jail term rather than merely dipping into the shareholders' profits to settle a suit. However, a system of criminal redress would lead to two consequences. First, it would affect the behavior of potential victims by encouraging untoward caution because they know that no monetary compensation will be available. Second, it would discourage quite legitimate business activity because of fear of criminal punishment.

We can better understand the significance of a civil code by considering what would happen in the absence of civil compensation, a circumstance that existed in socialist economies where the law of liability was likened to military law. Blame, when it could be assigned, was a criminal matter and would be redressed by the punishment of the offender rather than by the compensation of the victim. **Tort law**, which deals with the redressing of private or civil wrongs through suit, did not exist in the centrally planned economies. Some may think that the United States suffers from a plague of lawyers, many of whom make their living through civil suits, and the prospect of a tort-free society might seem attractive. However, the threat of suit can clearly have positive influences; a firm found guilty of injury will ameliorate its behavior in the future, the more so if forced to pay punitive damages. Consider a Western business engaged in for example an extractive industry, wishing to start operations in, for example, Russia. The technique is not without risk either to the business's own workers or other nearby individuals. In the West, the businessperson would know that he or she is subject to civil suit in the case of accidents, but to criminal liability only in the case of gross negligence. In Eastern Europe and the former Soviet Union, it is quite possible that the redress would occur only through criminal proceedings. What is true for the Western investor is also true for the domestic Russian businessperson. Removing the greatest problems to investment while retaining some censure over dangerous behavior, and ensuring the ability of the victim to be compensated, requires the development of a civil liability code.

THE FINANCIAL SYSTEM

The role of a financial system in a mixed capitalist economy is paramount. It can be argued that, since it does not "produce" any final good, the financial superstructure of an economy is to some extent "unproductive," but the evidence of recent years seems to be that those countries with the least regulated and most competitive financial systems have been the ones that have prospered. This situation contrasts sharply with that of the 1970s and 1980s, when the economies with highly controlled (Japan and Korea) or noncompetitive (Germany) financial systems seemed to perform best in terms of economic aggregates.

The Central Bank

At the heart of the financial system is the central bank. The linchpin of monetary policy, the central bank has several important functions to discharge. Generally speaking, these include the following:

1. To act as a clearing bank for other banks
2. To act as the promulgator and enforcer of financial regulation, designed to enhance the stability and efficiency of the financial system
3. To act as a lender of last resort
4. To control the overall stock of money in the economy, and hence the interest rate
5. To monitor the foreign exchange value of the currency

The central bank has at its disposal several tools with which to influence the stock of money in the system:

1. Open-market operations, by which the central bank buys or sells government bonds to and from the public
2. Reserve requirements, which constitute controls on the minimum amount of liquid reserves that a bank must hold against the liabilities that it owes its depositors
3. The discount rate, which is the interest rate at which the central bank lends money to banks to provide the reserve base against which banks can lend to borrowers

In addition to these tools of the central bank, the money supply can also be changed by the obvious device of printing more money, although that is usually the activity of the treasury or finance ministry rather than the central bank.

The Independence of the Central Bank A key issue in comparing economic structures lies in the relative degree of **central bank independence.** In the United States and, for example, Germany, the central banks have constitutions and hold powers that insulate them to a high degree from the government and the political system. In other countries, autonomy is not the case. The Bank of Japan and the Bank of France are highly controlled by the government. The Bank of England, which was for most of the postwar period an obedient arm of the British government, has now been granted practically total independence.

A seven-member board of governors determines monetary policy in the United States. Each governor is appointed by the president of the United States and confirmed by the Senate. Vacancies occur on average about every two years, and during a maximum of two terms in office a president is likely to appoint at most four governors. Thus a president can structure the board of governors to his ideological liking only at the point at which his second term ends.

The argument for independence largely rests on the fact that central bankers have a tough job to do. Their expertise allows them to make impartial decisions and "do the right thing" if politicians are prevented from influencing them. After all, the prime job of the central bank is to preserve the value of the currency and it should therefore frequently take a restrictive and conservative line on credit creation. If politicians were given control over the central bank, monetary policy would tend to be too relaxed. The hard job of squeezing credit and watching enterprises fail, while unemployment mounted, would be avoided.

The opposing view argues is that a totally independent central bank answers to no one. In a market economy it is an institution of great power,[10] and it is odd that in a representative democracy the people have no say in this vital dimension of policy making. In this view the central bank responds largely to the narrow financial community from which members of the board of governors are likely to spring. As such, an independent central bank might be unduly austere, placing burdens on the less well off, and hence jeopardizing political stability by pursuing its own brand of financial rectitude.

This debate ultimately fails to produce a right or wrong answer. Politicians are adept at judging the public will, and when they control the central bank we could say that a form of representative democracy prevails. On the other hand, politicians do tend to have a short-term outlook and are prone to shallow compromise, where the financial experts insulated from pressure might effect the correct long-term policies.

Depository Institutions

The important tasks of the financial system are the pooling of savings, the assessment of borrowers, and the lending of funds at appropriate interest rates. The gathering of the savings of small savers is largely a task of the **depository institutions**: commercial banks, savings and loans (also known as thrifts, building societies, etc.), credit unions, and (in many countries) the postal savings system.

Commercial Banks Commercial banks are characterized mainly by the fact that they accept deposits from individuals and firms, they allow the transfer of funds by check from account to account, and they lend out money to individuals and businesses. Within these broad parameters they can take a variety of institutional forms. In most market economies they are privately owned (rather than nationalized) institutions, they are organized as limited liability corporations, and they are profit seeking. However, a quick glance at the commercial banking structure of various countries reveals wide differences. The United States is characterized by a large number of commercial banks, and this is a product of regulation. Banking is governed by state law, and interstate branching of banks was for a long time prohibited. Consequently, while other countries witnessed their banking system consolidated by mergers and takeovers, in the United States a large number of independent commercial banks survive to this day. There are some 12,000 commercial banks in the United States, a clear contrast to the much more concentrated systems in, for example, England or Canada, where only a handful of institutions dominate commercial banking.

Depositors use commercial banks largely as a matter of convenience and security. Demand deposits usually carry no, or a low, interest rate, but this rate is offset by accessibility and the safety provided by the banks' diversified portfolio of assets. Borrowers use commercial banks as a source of funds because transaction costs are likely to be lower than having direct access to the stock or bond markets.

---

[10]If confirmation of its power were required, we would only need to take note of the army of "Fed watchers" in the United States, who are concerned with predicting the Fed's behavior.

In most industrialized countries commercial banks are the dominant form of corporation finance for small and middle-sized companies. Stability and probity are essential in the commercial banking system. For those reasons, most commercial banking systems are heavily regulated, to avoid the prospect of bank failure, and the deposits of customers are often insured by the government to guard against runs on a bank.

Savings and Loan Banks Savings institutions (otherwise known as thrifts or, in some countries, building societies) evolved largely as a means to finance home construction and ownership. They accept interest-paying deposits from savers and lend money to home buyers as mortgages. These activities can lead to a serious mismatch in the term structure of their assets and liabilities. Interest rates on mortgages are long-term and represent illiquid assets.[11] Deposits, the thrift's liabilities, on the other hand, are liquid. In the United States in the late 1970s and 1980s deposits flowed from the thrifts to the rapidly growing money market mutual funds, creating a shortage of liquidity that was popularly known as the "savings and loan" crisis.

Credit Unions A growing alternative institution for savings and lending in the United States has been the credit union. One of the problems of lending to individuals is the difficulty of gathering information on the characteristics of the borrower and hence assessing the appropriate level of risk to assign. Credit unions tackle this problem by lending only to people who share some characteristics (generally occupation or employer). This familiarity reduces risk and makes the problem more tractable.

Postal Savings Banks Although they are not found in every country, many economies make use of an extensive postal savings bank as a vehicle for mass banking. Such a system uses the wide distribution of post offices to create a highly accessible banking network, which provides a highly liquid form of savings but pays low interest. Post office banks do not make loans, but the accumulated and pooled saving is generally passed upward to the government. It is, therefore, either a way of subsidizing the general government deficit or a source of pooled savings to be used on some investment project. In Japan, for example, such saving is received from the post office and channeled by the Ministry of Finance to fund, via the major banks, chosen industrial projects.

Nondepository Institutions

Investment Banks Investment banks are not depository institutions. Their principal function is to assist larger businesses in acquiring new capital by issuing and underwriting new stock or bond issues into the primary financial markets. In this underwriting function, **investment banks** guarantee a price to the issuer and try to

[11]In the United Kingdom, building society mortgages almost universally use a variable rate, and U.K. building societies were not placed in the squeeze that their counterparts in the United States experienced.

profit by selling the stock at a level above the guaranteed price. The difference between the guaranteed price and the sale price is known as the *spread*.

Investment banks increase the efficiency of the financial system by reducing information costs. A buyer of securities can rely on the name and reputation of the investment bank as a proxy for expensive research about the reliability of the issuer. Investment banks offer advice and help in the restructuring of firms and merger acquisitions. They also engage in merchant banking by lending their own capital to firms in the process of reorganization.

Mutual Funds Mutual funds are financial intermediaries that allow individual investors to take advantage of the returns and security offered by investing in diversified portfolios of stocks, bonds, or other instruments, such as short-term corporate debt. The mutual fund industry experienced enormous growth in recent years, especially in the United States, as smaller savers use it to gain access to stocks with the security of diversification. This growth meant negative implications for other parts of the financial system. Thrift institutions (i.e., savings and loans in the United States) found themselves fighting harder for deposits and raising interest payments to compete with mutual funds.

Venture Capital Funds In recent years venture capitalism made a strong comeback and can be credited with providing much of the finance for the small and medium-sized firms that powered the great expansion of the United States economy in the 1990s. Venture capital companies generally raise risk capital from private sources and grant it to start-up firms in return for a portion of the share capital. In general, venture capital companies prove more flexible and innovative than commercial or investment banks.

Insurance Companies Although one function of insurance is to protect individuals and companies from risk, the accretion of the premiums paid by policyholders puts a great deal of capital in the hands of the insurance companies and makes them important players in financial markets. As Table 5.3 shows, in the United States, insurance companies hold about 4 percent of all common stock. In other countries, Japan and the United Kingdom especially, the share is much greater.

The Market for Financial Assets

The financial sector concerns itself primarily with the transfer of the various forms of financial assets: stocks (or shares), which indicate ownership of corporations, or bonds or other forms of debit instruments that may be issued either by corporations or by any level of government. The action of the financial markets by and large determines which companies should grow and which should contract or become defunct by regulating access to investment capital.

The Ownership of Stock Financial structures vary between countries. One aspect of this variation can be found in how dispersed share ownership is within the population. Table 5.3 gives data on the major capitalist economies. One immediately

TABLE 5.3

Ownership of Common Stock: An International Comparison (percentage at year-end)

	United States	Japan	Germany	France	United Kingdom	Italy	Sweden
	1994	FY 1994	1993	1993	1993	1993	1993
Financial Sector	**45**	**44**	**29**	**8**	**62**	**19**	**24**
Banks	3	26	14	3	1	10	1
Insurance companies	4	16	7	1	17	2	8
Investment funds	0	0	0	0	0	0	8
Pension funds	26	0	0	0	34	0	0
Mutual funds	12	0	8	2	7	6	6
Other financial institutions	4	2	0	2	3	1	0
Nonfinancial Sector	**55**	**56**	**71**	**92**	**38**	**81**	**76**
Nonfinancial enterprises	0	24	39	59	2	32	34
Public authorities	0	1	4	4	1	28	7
Individuals	48	24	17	19	18	17	16
Foreign	6	7	12	11	16	5	9
Other	1	0	0	0	2	0	10
Total	**100**	**100**	**100**	**100**	**100**	**100**	**100**

NOTE: Due to rounding, the figures may not add up to the total. Pension funds in Japan are managed by trust banks and insurance companies. The assets in these funds are included under banks and insurance companies. No data are available on the extent to which mutual funds own shares. Security houses do manage such funds; these companies are included under other financial institutions.
SOURCE: Board of the Federal Reserve System. Round Table of National Stock Exchanges, "Survey of Stock Ownership Distribution," *Flow of Funds,* August 1995; Deutsche Bundesbank, Banque de France, CSO, Consob, Banca d'Italia, Statistika Centralbyran, Sweden. Quoted in OECD (1995b); Annual Security Statistics (1995); OECD Economic Surveys, 1995–1996, Japan, p. 152.

apparent feature is the wide distribution of stock in the United States relative to other countries. Individuals hold almost half (48%) of the total market capitalization, and a further 12 percent lies in mutual funds, generally as a proxy for individuals. Financial institutions, such as insurance companies, banks, and pension funds, own only one-third of total shares. This "popular capitalism" is an important feature of the U.S. system. It ensures broad support for the capitalist system (implying, for example, a resistance to high rates of capital and capital gains taxation). It also means that stock market movements directly affect the income and wealth of individuals, providing a much more direct link between financial performance and, say, consumer expenditure than in other countries. It also probably contributes to the stability of the system because a fall in the value of shares does not immediately endanger the financial well-being of other financial and nonfinancial corporations. The wide ownership of shares does, however increase the macroeconomic significance of stock market fluctuations via the "wealth effect." Families that watched the value of their portfolio shrink are likely to raise their savings rate to rebuild their assets, implying a recessionary fall in real demand following a stock market fall. The reverse is also true. Surging stock prices can fuel demand for real goods and services.

In Europe the level of stock ownership by individuals is much lower; the household sector holds roughly 18 percent of stock. In Germany, banks hold control of a sizable part of total shares, while in the United Kingdom pension funds and insurance companies predominate. In Japan the corporate sector is largely owned by banks and other corporations through cross-share holding within the large industrial groups, or *keiretsu*. In recent years this arrangement proved to be a source of great instability for the Japanese financial system. A fall in the price of shares puts pressure on the balance sheets of banks and raises the risk of cumulative collapse, which was nearly the case in the crisis of 1997.

How Financial Markets Provide Corporate Governance In most Western nations the exchange of both shares and bonds is handled by brokerage houses that are members of exchanges. Traditionally brokerages performed not only the functions of buying and selling for a customer, but provided extensive research departments, as do mutual funds companies and pension funds. In addition, specialist institutions also sell data useful to market participants. Of particular importance are the bond-rating services, which are influential in determining the interest costs faced by corporations and government. These institutions focus on the performance of firms, agencies, and municipalities, and draw attention to missteps of management, which provides a constant check on management performance, and is a force for good **corporate governance**.

The Market for Corporate Control Firms that perform badly in the eyes of financial analysts face two problems. First, they face an inability to raise loans, either directly from banks or in the debt markets. This obstacle places a serious and hard budget constraint on the firm and may curb expansion, force it to improve the efficiency of its operation, or possibly drive it to bankruptcy if it cannot ensure the credit it needs to survive. The other consequence comes when the value of a firm's shares falls on stock markets, making it vulnerable to an outside takeover bid. In such a case, the assets would fall under new management that would better realize the potential. This active **market for corporate control** is an important feature of capitalism in the United States and Britain.

THE ORGANIZATION OF BUSINESS

The Corporate Form

One of the most important innovations of Western economies is the ability to create corporations, legal entities that can, through the sale of stock, raise capital from a large number of individuals, each of whom shares in the profits of the firm. The corporation provides a second important feature; each investor is liable only for the amount of money that he or she invested. Thus, the overall liabilities of the firm are limited to the net worth of the firm, rather than its total debts and obligations. Consequently, the downside in a corporate venture is less than that in an equivalent partnership or proprietorship, where the owners would be liable for the full value of the obligations.

STOCKS, OPTIONS, AND CORPORATE GOVERNANCE

The rise of global stock markets in the 1990s had a strong impact both on stock ownership and on corporate governance. Several trends were at work. First the rise of the markets tended to attract first-time owners of shares. Second the wider use of vested stock ownership plans to replace traditional pension schemes broadened share ownership further. Perhaps most startling was the acceleration in the use of stock options as a means of compensating both management and worker. Two implications arose. One was that the ownership of the corporations was progressively transferred from the preexisting group of shareholders toward the management and workers. Although this shift might in some respects be a solution to the principal/agent problem by making management more closely identified with the profitability of the firm, it did represent a transfer of wealth from shareholders to management. There is now public pressure to ensure that the issuance of options be more carefully documented and reflected as an expense in the reporting of financial results. A serious problem was revealed when it became clear that too frequently the reward of management with options encouraged a short-term view of the future. It became in management's interest to manipulate the stock price higher, cash out options, and leave the firm. What appeared to be a positive device to reward management for a firm's success, by putting too much emphasis on the short run (and perhaps by allowing the reward to be great enough to facilitate premature retirement), actually encouraged the pillaging of the corporation. Having survived the challenge of the Marxists, people began to wonder whether capitalism was strong enough to survive the capitalists.

The development of the corporate form in Western economies was crucial in providing a means to raise large sums of capital and limiting the risk of each investor, particularly when the number of investors is large and no one investor can be responsible for oversight of the firm's operations. Without access to the corporate form it is difficult to gather the finances necessary to undertake large-scale operations. Corporations may be either privately held, in which the shares are not traded on stock markets, or publicly held, in which ownership is liquid and traded on stock markets. To be successful, economies in development or transition must establish stock markets and overcome the considerable barriers to their rapid expansion. It should be noted that although the corporation is efficient in encouraging large and risky ventures, its presence does limit the effectiveness of contract law. A corporation's liability is limited to the extent of its assets, and situations may result in which its liability under a contract exceeds those assets.

The Behavior of Firms

The corporation is undoubtedly the dominant form of enterprise in the major market economies. It accounts for most of output, most employment, and most research and development. In the United States, for example, some 3 million corporations make up almost 90 percent of total sales. Within that group, large publicly held corporations constitute the majority of employment and output.

However, the very existence of the modern corporation presents the theory of the market economy with some serious problems. The first is that large corporations necessarily require a separation between the ownership of the firm and its management. This separation causes a principal/agent problem. How can the owners of the firm—the shareholders or principals—be sure that management (the agents of the shareholder-owners) in fact pursues the shareholders' interests rather than its own? (This issue, of course, is in addition to a more general principal/agent issue—how do managers get workers to maximize their effort?)

This problem raises a further question. The whole paradigm of free enterprise and the market system relies for its efficiency on the idea of pursuit of profit maximization. If the corporate sector fails to ruthlessly pursue profit and settles instead for other objectives, then how efficient can the market system be? One clear way of resolving the issue is to make managers' interests more closely coincident with those of the owners. In large part, this attempt to merge interests accounts for the rapidly growing popularity of stock options as a form of remuneration, because rising share prices earn money for the managers and hence ensure that they will tend to pursue policies that will maximize share values.

The other constraint on the behavior of management comes from a contested market for corporate control. In theory, shareholders can band together to get rid of management that is underperforming, but in reality such "revolutions" are rare. It is more likely that a corporation that is underperforming will find itself the target of takeover interest from other companies or entrepreneurs who feel that the assets are underused. Because top management is likely to be ejected as a result of hostile takeover, this possibility provides a constraint on management behavior.

THE LABOR MARKET

An important set of institutions in most developed market economies emerges from the labor market. On one side are the workers, who can join together to form unions; on the other side are employers, who frequently unite to form a collective bargaining agency. A third agent, the government, can regulate the labor market by controlling the age of workers, the length of workweeks, and the minimum wages. It can also maintain institutions that improve the efficiency of labor markets through job exchanges and retraining policies. Government income support policies are also relevant. They affect the reservation wage of workers and so can tend to increase the unemployment rate.

Types of Labor Unions

In all industrial democracies, union power grew with the rise of large-scale industrial enterprise. A lag often occurs in this process, because in many countries unionization was opposed by employers and was initially illegal. Subsequently, unions were granted legal status, and in some countries they became important institutions in overall economic decision making. In the United States, the 1930s were decisive in union growth. The Wagner Act gave unions rights to organize, and the Congress of Industrial Organization (CIO) provided a powerful umbrella organization embracing all workers, skilled and unskilled. Union membership in U.S.

nonagricultural employment rose sharply in the 1930s and 1950s, reaching a high in 1955 when about one-third of the workforce was unionized.

American unions tend to be organized along industry lines. Thus, for example, almost all unionized workers in the automobile industry are members of the United Automobile Workers (UAW). Wage negotiation functions on a firm-by-firm basis, rather than being determined for the entire industry. In other countries unionization took a different path. Although the picture has changed somewhat in recent years, unions in Britain are organized along occupational rather than industrial lines. Thus all electricians belong to an electricians' union, irrespective of the industry in which they are actually employed. This structure makes labor negotiation more difficult and labor peace more fragile because each employer must negotiate with several unions within an individual factory or work site. In Germany, as in the United States, unions are organized on an industry basis, but labor negotiations occur between a union and a confederation of employers. Thus wages and conditions are broadly the same across industries. In Sweden a similar system now exists, although until recently unions, through the national labor federation, were an important part of national wage determination procedures. In Finland and Portugal this kind of system is still in place. In Japan unions are organized along company lines and represent both white- and blue-collar workers. As an established part of the enterprise they are characterized by considerable docility.

Relative Rates of Unionization

The Scandinavian countries are the most highly unionized societies in the world, with some sources giving unionization rates in Sweden at over 90 percent. The United States in contrast has the lowest rates, with an aggregate economy-wide rate of 19 percent. Although Japan's overall rate hovers at about 28 percent, as noted earlier, its unions tend to be rather nonmilitant because they are company unions. Most other industrialized countries' union rates for full-time workers fall between 33 percent and 50 percent (Table 5.4).

In industrial countries the rate of unionization in the private sector fell sharply in recent years. In part this decline stems from the contraction of large-scale "rust-belt" industries—steel, textiles, rubber, ceramics—and the growth of the service sector, which proved historically more difficult to unionize. Federal, state, and local government remain an exception. Unionization among governmental employees increased sharply with important ramifications for overall political economy. One reason that explains the difficulty in restricting the growth of government sector unionization lies in the high level of organization among government workers and their opposition to initiatives designed to reduce public-sector employment.

Income Support

The extent and generosity of the "social safety net" varies considerably from country to country. In the United States, although comprehensive and relatively generous in supporting retired workers, the level of support for the unemployed (especially long-term unemployed) and single parent families tended to decline,

■ TABLE 5.4

Union Membership, Selected Countries, 1987–1989 (membership as a percentage of total employment)

Country	Nonagricultural Employment	Full-Time Employment	Full-Time Manual Workers
Sweden	96	n.a.	n.a.
Austria	61	52	57
Australia	56	70	69
Ireland	51	48	49
United Kingdom	50	47	53
Italy	45	33	37
Germany	43	34	39
Canada	36	n.a.	n.a.
Netherlands	35	42	47
Switzerland	33	37	37
France	28	n.a.	n.a.
Japan	28	n.a.	n.a.
United States	17	19	27

SOURCE: David G. Blanchflower and Richard B. Freeman, "Unionism in the United States and Other O.E.C.D. Countries," *Industrial Relations* 31 (Winter 1992), pp. 56–79; Richard B. Freeman, "American Exceptionalism in the Labor Market: Union-Nonunion Differentials in the United States and Other Countries," in *Labor Economics and Industrial Relations: Markets and Institutions*, ed. Clark Kerr and Paul D. Staudohar (Cambridge, MA: Harvard University Press, 1994), p. 279.

while in Europe the level of support for the unemployed remains high. In the European Union take-home pay after losing a job can frequently be as much as 80 percent of the working rate. Consequently, there tends to be little downward flexibility in wages, and the consequence is high unemployment. Japan's income support systems are not generous, but whether they are the cause or the effect of low levels of unemployment is debatable. What is clear is that the difficulties currently encountered by large corporations in maintaining the system of "nenko" or lifetime employment are particularly important, given the low level of income support.

INDUSTRIAL POLICY

Industrial policy is a general term that encompasses the involvement of the government in the promotion of economic growth. As such, it involves both macroeconomic and microeconomic aspects. In its macro form, industrial policy involves the successful pursuit of economic stabilization, the determination of exchange rates and interest rates calculated to support economic growth and due attention to infrastructure and human capital development. Normally, however, when we speak of industrial policy we mean particular policies that aim to affect the prospects of specific sectors of the economy or even individual firms within these sectors. This microeconomic form of industrial policy is widely practiced in many countries, although considerable debate continues over its effectiveness. Industrial policy can either promote the growth of an industry, seek to stabilize against (for example) inroads of foreign competition, or assist in the orderly decline of an industry, mitigated by the consequences for unemployment or the waste of social infrastructure and human capital.

Government may pursue a variety of measures in forming its microindustrial policy. These measures include direct subsidy payments to firms, government funding of research and development, discriminatory tax relief, government-subsidized or government-directed finance, and the use of tariffs or quotas to protect domestic products. The most aggressive example of industrial policy in recent years can be found in the late industrializing countries of East Asia. Slightly earlier, comprehensive industrial policy was practiced in Germany and France. These examples point out immediately a relevant fact: The most successful industrial policy is practiced by those economies that are well behind the frontier of best practice and advanced technology and have ground to make up.

Consequently, Japan was able to use industrial policy successfully in its transformation after the Meiji restoration in the 1860s as well as in the post–World War II "miracle" period. Similarly, German industrialization relied a great deal on state intervention and direction in both the late nineteenth century and during the 1950s and 1960s. The success of Germany and France in the 1950s, Japan in the 1960s, and Korea in the 1970s attracted favorable attention to the concept of industrial policy, and some advocated the institution of more extensive industrial policy in the United States. However, the rationale behind any government intervention in the economy must be based on the existence of some form of market imperfection, and it is difficult, in the context of the United States today, to imagine the bureaucracy performing better than the market.

Thus while macroindustrial policy might be used to address, for example, the incompleteness of capital markets or failures of coordination due to poor information, justifying microindustrial policy is more difficult. When an economy is behind cutting-edge technology and the government can see the "state of the art" and is knowledgeable about its structure of comparative advantage, it might be able to outperform the market because of this superior information. However, the closer an economy gets to the "frontier," the more difficult the task of "picking winners" becomes. Moreover, intervention in credit markets, frequently a facet of industrial policy, carries with it the loss of the independent impartiality and of the financial system. Industrial policy might be valuable in encouraging growth of specific geographical regions where the preservation of infrastructure might carry externalities that the market fails to reflect.

TRADE POLICY

The postwar years saw a concerted and sustained effort toward liberalization in trade. These efforts led to the burgeoning of international commerce, and practically all economies opening up more than they used to be. Consequently, the implications of trade for growth and employment loom greater, and despite lower tariff levels, trade policy now plays an active part in economic diplomacy.

Trade policy has two clear dimensions: assisting exports and protecting the home market. In some countries, economic agencies act aggressively in export promotion. In Japan, for example, the Ministry of International Trade and Industry (MITI) took an active and strong role in coordinating Japanese exports abroad. The other side of trade policy centers on the protection of the home market and employment. This kind of policy has its roots in the mercantile doctrines of the sixteenth and seventeenth centuries that sought protection for domestic industries against colonial and other competition. Economists generally believe that restraints on trade not only lower global welfare but also reduce the welfare of the countries that impose them. They are therefore explicable largely in terms of politically motivated redistribution.

DEVELOPING HUMAN RESOURCES

We saw in Chapter 1 that the greatest source of the wealth of nations lies in the stock of human capital embodied in its population. We should also give thought to the role of the institutions responsible for the development and maintenance of human capital—the educational system and the health care system.

TRADE AND PROTECTIONISM

The United States traditionally views itself as a strong advocate of free trade and it has been largely responsible for pushing international trade liberalization agreements since World War II. Most economists believe that free trade enhances both world welfare and the aggregate welfare of countries that engage in it. However, within a country international trade results in costs to particular groups. In general we may say that the broad consuming public benefits from liberalization because it provides access to lower-cost imports. However, the labor and capital engaged in the industries at home with which the imports compete are likely to bear the costs. As a rule the broad benefits to the consuming public are greater than the narrower losses to specific labor and capital. However, trade policy is almost always a political issue, which was demonstrated clearly in March of 2002 when President George W. Bush announced tariffs on steel of up to 30 percent. Bush generally sided with the antitax, antitariff wing of the Republican Party, which was disconcerted by the measures. Moreover, the shift put the president at odds with many of his steel-producing allies. Generally speaking economists accept few arguments in favor of tariffs—the chief being the protection of infant industries and the preservation of strategic assets. Protection of steel might be seen as strategic consideration but it is more likely that protectionism was promoted by domestic political considerations than by long-run strategic concerns. The point is that protectionism always exacts a cost, and in this case will raise the costs in every industry that uses steel as an input. As such it will negatively affect the United States' competitive position in industries such as automobiles and machinery. It will raise the costs of U.S. construction and have knock-on effects in every corner of the economy. It might succeed in saving some jobs in steel but the downside clearly shows a likelihood that those jobs saved will be offset by the increase in prices and the effect on competitiveness in other industries.

The Educational System

In most developed market economies, the government makes much of the educational investment. As we noted earlier, education is not a pure public good because it is both excludable and diminishable. Its public provision can probably best be justified on grounds of externalities. An educated individual provides **spillovers** that increase the productivity of those around him or her (and often other measures of welfare, too). A high degree of variance exists even among the wealthier nations in the delivery of education: who pays, who sets standards, who evaluates, and who receives the greatest level of service. In most European nations education represents a social expense, and the school and university systems are almost entirely public. Access is frequently determined by national examination and purports to be largely meritocratic—though clearly class, background, and wealth play a role. In "Anglo-Saxon" nations a greater role is played by the private sector, especially in the United States, implying that education is more a personal rather than social investment.

The scope, efficiency, and finance of educational systems are vital because education is a major determinant of economic outcomes. The performance of the educational system is crucial in understanding the functioning of the larger economic system. A particular puzzle is the performance of socialist countries, where universal literacy and high participation in tertiary education was the rule, but economic performance lagged. Today we must ask what implications the large stock of well-educated workers has for successful transition to a market economy?

The Health Care System

The health care system shares many characteristics with education. It is not a pure public good, but it is frequently supplied by the government, particularly in Europe, where national health services are the norm, and less so in the United States. The importance of health care is likely to increase in the next decades. In most developed economies, including Western Europe, Japan, the United States, and Eastern Europe, the populations are aging rapidly. The burden of health care is likely to grow and may represent a potentially suffocating load for the economies of these countries.

A debate also focuses sharply on the advantages and disadvantages of market provision versus public supply. Europe continues to follow a public model that proved itself both more effective in containing costs of medical services and pharmaceuticals and in providing a more equitable distribution of medical care. Cost containment results mainly from the government's considerable monopsony power that it exerts against physicians, nurses, and pharmaceutical companies. The equitable access to health care in turn reveals that basic indicators of health fail to correlate highly with income. The early years of the Clinton administration saw an attempt to introduce aspects of publicly provided national health care into the United States. It was soundly rejected by the configuration of political forces, though medical costs ballooned in the aftermath.

KEY TERMS AND CONCEPTS

allocation function
central bank independence
civil compensation
corporate governance
depository institutions
distribution function
fiscal policy
industrial policy
investment banks
market for corporate control
merit goods
monetary policy
progressive tax
quasi-public goods
redistribution in-kind
spillovers
stabilization function
tort law
voucher systems

QUESTIONS FOR DISCUSSION

1. Tax systems become less progressive in many societies even as transfers continue to rise. Can you account for these apparently contradictory trends?
2. Why is contract enforcement necessary for the functioning of a modern market system?
3. Why should central banks be independent of the political process?
4. Excessive management compensation and "perks" are the inevitable result of the separation of ownership from management. Discuss.
5. Does the widespread holding of shares in the United States influence the effectiveness of corporate governance? Why?
6. The corporate form enables businesspeople to escape the full consequences of their actions. Discuss.
7. Do you think that the abuse and fraud revealed in the U.S. economy provide a full justification for a return to much heavier regulation?
8. The low level of unionization in the United States is a key reason for the low rates of unemployment relative to Europe. Discuss.
9. Why does domestic political agenda make it difficult for any regime, no matter how committed to the market, to stick to a policy of free trade?

RESOURCES

Web Sites

Mark Bernkopf's Central Banking Resource Center.. http://patriot.net/~bernkopf/

This site offers a comprehensive series of links to almost every central bank and ministry of finance in the world, as well as ministries of finance, research departments, and an excellent page on the history of central banking. The site is a first step for any research on comparative central banking.

The Cato Institute .... http://www.cato.org/
The home page of this conservative think tank and lobby organization contains a great deal of information and papers on the introduction of markets into public service provision (health and education), welfare reform, and the privatization of social security. All the work conforms to the institute's agenda but it is comprehensive and useful, and much can be downloaded free of charge.

The Milken Institute .... http://www.milkeninstitute.org/
This site also contains some useful books and position papers.

Books and Articles

Alstenstetter, Christine (ed.). *Health Policy Reform: National Variations and Globalization.* London: St. Martin's Press, 1997.

Blanchflower, David G., and Richard B. Freeman. "Unionism in the United States and Other O.E.C.D. Countries." *Industrial Relations* 31 (Winter 1992), 56–79.

Crumper, George. *Evaluation of National Health Systems.* Oxford: Oxford University Press, 1991.

Freeman, Richard B. "American Exceptionalism in the Labor Market: Union-Nonunion Differentials in the United States and Other Countries." In *Labor Economics and Industrial Relations: Markets and Institutions,* Clark Kerr and Paul D. Staudohar (eds.). Cambridge, MA: Harvard University Press, 1994.

Friedman, Milton, with Rose Friedman. *Free to Choose.* Fort Worth, TX: Harcourt Brace, 1990.

Goodhart, Charles. *The Central Bank and the Financial System.* Cambridge, MA: MIT Press, 1995.

Kwoka John E., and Lawrence J. White (eds.). *The Antitrust Revolution: Economics, Competition, and Policy,* 4th ed. New York: Oxford University Press, 1997.

Lippo, Francesco. *Central Bank Independence: Political and Economic Aspects of Delegating Arrangements for Monetary Policy.* White Plains, NY: Edward Elgar Press, 1999.

McGroarty, David, and William J. Bennett. *Break These Chains: The Battle for School Choice.* Rocklin, CA: Prima Publishing, 1996.

Musgrave, Richard, and Peggy Musgrave. *Public Finance in Theory and Practice.* New York: McGraw-Hill, 1984.

Nester, William R. *American Industrial Policy: Free or Managed Markets?* New York: St. Martin's Press, 1997.

Okimoto, Daniel I. *Between MITI and the Market: Japanese Industrial Policy for High Technology*. Stanford, CA: Stanford University Press, 1990.

7

SWEDEN AND SOCIAL DEMOCRACY

SWEDEN		
	Area (thousand sq. km.)	450
	Currency	krona
	Exchange Rate	SEK 9.16 = US$1
	Population 2000 (millions)	9.00
	Population Growth Rate	0.4%
	GNI per Capita, 2000	$26,780
	GNI per Capita, PPP	$23,770
	GDP Growth 1990–2000	1.8%
Value Added as % of GDP 2000	Agriculture	2%
	Industry	29%
	Services	69%
% of GDP	Government Expenditure	53%
	Exports	38%

FUNDAMENTAL FEATURES OF THE SWEDISH MODEL

In Chapter 4 we discussed the operation of a market economy and some of the failures that might result. The problems of externalities and public goods differed in type from concern that income distribution resulting from the operation of a market economy might not be equitable or "fair." In a pure market system, an individual's income depends on his or her ownership of factors of production. The pattern of economic well-being generated might be considered unsatisfactory from a variety of points of view, which may provide a motivation for government action. In fact, one of the principal activities of governments in modern market economies involves modifying the income distribution. This involves the use of transfer payments, the public provision of goods that might otherwise be supplied privately and the finance of both these expenditures out of taxation. We generally refer to this activity as the operation of a "welfare state."

Sweden is generally regarded as the quintessence of the welfare state; the state guarantees everyone who is prepared to work a high standard of living, and provides the entire population with access to a wide range of services. These services include free education at all levels (with stipends for students above the high school level), free health care, and a comprehensive retirement scheme. Such policies ensure a high profile for the government in many aspects of economic life. Total government expenditures in Sweden are more than half of total gross domestic product. Payroll taxes amount to more than one-third of the total payroll, and most blue-collar workers pay a marginal income tax rate greater than 40 percent.

As a further feature of the "Swedish model," government maintains a high level of activity in the labor market. This has two aspects. In macroeconomic terms, the government aggressively uses monetary, fiscal, and exchange rate measures to maintain a high level of employment. On the microeconomic side, the government offers a comprehensive system of assisted job search and retraining programs to keep the level of frictional unemployment low.[1] These policies ensured that the rate of unemployment in Sweden until recently remained consistently below that of most other market economies.

By maintaining low unemployment and high levels of social goods and social insurance, Sweden has avoided the sharp contrasts between the affluent and the poor that can characterize pure market capitalism. The Swedish model also went a step further by its use of highly centralized collective bargaining practices. Negotiations between representatives of labor and employers on the national level largely determine wages. These negotiations, undertaken under the stewardship of the government, involve the various parties in the most heavily unionized society in the world. In Sweden, where some form of collective bargaining agreement covers 85 percent of workers, such central bargaining determines to a great extent the distribution of the social product.

One objective of this collective bargaining system has been the elimination of social waste by arriving at settlements without resort to socially and economically damaging strikes and labor disputes. Another objective has been the promotion of "wage solidarity," which involves an overt attempt to keep the earnings of all workers more closely grouped than is the case in less socially conscious societies. This aspect of policy aims to produce a higher degree of social cohesion within the population, and the consequent elimination, or at least minimization, of class conflict.

Although government strongly shapes the distribution of income and goods in kind in Sweden, ownership of the means of production falls almost entirely within

[1]Frictional unemployment results when a worker engages in some form of job search while out of work and represents behavior compatible with a high level of demand in the labor market.

the private sector. Thus, many authors describe Sweden as being representative of a "middle way"—socialist in terms of its distribution policy but capitalist (relying on markets and competition) in production. Because of its approach, and the apparent elimination of the "market failure" of highly skewed distribution of well-being, the Swedish model appears, at first sight, highly attractive. However, critics point to the high level of taxes required to finance redistribution policies, and the consequent erosion of incentives, as the flaw that ultimately hobbled the Swedish system. Moreover, although Swedish firms are capitalist in terms of ownership, the strength of unions, powerful labor laws, and other government restrictions place constraints on Swedish managers' ability to operate. In the long term, these constraints may adversely affect international competitiveness. This chapter looks at the key features of the Swedish model and asks whether other countries—developed, developing, or in transition from some form of socialism—might profitably learn from the Swedish experience.

Characteristics of Swedish Society

First, one tends to note Sweden is a small country. Its population of only 9 million is remarkably homogenous, both politically and ethnically. Without any great racial or class conflict, the political debate remains rather localized in terms of the ideological spectrum. Most Swedes accept the essential propositions of Swedish society, a commitment to wage solidarity and social cohesion.

Whether this consensus comes as a product of the Swedish economic model or is a cause of it represents an open question. The Social Democratic Party has been in power for 61 of the last 70 years. It won its third successive general election in September 2002. Although the Social Democrats received only 40 percent of the popular vote, they enjoy a stable majority in Parliament because of the support of the Greens and several left-wing former communists. No matter which party held power, the political system remained highly corporatist. Decision making is collective, but only through institutions sanctioned by the state and granted access to the process. Groups outside of those formally recognized by the government (and therefore policy making) have only a small voice. Although individuals enjoy a relatively high level of liberty, they also live within an expectation of conformity to the basic objectives of society.

Sweden is also a prosperous society. Only Switzerland, the United States, and Japan score significantly above Sweden in terms of income measured by purchasing per head. The Swedish economy distributes income quite equitably. The ratio of the income share of the most affluent quintile to the least affluent is only 3.5 to 1, thus Sweden may be thought of as about twice as "equitable" as the United States. This equality owes much to the strong role of the government; general government total outlays were 52.7 percent of GDP in the year 2000, the highest in the world.[2] Although down from a peak near 67 percent in 1993, this percentage is well above the average for the European Union (EU), which sat at only 44.2 percent, and

[2]See OECD *Economic Outlook*, June 2001.

almost twice the relevant U.S. figure of 29.6 percent. Social security transfer payments alone account for 19 percent of GDP, against an average of 10 percent for the industrialized world as a whole and only 7 percent for the United States. However, although the Swedish government experienced a considerable deficit in the early 1990s, as much as 8 percent of GDP, fiscal prudence, falling unemployment and a growing economy restored the balance.

Contrary to popular wisdom, Sweden does not attract a plethora of social problems, and statistics show it does well on most measures. It records one of the highest life expectancies in the world (second only to Japan) and one of the lowest infant mortality rates. Fewer people populate Sweden's prisons than the average in the industrial world; in fact, its incarceration rate equals only about 11 percent of that of the United States. Suicides rank at about the mean for developed nations. In terms of overall "human development,"[3] as defined by the United Nations Development Programme (UNDP), Sweden ranked fourth in the world in 2001. The divorce rate is about the same as that of the United States, though births outside of matrimony are higher. Alcohol consumption is low, and injuries due to traffic accidents (perhaps not coincidentally) occur at one-fifth of the U.S. level. Sweden's population continues to age—now one of the oldest populations in the world—with 18 percent of the population above the age of 65. This growing share of elderly gives Sweden one of the highest dependency ratios in industrialized countries, and the necessity of providing for an increasing proportion of retired further strains the public finances.

Although it is a member of the European Union, Sweden has so far declined to be a part of the common currency system. It has traditionally guarded its sovereignty and continues to regard the exchange rate as a means of promoting the high levels of employment essential to its system. However, sentiment is shifting in favor of the Euro. Sweden, a small and highly open economy, would gain a great deal from the common currency. Prime Minister Persson will probably try to prod the country in the direction of monetary accession during 2003.

SOCIAL DEMOCRACY

Even after the reforms of the early 1990s, which curtailed some aspects of public spending, Sweden remains the best example of **social democracy.** Henry Milner defines a social democratic system in terms of six basic principles governing the interaction of government and citizens.[4] These principles can be summarized as follows:

1. *A fair distribution of economic well-being.* The fruits of economic prosperity are to be distributed fairly, but in such a way as not to undermine that prosperity. In other words, taxes and transfer payments must be used but care should be

[3]The World Bank's Human Development Index uses a weighted average of life expectancy, literacy, higher education, and income per head.

[4]This section on the underlying principles of social democracy is taken and modified from Henry Millner's *Sweden: Social Democracy in Practice* (New York: Oxford University Press, 1989), pp. 4–5.

taken lest high tax rates or overgenerous transfers create substantial disincentives to effort.

2. *Work for all as the primary means of eliminating deprivation.* Because human beings seek to live productively, fair distribution is to be effected through decently remunerated employment rather than simply cash or services.
3. *A high degree of social solidarity to bind individuals to a common purpose.* Individuals are members of communities through ties of culture and history. Members enjoy reciprocal rights and obligations over and above the right of all human beings to be treated with tolerance and compassion without distinction as to race, sex, disability, and so on.
4. *Rules to be made by a democratic process.* A society of justice must follow rules, without which it degenerates into a jungle in which the "fittest" prosper. Democracy entails that the rules to be obeyed—by leaders and followers alike—result from decisions made by the people themselves through free elections that fully safeguard fundamental political freedoms.
5. *Participation must extend beyond electoral democracy.* Especially in modern societies with complex systems of economic coordination, democracy entails active decentralized decision making and employee participation in management.
6. *Access to information for all citizens.* Democratic participation requires open and informed discussion—that is, a free and responsible press; an informed, well-educated citizenry; full public access to information based on data reliably gathered and presented; and publicly accountable independent boards of inquiry into matters of controversy.[5]

Although Sweden provides perhaps the best real-world example of a social democracy, it falls short of these defining characteristics in key ways. In particular, the first principle's drive for egalitarianism clashes with economic efficiency, hampering the operation of the labor market, reducing saving, and leading to high rates of absenteeism. This conflict has led to rising unemployment and a falling sense of solidarity. Although democratic in terms of its electoral policies, real power in Sweden is held by a small group of individuals within a limited set of institutions. This chapter asks, among other things, whether egalitarian labor market policies and a high degree of redistribution through transfer payments are compatible with relatively high rates of economic growth in the long run.

THE TAX AND TRANSFER SYSTEM

Sweden's comprehensive system of social insurance and redistribution forms the cornerstone of its social solidarity, which ensures that a worker who is willing to work will not be unduly harmed by involuntary job loss, injury, sickness, or even family responsibilities. The Organization of Economic Cooperation and Develop-

[5]A final principle could be added: respect for the environment. Through creative decentralized planning, social democracy ideally protects and enhances the natural environment as vital to human existence.

ment (OECD) calls it "[a] universal and generous system of social protection [that] has combined with progressive income taxes to achieve a high degree of poverty alleviation and equalization of incomes." Sweden outperforms most other countries in terms of relative income levels for key groups such as families with children and old-age pensioners.[6] A full 35 percent of all household income in Sweden results from transfer payments, up from only 15 percent in the mid-1960s. Table 7.1 shows that today Swedish workers lose little of their take-home pay for most unwelcome circumstances, and on the whole fare much better than the other countries illustrated, all of whom can be called something of a welfare state.

Although government financed, unemployment insurance funds are administered by the powerful and omnipresent labor unions. Membership is voluntary and open to all members of the labor force. Members may claim benefits after 12 months of membership with a replacement rate of 80 percent of gross earnings. Younger workers exhaust benefits after 300 days. If the worker remains out of work for a year, the last 65 days carry no unemployment benefit. Hence the **replacement wage** for a full year's unemployment is only 71 percent, as seen in Table 7.1, though workers over 55 can receive benefits for a total of 450 days. The same table also shows Sweden's generous sickness, injury, maternity, and retirement schemes.

Households unable to reach a reasonable living standard can claim social assistance benefits, administered by local authorities, although access is subject to strict

TABLE 7.1

International Comparison of Social Insurance Scheme (percentage change in annual disposable income for the average production worker in moving from employment to social insurance, 1996)

Benefit	Sweden, 1997[a]	Denmark	Finland	Germany	United Kingdom	Netherlands	Canada
12 months unemployment, insured	–29	–35	–38	–42	–79	–27	–44
Sickness, 1 week[b]	–0.8	0	0	0	–0.4	0	–1.5
Work injury, total incapacity	0	+26	–8	+15	–57	–27	–10
Maternity leave, common duration	–2	–3	–2	0	–3	0	–4
Old-age pension,[c] full work record	–36	–44	–33	–25	–47	–53	–45

[a]Based on a general replacement rate of 75 percent in social insurance, the increase to 80 percent in unemployment insurance in the fourth quarter is taken into account.
[b]Includes occupational pensions.
[c]Maximum (and not average) benefit in public schemes but without additions from occupational schemes.
SOURCE: OECD *Economic Survey of Sweden*, 1999, p. 125.

[6] OECD *Economic Survey of Sweden*, 1999, p. 16.

means testing, requiring recipients to sell capital assets. Housing benefits are means tested too and availability depends on the number of children, the income of the household, and the level of housing costs. Weekly cash payments are issued for each child in the family, with a higher rate effective from the third child on. Family benefits compensate parents for staying at home to take care of their children during the period immediate after their birth. The replacement rate amounts to about 80 percent (as elsewhere in the social insurance system) for the first 12 months. Day care for children is provided at prices below cost and dependent on parental income. Transfers are taxed on a par with labor income when they substitute for a short- or long-term earnings loss to avoid tax considerations playing into the take-up of benefits. Social insurance benefits are thus generally provided gross of taxes, the exception being social assistance. Child and housing benefits are consequently provided net of taxes.

This comprehensive welfare system does not come cheaply, making Sweden notorious for its high level of personal taxation. However, concerns about the disincentive effects of high taxation brought about a comprehensive reform in the tax system. The top rates of tax on unearned income remain high because reforms only cut the effective tax rate[7] from about 63 percent in 1989 to 60 percent today, still almost twice the U.S. rate of 35 percent. Table 7.2 shows that capital taxation in

■ TABLE 7.2

Dimensions of Capital Income Taxation

	Highest Tax Rate on Interest Income	Corporate Tax Rate	Total Dividend Taxation	Taxation of Capital Gains	Rate	Threshold
Sweden	30	28	50	30	1.5	0.9
Austria	25	34	50	0	0	
Belgium	15	40	49	0	0	
Denmark	59	34	60	0–40	0	
Finland	28	28	28	28	0.9	1.65
France	25	33	66	26	0.5–1.5	6.25
Germany	56	58	49	0	0	
Ireland	48	32	55	40	0	
Netherlands	60	35	74	0	0.7	0.77
Norway	28	28	28	28	0.7–1.1	0.13
United Kingdom	40	31	48	0–40	0	
United States	47	35	68	0–20	0	

NOTES: Tax rates are in percentages and thresholds are in SKr million.
SOURCE: OECD *Economic Survey of Sweden*, 1999, p. 133.

[7]Defined as employees' social security contributions plus personal income taxes as a percentage of gross labor costs.

Sweden compares favorably with the United States, although Sweden does impose a wealth tax of 1½ percent per annum in principle levied on all personal wealth greater than about $110,000 (however, loopholes abound and evasion is common).

CORPORATISM

Though ideally social democracy gives everyone a role in the decision-making process, in reality Sweden is a highly corporatist state with much of the power, especially in economic matters, being located in the government (with power held by the Social Democrats for most of the postwar period), the employers' federations, and the labor unions. The discussion of **corporatism** in Chapter 5 showed Sweden as the most highly unionized society in the world with the vast majority of workers represented by unions. However, this concentration of power by labor is matched by a similar centralization in capital. A disproportionately large number of major companies calls Sweden home. Table 7.3 shows it has the highest density of large companies of any European nation. Moreover, because of a limited domestic market, those companies must be globally competitive and reach markets beyond Sweden's seven million consumers. These export-oriented industries are vital for Sweden's well-being and play a key role in wage negotiations. Government's close relationship with the few business leaders who dominate Swedish industry is one reason why rates of taxation on capital are relatively modest compared to those falling on labor income—28 percent for corporate taxes as opposed to more than 60 percent for wage income under the personal income tax.

Not only is Swedish industry dominated by large firms, the corporatist structure of the country is more pronounced because of the dominance of a single holding company, Investor AB, which holds controlling interests in many of the big companies. Firms either controlled by Investor or in which it maintains a dominant interest make up about 40 percent of the Stockholm stock market's capitalization. In addition, 40 percent of Investor AB is owned by members of, or trusts controlled by, the Wallenberg family. Economic power in Sweden, more centralized than in any other

TABLE 7.3

Large Companies per Million Inhabitants, 1998: Number of Companies Among Europe's 500 Largest Companies

Country	Number of Companies	Country	Number of Companies
Sweden	3.6	Ireland	1.7
Switzerland	3.5	Denmark	1.3
United Kingdom	2.7	Portugal	1.1
Belgium/Luxembourg	2.3	France	1.1
Netherlands	2.1	Norway	0.9

SOURCE: *Financial Times*, 1999.

SWEDEN'S MISSING ENTREPRENEURS

Sweden's deserved reputation as welfare state with an industrial sector dominated by a few large firms may be a problem for its long-term growth prospects. Despite Sweden's excellent education system and the high level of human capital embodied in its workforce it may lack one specific factor of production that has been found to be important in furthering growth—entrepreneurship. In 2000 two economists at the Stockholm School of Economics undertook a study of the determinants of the start-ups and high-growth firms. With the Internet and communications revolution being led by the small growth firms of Silicon Valley and the success of other small companies and services and retailing, it was thought to be on the keys to economic growth. They tried to measure entrepreneurship, and also the economic and cultural environment, by establishing by survey the number of people who actually tried to start their own company. They found that Sweden was the lowest of any of the European countries that they studied; only 2.2 percent of Swedish adults indicated experience as entrepreneurs against 3.1 percent in the United Kingdom and 3.8 percent in Norway. Europe as a whole, however, fared poorly against the United States where 8.4 percent of adults had, at one time or another, tried to start a business. Whether this contrast is due to "national character," the tax regime or other aspects of government policy is not clear. It can be used to support a general thesis that provision of job security does deplete initiative.

SOURCE: Magnus Henrekson and Per Davidsson, "Determinants of the Prevalence of Start-ups and High-Growth Firms," *Small Business Economics* 19, no. 2, 2002.

major capitalist country, facilitates the operation of the troika of employers, unions, and the Social Democratic Party that has controlled Sweden for decades.

THE SYSTEM OF LABOR RELATIONS

The Basic System

One of the most distinctive features of the Swedish economy, and the one we wish to focus on here, is its system of collective bargaining and industrial relations. This system originated in the late 1930s in discussions motivated by the need to reduce the then high degree of industrial unrest that Sweden experienced in the 1930s. In 1938, the employers' federation (the SAF) and the Swedish Trade Union Confederation (the LO) signed the basic agreement in the resort town of Saltsjöbaden, near Stockholm. The **Saltsjöbaden agreement** is the cornerstone of the system, providing a mechanism of collective bargaining to determine the rate of wage increase across industry and placing limits on the nature of industrial action by the unions.

As we noted, Sweden is one of the most heavily unionized societies in the world. Some 85 percent of workers claim membership of some union.[8] The LO represents

[8]United Nations Development Programme, *Human Development Report*, 1995, p. 201.

only blue-collar workers and now has about 2.2 million members. White-collar workers, a growing percentage of the workforce, are represented by their own confederations, the largest of which is the Swedish Confederation of Professional Associations (TCO). The SAF now represents some 42,000 firms of all sizes including all of the major employers. Government-sector employees are represented by their own agency.

Throughout the entire postwar era, until the end of the 1980s, national-level negotiations between the SAF and the LO provided the framework for changes in wage costs. Both sides saw benefit in this arrangement. The employers viewed the agreements as being able to deliver lower increases in labor costs, and lower prospects of strike activity, than might result from disaggregated bargaining. The unions supported the policy because it offered an avenue toward their overall political goal of **wage solidarity** (discussed later). Negotiations conducted at the national level hammered out a framework agreement that determined the overall increase in the wage bill. This framework was subsequently supplemented by industry agreements, which translated the total settlement with norms for the various sectors of the economy.

The EFO Model

A primary constraint on the system of wage settlement came from the need to maintain international competitiveness. Sweden, a small and relatively open economy, exports roughly one-quarter of its GDP, and wage cost inflation could not be allowed to jeopardize international competitiveness. The system of negotiation therefore explicitly differentiated between a competitive ("exposed") sector (comprised of firms such as Volvo, Saab-Scania, and Electrolux) which operated in world markets, the price structure of which lay beyond the control of anyone within Sweden, and a domestic ("protected") sector in which prices might be endogenously determined.[9] The rate of wage increase in the competitive sector was determined first on the proposition that the rate of growth of unit labor costs (basically wage cost increases less any anticipated productivity gains) should not outpace the rate of growth of prices for Swedish exports, as determined in world markets. This implies that:

$$\dot{W}_X = \dot{P}_X + (\dot{Q}_X - \dot{L}_X)$$

where $\dot{W}$ is the rate of change of wages; $\dot{P}$ is the rate of change of prices; $\dot{Q}$ is the rate of change of output; and $\dot{L}$ is the change in the use of labor. $\dot{Q}_X - \dot{L}_X$ therefore indicates the change in productivity; subscript x denotes the **exposed sector**. Any wage increase above this rate harms international competitiveness, resulting in a fall in exports, balance of payments problems, depreciation of the currency, and

[9]This procedure is known as the EFO model after the Gösta Edgren, Karl-Olaf Faxen, and Clas-Eric Odhner, who were the chief economists for the SAF, LO, and TCO, and who literally wrote the book on Swedish collective bargaining, *Wage Formation and the Economy.*

serious inflation in an open economy like Sweden's. An arithmetic example of the process is useful. If world prices for Swedish exports are expected to advance by 4 percent and productivity gains in Swedish industry are predicted to lower costs by 2 percent, the maximum increase in unit wages compatible with sustained export competitiveness is 6 percent. This calculation determined the wage settlement in the exposed sector. Subsequently, the rate of wage increases in the protected (i.e., nonexport) sector would be fixed at a rate comparable to that determined for the exposed sector. Such agreements were truly national and employees in the nontradable service and government sector enjoyed a rate of increase of wages predicated on the rate of price increases and productivity gain in the most competitive sector.

Wage Solidarity

This model enabled the trade union movement to pursue one of its most cherished objectives—wage solidarity—with the underlying idea that the wage rate for all jobs requiring comparable effort and comparable skills should be the same across all industries. To put it another way, the unions committed to equal pay for equal work and to the notion that one's wage should not depend on the profitability of the industry in which one works. This proposition conflicts with the market logic that links wages to the marginal value product. Critics predicted that adherence to wage solidarity would lead to a variety of problems. Growing firms would find it hard to attract labor. Work incentives would be lowered, and the workforce would be inefficiently allocated between occupations and industries. Nevertheless, the unions experienced considerable success in eroding wage differentials between industries. In 1959 the spread between average wages in the highest and the lowest paid industries stood at 39 percent. By 1964 it had fallen to 26 percent and by 1981 was only 12 percent. A similar narrowing occurred in terms of wage differentials by sex. An average female worker in Sweden earns 90 percent of the male level, considerably above the "60 cents on the dollar" experienced in the United States.

The sustained growth of the government's role in the Swedish economy and the extensive provision of social goods made the public sector Sweden's largest employer. The Municipal Employees' Union is now the largest union in Sweden. The workforce actually engaged in the exposed sector shrank as a share of total employment as the services and government sectors grew. Furthermore, because any increase in pay for government-sector workers must be financed from taxes, a system where public-sector wages shadowed those of the most competitive sector embodied a serious problem. Simply, whenever productivity or prices rose in the export, or exposed, sector, wages for the workers in that sector would increase. The system of national wage negotiation meant that a wage increase in the service and government sectors would inevitably follow. This wage increase implied domestic inflation, as well as tax increases to pay the increased wages in the government sector, both of which resulted in ultimately injurious consequences for competitiveness in export markets.

The Breakdown of National Agreements

Although praiseworthy in terms of equity, attempts to ensure that equal work meant equal pay dulled the efficiency of the labor market. Wages in a market system, like other prices, act as signaling devices that indicate shortages; rising wages set in motion shifts that act to eliminate shortages. Because Swedish policy explicitly tried to eliminate wage differentials, the labor market could not adjust to rectify shortages in particular industries or sectors. With high demand for Swedish products in world markets, employers in the exposed sector found themselves short of labor and unable to increase wages to attract new workers. Expansionary macroeconomic policies ensured that the aggregate level of employment stayed high, and because of the national agreements, wages in **protected sectors** roughly equaled those in the exposed sector, making workers reluctant to change jobs.

Initially, employers in firms short of labor attempted to attract new workers while nominally living within the wages determined by the national agreement. Because nominal wage rates could not be raised at a rate above the agreed level, employers introduced special "perks" and fringe benefits as inducements to retain the workforce and attract new recruits. These incentives included productivity-related bonuses, premiums for shift work, shorter hours, and longer vacations. This phenomenon of raising the effective wage per unit labor while leaving the nominal hourly wage unchanged is known as **wage drift**. During the 1980s, an estimated 50 percent of effective wage increase could be attributed to wage drift. Wage drift is still present but has fallen to a smaller share of overall wage increase; in 1998 it represented less than 25 percent of the total changes. (See Table 7.4.)

Nonetheless, the employers in firms facing high product demand still felt shackled and in 1983 the Engineering Employers' Association (VF), a member unit of the SAF, decided to go alone and concluded its own set of wage agreements with the Metal Workers Union signaling the end of effective national wage determination. Since 1983, no national agreement on wage increases has been reached, although in some years the LO and the SAF recommended a nonbinding norm to their membership. The role of the union confederation now involves one of coordination and oversight rather than that of lead negotiator.

TABLE 7.4

Aggregate Wage Growth (percent)

	1994	1995	1996	1997	1998
Aggregate wage growth	2.4	3.3	6.0	4.5	3.6
Contribution from					
Central bargaining	1.5	2.1	4.4	3.8	2.8
Wage drift	1.0	1.2	1.7	0.7	0.8

SOURCE: Statistics Sweden; National Institute of Economic Research; Ministry of Finance, in OECD *Economic Survey of Sweden*, 1999, p. 68.

Other Aspects of Labor Market Policy

Although centralized wage negotiation formed the centerpiece of the labor market policies, it did not tell the whole of the story. Sweden's highly **active labor market policy** remains in place despite the demise of centralized wage bargaining and the consequent slippage of wage solidarity. This policy embraces relocation grants, training, and retraining schemes, private-sector employment subsidies, and where necessary, public-sector job schemes.

Active labor market policy supplied the necessary complement to centralized wage bargaining. In a free labor market, wage differentials between industries and occupations provide the incentives for workers to change jobs and so resolve shortages. This interaction ensures the flow of labor between occupations and a consequent microeconomic equilibrium, while real wage flexibility maintains full employment. Because the Swedish system for many years actively discouraged the development of wage differentials, the government resorted to active labor market schemes to solve the problem.

"Labor exchanges," government offices that assist in matching displaced workers with vacancies are the first point of intervention. In Europe, active labor market policy plays a more important role than in the United States, but in most countries labor exchanges operate with high levels of caseloads per staff worker. In Britain, for example, the ratio is 375 cases per employee; in Germany it is 370, and in the Netherlands 160. In Sweden, in contrast, it varies between 15 and 30, depending on the region and as a result offers high individual attention to each job seeker. The law requires that employers must report all vacancies to the authorities, and the labor exchange professionals know all essential information concerning all job openings in the country. Consequently they can work actively with the human resource departments of firms to find the best match between job seekers and vacancies. To further decrease rigidities and frictional cost to the unemployed, the government makes available funds for site visits and, should a job seeker accept a distant vacancy, for relocation expenses. If no suitable openings can be found for a job seeker, then the job seeker can participate in retraining funded by the government. Furthermore, in order to cope with potentially large crises, the authorities require that they be told well in advance about plant closings and downsizing, allowing forward thinking on strategies to address the problem and the institution of retraining schemes even before plant closings occur.

Generous unemployment benefits in Sweden result in only small reduction of take-home income consequent to a job loss. However, benefits are contingent on active job search and subject to strict time limits. Should an individual's benefits run out, the government acts as an "employer of last resort" and will provide a job for at least six months. As a result of this combination of policies, unemployment rates in Sweden remained low until recently, generally between 1 and 1.5 percent, but rose to more than 8 percent by the mid-1990s.

In August 2001 the government introduced a system of "activity guarantee." This plan requires that any person registered with the public employment to receive unemployment or social benefits must enroll in some education program if his or her unemployment lasts for more than six months. The nominal objective of this policy is to augment human capital, but the effectiveness of the policy is under question; it might merely serve to reduce the recorded rate of unemployment.

Attempts to Socialize Capital

The policy of wage solidarity resulted in the repression of wages in the profitable, exposed sectors of industry, and although this policy contributed to managers' problems by lessening their ability to recruit qualified labor, it positively affected profits by keeping wage costs low. Workers in these industries felt that they should share in the excess profits generated by their restraint. In 1976 the Congress of the LO adopted a resolution proposed by Rudolf Meidner, their chief economist, to establish **wage earner funds**. The ambitious original plan prescribed that each year all firms that employed more than 500 workers would hand over 20 percent of their pretax profits to a union-controlled fund specific to that industry. Under the plan these monies would be used by the union to purchase (at book value) shares of the firm in which the "excess" profits were made. Consequently, the share capital of the large, profitable elements of Swedish industry (which were concentrated in the exposed, export sector) would be increasingly accumulated by the unions. In the limit the unions might control all industrial capital, with the most profitable firms passing most quickly to union control. When the union share holdings represented a majority, they would be in a position to appoint management and assume strategic control of the firm. Had the **Meidner plan** been followed the Swedish system would eventually resemble the Yugoslav system of worker management, except for two important differences:

1. Union workers, rather than society as a whole, would be owners of capital.
2. Control of the firm would pass to industry-wide unions, rather than to the workers in the specific enterprise.

The Swedish parliament balked at enacting the Meidner plan into law, despite aggressive union lobbying. Such a radical idea would transform the Swedish model by progressively eliminating private capital, leading to union control of both sides of the labor process. It proved too ambitious, even for the ruling Social Democrats, and Sweden's tight group of capitalists staunchly opposed it. As a compromise Parliament went for a watered-down version, establishing five regional funds financed by a 20 percent tax on "excess profits," which were empowered to buy shares not at book value but at the much higher market value. This legislation also restricts accumulation to no more than 8 percent of the capital of any one firm, and total ownership by all of the funds together must not exceed 49 percent, thus denying the possibility of union control of business.

Recent Labor Market Developments

A startling development in Sweden in the early 1990s was a sharp rise in unemployment, shocking in an economy predicated on the idea of a universal right to work. Unemployment peaked at about 8 percent between 1994 and 1997, and has fallen back considerably since, at least in measured terms.

Table 7.5 shows recent developments in the labor market. The unemployment rate fell from its highs of greater than 8 percent in 1996 to about 5.5 percent in the year 2000. However, the government achieved this reduction by providing occupations to the potentially unemployed rather than by increasing the number of people in jobs actually created without overt government intervention. Thus the percentage of the workforce that is actually covered by unemployment, make-work, and special education programs together remained almost constant at 14.3 percent. Because more people enroll in education programs (especially in the adult education initiative introduced in 1997), fewer actually remain idle or in a make-work program. In theory this approach should lead to a better-trained and more productive workforce, though there is too little evidence to judge the effectiveness of job retraining schemes. The OECD reports that:

> The authorities have launched an extensive adult education programme. This is aimed at those with inadequate qualifications and has now been running, in line with the quantified objectives set, for two years. Insofar as educational qualifications are closely linked to unemployment risk, an emphasis on human capital enhancement is a key ingredient in the long-term improvement of labour-market outcomes.[10]

In February 2001 government, unions, and employers readied a guideline agreement to cover the entire labor sector for three years. The agreement specified hourly wage increases of 2.8 percent per annum, and a reduction in working hours added roughly another 0.5 percent to labor costs. Most analysts expect the pace of unit labor cost increases to be somewhat more rapid over the previous three years. Although still coordinated at the national level, Swedish labor negotiations show movement toward decentralization with more agreed upon at the plant or office level. This trend means greater difficulty in distinguishing between the agreed "official settlement" and "wage drift" as more deviations from the national agreements

■ **TABLE 7.5**

Labor Market Developments, 1996–2000

	1996	1997	1998	1999	2000
Labor force, 1,000 persons	4,310	4,264	4,255	4,308	4,364
Unemployment rate	8.1	8	6.5	6.4	5.6
Unemployed and covered by government programs (%)	14.3	14.8	13.8	16.3	14.3
Covered by make-work programs	4.5	4.3	3.9	3.3	2.8
Covered by education programs	1.7	2.4	3.4	6.6	5.9
Of Which: Adult Education Initiative	n.a.	2.7	3.3	3.3	3.1

SOURCE: OECD, *Economic Survey of Sweden*, 2001.

[10]OECD, *Economic Survey of Sweden*, 1999, pp. 13–14.

become codified into a local arrangement. The successful conclusion of this round of collective agreements represented in many ways "the ultimate test of the wage formation system in Sweden to deliver appropriate outcomes.[11]

Generally speaking, the agreement "passed" this test. The size of the increase, however, might pose a certain amount of difficulty for Swedish industry. The pace of labor cost increases during the period 1995–2001 led, in a competitive pricing environment, to a fall in the profit share of value added. As indicated in Table 7.6, labor gained considerably at capital's expense, averaging 4 percent of value added per annum over a six-year period. In manufacturing industry ("the exposed sector"), a healthy pace of productivity increase (4.7% per annum) did minimize the rate of labor cost increase, but the slow rate of price increases for manufactured goods in international markets still squeezed profits.

LESSONS OF THE SWEDISH MODEL

During the period from the establishment of the system of centralized wage bargaining in the late 1930s to the early 1980s, Sweden compiled an enviable record of labor peace and economic growth. However, during the 1980s recurrent economic problems called the success of the corporatist Swedish model into question.

Swedish experience in the labor market exemplifies the problems that confront a society's attempts to suspend the role of wages in furthering an efficient allocation of labor. Even though the convergence of wages toward equality might be regarded as a laudable social goal, without differential wages to encourage worker mobility the labor market cannot function smoothly. The conflict between the drive for equity in society at large and the needs of export-oriented industry caused the

TABLE 7.6

Costs, Prices, and Profitability in the Business Sector (average annual increase in percent, 1995–2001)

	Total	Manufacturing	Construction	Nonfinancial Services
Unit labor costs	2.5	0.2	4.2	3.3
Hourly compensation	5.0	4.9	4.0	5.4
Labor productivity	2.5	4.7	–0.2	2.1
Output price	1.3	0.8	2.9	2.2
Profit share in value added (% change)	–4.0	–4.4	–3.5	-1.4

SOURCE: National Institute of Economic Research.

[11]OECD, *Economic Survey of Sweden*, June 2002, p. 26.

ABSENTEEISM, TAXES, AND HEALTH

Sweden's population can be considered healthy by most measures. Swedes smoke less, drink less, and weigh less than the European average. It is curious then, that the Swedish workforce leads the world in staying home sick. In the European Union as a whole, only 1.9 percent of workers stay out sick for an entire week in any given year; in Sweden the figure is 4.5 percent. On any working weekday almost 10 percent of the workforce is out sick, and the figure doubled in the last ten years. The question is why. One possible answer is that the Swedish workforce, which is older than most other nations with high participation rates for workers over 60, actually is more illness prone. Another is that the Swedish work ethic has collapsed as workers become more alienated from the large firms and governmental organizations in which they work. Another is fiscal; the supportive welfare state almost completely protects workers' income from the consequence of being off work. For most factory and office workers the worker loses all pay for the first day but subsequently receives 80 percent of wages up to $2,600 per month. After two weeks the employer is relieved of most burden and the state pays the bulk of support which can be up to 90 percent of the work wage. Some workers actually see their take-home pay increase as a result of tax changes and the elimination of commutation expenses. The policy response largely depends on the diagnosis of the problem. The government has now created a ministerial post charged with reducing absenteeism, which costs the government more than $12 billion annually in lost taxes and support payments, to one half the current level by 2008. That level will put the incidence back where it was in 1996, when unemployment was at a post-war high.

SOURCE: *The Economist*, October 26, 2002, p. 49.

breakdown in the national system of wage bargaining. The question remains: Can it be put back together, or is it permanently consigned to history? Both parties to the labor agreement seem to be optimistic:

> Whether the social partners will be able to act in concert in order to get the economy moving again is something we cannot yet tell. . . . We can only express the hope that out of the present labor pains a new Swedish model will be born, resembling its forerunner. There are, in fact, good chances of this. Despite the adverse trends . . . there are many sound elements of the Swedish economy and industrial relations system that have survived and can be built on. . . . In their hearts the Swedes share a deep community of values. The representatives of labor and management can still mix with each other centrally and locally in a spirit of trust and are capable of working together on matters of common interest. Promising signs are the agreements that have been concluded in recent years on such collaboration and, above all, the fact that the debate on wage policy is now being conducted in the broader context of the nation's economic health.[12]

A similar guarded optimism came from the union side:

> Many people in Sweden see . . . the frequent breaches of labor peace as linked to the departure from the centralized bargaining system. At the same time there is widespread agreement that prosperity must be safeguarded and equitably shared. This is why I

[12]Both this and the following quote were from the *International Labour Review*, 1986, cited in Milner, pp. 225–226. The employer's view is from L. G. Albåge, and the union position from Harry Fjällström.

> believe that the pressures favoring the return to coordinated central negotiations will prevail, even if slight changes may be expected in the unions' distribution policy. The bargaining system that has come to be known as the Swedish model of industrial relations has stood the test of time and I am confident that given the opportunity it will continue to serve both sides of industry well for many years yet.

Whatever the future of national labor negotiations, most analysts seem to agree that the umbrella nature of the Swedish social welfare system hurt macroeconomic performance. The high rates of taxation required to finance the welfare state probably cast a disincentive effect over both worker effort and savings, retarding growth to a rate that was in the 1970s half the OECD average. It represents perhaps the most important issue to be addressed in a comprehensive welfare state. Milner noted it in the 1980s:

> The most important and difficult question raised by critics of the welfare state concern the system of rewards resulting from the combination of wages, taxes, transfers, and other sources of income on individuals and, ultimately, its effect on the workings of the economy. They are perhaps most fully explored in the work of the distinguished and increasingly critical Swedish economist Assar Lindbeck. In Lindbeck's recent work is found perhaps the most sophisticated expression of the often-made argument that somewhere in the 1970s the excessive redistributiveness of Swedish welfare policy began to actually decrease the aggregate quantity of socially useful work by significantly increasing leisure through shorter work years and absenteeism and pushing activity into the "unofficial economy" in the form of barter, do-it-yourself work, and other forms of tax avoidance.[13]

Disincentive effects of high benefits and taxes manifest themselves in a variety of ways. A 1986 report by the engineering employers' association found that blue-collar Swedish workers were on the job less—putting in only 1,546 hours a year compared to 1,654 in West Germany and 1,930 in the United States—in part due to increased absenteeism and "sick outs." High tax rates forced activity into the black economy. One study found that between 12 and 25 percent of income in Sweden was unrecorded.[14]

An OECD report a decade later addressed the issue of incentive and came to the following conclusion:

> A universal and generous system of social protection has combined with progressive income taxes to achieve a high degree of poverty alleviation and equalisation of incomes. Sweden outperforms most other countries in terms of relative income levels for key target groups such as families with children and old-age pensioners. This redistribution has been accompanied by a continuous extension of transfers, from 15 per cent of household incomes in the mid-1960s to 35 per cent in the late 1990s, with the result that as much as two-thirds of transfers reflect redistribution over the life-cycle of individuals and only one-third interpersonal ("pure") redistribution.

---

[13]Henry Milner, *Sweden: Social Democracy in Practice* (New York: Oxford University Press, 1989). The best example of Lindbeck's views may be found in Assar Lindbeck, *Swedish Economic Policy* (Berkeley: University of California Press, 1974).

[14]Edward Feige, "Sweden's Underground Economy," in *The Economics of Institutions and Markets,* Gunnar Eliason, ed. (Stockholm: UIU, 1986), p. 127.

> High tax rates and generous replacement rates, with a *de facto* indefinite duration of unemployment and sickness benefits, have worked to this effect. Income taxes and social security contributions combine with means-tested housing and day-care benefits to reduce substantially the return from taking a better-paid job or increasing hours worked. The added effect of the internationally high 80 per cent replacement rate in benefits actually produces a substantial penalty for many on moving from unemployment to employment. Close to 40 per cent of unemployed would see no or insignificant increases in disposable incomes from moving back into work.[15]

Troubling problems arise from the high levels of distribution as well as from the high level of taxation that such redistribution requires. Material incentives, thought by many to be crucial to the prosperity of any economic system, are undeniably dulled. However, Sweden's relative economic success over many years demands that we take the "Swedish model" seriously. Despite the dip in the middle and late-1990s, Sweden reemerged as one of the most prosperous economies in the world. An active debate currently centers on the measurement and evaluation of Sweden's performance.[16] A few years ago the picture turned somewhat grim as Sweden fell in most cross-country comparisons of well-being, but in recent years it experienced higher growth and lower inflation than in most of the developed world. To what extent this performance results from the durability of the Swedish model and to what extent the revival may be attributed to promarket reform is still open to question.

KEY TERMS AND CONCEPTS

- active labor market policy
- corporatism
- EFO model
- exposed sector
- labor exchanges
- means testing
- Meidner plan
- protected sector
- replacement wage
- Saltsjöbaden agreement
- social democracy
- wage drift
- wage earner funds
- wage solidarity

QUESTIONS FOR DISCUSSION

1. Why is the concept of wage solidarity central to Swedish society?
2. How does an attempt to limit the distribution of wages lessen the effectiveness of the labor market?
3. Why is an active labor market policy a possible remedy for the absence of wage signaling?

---

[15]OECD, *Economic Survey of Sweden*, 1999, pp. 16–18.

[16]See Magnus Henrekson, "Swedish Economic Growth. A Favorable View of Reform," *Challenge* 44, no. 4 (July–August 2001).

4. In what ways does Sweden as a society differ from an "ideal" social democracy?
5. Is it appropriate to describe Sweden as corporatist? Why?
6. What pressures from the exposed sector led to the breakdown of national agreements?
7. What sort of socialism would the extensive use of wage funds lead to?

RESOURCES

Web Sites

Central Bank .... http://www.riksbank.com/
Swedish Municipal Workers Union .... http://www.kommunal.se/
Investor AB .... http://www.investorab.se/
Stockholm School of Economics .... http://www.hhs.se/
Swedish Confederation of Professional Employees .... http://www.tco.se/
Swedish Employers Federation (SAF) .... http://www.saf.se/
The Swedish Trade Union Confederation, LO .... http://www.lo.se/
Swedish Government Web site .... http://www.sweden.gov.se/

Books and Articles

Bosworth, Barry P., and Alice M. Rivlin (eds.). *The Swedish Economy.* Washington, DC: Brookings, 1987.

Davies, Steven, and Magnus Henreksen. "Wage-Setting Institutions as Industrial Policy." NBER Working Paper No. 7502 and SSE/EFI Working Paper No. 352, January 2000.

Davidsson, Per, and Magnus Henrekson. "Determinants of the Prevalence of Start-Ups and High-Growth Firms." *Small Business Economics,* 19, no. 2 (2002).

Calmfors, Lars (ed.). *Wage Formation and Macroeconomic Policy in the Nordic Countries.* Oxford: Oxford University Press, 1990.

Canova, Timothy A. "The Swedish Model Betrayed." *Challenge,* May–June 1994, 36–40.

Cohen, Peter. "Sweden: The Model That Never Was." *Monthly Review,* July–August 1994, 41–59.

European Parliament. *Social and Labour Markets Policy in Sweden.* Directorate-General for Research, Working Papers, Social Affairs Series, July 1997.

Henrekson, Magnus. "Swedish Economic Growth. A Favorable View of Reform." *Challenge,* 44, no. 4 (July–August 2001).

Lindbeck, Assar, Per Molander, Torsten Persson, Olof Peterson, Agnar Sandmo, Birgitta Swedenborg, and Niels Thygesen. "Options for Economic and Political Reform in Sweden." *Economic Policy,* October 1993, 219–263.

Maccoby, Michael (ed.). *Sweden at the Edge: Lessons for American and Swedish Managers.* Philadelphia: University of Pennsylvania Press, 1991.

Milner, Henry. *Sweden: Social Democracy in Practice*. New York: Oxford University Press, 1989.

Palme, Marten O., and Robert E. Wright. "Gender Discrimination and Compensating Differentials in Sweden." *Applied Economics* 24 (1992), 751–759.

Persson, Inga (ed.). *Generating Equality in the Welfare State: The Swedish Experience.* Oslo: Norwegian University Press, 1990.

Ramaswamy, Ramana. "Wage Bargaining Institutions, Adaptability, and Structural Change: The Swedish Experience." *Journal of Economic Issues* 26, no. 4 (December 1992), 1041–1061.

"A Survey of the Nordic Countries: Happy Family?" *The Economist,* January 23, 1999, 50.

"A Survey of Women and Work." *The Economist,* July 18, 1998, 48.

"The Entrepreneur and the Swedish Model." In M. Henrekson, M. Larsson and H. Sjögren, eds., *Entrepreneurship in Business and Research. Essays in Honour of Håkan Lindgren*. Stockholm: Probus Förlag and Institute for Research in Economic History, 2001.

10

THE EUROPEAN UNION: HISTORY AND INSTITUTIONS

THE CREATION OF THE EUROPEAN UNION: A BRIEF CHRONOLOGY	
Date	**Event**
1947	Initiation of the Marshall Plan to promote the economic revival of a Europe devastated by war
1948	Benelux Treaty creating the common economic space of Belgium, the Netherlands, and Luxembourg enters into force
1948	Creation of the Organization for European Economic Cooperation (OEEC) to administer the Marshall Plan
1949	Creation of the Council of Europe located in Strasbourg
1950	Schuman Declaration
1951	The Treaty of Paris establishes the European Coal and Steel Community (ECSC)
1952–1954	Preparation, and failure, of plans for a European Defense Community (EDC)
1955	Renewed vitality for the idea of European unity provided by the Messina Conference
1957	Signing of the Treaties of Rome establishing the European Economic Community (EEC) and the European Atomic Energy Community (Euratom)
1967	Merger of the institutions of the three communities (ECSC, EEC, and Euratom)
1968	Completion of the customs union
1972	Treaties of Accession of Denmark, Ireland, Norway, and the United Kingdom
1973	Denmark, Ireland, and the United Kingdom join the European Community; Norway chooses to stay outside
1979	Signing of the Treaty of Accession of Greece
1979	First election of the European Parliament by direct universal suffrage
1981	Greece joins the Community
1985	Signing of the Treaties of Accession of Portugal and Spain
1986	Portugal and Spain join the European Community
1987	Signing of the treaty and entry into force of the Single European Act
1989	Signing of the Social Charter by all members except Britain
1990	Unification of Germany
1992	Signing of the Treaty on European Union (the Maastricht Treaty)
1993	Introduction of the single European market and the European Economic Area
1993	Maastricht Treaty becomes effective creating the European Union; Austria, Finland, and Sweden join the European Union
1997	Signing of the Amsterdam treaty
1999	Economic and Monetary Union established: Sweden, Britain, and Denmark opt out, and Greece is denied entry.

1999	The European Parliament comes of age. It calls for investigation of corruption and fraud at the Commission leading to the resignation of the Commission in March. A new Commission formed in August.
2000	Treaty of Nice is signed redefining voting rules in the EU.
2001	National currencies are phased out in "euro zone"; Greece joins as the twelfth member.
2002	Agreement that Poland, the Czech Republic, Hungary, Slovakia, Lithuania, Latvia, Slovenia, Estonia, Cyprus, and Malta could join in 2004. Bulgarian and Romanian accession in 2007 an "objective." Turkey snubbed again.

PRECURSORS TO THE EUROPEAN UNION

Many visionaries sought the peaceful unification of Europe, and a few dictators looked to do the job by force, but serious planning for economic and political unification in Europe did not occur until after World War II. The damage caused by nationalism and war in the three decades between 1914 and 1945 created a strong impetus for change. Even after the war, raised tensions contributed to the dispute between the conflicting and, to many eyes, largely bankrupt ideologies of nationalism, communism, and fascism. "Europeanism" offered an alternative, which could both influence domestic political agendas and provide a supranational goal to diffuse nationalist tensions. The potential economic rewards of a united Europe, although appreciated from the beginning, initially carried less importance than the prospect of political gain.

A further push toward unity came shortly after the war by the creation of the American-financed **Marshall Plan** and the institution created to administer it, the Paris-based **Organization for European Economic Cooperation (OEEC)**.[1] Today the Marshall Plan is almost universally remembered and revered as a rare example of enlightened altruism on the part of the United States. Rather than extracting revenge and reparations from the defeated powers in the manner of the Treaty of Versailles, which concluded the First World War, the Marshall Plan contributed to the reconstruction of Europe by helping both victor and vanquished. As well as administering project aid, the OEEC actively alleviated the dollar shortage, financed the bilateral currency imbalances, and helped to remove the trade barriers instituted in the prewar periods. After three years of slow growth across the continent, the OEEC efforts began to bear fruit. American exports to and investment in Europe soared and prosperity began to return to the continent. Some scholars view the Marshall Plan, even though often credited with the revival of Western Europe, as a decisive step in the division of postwar Europe. Stalin rejected the invitation to the Soviet bloc participation in the Marshall Plan because of its condition of

[1]This body with a larger membership is now known as the Organization for Economic Cooperation and Development, or OECD.

extensive information sharing. The exclusion of Eastern Europe helped draw the "iron curtain" that divided the nations of Europe until 1989.

In 1948, a conference attended by all the major Western European nations convened at The Hague. Originally called the Congress of Europe, this body became known as the Council of Europe and made its permanent home in Strasbourg in eastern France. It became a useful forum in which to debate and define the competing models of European integration. Britain's role became an important issue. Britain emerged from the war with a great deal of moral authority and might have taken the leadership role on European unity had it not favored European integration through intergovernmental cooperation rather than by creating supranational organization. In retrospect we can see that the British leadership failed to appreciate that major changes had occurred in the global political landscape. It viewed World War II as merely the latest in a series of continental conflicts requiring British intervention to restore the balance of power. At the end of the war, Britain turned to concentrate on world trade and the remnants of its empire to the neglect of its interests in Europe. The Scandinavians supported Britain's position of cooperation without political integration, and the Council of Europe remained unable to offer a clear path toward the federal solution preferred by the other West Europeans.

The real precursor of the contemporary European Union (EU) came in the form of the **European Coal and Steel Community (ECSC)**, first suggested by **Jean Monnet** and later advanced by another Frenchman, **Robert Schumann**. The fear that revival of the German economy might cause German military power to rise once more originally prompted its proposal. The ECSC created a "common market" in coal and steel, which would remove the basic ingredients of a war machine from national control and place oversight with a "high authority," independent of national governments. Initially the ECSC consisted only of France and Germany, but the Benelux countries and Italy joined to form "the Six," signing the Treaty of Paris in 1951. The ECSC not only succeeded in reducing tensions in Western Europe, but it also provided a compelling model of the value of pooling national markets.

Buoyed by the success of the ECSC, the Six tried to move toward political unity at an unrealistic pace. In 1952 representatives drafted a treaty establishing a European Defense Community (EDC), followed in 1953 by the draft of a treaty creating a European Political Community (EPC). Although five of the members of the ECSC happily went along with these proposals, in 1954 the French National Assembly failed to ratify the EDC, a move that proved fatal for the EPC as well. Persuading European governments to yield sovereignty in the defense and political arenas always presented a tougher task than harmonizing economic arrangements.

The Treaty of Rome

The failure of the EDC and EPC initiatives set back the European movement; Europeanists shifted their emphasis from rapid political unification toward consolidating economic integration. The foreign ministers of the Six met at Messina in 1955 and began a process that culminated in the **Treaty of Rome**. This agreement established two new bodies: the European Economic Community (the EEC, often called the European Common Market), and Euratom, the European Atomic Energy Community. Together with the ECSC, these bodies constituted the European Communities (EC).

The most important body was the EEC. The success of the ECSC demonstrated that economic gains could be made by increasing the size of the market, thereby allowing both greater competition (with a long-term impact on efficiency and dynamism) and a greater degree of specialization. Moreover, confidence in the power of economies of scale characterized the 1950s. National firms might be uncompetitive in global terms because of the limited size of the domestic market, but European firms could amass the size to compete internationally.

Although generally accepted that economic integration offers benefits to all participants, there are different degrees of economic integration. At the lowest level, a **free trade area** allows the movement of goods between countries without the hindrance of tariffs or quotas. A **customs union** not only provides for such movement but also requires that the members apply a **common external tariff (CET)** to their imports from third-party countries. A **common market** encompasses a customs union with the additional commitment to the free movement of factors of production within the member states. The member countries held as their ultimate goal a common market, but the first step toward this common market required completion of a customs unions and the establishment of a common external tariff.

The Community of Six

The Community of Six, established by the Treaty of Rome, gave itself a 12-year adjustment period to establish a customs union. During this time, members worked to progressively reduce internal tariffs between constituent nations were to be to zero and to harmonize the tariffs on goods originating outside the community. By 1968 the members had completed this customs union, although progress toward the liberalization of factor movements, required for a true common market, proceeded at a much slower pace and would, in fact, take another quarter of a century to complete.[2]

Outside the EC concern grew about the prospect of **fortress Europe**, a market shielded by high tariffs, which went against the prevailing trend of multilateral tariff liberalization. However, despite the threat to its economic interests, the United States supported the development of the EC because it offered the political reward of European stability. Fears on the economic front subsided when it became clear that the final external tariff structure of the EC would be more liberal than that of the original members. Trade relations between the EC and the United States sometimes can be described as less than harmonious, and fears of restricted access to the European market remain chronically recurrent. Nevertheless, the tariff reductions negotiated in both the Dillon and Kennedy rounds of General Agreement on Tariffs and Trade (GATT) translated into cuts in the common external tariff.

[2]The common market was finally completed in 1993 due to the Euro-92 program.

Although economic aspects of the Europeanism thrived, progress toward a politically united Europe lagged, with both defense policy and foreign policy remaining the domain of national governments. However, the stances of Germany and France, the two most powerful nations, became increasingly coordinated as German Chancellor Konrad Adenauer and French President Charles de Gaulle cooperated closely in "the Bonn-Paris axis," and their interaction frequently determined European policy. However, despite increased cooperation such policy making took place at the national and not the Community level.

Shortly after the Treaty of Rome, Britain rethought its position on EC membership. With the remnant of its empire, the British Commonwealth, largely dispersed and the treasured "special relationship"[3] with the United States dissipating, Britain took the lead in 1959 in the creation of the **European Free Trade Area (EFTA)**, otherwise known as the "outer seven," consisting of Britain, three Nordic nations (Sweden, Denmark, and Norway), Austria, Switzerland, and Portugal. It was designed to capture the benefits of a free trade area without any commitment to social expenditures or to political union. The British came to regret that each of its small partners gained much more in terms of market access than did Britain. Quickly recognizing the limitations of EFTA, Britain formally reversed its position on the EC, announcing in 1961 its interests in full European membership, but French President de Gaulle unilaterally terminated negotiations using the French veto to deny entry.

Expansions of the 1970s and 1980s

After de Gaulle resigned in 1969, British entry became a possibility once more. In December 1969 talks began to admit not only Britain, but also Ireland, Norway, and Denmark. Britain secured entry, but paid a price in terms of budget contribution that required a higher share of gross national product (GNP) than that of any other member. Ireland and Denmark also joined, but Norway, although admitted, rejected membership in a national referendum, influenced by the fear that its valuable fisheries would be opened to wider exploitation. The short-term consequences of membership proved unfavorable for Britain. Food prices soared as a result of the protectionist **common agricultural policy (CAP)** that ended cheap imports from Australia and New Zealand.[4] The lack of competitiveness in British industry resulted in lost market share at home without significant expansion of exports to continental Europe. In the early 1980s the Thatcher administration eventually negotiated a lower British budgetary contribution and even secured a modest refund, but the British population remained skeptical about the benefits of membership.

Greece joined the EC in 1981 and Spain and Portugal in 1986. These new members, noticeably poorer and less developed than the existing EC nations, increased the population of the community by one-fifth but its income by only one-tenth.

---

[3]The Suez crisis and the U.S. insistence that Britain withdraw from Egypt or face economic sanctions was, in some ways, the final straw in pursuit of the special relationship.

[4]See Chapter 11 for a discussion of the CAP.

They therefore acted as a net drain on EC finances. Membership for these nations involved a different calculus of gains and losses. Although the newcomers did contribute something in terms of increasing the accessible market for existing members, the main gains were political. Popular thinking believed entry into the EC created a centralizing impact on the domestic politics of member nations, and many hoped that membership would put these countries, all of them recently under fascist regimes, on the road to moderate politics.

EC-1992: Completing the Internal Market

Experience showed that deepening the political links of the EC to be a difficult operation because it involved the sacrifice of domestic sovereignty. Liberalizing the internal economy of Europe, on the other hand, felt less contentious. In 1985, with the absorption of Spain and Portugal almost complete, the European Commission issued a White Paper containing 300 proposals for the "completion of the internal market." In 1987 the passage of the **Single European Act** amended the Treaty of Rome. This most important proviso ended any individual country's power to veto economic legislation on the grounds of national interest. It cleared the way for the project known as **EC-1992**, the completion of the internal economic space to allow totally free movement of goods, persons, services, and capital.

Total liberalization of trade within the EC required the elimination of three types of trade impediment. The first were the physical barriers at national borders. Preexisting arrangements resulted in excessive customs regulation and paperwork that wasted a good deal of resources and time at borders. EC-1992 sought to eliminate these barriers by harmonizing both product standards and value-added taxation. A second set of barriers related to the procurement patterns of national and local government, which tended to favor local firms with resultant anticompetitiveness and efficiency loss. The third group of barriers lay in the financial services industries and their slow integration, protecting inefficient national markets. The elimination of these barriers would bring substantial gains, but they would also produce so-called supply-side effects by fostering increased competition and facilitating economies of scale.

Table 10.1 summarizes the European Commission's official estimates of the gains of EC-1992. The Commission thought that the elimination of border controls would yield a once-and-for-all increase in gross domestic product (GDP) of 0.4 percent, cut consumer prices by 1 percent, and lead to the creation of an additional 200,000 jobs within the Community. Similar gains were seen to result from increased integration of financial services and a "level playing field" for public procurement. The estimated supply-side effects of the extended market—resulting from economies of scale formerly constrained by national market size and increased transnational competition—would raise GDP by 2.1 percent, cut consumer prices by 6.1 percent, and lead to the creation of 1.8 million jobs. The single market program also held the potential to cut the budget deficits of the member countries by 2.2 percent and improve external position of the EC vis-a-vis the world. In addition to these medium-term consequences, predicted second-order effects included a virtuous circle of high investment, stable prices, and rapid growth.

■ **TABLE 10.1**

Medium-Term Prospective Gains from the Completion of the Internal Market, EC-1992 (% of GDP)

	Border Controls	Public Procurement	Financial Services	Supply-Side Effects*	Total Average Value
GDP	0.4	0.5	1.5	2.1	4.5
Inflation	21.0	1.4	21.4	22.3	26.1
Budgetary balance	0.2	0.3	1.1	0.6	2.2
External balance	0.2	0.1	0.3	0.4	1
Employment (in thousands)	200	350	400	850	1800

*Due to economies of scale and increase in competition.
SOURCE: Paolo Cecchini, *The Cost of Non-Europe* (Brussels: European Commission 1988).

Despite slow progress, by 1993 most of the legislation to complete the internal market was finished. The Commission encountered its most serious problems in service industries where complex national rules, many ostensibly designed for consumer protection, required attention. Although public procurement was, in theory, liberalized, strong indications of national bias still persist. Integrating labor markets also proved difficult, but EU members no longer required passports within the EU for EU citizens.[5]

The growth and success of the EU overshadowed the modest achievements of EFTA, whose members saw that the free trade area could never offer a market of the size and depth of the EU. Consensus favored a closer alliance with the EC, and several EFTA members actually applied for full membership. In 1991 EFTA and the EC combined to establish a common free trade area, for manufactured but not agricultural goods, an institution that became known as the **European Economic Area (EEA)**.

Gauging the success of the internal market project is difficult. It has failed to deliver the promised economic gains, with only lackluster EU growth since the completion of the market. In the period 1993–2002, GDP growth in the EU averaged 2.3 percent per annum, faster than stagnant Japan but well below the pace of 3.5 percent set by the United States (see Table 10.2). European employment showed even slower growth during this period with job creation lagging behind the labor market entry rate; rising unemployment now stands as one of Europe's largest social problems. Whether the position would be even more dire without EC-1992 is impossible to tell.

[5]The Maastricht Treaty was responsible for formally changing the European Communities to the European Union, hence the acronym from EC to EU.

■ TABLE 10.2

Economic Growth in Europe, Japan, and the United States (average annual percentage changes)

Real GDP Growth

	1974–1985	1983–1992	1993–2002
European Union	2.0	2.6	2.3
United States	2.3	3.4	3.5
Japan	3.4	3.9	1.2

Employment Growth

	1974–1985	1983–1992	1993–2002
European Union	0.0	0.6	0.8
United States	1.8	1.8	1.4
Japan	0.7	1.3	0.1

SOURCE: Eurostat, *IMF: World Economic Outlook,* May 2001.

The Social Charter

The heads of state or government of 11 member states of the European Community[6] adopted the **Social Charter** (officially the "Community Charter of Fundamental Social Rights of Workers") declaration at the meeting of the European Council in Strasbourg in December 1989. It set out broad principles shared by the signatories and constituted a first step in the harmonization and establishment of consistent labor law across the EU. The Conservative British government of that time, committed to the interests of business, felt that the clauses in the Social Charter designed to strengthen the power of labor in the workplace would both lessen the freedom of management and the mobility of labor.

The rights expressed in the Social Charter are quite general and involve shared commitment to a safe workplace and social protection. One clause asserts the right of all workers to a paying job, clearly a dead letter given the high rates of unemployment in the Community. Three specific sets of provisions were obnoxious to the British Conservatives. The first protects labor unions and guarantees their right to engage in collective bargaining. This provision might have been palatable, but the charter went beyond this point in providing that workers must be informed about the activities and plans of the management and that workers participate in

[6]The EU included 12 member states at that time, but the United Kingdom "opted out."

the running of the company through representation on the board. To the business-oriented Conservatives, it seemed to allow the unions to usurp management prerogatives and was styled by Margaret Thatcher as "backdoor socialism." A second set of provisions guarantees the absolute freedom of workers to move within the EC, and a third guarantees the equal treatment of men and women, including equal pay for comparative work. The Social Charter presents a statement of general commitment but does not impose any specific action on a member country.

The Maastricht Treaty

Following the relative success of EC-1992 in completing the economic space, the EC faced new challenges in both economic and political spheres. Progress toward an ever-closer political union was put on one side while leaders pursued the single market project. The economic sphere offered clear and sometimes quantifiable benefits. It involved less sacrifice of sovereignty than the political agenda and was supported even by "euroskeptics" like Margaret Thatcher. However, the next and more controversial step toward full economic integration involved the creation of a single currency, which, Europeanists argued, would tie the European economy closer together in the way that the common dollar ties together the elements of the United States.

In December of 1991 the European Council, consisting of the heads of state and of government of the member nations, met in the previously obscure Dutch town of Maastricht and drafted the **Treaty on European Union**, almost always referred to as the **Maastricht Treaty**. This document was the foundation of the next stage of the European project, even changing the name of the community to the **European Union (EU)**.

In a rather ponderous architectural metaphor, the treaty defined the Union as resting on three "pillars." Pillar One concerns economic matters and covers agriculture, transportation, the environment, energy, research and development, and regional policy. Pillar Two establishes a common foreign and security policy, a priority objective for some time, but achieving a halting sort of progress. Joint Community policy failed to emerge in either the conflict in the former Yugoslav territories or in the response to the first or second Gulf Wars. Pillar Three focuses on cooperation in the fields of justice and home affairs and aims to achieve the free movement of persons inside the Union and to promote measures of common interest in the fields of external border control, asylum policy, immigration policy, terrorism, drug trafficking, and other serious forms of international crime. Because Britain refused to sign the Social Charter, the Maastricht Treaty embodied those principles in a separate protocol entitled "The Agreement on Social Policy," usually referred to as "the Social Chapter."[7] In a sense, therefore, the "social chapter" provides a fourth pillar of the Union.

[7]The current Labour government led by Prime Minister Tony Blair finally committed Britain to the Social Charter and the agreement on social policy.

The Principle of Subsidiarity

One of the most difficult political issues facing the EU centers on how much sovereignty and power should be gathered in Brussels and how much should be allowed to remain with the governments of the member nations or some lower regional authority. Citizens of member nations frequently criticize the EU as being remote, dictatorial, and bureaucratic, laying down directives impinging on the local culture and economy without due regard to circumstance. The Maastricht Treaty sought to meet this criticism by establishing limits to EU action. Article 3b of Title II of the treaty requires that

> [i]n areas which do not fall within its exclusive competence, the Community shall take action, in accordance with the principle of subsidiarity, only if and in so far as the objectives of the proposed action cannot be sufficiently achieved by the Member.

In short, this **principle of subsidiarity** affirms that all issues must be handled at the lowest level that can effectively deal with them. Any organ of the EU (including the European Council, the European Parliament, and the Commission) can intervene only in areas of common concern when the individual states cannot act effectively on their own. Even then, impositions from above must respect the specific characteristics of the states and regions and highlight their diversity. Any item of EU legislation proposed in Brussels must therefore satisfy three key criteria: that the item acts at the all-union level, that the EU's action is not excessive, and that any legislation is clear and transparent.

The principle of subsidiarity is relevant in many areas, not all of them specifically economic. For example, one issue in the news concerns the protection of migratory birds, and in fact the EU itself used this matter as an example of how the principle might work. The Commission determined that it is not for the European Union to set the dates for the opening and closing of hunting seasons in specific EU regions. Hunting seasons should be decided on according to local hunting traditions, with agreement reached on how each of the EU's member states complies with the overall objectives of bird protection. However, classic "externality" problems remain. France allowed generous hunting rules, extending into breeding seasons, which threatened the continent-wide bird population. Other countries demanded action by Brussels as France resisted, citing the principle of subsidiarity. In more strictly economic matters, the principle emerges in other important ways. Two examples are worth mentioning here, though they will be dealt with in more detail in Chapter 11. The first deals with competition and merger policy, traditionally handled at the national level. The introduction of the single market requires, for some industries at least, Union-wide treatment. The other issue revolves around the expenditure of monies granted through the structural funds. The recipient nations feel that they know better how such monies should be spent, while the Commission as grantor feels it deserves a say in its use.

The Treaty of Amsterdam

The Treaty of Amsterdam, concluded in 1997, did not fundamentally change the nature of the union but rather highlighted some specific issues for action. It included four main objectives:

1. *To place employment and citizens' rights at the heart of the Union.* Although no specific policy measures accompanied the treaty, it committed the European Union to the achievement of full employment within the member states.
2. *To sweep away the last remaining obstacles to freedom of movement and to strengthen security.* A long-standing concern of member states in increasing elimination of barriers to movement within the EU centers around the issue of loosening the control of member states over criminal activity and illegal immigration. The treaty committed the Union to continue to remove barriers to the movement of people and at the same time strengthened the cooperation between police and security forces and promoted the growth of "Europol," the European police network.
3. *To give Europe a stronger voice in world affairs.* Committing the Union to the development of a unified foreign policy, one of the most serious stumbling blocks in the drive to unity, increases its power in influencing international policy.
4. *To make the Union's institutional structure more efficient with a view to enlarging the Union.*

The Treaty of Nice

The Treaty of Nice, concluded in 2000, makes the last objective of the Treaty of Amsterdam more concrete by modifying the structure of the EU to render policy making tractable as the Union expands from 15 members to 25 in the year 2004, and then, probably, to 27 in 2007. As the number of members increases, so does the difficulty of enacting legislation. Although the Maastricht Treaty stripped member countries of the power of veto in the economic sphere and substituted qualified majority voting (QMV), the Treaty of Nice changed the rules again.

Enlargement of the EU in 2004 and 2007

Over the last five years the EU defined its strategy for future enlargement to the east, which will give rise to many difficulties. Unlike the last expansion, which admitted three rich nations (Austria, Finland, and Sweden), all prosperous with a long market tradition, the next expansion allows relatively poor nations emerging from a 55-year history of socialism and central planning.[8] These potential members will create a drag on the budget as well as the concern that the cheap labor available in Eastern Europe will draw investment away from current members and aggravate the high levels of unemployment now endemic through continental Western Europe. However, expansion offers clear political gains by ensuring the stability and moderation of the countries to the east.

[8]Two of the entrants, Malta and Cyprus, do not fit this description, but have pronounced singularities of their own. Cyprus remains partitioned, and only the Greek Cypriot part is destined to enter, while Malta is a small island economy.

The European Union opened negotiations with six countries in October 1998 and broadened the field to 12 a year later. Enlargement raises a number of thorny issues, including how soon new members should join the euro, immigration, agricultural subsidies, and concern about border security in the East.

In 1997 the European Commission conducted a comprehensive evaluation of each candidate country's political and economic readiness for EU membership. Initially it seemed that only five Central European countries (Hungary, Poland, Estonia, the Czech Republic, and Slovenia) were favored for "fast-track" entry. They, in the words of the Commission's report, "came closest to satisfying the membership eligibility criteria of having secure democratic government, a well-functioning market economy and the ability to take on the obligations of EU membership."

However, in 2002, the Commission decided to go ahead and start the admission process for a total of 10 nations (the above group plus Latvia, Lithuania, Slovakia, Cyprus, and Malta) with entry in 2004. Two other countries—Bulgaria and Romania—were listed with a target entry in 2007. Turkey, the thirteenth candidate, is the last in the queue, ostensibly because of concerns about its human rights record, though there are other factors. The original Treaty of Rome defined the Communities as being made up of European nations, and the bulk of Turkey's land area lies geographically in Asia. Other factors include its population, its relative poverty, and its non-Christian culture. This last point was emphasized by the former French President Valery Giscard d'Estaing who currently chairs a constitutional commission on the future of the EU. Even though politicians moved quickly to dissociate themselves from his comments, it left little doubt that Turkey faces an uphill struggle. The election of an Islamist government in the fall of 2002 did not advance Turkey's case, although the United States, with a eye on the geopolitical situation in the Middle East, continues to push hard to anchor Turkey firmly in Europe.

THE INSTITUTIONS OF THE EUROPEAN UNION

The European Union can be a confusing political entity to an outsider.[9] Its powers consist of issuing directives and regulations that are binding on members to various degrees, managing a budget, and making a limited number of agreements in the international sphere. Common institutions residing in Brussels, Strasbourg, and Luxembourg, with complex structures unfamiliar to most non-Europeans and baffling to many Europeans as well, exercise EU powers. Therefore it is useful to outline the distribution of decision-making authority in some detail. This analysis looks at the relationships of the nation-states to the EU, the "democratic" structure of the EU, and the direction of further integration.

[9]Madeleine Albright, U.S. Secretary of State under Clinton, once remarked that to understand the EU one "had to be either a European or a genius."

The European Council

The overall agenda of the European Union is determined by the **European Council**, composed of the political leaders ("the heads of state and government") of the 15 member nations. It sets the key policy guidelines and provides the impetus on the most important subjects. It also arbitrates disputed questions in which agreement has not been reached within the European Union Council of Ministers. Each member country presides over the European Council in turn for a six-month period (e.g., Greece and Italy in 2003, Ireland and the Netherlands in 2004, and the United Kingdom and Luxembourg in 2005). During the six-month presidency, therefore, each country holds the power to determine the agenda of what is discussed and to some extent what is pushed forward.

The European Commission

The **European Commission** is the Brussels-based permanent bureaucracy of the EU, employing some 17,000 people. The Commission draws up common projects and, after the European Union Council of Ministers makes a decision, sees that it is properly implemented.

Twenty commissioners, led by a permanent president, now Romano Prodi of Italy who replaced Jacques Santer of Luxembourg, direct the work of the Commission. As one of its important principles, the Commission operates independently of the national governments. Each commissioner takes an oath of office by which he or she forswears consideration of national interest in favor of a European perspective. Despite this ideal, the commissioners are not selected from the member nations strictly according to ability. Each nation sends at least one commissioner, and the larger nations send two, and because commissioners are appointed by national governments, the job frequently goes as a reward for loyal political service. Despite the rhetoric, commissioners are likely to act to some extent in the interests of the government of their home nation.

Commissioners are politically appointed, but the bureaucracies of the various directorates general that compose the Commission are long-serving permanent officials, which provides them with considerable power. Their commissioners rely on them as the repository of experience and knowledge, which allows them to control information flows and to some degree the agenda. The function of the Commission is to implement the common policies of the Union: agriculture, fishing, research, energy, environment, and so on. Also, when it is mandated by the member countries, it negotiates international agreements on cooperation and trade.

The Commission, not merely a passive body, also holds the power to initiate reform. For that reason the principle of subsidiarity, which places power whenever appropriate on a lower level of government, carries great significance. On its own initiative or in response to a citizen's complaint, it may bring an action before the European Court of Justice should the Union's laws not be respected in member states. The Commission also manages the Union's annual budget (ECU 86 billion in 1996), which is dominated by farm spending allocated by the European Agricultural Guidance and Guarantee Fund and by the Structural Funds, designed to even out the economic disparities between the richer and poorer areas.

The European Parliament

The EU's directly elected parliament consists of 626 members who serve five-year terms to sit in Strasbourg. The powers of the **European Parliament** are limited and, although its responsibilities have grown, it remains largely a symbolic and consultative group rather than an embodiment of representative democracy.

All of Europe's major political currents are represented in the Parliament, ranging from far left to far right. Members of the European Parliament (MEPs) come from nearly 100 political parties and are organized in a limited number of groups (presently eight) along ideological, not national, lines. Parliament conducts much of its effective work in its 20 committees that cover all areas of the European Union's activities, ranging from agriculture to common foreign and security policy, from legal affairs and citizens' rights to overseas cooperation and development. Parliament maintains friendly relations with elected assemblies all over the world and MEPs meet regularly with representatives from the parliaments of member states in interparliamentary committees and delegations.

The Powers of the Parliament The European parliament's powers fall into three areas:

1. *Legislation.* The original Treaty of Rome gave the European Parliament only a consultative role, providing at best a "talking shop" on legislative matters. However, subsequent amendments (through to the Maastricht Treaty) extended its authority, and now the Parliament holds the power of codecision (with the European Council) over policy areas, such as the free movement of workers, consumer protection, education, culture, health, and trans-European networks. Many legislative proposals now require an opinion from Parliament before they can be resolved by the Council. In the event of a conflict, a conciliation committee made up of equal numbers of MEPs and Council members is formed to seek a compromise. In the case of insoluble conflict, Parliament can pass a motion of censure on the Commission and force it to resign.
2. *The Budget.* The Parliament approves the EU's budget each year and can propose modifications or amendments to the Commission's initial proposals. The Council has the last word on agricultural spending and costs arising from international agreements, but the Parliament decides on other expenditures in, for example, education, social programs, regional funds, and environmental and cultural projects. In exceptional circumstances, the European Parliament can vote to reject the budget if it feels that its wishes were not adequately respected.
3. *Supervision of the Executive.* The Parliament exercises overall political supervision over the conduct of the European Union's policies. Executive power in the EU is shared between the Commission and the Council of Ministers, and their representatives appear regularly before Parliament. Parliament is also responsible for selecting a new president of the Commission every five years.

For many years the Parliament carried the reputation of a toothless body within the EU; but in 1999, it tackled the Commission with some effectiveness. It questioned the budget and required an independent committee to examine the behavior of the Commission, singling out two commissioners for special scrutiny. The committee's finding suggested fraud, nepotism, and corruption in the Commission's behavior. In March of 1999, the entire Commission of 20 members resigned. In August of 1999, Parliament approved a newly reformed Commission.

The European Union Council of Ministers

Most of the day-to-day decision-making power within the European Union lies in the **Council of Ministers** and in its permanent bureaucratic counterpart ***Coreper*** (the French acronym for the Council of Permanent Representatives). Each member state sends a national delegation to Brussels headed by permanent representatives, normally senior diplomats. Though nominally only an administrative adjunct of the Council of Ministers, Coreper exercises a great deal of power in day-to-day matters, leaving only the most sensitive matters to be handled by the Council of Ministers.

Actions of the Council take several forms:

- *Regulations* are binding and directly applicable to all citizens.
- *Directives,* a level of compulsion below the regulations, are binding on all, but they are indirect. They must be first "transposed" into the law of each country in a way that satisfies the intent of the directive.
- *Decisions* are binding and directly applicable but only to the institutions, bodies, businesses, or citizens specifically named.
- *Recommendations, advisory opinions,* and *resolutions* offer consultative or guidance texts addressed to the states.

Other European Bodies

The Economic and Social Committee and the Committee of the Regions are major consultative committees that relay the advice of professional groups and local bodies to the Commission, the Council, and the Parliament. All the guidance documents (known as White Papers and Green Papers) and all the proposed European laws are submitted for consultation to these two committees. The Economic and Social Committee consists of representatives of the workers, large and small businesses, farmers, families, and consumers of each country. The Committee of the Regions represents the voice of the municipalities, departments, and regions of the European Union.

The European Court of Justice is responsible for the proper implementation of the treaties and community legislation. It consists of judges and independent advocates general. Citizens may appeal to it through the European Commission (complaint) or a national court. The European Court of Auditors examines the legality and regularity of EU revenues and expenditures.

The **Ombudsman** is a peculiar European institution, the name and function of which are Scandinavian in origin. As its purpose, the office provides a clear avenue for any European citizen or resident of the EU with a complaint against a policy or institution of the EU. The Ombudsman hears grievances and holds authority to investigate and if necessary take action on them. In the United States, the function would be achieved by bringing suit against the federal government or its agency, but the Ombudsman is less formal and less expensive. The European Parliament names the Ombudsman after each Parliamentary election for the duration of that legislature.

MAKING DECISIONS IN THE EUROPEAN UNION

One of the most important features of the Maastricht Treaty was to reduce the power of any single member state to frustrate change within the Union. For matters within Pillar One, action generally starts with a proposal from the Commission, which, after consultation with Parliament and the Economic, Social, and Regional Committees, the Council of Ministers can adopt, amend, or ignore. In most cases (including issues that involve agriculture, fisheries, internal market, environment, and transport), the Council decides on the basis of a "qualified majority vote," with member states exercising voting power as shown in Table 10.3. Under the current pre-expansion arrangements a proposal needs the support of 62 votes (71.26 percent of the total of 87), which must be cast by at least 10 different member states. In practice the Council tries to reach the widest possible consensus at the committee stage before taking a vote, and historically only 14 percent of the legislation adopted by the Council was the subject of any negative votes or abstentions. Other policy areas within Pillar One (including taxation, industry, culture) remain subject to unanimity. In Pillars Two and Three unanimity (and therefore the veto) remains the rule.

The enlargements proposed will inevitably change this situation, and the **Treaty of Nice** determined the new allocation of voting among the members of the expanded EU. This structure is illustrated in Table 10.3. In the future, the sum of the votes in the European Council will rise to 345 and the number of votes needed for the acceptance of a measure will be 258. The Big Four (Germany, France, Italy, and the United Kingdom) will continue to have the same number of votes, but their share of the total will fall from the current 11.49 percent each to 8.41, which reduces their power. Formerly, if the four agreed, they already held nearly 46 percent of the vote and needed only to attract six other countries to assure passage of legislation. Now they start with less than 34 percent of the vote, and a winning coalition must include at least 14 countries. Consequently, passing legislation becomes more difficult.[10] The number of MEPs also increases with enlargement, from 626 to 732.

Table 10.3 also illustrates an important aspect of governance and democracy within the EU that did not change a great deal with the Treaty of Nice. Citizens of small states hold a disproportionately large say in the workings of the Union. For example, Germany with 17 percent of the population of the expanded union holds only 8.4 percent of the council votes and 13.5 percent of the representation in Parliament. Finland, with 1.1 percent of the population, holds 3.45 percent of the council votes and 2.56 percent of the representation in Parliament. Luxembourg has an even more privileged position.

[10]Other simpler procedures were rejected, including the so-called double majority consisting of a majority of nations and at least 50 percent of the council votes.

■ TABLE 10.3

Voting in the European Union Council and Parliament Before and After Expansion

	Population (2000)		In the Council				In Parliament			
	Share in EU 15	Share in EU 27	Current Votes Number	Current Votes Share	Votes in EU 27 Number	Votes in EU 27 Share	Current Votes Number	Current Votes Share	Votes in EU 27 Number	Votes in EU 27 Share
Germany	21.8	17	10	11.49	29	8.41	99	15.81	99	13.52
United Kingdom	15.8	12.4	10	11.49	29	8.41	87	13.90	72	9.84
France	15.7	12.3	10	11.49	29	8.41	87	13.90	72	9.84
Italy	15.3	12	10	11.49	29	8.41	87	13.90	72	9.84
Spain	10.5	8.2	8	9.20	27	7.83	64	10.22	50	6.83
Poland		8			27	7.83			50	6.83
Romania		4.7			14	4.06			33	4.51
Netherlands	4.2	3.3	5	5.75	13	3.77	31	4.95	25	3.42
Greece	2.8	2.2	5	5.75	12	3.48	25	3.99	22	3.01
Czech Republic		2.1			12	3.48			20	2.73
Belgium	2.7	2.1	5	5.75	12	3.48	25	3.99	22	3.01
Hungary		2.1			12	3.48			20	2.73
Portugal	2.7	2.1	5	5.75	12	3.48	25	3.99	22	3.01
Sweden	2.4	1.8	4	4.60	10	2.90	22	3.51	18	2.46
Bulgaria		1.7			10	2.90			17	2.32
Austria	2.2	1.7	4	4.60	10	2.90	21	3.35	17	2.32
Slovak Republic		1.1			7	2.03			13	1.78
Denmark	1.4	1.1	3	3.45	7	2.03	16	2.56	13	1.78
Finland	1.4	1.1	3	3.45	7	2.03	16	2.56	13	1.78
Ireland	1	0.8	3	3.45	7	2.03	15	2.40	12	1.64
Lithuania		0.8			7	2.03			12	1.64
Latvia		0.5			4	1.16			8	1.09
Slovenia		0.4			4	1.16			7	0.96
Estonia		0.3			4	1.16			6	0.82
Cyprus		0.1			4	1.16			6	0.82
Luxembourg	0.1	0.1	2	2.30	4	1.16	6	0.96	6	0.82
Malta		0.1			3	0.87			5	0.68
Total	100	100			345	100.00	626	100.00	732	100.00
Votes required for:										
QMV			62	71.26	258	74.78				
Blocking Minority			26	29.89	91	26.38				

SOURCE: Draft Nice Treaty, Annex II (as published on December 12, 2000), Eurostat, OECD, in OECD Economic Surveys: Euro Area, 2001.

CONCLUSION

With this historical background to the development of the European Union and some analysis of how it functions, we now turn in the next chapter to the consequences of evolution in the EU, how it affected the economic systems of its member states, and what economic outcomes resulted.

KEY TERMS AND CONCEPTS

common agricultural policy (CAP)
common external tariff (CET)
common market
Coreper
Council of Ministers
customs union
EC-1992
European Coal and Steel Community (ECSC)
European Commission
European Council
European Economic Area (EEA)
European Free Trade Area (EFTA)
European Parliament
European Union (EU)
fortress Europe
free trade area
Maastricht Treaty
Marshall Plan
Monnet, Jean
Ombudsman
Organization for European Economic Cooperation (OEEC)
principle of subsidiarity
Schumann, Robert
Single European Act
Social Charter
Treaty of Nice
Treaty of Rome
Treaty on European Union

QUESTIONS FOR DISCUSSION

1. Why did Britain perceive it gained little from EFTA and needed the larger market afforded by the EU?
2. Why was the ending of the veto by the Maastricht Treaty important for the development of the EU?
3. What is the principle of subsidiarity and how might it lessen the popular fear of Brussels bureaucrats?
4. Why will admitting the poorer nations of Eastern Europe be a challenge to the EU?
5. What are the particular problems of Turkey's application to the EU?
6. In what sense is the EU a democracy?

7. How do the new voting rules in the Treaty of Nice reduce the power of the larger nations?
8. For what are the reasons do existing members of the EU favor the admission of new nations from the former Soviet Bloc?

RESOURCES

Web Sites

Europa .... http://europa.eu.int/
This site acts as front door to all of the official sites of the European Union. It gives access to Eurostat, the statistical agency, and the Web sites of the Commission, Parliament, the Court of Justice, the Court of Auditors, all of the secretariats, and the Economic and Social Committee.

European Central Bank .... http://www.ecb.int/
This useful is for statistics, policy statements, and working papers will grow in importance in the years ahead.

Center for West European Studies, University of Pittsburgh .... http://www.ucis.pitt.edu/cwes/CWES/cwes.html
This useful site for research provides many links.

The EU Information Society Web site .... http://www.europa.eu.int/ISPO/
This English-language site in Belgium addresses issues concerning the EU and the "information society."

The European Parliament .... http://www.europarl.eu.int/

European Union in the United States .... http://www.eurunion.org/
The official site of the EU delegation in the United States offers good information and useful links.

European Parliament .... http://www.europarl.eu.int/

Policies and Legislation of the European Union .... http://www.eurunion.org/legislat/index.htm

The Texts of Treaties .... http://www.europa.eu.int/eur-lex/en/treaties/

Books and Articles

Britton, Andrew, and David Mayes. *Achieving Monetary Union in Europe.* London: Sage Publications, 1992.

Calleo, David, and Richard Leone. *Rethinking Europe's Future.* Princeton, NJ: Princeton University Press, 2001.

Cecchini, Paolo. *The Cost of Non-Europe.* Brussels: European Commission, 1988.

Devinney, Timothy M., and William C. Hightower. *European Markets after 1992.* Lexington, MA: D. C. Heath and Co., 1991.

Fossati, Amedeo, and Giorgio Panella (eds.). *Fiscal Federalism in the European Union.* Vol. 9 of *Routledge Studies in the European Economy.* New York: Routledge, 1999.

Giordano, Francesco, and Sharda Persaud. *The Political Economy of Monetary Union: Toward the Euro.* New York: Routledge, 1998.

Gros, D., and N. Thygesen. *European Monetary Integration.* New York: St. Martin's Press, 1992.

Kluth, Michael F. *The Political Economy of a Social Europe: Understanding Labour Market Integration in the European Union.* New York: St. Martin's Press, 1998.

Leonard, Dick. *Guide to the European Union*, 8th ed. London: Economist Books, 2002.

Milward, Alan S. *The Reconstruction of Western Europe: 1945–51.* London: Methuen & Co., 1984.

Nevin, Edward. *The Economics of Europe.* New York: St. Martin's Press, 1990.

Padoa-Schioppa, Tommaso. *Efficiency, Stability and Equity: A Strategy for the Evolution of the Economic System of the European Community.* Oxford: Oxford University Press, 1987.

Pinder, John. *European Community: The Building of a Union.* New York: Oxford University Press, 1991.

Pinder, John. *The European Union.* New York: Oxford University Press, 2001.

Pohl, Gerhard, and Piritta Sorsa. "Is European Integration Bad News for Developing Countries?: A Comment on Hughes Hallet." *World Bank Research Observer,* January 1994, 147–155.

Price, Victoria Curzon, Alice Landau, and Richard Whitman. *The Enlargement of the European Union: Issue and Strategies.* Vol. 7 of *Routledge Studies in the European Economy.* New York: Routledge, 1999.

Story, Jonathan, and Ingo Walter. *Political Economy of Financial Integration in Europe: The Battle of the Systems.* Cambridge, MA: MIT Press, 1997.

"A Survey of EMU: An Awfully Big Adventure." *The Economist,* April 11, 1998, 42.

"A Survey of the European Union: Europe's Mid-life Crisis," *The Economist,* May 31, 1997, 52.

"European Enlargement," *The Economist,* May 19, 2001.

United Nations. *Economic Commission for Europe Annual Reports.*

11

THE EUROPEAN UNION: ECONOMIC CONSEQUENCES

THE MAKEUP OF THE EU

Since its last expansion on January 1, 1995, the European Union (EU) includes 15 member states with a total population of 371 million persons. Its average gross national income (GNI) per head measured at current exchange rates is a prosperous $23,000 (Table 11.1). Calculations based on the purchasing power of domestic currencies places it slightly higher at $25,231. The total GNP of the EU (the sum of the national GNPs) is about $8.9 trillion at current exchange rates making it a larger economic entity than the United States and, therefore, a formidable global force. Although economic growth in Europe was strong during the early days of the European Economic Union (EEC), the pace slackened recently as the EU grew more slowly than North America, although it turned in a better performance than slumping Japan. Few Europeans regard the growth rate of income per head of 2.1 percent per annum, exhibited between 1980 and 1999, as creditable, especially as slow growth in output has led to an increasing unemployment. The causes of this poor performance are much debated, but most observers place some blame on inflexible labor markets and a lag in the pace of technological innovation relative to other nations.

THE WELFARE EFFECTS OF THE COMMON MARKET

The theory of the economic consequences of the creation of the EEC, and its successor the European Union, is well developed. The impact can be divided into static effects, which are examined formally next, and the longer-term dynamic effects, looked at in the following section.

Static Effects

The static effects of a common market, or customs union, are shown in Figure 11.1. Let us start with the assumption that the same good is produced in three countries: A (the domestic economy), B (its neighbor and ultimate partner in a customs union), and C (the lowest cost producer in the world). For simplicity we assume that Country C can supply effectively unlimited quantities of the good to Country A, which is relatively small, at a constant price of P_C. Under these conditions all of A's

TABLE 11.1

Selected Macroeconomic Indicators for EU Members

	Population (millions)	GNI per Capita, 2000	GNI per Capita PPP, 2000	GDP, 1999 (billions)	Real GDP Growth % per Annum 1990–1999	Inflation % per Annum 1991–2001
Germany	82	$25,050	$25,010	$2,112	1.00	2.0
United Kingdom	60	$24,500	$23,550	$1,442	2.10	3.4
France	59	$23,670	$24,470	$1,432	1.10	1.7
Italy	58	$20,010	$23,370	$1,171	1.20	4.1
Spain	39	$14,960	$19,180	$ 596	2.00	4.4
Netherlands	16	$25,140	$26,170	$ 394	2.10	2.4
Greece	11	$11,960	$19,640	$ 125	1.80	10.0
Belgium	10	$24,630	$27,500	$ 248	1.40	2.1
Portugal	10	$11,060	$16,880	$ 114	2.30	6.2
Sweden	9	$26,780	$23,770	$ 239	1.20	2.8
Austria	8	$25,220	$26,310	$ 208	1.40	2.1
Finland	5	$24,990	$24,610	$ 130	2.00	2.2
Denmark	5	$32,020	$27,120	$ 174	2.00	2.4
Ireland	4	$22,960	$25,470	$ 93	6.10	3.3
Luxembourg	0.438	$44,340	$45,410	$ 19	3.80	2.5
European Union	376.438	$23,819	$25,231	$8,497	2.10	3.0

SOURCE: World Development Report 2002; Human Development Report 2001.

imports of the good (an amount shown by gh in the diagram) originate in C, and the balance of consumption Q_1. B is by and large a lower cost producer than A, selling at P_b, but it cannot compete with C's price of P_c. Now let us consider the effect of a protective tariff of magnitude t. Because of the small country assumption, C's output remains at the same price on world markets, but within A is increased by the full amount of the tariff. Therefore the price within A's economy rises from P_c to P_t. The output of neighboring Country B is, in the presence of the tariff, priced at P_b + t, which is still above C's price of P_c + t or P_t. Imports, therefore, come exclusively from the lowest cost producer country C, but they are now restricted by the tariff to a level of ab. The balance of domestic consumption is supplied by A's own protected producers, who are able to expand production behind protective barriers. Revenue from the tariff is the rectangle abji—that is, the volume of imports, ab, multiplied by the tariff, t. The welfare consequences of this tariff are a fall in consumers' surplus of $P_c$hbP_t, and the protection raises producers' surplus by an amount $P_c$gaP_t. Total deadweight loss is given by the two triangles aig and bjh.

From this point we can consider the results if the neighboring countries A and B form a customs union. They agree to eliminate all tariff and quota restrictions between each other but maintain a common external tariff of size t with respect to the rest of the world. Now tariff-free goods from B are cheaper than the tariffed goods that originate in C. As a result, imports from the rest of world are eliminated,

■ FIGURE 11.1

The Static Effects of a Customs Union

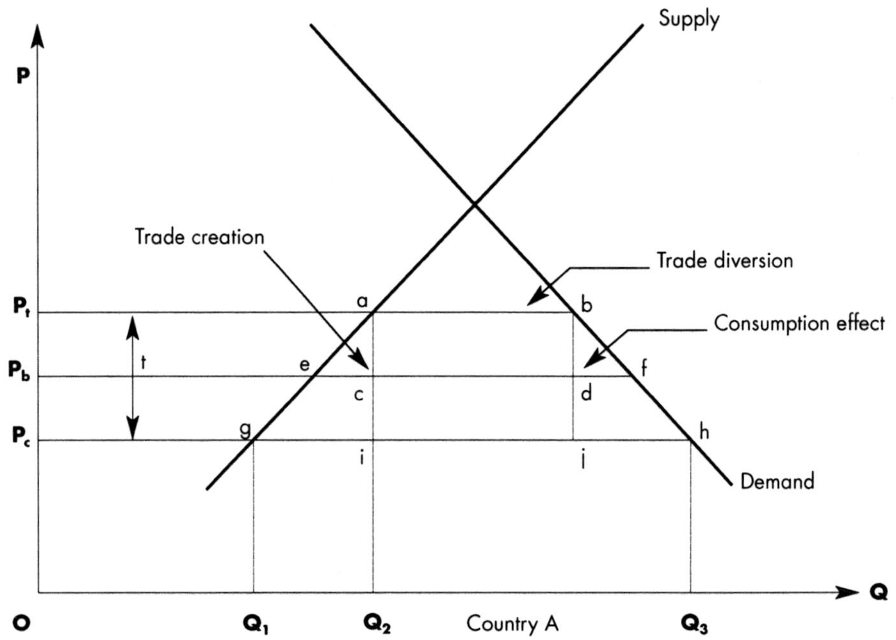

and instead they originate in B. The price of the good established in A is the production cost of B, (i.e., P_b). Total imports are of a magnitude ef. Part of this total, an amount cd (= ab), replaces the imports from C. This result is called the **trade diversion effect** of a customs union. However, total imports are greater than in the case of a general tariff. An amount ec replaces a part of domestic production and is termed the **trade creation effect**. The amount ef is an increase in consumption brought about by lower prices and is termed the **consumption effect**.

Compared to the situation in which A imposes a tariff on imports from all sources, the customs union does represent a welfare gain. Consumers in A gain access to goods at a lower price, P_b, than would be the case if tariff barriers were imposed on all imports. The gain in consumers' surplus is $P_b$fbP_t and is clearly greater than the sum of the loss of producers' surplus $P_b$aeP_t and the foregone tariff revenue abdc. However, these welfare gains are smaller than those that would result under free trade. The largest benefit from A's entry into the market in this example goes to the producers, and workers, of B who gain access to A's market; they see their production increase by an amount ef to meet the demand from A. Compared to free trade, A's consumers are losers, and the only gainers are the producers of B.

Consequently, viewed in a strictly static way, A would only join a customs union if it felt that in some industries it was in the position of lowest cost producer of the member nations. In reality this outcome does reflect the perceived benefits of joining the EU. The greater overall size of market allows greater specialization and division of labor. Economies become more open and trade flows increase. Some domestic industries are likely to decline as imports from other member countries cut into the market, while the output of other industries increases.

Dynamic Effects

Even though the static effects of a customs union are important, long-term dynamic considerations are probably more significant in providing a rationale for the creation of a common market than the static ones. Certainly from the inception of the EEC, one driving motivation was the beneficial effects of exposure of European firms to greater competition from its partners within the common market. A second was the ability to grasp economies of scale from the larger domestic market.

Table 11.2 indicates some of the changes in trade volumes that occurred following the formation of the EEC and its successor the EU between the 1960s and 1990s. In terms of the openness of the whole Community as a bloc of economies,

TABLE 11.2

Openness of EU Economies, 1960–1994
(average of imports and exports of goods as a percentage of GDP)

	1960–1967		1991–1994	
	World	Intra-EU	World	Intra-EU
Belgium and Luxembourg	37.5	64.8	53.3	70.0
Denmark	27.0	52.3	25.4	53.0
Germany	15.9	44.8	20.7	52.2
Greece	12.7	50.6	17.0	59.2
Spain	8.1	47.8	15.2	62.9
France	11.0	45.8	18.7	63.3
Ireland	33.6	72.2	50.3	68.8
Italy	11.7	42.9	15.9	56.4
Netherlands	37.7	62.7	43.9	65.9
Portugal	19.8	48.3	28.5	73.3
United Kingdom	16.0	26.7	20.2	52.1
EU-12	**8.8**	**45.0**	**8.9**	**58.6**
Austria	—	—	25.6	66.1
Finland	—	—	22.4	46.7
Sweden	—	—	23.6	54.9

NOTE: For the member states, these figures include intra-Union trade; for EU-12, intra-Union trade has been excluded. Intra-EU trade is given as a percentage of total trade.
SOURCE: Eurostat; Loukas Tsoukalis, *The New European Economy Revisited*, p. 182.

little changed during this 30-year period. Between 1960 to 1967, about 8.8 percent of the GNP of the 12 nations, then part of the EEC, was traded. The comparable figure for the same group of countries between 1991 and 1994 was 8.9 percent. This stability is surprising, especially in light of the sharp increase in the openness of most of the economies in the world during this time, as the trade-to-GNP ratios rose rapidly on a global basis. Although trade with nations outside of the EU only kept pace with the growth of output, trade within the EU grew considerably more rapidly. On average the nations of the EU conducted 45 percent of their trade with other members in 1960; by 1991–1994 level this had risen to 58.6 percent. The evidence therefore points to substantial trade creation and trade diversion effects.

THE EXTERNAL TRADE POLICY OF THE EU

Developed Nations

After the end of World War II, the United States directed its energy into creating a nonpreferential system of world trade predicated on the most favored nation principle of the General Agreement on Tariffs and Trade (GATT). The creation of customs unions like the European Community (EC) was facilitated by a special clause in the GATT (Article XXIV), which allowed the establishment of formal free trade areas. The United States allowed and even encouraged this development because it felt a strong Europe was essential to contain an expansionist Soviet Union. Nevertheless, many Americans held on to a certain ambivalence because of a recurrent fear that Europe might choose to close itself behind high tariff or walls.

Fortunately, the trade policy of the EU remained in line with GATT policy. The fears of Fortress Europe have been soothed by successive reduction in the **common external tariff (CET)**. The EU also sought to extend the free trade area beyond its core membership. The first extension was the creation of a free trade area linking the EC and the European Free Trade Area (EFTA) called the **European Economic Area (EEA)**. Subsequently the central and east European economies in transition were afforded special status through the signing of economic agreements (EAs) committing the parties to move toward a zero-tariff status over a 10-year period. After U.S. pressure, and in partial compensation for the stalling over its full membership, Turkey was admitted into the customs union without participating in the other aspects of the EU.

Trade Wars

Despite overall conformity with the rules of the GATT, the EU often uses nontariff barriers to protect sensitive industry. These barriers have led to frequent disputes, especially between the EU and the United States. The biggest problem has been related to agricultural products, not surprising given that agriculture lay beyond the purview of the GATT and the highly protectionist postures of both Europe and the United States. One outburst in 1997 erupted over new European Union rules requiring that exporting countries comply with the EU's food hygiene standards.

The EU blocked the import of U.S.-raised chickens and turkeys, and the Clinton administration responded by promising to block $300 million worth of meat imports annually. Like other disputes before it, it was resolved; but an undercurrent of mutual suspicion endures.

Policy toward Developing Nations

The EU's relationships with the "developing" world are governed by the **Lomé agreements**; the latest of these (Lomé IV) was signed in 1989 and subsequently modified in 1995. The signatories of the Lomé pact include the 15 nations of the EU and some 70 Third World countries known as the African, Caribbean, and Pacific (ACP) nations, many of which have historic colonial ties to members of the EU. The agreements allow virtually tariff-free access into the EU for most exports of the ACP nations without any reciprocal obligation. Furthermore, the Lomé arrangements were backed by the stabilization of prices of agricultural exports (Stabex) and mineral exports (Sysmin). In addition, the European Development Fund disburses about 6 percent of European Union revenue in aid to the ACP nations.

However, despite their apparent generosity, the Lomé agreements have done little to assist either development in, or exports from, the ACP group. In fact, EU imports from the ACP countries fell sharply between 1970 and 1994, from more than 8 percent of total non-EU imports to about 3 percent. Even though the pure transfer element of the grants-in-aid and the stabilization schemes is still important, the trade concessions have become less valuable over time as the size of the common external tariff has fallen.

THE ECONOMICS OF A SINGLE CURRENCY

The biggest recent change in the European Union is the adoption of a single currency. The launch of the euro must surely be ranked one of the most important events of the late twentieth century, both for its ramifications for the global system of finance and for its impact on the policies of the member countries of the EU. The single currency remains, however, a controversial issue. On balance, most studies find economic gains from the creation of a single currency, but they also note substantial attendant costs that must be balanced against those gains.

Economic and Monetary Union

In March 1971, the member states of the EC expressed "their political will to establish an economic and monetary union." The first step toward this **Economic and Monetary Union (EMU)** was the adoption of the "currency snake" linking the European currencies through fixed exchange rates while the rest of the industrial world moved toward floating rates. The next step, in 1979, was the creation of the **European Monetary System (EMS)** and the **European currency unit (ECU)**. The EMS was a fixed exchange rate scheme in which most currencies were held in a narrow band against each other (2.25 percent either side of the central parity). Rates were not totally stable, and considerable realignment resulted from differential inflation rates. The ECU was used as a unit of valuation only.

In June 1989, the European Council adopted the proposal of Jacques Delors, then president of the Commission, to embark on a three-stage program leading to a single currency. The first step beginning in 1990 consisted of closer coordination in monetary policy under the supervision of the Committee of Governors of the EC Central Banks.

In late 1992, progress to monetary union was set back by the consequences of German reunification. The need for income support and reconstruction assistance required that the German government pour some DM100 billion per year into the territories of the former East Germany. This expenditure depleted federal finances and led to increased borrowing by the German government, which raised interest rates and pushed up the value of the mark, severely straining the fixed exchange rates of the EMS. The maintenance of existing parities within the EMS required other countries to increase their own interest rates. Both Britain and Italy were unwilling to surrender monetary policy to the EMS in this way and left the system. For the countries remaining, the bands around parity were widened to 15 percent, and their width meant that although the EMS survived, it could no longer be regarded as a truly fixed parity arrangement.

Despite the disruption to the system and the threat to the EMU, the leaders of the member nations resolved to initiate the second stage at the beginning of 1994. The most visible development was the establishment of the **European Monetary Institute (EMI)** in Frankfurt. This location was the subject of some contention because Britain felt that the EMI should be located near the European Union's largest financial market, London. However, the fact that the United Kingdom had removed itself from the EMS, and the political reality that the mark dominates the EMS, favored a German site.

Proponents of the EMU felt that the key to a successful common currency lay in the economic convergence; the so-called **Maastricht criteria** were adopted to ensure that the economies were on a similar path. No state was to be admitted into Stage 3 of monetary union unless it met the following criteria:

1. Its inflation rate did not exceed by more than 1.5 percent that of the average of the three member states with the lowest inflation.
2. Its long-term interest rate did not exceed by more than 2 percentage points that of the three best states in terms with the lowest inflation rates.
3. Its current public sector deficit was less than 3 percent of GDP.
4. Its public sector debt was less than 60 percent of GDP, or approaching 60 percent at a satisfactory pace.
5. Finally, a member state's exchange rate must have been stable over the two preceding years, showing no more than "normal variation."

As late as 1997 no EU nation (exception tiny, wealthy Luxembourg) met these criteria, and a desperate drive to conform (especially to items 3 and 4) initiated a period of fiscal austerity that slowed growth of the EU economies. In March 1998 the European Monetary Institute produced an assessment of each country's performance in meeting the criteria, which was to be the basis for accession to the EMU. When it came to the crunch, only Greece was found to have failed to meet the criteria, although Britain, Denmark, and Sweden were skeptical about monetary union and opted not to enter the system at its initiation in 1999. Only three nations met the strictest definition of condition 4, all the other nations were found to be reducing their ratio of public debt to GDP at a "satisfactory" pace. This interpretation was something of a stretch. Belgium (with a debt/GDP ratio of 122.2 percent) and Italy (121.6 percent) were on the face of it well beyond the limits, but political considerations led to their inclusion under the generous "fudge factor." Consequently, a group of 11 nations (styled Euro-11) were admitted to initiate the monetary union. Subsequently in 2001, Greece was accepted into Euroland as the twelfth member. It now seems only a matter of time before Sweden joins, leaving only the United Kingdom and Denmark on the outside.

The Benefits of a Single Currency

Currency union is expected to bring several benefits. The most obvious is the elimination of currency conversion, releasing substantial resources in the banking sector.[1] Another is the end of exchange rate uncertainty, which should encourage trade and allow more efficient allocation of resources within the EU, through specialization and economies of scale.

A third benefit is that participating nations can largely eliminate their holdings of international currency and bullion reserves. The combined reserves of the members of the EU in 1990 was about ECU 200 billion, while the United States with an economy similar in size had reserves of only about ECU 40 billion. Although the special position of the dollar as a reserve and intervention currency means that the United States can keep lower reserves than other economies, a substantial reduction in overall European reserves can be anticipated.[2] Finally, the creation of a common European currency unit will increase the importance of European currency in world markets. More of the world's reserves will be held in euros and the EU will be able to benefit from seigniorage (the process of creating money to be held by others) and lower interest rates than would otherwise be the case.

The Costs of a Single Currency

Adopting a single currency, however, involves costs, the chief of which is the elimination of exchange rate policy as a means of accommodating shocks and balancing the external accounts. To understand this loss, consider a country that experiences a sudden fall in the demand for its exports. If it has its own currency, it can devalue,

[1]The quantification of these benefits involves making some assumptions but the adoption of a single currency is estimated by the European Commission as providing cost savings equivalent to some ECU 15 billion per annum, capable of creating a boost to the GNP of the participant countries of about 0.4 percent if, of course, the unemployed resources are put to use.

[2]Most of these reserves are currently held in interest-bearing assets, which means the actual degree of saving might well be small.

or allow it to depreciate, and can regain international competitiveness at lower real incomes without causing a fall in nominal income or a rise in unemployment at home. If it is part of a currency union, it must absorb the shock in terms of lower income and higher short-term unemployment. The size and openness of the economy determines the seriousness of losing currency flexibility. Small countries have relatively large propensities to import and therefore are able to achieve external balance through proportionately small changes in GDP. Bigger countries, which are generally more closed, require a larger movement of output to rectify external imbalances. As a rule therefore small countries incur lower costs in joining a fixed-rate system and especially a monetary union.

A second factor is the exposure of a national economy to an asymmetric shock, one affecting it more severely than the rest of the monetary union. If all parts of the union are hit similarly by an economic shock, it can be accommodated by coordinated union-wide monetary, and possibly fiscal, policy. The relationship between the economic structure of each member country and the whole of currency union becomes key. The more a country resembles the union-wide average, the less harmful is the loss of an exchange rate flexibility. The greater the similarity between the structures of all the member countries, the more likely is it that it comprises "optimum currency area." Table 11.3 shows that even though considerable variance characterizes the industrial structure of the members of the Europe Union, it

■ TABLE 11.3

European and American Industrial Structure: Europe by Nation, United States by State

	European Community		United States	
Sector	Mean Percentage Share	Variance	Mean Percentage Share	Variance
Food, beverages, and tobacco	11.2	11.3	8.3	3.9
Textiles, clothing, and leather	8.1	25.9	4.8	15.9
Wood and wood products	3.8	1.4	4.3	3.1
Paper and paper products	7.4	5.9	8.8	8.6
Chemical and chemical products	17	5.8	17.1	33.9
Nonmetallic mineral products	4.8	1.4	2.7	0.3
Basic metals	6.2	2.4	4.1	3.7
Metal products	9.3	2.9	7.4	5
Nonelectrical machinery	10.1	12.9	19.8	27.2
Electrical machinery	10.5	8.6	10.3	9.6
Transport equipment	11.7	7.5	12.5	26.4
Totals	100.1	8.4	100.1	18.0

SOURCE: Bini Smaghi, L. Vori, and S. Vori, "Rating the EU as an Optimum Currency Area," *Banca D'Italia Temi do Discussione*, January 1982.

is actually less than that between the states of the United States, which share a common currency.

The degree of mobility factor also affects the desirability of a currency union. Highly mobile labor or capital helps adjustment to a negative shock by moving quickly from the impacted region to areas where they are in higher demand. Consider an example from the United States. The state of Maine had a high proportion of employment in footwear manufacture, much higher than the U.S. average. When cheap shoes from low labor-cost countries began to flow into the United States, unemployment mounted in Maine. If the state had its own currency, we would see a depreciation of the "Maine $" and a movement toward restoring external balance. However, the shock was absorbed by lower real wages in Maine, which prompted an outflow of labor to states where wages were higher, and some investment in new industry in Maine to take advantage of the cheap labor. Labor mobility between the EU nations is, however, much lower than interstate mobility in the United States. Language and cultural factors, as well as generous unemployment assistance, tends to keep people at home. Net regional migration in the EU represented only 0.2 percent of the total population in the five-year period from 1980 to 1985, only 25 percent of the level in the United States.

Who Gains and Who Loses from a Single Currency?

Because of the complexity of these considerations, it is difficult to establish whether a particular group of countries does indeed constitute an **optimum currency area**, or even which countries will benefit from membership. Nevertheless, using heroic assumptions it is possible to get a quantitative handle on the issue. Table 11.4 shows one attempt to forecast the gainers and losers for the EC-12.[3] The measure of benefits consists of the proportion of GDP that is traded within the community. The measure of cost is the degree to which the industrial structure of the member countries differs from the community average, a gauge of the degree of susceptibility to asymmetric shocks. In general, the smaller, more open economies show the greatest gains. However, these same countries also tend to have less diversified industrial structures, differing from the community average. However, net benefits seem to be enjoyed by all potential members except Greece.

Such a two-dimensional representation of the costs and benefits is potentially misleading. In reality, the economic implications of the EMU are still shadowy, and it is probable that political factors dominated economic in its formation. Some suggest that, like a bicycle rider, the EU needs forward momentum to maintain its stability. After the completion of the internal market, a new project was needed and it was found in monetary unification. Although it maintains the momentum of EU integration, the current two-tier structure creates a rift between the fast-track members of the monetary union (Euroland 12) and the more cautious or less integrated remainder (Denmark, Sweden, United Kingdom).

---

[3] D. Gros and N. Thygesen, *European Monetary Integration* (New York: Addison Wesley, 1998), p. 258.

▪ TABLE 11.4

Estimates of Net Benefits of EMU Membership (EU of 12)

	Benefits	Costs	Net Benefits
Belgium/Luxembourg	44.5	-1.39	43.11
Denmark	13.65	-6.47	7.18
Germany	14.35	-1.81	12.54
Greece	13.25	-14.01	-0.76
Spain	8.95	-2.07	6.88
France	12.95	-0.71	12.24
Ireland	38.85	-8.48	30.37
Italy	9.7	-2.02	7.68
Netherlands	34.2	-5.14	29.06
Portugal	24.55	-10.31	14.24
United Kingdom	10.7	-8.4	2.3

BENEFITS: Intra-EC trade as a percentage of GDP.
COSTS: Difference between nation's economic structure and the EC average.
SOURCE: D. Gros and N. Thygesen, *European Monetary Integration* (New York: Addison Wesley, 1998), p. 258.

The Stability and Growth Pact

Although all the members of the EU, including ultimately Greece, "satisfied" the Maastricht criteria, much was owed to the generous use of the "fudge factor." However, the new monetary union needed a way to ensure that the convergence required for countries to enter the system is maintained into the future. Given the rigors that some countries underwent to meet the criteria, or at least to appear to be moving in that direction, and the high level of unemployment throughout the EU,[4] the temptation is now for countries to indulge in expansionary fiscal policy. All members of the EMU have committed themselves to a stability and growth pact requiring the continued enforcement of the Maastricht criteria. Germany, which traditionally had the strongest and most stable currency in Europe, was justifiably nervous about entering into a union with countries such as Italy, renowned for its mountainous government debts and consequent inflation. It therefore insisted on the **stability and growth pact**. The pact stipulates that all EU countries will run balanced budgets in normal times. If any of the 12 that adopted the euro ever lets its budget deficit exceed 3 percent of GDP, it will be forced back into line with the threat of substantial fines. However, recent tough times have cut central government tax revenues, and standard "Keynesian" economic theory insists that the correct way out of a recession is to increase the size of the deficit. Portugal became the

[4]The levels are high except, somewhat ironically, in Britain, which has the lowest EC joblessness rate and has chosen not to be a member.

first to break the deficit limit by notching up 4.1 percent for the 2001 tax year. Italy and France are coming dangerously near the trigger point, and Germany crossed the 3 percent threshold during 2002.

In the fall of 2002, the president of the Commission, Romano Prodi, an Italian former economics professor, publicly characterized the pact as "stupid." When the EU recovers from this iconoclasm it is probable that some form of flexibility will be built in to take account of the need for deficit-based reflation in tough times. Three main suggestions for reform are being considered. The first is that countries with low debt to GNP ratios (such as Germany) may be allowed to exceed the deficit limit. Another is to reclassify public outlays into "current" and "investment" expenditures, and allow some latitude for the latter. This approach would allow extensive public works projects to escape the guillotine. The final possibility is to recognize that 3 percent was too low and raise it to 5 percent while still insisting on balancing budgets over a longer-term (10-year) horizon. Because any shift would require the unanimous consent of participants, change is unlikely. It does not mean that the 3 percent limit will be adhered to, but rather that transgressors and the other members will likely deal leniently with their failures. The more who fail to keep the line, the lower will be the fines.

The Independence of the European Central Bank

In theory, the new **European Central Bank (ECB)** will be highly insulated from political pressure from member governments. If this theory proves to be the reality it will be an unusual European institution, because the European Council or the Council of Ministers, both of which are responsible to the national governments, decide most of the major issues. The rationale for independence is clear. Only in the absence of direct political pressure will the president of the ECB and the members of its executive board be able to make decisions based on expertise rather than on political exigency. Therefore, both the board and the president are appointed to eight-year nonrenewable terms. The Council of Ministers, the Commission, and the European Parliament can make their views known to the ECB through defined avenues, but the bank is under no obligation to respond. However, despite its theoretical independence, the status of the ECB was undermined at the outset by the French insistence on their own candidate, the governor of the Bank of France, as president of the ECB, and their refusal to accept the consensus candidate, Wim Duisenberg, the president of the ECB's precursor, the European Monetary Institute. A compromise was achieved by splitting the eight-year term into two four-year terms, but the prospects for independence are not good. Things were complicated in 2002 when the prime French candidate was accused of malfeasance in his dealings as a private banker.

THE UNION BUDGET

The European Union has a surprisingly modest budget, but it does not provide many services. In 2002 it amounted to €96 billion ($97 billion at the current exchange rates), little more than 1 percent of total GDP of the member states. Expenditures averaged 2.4 percent of total public expenditure of member states—€314 per head per year.

Finance comes from four sources, as shown in Figure 11.2. The first is the levies imposed on imported agricultural goods. These tariffs are an integral part of the common agricultural policy (CAP) and are designed to bring the price of imported food into line with European costs. It is a useful source of revenue, although one raised at considerable cost, with a high excess burden that falls on the European consumer. It represents only 1.48 percent of total EU revenue and will probably decline in the future as a result of the Uruguay accords of the World Trade Organization, which require the EU to bring agricultural prices into closer alignment with world prices. The second source of revenue consists of tariffs levied on industrial goods as they enter the EU. This source contributes about 15 percent of the budget. The third source of income is the proceeds of a 1.4 percent surcharge, levied as a part of the member countries' value-added tax (VAT), which brings in 38 percent of revenue. Finally, and now most importantly, an additional contribution is demanded of members to bring their budget contribution to 1.27 percent of their GDP, known as the "fourth resource."

The common agricultural policy is the largest element of expenditure in the EU. It currently represents 45 percent of the total budget expenditures, about €44 billion. The second largest component is broadly grouped as structural measures, consisting primarily of regional development and income transfer measures. They account for an additional 34 percent (€30 billion). Industry, research, the environ-

▪ FIGURE 11.2

Sources of EU Revenue, Budget 2001

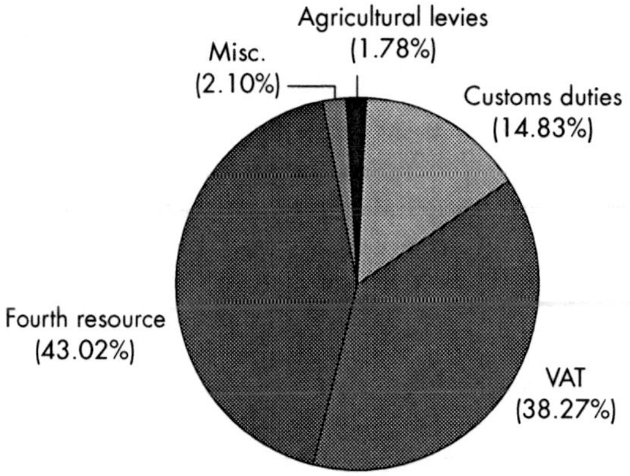

SOURCE: Eurostat.

ment, and transport share 6 percent of the budget. External activities (emergency aid and cooperation) correspond to 8 percent of the budget. Of this portion, about 3 percent is allocated as pre-accession to the countries of Eastern Europe. Other foreign activities account for 5%. Administrative expenses represent 5 percent of the budget. In all, 92 percent of the EU budget expenditures benefit the member countries themselves. The 1995 enlargement of the European Union from 12 to 15 members (after the accession of Austria, Sweden, and Finland) resulted in an increase of 6 percent in the budget, and expansions in 2004 and 2007 will increase it again. Whereas the last group of entrants were net contributors to the EU finances (the taxes and levies they contribute to the budget are greater than the direct expenditure received) that will not be true of the group of countries to join.

The financial management of the European Commission is overseen internally by financial auditors and externally by the European Court of Auditors and the European Parliament. Fraud is a persistent charge in EU institutions, and concern in the European Parliament and in member states forced the Commission to step up the fight against it.

THE COMMON AGRICULTURAL POLICY

As Figure 11.3 shows, about 45 percent of the budget goes to support agriculture. Although its share of total expenditure fell over recent years and will fall further in the near future, the dominance of the **common agricultural policy (CAP)** is still

FIGURE 11.3

Expenditures of the EU, Budget 2002

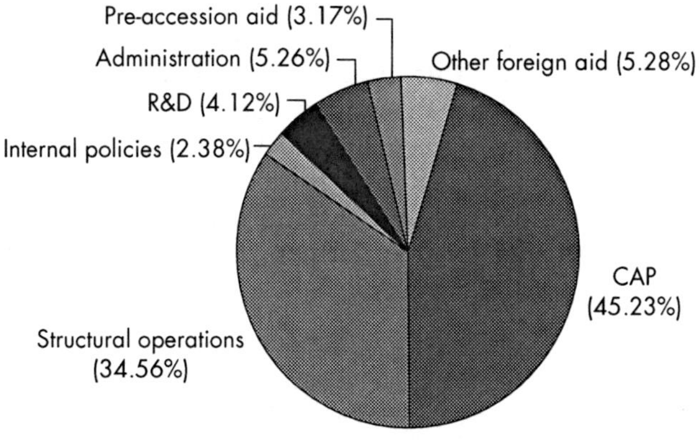

SOURCE: Eurostat.

obvious. The system is complex and varies from commodity to commodity, but in essence it consists of manipulating prices within the EU to produce a desired level of farm income. This manipulation is achieved by both high intervention prices (at which the EU buys excess produce) and various output restriction schemes. Excess production is stored (in "butter mountains," "oil lakes," etc.) and exported to other countries, often at low prices.[5] To keep EU prices above world levels, agricultural goods entering the EU pay a variable import levy, which bridges the difference between world and EU prices. The main beneficiaries of CAP are the producers within the EU, and to some extent foreign consumers, while the losers are consumers within the EU and foreign producers. The system certainly imposes substantial deadweight losses.

At one level, CAP transfers income from country to country. A big agricultural sector leads to an inflow of funds, and because the CAP guarantees prices, nations with efficient agricultural sectors, relative to the European average, gain most. "Winners" fall into two groups. One consists of Greece, Ireland, and Spain, relatively poor countries with large, low productivity agricultural sectors. The other is made up of France and Denmark, rich countries with high productivity in agriculture. The rest of the countries are losers with the largest being Germany, Italy, and the United Kingdom. These transfers are no accident. Freeing trade in manufactured goods benefitted Germany's expanding industrial machine, and CAP was a political counterweight, ensuring membership benefits for France, which had a large agricultural sector. Support is more generous for meat, dairy, and cereals than for "Mediterranean produce," which in part explains why both Italy and Portugal with large agricultural sectors are net losers.

However, viewing redistribution as a national issue alone misses much of the picture. CAP involves subsidies that enable poorer farmers in Scotland, Ireland, Finland, and the "Club Med" countries to stay in business. These subsidies provide several benefits, including the maintenance of a basic level of prosperity in remote regions, contributing to one of the objectives of regional policy. However, the system also favors rich, efficient farmers, and the overall distributional effect of CAP is regressive, moving funds from relatively poor urban consumers (who spend a large proportion of their income on food) to the wealthier farmers of northern France, East Anglia, and Denmark. This pattern of transfers lowers social support or cohesion within the EU by taking from the poor and giving to the more affluent. Partly to rectify this undesirable consequence, but also to meet the objectives of the Uruguay agreement and the World Trade Organization, the EU will shift the emphasis of CAP from price support (which not only is a drain on the budget but also increases agricultural prices and the cost of living[6]) to targeted income maintenance for poor farmers. By eliminating the subsidies to the "rich"

[5]At one point in the late 1980s, the then-Soviet Union was able to buy European butter at 12 cents a pound. Stocks of beef were so high in 1986 that the Commission had to hire refrigerated ships lying in Rotterdam harbor to store the surplus. See Dennis Swann, *The Economics of the Common Market*, 6th ed. (London: Penguin, 1988), p. 219.

[6]The OECD reckons that the CAP adds 15 to 20 percent to the cost of food in the EU.

farmers of northern Europe, the cost of CAP will be reduced, European prices will be more in line with world prices, and the expensive and inefficient system of purchasing, inventory, and resale at a loss will be eliminated.

The German Commissioner for Agriculture, Franz Fischler, outlined his proposals for CAP reform in July 2002. His chief proposal was to delink the subsidies from production and direct them instead toward the income support of poor farmers and to investment in rural development. He was strongly backed by Britain, the Netherlands, and Germany, countries which, although they receive substantial CAP aid, are net losers to the scheme because of their high contributions to the EU budget. Predictably France and Spain, big net gainers, protested and French president Jacques Chirac was able to extract support from the Germans to maintain the current system in place until at least 2007. After that, when the accession of the Eastern European countries is complete, the aid to the new members will be limited to just 20 percent of the total. Given the poverty and heavy dependence on agriculture of the newcomers, this policy is far from what would appear to be fair.

The success of CAP as a policy is debatable, and the verdict depends largely on one's viewpoint. One objective was to stabilize prices with the Community, which was achieved. Less price volatility occurred in the Community than in world markets or even within the United States, which also maintains an extensive and expensive system of supports. However, the cost of stability is the most expensive food in the world, except perhaps in Japan. A second goal was certainty of supply. With the EU now self-sufficient, this target has been met. However, one might question the value of the objective itself. Food is easily available from a variety of producers, most of whom can reasonably be expected to remain politically friendly to Europe. Therefore it is hard to make a case for strategic self-sufficiency. (This state of affairs contrasts with, say, the energy sector, which has fewer supply points, many of which are beset with political problems.) Moreover, self-sufficiency has been more than achieved; overproduction and the disposal of excess now constitute a major preoccupation of the EU. A third objective was to raise agricultural productivity in Europe. The existence of CAP did coincide with a sharp improvement in agricultural productivity, though a cause-and-effect relationship is unclear. All developed countries have seen in the last 40 years an increase in both yield per acre and labor productivity. It can be argued that by guaranteeing the incomes of marginal farmers, CAP shielded producers from market discipline, an effect that will become stronger when CAP's emphasis shifts from price support to income guarantee.

Thus CAP's success lies in the eye of the beholder. Farmers like the policy, while consumers in general suffer, but in a surprisingly uncomplaining manner. The policy contributes to the cohesion of the EU, by winning the support of the poorer nations at the periphery. It is no coincidence that Ireland, a significant gainer from CAP, was the first country to enthusiastically embrace the Maastricht Treaty in a popular referendum. Moreover, CAP is instrumental in preserving an economic pulse in depressed regions. However, it may not provide such a cohesive effect if agricultural aid to the 12 countries due to join between 2004 and 2007 are subject to a different and less generous formula than that enjoyed by the current membership. It would instead be a recipe for resentment and disunity.

THE STRUCTURAL FUNDS

Composed of 15 nations, many of whom have wide regional differences within themselves, the EU is characterized and enriched by diversity. These differences include language, culture, and landscape between nations and between regions of nations. While Europe celebrates these differences, concern continues to grow that socioeconomic disparities may prove harmful to the unity of the EU. Now, policy makers regard economic and social cohesion as a prerequisite for both political stability and economic efficiency.

In the 1960s and 1970s most member countries of the EU developed aggressive "regional policies" designed to foster convergence in regional incomes and employment. Over time, these policies became discredited as expensive, achieving little of lasting consequence, and attempting to overrule the market as arbiter of efficiency. Far from producing national cohesion, regional policy often led to resentment in the territories that had been "net payers." Italy provides a significant example. Despite a battery of policies designed to encourage growth in the "Mezzogiorno," or South, regional disparities persisted and grew. The burden of the expense of redistributive transfers led to the emergence of a political party (the Northern League) devoted to promoting regional separatism.

However, the Single European Act brought regional policy to the fore. This act added a new title to the Treaty of Rome specifically stressing economic and social cohesion and providing specific instruments—the **structural funds**—to address it. Structural funds were not themselves new.[7] What changed was the willingness of the EU to finance regional development. In 1993, ECU 21 billion ($25 billion) was spent on the structural funds, and this amount rose to €34 billion ($33 billion) by 2001, including €3 billion in a specially established cohesion fund directed to the poorest members of the EU known as the "cohesion four": Greece, Ireland, Spain, and Portugal.

The structural funds have clear objectives:

1. To promote development and economic adjustment in regions whose GDP per head is less than 75 percent of the EU average[8]
2. To radically improve the economic base of regions most seriously affected by industrial decline
3. To combat long-term unemployment
4. To address the labor market problems of young people

---

[7]The European Social Fund (ESF) existed since the beginnings of the Europe of Six. The European Regional Development Fund was established in 1975, in the aftermath of the expansion of the early 1970s. The third structural fund was made up of the guidance component of the CAP. A fourth structural fund was added in 1993—for fisheries.

[8]This single objective absorbed three-quarters of total regional expenditure in 1999, and practically all goes to Portugal, Spain, Southern Italy, Eastern Germany, and the overseas departments of France.

5. To promote rural development and structural adjustment in agriculture and fisheries
6. To assist regions with an extremely low population density

Expenditure on the structural funds will necessarily rise with the accession of the poorer countries of eastern Europe. Although the Czech Republic and Slovenia are relatively prosperous, their per-head income is less than 50 percent of the EU average, even when measured in purchasing power terms. Other potential entrants have incomes as low as 20 percent of the average.

INDUSTRIAL POLICY

Although much smaller than the agricultural or the structural funds, the next largest item in the EU budget is expenditure on internal policies, embracing research and development, industrial subsidy, and transportation. Together these activities take almost 6 percent of the total budget.

General Trends in European Industrial Policy

European nations have traditionally taken an interventionist stance on economic development, a feature that distinguished a "continental school," more inclined to government intervention than the **laissez faire** Anglo-Saxon school more dominant in Great Britain and the United States. Furthermore, since the early 1970s Europeans have been concerned that the EU lags behind the United States (and Japan) in technology, in the ability to grasp scale economies, and in finance. Finally, many Europeans feared that U.S.-based multinational corporations had established an almost irresistibly dominant position.[9] These concerns nurtured a series of initiatives specifically directed to putting European industry on a more competitive footing.

National Industrial Policy and the Era of National Champions

As the single market in Europe emerged, member nations instituted industrial policy that favored the promotion of "national champions" with the size and resources to compete in the European arena. National antitrust policy was jettisoned in the face of growing competition from other European firms, and governments engaged in brokered mergers designed to grasp the largest share of the European market. This "new mercantilism" ran counter to the logic of division of resources and comparative advantage that underpinned the idea of the common

[9]This belief was articulated in a popular book authored by Jean Jacques Servan-Schreiber, *The American Challenge (Le Defi Americain)* (New York: Athenaum, 1968).

market. It was also a limited and expensive policy, and one doomed to failure if, as indeed seemed to be the case, the European high-tech and communications industry lost to rivals in North America and the Far East. The use of nontariff barriers and subsidies to promote national champions in each of the countries led to a fragmentation of the market, and the consequent reduction in competition within Europe was itself a key ingredient in the loss of global competitiveness and the failure to innovate.

The Industrial Policy of the EU

As barriers to trade and investment came down within the EC, it became apparent that a truly European stance on industrial policy was necessary. One possibility involved the Commission working to promote the development of "European Champions" able to compete against the giants of North America and Japan in the same way that national governments had acted in the 1960s and 1970s. This approach had several potential defects. First, it favored creating great market power within the Community, to the probable detriment of European consumers. It also failed to give European industry access to advanced technology from Japan and the United States while many companies looked to mergers and joint ventures with non-European firms as a more attractive avenue. Rather than risk these outcomes, the Commission assumed a facilitating, but not an active role, limiting its activities to the removal of fiscal and legal impediments to cross-border mergers.

EU industrial policy is based in the belief that public authorities can play a vital role in promoting successful competitive strategies and that comparative advantage can be created by policy initiative rather than being the result of factor endowment alone. However, in theory at least, EU industrial policy rejects outright protectionism and favors market orientation.

Its most important dimension is fostering collaborative research and development initiatives. These policies started in the early 1980s when the "technological gap" by which Europe lagged the United States and Japan was estimated at between one and two years. The Commission considered two broad strategies to catch up. One, strongly preferred by the French, was to erect protective barriers around the markets for sensitive products; behind these walls European firms would grow strong enough to meet potential international competition. This strategy was rejected by the majority of nations because it would have insulated Europe from the global competitive trends. Instead a policy of promoting Community-wide cooperation and collaboration in research and development was adopted. First the Commission would identify industries that were at risk of falling further behind, then a jointly funded international research effort involving all of Europe's leading firms in the industry would be established.

Information technology was seen as the greatest risk, and in 1982 the European commissioner for industrial affairs, Viscount Davignon, succeeded in getting the heads of the 12 largest European electronics firms around one table. As a result, the **European Strategic Programme for Research in Information Technology**

(ESPRIT) was born. The program's emphasis was on precompetitive basic research, and it operated on a multiyear planned basis. Its success is questionable. It initiated cross-border cooperation and established agreement on basic standards and protocols, but it has not succeeded in closing the technology gap, although it can be argued that the gap would have widened in its absence.

Despite the uncertain record, ESPRIT's promise was enough to encourage imitators, notable for the subtlety of their acronyms, if not for their results. A new program for **Basic Research in Industrial Technology (BRITE)** and another that sought to perform Research in Advance Communications for Europe (RACE) were two examples. Finally, collaborative research was sought even beyond the borders of the EC. The **European Research Coordinating Agency (EUREKA),** an agency to institute shared research throughout western Europe, was established in 1985.

In most industries, heavy-handed protectionist and national champion policies were abandoned in favor of greater market logic, augmented and rationalized by the use of collaborative research; the exceptions to this were the defense and aerospace industries. These industries, not subject to initiatives from the European Union itself, were organized and promoted by agreements between national governments and companies acting through consortia. The most prominent of these is the Airbus Industrie, which is a subsidized and aggressive attempt to maintain European production of civilian air transport and to seize part of the global market from Boeing, which as a result of growth and merger had a near global monopoly.

European industrial policy has been most evident not in the promotion of growth but in easing the death throes of industrial contraction. The ancestor of today's EU was the European Coal and Steel Community, largely concerned with managing a downturn in demand in those basic industries. In steel, for example, the Commission considered itself faced with a crisis. It has at times organized the cartelization of the industry, used quotas to divide output between national firms, and adopted both price guidelines and required minimum prices to avoid "excess" competition between producers and to coordinate an orderly reduction in overall output. The EU has also interceded with foreign suppliers to initiate voluntary export restraint. However, it also acted in both steel and textiles to prevent the subsidy of output by member governments. Any government grants to industry were only allowable if they were a part of a systematic industrial restructuring designed to reduce output in the medium term.

Competition Policy

In its early years the EC lacked a centralized competition policy. Each member country had its own approach, but only Britain, France, and Germany had effective antimerger legislation. The growing integration of the European market brought with it the need for a European policy, although member countries were reluctant to relinquish their authority to Brussels. As a compromise it was agreed that only large mergers would be an issue for the EU. If the combined annual turnover of the merging firms was in excess of ECU 5 billion, and at least ECU 250 million of that

THE GE-HONEYWELL MERGER

In 2001, the EU Competition Directorate headed by its Italian Commissioner Mario Monti, earned the distinction of squelching the world's largest ever industrial merger—the $42 billion offer of General Electric for Honeywell. These companies, both of which had considerable markets in aviation-related industry, were set to merge and already had secured the approval of U.S. authorities. However, the European authorities saw in the merger strong anti-competitive elements and produced a series of theories of how the merger might harm competition. One was that the merged entity would enjoy dominance in avionics; another was that the "bundling" of GE's financial might with Honeywell's expertise in instrumentation would force customers to buy packages of products rather than supporting independent suppliers.

The American attitude was that the competition agency's antagonism lay more in seeking to protect European producers than in protecting European consumers. GE offered to divest a substantial part of the avionics production of the merged firm, but balked at the amount demanded by the EU. In the end GE walked away from the deal to the dissatisfaction of Honeywell shareholders, giving ample proof of the effectiveness, though perhaps not the benefits, of EU competition policy.

turnover was in nations of the EU, Brussels could act; otherwise action would be guided by national regulations.

These rules give European regulators a reach well beyond Europe's borders. For example, when the world's largest aircraft manufacturer, Boeing, sought to merge with McDonnell Douglas in 1997, the joint turnover and European sales put the case within the EU purview, and the deal was saved only by an eleventh-hour compromise but the 2001 GE-Honeywell merger was prevented (see the boxed feature). One of Europe's merger problems stems from an asymmetry in the ease of hostile takeovers between countries. Takeovers are more feasible where an active **market for corporate control** is present. When most companies are publicly traded, rather than held by large institutional or family investors, the chance of rivalry for control increases, which can be an effective means of correcting managerial failure and ensuring that investors get full share value. Within the EU, the market for corporate control is most active in the United Kingdom, which has a high ratio of stock capitalization to GDP (112 percent in 1994) and an active stock market. As barriers to international mergers fall, takeovers and industrial restructuring are occurring in the United Kingdom at a rapid pace. In countries characterized by low market capitalization (34 percent of GDP in France and only 26 percent in Germany in 1994), the scope for mergers is much more limited.

In many countries, other factors augment the barriers to takeovers caused by low stock market activity. These factors included the predominance of family holdings in Italy, the important role of banks as shareholders in Germany, and legislation against hostile takeovers in France. Thus merger policy represents another example of the clash between an Anglo-Saxon market-reliant approach and a continental model (which we also see in Japan) that puts greater emphasis on long-term relations between investors, managers, and employees.[10] A certain irony arises as the lowered barriers to intra-European mergers make firms in the market-oriented United Kingdom easy takeover targets for German and French companies that subscribe to an approach that puts much less reliance on short-term value realization. The British in turn lobby for a level playing field that would make continental European firms easier to acquire. Although it is conceivable, and even likely, that specific legislation that impedes mergers will be removed, the takeover barriers imposed by low capitalization, or block holding, are not easy to legislate away.

As well as being able to deny or modify mergers, the Commission also holds the power to investigate any anticompetitive arrangement and levy fines for such issues as price fixing or supply constraint. For example, it charged that a cartel existed in the cement industry and imposed fines totaling ECU 248 million on 33 producers. The Commission also tried to deny the use of subsidies for national firms and acted several times especially against "flag" airlines—including Air France, Iberia, and Olympic.

Competition policy in the EU is currently under revision. The GE-Honeywell affair (see the boxed feature) ruffled some feathers and in the summer of 2002 the Commissioner was roundly attacked, and some decisions reversed, by the European Court for overstepping its authority. The most substantial criticism is the lack of a clear theoretical underpinning to competition policy that allows the individual case officers too much discretionary authority. Reform will seek to establish clearer guidelines as to what constitutes harm to the consumer and is likely to employ the more transatlantic concepts of dynamic markets and contestable markets. It will also probably see an increase in staffing for the agency, which currently reviews about 300 mergers annually with a professional staff of only 100.

SOCIAL POLICY

What should be apparent from much of this discussion is that the prevailing social philosophy of the European Union is concerned with the construction and maintenance of what is now referred to as **cohesion**, and this approach frequently has adverse consequences for competitiveness. In some ways the debate that occupied economists in the 1960s—the two "Es," equity versus efficiency—has become within the EU the conflict of two "Cs," cohesion versus competitiveness.

[10]The clash of cultures was vividly illustrated in November 1999 when Vodafone of the United Kingdom attempted the takeover of Mannesmann. It was not only the biggest ever hostile takeover, it was also the first attempted hostile acquisition of a German company. The takeover was even opposed by German Chancellor Gerhard Schroeder, who opined, "Hostile takeovers destroy the culture of the company . . . those who launch such ventures in Germany underestimate the virtues of our joint [union-management] codirection. . . . For these reasons I am warning those who want to jump into such an adventure to be careful." Following a considerable increase in the offer price, Vodafone was ultimately successful in acquiring the German company (*The Economist*, February 12, 2000, p. 68).

The Problem of Unemployment

The most serious problem undermining the cohesion of the European Union as a whole is unemployment. For the bulk of the postwar period, unemployment within the countries that now make up the EU was low, especially relative to the United States. Through the 1960s and until the middle of the 1970s the rate was between 2 percent and 2.5 percent of the active workforce. However, global stagnation of the late 1970s and early 1980s saw a sharp rise to almost double digits, and despite a decline in the activity rate, it failed to fall significantly since. By 1996, more than 17 million people were registered as unemployed (see Table 11.5). In comparative terms the situation may have been worse because activity rates (the number of people in work or seeking work) fell relative to the 1960s and were even lower relative to the United States and Japan. One study estimated that the "employment gap," the difference between the employment required to employ everyone who actually wanted a job (including "discouraged workers") and actual employment was as high as 26 million. Since 1996 the situation improved but remains high at 13.5 million workers within the labor force. Add to that discouraged workers, premature retirees, and those on make-work projects and the figure is probably close to 20 million.

Causes of Unemployment in Europe

Whatever measure is used, it is clear that Europe's employment performance gives cause for alarm. It represents a nexus of problems with no easy solutions, and threatens, because of its cost, the very nature of the welfare state in the EU. Europe (as a group of nations) and the European Union (as an institution) are committed to an idea of a high degree of social stability and social cohesion. These goals indicate a strong preference for maintaining a substantial degree of social protection, guaranteeing incomes and services for those out of work, and to maintaining a commitment to a principle of "equal pay for equal work," rather than relying on the unfettered operation of a labor market. Both of these objectives tend to lessen labor

■ TABLE 11.5

Employment and Unemployment in the EU, 1985–2001 (millions)

	1985	1991	1996	2001
1 Labor Force	151.0	167.0	168.8	178.2
2 Employment	136.0	154.0	151.5	164.7
3 Unemployment	15.0	12.9	17.3	13.5
4 Unemployment rate (%)	9.9	7.5	10.3	7.6

SOURCE: OECD.

market flexibility, creating unemployment. The high degree of joblessness entails a high degree of expenditure on social protection.

> Public expenditure on social protection averages 22 percent of GDP in EU-15 on the basis of 1990 data, approaching 35 percent in some Northern European countries, as opposed to 15 percent in the U.S. and only 12 percent in Japan. The difference in the amount spent by governments is reflected in different popular expectations; a very large majority of Europeans seem to expect their governments to provide a basic income for all, including income support for the unemployed. . . . Solidarity has become a key word in the political culture of European societies; is it likely to change in the new economic environment characterized by high rates of unemployment and the growing financial pressures on the welfare states.[11]

The System of Collective Bargaining In Western Europe most workers are covered by national wage agreements negotiated at the industry-wide level, as opposed to being subject to more flexible plant or enterprise agreements more common in the U.S. context. Individual employers, therefore have remarkably little control over what they pay their workers, a source of labor market inflexibility contributing to joblessness. The rising unemployment rates in EU countries favor the trend toward decentralization, and national and industry-wide bargaining are now losing ground. Even in countries such as Germany, where industry-wide negotiations are still the norm, an increasing recourse to "opening clauses" allows works councils and employers to negotiate amendments to these agreements at the enterprise level.

Despite these trends, decentralization is still limited in most western European countries. An International Labour Organization (ILO) report found that

> In 1995, enterprise agreements covered only 8 percent of the private sector in the Netherlands (compared to 75 percent for industry-wide agreements), 14 percent in Spain (compared to about 70 percent for industry-wide agreements) and 25 percent in France (compared to over 80 percent for industry-wide agreements). In Sweden, while central wage agreements are no longer the order of the day, bargaining at industry level remains a current practice. Even in Germany, considered a bastion of the European model, employers in the chemical and metal industries continue to favor industry-wide bargaining. The major change that has occurred is that industry-wide bargaining now offers much more scope for enterprise negotiation on day-to-day productivity issues.[12]

Although most bargaining is at the industry—not the firm—level, works councils are increasingly relied on to encourage dialogue and cooperation within the enterprise. The goal of these councils is, in most cases, to restructure work assignments in line with technological changes and competitive pressures and to maintain employment. The ILO report concludes that "with very few exceptions,

[11]Tsoukalis, *The New European Economy Revisited* (Oxford: Oxford University Press, 1997), p. 115.
[12]International Labour Organization, *World Labour Report*, 1996–1997.

collective bargaining in Europe focuses primarily on the issue of working time (taken here in the broadest sense: reduction, organization, job sharing, retirement, etc.) and related means of saving jobs." The same report finds that both industry-wide and enterprise level agreements show similar preoccupations: "The most frequent job-related topics are wage moderation or even reduction, reduction in working time with a corresponding drop in wages, and payment of overtime at the base rate or in the form of compensatory leave." Measures to ease access to employment, including hiring at reduced rates and increasing the number of apprenticeship places, are often parts of the agreements.

High Reservation Wages The high degree of social protection in Europe means that the cost of losing a job is much less than elsewhere, which has an impact on productivity. Furthermore, the generous income support for the unemployed means that a job search tends to be less pressured than in, say, the United States; this degree of support leads to workers adopting a high **reservation wage**, defined as the lowest wage that will induce an unemployed person to accept a job. The "replacement" rate (the percentage of take-home pay that continues to be received after loss of employment) varies from country to country within the EU and according to family circumstance, as well as with the duration of unemployment. In France, for example, a married person with two children receives 88 percent of take-home pay when first unemployed. The Organization for Economic Cooperation and Development (OECD) average is a more modest 77 percent, largely because of low replacement levels in the United States. Even by the 60th month of unemployment, a French worker would still receive 83 percent of initial in-work take-home pay.[13] Recognizing these high levels of support as being in part responsible for unemployment, European governments struggle to contain the costs of social protection and to lower benefit levels. Until 1993, an unemployed worker in Sweden would receive more than 90 percent of in-work pay when first unemployed. Reforms in 1993 reduced that amount to 80 percent and in 1996 it was further reduced to 75 percent.[14]

A case can be made for the economic efficiency of more protracted periods of unemployment, because a longer period of search should ultimately ensure a better match between the requirements of the vacancy and the skills of the applicant. Moreover, European nations tend to pay close attention to active labor market policy, using government institutions to place the unemployed and using job training schemes and public employment as a means of changing the skills of the unemployed. However, while labor exchanges might speed up the process somewhat, the high level of income protection means a loss of urgency on the part of the job seeker and leads to higher rates of unemployment and a less flexible labor market.

---

[13]OECD, *Economic Survey of France*, 1996–1997, p. 81.

[14]European Parliament, Directorate General for Research, "Social and Labour Market Policy in Sweden," W-13, 39, July 1997.

Nonwage Costs Even though the maintenance of social solidarity is a priority in the EU, concern about its cost is growing. Transfers to the unemployed, the disabled, and the elderly are generally financed by heavy payroll taxes, nominally shared by employers and workers, although the real incidence drives up the cost of labor and acts as a deterrent to taking on more workers. The actual burden varies from nation to nation within the EU. France, for example, with its generous social protection scheme, has experienced one of the sharpest increases in the level of unemployment. This shift has instituted a vicious cycle: rising unemployment pushes up the total cost of social protection, causing in turn an increase in the payroll taxes. However, because payroll taxes are levied on a shrinking workforce and must support more dependents, the tax rates must rise, discouraging employment. By the mid-1990s the combined payroll tax on the lowest paid, and least skilled, workers was about 62 percent, with employers paying social security contributions of about 40 percent of gross wages and the employees contributing an additional 22 percent.[15] Thus, although increases in wages themselves were moderating, real costs for unskilled labor in France were about 40 percent higher than in the United States.

Table 11.6 shows the total taxes (payroll—both employers' and employees' shares—and income taxes) that fall on wage income of the members of the EU. The various components of the total tax bite vary by country,[16] but in every country a sizable "wedge" distorts the labor-leisure decision and raises costs to employers, creating a bias for off-shore production and capital intensity.

Fragmented Labor Markets Although the European Union constitutes a single economic space, its labor market is highly fragmented because regional, national, cultural, and linguistic differences cause pockets of high unemployment to coexist with areas of tight labor demand. This fragmentation occurs even within a single member country. For example, unemployment in northern Italy's Alto Adige region is only 3.4 percent, a figure that would be regarded as close to full employment by most economists, whereas in Campania and Calabria in the south (barely a day's drive), the rate is more than 25 percent. Within the EU as a whole even wider differences exist. Luxembourg has a jobless rate of 3.2 percent, while Andalucia, a poor region of southern Spain, experiences 32 percent unemployment, an unusually pronounced difference in the absence of legal barriers to the movement of labor. In fact labor flows among the nations of the EU actually decreased as the barriers to movement have been removed. "The internal market programme seems to have had very little effect on Intra-EU labour flows which remain very small. Thus, labour mobility should not be expected to play a significant role as a means of economic adjustment in the context of a . . . monetary union."[17]

---

[15]OECD, *Economic Survey of France* 1996–1997, p. 71.

[16]Denmark, for example, provides generous social protection, but finances it almost entirely out of general tax revenue and has only a small social insurance tax.

[17]Tsoukalis, *The New European Economy Revisited* (Oxford: Oxford University Press, 1997), p. 120.

■ TABLE 11.6

Total Taxes on Labor in the EU

	Income Tax	Employee	Employer	Total SSCs	Total
Belgium	21.4	10.5	24.7	35.2	56.6
Denmark	32.4	11.7	0.4	12	44.4
Germany	17.3	17	17	34	51.3
Greece	1.8	12.4	21.9	34.3	36.1
Spain	9.3	4.9	23.4	28.3	37.6
France	10.4	9.6	28.1	37.7	48.1
Ireland	13.6	4.6	10.7	15.2	28.8
Italy	14.2	6.9	25.3	32.2	46.4
Luxembourg	11.2	12.1	12	24	35.2
Netherlands	5.3	25.3	13.9	39.2	44.5
Austria	7.4	13.8	24	37.7	45.1
Portugal	5.4	8.9	19.2	28.1	33.5
Finland	21.4	5.6	20.6	26.2	47.5
Sweden	19.5	5.3	24.7	30	49.5
United Kingdom	14.5	7.2	8.5	15.8	30.3
EU15	14	11.4	19.6	31	45
United States	16.6	7.2	7.1	14.3	30.9
Japan	6.3	9.1	9.4	18.5	24.8

SOURCE: Eurostat.

The Antiemployment Bias of Growth Europe's performance was not strong during the 1990s, and certainly unemployment would be lower had the aggregate growth rate been higher. But as Table 11.7 shows, Europe's growth, at least through the mid-1990s, remained "antiemployment" in its character, both in the absolute and when compared to the United States and Japan. At 1.4 percent per year, European growth rate was slower than that of the United States, which averaged 2.3 percent per year over the same period. However, the residual growth of GDP that cannot be explained by increases in the employment of factors of production was more rapid than in the United States. Such growth, so-called total factor productivity growth (TFP), is generally ascribed to technical progress and innovation. TFP alone accounted for 1 percent of Europe's 1.4 percent average growth performance. In addition, the European economies substituted increased capital for labor, and this increase in capital accounted for a further 1.1 percent annual expansion. Labor employed actually fell. Although economists regard growth due to both technical change and capital deepening as a positive long-term development for an economy, the consequence for Europe in the medium term is growing unemployment.

In short, Europe's slow pace of growth is biased toward economizing on labor, which results in growing joblessness. The data of Table 11.7 are merely an accounting

■ TABLE 11.7

Output, Productivity, and Capital Labor Substitution (annual percentage rates)

	1961–1973	1974–1985	1986–1995	1986–1990	1991–1995
1. Technical Progress = TFP Growth					
European Union	2.8	1.0	1.2	1.5	1.0
United States	0.6	0.9	0.8	0.6	0.9
Japan	6.3	1.1	0.9	2.3	–0.5
2. Macroeconomic Capital-Labor Substitution = Labor Saving Growth (2 = 3 — 1)					
European Union	1.5	1.0	0.7	0.4	1.1
United States	0.3	0.1	0.1	0.0	0.2
Japan	1.8	1.6	1.1	1.2	1.1
3. Apparent Labor Productivity Growth (3 = 5 + 2)					
European Union	4.4	2.0	1.9	1.9	1.9
United States	1.9	0.5	0.8	0.6	1.1
Japan	8.2	2.7	2.0	3.6	0.6
4. Employment Creating Growth (4 + 5 = 3)					
European Union	0.3	0.0	0.4	1.3	–0.5
United States	1.9	1.8	1.7	2.1	1.2
Japan	1.3	0.7	0.9	1.0	0.7
5. Actual GDP Growth (5 = 1 + 2 + 4)					
European Union	4.7	2.0	2.3	3.3	1.4
United States	3.9	2.3	2.5	2.8	2.3
Japan	9.7	3.4	2.9	4.6	1.3

SOURCE: European Commission.

of this process; the causes include the system of collective bargaining, the high reservation wage brought about by generous social protection, high nonwage costs, and fragmented labor markets. To this list should probably be added another factor: the shift to more restrictive fiscal policy occasioned by the Maastricht criteria and the growth and stability pact.

The EU Program on Unemployment

The Commission and the European Council are aware that unemployment threatens social cohesion, despite the paradox that joblessness has been created by an attempt to promote social cohesion through highly redistributive policies. At the 1994 meeting of the European Council in Essen, an outline plan to address unemployment was presented, building on a 1990 White Paper on Employment and Growth. The plan envisaged five sets of policies to tackle the joblessness problem.[18]

Some of these are rather "old hat" and represent the repetition of long-held beliefs rather than a true change in policy. Among these policies is a faith in **vocational training** and **life-long education**, and aid for groups most hard hit by unemployment. It also establishes a commitment to "increase the **employment-intensiveness** of growth." However, among the more innovative ideas is a wage policy that encourages labor-intensive investment by moderating wage increases to a rate below the growth of productivity. Another is a series of initiatives, particularly at regional and local levels, that create jobs in the environmental and social services spheres. The European Council also attempted to come to grips with some of the root causes of unemployment—high nonwage labor costs and income support policies that are "detrimental to readiness to work."

REDISTRIBUTION AMONG NATIONS IN THE EU

The European Union is a redistributive organization. A variety of programs redistribute income among individuals and nations. Table 11.8 gives some estimates of the extent of that redistribution. Because of administrative operations costs and the provision of foreign aid, the costs of the EU outweigh the allocated benefits by about 5 percent. Some countries benefit from administrative operations more than others. Belgium has the benefit of the Commission being located in its capital, a considerable gain to the economy of the Brussels region. Luxembourg and France also gain from the Court of Justice and the Parliament, respectively. Given these limitations we can see five consistent gainers: Greece, Ireland, Portugal, Spain, and Denmark. The first four are the poorest nations in the Union at present. The gains of some of these countries are considerable, with 2 to 5 percent of national income coming from Brussels. Denmark is relatively well off but gains disproportionately because of its higher share of subsidized agriculture in its GDP. The five consistent payers then are Germany, Britain, France, Austria, and Luxembourg. The other five members drift between being receivers and givers.

The entry of the additional twelve countries in 2004 and 2007 will change this balance. All of the newcomers are relatively poor and most are highly agricultural. Although the deal on agricultural aid cut between Germany and France will limit agricultural aid to the new members, they will inevitably be net gainers, which means the countries in the middle will doubtless have to contribute more.

[18]"The Presidency Conclusions" of the European Council Meeting, Essen, Germany, December 1994, available at http://www.europarl.eu.int/summits/ess1_en.htm?redirected=1.

▪ TABLE 11.8

Net Transfers through the EU Budget, 1994–2000 (receipts minus contributions expressed in € millions and as a percentage of national GDP)

	1994 ECU (in millions)	Percentage of National GDP	1997 ECU (in millions)	Percentage of National GDP	2000 ECU (in millions)	Percentage of National GDP	Share of Total EU Receipts
Austria	–	–	−886.1	−0.49	−543.5	−0.27	2.5
Belgium	−138.6	−0.07	−505.5	−0.24	−327.3	0.13	4.0
Denmark	388.7	0.32	61.8	0.04	169.1	0.10	2.0
Finland	–	–	−12.4	−0.01	216.9	0.17	1.5
France	−1,900.9	−0.17	−1,486.7	−0.12	−1,415.3	−0.10	16.7
Germany	−11,302.2	−0.65	−8,962.7	−0.48	−9,273.2	−0.47	24.4
Greece	3,934.4	4.68	4,312.5	4.05	4,373.9	3.61	1.6
Ireland	1,938.8	4.65	2,788.0	4.40	1,674.6	1.83	1.4
Italy	−1,881.3	−0.23	−1,888.2	−0.18	713.4	0.06	13.0
Luxembourg	−64.5	−0.46	−62.8	−0.39	−65.1	−0.35	0.2
Netherlands	394.5	0.32	1150	0.6	−1,224	−0.38	6.5
Portugal	–	–	514.9	1.45	2,675.4	3.07	1.5
Spain	3,354.1	0.81	5,512.2	1.15	5,055.9	0.86	7.7
Sweden	–	–	−1,210.2	−0.60	−1,177.4	−0.50	2.7
United Kingdom	1,078.3	0.13	−3,547.7	−0.05	−3,506.8	−0.25	14.3
Total	−3,143.8	−0.05	−3,802.9	−0.05	−3,998.5	−0.05	100.0

NOTE: Approximately 5 percent of all expenditure is absorbed by administrative costs or is used for development aid. These outlays cannot be apportioned among the member states and consequently the aggregate of member states' contributions to the EU budget exceeds the total for receipts.
SOURCE: Court of Auditors.

KEY TERMS AND CONCEPTS

Basic Research in Industrial Technology (BRITE)
cohesion
common agricultural policy (CAP)
common external tariff (CET)
consumption effect
Economic and Monetary Union (EMU)
employment intensiveness
European Central Bank (ECB)
European currency unit (ECU)
European Economic Area (EEA)
European Monetary Institute (EMI)
European Monetary System (EMS)
European Research Coordinating Agency (EUREKA)
European Strategic Programme for Research in Information Technology (ESPRIT)
laissez faire

life-long education
Lomé agreements
Maastricht criteria
market for corporate control
optimum currency area
reservation wages
stability and growth pact
structural funds
trade creation effect
trade diversion effect
vocational training

QUESTIONS FOR DISCUSSION

1. Do you think that the creation of regional organizations like the EU will hasten or impede moves to freer global trade?
2. Why does the trade creation effect enhance welfare, while trade diversion lessens it?
3. Are you surprised that the openness of the EU with respect to the rest of the world has not changed since the 1960s? What accounts for this lack of change?
4. Why was it thought necessary to improve the Maastricht criteria on potential entrants of the EMU?
5. How is the convergence issue to be handled after the creation of the EMU?
6. Is Europe an optimum currency area?
7. Why is it important to have an independent central bank for Europe?
8. Has the common agricultural policy been a success? How would you reform it?
9. Why is cohesion now the most important issue in the EU? How will enlargement change it?
10. Discuss the evolution of competition policy in the EU. Why is the EU concerned at the merger of two U.S. firms like GE and Honeywell?
11. What are the root causes of growing unemployment in the EU? Are they the result of the economic system?

RESOURCES

See Chapter 10 for useful Web sites concerning the EU.

Books and Articles

Britton, Andrew, and David Mayes. *Achieving Monetary Union in Europe.* London: Sage Publications, 1992.

Buiter, Willem, Giancarlo Corsetti, and Nouriel Roubini. "Excessive Deficits: Sense and Nonsense in the Treaty of Maastricht." *Economic Policy,* April 1993, 58–100.

Devinney, Timothy M., and William C. Hightower. *European Markets after 1992*. Lexington, MA: D.C. Heath and Co., 1991, 52.

El-Agraa, Ali M. (ed.). *The Economics of the European Community*. 3rd ed. New York: St. Martin's Press, 1990.

Field, Graham, *Euroland: Integrating European Capital Markets*, London: Euromoney, 2000.

Fossati, Amedeo, and Giorgio Panella (eds.). *Fiscal Federalism in the European Union*. Vol. 9 of *Routledge Studies in the European Economy*. New York: Routledge, 1999.

Frieden, Jeffrey, Daniel Gros, and Erik Jones (eds.). *The New Political Economy of EMU*. London: Rowman and Littlefield, 1998.

Molle, Willem. *The Economics of European Integration (Theory, Practice, Policy)*. Aldershot, England: Dartmouth Publishing, 1990.

Nevin, Edward. *The Economics of Europe*. New York: St. Martin's Press, 1990.

"A Survey of Business in Europe: Present Pupils." *The Economist*, November 23, 1996, 1–16.

Swann, Dennis. *The Economics of the Common Market*, 6th ed. London: Penguin Books, 1988.

Tsoukalis, Loukas. *The New European Economy Revisited*. Oxford: Oxford University Press, 1997.

United Nations. *Economic Commission for Europe Annual Reports*.

PART FOUR

Asian Economies

12

JAPAN: FINANCIAL PROBLEMS AND THE CORPORATE ECONOMY

	JAPAN	
	Area (thousand sq. km.)	378
	Currency	yen
	Exchange Rate (August 2002)	¥120 = US$1
	Population 2000 (millions)	127
	Population Growth Rate	0.3%
	GNI per Capita, 2000	$34,210
	GNI per Capita, PPP	$26,460
	GDP Growth 1990–2000	1.3%
Value Added as % of GDP 2000	Agriculture	2%
	Industry	36%
	Services	62%
% of GDP	Public Revenue	28.9%
	Exports	10.8%

INTRODUCTION

With a population of 127 million and a GDP of roughly well over $4 trillion,[1] still the second largest in the world, Japan undoubtedly remains a formidable economic power, though much diminished from a decade ago. In the late 1980s, many politicians and economists regarded the Japanese economic system as a juggernaut on

[1]This figure was determined by using the current official exchange rate.

an inexorable course to being the world's leading economy. Western commentators were prone to see in Japan's interventionist policies an advantage that would lead to the eclipse of U.S. business unless strong countermeasures were enacted or Japanese practices imitated.[2] The situation is now differs significantly. In recent years, growth of real gross domestic product (GDP) in Japan lagged behind that in the United States and much of Europe; between 1990 and 2000 it was a mere 1.3 percent per year. Japan's financial system, the core of its industrial policy, is under great pressure; most banks need refinancing, and many need closing. Perhaps most important, Japan has lost self-confidence, reflected in indecisive policy making while consumers and investors lack faith in the future. Admired, envied, and imitated a decade ago, the Japanese system is now openly questioned, and reform demanded at the most fundamental level. This chapter provides an overview of the development and operation of the Japanese system and examines its prospects for success and reform.

HISTORICAL BACKGROUND

Early Development

The modern development of Japan dates from the appearance of the so-called black ships of the American Commodore Matthew Perry in Tokyo Bay in 1853. This intrusion of the world into Japan's isolationism prompted rapid social and economic change, fostered and accelerated by the restoration of the Meiji dynasty in 1868. The feudal system, which had been preserved in Japan, was brushed aside, and the warrior **Samurai** class was integrated into the civil society. Most important, the government initiated a program of state-led industrialization and modernization, which not only transformed Japan's economic base but also imbued Japanese capitalism with many of the distinctive characteristics visible today. A strong governmental role in industrial development remains a characteristic of the Japanese model. Aggressive public investment provided the basic infrastructure for growth through spending on communication, railways, postal services, and education. The government also entered direct production in many industries including steel, engineering, and shipbuilding. The financial sector to this day is dominated by the publicly owned Bank of Japan, established in 1882.

Alongside the growth of the state-sponsored industries, social pressure was used to stimulate the growth of the private sector. The government assisted and guided development, encouraging the acquisition of foreign techniques and the imitation of western industrial and military technology. The members of the Samurai aristocracy, who were at best an anachronism in Japan and who constituted a potential deterrent to progress, were financed and encouraged to undertake industrial ventures. Although not all of the new industrial class had Samurai roots, the effect of government sponsorship of a

[2]See, for example, Clyde Prestowitz, *Trading Places: How We Are Giving Our Future to Japan and How to Reclaim It* (New York: Basic Books, 1993).

limited number of leading families was to be one of the important features of Japanese economic development for the succeeding century.

The favored family industrial groups grew into ***zaibatsu***—closely held diversified industrial and financial combines that dominated economic activity. Each combine was composed of roughly 20 to 30 firms that generally spanned the gamut of economic activity—coal mines, steelworks, shipyards, banks, trading companies, insurance, and so forth. This system led to the substantial concentration of economic power in a relatively small number of diversified groups. Mitsui, the largest of the prewar *zaibatsu*, employed about 1.8 million workers; Mitsubishi, the second largest, employed more than 1 million.

Class links between the leaders of industry and the members of the government, and the great concentration of economic power, led the Japanese political system toward corporatism, a close alliance of government, finance, industry, and, importantly in the Japanese case, the military. Economic growth in Japan was rapid, shown in Figure 12.1, which depicts an index of real gross national product (GNP) from 1885 to 1930. The early part of this period might well be termed the first

▪ FIGURE 12.1

Japanese Economic Growth 1887–1930

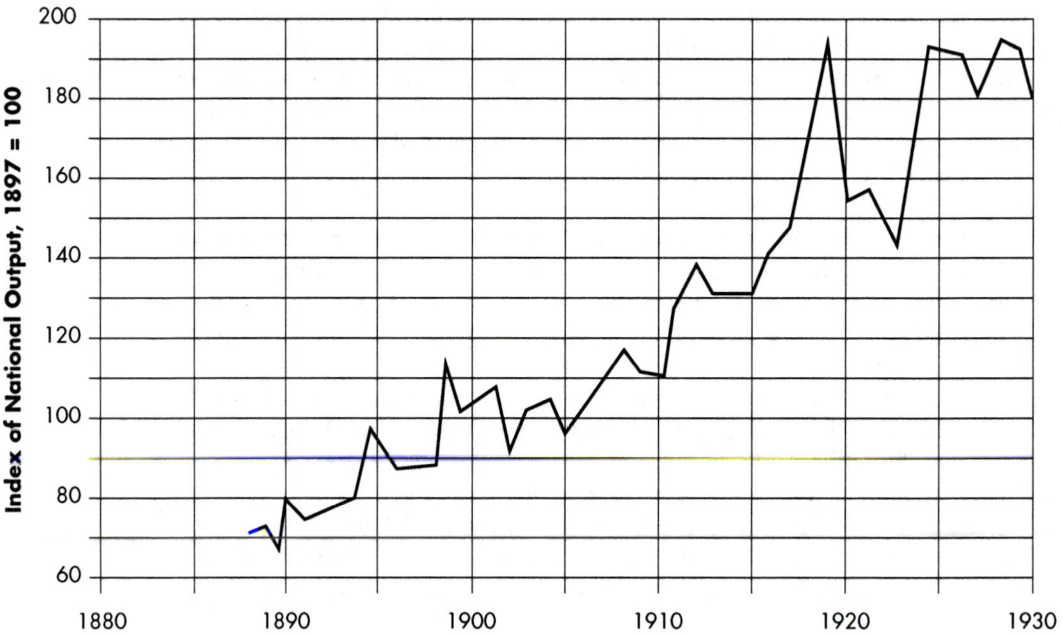

SOURCE: Data from Boulding and Gleason, "War As Investment," in *Economic Imperialism* (Ann Arbor, MI: University of Michigan Press, 1972), pp. 242–243.

Japanese economic miracle, during which time Japan established itself as an industrial power. Real GNP rose by 60 percent between 1887 and 1897. Despite some setbacks between 1898 and 1904, GNP doubled once again between 1905 and 1917. Growth was spurred by the onset of World War I in 1914, which sharply raised global demand for heavy industrial goods. The Japanese metal, defense, and engineering industries all benefited, and the resultant surge in exports spilled over into all sectors of the economy. The collapse of demand after 1918 hurt output in the short run, but the economy recovered by the late 1920s.

In contrast to the rest of the world economy, Japan continued to expand throughout the global depression of the 1930s. Growth was led by the surge in military purchases required for the military occupation of Manchuria and China, and continued until the onset of more general warfare in 1939, when the military burden began to crowd out industrial investment. The destruction and economic dislocation caused by the conclusion of World War II led to the complete collapse of the Japanese economy. Figure 12.2 shows that by 1946 output was well below the levels of 1930.

■ FIGURE 12.2

Japanese Growth 1930–1960

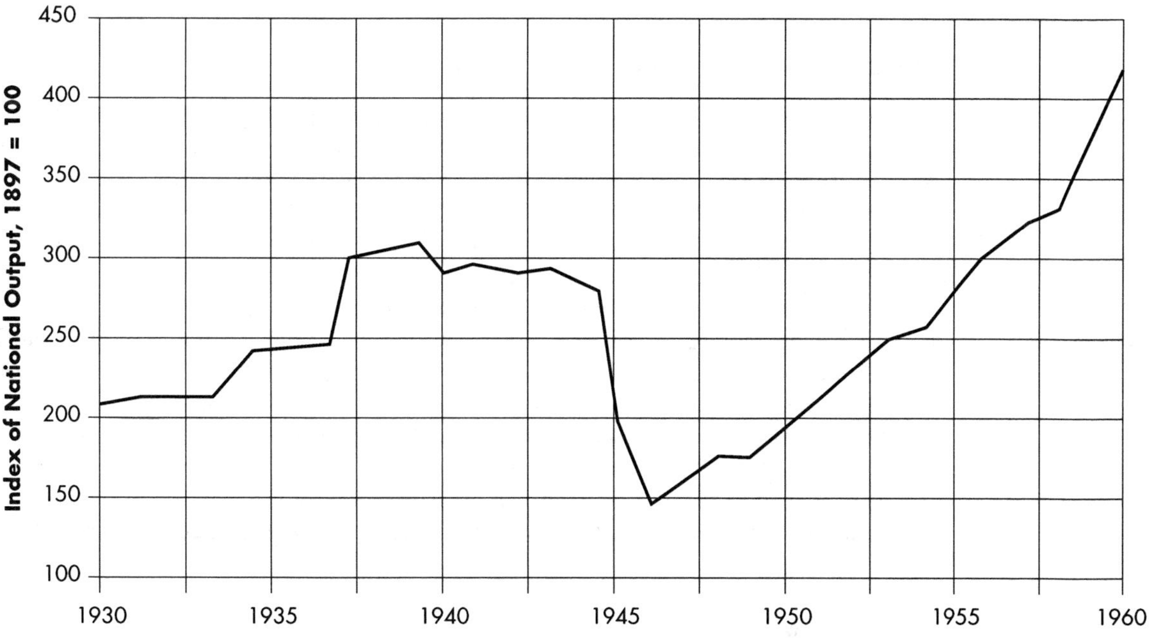

SOURCE: Data from Boulding and Gleason, "War As Investment," in *Economic Imperialism* (Ann Arbor, MI: University of Michigan Press, 1972).

Postwar Reconstruction

After the war, the U.S. occupation authorities radically restructured the Japanese economy. The *zaibatsu* and the close relationship between industry and state were considered by the Americans at least partly responsible for Japanese military adventurism in China and the Pacific.[3] Therefore the occupation authorities decided that breaking up the *zaibatsu* was essential to curbing future expansionism.

Subsidiary enterprises of parent holding companies were converted into independent entities and their share capital sold off. For example, the Mitsui *zaibatsu* was split into 180 nominally independent firms whose shares were then sold into and traded on an open market. However, the destruction of the Japanese economy during the war left little wealth in the hands of individuals. Most of the demand for shares of the newly independent enterprises necessarily came from other corporations, often in the form of exchange for their own shares. In fact, much of the stock in many firms was acquired by companies that were themselves former members of the same *zaibatsu*. Such "sister" companies held historical allegiances, trading links, and a high degree of proprietary information that naturally gave them interest in each other. The dissolution of the *zaibatsu* was accompanied by antitrust regulation, which was modeled on U.S. policy, but in actuality was weakly enforced. The result was that the *zaibatsu* were not eliminated but rather were transformed into ***keiretsu***—diversified industrial groups similar to the *zaibatsu* but held together by interlocking shareholding rather than being held by a single parent. (More on the structure of these *keiretsu* is presented later.)

The Emergence of the "Iron Triangle"

The late 1940s and 1950s saw rapid and sustained economic growth, mostly attributable to the reemployment of the labor and capital idled at the end of the war. Japan exploited its comparative advantage in labor-intensive goods, and by 1955 output once more reached the levels of the 1930s. By 1960 the "gap" created by the war and its aftermath was largely eliminated. (See Figure 12.2.) Although expansion was rapid in the 1950s, Japan was far from a harmonious society.

Labor/management relations were contentious and strikes, frequently quite violent, were common. The government threw its weight behind the employers and helped them break the more radical labor unions, especially in the coal-mining industry. This period saw the modern model of Japanese economic system evolve more clearly. Power rested on three supports: the politicians (principally those of the Liberal Party, which held a near monopoly of government throughout the postwar period), the leadership of industry (primarily the heads of the *keiretsu*), and the planning and financial technocracy, mainly in the **Ministry of International Trade and**

[3]In fact, later scholarship found that the link between the traditional *zaibatsu* and the expansionist policy of the 1930s was questionable. The highest involvement seems to have been with a collection of new firms with specific interests in Manchuria and China. See Boulding and Gleason, "War as Investment," in *Economic Imperialism*, K. Boulding and T. Mukherjee, eds. (Ann Arbor, MI: University of Michigan Press, 1972), p. 253.

Industry (MITI) and the **Ministry of Finance (MoF).** This constellation of power is usually called the "iron triangle." In Japan, in contrast to most West European countries, labor took a backseat. Docile company-organized unions emerged, and aggressive collective bargaining was abandoned in return for the paternalistic principle of "life time employment."

Success of the Japanese Economy

Throughout most of the postwar period, Japan must be regarded as an immensely successful economy. From the low point of 1945, Japan enjoyed rapid and sustained year-on-year economic expansion for more than 50 years. Growth slowed over time as the potentialities for expansive growth, using underemployed factors of production, and "catchup," facilitated by importing more advanced technology from abroad, became exhausted. From an average of 4.3 percent per year in the 1970s, growth of GDP slowed to 4.0 percent in the 1980s. The pace slackened further in the 1990s and turned negative by 1998. However, Japan is today still the second largest economy in the world and is also second in terms of gross national income per head, which in 2001 measured about $35,610 in current exchange terms.[4] Unemployment remains low by international standards, although it has risen recently to levels that are uncomfortable in the Japanese context. In 2002 it reached 5.6 percent, the highest since the 1950s. For the past three decades, Japan enjoyed a balance of payments surplus and is currently the world's largest overseas investor in terms of annual capital flows, with its net creditor position fast becoming the world's largest. The distribution of income in Japan is quite even in comparison to most developed market economies, close to the social democracies of northern Europe. The average income of the top 20 percent of households is only 4.3 times that of the lowest. Japan also performs well in social terms. Conventional measures of social dislocation (crime rates, incarceration rates, etc.) are all modest relative to other developed market economies.

No single cause explains Japan's growth, and many different policy lessons can be drawn from the country's experience. Success has been attributed to the system of labor management, the determining role of industrial policy, the system of directed credit, respect for social order, and the absence of large defense expenditures that perhaps allowed for high investment rates. Nevertheless, the current slow growth of the economy sparked a critical reassessment of the Japanese model, and a skeptical reappraisal of the lessons to be learned, particularly with regard to the financial sector.

SOCIAL CHARACTERISTICS

The Japanese economy and its performance must be viewed in the context of a broader society. Westerners, particularly those in the Anglo-Saxon tradition, value

[4]Data are from the *World Development Report.* Comparisons are less favorable in terms of purchasing power parity because of the high cost of living in Japan, particularly for food and accommodation. In this measure Japan ranks sixth with per-head GDP of $23,400. The comparable figure for the United States is $28,740.

a market system, in part at least, for its impersonal rationality. This view is not the case in Japan. A deep sense of interpersonal responsibility permeates both society and the economy. In some ways Japanese society still resembles the vertical and reciprocal personal obligations that characterized feudalism. Relations within the firm tend to be hierarchical and, by and large, respectful. This behavior also reflects Confucian thought, which stresses personal respect for authority and mutual obligation between members of society. Consequently, while bureaucrats tend to be mistrusted in the United States, in Japan they enjoy great respect because they are the immediate embodiment of authority. Strangely to western eyes, similar respect is also often afforded to politicians, despite the almost ceaseless corruption scandals that characterize recent political life in Japan.

In Japan a high degree of individual identification with a variety of collective institutions reinforces the system of reciprocal obligation. The family is of prime importance. Children, for example, are expected to care for their parents, and they do to a much higher degree than in the United States. In Japan more than half of all retired persons live with their offspring, although this tendency is declining with time. School and university affiliations tend to be long lasting. The workers of the major firms identify with their employers to a higher degree than would be found in the United States. When asked for their occupation, Japanese are prone to tell you whom they work for, rather than what they do. This close identification is a result of the "lifetime employment" obligation of the employers to some workers (discussed later), is a relationship has come under some pressure as Japanese firms respond to economic problems by downsizing. Within firms, workers are organized in groups, or cliques, that again are characterized by personal obligation and mutual assistance.

INDUSTRIAL GROUPS—THE *KEIRETSU*

Because the prewar *zaibatsu* were considered by the United States to bear some responsibility for the aggressive nationalism that led to World War II, the U.S. occupying authorities insisted on their dissolution and, to prevent their reemergence, a ban against holding companies was written into antimonopoly legislation. The *keiretsu* groups that emerged are looser in structure than the *zaibatsu* and are held together by a variety of devices including cross-holding of shares, the use of a single group bank, reliance on a group trading company for sales and project coordination, consultation between CEOs in a presidential council, and the foundation of joint subsidiaries.

Figure 12.3 shows the eight largest conglomerate *keiretsu* in Japan, of which six are traditionally considered to be major. Three are linear descendants of the prewar *zaibatsu:* Mitsubishi, Mitsui, and Sumitomo. Each is grouped around a ***sogo sosha***, or major **trading company** (discussed later) that creates a center for the group. An example of the operation of the various companies within a single "conglomerate" *keiretsu,* the Mitsubishi Group, is given in Table 12.1. This table gives only figures for the largest members of the group, the ones that themselves showed up in the *Fortune* 500 listings in 2002. The group, or "Community of Companies," as Mit-

■ FIGURE 12.3

Japan's Industrial Groups: The *Keiretsu*

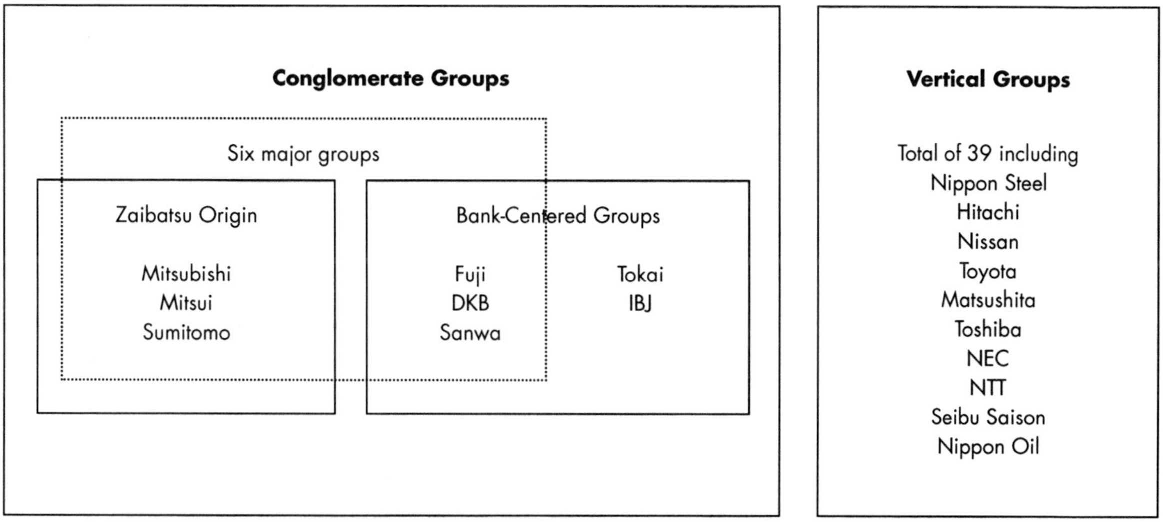

SOURCE: Nanto, "Japan's Industrial Groups," in *Comparative Economic Systems* (Burr Ridge, IL: Irwin, 1994), p. 238.

subishi likes to call itself, is much larger, embracing 40 major corporations in Japan and literally hundreds of overseas subsidiaries and joint ventures.

The principal way in which these groups are held together is by the cross-holding of equity capital, a practice that became prevalent immediately after the war, during the division and disposition of the *zaibatsu.* A further impetus to cross-holding of shares within a *keiretsu* was provided in the 1960s and 1970s when fears of hostile takeovers (possibly from foreign firms) arose and cross-holding presented an effective defense.

Table 12.2 shows the extent of cross-holding of shares in the major *keiretsu,* the conglomerates illustrated in Figure 12.3. These data show that 38.2 percent of the capital of all the constituent members of the Mitsubishi group is held by firms that are themselves a part of the group. It is the highest rate of cross-holding of shares of any of the major *keiretsu.* The comparable figure for the Sumitomo Group, for example, is 28.0 percent, and that for Mitsui is only 19 percent. For the **bank-centered *keiretsu*** groups (Fuji, Sanwa, and DKB), the percentage is uniformly lower. The same table also shows a greater than 55 percent probability that any one firm within a major *keiretsu* will hold shares of any other firm within the group. For the economy as a whole, Hugh Patrick, a well-known authority on the Japanese economy, estimates that the cross-holdings amount to as much as 22 percent of total paid-up capital.

■ TABLE 12.1

The Seven Largest Components of the Mitsubishi *Keiretsu*, 2001

	Revenue ($ millions)	Profits ($ millions)	Assets ($ millions)	Stockholder's Equity ($ millions)	Employment
Mitsubishi	10,5813.9	481.7	61,455.1	7,761.1	43,000
Mitsubishi Electric	2,9183.2	–623.6	30,613.5	4,087.3	116,192
Mitsubishi Tokyo Financial Group	2,6091.0	–1,218.2	750,713.5	25,083.3	22,261
Mitsubishi Motors	2,5598.0	90.0	21,839.7	2,042.2	64,000
Nippon Mitsubishi Oil	2,3520.6	192.0	25,990.9	6,972.7	14,368
Mitsubishi Heavy Industries	2,2905.0	211.5	29,541.1	9,678.3	62,753
Mitsubishi Chemical	1,4238.5	–361.9	16,947.4	2,593.6	38,617

SOURCE: *Fortune* 500, 2002.

This cross-holding not only leads to close relationships within the group, but also creates a mutuality of interest and a reason to look to group members as both suppliers and customers. On the downside, however, the impact of cross-holding is to insulate management from an impartial "market for corporate control." Shares held within the group are rarely sold, and consequently executives are largely safe from outside takeover bids. Hence a depressed share price, the failure to realize a firm's potential, does not trigger the hostile mergers and asset stripping that occur in more aggressive capitalist markets. Table 12.3 contrasts the structure of shareholding in the United States and Japan, showing why the market for corporate control is likely to be more active in the United States.

■ TABLE 12.2

Intragroup Shareholding of the Six Major *Keiretsu*

	Average Linkage to Other Members*	Average Stake Size	Ratio to Total Capitalization
Mitsubishi	75.3%	1.8%	38.2
Sumitomo	94.5	1.6	28
Mitsui	57.6	1.3	19.3
Average of the prewar *zaibatsu*	75.8	1.6	28.5
Fuji	46.8	1.3	16.9
Sanwa	27.5	1.4	16.7
DKB	29.4	1	14.2
Average of the bank-centered groups	34.6	1.2	15.9
Average of the six major groups	55.2	1.4	22.2

*Average linkage is the percentage probability that any member firm of the group holds shares in another firm within the group.
SOURCE: OECD, *Economic Surveys of Japan*, 1995–1996, p. 156.

TABLE 12.3

Shareholding of Public Companies: Japan and the United States Compared by Category

Category	U.S. Companies	Japanese Companies
Institutional investors	71.7	12.9
Financial institutions with business relationships	1.9	35.6
Nonfinancial institutions with business relationships	1.9	9.4
Parent companies or companies in same group (*keiretsu*)	1.9	30.7
Owner families	15.1	5.4
General investors	5.7	2.5
Other	1.9	3.5

SOURCE: OECD, *Economic Surveys of Japan*, 1995–1996, p. 153.

Cross-holding is not the only means by which *keiretsu* are held together. Cohesion within the group is enhanced by the operation of presidential councils, made up of the chief executive officers of the larger firms of the group. They generally convene once a month, and though they are not in theory policy-making bodies, they do discuss the current economic outlook, investment policies, market research, R&D, and other factors with a direct bearing on the efficient operation of the firms, as well as the potentialities of new business ventures. At a slightly lower level, *keiretsu* solidarity is further enhanced by the reciprocal representation of company officers on the boards of sister companies. Furthermore, startup companies to exploit new areas of business activity are often established as joint enterprises between group members, with equity capital put up by member companies, and a board including officers from the parent companies.

Conglomerate *keiretsu* groups (those with activities in a broad range of industries) are frequently grouped around a core company, which plays a leadership role in group management. Such a company may be a general integrated trading company or it may be a bank. Trading companies that specialize in sales and marketing, especially overseas, are, on this scale, institutions largely unique to Japan. Not only are the general trading companies themselves among the largest commercial operations in the world, but also each of the groups that are led by these companies has several major corporations that stand high in the *Fortune* 500 list. The *keiretsu* with origins in the prewar *zaibatsu* are also quite old, tracing their history back some hundreds of years. The boxed feature titled "The Mitsui Group" traces the history of that organization from its origins in 1568.

Other conglomerate groups are best described as bank centered. (Although the *keiretsu*, of *zaibatsu* origin, include a group bank, the lead company in these cases is the general trading company.) These groups are Fuyo (centered on Fuji Bank), DKB (Dai-Ichi Kangyo Bank),[5] and Sanwa (Sanwa Bank). These banks at the core of these

[5]These relationships became more complex in 1999 when Fuji Bank acquired both Dai-Ichi Kangyo Bank and the Industrial Bank of Japan. See Table 12.8 for details on this and other bank mergers.

THE MITSUI GROUP

The Mitsui Group is perhaps the largest business enterprise in the world. Its flagship company claims the world's oldest general trading concern, Mitsui & Co. Ltd. The group, or *keiretsu,* consists of 842 companies, of which 333 are located outside Japan. The group has major operations in construction, investment, finance, transportation, machinery, chemicals, nonferrous metals, and foodstuffs. Japan's largest liquid propane gas transport fleet is operated by a Mitsui company, and Mitsui & Co. dominates the Japanese import market for cigarettes and sports and hobby goods. The economic slowdown in Japan and the strong yen prompted Mitsui management to pursue a range of projects overseas, particularly around the Pacific Rim.

A Brief History

After they were defeated by the Japanese shogun Nobunaga, the Mitsui family fled Omi Province in 1568. Unemployed, the samurai Sokubei Mitsui opened a sake and soy sauce brewery at the urging of his wife, who eventually took over management of the business. She encouraged her sons to enter business and the youngest, Hachirobei, went to Edo (now Tokyo) and opened a dry goods store in 1673. Breaking with Japanese retailing tradition, the store offered merchandise at fixed prices on a cash-and-carry basis.

In 1683 Hachirobei started a currency exchange that ultimately evolved into Mitsui Bank. The business received a boost in 1691 when it became the Osaka government's official money changer. The bank introduced money orders to Japan and profited by securing up to a 90-day float on funds transfers between Osaka, Edo, and Kyoto. Before he died in 1694, Hachirobei wrote a non-traditional will, by which control of the business passed to all related family members, not just to the eldest son's family.

In the mid-1800s the Japanese government ordered Mitsui to help finance its war with rebels. The family hired an outsider with government links, who managed to protect Mitsui from increasing demands for cash. The company then made a timely switch of support to the victorious rebel side and Mitsui became the bank of the Meiji government at the time of the restoration. The new government encouraged, as part of its industrialization drive, and supported Mitsui's diversification into paper and textiles, and a machinery business that was an antecedent of Toshiba. Expansion in foreign trade and banking led to the creation of Mitsui Bussan (now the Mitsui & Co. trading company) in 1876. In the late 1800s the Mitsui *zaibatsu* profited from Japanese military activity, and also moved into shipping, challenging Mitsubishi's monopoly. The Mitsui family withdrew from management of the company in 1936, following a violent campaign by nationalist, expansionist fanatics against the more liberal members of the capitalist establishment.

Prior to World War II the group benefited from the Japanese military buildup. After the war, the U.S. occupation forces split the Mitsui *zaibatsu* into more than 180 separate entities. However, in 1950, 27 leaders of former Mitsui companies began meeting and the Mitsui group became established. The group has expanded rapidly in petrochemicals and metals. In 1990 Mitsui Bank and Taiyo Kobe Bank merged to form the world's second largest bank. Its recent emphasis has been on China.

keiretsu still remain, despite their present difficulties, among the most powerful financial institutions in the world. (See Table 12.8, presented later in the chapter.) Today both legislation and practice place limits on the role of the bank within the group. The law prohibits *keiretsu* banks from lending exclusively within the group and requires that nongroup borrowers receive equal access. Similarly, companies increasingly sought financing from outside the group. Both of these changes represent prudent risk diversification. Nevertheless, the role of the bank within the group continues to be important, and this aspect may be a source of inherent weakness in the Japanese system. The group bank is likely to be more compliant in granting loans to member companies and might as a result end up with a badly performing loan portfolio, reflecting a form of soft-budget constraint. Moreover, banks are unlikely to force group members into liquidation, although it may be rational for them to do so. On the other hand, proximity offers an opportunity for close monitoring of creditworthiness and loan performance.

Distinct from the conglomerate *keiretsu* are the groups that are vertically integrated and oriented around the production of a single product. Patrick identified 39 of these vertical *keiretsu,* the largest of which is the Toyota Group, focused on automobiles and parts, with involvement in distribution and finance. In 2002 Toyota was the tenth largest company in the world in terms of turnover, and its structure differs little from other automobile firms such as General Motors, which is ninth, Ford, which is fifth, or even Fiat, 49th. They are all complex groups involving all stages of manufacturing and distribution.

Despite the intent of U.S.-inspired legislation to break up the groups, tight-knit linkages reemerged in Japanese industry. Rather than a holding-company/subsidiary structure, the case in the *zaibatsu,* linkages within a *keiretsu* are subtler and more "around a circle." Successive Japanese governments took a lenient view toward the reemergence of highly concentrated power in the corporate sector. This tolerance is not surprising because the government, too, was part of the "triangle" of power and saw the existence of a relatively few groups as an easy way to facilitate policy making and implementation. Moreover, recent scandals showed that leading politicians, predominantly those of the dominant Liberal Democratic Party (LDP), received substantial bribes and illegal political contributions. However, the effect of the reemergence of the major groups on consumer welfare and economic growth is unclear. Even though the trend toward concentration did lessen competition as traditionally measured in some markets, as we will discuss in more detail later, Japanese industrial policy did foster effective competition albeit between a limited number of participants in a wide range of product markets.

The *keiretsu* system implies a closer relationship than exists between purchaser and supplier in most countries. The relationships are long term and largely nonmarket. Mutual reliance and trust replace detailed contracts (thus economizing on the services of lawyers), and an enduring sense of dependence and obligation is key. This form of relationship also extends to the many suppliers and subcontractors who are not group members but whose businesses are tightly dependent on the group. The Japanese economy contains many small and marginally profitable firms as well as global giants (a feature often termed **duality**). The impression of Japan from the outside is that most employment is within the large firms, but in fact most Japanese work in firms that employ fewer than 200 employees, which exist as suppliers to the big companies. Again, this proximity offers mixed blessings. Closeness enables stability, coordination, and such productivity-enhancing systems as **just-in-time (JIT) inventory control**. It also is conducive to tight quality control, as the ultimate user is closely involved with the supplier. Moreover, supply contracts in Japan often call for prices to fall over time based on the expectation that the amortization of capital and a leaning curve will enable costs to be cut over the long run.

On the other hand, the system entails certain costs that proponents of market coordination see as important. First, it is difficult for a new supplier to break into this tight circle. Even innovations to improved products, or lower costs, might be slow to be introduced into production. Second, the close relationships necessarily involve a high degree of interdependence and the potential for one firm's failure having repercussive effects is high. In the past the strength and dynamism of the Japanese economy made such contingencies unlikely; however, today the stability of the Japanese system is more open to question, and the risk is greater.

Distribution *Keiretsu*

A feature of the group structure in Japan is its extension into the retail market. Major manufacturers frequently establish a network of stores to handle their own products exclusively. This structure is unusual; in the United States, though a system of exclusive outlets dominates in automobile retailing, it would not be acceptable in most product lines. In some industries the groups are almost totally dominant. For example, in electronics, Matsushita owns 24,000 shops, Toshiba 11,000, Hitachi 9,000, Sanyo and Sharp, 5,000 each, and Sony 3,000. Clearly this structure can be regarded as anticompetitive, and it makes changing the existing balance of market share extremely difficult. New firms and foreign imports are at a particular disadvantage because of these substantial barriers to entry.

Trading Companies

A unique and significant feature of the Japanese economic system is the existence of the "general, integrated trading companies" or *sogo shoshas.* Although some companies operate with similar ranges of activities in western economies, they do not have the same centrality to the overall economic system as in Japan.

Among the eight major trading companies in Japan are the largest companies in the world.[6] Table 12.4 shows that in 2001 Japanese general trading companies made up 3 of the 20 largest companies in the world when measured in terms of revenues.[7] It is important to emphasize, however, that such revenue comparisons overstate the importance of these firms. In terms of assets or employment, the companies are by no means as significant. Mitsubishi, for example, ranks 12th in revenue, 103rd in assets, and 295th in terms of employment. However, purely because of its turnover, which represents enormous buying power and selling ability, the company carries great importance. Three of the largest general trading companies (Mitsui, Mitsubishi, and Sumitomo) form the core of three of the largest *keiretsu.* The trading

[6]The integrated Japanese trading companies are Mitsubishi, Mitsui, Itochu, Sumitomo, Marubeni, Nissho Iwai, Tomen, and Nichimen.

[7]The rankings have, in fact, been greatly altered by poor Japanese economic performance and by the "Asia crisis." In 1995 Japanese general trading companies made up five out of the six largest companies in the world measured by revenue, but by 1997 had fallen to six out of the top 20. Two other trading companies, Sumitomo and Marubeni, figure in the top 25 firms in the world.

TABLE 12.4

The 20 Largest Global Companies by Revenue, 2001

Rank Company		Revenue ($ billion)	Profits ($ billion)	Assets ($ billion)	Stockholders' Equity ($ billion)	Employees
1 Wal-Mart Stores	Retail	219,812	6,671	83,375	35,102	1,383,000
2 Exxon Mobil	Petroleum	191,581	15,320	143,174	73,161	97,900
3 General Motors	Autos	177,260	601	323,969	19,707	365,000
4 BP	Petroleum	174,218	8,010	141,158	74,367	110,150
5 Ford Motor	Autos	162,412	–5,453	276,543	7,786	352,748
6 Enron	Energy	138,718	—	—	—	15,388
7 Daimler Chrysler	Autos	136,897.3	–592.8	184,671.4	34,727.9	372,470
8 Royal Dutch/Shell Group	Petroleum	135,211	10,852	111,543	56,160	91,000
9 General Electric	Machinery	125,913	13,684	495,023	54,824	310,000
10 Toyota Motor	Autos	120,814.4	4,925.1	150,064	55,268.4	246,702
11 Citigroup	Banking	112,022	14,126	1,051,450	81,247	268,000
12 Mitsubishi	Trading	105,813.9	481.7	61,455.1	7,761.1	43,000
13 Mitsui	Trading	101,205.6	442.8	50,313.5	6,903.5	36,116
14 Chevron Texaco	Petroleum	99,699	3,288	77,572	33,958	67,569
15 Total Fina Elf	Petroleum	94,311.9	6,857.7	78,886.7	30,212	122,025
16 Nippon Telegraph &Telephone	Communications	93,424.8	–6,495.5	157,550.7	44,563.7	213,000
17 Itochu	Trading	91,176.6	241.5	35,856.7	3,000.4	36,529
18 Allianz	Insurance	85,929.2	1,453.4	839,551.1	28,192.6	179,946
19 International Business Machines	Technology	85,866	7,723	88,313	23,614	319,876
20 ING Group	Insurance	82,999.1	4,098.7	627,816	19,155.4	113,143

SOURCE: *Fortune* 500, 2002.

companies played a formative role in Japanese growth and development, and they constitute a formidable force for nonmarket-based economic coordination. First and foremost the trading companies are the eyes and ears of the *keiretsu* and the Japanese industrial base. They have been influential in identifying market demand as they scour the globe for sales opportunities, inputs, and raw materials. They also bring companies together to form joint ventures to produce new products. In short, they perform market research, provide a window on the world, take a stand on the future, and provide coordination within a group.

LABOR RELATIONS

Conventional wisdom sees the Japanese workplace as characterized by an absence of conflict revealed in a low rate of strikes, shared objectives for the firm, and a generally harmonious and consensual set of on-the-job relationships. Like many of our preconceptions about Japanese life, this picture is only partly true. Moreover, harmonious industrial relations in any real sense have only been a feature of the past 35 years. The 15 years immediately after the end of World War II were characterized by deep acrimony and even violence. However, since 1960 strike incidence was relatively low, certainly less than in the United Kingdom or the United States, but on a par with Germany.

Although the Japanese system of wage determination is in theory decentralized, it contains strong elements of national coordination. The International Labor Organization considers the state a major protagonist in industrial relations, intervening both through legislative action and the conduct of industrial policy. The most prominent form of national coordination is the ***shunto***, organized annual wage bargaining, the outcome of which directly affects about 25 percent of Japanese workers and which sets a benchmark for wage increases in small and medium-sized enterprises where unionization levels are low.

Japanese industrial relations are often referred to as having three "treasures": **lifetime employment**, known in Japanese as ***sushin koyo***, which protects many of the workers from being laid off; **seniority wages *(nenko)***, which ensures that compensation increases in terms of an employee's age rather than one's responsibilities; and the widespread reliance on **company unions**. In fact, however, although these institutions are very important in some spheres of Japanese economic life, they are by no means universal. Moreover, as well as constituting advantages that have assisted Japan's remarkable growth, these so-called three treasures also entail limitations and may be detrimental to the long-term development of the economy.

Lifetime Employment Policies

Lifetime employment refers to the practice that, once employed, the firm has an obligation to retain a worker despite downturns in business activity. In return the worker recognizes his or her responsibility to work productively and to show loyalty to and identify with the company. Lifetime employment is an important feature for those who enjoy it, but it applies to only roughly 30 percent of the total workforce. It is another feature of the duality of Japanese industrial structure. Only 15 percent of all workers are employed in organizations of more than 1,000 persons, and only these larger firms offer guaranteed lifetime employment to most workers. Moreover, they exclude from coverage part-time employees and a growing force of "contract workers." The 40 percent of Japanese workers employed by firms of fewer than 30 workers never receive any explicit or implicit lifetime guarantee. A second caveat relates to the worker's age of retirement from primary lifetime employment. Lifetime employment is guaranteed only to the age of 55, but most workers need to work at least another decade. Thus even the most privileged of the workforce must find a new occupation for the last 10 years before retirement.

Table 12.5 shows that the Japanese labor market is considerably less fluid than that of other Organisation for Economic Cooperation and Development (OECD) countries. Approximately 63 percent of Japanese workers have been with their employer for more than five years compared with about 50 percent for the OECD average and less than 40 percent for the United States, which is the most labor mobile economy. The same trend is confirmed by Table 12.6, which shows that in 1995 more than 45 percent of Japanese workers aged 40 had only had one employer. Smaller Japanese

TABLE 12.5

Average Employment Longevity in Selected OECD Countries (percentage of workforce)

	Less Than 1 year	1–5 years	5–10 years	10–20 years	More Than 20 years
Australia	21.4	39.2	16.2	15.2	8.1
Canada	23.5	31.9	15.2	19.4	10.0
Finland	11.9	37.3	16.7	21.4	12.8
France	15.7	26.3	16.2	25.6	15.8
Germany	12.8	28.2	17.8	24.5	16.7
Japan	9.8	27.6	19.7	23.7	19.3
Netherlands	24.0	38.4	11.4	15.2	11.0
Norway	14.9	29	19.7	24.1	12.3
Spain	23.9	22.5	14	21.3	18.4
Switzerland	17.6	32.3	16.8	18.8	13.8
United Kingdom	18.6	36.2	16.1	19.3	9.6
United States	28.8	32.9	11.7	17.8	8.8
Unweighted average	18.6	31.8	16	20.5	13

SOURCE: OECD, *Economic Surveys of Japan*, 1995–1996, p. 98.

firms, however, those that constitute the secondary sector, experience greater mobility, and the labor market is fluid, with flexible employment and wages.

Downsizing, a common phenomenon in the United States today, is much more difficult in Japan, because a sizable proportion of employees of large firms enjoy lifetime guarantees. But it is not the only cost of *sushin koyo.* Lifetime contracts are also an impediment in getting the "right people to the right job." They present a barrier to promotion based on ability and may stifle corporate innovation and progressiveness. Deadwood accumulates at the middle management level, and it is difficult to reward the productivity and initiative of younger workers. This

TABLE 12.6

Percentage of Male Graduates in Japan with Only One Employer

	Age			
	40	45	50	55
1980	37.6	30.9	20.2	6.3
1985	45.4	34.4	24.8	12.5
1990	42.9	42.5	29.1	16.2
1995	45.3	40.4	35.3	21.7

SOURCE: OECD, *Economic Surveys of Japan*, 1995–1996, p. 100.

problem is in part resolved by the fact that the lifetime contract covers workers only into their early fifties, rather than their middle sixties, the normal retirement age in the United States. Workers are expected to move on at that time to another post if they have not risen appropriately in the company. Here another feature of the Japanese system comes into play—the close relationship between a firm and its suppliers. Many larger companies try to place their senior workers and middle management with their suppliers, who often cannot refuse for fear of upsetting an important business relationship and who sometimes see it as an advantage for deepening relations.

Seniority Wages

In some sectors of the Japanese economy, wages are more dependent on length of service than is the common practice in other developed economies. Managerial pay is less a function of perceived individual productivity than the number of years an employee already spent with the firm. Like guaranteed employment, the scope of this *nenko* system is limited and generally applies only to those privileged workers who have a lifetime commitment with the firm.

The combination of lifetime employment and seniority wages presents larger Japanese firms with serious problems. Because the natural management structure in most organizations is pyramidal, the upper echelons of Japanese management tend to become crowded as a cohort advances. Enough productive upper management positions are simply not available for those whose seniority with the company would qualify them. Moreover, a seniority wage demands that these employees be paid more than their younger colleagues, who because of their education, energy, and competence might logically be better paid and faster advancing. The net result is an overcrowded, and overpaid, management structure that is a drag on profits in good times and is dangerous to the livelihood of the company in recessions.

Company Unions

The third of Japan's "treasures" is the institution of company unions. More than 80 percent of unionized workers are organized in unions that are unique to the organization for which they work. In other countries, occupational unions organized across firms are more often the rule. From the perspective of collective bargaining, the system is not altogether unique, however. Where Japanese practice does differ is in the close consultation and information flow between the unionized workers and management that usually takes the form of a consultation meeting, held monthly, in which issues of management policy, production plans, and work practices are raised. This high degree of consultation means that unions, and their workers, operate closely in line with the company and tend to identify with it.

This system of company unions and consultation was introduced during the 1950s in an attempt to reduce militancy, lower the high degree of labor conflict, and combat the possibility of rising communist power. The government and employers confronted the unions in a series of important industrial actions in the steel and coal industries. In the aftermath of the 1970's oil shocks, many more large companies established worker-employer cooperation committees, which continue today and which many non-Japanese enterprises have sought to imitate. Unions are a major factor in facilitating the committees. In 1994, 56 percent of enterprises maintained such committees, but in enterprises where labor unions are present, the figure was 81 percent, versus 32 percent for nonunion enterprises.

The degree of unionization in large enterprises remains high in Japan, but it is balanced by low levels of union representation in small firms. In 1993, trade union membership in enterprises with more than 1,000 workers stood at an average of 58.2 percent, compared to only 1.8 percent in enterprises with fewer than 100 employees. Although the large company union is under no real threat, the pressure felt by the union movement worldwide is also apparent in Japan. The problem of getting a job amid mounting unemployment makes Japanese workers in second-tier labor markets increasingly individualistic. Nearly half of all small and medium-sized enterprises encourage alternative forms of representation for determining conditions of employment.

Active Labor Market Policy

One consequence of the high longevity of job occupancy and the low level of unemployment is that the scope of active labor market policy (those policies designed to retrain workers, match applicants and vacancies, and provide public-sector employment) in Japan is limited, as shown in Table 12.7. In a highly interventionist state, this aspect is surprising. Japan spends only one-tenth of 1 percent of its GDP on active labor market policy, about the same as the United States. Germany, in contrast, spends more than 1.3 percent of its GDP on active labor intervention, which is still low compared to the Nordic countries, especially Sweden. This difference is in part explained by the historically low unemployment rate, but Japan also displays a low intensity of expenditure. The share of GDP expended per unemployed worker is also very low—about one-half the OECD average.

TABLE 12.7

Expenditure on Active Labor Market Policy: Selected OECD Countries, 1995

	Expenditure (percentage of GDP)	Unemployment Rate (percentage of labor force)	Expenditure Intensity
United States	0.2	5.6	0.04
Japan	0.1	2.9	0.04
Germany	1.3	9.4	0.14
France	1.2	12.3	0.1
Italy	0.9	10.5	0.09
United Kingdom	0.5	8.2	0.06
Canada	0.6	9.5	0.06
Average (unweighted)	0.7	8.3	0.07

SOURCE: OECD, *Employment Outlook.* OECD, *Economic Surveys of Japan,* 1995–1996, p. 125.

FINANCIAL STRUCTURE

The Japanese financial system is characterized by four essential features. First, the central bank, the Bank of Japan, with only limited independence, functions largely as an arm of government policy rather than an independent balance to the administration. Second, the highly concentrated system of commercial banks operates closely with the government, which has strongly influenced their lending patterns while limiting competition between them. Third, a high degree of functional separation between the various forms of financial intermediaries is maintained. The government promised to deregulate the financial sector to lower these barriers (discussed later), but so far achieved little. Fourth, the high rate of household saving finds only a limited choice of investment instruments. Most household saving, and 20 percent of all saving in Japan, is gathered through the postal savings system, universal across Japan and the prime means of saving for the less affluent. The postal savings bank has more than $1 trillion in assets. Savings are accumulated by the postal savings system and then passed through the Bank of Japan, the central bank, to the city banks.

Unlike the European Central Bank or the U.S. Federal Reserve, the Bank of Japan (BoJ) has no pretensions to independence and generally acts in concert with the government. Its importance as a tool of macroeconomic policy is not especially surprising or unique. However, unlike most other central banks, the BoJ plays an important role in microeconomic industrial policy because it enables the system of directed credit to priority industries to function.

The Banks

The large commercial banks of Japan are known as the city banks. The late 1990s saw a period of aggressive consolidation, the largest instance of which was the merger of the Industrial Bank of Japan (IBJ) with Dai-Ichi Kangyo Bank (DKB) and Fuji Bank, which produced Mizuho Holdings, the largest financial corporation in the world as measured in assets.[8] The remaining six banking groups, and the recent mergers are shown in Table 12.8.

City banks play a key role in fostering and financing the projects that are favored by the Ministry of International Trade and Industry (known as MITI). The process of industrial policy in Japan is more fully discussed later, but the essential procedure is that a dialogue between MITI and industry determines the sectors and projects that are to receive priority treatment. MITI then determines exactly which companies are to have the central role, and the next step is to ensure that the required finance is available. At this point, MITI consults with the Bank of Japan and the Ministry of Finance, and the BoJ provides the necessary liquidity to the banks that will be responsible for providing the financing, under the general umbrella of the Fiscal Investment and Loan Program.

[8]At the time of the merger in 1999 assets were ¥141 trillion ($1,270 billion), and it had 645 branches, and 34,000 employees. Assets fell after the merger, the result of bad loans, but it is still the largest bank in the world in terms of assets with $1,419 billion.

■ TABLE 12.8

The Major Japanese Banks, 2001

	Previously	Revenues ($ million)	Profits ($ million)	Assets ($ million)	Stockholders' Equity ($ million)	Rate of Return on Assets 2001
Mizuho Holdings	Fuji Bank Dai-Ichi Kangyo Bank Industrial Bank of Japan	41,445.1	–7,806	1,141,667	35,699	–0.68%
Sumitomo Mitsui Banking	Sakura Bank Sumitomo Bank	30,228.6	–3710	814,908.5	21,976	–0.46%
Mitsubishi Tokyo Financial Group	—	26,091	–1,218.2	750,713.5	25,083.3	–0.16%
UFJ Holdings	Sanwa Bank Tokai Bank Tokyo Trust	25,299.9	–9,816.5	601,895.1	19,623.1	–1.63%
Norinchukin Bank	—	12,939.1	564.7	434,446.7	14,198	0.13%
Daiwa Bank Holdings	—	10,887.5	–7,425.8	339,171	9,726.1	–2.19%

SOURCE: *Fortune* 500, 2002.

A fundamental criticism of this system is that the banks in Japan are simply not allowed to act as rational and profit-maximizing entities, which is essential to market discipline, but are rather the tools of the bureaucracy. This limitation implies that they cannot fulfill the impartial role in assessing the viability of investment projects, which is essential for the capital market to do its job. It has now become clear that the MITI officials frequently erred in their assessment concerning which projects to support; as a result they induced banks to make loans to enterprises that failed to show the appropriate economic viability. This failure saddles the banks with nonperforming loans and jeopardizes their financial stability.

As Table 12.8 shows, Japanese banks are still large and powerful in terms, but their poor performance in recent years certainly reduced their stature as global players. A few years ago 8 of the world's 10 largest banks measured in terms of assets were Japanese. However, their assets shrank because of the high number of nonperforming loans in their portfolios. Five out of the six major banking groups actually incurred losses in 2001, and the rate of return on assets of the other was only 0.13 percent. Japan's banks are not particularly inefficient in their day-to-day operations, and the revenue from loans exceeds borrowing and other costs. However, the need to perpetually increase the bad loan provisions swamps operating profits and leads to overall losses. The OECD estimates that the Japanese commercial banking sector lost ¥70.5 trillion in bad loans in an seven-year period from 1994 to 2000.[9] This amount is roughly equivalent to 13 percent of Japan's current annual GDP. Most of these bad loans entered the bank's portfolio because of the system of directed credit of the government influence on the banks' lending decisions. In turn the problems of the banks contributes to financial instability in Japan and lay behind the larger Asian banking crisis. The Japanese government publicly estimates that non-performing loans in the asset sheets of banks stand at ¥37 trillion (about 7% of GDP). Many observers think that this figure is optimistic, and a consensus is closer to ¥80 trillion. *The Economist* reports that Goldman Sachs, the U.S. investment bank, put the likely total of bad debts as high as ¥170 trillion in 2000.[10] Conditions worsened since then, with both industrial companies and real estate loans turning bad.[11] If the higher figure is true, then bad debt amounts to almost one-third of Japan's GDP, in addition to the 13% of GDP that the banks have already conceded as lost.

Deregulating the Financial System

Japan still relies heavily on a system of **directed credit** that requires the banking sector to be responsive to and complicit in the government's investment plans, largely through the Fiscal Investment and Loan Program (FILP), probably the largest government-sponsored loan program in the world. As a result, the financial system in Japan was highly regulated by a plethora of rules designed to control the banks and to limit competition, especially from abroad. Critics inside Japan and overseas increasingly regarded this protectionism as a weakness of the Japanese system, and they intensified pressure for a comprehensive package of financial-market reforms. The government launched such a reform package in June 1997. It was known as the **big bang**, because it was similar on paper to the reforms known by the same name in the United States in the 1970s and in Britain in the 1980s. Measures phased in over a five-year period ending in 2002 were expected to transform the Japanese financial landscape. However, in reality the reforms were more cosmetic than substantive and a weak and over-regulated financial sector still lies at the heart of the troubled economy. When Prime Minister Koizumi assumed office in April 2001 he promised a renewed reform effort. However, entrenched opposition from within the LDP, the bureaucracy, and the banks delayed the onset of reform. Subsequently, Koizumi's prestige slipped while the required reform failed to occur. The creation of a modern efficient financial sector depends on reform in several areas.

Reducing Financial Repression An advantage enjoyed, and exploited, by Japanese firms is cheap capital, the result of **financial repression**. The government limits the opportunities for small savers and forces them to put their money in low-yielding deposit accounts, generally in the postal savings system (PSS). Deposit insurance in the private sector is much more limited than in the United States and for safety the majority of small savers turn to the PSS because of the security it offers, despite the extremely low interest rates. These savings are recycled through the

[9]See *OECD: Economic Survey of Japan*, November 2001, Table 11, p. 53.

[10]"Survey of Japan," *The Economist*, April 18, 2002.

[11]Average commercial real estate prices in Japan's 10 biggest cities fell by 84 percent between 1991 and 2001.

Bank of Japan and the city banks to become the source of low-interest investment funds for prioritized sectors through the FILP. The "big bang" legislation proposed the end of repression, allowing small savers access to higher interest instruments.

Critics were skeptical of the outcome, and their suspicion proved well-founded. For one thing, the end of repression would have created a mismatch in the term structure of bank balance sheets. The assets of banks are long term, consisting largely of industrial and housing loans). The withdrawal of savings in pursuit of higher interest would potentially exacerbat the crisis in the banking sector, just as parallel reforms in the United States crippled the savings and loan industry. Given the fragile state of banking in Japan at present, the reform can proceed without the commitment of extensive government subsidies to banks in the short to medium term. Moreover, the essence of the Japanese industrial policy lies in the use of directed credit. Opening opportunities for small savers would inevitably reduce the leverage of the bureaucrats and the LDP to favor prioritized projects. Although this option might enhance efficiency, it would also involve a reduction in bureaucratic power that the authorities might be unwilling to allow.

Cutting Financial Market Segmentation The Japanese system follows a "Glass-Steagall" style of regulation, creating legal barriers between commercial banking, investment banking, brokerage, and insurance. Everywhere in the world market forces are tending to erode these distinctions, and changes in technology are making them obsolete. In Japan, regulatory change must accommodate these shifts, but the fragile banks need continued protection from competition.

The Role of Foreign Financial Intermediaries The weakness of Japanese banking forced the government to recognize that foreign financial intermediaries perform better than their domestic counterparts. The big bang in theory allowed a more level playing field and should have let foreign banks, brokerages, and insurance companies into the Japanese market. One substantial problem is that the efficiency differential between "best worldwide practice" and average Japanese performance is huge. It may force Japanese companies to the wall or open them to acquisition by foreign firms. Given the traditional protectionist bent of Japanese policy, the government's move to preserve the essentially Japanese character of the banking sector remains somewhat slow.

INDUSTRIAL POLICY

The Japanese system embodies a high degree of "industrial policy," the active intervention of the government to promote or change the course of industrial development. Of course, Japan is not alone. Many countries actively institute policies to promote industrial growth, and many examples may be taken from history. However, in Japan industrial policy assumes a comprehensiveness that prompted some observers to use the rather biting sobriquet of "Japan Inc." It is useful to distinguish, however, between what Hugh Patrick has termed **macroeconomic industrial policy** and its microeconomic counterpart.

Macroeconomic Industrial Policy

This category embraces measures designed to increase the pace of overall industrial growth, while having only a limited impact on industrial structure. Such policies include measures to promote savings, to provide universal and accessible education, to protect industry from overseas competition, and to stimulate exports. All of these measures, as long as they provide a level playing field across industry and do not favor any particular sector or type of firm, are not particularly invasive. They have long been a part of the Japanese scene and led to a large share of the country's savings finding its way to the industrial groups, rather than to consumer spending or investment in social projects—like housing. On the whole, such macroeconomic industrial policy successfully accelerated the pace of industrial growth, albeit at the expense of the consumer.

Microeconomic Industrial Policy

When we talk of industrial policy, however, we generally envisage its microeconomic form. Indeed, one prominent economist, Richard Cooper, has defined industrial policy as action "whose intended purpose is to affect the structure of output." In this sense, industrial policy is designed as a substitute for the allocative function of the market and may be justified by the existence of some form of market failure. Again a broad range of policy instruments are available: access to investment funds, direct subsidies, differentially favorable tax treatments, tariff or quota protection, and so forth. The success of **microeconomic industrial policy** in Japan is open to question. Despite notable successes, in equally notable examples promotion of a specific industry or products led to failure and wasted investment. It is important to bear in mind that microindustrial policy has two faces. The more glamorous aspect is the promotion of industries selected as candidates for growth; however, equally important, especially as older "rust-belt" industries lose markets, is the rationalization of industries that are inevitably in decline.

Picking Winners If microeconomic industrial policy is to improve economic performance, it requires an economic justification as to why bureaucrats are able to outperform the market. Industrial policy in Japan originated with the Ministry of International Trade and Industry (MITI), which gives several rationales for intervention.[12] First is a belief that the Japanese economy is characterized by substantial market failure, including the existence of significant economies of scale, the strong linkages between industries, public good effects, and capital market imperfections. In addition to these general justifications, MITI also took the view that the *keiretsu* system actually encourages unhealthy competition because each of the major groups feels that it must have a presence in practically every product line. This concern about the wasteful duplication of investment results in the belief that restraint on competition can be socially beneficial. Hence government intervention to shape market structure can lead to a more efficient use of capital. A further rationale for

[12]This bureaucracy has now been renamed the Ministry of Economy Trade and Industry, or METI but the rest of the chapter will use the acronym by which it became famous.

industrial policy is that markets are myopic and left to themselves, they fail to assume the long-run optimal level of risk. By anticipating the direction of change, industrial policy can actually speed up the operation of the market. MITI also took a long-term view on the industrial mix required to raise Japan to the level of a first-class economic power and keep it there.

The interventionism of MITI started in the early 1950s and initially relied on four measures—import restrictions, directed credit, tax incentives, and foreign exchange controls. The Export and Import Trading Act of 1953 legalized the formation of cartels and price fixing and limited imports. In these early years the system of directed credit consisted of funneling the savings gathered through the postal savings system and civil service pension surpluses into Japan Development Bank (JDB) and other trust funds created under the **Fiscal Investment and Loan Program (FILP)** that were functionally oriented toward industrial finance. Between 1952 and 1955, 28 percent of total finance to Japanese industry was through the FILP trust programs. A discretionary tax system enabled the adoption of discriminatory tax rates and depreciation codes. Finally, because foreign exchange control existed throughout the period, MITI was able to control the access to foreign technology and scarce imports, allocating the required permits only to favored firms whose projects received approval.

As well as using material incentives and restrictions, MITI also made use of propaganda and moral suasion. Such jawboning was not always successful. In 1955, MITI put forward a plan to create a single automobile company in Japan, believing economies of scale to be so strong as to prevent multiple Japanese firms from competing in the world market. It was forced to abandon the scheme in the face of protest from the various *keiretsu*. After this episode, vigorous competition between the various companies ensued, and ultimately four strong, exporting motor companies resulted.

In the late 1950s, MITI was forced to modify its policies. After Japan became a signatory of the General Agreement on Tariffs and Trade (1955) and joined the OECD (1964), Japanese economic policy was subject to international regulation. Trade was required to be liberalized and foreign exchange convertibility increased. It removed some weapons from MITI's arsenal, and greater reliance began to be placed on moral suasion and the establishment of consensus. The importance of the FILP trust funds began to recede, and more emphasis was placed on directing credit through the private banks.

The 1960s saw MITI make another misstep in promoting the development of an oil and petrochemical industry. This effort failed as world energy prices rose sharply following the OPEC oil crises. MITI then took a hard look at the future and decided to promote "knowledge-intensive industry," especially computers and communications. The Agency for Industrial Science and Technology (AIST) was created within MITI. Its purpose was to conduct and finance basic and applied research to assist in the development of the computer, communications, ceramics, and computer-aided manufacturing systems (robotics).

Planning the Decline of Losers Japan's success in the 1960s was to a large extent based on the development of industries that comparative advantage favored while Japan's labor costs were low—textiles, steel, rubber, shipbuilding. Now, as in the United States and Europe, these industries are in decline. An issue is whether the market should be allowed to be the arbiter of who survives and who sinks, or whether government can play a constructive role. Japan has taken the latter tack. Using legislation that dates back to the early 1950s, MITI frequently sponsored the cartelization of declining industries so as to see an orderly restructuring of output. The Japanese believe this approach proved more beneficial in terms of the preservation of industrial capital, social infrastructure, and healthy communities than merely allowing the market to choose the losers.

The Efficacy of Industrial Policy It is not easy to evaluate the success of Japanese industrial policy because of the difficulty in establishing a counterfactual, a consensus on what kind of path Japan would have followed in the absence of industrial policy. Japan indeed demonstrated impressive growth since the war, but what Hugh Patrick characterizes as "myths" are frequently wrongly credited for the success and in his opinion the biggest myth is that of industrial policy, which he finds to be the subject of facile and misleading generalizations. He considers that the macroeconomic elements of industrial policy that created a platform for growth without favoring any particular industry or initiative have been successful, while microeconomic industrial policy ("picking winners") resulted in a much more mixed record. Although the successes might be the ones that catch the eye, several conspicuous failures occurred as well. Patrick documents the ill-starred, energy-intensive industry drive in the 1950s and 1960s and MITI's aborted attempt to promote concentration in the automobile industry in the 1950s. A more recent case is the promotion of the analog system of high-definition television (HDTV), which lost out to a digital version, a misjudgment that perhaps cost as much as $10 billion. Moreover, many of Japan's most impressive achievements were brought about without MITI's help, and in some cases over MITI's objections. The performance of the Japanese economy in the 1990s and the fragility of the banking system (caused in large part by the system of microeconomic industrial policy and directed credit) have thrown the validity of the entire system into doubt. Now the winning strategies promoted by MITI seem to be fewer and the losers more conspicuous. Popular wisdom is moving toward favoring a less prominent role for the now renamed Ministry of Economy Trade and Industry (METI) and a greater reliance on market logic.

WHAT'S WRONG WITH THE JAPANESE SYSTEM?

The Japanese economy seemed only a decade ago to be the success story of the second half of the twentieth century. In the early 1990s, a debate, key to the election of Bill Clinton, centered on how the United States might compete in the long run with the Japanese. Now Japan seems to be almost universally regarded as the sick economy of the developed world. The close relationships between business, bureaucracy, and politics, once lauded as the key to stable and sustained long-term growth, are now decried as the basic cause of the longest recession among major developed economies in the last 50 years. The Japanese economy has been depressed for some

12 years and is not only failing to grow but it is failing to fully utilize its industrial capacity to the detriment of its population. Unless the corner is turned soon, it is likely that the situation will unravel further.

The situation is a compound of problems. First and foremost is the financial sector. It was once seen as a source of great power as, under government direction, cheap investment funds were funneled into industries identified by the bureaucrats of MITI as the source of future growth. Now, the banks wallow in a sorry state; because of bureaucratic intervention they are saddled with loans to corporations who simply cannot repay them, while the value of equities on their balance sheets plummeted. Despite mergers and consolidation, and the continued flow of savings, the banks are fundamentally insolvent.

Secondly, the labor system, particularly lifetime employment and seniority wages, an asset in a growing economy, cannot deal with contraction or even stability, and leaves many of the corporations top-heavy and unresponsive. The non-export sector, sheltered from foreign competition by the government shows little in productivity growth and is inefficient by world standards. The duality of the Japanese system has increased over time.

Third, the population as a whole is fearful of the future and yet conservative in outlook and unwilling to change. Consumer confidence is low and as a result consumer spending suffers. Saving, an individual virtue, is a collective problem as demand lags behind capacity. The conservatism also reflects itself in a fear of changing government. Despite the manifold economic problems, the Liberal Party still holds a virtual monopoly on power. The prime ministership changed hands with considerable regularity and speed, in 11 of the last 12 years, but structural reform remains halting and incomplete, largely because of the power and permanence of the bureaucracy that determines policy.

Fourth, policy options are limited. Inflation in Japan is currently nonexistent. Both producer prices and consumer prices are falling at a rate of just less than 1 percent. Short-term interest rates are zero in both short-term money markets and on two-year government bonds; 10-year government bonds pay only 1 percent interest, which is a real rate of only about 0.25 percent. The economy cannot be stimulated by lowering the nominal rates, and it is possible that highly aggressive government policy can be used to accelerate the rate of inflation and hence drive the real interest rate into negative territory.

Fiscal policy is similarly problematic. None of the 11 different fiscal stimulus packages in the last decade has worked, probably because each was too small to have a dramatic impact on consumer sentiment. However, the effect on government finance has been profound. The deficit grew inexorably and the national debt is more than 130 percent of GDP, more than twice the level imposed on European countries by the Maastricht treaty. However the economy remains stubbornly immobile.

Japan needs both fundamental restructuring, especially in the finance sector, and consumer sentiment must be turned around. Until Japanese feel more confident in the future and start to spend appropriately, the recession will drag on. Japan Inc., once so strong, could be stalled in a perpetual state of low growth, low confidence, and stagnation.

KEY TERMS AND CONCEPTS

bank-centered *keiretsu*
"big bang"
company unions
directed credit
duality
financial repression
Fiscal Investment and Loan Program (FILP)
just-in-time (JIT) inventory control
keiretsu
lifetime employment
macroeconomic industrial policy
microeconomic industrial policy
Ministry of Finance (MoF)
Ministry of International Trade and Industry (MITI)
nenko
Samurai
seniority wages
shunto
sogo sosha
sushin koyo
trading company
zaibatsu

QUESTIONS FOR DISCUSSION

1. What are the *keiretsu?* In what ways do they resemble and in what ways do they differ from the *zaibatsu?* How are *keiretsu* held together?
2. How general is the system of lifetime employment? In what ways does it help and in what way does it hurt productivity?
3. How are Japanese trade unions organized? Does this structure contribute to labor peace?
4. How does a system of "seniority wages" differ from the normal assumptions of microeconomic theory? Can you see any advantages?
5. How has Japan's system of directed credit harmed its financial sector?
6. What constitutes "macroeconomic" industrial policy in Japan? Has it been successful?
7. Is microeconomic industrial policy just about "picking winners"? What else is important?

RESOURCES

Web Sites

Ministry of Finance .... http://www.mof.go.jp/
Central Bank .... http://www.boj.or.jp/
Ministry of Economy, Trade and Industry .... http://www.meti.go.jp/
Statistics Bureau .... http://www.stat.go.jp/

National Tax Agency .... http://www.nta.go.jp/
Tokyo Stock Exchange .... http://www.tse.or.jp/
Development Bank of Japan .... http://www.dbj.go.jp/
Japan External Trade Organization .... http://www.jetro.go.jp/top/
Mitsubishi Companies .... http://www.mitsubishi.or.jp/
***Japan Times* National Newspaper** .... http://www.japantimes.co.jp/
Embassy of Japan in the United States .... http://www.embjapan.org/

Books and Articles

Abe, Etsuo, and Robert Fitzgerald. "Japanese Economic Success: Timing, Culture, and Organizational Capability." *Business History,* April 1995, 1–31.

Alam, M. Shahid. *Governments and Markets in Economic Development Strategies: Lessons from Korea, Taiwan, and Japan.* New York: Praeger, 1989.

Aoki, Masahiko. "Toward an Economic Model of the Japanese Firm." *Journal of Economic Literature* 78, no.1 (March 1990), 1–27.

Boulding, Kenneth, and Alan Gleason, "War as Investment: The Strange Case of Japan." In *Economic Imperialism,* Kenneth Boulding and Tapan Mukherjee (eds.), 240–261. Ann Arbor, MI: University of Michigan Press, 1972.

Calder, Kent E. *Strategic Capitalism: Private Business and Public Purpose in Japan.* Princeton, NJ: Princeton University Press, 1993.

Callon, Scott. *Divided Sun: MITI and the Breakdown of Japanese High-Tech Industrial Policy, 1975–1993.* Stanford, CA: Stanford University Press, 1997.

Carlile, Lonny E., and Mark Tilton (eds.). *Is Japan Really Changing Its Ways?: Regulatory Reform and the Japanese Economy.* Washington, DC: The Brookings Institution, 1998.

Drucker, Peter F. "The End of Japan, Inc.?: An Economic Monolith Fractures." *Foreign Affairs,* Spring 1993, 10–15.

Fingleton, Eamonn. "Japan's Invisible Leviathan." *Foreign Affairs,* March/April 1995, 69–85.

Francks, Penelope. *Japanese Economic Development: Theory and Practice.* London: Routledge, 1992.

Gerlach, Michael L. *Alliance Capitalism: The Social Organization of Japanese Business.* Berkeley, CA: University of California Press, 1993.

Gibney, Frank. *Unlocking the Bureaucrat's Kingdom: Deregulation and the Japanese Economy.* Washington, DC: The Brookings Institution, 1998.

Grabowski, Richard. "The State and Economic Development." *Studies in Comparative International Development,* Spring 1994, 3–17.

Hart, Jeffrey A. *Rival Capitalists: International Competitiveness in the United States, Japan and Western Europe.* Ithaca, NY: Cornell University Press, 1992.

Hobday, Michael. *Innovation in East Asia: The Challenge to Japan.* Aldershot, England: Edward Elgar Publishing, 1995.

Hollerman, Leon. *Japan, Disincorporated: The Economic Liberalization Process.* Stanford, CA: Hoover Institution Press, 1988.

Ito, Takatoshi. *The Japanese Economy.* Cambridge, MA: MIT Press, 1992.

Japan Science Foundation. *U.S.–Japan Comparison in National Formation and Transformation of Technology Centering around Mass Production Systems, 1900–1990.* Tokyo: Japan Science Foundation, 1992.

Johnson, Chalmers. *MITI and the Japanese Miracle: The Growth of Industrial Policy, 1925–1975.* Stanford, CA: Stanford University Press, 1982.

Johnson, Chalmers, Laura D'Andrea Tyson, and John Zysman. *Politics and Productivity: The Real Story of Why Japan Works.* Cambridge, MA: Ballinger Publishing, 1989.

Katz, Richard. *Japan, The System That Soured: The Rise and Fall of the Japanese Economic Miracle.* Armonk, NY: M.E. Sharpe, 1998.

Kikkawa, Takeo. "Kigyo Shuda: The Formation and Function of Enterprise Groups." *Business History,* April 1995, 44–53.

Komiya, Ryutaro, Masahiro Okumo, and Kotaro Suzumara (eds.). *Industrial Policy of Japan.* Tokyo: Academic Press, 1988.

Kosai, Yutaka, and Yoshitaro Ogino. *The Contemporary Japanese Economy.* Armonk, NY: M.E. Sharpe, 1984.

Lee, Chung H., and Ippei Yamazawa (eds.). *The Economic Development of Japan and Korea: A Parallel with Lessons.* New York: Praeger, 1990.

Lincoln, Edward J. *Japan: Facing Economic Maturity.* Washington, DC: The Brookings Institution, 1988.

Lincoln, Edward J. *Japan's Unequal Trade.* Washington, DC: The Brookings Institution, 1990.

Morikawa, Hidemasa. *Zaibatsu: The Rise and Fall of Family Enterprise Groups in Japan.* Tokyo: University of Tokyo Press, 1992.

Morishima, Michio. *Why Has Japan "Succeeded"?: Western Technology and the Japanese Ethos.* Cambridge, MA: Cambridge University Press, 1982.

Mosk, Carl. *Competition and Cooperation in Japanese Labour Markets (Studies in the Modern Japanese Economy).* New York: St. Martin's Press, 1995.

Nanto, Dick K. "Japan's Industrial Groups: The *Keiretsu.*" In *Comparative Economic Systems: Models and Cases,* 7th ed., 236–251, Morris Bernstein (ed.). Burr Ridge, IL: Irwin, 1994.

Nester, William R. *The Foundation of Japanese Power: Continuities, Changes, Challenges.* Armonk, NY: M.E. Sharpe, 1990.

OECD. *Economic Survey of Japan,* November 2002.

Odagiri, Hiroyuki. *Growth Through Competition, Competition Through Growth: Strategic Management and the Economy in Japan.* Oxford: Oxford University Press, 1992.

Okazaki, Tetsuji. "The Evolution of the Financial System in Post-War Japan." *Business History,* April 1995, 89–106.

Oppenheim, Phillip. *Japan without Blinders: Coming to Terms with Japan's Economic Success.* Tokyo: Kodansha International, 1992.

Patrick, Hugh T., and Yung Chul Park. *The Financial Development of Japan, Korea and Taiwan: Growth, Repression and Liberalization.* Oxford: Oxford University Press, 1994.

Pempel, T. J. *Regime Shift: Comparative Dynamics of the Japanese Political Economy (Cornell Studies in Political Economy).* Ithaca, NY: Cornell University Press, 1998.

Sato, Kazuo. *The Transformation of the Japanese Economy.* Armonk, NY: M.E. Sharpe, 1999.

Shichihei, Yamamoto. *The Spirit of Japanese Capitalism and Selected Essays.* Lanham: Madison Books, 1992.

Shigeto, Tsuru. *Japan's Capitalism, Creative Defeat and Beyond.* Cambridge, England: University of Cambridge Press, 1993.

Shimotani, Masahiro. "The Formation of Distribution Keiretsu: The Case of Matsushita Electric." *Business History,* April 1995, 54–69.

"Survey: Japan." *The Economist,* April 18, 2002.

Tai, Hung-chao (ed.). *Confucianism and Economic Development: An Oriental Alternative?* Washington, DC: The Washington Institute Press, 1989.

Takenaka, Heizo. *Contemporary Japanese Economy and Economic Policy.* Ann Arbor, MI: University of Michigan Press, 1991.

Tatsuki, Mariko. "The Rise of the Mass Market and Modern Retailers in Japan." *Business History,* April 1995, 70–88.

Teranishi, Juro. "Economic Recovery, Growth and Policies: 'Gradualism' in the Japanese Context," *Economic Policy,* 19 supp. (December 1994), 137–154.

Udagawa, Masaru. "The Development of Production Management at the Toyota Motor Corporation." *Business History,* April 1995, 107–119.

Werner, Richard. *Princes of the Yen: Japan's Central Banks and the Transformation of the Economy.* Armonk, NY: M.E. Sharpe, 2003.

Whitehill, Arthur M. *Japanese Management: Tradition and Transition.* London: Routledge, 1991.

15

THE ASIAN MIRACLE AND THE ASIAN CRISIS

INTRODUCTION

In the aftermath of the Asian financial crisis, and the short-term collapse of many economies in the region, one can wonder if there was only "mirage" rather than a "miracle." However, a facet of the crisis was that recovery in most nations was rapid. For the region as a whole, the only year in which a contraction of real GDP occurred was immediately post-crisis in 1998.[1] Although growth sagged again in 2001, some gains were still made. It goes without question that the growth performance of the East Asian economies had been extraordinary between the early 1970s and the late 1990s. The widely used and authoritative Summers and Heston data set shows that in the 25-year period from 1960 to 1985, no fewer than six East Asian countries placed in the top seven economies of the world in terms of growth of gross domestic product per head of population. The region of East Asia as a whole achieved growth greater than 5.5 percent annually for this same period. This record was significantly better than both that of the industrialized West and developing nations located in other parts of the world, including the petroleum-rich countries of the Middle East and North Africa, despite their rapid resource-driven growth in the 1970s and early 1980s. In this chapter we will review the nature of this growth, and try to account for it. In the final section we will review the nature of the Asian financial crisis of 1997–1998 to see how it relates to and what impact it had on the particular economic model pursued in East Asia.

The strength of East Asia's record is visible in a variety of measures; for example, exports grew even faster than gross domestic product (GDP). Moreover, economic expansion in East Asia was accompanied by a more equitable pattern of wealth and income distribution than in rapidly growing economies elsewhere. The financial crisis of 1997–1998 took some of the gloss from this spectacular performance, but it would take many years of declining GDP to erase the gains of the past quarter-century.

Because of this speedy expansion, much has been written on "the Asian Miracle," a catchphrase that, taken literally, implies that the path of economic development in these countries cannot be explained by the action of human agency or the normal laws of economics, but rather must be attributed to some extranormal factor, even

[1] World Bank, *East Asia Update*, November 2002, p. 5.

divine intervention.[2] Paradoxically, many of the authors who favor the "miraculous" description also seek to draw lessons from the East Asian experience and recommend the same policies and institutional structure to other countries pursuing growth.[3]

Hyperbole aside, analysts, policy makers, and politicians share the perception of the Asian experience as being out of the ordinary. If growth records for 1960 to 1985 were randomly distributed across the countries of the world, the chances would be less than 1 in 10,000 that the East Asian Group would enjoy such high and similar growth trajectories. The World Bank devoted considerable attention to the performance of eight **high-performing East Asian economies (HPAEs)**: Japan, Hong Kong, South Korea, Singapore, Taiwan, Indonesia, Malaysia, and Thailand. Also performing remarkably well, although mostly outside of the purview of the World Bank study (because of its different starting point as an economy in transition from planned socialism), has been the People's Republic of China.

This chapter examines four closely related issues. First we look at the characteristics of the Asian Miracle—what it achieved in terms of economic change and higher levels of economic welfare. Next we examine the economic factors associated with such growth. In some analyses these associated factors are termed *causes*, but as we shall see, the relationships are often complex and reciprocal. In the third section we discuss two aspects of a current and lively debate. One is the extent to which credit for growth should be given to market forces, rather than interventionist government policy. The other is whether the outcomes in Asia are explicable by looking at changes in the quantities of factors of production (primarily labor and capital) that are used. The fourth section examines the sustainability of recent growth performance in the light of the financial collapse of 1997–1998 and the changes that it wrought upon the environment in East Asia.

THE CHARACTERISTICS OF THE MIRACLE

Economic variables are often highly correlated, and it is difficult to identify cause and effect. To one observer, for example, high savings cause high investment and therefore rising incomes, while to another rising incomes are the consequence rather than the cause of rapid growth. Standard statistical tests provide some help but will not give unambiguous answers. In this section we identify the characteristics of the "miracle" and leave until later in the chapter an examination of the extent to which it is attributable to policy and institutional factors.

High and Persistent Economic Growth

The most obvious change in East Asia during the last 25 years has been the growth of gross domestic product. The nine East Asian economies all placed in the top 20

[2]The World Bank has been particularly fond of the miracle analogy. See, for example, the World Bank Policy Report, *The East Asian Miracle: Economic Growth and Public Policy*, and Joseph Stiglitz and Arilou Uy, "Financial Markets, Public Policy and the East Asian Miracle," *World Bank Research Observer*, 1996.
[3]See Joseph Stiglitz, "Some Lessons from the Asian Miracle," *The World Bank Research Observer* 11, no. 2 (August 1996), pp. 151–177.

economies in terms of growth of GDP over a 25-year period.[4] Growth in almost every case has been sustained and steady. Until the recession of 1998 each year built on the last and saw a record GDP. This pattern of continuing growth contrasts with the experience of other countries in the same time period—for example, Brazil or Mexico—and the experience of the East Asian group at other times. It is common for a nation to experience rapid growth for a limited period of time, when it is "bouncing back" to a level of income—or even to a growth trajectory—from which it had fallen as a result of war, disasters, or inept economic management. Economists generally view this bounce as a return to the production possibility frontier, bringing unused capacity back into production after a shock. Such was the case, for example, for Japan in the 1950s, when it struggled to reach the levels attained in the 1930s after a fall due to the war and its aftermath. Similarly, many economists expect a period of sustained growth in the Eastern European and former Soviet countries, which saw dramatic contractions in output from late 1980s to mid-1990s, largely as a result of the disarticulation of the former Soviet system.[5] However, in East Asia, with only a brief interruption following the crisis, growth has been consistent with the production possibility envelope pushing steadily outward.[6]

Growth with Increasing Equality

The relationship between the distribution of income and economic growth is a complex one. At least two causalities are at work. One is the extent to which inequality in income distribution favors economic growth, while the other is the effect that growth has on the distribution of income. East Asian economies have combined high growth performance with increasing equality in distribution. This relationship is illustrated in Figure 15.1, which shows that in the East Asian countries high rates of growth have been associated with a falling Gini coefficient.[7] In contrast, in Latin America lower growth rates are accompanied by increasing inequality.

In conventional analysis the increasing inequality of income that often accompanies rapid growth is brought about by rising incomes in a dynamic sector, while traditional sectors lag behind. Such dispersion can assist the process of economic growth because the affluence is biased toward wealthier families who show a higher propensity to save, and increased savings can generate funds for investment. Nevertheless, East Asia experienced rapid growth and high propensities to save, despite a narrowing of the dispersion of income.

Another way of looking at the issue of economic inequality is to see what happened to the percentage of the population, and the numbers of individuals, who are subsisting on incomes less than the poverty level. Poverty is a relative measure defined by the World Bank as an inability to maintain a minimal standard of living. In all of the East Asian countries, rapid economic growth has been accompanied by

[4]These nine economies consist of the eight World Bank HPAEs plus the People's Republic of China.
[5]So far, however, as we shall see later on, only Poland is currently living up to this expectation.
[6]The exception is the crisis of 1998, which put many Asian economies into contraction.
[7]We discussed the Gini coefficient in Chapter 1. In technical terms, it measures the area between an observed Lorenz curve and the line represented by absolute equality. Consequently, a high Gini coefficient indicates greater inequality.

■ FIGURE 15.1

Income Distribution and Growth

This figure plots the relationship between the average per-head change in income and the change in the Gini coefficient for each of the economies. A fall in the Gini coefficient indicates increasing equality.

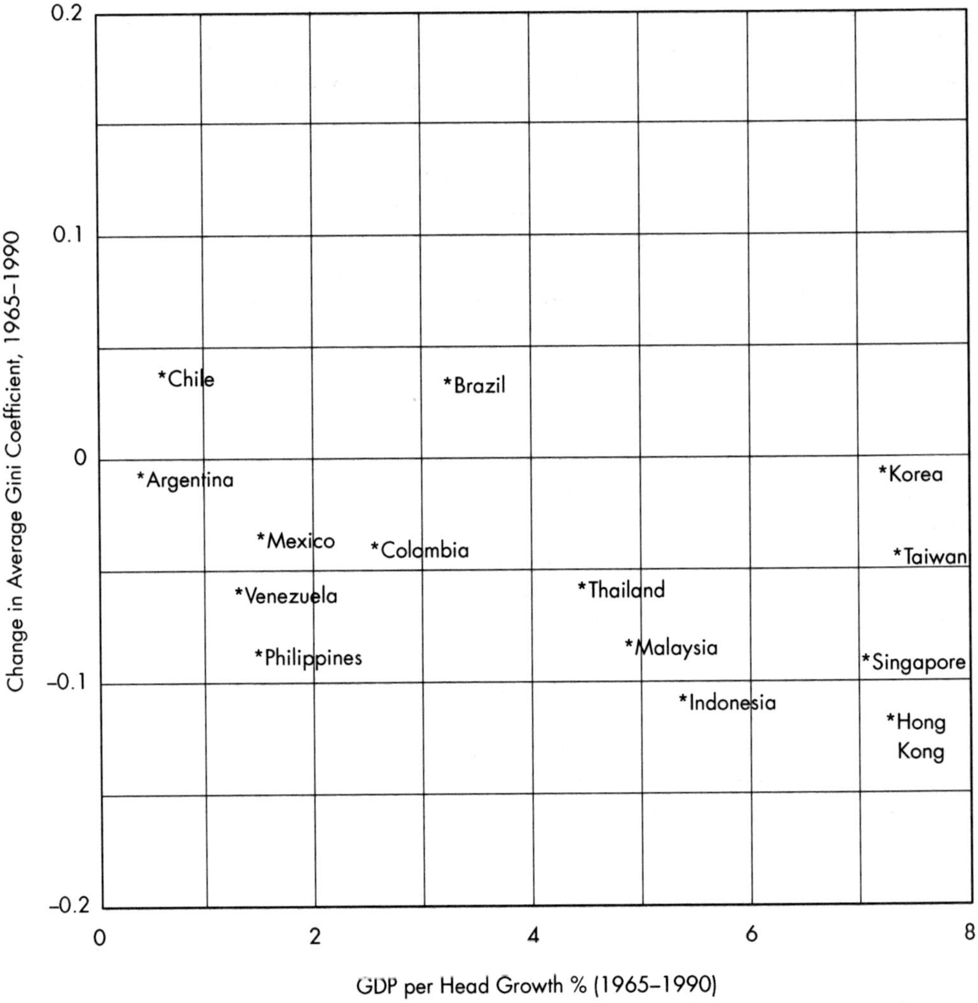

sharp declines in both the poverty rate and the absolute numbers living below the poverty level. In most other countries of the developing world, the poverty rate has fallen (Africa provides frequent exceptions), but a high population growth rate keeps the numbers in poverty growing.

ECONOMIC FEATURES OF THE MIRACLE

A Rapid Demographic Transition

Traditional societies are characterized by high and quite stable birthrates and high, though fluctuating, death rates. Industrialized societies, in contrast, are typified by low and relatively stable death rates, accompanied by low and occasionally fluctuating birthrates. The shift in these parameters from the traditional to the developed pattern is known as the **demographic transition**. Generally speaking, improved public health measures that eradicate catastrophic epidemics lead to a falling death rate, followed later by a fall of the birthrate as the cultural norms that favored larger families adjust to a changed environment. The lag between the two shifts is commonly called the "demographic gap" and results in a rapid increase in population as a low death rate is accompanied by a high birthrate for a generation or so. The longer the transition, the greater the population increase, and the greater the strain on the economy as population growth makes it more difficult to raise living standards. Gains in aggregate output fail to yield higher average welfare because the growing pie must be shared by a rapidly growing population.

The demographic transition in East Asia has been unusually rapid, and the fall of death rates has almost coincided with the drop in birth rates. Average birth and death rates both fell by about 50 percent between 1965 and 1980. This demographic shift contrasts sharply with sub-Saharan Africa, where a fall in the death rate comparable to East Asia was accompanied by a drop in the birth rate of less than 10 percent, resulting in rapid population expansion. Similar rapid population increases occurred in South Asia and Latin America.

A Rapid Accumulation of Human Capital

One cause of rapid demographic transition has been the sharp increase in human capital through education and the swift erosion of differential educational achievement between girls and boys. The success of HPAEs in narrowing this gender gap, especially in primary education, produced two consequences. First, it led to an increase in the available workforce equipped with basic tools of literacy, paving the way for a speedy increase in the female activity rates. Second, it is one factor responsible for the falling birthrate; an effect confirmed by many studies, though the causation is not simple and takes several paths. For example, more educated women are likely to marry later, are more likely to be engaged in paid employment (which increases the opportunity cost of children), and are likely to be more informed about contraceptive technologies. Moreover, as rising educational levels speed the demographic transition, falling birthrates themselves allow for rapid increases in human capital per individual. In countries where the birthrate remains high, the growth of the school-age population absorbs more educational resources, slowing the growth of enrollment rates and years of schooling per pupil. East Asian countries experienced a virtuous cycle: sharply lowered population growth fostered higher average educational attainment, which in turn results in further lowered birthrates. Enrollment rates in both primary and secondary education in

East Asian countries exceed the global average, even when controlling for income levels. Not only have more public resources been expended on education in East Asia than in other countries of similar affluence, but the education itself has been more effective than elsewhere. In all of the reliable international comparisons of educational achievement, East Asian children tend to perform better, perhaps explained by strong support for education in the family and the culture as a whole.

Sharp and Sustained Increases in Savings Rates

Another feature of East Asian economic performance is a rapid increase in savings rates, now the highest in the world. In 1965 average saving in East Asian economies was about 17 percent of GDP, a point or two less than in Latin America. During the following 25 years, savings rates more than doubled in East Asia, while they remained unchanged in Latin America. It is tempting to attribute the sustained increase in investment and the consequent increase in income to this high savings rate, but what caused this shift in savings behavior? One explanation is the government's role in creating and maintaining stable and accessible financial institutions, giving savers confidence that their money would be safe with financial intermediaries and raising the expected rate of return by eliminating risk associated with possible bankruptcy. However, whether the rapid increase in savings is the cause or the consequence of rapid income growth is still an important issue. Considerable evidence suggests that when income grows unexpectedly rapidly, consumption lags behind, creating increased savings that are in a sense unplanned. Another explanation lies in demographic factors. Falling birthrates and rapid increases in economic participation reduce the **dependency ratio**—the ratio of the nonworking population (who must be supported) to those who work. Life cycle savings theories support the idea that middle-aged workers save more in order to maintain a relatively stable consumption stream into retirement and old age.[8] This provides one explanation for a fall in savings rates. The greater the percentage of the population in retirement, everything else being equal, the lower the savings rate will be: a powerful reason for falling savings rates today in the aging societies of North America, Europe, and Japan.

Although both rapid income growth and demographic factors played a part in increased savings, public policy and institutional change also had an effect. The most important macroeconomic factor in encouraging savings is the maintenance of positive real interest rates. If inflation outpaces the nominal interest rate, the real return to savings is negative, and incentives to save, rather than to consume or invest in goods and real estate, are reduced. Taming inflation, through fiscal and monetary conservatism, can be important. By and large (although not universally) the HPAEs have been successful in restraining inflation and maintaining positive real interest rates. The average real rate in the HPAEs for the late 1970s and 1980s was 1.59 percent.[9] Most other regions of the less-developed world showed negative

[8]Ando, Albert, and Franco Modigliani, "The Life Cycle Hypothesis of Saving: Aggregate Implications and Tests," *American Economic Review* 53, no. 1 (1963), pp. 55–84.

[9]Of the HPAEs, only Hong Kong and Japan showed negative real rates during this period.

real interest rates and lower savings rates. Moreover, real interest rates in all HPAEs showed a low standard deviation, giving an element of predictability important for savings behavior.[10]

East Asian governments also created a system that favors savings by reducing the risk to bank depositors and ensuring that they share in the increased demand for funds. One approach focuses on bank regulation and relatively successful supervision of the problem banks. Such regulation reduces the probability of bankruptcy and loss of deposits, the high incidence of which is a strong disincentive to savings in the formal sector. Banking crises have occurred in all of the HPAEs, and they are probably inevitable in rapidly growing economies, but their severity and duration even in the crisis years of 1997–1998, were curtailed by intervention.

Most East Asia nations established regulations that limit competition and keep banking the preserve of a few correspondingly larger banks. Hong Kong, Indonesia, and Singapore are notable exceptions and welcome new financial institutions. (Indeed the livelihood and development strategy of both Hong Kong and Singapore depend in large part on the attraction of financial intermediaries, while Indonesia prior to its collapse was notable for the rapid—and, in some eyes, premature—liberalization of its capital markets.)[11] The success of a restrictive policy depends on a trade-off between the beneficial effects of greater stability (which tends to increase savers' confidence in the safety of their assets and, therefore, raises the savings rate) and the potential for inefficiency and higher costs because of monopolistic practices (tending to reduce the return to savers and thus lower savings). The evidence is ambiguous, though it is probable that enough oligopolistic competition is present to limit inefficiency and protect the saver.[12]

As an additional guarantee for the saver, the governments of the HPAEs (with the exception of Hong Kong and Singapore) resort to a policy of regulating interest spreads from time to time. Such a policy limits the amount of economic rent that the banks earn from the monopoly power created by regulatory limitations on entry. Margins, when regulated, have generally been set at levels comparable to those in developed nations, and lower than those commonly found in developing countries. Savings by small savers were generally encouraged by the existence of state-owned **postal savings institutions**. Before this institutional innovation (which was a common feature of virtually all Western European economies) was applied to Asia, high transaction costs, poor access, and minimum deposit requirements prevented many rural savers from access to top financial intermediaries. The postal savings institutions gathered and aggregated small savings and used them to finance development and private bank loan activity.

---

[10]The exception that should be noted is Latin America, which, largely because of strongly positive real rates in Bolivia and Chile, showed regional positive averages. However, the standard deviations in Latin America were very large, indicating a low level of predictability in the real return and a consequent disincentive for saving by the risk averse.

[11]See World Bank, *The East Asian Miracle* (New York: Oxford University Press, 1993), pp. 238–239.

[12]In fact, the concentration ratio in the banking sector in East Asia is similar to that of developed countries, where we assume adequate competition is at work. However, the paths taken to arrive at that point are quite different. In most developed countries, high concentration ratios were arrived at through merger and consolidation, not barriers to entry.

Finally, it should be noted that three of the HPAEs (Malaysia, Japan, and Singapore) required forced savings through comprehensive and mandatory pension plans or provident funds. The evidence on whether these plans increased total saving is mixed, and, to some extent at least, they act as a substitute for private saving. One study of Japanese savings patterns concluded that total savings were reduced by the mandatory pension scheme.

A High Rate of Private Investment

Throughout their period of rapid growth, East Asian economies maintained the investment share of GDP at a level 7 percent higher than that of other low- and middle-income economies, and saving takes some of the credit. In a world of mobile capital, domestic savings are not the only source of investment finance, nor need all domestic savings necessarily be used for capital formation at home; some may be invested or loaned abroad. However, it is a fact that refraining from consumption provides a source of funds that can be channeled for domestic investment.

High investment has other causes. First, credit must go to credible and defensible property rights. Experience from other parts of the world (especially the transition economies of Eastern Europe) indicates that one of the largest deterrents to investment is uncertainty about whether the property will be secure from expropriation by the government or others in the future.[13] Second, the East Asian governments generally provide the physical infrastructure and human capital to make investment both possible and attractive. Transportation facilities and access to electrical power are particularly important aspects of economic infrastructure and the available evidence suggests that large strides have been made in these areas. An adequate supply of appropriately skilled labor is also complementary to investment, and the efforts and results of the aggressive increase in primary school education provides East Asia with an attractive labor force, which increases the efficiency of domestic capital and is a lure for foreign capital.

Providing Access to Capital These government policies all have played a role in increasing the level of domestic activity and are relatively uncontroversial in their effect. More contentious is the active intervention in credit markets, which has been a feature of East Asian governmental policy. In general, economic efficiency is fostered by reliance on market mechanisms to allocate factors of production among competing uses. Intervention in the operation of markets is justified only by market failure, or when it can be clearly demonstrated that the social rate of return on investment differs substantially from the perceived private rate. With respect to the credit markets, in the HPAEs the two causes of market failure most generally adduced are information failures and coordination problems.

Directed Credit One feature of the East Asian system is government policies of **directed credit**, frequently extended at below-market interest rates, to industries

[13]Maxim Boycko, Andrei Shleifer, and Robert Vishny, *Privatizing Russia* (Cambridge, MA: MIT Press, 1996).

deemed vital and selected by the authorities as being strategically important for growth. The specific mechanisms of directing credit differ from country to country. In Korea, where the banking sector was almost totally nationalized during the period of the most rapid growth, selective financing was achieved *directly*. In other countries the government "leaned" on the banking sector to provide the loans to the targeted sectors. If a directed credit policy is to result in a higher aggregate rate of investment rather than merely to affect the distribution among industries, the government action must correct some imperfection in the capital market, perhaps the reluctance of the banking sector to shoulder loans in long-term industrial projects rather than real estate or commerce.

Development Banks In addition to directing the credit policy of private banks, some HPAEs (particularly Japan, Korea, and Taiwan) created specialist publicly owned development banking institutions whose exclusive purpose is to make long-term loans to industry. Frequently these institutions focus on small and medium-sized industry because that sector is often neglected by the private banking sector as too risky or too costly to operate in. In these countries the development banks played an important role, especially in the early stages of development, tending to be less vital as later development produced financial deepening.

The Limited Role of Stock and Bond Markets The role of equity and bond markets in providing investment capital to industry in the East Asian economies has been modest, though it increased with economic and financial maturity. In the Asian context, the expansion of both bond and stock markets should be seen as a result of growth rather than the cause of it. In part this minimal role is due to a policy decision; government control of the financial sector repressed all the forms of financial deepening, including debt and equity markets. In Japan, for example, the government gave the banks a monopoly in the issuance of long-term debentures, which suppressed the growth of corporate bond trading. Stock markets provided only limited capital in the early stages of industrialization in Japan and have grown to some degree subsequently. Joseph Stiglitz, formerly chief economist at the World Bank, finds the evidence suggests that equity markets play only a small role anywhere in Asia.[14]

Tax Policies Taxation affects the attractiveness of private investment by changing the after-tax, or net return. High rates of corporate or profits taxes reduce the net return on investment and tend therefore to lower investment rates. Lower business taxes, or preferential personal tax rates for business-related income, increase investment rates by raising the after-tax yield. Two broad alternative strategies are open to governments in determining the appropriate taxation on investment income. On the one hand, they may pursue a policy of generally low and nonselective rates. This approach will tend to make investment relatively attractive, but it will leave the composition of investment between the different sectors to be determined by private market forces. The alternative strategy is to use the tax

[14]See Stiglitz, "Some Lessons from the Asian Miracle," *The World Bank Research Observer* 11, no. 2 (August 1966), pp. 151–177.

system to discriminate between sectors and hence encourage those activities that the government, rather than the market, prizes most highly.

In general, East Asian governments opted for the latter approach, adopting quite high basic corporate tax rates and using a complex system of investment credits, tax holidays, and discriminatory rates to encourage particular industries. In the eyes of most economists such discriminatory policy is *a priori* dangerous and can be justified only in the case of market failure. Such failure may occur, for example, when the government has more information than is available to the actors in the financial market or when social returns deviate substantially from private returns. Even when convincing evidence of market failure is seen and discrimination justified, the tax scheme must be well designed and efficiently managed to achieve the intended results. Japan, South Korea, Taiwan, Malaysia, Thailand, and Singapore all offer examples of highly interventionist tax policy, and much evidence suggests that it has often been counterproductive. One study of South Korea found that only about 6 percent of total Korean growth between 1962 and 1982 could be attributed to interventionist tax policy. Such a yield probably does not justify the uncertainty introduced into the system, nor the resources that the constantly changing system absorbs. Hong Kong, with its generally low rates, stands as an exception to the tinkering of most other Asian governments and may be the preferred model.

Low Capital Goods Prices The real level of investment is determined both by the nominal resources committed to capital formation and the price of investment goods. East Asian countries have been successful relative to other nations in keeping down the domestic price of imported investment goods. During the 1960s most low- and middle-income countries saw more rapid inflation in the price of investment goods than in GDP as a whole, which was achieved through the management of tariff policies and exchange rate movements. Most important was the policy of allowing investment goods to enter virtually tariff free. A cost of this policy was that a protective strategy for the domestic investment goods sector was impossible, but cheaper access to capital goods benefited a broader range of industries.[15]

Bounding Risks The rate of investment is largely determined by the expected rate of return, which is itself a composite of upside and downside risk. By **bounding risks**, government programs placed limits on the downside risk for many industries by granting subsidies to those firms that undertook risky projects and by allowing firms to combine into cartels to resist the impacts of downturns in demand.

Controls on the Export of Capital One way of encouraging domestic investment is to place controls on the outflow of capital. The governments of Japan, Korea, and Taiwan all formed policies that deterred or prevented private capital from leaving, tying the hands of domestic investors and forcing them to choose between investing at home or not investing at all. In the long run such **capital controls** might lower the rate of return on capital and hinder the growth of gross national product, but in the short term they do create positive effects on domestic capital formation and therefore employment and labor productivity.

---

[15]World Bank, *The Asian Miracle*, p. 232.

Repression of Interest Rates A feature of East Asian growth has been the moderate **repression of interest rates**. This policy means that the rate of interest paid to the saver is kept low, consequently making funds available for capital investment at correspondingly lower rates. Repression is most common when inflation rises without a corresponding adjustment in government-regulated interest rates. This situation could lead to low and possibly negative interest rates for savers, which might result in a serious and depressing impact on savings. The key therefore is "moderation." Several Asian economies successfully kept the real rate for savers relatively low, and, arguably, thereby increased the rate of investment and growth.

Export Growth

No discussion of the characteristics of East Asian growth can omit the extraordinary emphasis placed on the export sector. As we noted earlier, the rate of growth of exports in the Asian economies as a group has been remarkable, and a case can be made for overall success originating in the export sector. However, while exporting has been important, it is essential to understand that export growth owed much to domestic reform.

High Labor Productivity Growth

The consistently high rate of labor productivity growth in the HPAEs can be attributed to several factors. Some of the growth is due to high rates of investment increasing capital per worker, and some may be owed to increased human capital as a result of schooling. However, some is the result of more efficient practices and the adoption of new technology, called **total factor productivity (TFP)** growth and conventionally measured as a residual, after allowing for the effects of increased physical and human capital. The World Bank finds that about two-thirds of HPAE productivity growth is due to capital accumulation and therefore about one-third is due to TFP growth, in its view, a high rate. However, this view has its critics who note that much of the increase of TFP resulted from movement of workers from sector to sector, and though this gain contributes to allocative efficiency, it is a general and predictable consequence of industrialization. We turn to this debate in the following section.

THE DEBATE OVER THE MIRACLE

The Market, or Neoclassical, Explanation

In the 1980s much of the literature concerned with East Asia's high levels of growth focused on reliance on market fundamentals and limited government intervention. This neoclassical view stressed the importance of markets in establishing prices that reflect scarcity and therefore lead to efficient resource allocation. The role of the state was crucial but largely limited to establishing macroeconomic stability and the framework (including the legal structure, property rights, and the provision of public goods) within which markets and businesses could operate.

In this view intersectoral distortions were limited:

> East Asia's success is due to the similar rewards for selling in the domestic and foreign markets. Because variation of incentives across sectors, as measured by the effective rate of protection of value added, has been limited, inputs have flowed to sectors roughly on the basis of static comparative advantage, and international competition has provided an impetus for cost discipline and technological upgrading. Traded inputs have been made available to exporters at international prices, and exporters have faced an international price regime in making their decisions. Finally, factor markets have been roughly competitive, so positive real rates of interest have prevailed, and there has been an absence of duality in the wage structure by size of firm or sector of production.[16]

The Revisionist Critique

In the late 1980s a series of criticisms of this neoclassical explanation began to be articulated stemming from detailed research on the operation of the Japanese, Korean, and Taiwanese economies, especially in the work of Howard Pack and Larry Westphal, Alice Amsden, and Robert Wade. These authors carefully documented that at least in Japan, South Korea, and Taiwan, the governments targeted particular sectors for growth, afforded these sectors protection from foreign competition, and granted subsidized access to capital, frequently on the basis of export performance. Far from providing a level playing field, the revisionists argued, government intervention favored specific sectors which enjoyed high growth and effectively powered the economy.

The revisionists stressed the high level of market failure in developing economies. In particular, information is lacking; spillovers are common, and the market is incomplete and therefore unable to fulfill the task of coordination. The government acted to lead the market and attempted to correct for these imperfections by manipulating key prices (especially in capital markets) in order to promote growth, presenting the vision of the government outperforming the market. This approach is, in some eyes, troublesome, particularly when the recent economic history of Korea, Japan, and Taiwan includes many instances of the bureaucracy leading industry into socially unproductive blind alleys. These range from the petrochemical drive in Japan to high-definition TV and the current financial chaos in Korea.

The "Market Friendly" Approach

To accommodate the idea that the market is in the long run efficient, yet gains may come from selective government intervention, the World Bank chose to stress the East Asian approach is neither market oriented nor wholly interventionist but is, in a phrase, a **"market friendly"** approach.

In the World Bank's view:

> The market friendly approach captures important aspects of East Asia's success. These economies are stable macroeconomically, have high shares of international trade in GDP, invest heavily in people, and have strong competition among firms. But the characteristics are the outcome of many different policy instruments. And the instruments chosen partic-

[16]See World Bank, *The Asian Miracle*, p. 82.

ularly in the northeast HPAEs, Japan, Korea, Taiwan, China, sometimes included extensive government intervention in markets to guide private sector resource allocation.[17]

Augmenting the Market Through Competition One of the principal problems of government interventionism is that it leads to a soft-budget constraint. The virtue of the market is that it is unsentimental and winnows out the weaker firms, forces firms to minimize costs, and focuses attention on producing goods that are in demand. In contrast, government subsidies become politicized, enabling underperforming firms to remain in business because of their access to forms of subsidy. As we have seen, one of the chief tools of government interventionism in East Asia is directed credit, accessed by firms at below-market rates. A key to successfully **augmenting the market** is to develop a system that performs the same job as the market—picks winners—and therefore determines the direction of subsidy.

One way to "pick winners" is to promote the development of several firms in an industry and conduct a form of contest among them to see who will enjoy further government support. In East Asia the yardstick, for which the prize of renewed subsidy is awarded, has frequently been export success. This type of contest serves two purposes. It provides the necessary foreign exchange to pay for imports of necessary raw materials, defense equipment, and capital goods. It also offers a more objective test of efficiency than the domestic market. Although exports might be helped by undervalued exchange rates, such an advantage would be common to all domestic firms and therefore relative export performance is a good index of relative competitiveness. In the World Bank's opinion, using exports as a performance yardstick generated substantial benefits because export success is a better indicator of economic efficiency than performance success in a protected domestic market.

Insulating the Bureaucracy The usefulness of any competition depends on a clear definition of the rules and effective arbitration of any disputes. In matters of trade policy it is largely up to the economic bureaucracy to articulate the rules, and, until recently, the conventional wisdom was that the East Asian bureaucracies were both competent and insulated from the pressures of politics and business. In most of East Asia, civil service posts are well paid and enjoy respect. However, the recent plethora of corruption led to questioning of bureaucratic honesty. Given the massive payments from business to politicians, something must have occurred in return, and that presumably was preferential access to some form of subsidy. Despite the World Bank's glowing comments about **insulating the bureaucracy**, the evidence suggests that in Japan and Korea substantial influence peddling was at work by both bureaucrats and politicians.

The Role of Trade We noted earlier that export growth has been a persistent feature of the East Asian success, and it is tempting to regard it as being fundamental to economic growth in the region. Certainly in the World Bank's eyes export success provided a proof of efficiency, a source of funds to purchase capital equipment and technology, as well as substantial employment.

[17]See World Bank, *The Asian Miracle*, p. 85.

However, several critics have taken the World Bank to task for overrating the role of trade. Alwyn Young asserts that the criterion to judge "miracles" is not the growth rate *per se*, because growth rate is largely a function of the accumulation of factors of production. The proper criterion for a miracle is an unusually rapid rate of growth of total factor productivity (TFP), the residual left in the growth rate where the contributions of increased quantities of capital and labor are all accounted for. Young shows in a series of articles that TFP growth in Asia has not been especially rapid despite surging exports; indeed, it has been lower than that in several economies that showed slower export growth. Consequently he finds that exporting in itself is no guarantor of growth. Indeed, restricting access to the domestic market (the opposite of openness) is arguably more crucial than export penetration of foreign markets.

Dani Rodrik argues with respect to Japan that it was this closure to the world, coupled with a high degree of domestic competition that contributed most to Japanese success. He cites Hiroyuki Odagiri and Akiri Goto:

> The restriction on imports and foreign direct investment [into] Japan was probably the most important policy until the early 1970s (as regards innovation). Restricting the growing Japanese market, already the second largest in the capitalist world in the late 1960s, to the Japanese firms who were competing intensively among themselves gave a strong incentive to invest in plants, equipment and R&D.[18]

THE SUSTAINABILITY OF THE MIRACLE

Despite the astonishing speed of growth in many Asian economies, an ongoing and vital dispute concerns the nature of the growth process. One school declared that it is no "miracle" at all: the rapid observed growth is explicable in terms of conventional economics; that is, most of the increase in output could be attributed to increases of factor inputs (labor and capital), the securing of economies of scale, and the redeployment of workers from sectors with low marginal products per worker (largely small-holding agriculture) to those with higher marginal products (the manufacturing sector). In our analysis of Korea, for example, we saw that most economic growth could be readily accounted for by the increase of factor inputs. The population has been mobilized, participation rates increased, and the capital input per worker raised. In the case of Korea, roughly 75 percent of the growth between 1963 and 1990 was accounted for by changes in factor inputs. The gain in the productivity of those factor inputs represented only a residual 25 percent. Moreover, most of the gain in output per unit of input was accounted for by the relocation of labor from low productivity agriculture to industry and well-documented, though limited, economies of scale. That leaves less than 1 percent of growth to be accounted for by improvement of technique, gains in skill, higher productivity due to supervision, and other factors not included elsewhere. This assessment led Paul Krugman to claim that, relying on increases in factors of production, East Asian growth is like the growth of Stalin's Russia, impressive but extensive, and therefore not sustainable.

---

[18]Dani Rodrik, "King Kong Meets Godzilla: The World Bank and the East Asian Miracle," in *Miracle or Design? Lessons from the East Asian Experience,* Albert Fishlow et al., eds. (Washington, DC: Overseas Development Council, 1994).

The subsequent work of Nicholas Crafts supports Krugman's claims. Crafts concludes that:

> First, factor accumulation has been much more important than total factor productivity growth, especially in comparison to earlier epochs of rapid catch-up growth in western Europe and Japan; nonetheless, productivity performance has been stronger than has been allowed by critics of the east Asian experience. Second, a temporary demographic advantage of rising labor force participation has given these economies an added boost to economic growth during recent decades. Third, development has taken place rapidly from an initial position of economic backwardness, which has generated its own legacy of financial and other institutions.[19]

In response to such objections, supporters of the view that Asian growth is a miracle argue that the conventional way of measuring total factor productivity systematically understates the real role of technology and technical change. Moreover, other considerations suggest that what happened in Asia was a profound and unusual change. First is the real achievement of breaking the cycle of inward-looking underdevelopment. Second, the elevation of savings rates from about 6 percent of household income to over 30 percent is a kind of miracle in itself, particularly when associated with a consistent ability to match saving with productive investments.

However, it is important to assess what has been undone by the financial crisis and its aftermath. Was the crisis a "bump in the road" or did it permanently change the growth prospects of the region, and at the same time call into question the viability of the "state-led development model."

What Caused the Asian Crisis?

In the midst of the debate about the causes of the crisis, there is some agreement. Sentiment about the region's prospects became rather too bullish in the mid-1990s and foreign investment capital flowed into the area. This surplus on capital account inevitably created a deficit in the current accounts of most of the east and southeast Asian nations. Confidence in the region was artificially promoted by the heavy involvement of governments in the investment process. Their role was taken by some as a guarantee of investment viability and increased the perception of repayment. Within nations a pervasive system of directed credit led domestic banks to take on excessive quantities of questionable loans. The result was overinvestment in productive capacity and overborrowing from abroad.

In early 1997 the problems began to unwind. Initial difficulties in Thailand and Korea raised warning flags, and foreign investors and lenders began to repatriate their capital as fast as possible. This flight led to a **run on the banks** and a credit crunch for many firms. Share values plummeted and bank balance sheets suffered as assets were wiped out. Panic set in and the situation became progressively worse.

Policy Response to the Crisis

In the aftermath of the crisis, a great deal of criticism was raised relating to the conduct of IMF policy during and after the crisis. The IMF response had two principal

[19]Nicholas Crafts, "East Asian Growth: Before and After the Crisis," IMF, working paper WP/98/137, 1998.

dimensions. On the one hand it extended a great deal of credit to the region, enabling the governments to recapitalize the banks (frequently taking them into public ownership) and assisting foreign investors to extricate some of their capital. At the same time it required policies of fiscal and monetary stringency as conditions of credit extension. The Fund has been criticized on both scores. The first charge is that the credit did little to assist the affected countries but primarily helped western lenders to get their money out. Critics charge that the capital had been committed under unstable conditions for profit and the lenders should have taken the consequences as they fell. Otherwise the **moral hazard** implications are worrisome. In the future, critics argue, banks and other lenders will fail to perform due diligence because they feel that the role of international bodies is to protect them against the consequences of unwise lending albeit in the name of preserving the viability of the international financial system. Moreover, it is said, countries will behave irresponsibly because they know that the IMF is there to bankroll them.

Stanley Fischer, then managing director of the IMF, tried to address these issues:

> Of course, not everyone agrees with the international community's approach of trying to cushion the effects of such crises. Some say that it would be better simply to let the chips fall where they may, arguing that to come to the assistance of countries in crisis will only encourage more reckless behavior on the part of borrowers and lenders. I do not share the view that we should step aside in these cases. To begin with, the notion that the availability of IMF programs encourages reckless behavior by countries is far-fetched: no country would deliberately court such a crisis even if it thought international assistance would be forthcoming. The economic, financial, social, and political pain is simply too great; nor do countries show any great desire to enter IMF programs unless they absolutely have to.[20]

The second criticism is that the fiscal and monetary policies urged on the governments in the region contributed to the crisis by causing a sharp drop in demand and creating more economic contraction, bankruptcies, and unemployment. In a potentially recessionary situation, the IMF's critics maintain, steps should be taken to bolster demand, not to reduce it.

Again, Fischer articulated the IMF position.

> Other observers have advocated more expansionary fiscal programs to offset the inevitable slowdown in economic growth. The balance here is a fine one. As already noted, at the outset of the crisis, countries need to firm their fiscal positions, to deal both with the future costs of financial restructuring and—depending on the balance of payments situation—the need to reduce the current account deficit. Beyond that, if the economic situation worsens, the IMF generally agrees with the country to let automatic stabilizers work and the deficit to widen somewhat. However, we cannot remain indifferent to the level of the fiscal deficit, particularly since a country in crisis typically has only limited access to borrowing and since the alternative of printing money would be potentially disastrous in these circumstances.

The Aftermath

As noted, the long-term effect of the crisis has been less than was feared at the time, an especially surprising outcome when viewed against the problems of the Euro-

---

[20]"The Asian Crisis: A View from the IMF," Address by Stanley Fischer, First Deputy Managing Director of the International Monetary Fund at the Midwinter Conference of the Bankers' Association for Foreign Trade, Washington, DC, January 22, 1998.

pean and U.S. economies during 2000–2002. These difficulties included a major U.S. market collapse and a sharp fall in all kinds of information technology-related equipment that dealt a sharp blow to the economies of Korea and Taiwan. Almost every country in the region experienced positive growth in every year except 2001. The exceptions are Taiwan and Singapore in 2001, and Japan in 1998, 2001, and 2002.

Foreign investment inflows are now positive into the region, although (except for China) they are running at about half of their 1996 and 1997 levels. The economies do still face major problems. The burden of **nonperforming loans** is still considerable; in Indonesia in early 2002, some 50 percent were nonperforming, with almost 30 percent in Thailand.

Nevertheless, it can be said that the region is on the road to recovery.[21] The question is whether the developmental model should change, and whether this change will occur as a natural consequence of the crisis or will require policy intervention.

THE LESSONS OF THE MIRACLE

The "lessons" of the miracle are complex, and the applicability of the East Asian experience to other countries (for example, in South Asia, Latin America, or in the successor states to the Soviet Union) must be in doubt; but some useful generalities about the role of systems and policy in establishing sustained development may be drawn out here:

1. Macroeconomic stability is an important prerequisite for sustained economic expansion. Growth is not possible in a hyperinflationary situation, or for that matter in one of widely fluctuating demand. However, single-digit inflation is not a necessity; moderately high inflation rates have been associated with rapid growth in South Korea and elsewhere.
2. Government action is essential in establishing the preconditions of growth, especially in transportation, communication, and education. As Patrick found in Japan, macroindustrial policy creating infrastructure and human capital does work.
3. The record of microeconomic industrial policy has been mixed. Some apparent successes have been counterweighted by some very notable failures. Problems are more likely the closer the economy gets to the cutting edge of new technology. In the early stages of industrialization it is easier to predict the most appropriate sectors to favor, since changes in the industrial structure can follow an established pattern of comparative advantage. In later phases of growth it becomes harder to "pick winners," as the Japanese experience with HDTV shows.
4. Reliance on directed credit may have adverse consequences for the banking sector, which can be left with a portfolio of losers. If they are not guided by bureaucrats, bankers will take care to assess the risks associated with a loan. The direction of credit by planning agencies distorts the allocative efficiency of financial markets and removes discretion from the bankers. Being forced to

[21]*East Asia: The Road to Recovery* (Washington, DC: World Bank, 1998).

lend to politicians' favorites, rather than the most potentially productive firms, can upset the stability of the financial sector, as experiences in South Korea and Japan showed in the Asian financial crisis.

5. Education expenditure is generally worthwhile, but is most effective when it is directed toward elementary education. Raising the literacy rate is cheap relative to producing a university graduate, and the greatest gains in workforce productivity are provided by a literate workforce.
6. The probity of financial markets is important. Individuals are less likely to save if they lack faith in financial intermediaries. Somewhat surprisingly the Asian financial crisis of 1997–1998 has not had a profound affect on personal saving.
7. Stock markets have not been an important element in the initial growth and development of Asian economies. Equity markets in early stages of development tended to be shallow, rather volatile, and more significant in the redistribution of wealth than in the creation of it. Even in the most developed of the Asian economies, Japan, the stock market has been manipulated and has been a potential source of economic instability.
8. Foreign direct investment has not been a dominant factor in Asian growth. Japan's success was financed to a large degree out of domestic saving; in Korea loans from multilateral agencies were a substantial factor. In Indonesia and Singapore foreign investment has been more vital. In fact, the greater the reliance on foreign finance the more vulnerable an economy was to the panic and capital outflow of the crisis years.
9. Competitions—for example, those predicated on export performance—can be useful ways to augment the market, but only if they are well designed and disinterestedly administered. Recent problems in Korea concerning the dominance of few major groups call into question how well Korean "competitions" helped the long-run growth of the economy. It is possible that the reliance on such competitions encouraged the overexpansion, and subsequent collapse, of the dominant *chaebol*.
10. Well-paid and respected civil servants lower the probability of corruption. For a long time the image of incorruptible and competent civil servants was a vaunted characteristic of the Asian model. American businesspeople, deeply mistrustful of government officials at home, attributed farseeing powers to those of Japan and Korea. However, more systematic studies of the Asian experience revealed a much higher degree of corruption and a lower degree of competence than once thought the case.

THE LESSON OF THE CRISIS

Finally, we should note that, whatever its other strengths, the Asia model of development has at its heart a legacy of weak financial institutions with its roots in the subservience of the banking sector to a powerful bureaucracy. This relationship, and consequent weakness, led in no small part to the financial crisis of 1997 and to the continuing overhang of nonperforming loans that will bedevil the financial sectors of some nations well into the new millennium, especially Japan, Korea, and Thailand. The Crafts study comes to the point:

> . . . despite its favorable attributes, such as effective mechanisms for technology transfer, outward orientation, and high savings, investment and human capital accumulation, there are downsides to the developmental state model, including a tendency to wasteful investment and the difficulties that it may pose for the transition to freer capital markets. These last are more attractive after the initial phase of development when coordination problems loom less large and diminishing returns are a bigger concern. Because the greatest successes of this managed development have come in the context of export-oriented manufacturing and industrialization, [I conclude] that an alternate model may be more appealing in the coming years of de-industrialization.[22]

The last point is a key one. The Asian nations' growth was predicated on the manufacture of tradable goods, and low labor costs were an important element of comparative advantage. As labor costs creep up, the economy must shift to high value services, and the "commodity" approach will not fit well to the new requirements. The problem is, how should a change be effected and what "alternate model" is suitable?

KEY TERMS AND CONCEPTS

augmenting the market
bounding risks
capital controls
demographic transition
dependency ratio
directed credit
high-performing East Asian economies (HPAEs)
insulating the bureaucracy
"market friendly"
moral hazard
nonperforming loans
postal savings institutions
repression of interest rates
run on the banks
total factor productivity (TFP)

QUESTIONS FOR DISCUSSION

1. How did a rapid demographic transition help growth in most East Asian economies?
2. How have high rates of investment been maintained in East Asian economies?
3. Have stock markets and foreign capital been important in Asian growth?
4. How has financial repression assisted growth?
5. What led to East Asian growth being described as "market friendly"?

[22]Nicholas Crafts, "East Asian Growth: Before and After the Crisis," IMF, working paper WP/98/137, 1998.

6. Is insulating the bureaucracy from political pressure a good thing? How is it done?
7. How can competitions for credit be said to be "market-augmenting"?

RESOURCES

Web Sites

Asian Crisis Information.......................................http://www.stern.nyu.edu/globalmacro/

The best Web site on the Asian Crisis is Professor Nouriel Roubini's at the Stern School, New York University**Association of Southeast Asian Nations** ...http://www.aseansec.org/

United Nations Economic and Social Commission for Asia and the Pacific ....http://www.unescap.org/

World Bank http://lnweb18.worldbank.org/eap/eap.nsf

More current material can be found on the East Asian and Pacific subsite of the World Bank.

Books and Articles

Adams, Gerard F., and Shinichi Ichimura (eds.). *East Asian Development: Will the East Asian Growth Miracle Survive?* New York: Praeger, 1998.

Amsden, Alice H. "Why Isn't the Whole World Experimenting with the East Asian Model to Development?: Review of *The East Asian Miracle.*" *World Development* 22, 1994, 626–633.

Arogyaswamy, Bernard. *The Asian Miracle, Myth, and Mirage.* Westport, CT: Quorum Books, 1998.

Bello, Walden, and Stephanie Rosenfeld. *Dragons in Distress: Asia's Miracle Economies in Crisis.* San Francisco: Institute for Food and Development Policy, 1990. Reviewed in *Journal of Contemporary Asia* 22, 1992, 546–551.

Campos, Jose Edgardo, and Hilton L. Root (contributor). *The Key to the Asian Miracle: Making Shared Growth Credible.* Washington, DC: Brookings Institution, 1996.

Chen, Xiangming. "The Changing Roles of Free Economic Zones in Development: A Comparative Analysis of Capitalist and Socialist Cases in East Asia." *Studies in Comparative International Development,* Fall 1994, 3–25.

Claessens, Stjin, Simeon Djankov, and Leora Klapper. "Resolution of Corporate Distress: Evidence from East Asia's Financial Crisis," World Bank working paper, 1998.

Claessens, Stjin, Simeon Djankov, and Larry H. P. Lang. "Who Controls East Asian Corporations?" World Bank working paper, 1998.

Crafts, Nicholas. "East Asian Growth: Before and After the Crisis." IMF, working paper WP/98/137, 1998.

Deyo, Frederic C. (ed.). *The Political Economy of the New Asian Industrialism.* Ithaca, NY: Cornell University Press, 1987.

Fishlow, Albert (ed.). *Miracle or Design? Lessons from the East Asian Experience.* Washington, DC: Overseas Development Council, 1994.

Garran, Robert. *Tigers Tamed: The End of the Asian Miracle.* Honolulu: University of Hawaii Press, 1998.

Goldstein, Steven M. *Mini Dragons: Fragile Economic Miracles in the Pacific.* New York: Ambrose Video Publishing, 1991.

International Monetary Fund. *East Asian Growth Before and After the Crisis.* IMF working paper, 1998.

Jomo, K. S. (ed.). *Tigers in Trouble: Financial Governance, Liberalisation and Crises in East Asia.* London: Zed Books, 1999.

Kwon, Jene. "The East Asia Challenge to Neoclassical Orthodoxy." *World Development,* 1994, 635–644.

Lall, Sanjaya. "The East Asian Miracle: Does the Bell Toll for Industrial Strategy?" *World Development,* 1994, 645–654.

Litonjua, M. D. "Outside the Den of Dragons: The Philippines and the NICs of Asia." *Studies in Comparative International Development,* Winter 1994, 3–30.

McVey, Ruth. *Southeast Asian Capitalists.* Ithaca, NY: Cornell University Press, 1992. Reviewed by Mike Moore, *The Journal of Development Studies,* April 1994, 724–725.

Park, Yung Chul, "Does East Asia Need a New Paradigm for Development?" Paper delivered at the Brookings Institution Trade Forum, 2002. Available at http://www.brookings.edu/dybdocroot/es/commentary/journals/trade/papers/200205_park.pdf.

Perkins, Dwight H. "There Are at Least Three Models of East Asian Development." *World Development,* 1994, 655–661.

Rodrik, Dani. "King Kong Meets Godzilla: The World Bank and the East Asian Miracle." In *Miracle or Design? Lessons from the East Asian Experience,* Albert Fishlow (ed.). Washington, DC: Overseas Development Council, 1994.

Sengupta, Jati K. "Growth in NICs in Asia: Some Tests of New Growth Theory." *Journal of Development Studies,* January 1993, 342–358.

Stiglitz, Joseph E. "Some Lessons from the East Asian Miracle." *The World Bank Research Observer* 11, no. 2 (August 1996), 151–177.

Stiglitz, Joseph E., and Arilou Uy. "Financial Markets, Public Policy and the East Asian Miracle," *World Bank Research Observer,* 1996, 249–276.

"A Survey of Business in Asia: The Search for the Asian Manager." *The Economist,* March 9, 1996, 1–26.

"A Survey of East Asian Economies: Frozen Miracle." *The Economist,* March 7, 1998, 58.

Tai, Hung-chao (ed.). *Confucianism and Economic Development: An Oriental Alternative?* Washington, DC: Washington Institute Press, 1989.

Tan, Gerald. *The End of the Asian Miracle?: Tracing Asia's Economic Transformation.* Singapore: Times Academic Press, 1999.

Terry, Edith Buchanan. *The Rise and Fall of the Asian Miracle.* Armonk, NY: M.E. Sharpe, 1999.

Wade, Robert (ed.). *Miracle or Design? Lessons from the East Asian Experience.* Washington, DC: Overseas Development Council, 1994.

Woo, Wing Thye, Stephen Parker, and Jeffrey D. Sachs. *Economies in Transition: Comparing Asia and Europe.* Cambridge, MA: MIT Press, 1997.

World Bank. *East Asian: The Road to Recovery.* Washington, DC: World Bank, 1998.

World Bank. *The East Asian Miracle: Economic Growth and Public Policy.* New York: Oxford University Press, 1993.

Young, Alwyn. "Lessons from the East Asian NICs: A Contrarian View." *European Economic Review,* April 1994, 964–974.

PART FIVE Socialist Economies

Chapter 16: The Command Economy

Why Study Planned Economies?

A Brief Overview of Russian Economic History

Chapter 17: The Operation of the Soviet Planned Economy

The Institutions of the Soviet State

The Mechanism of Planning

The Determination of Prices

Labor Markets

Market Clearing

Monitoring Plan Fulfillment

Incentives in Soviet-Type Systems

Conclusion

Chapter 18: The Participatory Economy: The Case of Yugoslavia

The Participatory Economy

Development of the Yugoslav State

Yugoslav Market Socialism

Problems of the Yugoslav Economy

Conclusion

Chapter 19: The Possibilities of a Third Way

Market Socialism and Social Markets

Market Socialism

The Social Market Economy

Conclusion

16

THE COMMAND ECONOMY

WHY STUDY PLANNED ECONOMIES?

At this juncture of history it is tempting to view both the theory and the experience of central planning as an irrelevant footnote. Both popular and academic opinion now consider command planning as a dead end, a mistake into which many nations were dragged for a few decades and from which they have now largely emerged. Today about 30 of the world's nations, with an aggregate population of about 1.6 billion people, who were previously committed to some form of central planning, are now regarded as **economies in transition**—converting from a socialist system to a capitalist one.[1] Indeed 20 years into the process we are entitled to wonder when the transition will be complete. It would, however, be premature merely to salute "the triumph of capitalism" and turn away from any consideration of the achievements and the shortcomings of socialism and central planning. A great deal can be learned from the careful examination of their history.

Central Planning Is Not Extinct As a System

Mark Twain once observed that "reports of my death have been greatly exaggerated," and the same may be the case for central planning. Despite current appearances and political trends, it is conceivable that some form of centralized planning will be reestablished, possibly emerging within the group of former socialist nations. Indeed, several of the largest nations are by no means so well advanced in the transition process that the situation is irreversible. China, for example, still retains the strong political control required to revert back to centralized planning if the social problems of greater liberalization continue to grow. Vietnam, despite some liberalization and incoming foreign investment, is committed only to an experiment in what its leadership calls **market Leninism**. Even within the nations of Central and Eastern Europe, former Communists have made strong showings at the polls. Though nominally committed to maintaining a path toward a full market economy, they still carry an ideological bias toward central control. In Western Europe a recent tilt in electoral sentiment put left-wing parties back into power.

[1]Of these, 15 were formerly republics that constituted the Soviet Union and four were part of Yugoslavia, which pursued a market socialist path that differed in some fundamental ways from that of the Soviet Union.

Finally, the chaos in the Asian markets during 1998 leaves some to wonder whether market capitalism is the most efficient system of economic organization.

Understanding the Planned Past Is the Key to a Successful Transition to a Market Future

An effective transition to a market economy depends on a full understanding of the constraints imposed by the legacy of the prior system. Although many economists advising the nations in transition seem to conceive of the task as building a system "from the ground up," in reality the culture, mores, institutions, and much of the distribution of power of the old system are very much alive. The direction of transition is contingent on the legacy of the socialist period in most countries, and change requires the acquiescence of the more privileged elite established by the prior order.

Most Economies Make Use of Some Form of Planning

As we noted previously, none of the world's economic systems are purely private. All nations pursue some mixture of both private and public systems. Studying the consequences of generalized planning in command economies can help inform our discussion of mixed systems, point to the limitations of government, highlight the need for incentives, and indicate when planning can be the best approach for meeting social needs.

There Are Lessons to Be Learned from Examining Failure

Finally, a clear idea of why centrally planned systems failed is necessary. "Those who fail to understand history are doomed to repeat it" is an overused expression, but in terms of choosing an economic system, this perspective may well be valid. Central planning was attractive because it offered a rational alternative to the repeated recessions and skewed income distribution that characterized capitalism. When, in the 1950s, Nikita Khrushchev declared that "we will bury you," he was talking in terms of systems, and at that time many in the capitalist world feared that he might be right. However, after watching the stagnation and relative decline of the socialist nations, we now know that socialism's apparent advantages are bought at a high cost.

A BRIEF OVERVIEW OF RUSSIAN ECONOMIC HISTORY[2]

For our example of central planning, we turn to the experience of the Soviet Union, the earliest example of comprehensive planning. Efforts in other countries, notably in Eastern Europe after World War II and in China, drew their expertise and inspiration from the Soviet model.

---

[2]This overview is indeed brief, and any interested student is referred initially to Paul Gregory and Robert Stuart, *Soviet and Post Soviet Economic Structure and Performance*, 5th ed. (Reading, MA: Addison-Wesley, 1999), for a much richer exposition.

The Czarist Economy

No system develops independently of historical influence, and the emergence of the planned Soviet state was no exception. The development of modern Russia, including the Soviet period, owes much to Peter the Great. As the first great modernizer, Peter aggressively imported Western technology and science, while simultaneously resisting the liberalizing influence of Western political thought. He began the process of Russian industrialization, founding a variety of state industries. He revolutionized public finance and increased the income of the treasury fivefold. However, he did little to reform serfdom, which was the basic institution of the labor market, and relied heavily on forced labor for his projects, the most enduring of which was the construction of his "European" capital, St. Petersburg. Consequently, the dualism of Russian society increased: a more affluent and westward-looking aristocracy contrasted increasingly with a backward and exploited peasantry.

The repressions of an absolutist monarchy, an elitist aristocracy, and a highly conservative Orthodox Church were formidable barriers to economic change, and Russia, despite its great potential, remained relatively poor. Failure to defeat a rather small Anglo-French force in the Crimean War of 1853–1856 underlined Russian backwardness. In 1861 this realization led Czar Alexander II to take the immense step of liberating the serfs, who then represented about three-quarters of the population. Emancipation was accompanied by land reform and after their manumission the peasants held, through communal organizations, about half of the country's agricultural land.[3] Predictably the aristocracy retained ownership of the best land, and the poorer acreage transferred to the serfs was not given but sold on mortgage, so from the start of their liberty the peasantry was encumbered by heavy debts.

The government set about modernizing the Russian infrastructure, with special emphasis on the transportation needs of the vast empire. More than 20,000 miles of railway track were built between 1861 and 1894, opening up the interior for export-oriented agriculture. The supply of grain for export was stimulated by the need of the peasants to sell much of their output for cash to meet their heavy debt obligations and taxes. By the 1890s Russia emerged as the world's largest grain exporter, and the hard currency revenues were used to finance the import of capital goods required for the aggressive industrialization scheme of the finance minister, Sergius von Witte. Industrial output tripled between 1880 and 1900 and after a brief dip due to the global recession in the first years of the twentieth century, industrial growth accelerated again, making Russia the world's fifth largest industrial power in 1913.

Living conditions remained grim for both agrarian and industrial workers. The peasants, "held in a vise of ruinous aggregate taxation," were forced to sell the bulk of their output to raise cash for taxes and debt service payments.[4] The conditions of industrial workers were little better and labor discontent led to political organization. Support grew among the industrial workers for the Russian Social Democratic

[3]Marx noted in the *Communist Manifesto* in 1882 that this form of "primeval communism" might make it possible for the Russian peasantry to pass more easily to a higher form of communist ownership.
[4]A. Gershenkron, "Russian Agrarian Policies and Industrialization," *The Cambridge Economic History of Europe*, vol. 6 (Cambridge, England: Cambridge University Press, 1965), p. 744.

Party, which held its first convention in 1903, but the party was from the first divided into two factions. The more moderate **Menshevik** wing consisted of social reformers, committed to piecemeal liberalization along the lines of Western Europe. The other wing, Lenin's followers—somewhat inaccurately termed the **Bolsheviks**, or majority—favored radical revolutionary change. The two factions of the party became increasingly alienated and formally split in 1912.

The Russo-Japanese war of 1904–1905 proved another rude shock to the czarist system. Russia was rapidly defeated by an Asian nation that, only 35 years previously, was isolated in a state of feudalism. The losing war effort led to privation at home, accompanied by rioting and strikes. A peaceful protest in front of the Winter Palace in St. Petersburg was fired on by the military, and sympathy for the regime fell, forcing the czar into a series of political reforms, among them the formation of a permanent parliament, the Duma. On the economic front, the **Stolypin reforms** (named for the finance minister) accelerated the rate of industrial growth, freed the peasants from the communes, and alleviated their crushing debt burden.

It is possible that in the aftermath of the Stolypin reforms Russian economic development might have followed the path of peaceful evolution taken in Western Europe, where feudalism gave way to industrial capitalism in a relatively leisurely and peaceful fashion. However, a look at the sources of Russian industrial growth during this period provides a reason to doubt a thesis of a gradually evolving market capitalism. Rapid expansion made Russia one of the world's major industrial powers, but growth in output came mostly from the increase of the industrial labor force and sustained growth in the volume of capital employed. Expansion was therefore highly extensive in character, the result of an increased use of factors of production, not of rising factor productivity. Total factor productivity growth (the residual increase in output, after allowing for the increase in labor and capital employed) was negligible. Industrial expansion could not under these conditions be accompanied by rising wages or living standards. One likely scenario is that prolonged capitalism in Russia would have led to the continued increase of a badly paid, and consequently angry, workforce, potentially provoking revolutionary tendencies at any time.

War Communism

Because of the turn of world events, we will never know whether the mold of extensive growth would have been broken or whether increasing labor demand would have ultimately resulted in burgeoning labor productivity and rising wages. In 1914 Russia became involved in a dispute with Austria and its ally Germany over the Balkans, and in August 1914 Russia was propelled into war along with its own allies, France and Britain. World War I was immensely costly to Russia as its massive but badly equipped and poorly led army absorbed enormous casualties—2 million dead in less than three years. At home even the barest essentials of life became unavailable for both the peasants and the urban poor, leading to food riots. In May 1917 the czar abdicated, and power passed to the Mensheviks, led by Alexander Kerensky. Menshevik policy was to continue the unpopular war, despite persistent failure on the battlefield and growing deprivation at home. Germany contrived to return the exiled Lenin from Switzerland to St. Petersburg where he led the Bolsheviks to power in the revolution of October 1917. Initially Bolshevik control was largely limited to the capital, with most of the countryside in dispute. Reunification of the country took three years of civil war.

The first decisive act of the new Bolshevik government was to end the war with Germany by the treaty of Brest-Litovsk signed in 1918 on terms close to capitulation. It consigned a large part of the czarist empire to German control, including much of Poland and the Ukraine, the industrial heart and breadbasket of the Empire. France, Britain, and the United States intervened in an attempt to restore the czar and bring Russia back into the war with Germany. However, their somewhat half-hearted efforts were fruitless and the Red Army slowly won control of Russia and ultimately of most of the former czarist territory.

The system of economic organization instituted by the Bolshevik administration during this period is known as **war communism**. Economic management was almost totally by command; food was "requisitioned" in the countryside by police and party officials and distributed in the cities. Thirty-seven thousand enterprises were taken into state hands, including every firm that employed more than 10 workers (5 in establishments where artificial power was used). The coordination of economic activity was ostensibly the preserve of the Supreme Council of National Economy (*VSNKh*), but effective action was fatally hampered by an almost total lack of meaningful information. Workers were conscripted and organized by military methods, and economic incentives for the industrial and agricultural labor forces alike were replaced by dictum and force.

Market economic relations were replaced by what the political leaders termed "natural" ones; housing, electricity, food, postal services, and transportation were all supplied to the public without charge. Interenterprise relations between the state-owned production units were of bookkeeping significance only. Obviously the system of war communism had many shortcomings, as efficiency suffered and corruption abounded. However, a dispassionate evaluation of this period as an economic system is not very meaningful. The country was in a state of civil war, struggling to recover from a disastrous defeat in war with Germany, the food and materiel shortage was acute, and desperate needs justified the desperate measures adopted. Moreover, from the Bolshevik viewpoint, the near-term objective was merely survival. The economic system of war communism enabled them to gather enough resources to defeat both White Russians and foreign interventionists.

The New Economic Policy

By 1920 the civil war was more or less over with Bolshevik rule firmly established not only within Russia itself but also in almost all of the former czarist empire, including areas conceded to Germany in the treaty of Brest-Litovsk. The economy fashioned by von Witte and Stolypin was reunited, and the Bolshevik leadership had an opportunity to develop a new economic system in relative peace.

The blueprint for development was the **New Economic Policy (NEP)** articulated by Lenin in 1921, which attracted recent attention because it has common features with the Soviet (and subsequently) Russian reforms of the late-1980s and early

1990s. It is important to understand that the early leaders of the Bolshevik state were working in a vacuum. To legitimize their revolution they created an alternative to capitalism that was not only superior in its theoretical rationale but also in its concrete results, at least in terms of the distribution of income and the avoidance of mass unemployment. Moreover, ideology required this system to be in some sense Marxian, although Marx's writings gave the Bolshevik leadership little guidance. An astute observer of capitalist societies and economies, Marx said little on the socialist future. Moreover, he predicted that the first socialist revolutions would occur in the most advanced capitalist societies (Britain and Germany the most likely candidates), and so revolution in Russia was somewhat anathematic to his theories. Lenin carefully established the orthodoxy of his revolution by a subtle reinterpretation of Marx, whose thought, he asserted, was really that revolution would occur in "the weakest link in the capitalist chain," rather than necessarily in the most advanced capitalist economies. Despite his care in establishing the Marxian pedigree of the Bolshevik Revolution, Lenin was surprisingly liberal in his design of the economic institutions embodied in the NEP. Although he allowed considerable economic freedom, he regarded the NEP as a pragmatic step backward to establish stability before the creation of socialism could proceed.

During its brief life, the NEP was a form of market socialism. The "natural" economic relations of war communism were terminated in favor of price mechanisms. Control of food production was returned to the peasantry, and market relations were reinstituted to regulate the flow of food to the cities. Small enterprises (defined as those employing fewer than 20 persons) were reprivatized, some were restituted to their former owners and others leased to new entrepreneurs. Most of large-scale industry remained in state hands. Sectors seen as strategically essential—the **commanding heights of the economy**, including fuels, metals, banking, transportation, and foreign trade—became an integral part of the state, dependent on budget allocations and controlled in all important dimensions by the government. The rest of industry was granted substantial subsidies by the state, but had no production quotas to meet, and was otherwise encouraged to act in a profit-maximizing fashion.

The NEP was not a planned economy. The state exercised considerable financial control, but enterprises were able to enter into contracts, fix their own prices, determine output levels, and decide on production techniques. Although **Gosplan**, the state planning agency, was founded in 1921, its functions in the early years of the NEP were limited to forecasting. Coordination in the economy relied increasingly on the concentration of economic power in the industrial sector, as individual enterprises combined to form "trusts," integrated production units promoted by the government. By 1923, 75 percent of all industrial workers were employed by the 478 government-chartered trusts. Subsequently, these trusts themselves combined into even larger units, known as syndicates, involving higher degrees of horizontal integration. By the late NEP period, production by the syndicates accounted for more than 80 percent of industrial output.

In terms of its primary goal of promoting stability, the NEP was a success. By 1926, output climbed back to and exceeded 1913 levels in most commodities. Agricultural output was the exception; it remained well below prewar levels, an ominous precursor of the problems in food production that would haunt the entire Soviet experience. Another sharp difference from the prewar world was the diminished role of trade. The Soviet economy was much less open to world trade than the czarist economy had been, in part because of the disappearance of the agricultural surplus, which constituted the czarist state's largest overseas earner. However, by the mid-1920s the days of the NEP were numbered. Its demise resulted from three factors:

1. *Dissent within the Communist party.* Most Bolsheviks believed that the NEP was a temporary concession, and the expectation grew within the party that, after stability was restored and the economy was stronger, the task of creating a truly socialist economy could commence in earnest.
2. *The "terms of trade" between the urban and the rural sectors.* The reform issue was brought to a head by the so-called **scissors crisis**, which occurred during 1922 and 1923 when the price of agricultural goods fell sharply while the prices of industrial goods rose.[5] When these indices were plotted graphically, they resembled the two blades of an open scissors (see Figure 16.1), hence the name. The Bolshevik leadership assumed that this fall in the real price of grain would cause the peasants to sharply reduce supply to urban markets and create famine in the cities. This presumption, based on little evidence, led the authorities to consider a return to a command economy entailing the forced requisition of agricultural goods. After intense debate, the government tried regulation and attempted to move real prices in agriculture's favor by imposing price ceilings on consumer goods. At the lower real prices consumer goods were in short supply, especially in rural markets. In the absence of effective rationing this "goods famine" led to a black market, with intermediaries from the cities reaping the rents from arbitrage between the official and the black market prices. This exploitation created resentment among the peasants, who at this point withheld much of their corn for their own consumption and shifted production to higher-value crops and livestock. Net sales of grain to the urban sector fell to close to 50 percent of the prewar level, creating famine in industrial areas and jeopardizing the whole development effort.
3. *The industrialization debate.* The scissors crisis brought home the difficulty of controlling the rate of industrial growth within the prevailing market framework of the NEP. The party leadership came to recognize that industrialization depended on an adequate and sustained flow of food and material from the rural sector and was a potential hostage to the *kulaks*, more prosperous peasants regarded by the party as a counterrevolutionary threat. The two sides of the debate were defined by the radical left views espoused by Evgenii **Preobrazhensky** and the more moderate agenda of Nikolai **Bukharin**. Preobrazhensky favored unbalanced development and saw a "big push" in heavy industry as necessary to close the gap with the West. Growth would be facilitated by forcing savings in the agrarian sector and transferring it to the

[5]This gap was due to the fact that agricultural output had risen to about 60 percent of its prewar level, while industrial goods output had recovered to only 35 percent.

FIGURE 16.1

The Scissors Crisis

SOURCE: Paul Gregory and Robert Stuart, *Soviet Economic Structure and Performance,* 4th ed. (Reading, MA: Addison-Wesley, 1997), 65.

industrial sector by "nonequivalent exchange," a program incompatible with the market mechanism of the NEP. Bukharin, while recognizing the need for rapid capital accumulation, especially in industry, feared that the divisiveness of discriminating against the agricultural sector would shatter the fragile alliance of peasants and industrial workers (the *smychka*). His predilection was for balanced growth, which would not only avoid discrimination against one sector or another, but also the bottlenecks that rapid expansion of one sector of the economy could produce.

Stalin and the Command Economy

After Lenin's death in 1924, **Stalin** rapidly consolidated power and by 1927 was unopposed. Stalin favored the rapid transformation of the economy by sustained expansion of the heavy industrial sector. Although initially allied with centrists like Bukharin, as soon as he secured his rule, Stalin shifted to Preobrazhensky's more radical position.

His economic strategy embraced two "reforms." One instituted command planning over the entire economy. The first **five-year plan** was formulated in 1928 and from this point forward the state would control the production and movement of all finished and intermediate goods. A debate arose within the leadership as to the degree of attention that any plan should pay to the demands of the general public. Some adopted what was termed the *geneticist* approach and saw the plan as an instrument to rationalize production along lines ultimately dictated by the consumer.[6] Stalin, however, envisaged a more proactive role for the state. Rather than responding to demand, the plan would be a tool for shaping individual tastes and behavior according to goals determined by the political authorities. This *teleological* approach dominated politics and planning throughout the history of the Soviet Union.

The second reform involved agriculture. Rapid industrialization depended on the availability of agricultural surpluses to the industrial sector to provide the raw material of investment, but the prospect of disruption due to movements in agricultural prices, remained real. Consequently Stalin terminated market relations between the industrial and agricultural sectors by collectivizing agriculture, a move designed both to increase the level of central control over the agricultural sector and to eliminate the counterrevolutionary potential of the rich peasants, the ***kulaks***. Individual land holdings were confiscated and the peasants forced into communes. Because the Communist Party lacked a rural power base, collectivization was effected by the dispatch of about 25,000 political operatives from the cities to impose it by force. *Kulaks* (and the definition was loose enough to include any peasant who had fallen foul of the political authorities) were dispossessed, but rather than becoming part of the communes, they were internally deported, usually to Siberia, or placed in penal labor camps. The collectivization program was rapidly instituted; in 1928 fewer than 2 percent of Soviet farm households were collectivized, but by 1931 this proportion had risen to 52 percent, and by 1938 it reached 94 percent. Many *kulaks* not just lost their livelihoods but also their lives; precise figures are unavailable, but deaths were certainly in the millions.

The Growth of Planning

Initially planning in the Soviet Union was little more than indicative. Gosplan started issuing **control figures**, which were basically tentative output targets, in 1925, and during successive years these figures assumed a greater importance. In the first five-year plan in 1928, control figures took on a more compulsive character, increasingly supported by detailed production and financial plans (***promfinplans***) at the sectoral level. As the system of materials balance planning, a response to shortages of key materials emerged, work by Russian economists on the precursors of input-output analysis gave Gosplan the technical basis for its work. Material balances for iron and steel were first compiled in 1925; energy products

[6] Such planning, generally called "geneticist," was advocated by, among others, N. D. Kondratiev, the founder of business cycle theory.

and building materials soon followed. By 1928 Gosplan was the primary coordinating agency for the whole process, preparing control figures that gave general direction to the economy while controlling a growing list of strategic materials by materials balance planning.

In the 1930s Stalin increased his power over the planning process and extended control into every aspect of the economy. Centralized price determination became an essential part of the overall procedure, and the manipulation of prices became a tool in the achievement of the overall goals. The emphasis was on heavy industrial growth, the First Plan calling for a 400 percent increase in investment in state industry.

Planning and the War

Despite the alliance of Germany and the Soviet Union, forged in the notorious Hitler-Stalin pact, the Nazis invaded the Soviet Union in 1941, making rapid inroads into the western industrial belt. The war's impact on the Soviet economy was profound and enduring. First, it prompted an extensive relocation of economic activity deep into the country beyond the Urals and into Central Asia. Economist Susan Linz estimated that 6 million persons were relocated along with some 1,500 large enterprises. Although this relocation led to widespread disruption and dislocation of output, much of the core of the Soviet industrial base was salvaged by this remarkable operation. Second, war led to a tightening of the system of planning, and by 1945 materials balance plans were drawn up for some 30,000 commodities.

The Postwar Period and Khrushchev

During the war, the Soviet Union lost between 10 and 15 percent of its population to military action, starvation, or exile to the ***gulag***. Thirty percent of the prewar capital stock was destroyed and most of the gains achieved during the industrialization program of the 1930s erased. Despite these heavy losses, postwar recovery was rapid, and by 1950 most indices of production exceeded their 1940 levels, a dramatic effort in difficult circumstances. Agriculture proved the most difficult area, due in part to the low priority assigned to it in the planning process, but also because of the lack of incentives on the collective farms. Lack of attention and investment led to generally depressed conditions throughout the rural sector. Heavy industry, on the other hand, which enjoyed a high priority in the investment allocation process, continued a strong performance, and light industry performed well too, doubling its 1940 output by 1950. Consistent with Stalinist orthodoxy, total capital investment grew at a double-digit rate throughout the 1950s. Stalin's last major initiative before his death was institution of the so-called transformation of nature, which called for massive projects of irrigation and engineering.

Stalin died in 1953 and, after a couple of years of joint rule, the party leadership was assumed by Nikita Khrushchev, who attempted fundamental change in economic and political life in the following ways:

1. Making the leadership aware of dissent, denouncing in 1955 Stalin's cult of personality, and drawing attention to Stalinist abuse of human rights.

2. Regionalizing the planning system, reversing the centralization that made the Moscow ministries not only centers of power but also sources of bureaucratic delay, and putting more authority into the hands of **regional economic councils** (*sovnarkhozy*).
3. Opening a debate on the management of the economic system. The most publicized reform proposals were those of Evsei Liberman, whose central idea was to replace physical targets for managers with an incentive system incorporating bonuses based on the enterprise's rate of profit. The central planning authority itself would have continued largely unchanged except that greater flexibility would be given to enterprises in the hopes of economizing on material. Though these proposals received front page treatment in *Pravda,* their importance, both in theoretical terms and in practical significance, may have been overstated.
4. Making a concerted effort to reform the agricultural sector. One aspect was the conversion of depressed and stagnant collective farms (***kolkhozy***), nominally operated by the peasants, to state farms (***sovkhozy***), which functioned like other enterprises, employing a workforce paid by weekly wages plus bonuses rather than a share of the profit. He also put more investment into agriculture, increased inputs of fertilizers, and raised the prices received by the collective farms as an incentive to increase output.

As Table 16.1 indicates, though the planners managed to achieve targets in basic industries (steel, electricity, coal), sophisticated manufacturing (motor vehicles and machine tools) and especially agriculture were serious problems. The inability of the Soviet Union to feed itself began to show during this time, and in the Seventh Plan, Khrushchev's ambitious plans for agriculture were underfulfilled by 32 percent, and meat output was 37 percent off target.

Table 16.2 shows some relevant growth rates. Growth of gross national product (GNP) and agricultural output accelerated during the Fifth Plan (1955–1960), but progress was not sustained. The service sector expanded quite rapidly, but the falling rate of industrial growth mirrored slippage in the growth of investment.

Brezhnev and the "Period of Stagnation"

Much of the communist leadership found Khrushchev's policies too liberal, and in 1964 he was ousted by other members of the Central Committee, power passing to the more conservative Leonid Brezhnev. Nevertheless, at the start of Brezhnev's regime parts of the reform initiated under Khrushchev continued and even yielded results. In 1965 Alexei Kosygin, the chief economic official, announced reforms to the system of targets given to enterprises by which managers were no longer to be held to physical targets established by the planners but were to be free to focus on maximizing what was called "realized output" (in western terms, the equivalent of the value of sales). Management was allowed to retain a large slice of the difference between the value of sales and the cost of materials (profit) to use to provide material incentives for themselves and their workers.

Greater freedom of initiative produced promising results, increased productivity in many enterprises, and sharply rising profits, but unfortunately the very success of

TABLE 16.1

Percentage Achievement of Plan in the Soviet Union

	Plan V 1951–1955	Plan VI 1956–1960	Plan VII 1959–1965
National income	107	97	97
Investment	103	101	106
Private consumption	104	95	98
Industrial production	109	99	102
Agricultural production	n.a.	89	68
Steel	91	96	103
Coal	105	86	95
Oil	101	110	104
Electricity	104	91	99
Gas	94	118	86
Machine tools	66	78	95
Motor vehicles	99	80	80
Textiles	94	88	91
Meat	70	67	63
Milk	83	74	71

SOURCE: Vera Lutz, *Central Planning for the Market Economy: An Analysis of the French Theory and Experience* (Harlow, England: Longmans, Green and Co., 1969).

TABLE 16.2

Aggregate Economic Performance, 1951–1970: Annual Percentage Change

	Plan V 1951–1955	Plan VI 1955–1960	Plan VII 1961–1965	Plan VIII 1966–1970
GNP	5.4	5.9	5.0	5.2
Industry	10.2	8.3	6.6	6.3
Agriculture	3.5	4.2	2.8	3.5
Services	1.9	3.5	4.4	4.2
Consumption	4.9	5.7	3.7	5.3
Investment	12.4	10.5	7.6	6

SOURCE: Gregory and Stuart, *Russian and Soviet Economic Performance and Structure* (Reading, MA: Addison-Wesley, 1997), pp. 128–130.

the measures alarmed the leadership. By allowing a substantial part of the profit to accrue to the enterprises and to workers in the form of bonuses, reform led to increased disparity in interenterprise wage differentials, a potentially disruptive development. Moreover, rising labor productivity would be followed by reductions in employment at the firm level and might lead to widespread unemployment. These fears led the leadership to be more tentative about reform, and the size of incentive funds and bonuses was limited. Although the initial intent of reformhad been to reduce the scope of planning and give initiative to managers, the tide soon ran in the opposite direction. Despite reformist rhetoric, the bureaucracy expanded and its powers strengthened. Khrushchev's reforms to devolve power to regional councils were reversed, and the Moscow ministries assumed the management of the enterprise on a union-wide scale. Despite a clear reluctance to enact serious reform, every year of the 1970s saw some new strategy to alter the performance of the system, always amounting to nothing. The fundamental problem lay in the structure of incentives embodied in the system of central planning, and remained unaddressed.

Hesitancy over reform led to the lackluster economic performance shown in Table 16.3. The growth rate of GNP, already down from more than 5 percent annually in the Khrushchev years, fell from 3.7 percent to 2.3 percent by the first half of the 1980s. During the 1970s the true state of the Soviet economy was disguised by the dramatic rise of oil prices, which benefited the Soviet Union as the world's largest energy producer, financing the import of needed technology and capital equipment, as well as consumption goods as basic as grain. However, bountiful energy and the failure of the Soviet price system to value it appropriately made Soviet industry wasteful in its use and ultimately uncompetitive in global terms. Labor productivity, which might have risen, had the proposed reforms in incentives been instigated, remained low. After the collapse of the Soviet Union, studies estimated that output per labor hour in the 1980s was only about 25 percent of the average in Western Europe, although Soviet planners were convinced that they were experiencing labor shortage and guest workers were brought in from North Korea and Vietnam.

Although the poor performance of the economy clearly indicated serious structural problems, the planners initially remained optimistic that growth could be maintained and even accelerated. Table 16.4 offers a comparison of the planned targets and the actual outcomes for the four five-year plans between 1965 and 1985. As the planners reluctantly factored in the underperformance of the early plans and lowered their sights, plan fulfillment slipped further. Agricultural performance was especially dismal and, compounded by severe shortcomings in distribution, led to serious food

TABLE 16.3

Aggregate Economic Performance, 1971–1987: Annual Percentage Change

	1971–1975	1976–1980	1981–1983	1984–1987
GNP	3.7	2.7	2.3	1.6
Industry	5.9	3.4	1.5	2.1
Agriculture	22.3	0.3	4.2	0.8
Services	3.4	2.8	2.1	—
Consumption	3.6	2.6	1.7	2.4
Investment	5.4	4.3	4.2	3

SOURCE: Gregory and Stuart, *Russian and Soviet Economic Performance and Structure* (Reading, MA: Addison-Wesley, 1997), p. 133.

shortages in many areas. Famine was avoided only by substantial grain imports from the United States and Canada, financed by energy exports. Considering that Russia led the world in grain exports in 1913, 50 years of socialism had yielded poor results.

Gorbachev

After Leonid Brezhnev died in 1982, he was briefly succeeded by two long-serving senior members of the party. However, neither Yuri Andropov nor Constantine Chernenko had either enough time in office or the resolve to take on the entrenched system of the Soviet privileged elite (***nomenklatura***) or to articulate a cohesive reform package. Andropov, a former head of the KGB, was convinced that the failures of the Soviet system were attributable to a lack of order and discipline. During his 16-month reign (from November 1982 to February 1984), he initiated campaigns against absenteeism, corruption, and excessive alcohol consumption, all with little effect. He also attempted to correct the deficiency of the Soviet quality control and product improvement by allowing enterprises to apply for price increases of up to 30 percent for "product improvement." Chernenko, an aging *apparatchik*, led the Soviet Union for only 13 months (February 1984 to March 1985) and followed the cautious Andropov line of exhorting greater efficiency and attempting to fine-tune the system of managerial incentives. By March of 1985 both men were dead and power was assumed by the relatively young and active Mikhail S. Gorbachev, an Andropov protégé.

Gorbachev, aware of the shortcomings of the Soviet economy, was resolved to change its direction. He will always be remembered for his introduction of twin reform tracks: ***glasnost***, usually translated as openness and signifying democratization and the tolerance of dissent, and ***perestroika***, or restructuring in the economic sphere. Although at the time Gorbachev's reforms were thought far-reaching,

TABLE 16.4

Plan Fulfillment: Planned versus Actual Growth

	Average Annual Growth			
	1966–1970	1971–1975	1976–1980	1981–1985
GNP				
Plan	6.5–7	5.8	5	4
Actual	*5*	*3.1*	*2.2*	*1.8*
Industry				
Plan	8.2	8	6.5	4.9
Actual	*6.3*	*5.4*	*2.6*	*1.8*
Agriculture				
Plan	5.5	3.7	5	5
Actual	*3.7*	*20.6*	*0.8*	*2.1*

SOURCE: Gregory and Stuart, *Russian and Soviet Economic Performance and Structure* (Reading, MA: Addison-Wesley, 1997), p. 135.

in reality they were timid, faltering, and based on inaccurate premises. Despite being highly critical of the reform efforts of the Brezhnev era (which he dismissed as an attempt "to improve things without changing anything"), his own reforms were similarly tentative, believing that substantial economic gains, in terms of increased output and efficiency, could be grasped by relatively modest changes in the economic system.

Gorbachev was, until his downfall, a member of the Communist Party. He sought reform of the system of central planning, selectively using prices and market incentives to iron out "bottlenecks," rather than trying to overthrow it. He was especially sanguine about the potential of imported technology to raise productivity and restore competitiveness. Although his program has been compared to the NEP of the 1920s, it was really the intellectual child of the piecemeal Kosygin reforms of the 1960s. His first steps moved to cut the power of the economic bureaucracy and give enterprise managers freedom and incentive to pursue their own initiatives; this shift resulted in the demolition of the old command system of allocating resources, but it did not allow enough freedom to permit a genuine market system to replace it, leading to a dislocation of the economy and a sharp fall in output, which made subsequent progress toward reform more difficult.

The Law on Enterprise Reform A second-phase of reform was ushered in 1987 with the **law on state enterprises**, which tried to put firms on a corporatized and accountable basis. The key concepts were **self-management** and **self-finance**. Under self-management, workers would take a more active role in the direction of the enterprise and would play a role in the selection of management. Under self-finance, capital was no longer allocated by the planners at subsidized interest rates, but rather each firm would finance investment either from retained profits or credit from banks by loans with "hard" interest payments. Investment funds from the government were to be used only for infrastructural improvements or the start up of new business sectors.

Gorbachev was also bent on the reform of the inflexible system of wage payments, which allowed little variation for worker productivity and therefore tended to reward indolence as much as effort. The reforms gave enterprises control over a **wages fund**, enabling them to reduce their workforces (though to avoid unemployment this could only be by attrition) and to use any money saved to increase the wages of remaining workers in line with productivity growth. By 1990, 75 percent of all industrial personnel were working under these new wage arrangements.

Although Gorbachev's reform plan had many commendable aspects, it was a gradualist agenda that attempted to increase enterprise freedom within the planned system of output quotas. This tinkering short of radical reform produced dislocation. Even though conditions improved for some, the Gorbachev era saw the start of a 10-year contraction of Soviet industrial output. Although modest growth in output was achieved during 1986–1988, in 1989 and 1990 the economy entered a phase of sharp contraction that continued until 1997. Even more dispiriting, despite the enterprise reforms, both labor and capital productivity fell throughout the period. During 1989 and 1990, the economic crisis became more intense. Acute shortages of basic consumer goods contributed to growing popular discontent with the reform effort.

Foreign Trade Reform Under central planning, foreign trade, as well as the domestic resource allocation, was controlled by planners. Within the area known in the West as the Soviet bloc, the procedures for international trade were broadly similar to those that governed the planning of domestic production. Trade within the bloc was conducted under the auspices of the **Council on Mutual Economic Assistance (CMEA)** (often referred to as COMECON, an acronym for Communist Common Market). Trade planning was made on the basis of physical units and prices were adjusted so that trade flows were roughly equalized in currency terms. No member of the CMEA therefore experienced a balance of payments problem because prices were soft and manipulated to equilibrate payments. Just as in domestic planning, the idea of economies of scale was important in structuring COMECON trade. Each nation within the CMEA was required to specialize in the production of certain goods, and the other members were expected to import all of their needs from them. Because trade was planned, comparative advantage, the basic underlying principle assumed to govern the direction and volume of trade between market economies, played a negligible role. Because the Soviet Union was rich in natural resources, especially energy, and the satellites were not, it supplied them with primary commodities at prices highly subsidized in terms of world levels and received manufactured goods in return. As world energy prices shot up during the 1970s, the prices charged within the CMEA system of trade adjusted only a little, and the terms of trade shifted sharply in favor of the satellite nations.

Trade outside the CMEA bloc was based on different principles, though they were no more rational in terms of basic economics. Decisions were made at the central level about the amount of foreign exchange required, generally a function of the amount of imports from the non-CMEA world. Special **foreign trade organizations (FTOs)** would purchase the export goods from Soviet suppliers and sell them at agreed upon, usually world, prices. The existence of FTO insulated domestic producers from world markets. The intercession of the FTO allowed the domestic producers no opportunity to profit from foreign trade, nor were they exposed to the competition in foreign markets.

This highly indirect system contributed to the inability of Soviet bloc enterprises to pursue international competitiveness through innovation and efficiency. Unlike the trading companies of Japan, which sought out foreign markets, educated domestic producers, and facilitated the import of ideas and technology, the FTOs were passive and formed a barrier between Soviet management and the world. Because no individual firm in the Soviet Union could benefit to any great degree from foreign trade, enterprise management held little interest. They conducted no global market research nor did they attempt to conform to international norms and standards.

In January 1987, the FTO monopoly of foreign trade was broken when 20 ministries and 76 large enterprises were allowed to initiate direct trade and to retain a substantial proportion of any hard currency earnings. The scheme was rapidly expanded and by the middle of 1990, more than 14,000 enterprises had the right to trade abroad on their own behalf. This liberalization was well intentioned and should have borne economic fruit, but it led instead to corruption and personal enrichment. Soviet-manufactured goods were of uncertain quality, poor design, and were much less likely to find markets than primary commodities such as petroleum and forest products. These commodities tended to be diverted from their planned use and sold abroad with the receipts frequently accruing to individual accounts offshore. The result was a lack of resources at home and problems in plan fulfillment.

The Failure of Perestroika Gorbachev's *perestroika* program fell between two stools. The reforms were too creeping for a rapid transformation to a market economy based on prices that reflected shortage and opportunity cost. However, they were enough to disrupt and create serious problems for the old system to which they were appended, leading to a collapse of output. More fatally for Gorbachev, they alarmed the old guard of the Communist Party.

The Coup of August 1991 Throughout 1990 and early 1991, the economic and political system of the Soviet Union teetered on the brink of reform. In August 1991, a coup by the old guard of the Communist Party supplanted Gorbachev, but the so-called *putsch* rapidly unraveled largely because it failed to neutralize Boris Yeltsin, the elected (and therefore legitimate) president of the Russian Federation. Yeltsin remained within the "White House," the Russian Parliament building, defying the authority of the Communist Party of the Soviet Union and communicating freely with other leaders, both in the constituent republics of the Soviet Union and the West. The failure of the *putsch* signaled the end of the Soviet Union as the constituent republics refused to recognize the Soviet authority. Within Russia, Yeltsin inherited power.

KEY TERMS AND CONCEPTS

- Bolsheviks
- Bukharin
- commanding heights of the economy
- control figures
- Council on Mutual Economic Assistance (CMEA)
- economies in transition
- five-year plan
- foreign trade organizations (FTOs)
- *glasnost*
- Gosplan
- *gulag*
- *kolkhozy*
- *kulaks*
- law on state enterprises
- market Leninism
- Menshevik
- New Economic Policy (NEP)
- *nomenklatura*
- *perestroika*
- Preobrazhensky
- *promfinplans*
- regional economic councils
- scissors crisis
- self-finance
- self-management
- *sovkhozy*
- Stalin
- Stolypin reforms
- wages fund
- war communism

QUESTIONS FOR DISCUSSION

1. Why did the economic situation of serfs liberated in 1861 lead to the rise of Russia as an agriculture exporter?
2. Why is Lenin's New Economic Policy often referred to as a kind of market socialism?
3. What was the importance of the scissors crisis? Why are the terms of trade between the rural and urban sectors so important in industrialization?
4. How did World War II affect the planning system and structure of the Soviet economy?
5. What was the thrust of Khrushchev's reforms? Were they successful?
6. How did the Soviet Union remain in the arms race and the space race despite faltering technology and slow growth?
7. How was trade conducted under the Soviet system?
8. Why did Gorbachev's policy of *perestroika* fail?

RESOURCES

Books and Articles

Bergson, Abram. *Welfare, Planning and Employment.* Cambridge, MA: MIT Press, 1982.

Carr. E. H. *The Russian Revolution: From Lenin to Stalin.* New York: Free Press, 1979.

Dunmore, Timothy. *The Stalinist Command Economy: The Soviet State Apparatus and Economic Policy, 1945–53.* New York: St. Martin's Press, 1980.

Goldman, Marshall I. *Gorbachev's Challenge: Economic Reform in the Age of High Technology.* New York: W.W. Norton, 1987.

Goldman, Marshall I. *U.S.S.R. in Crisis: The Failure of an Economic System.* New York: W.W. Norton, 1983.

Gregory, Paul R. *Before Command: An Economic History of Russia from Emancipation to the First Five-Year Plan.* Princeton, NJ: Princeton University Press, 1994.

Gregory, Paul R., and Robert C. Stuart. *Russian and Soviet Economic Performance and Structure (Addison-Wesley Series in Economics).* Reading, MA: Addison-Wesley, 1997.

Guroff, Gregory, and Fred Castensen (eds.). *Entrepreneurship in Imperial Russia and the Soviet Union.* Princeton, NJ: Princeton University Press, 1983.

Hewett, Ed A. *Reforming the Soviet Economy: Equality versus Efficiency.* Washington, DC: Brookings Institution, 1990.

Hewett, Ed A., and Victor H. Winston (eds.). *Milestones in Glasnost and Perestroyka: The Economy.* Washington, DC: Brookings Institution, 1991.

Hochschild, Adam. *The Unquiet Ghost: Russians Remember Stalin.* New York: Penguin, 1995.

International Monetary Fund. *A Study of the Soviet Economy.* Washington, DC: International Monetary Fund, 1991.

Jones, Anthony, and William Moskoff (eds.). *Perestroika and the Economy: New Thinking in Soviet Economics.* Armonk, NY: M.E. Sharpe, 1989.

Lavigne, Marie. *Financing the Transition: The Shatalin Plan and the Soviet Economy.* New York: Institute for East-West Security Studies, 1990.

Nove, Alec. *The Soviet Economy, an Introduction,* 2d ed. New York: Praeger, 1968.

Remnick, David. *Lenin's Tomb: The Last Days of the Soviet Empire.* New York: Random House, 1993.

Stuart, Robert C. (ed.). *The Soviet Rural Economy.* Totowa, NJ: Rowman and Allanheld, 1984.

Ulam, Adam Bruno. *The Bolsheviks: The Intellectual and Political History of the Triumph of Communism in Russia.* Cambridge, MA: Harvard University Press, 1998.

17

THE OPERATION OF THE SOVIET PLANNED ECONOMY

THE INSTITUTIONS OF THE SOVIET STATE

Because the economic and political systems of the Soviet Union were so closely interwoven, understanding the operation of the economy and the planning system requires some knowledge of the institutional makeup of the Soviet state.

The Communist Party of the Soviet Union

The dominant force in Soviet society was the Communist Party of the Soviet Union (CPSU). All important strategic decisions relevant to the operation of the economy were ultimately made by the party. The most powerful figure in the country was therefore the general secretary of the Communist Party, the post occupied by Stalin, Khrushchev, Brezhnev, and Gorbachev. The general secretary of the CPSU was *ex officio* leader of the **politburo**, the governing body of the party, whose other members represented the major regional party organizations, the officials responsible for foreign affairs, the organs of state security, and the major ministries. Although to the outside world the Soviet Union seemed to be a single-person dictatorship, in reality, at least for most of the post-Stalin period, a great deal of power resided with the other members of the politburo. They held the power to remove the general secretary from that post when his policy preferences deviated from those of the party, which happened in the case of Khrushchev.

The Legislature

Viewed through Western eyes, the legislature of the Soviet Union seemed weak. It was composed of two chambers: the Supreme Soviet and the Praesidium. The 370 members of the Supreme Soviet were nominally elected by popular vote, but in effect were appointed by the party, which retained tight control over the slate of candidates. The Supreme Soviet met twice a year, when its members, who served part-time and had other jobs, would assemble in Moscow essentially to rubber-stamp the legislative changes and the appointment of officials determined by the party bureaucracy. The Praesidium, which might be regarded as the upper house, was more compact and enjoyed more responsibility. Its members were mainly government officials, and it met twice monthly under the leadership of a chairman, who performed the function of head of state.

The Judiciary

The judicial branch in the Soviet state was even weaker than the legislature. It had little independence from the political process, a fact reflected by Nikita Khrushchev's now infamous remark "who is the Boss, us or the Law: we are the masters over the Law, not the Law over us."[1] This observation was true at two levels. In most developed market economies, particularly in the United States, a constitution, guarded by an independent judiciary, exercises ultimate authority over the political system and constrains the type of laws that the legislature might pass. This system of checks and balances was absent in the Soviet Union. Although a written constitution existed in the Soviet Union (in fact, it closely resembled that of the United States), in effect it was inoperative, because no independent judiciary enforced it. Moreover, the structure of power led to capricious and politically determined implementation of whatever laws were on the books. Thus the Soviet Union was characterized by what John Litwack has called an absence of **legality**, in which "*Legality* is associated with *rule by law* as opposed to the discretion of leaders."[2]

This absence of legality was especially important in economic matters, as Litwack points out:

> Recent research in economic history has emphasized the importance of the replacement of legal for discretionary rule in explaining the rapid economic development of the western world, as well as the disparities in wealth between the advanced capitalist and underdeveloped countries. . . . [The Soviet system] contains particular mechanisms of coordination, incentives, and distribution that function in the virtual absence of economic legality. The fundamental features that explain how the system actually works are the discretionary power of bureaucrats over subordinates, enforced by the political dictatorship of the Communist Party, and the reputation effects from personal, often informal, long-run ties.

THE MECHANISM OF PLANNING

The politburo and the party determined the basic direction in which the economy was to move and the policies to be followed. Thus the fundamental economic questions of what, how, and for whom were all answered by the political leadership. The broad directives of the party were embodied in the plan by the bureaucrats of the State Planning Commission, **Gosplan**, which although only one of more than 20 state committees, had the preeminent role in economic planning. Other committees with an economic function were **Gosbank** (the state bank), Gosstroi (the state committee for construction), Gosten (the state committee on prices), Gossnab (the state committee for material and technical supply), Goskomstat (the statistical service), and MinFin (the Ministry of Finance).

[1]Quoted in K. Simis, *The USSR: The Corrupt Society* (New York: Simon and Schuster, 1982).

[2]J. Litwack, "Legality and Market Reform in Soviet Type Economies," *Journal of Economic Perspectives* 5, no. 4 (Fall 1991).

The Time Frame of the Planning Process

Early in the planning year, Gosplan collected information on the performance in the previous year from the various actors in the economic system, with most information coming from the production side of the economy because Soviet planners gave little weight to the opinions of consumers.[3] Even if any desire to cater to consumers' demands to a greater degree were present, little could be done about quantifying consumers' concerns. In a supply-deficit economy with fixed prices such as in the Soviet Union, most goods found some buyer, even if it was an unhappy one. Goods in high demand were actively sought through bribery or queuing, symptoms that could not be expressed quantitatively to Gosplan. Thus at best any estimation of demand from consumers was likely to be highly anecdotal.

After analyzing this information, Gosplan reported to its political masters in the Praesidium of the party's central committee, which studied both the achievements and the problems experienced in the previous year and then set down broad directives for the following year. These directives included general statements such as "raise housing construction" or "increase the quantity of clothing available." For example, in April 1985 the plenary meeting of the CPSU central committee determined that

> It is planned to increase the national income used for consumption and accumulation by 19–22 percent. Ensure that the entire increase in the national income is reached by enhancing social labor productivity. Reduce its inputs of materials by 4–5 percent, power by 7–9 percent and metals by 13–15 percent.[4]

Gosplan took note of such party directives and during the summer drafted a preliminary planning balance for the economy, a first attempt at accounting for all sources and uses of the principal products produced or required in the economy. At the height of central planning this exhaustive and time-consuming operation covered some 30,000 different commodities; for each one, production sources and users were identified and quantified. This tabulation constituted the material balances for the economy. As an illustrative tool, Table 17.1 shows this kind of initial tabulation giving a hypothetical listing of the sources and uses of steel. It is highly simplified; in reality many different types of steel (construction, sheet, pipe, etc.) had to be planned for. Such a table had to be prepared for each major commodity, and it was vital that the supply and use totals balanced. The need of all the other industrial sectors for any commodity had to match its production, net import, and inventory change.

Demands and uses of commodities are interdependent, and the next task for the planners was reconciliation of the tables. If it was found that the projected needs for steel were greater than planned supply, the output of the steel had to be raised accordingly. This projection required the increased use of other inputs—steel itself,

[3]This policy goes back to the triumph of the "teleologists" over the "geneticists" in the late 1920s, which was discussed in Chapter 16.

[4]*Guidelines for the Economic and Social Development of the USSR for the period 1986–1990, and for the Period Ending in 2000* (Moscow: Novosti Press, 1985), pp. 21–22.

■ TABLE 17.1

Schematic Representation of Materials Balance for Steel (millions of metric tons)

Sources		Uses		
Production	150	Industry		165
Imports	20	(a) Mining	20	
Starting inventory	20	(b) Machinery	80	
		(c) Railways	10	
		(d) Steel	10	
		(e) Agriculture	5	
		(f) Construction	20	
		(g) Shipbuilding	20	
		Households		0
		Government		5
		Export		10
		Year-end inventory		10
Total Sources	190	Total Uses		190

iron ore, coal, limestone, and so forth—so the output in all these other industries had to be raised, requiring yet a further adjustment in steel output.

Soviet planners were helped in this iterative reconciliation by input/output tables, prepared in matrix format as illustrated by Table 17.2. Resolving this system requires the solution of a system of simultaneous equations. Each product group is represented by a row, with the possible sources represented on the left-hand side and the uses on the right. The right-hand side can be separated into intermediate uses (where the product is an input for the production of some other good) and final uses (where it is destined for consumption, use in investment, or for export). The columns represent the demands for intermediate goods that must be supplied by other industries to achieve the indicated level of production, according to the norms of the planners. For example, if product 1 is steel and products 2 and 3 are coal and electricity, then the attainment of an output level of X_1 of steel requires $a_{11}X_1$ of steel, $a_{21}X_2$ of coal, $a_{31}X_3$ of electricity, and so forth.

Where X_i is the output of the ith industry, a_{ij} is the requirement for input X_i per unit of output in the jth industry, S is the change in the stocks, M represents planned imports, C is consumer use, I is investment use, and Ex is planned exports.

The coefficients used to estimate the amount of input required are calculated by the planners using fixed-proportion production functions, based on the average "good practice" needs of industry. A matrix of this kind was maintained by the Soviet planners for about 250 of the most important product groups, which potentially required establishing 6,250 coefficients. In actuality, a substantial proportion of the coefficients would be zero, because many goods are not demanded as inputs by other industries. For example, fertilizers are not directly required by the mining industry or cereals by aluminum smelters. Thus the matrices can be solved in many

■ TABLE 17.2

Representation of Input-Output Analysis

Sources		Intermediate Uses	Final Uses
1. $X_1 - S_1 + M_1$	=	$a_{11}X_1 + a_{21}X_2 + a_{31}X_3 + a_{41}X_4 + \ldots a_{1n}X_n$	$+ C_1 + I_1 + Ex_1$
2. $X_2 - S_2 + M_2$	=	$a_{21}X_1 + a_{22}X_2 + a_{32}X_3 + a_{42}X_4 + \ldots a_{2n}X_n$	$+ C_2 + I_2 + Ex_2$
3. $X_3 - S_3 + M_3$	=	$a_{31}X_1 + a_{23}X_2 + a_{33}X_3 + a_{43}X_4 + \ldots a_{3n}X_n$	$+ C_3 + I_3 + Ex_3$
4. $X_4 - S_4 + M_4$	=	$a_{34}X_1 + a_{24}X_2 + a_{34}X_3 + a_{44}X_4 + \ldots a_{4n}X_n$	$+ C_4 + I_4 + Ex_4$
n. $X_n - S_n + M_n$	=	$a_{n1}X_1 + a_{2n}X_2 + a_{3n}X_3 + a_{4n}X_4 + \ldots a_{nn}X_n$	$+ C_n + I_n + Ex_n$

cases by separating them into subsystems. Nevertheless, the task of compilation was huge, and many of the problems of the planners were technical. Data management and computer systems in the Soviet Union during this period were not highly advanced, which handicapped the operation of the planning system. However, the bigger problem was getting reliable information to the center, a topic to which we will return.

At the height of its coverage and complexity, Soviet planning embraced some 30,000 commodities and thus a complete **input-output matrix** would have some 900 *million* cells, clearly an impossible task. Industrial groups were planned using the materials balance sheets like that in Table 17.1. These balance sheets could be more aggregated than the I-O matrices and did not have to rely on assumptions of fixed input proportions and the absence of economies of scale.

The Draft Plan

These preliminary estimates of both target outputs and planned inputs were called **control figures**. In the next step Gosplan disseminated them to the lower levels of the planning bureaucracies: the ministries and the regional planning centers. From there they were further disaggregated, and passed down to the enterprise level—the units actually responsible for the work—in the form of a **draft plan**. The breakdown among enterprises was, by and large, based on past performance, the **level previously achieved**.

The idea of basing targets on previous achievements is an important feature of central planning. Senior enterprise management in the Soviet system received a large part of their total remuneration in the form of bonuses paid to reward the realization of plan targets. Senior management could receive bonuses of as much as 50 percent of their basic salary for meeting their target and up to 4 percent more for each percentage point by which the plan was overachieved. Thus any effort expended by managers in lobbying the planners to hold the output targets low, while receiving a high allocation of inputs, was probably well spent in terms of the likely outcome on managerial salaries. However, although the bonuses paid for overfulfillment of plan targets were substantial, management in many cases chose to be cautious in determining by just how much to exceed their targets. If output is exceeded by a large margin in the current year, planners would likely raise output targets for successive years, because they based targets "from the level previously achieved." Overperformance with respect to one year's target might be praised at the time, and might lead to a big bonus in that year, but it is likely to lead to problems for the enterprise managers in the succeeding year because the output target will be ratcheted up. Thus the incentive to overachieve was limited. David Dyker, an authority on Soviet planning, called it the Micawber principle, after the Dickens character whose maxim was "Income one pound, expenses nineteen shillings and sixpence, result happiness. Income one pound, expenditure twenty shillings and sixpence, result misery." Considerable evidence confirms that a wise manager tried to meet the target and overachieve a little, but did not exert himself to achieve dramatic growth because of the consequences of having to achieve an elevated target the year after.

After the enterprises received their targets for the following year and their allotment of inputs, the direction of planning reversed. Enterprises turned to their immediate bureaucratic superiors and disputed their ability to meet the targets with the inputs allotted, arguing with all of the influence at their disposal for lower output targets and greater inputs. It is important to recognize that this part of the planning exercise was personal and involved an intense bargaining exercise. One way of describing this process is as "struggle," but it was generally a polite affair in which the participants sought to capitalize on their contacts, influence, and reserve of favors.

When some form of resolution was reached, the *draft plan* was then passed back up the hierarchy and was appropriately modified until it arrived at Gosplan again. At every point, the planners attempted to establish a reconciliation, or compromise, between the higher authorities (who tried to preserve compliance to the original draft plan, which represented conformity with Gosplan's control figures) and the lower authorities, who had the responsibility for meeting the targets. This process of reconciliation coincided with the "tightening" of the plan as production responsibilities became more and more precisely defined. On occasion, of course, all the loose ends could not be tied up and Gosplan adjusted the basic structure of the plan in order to take account of the problems.

Making the Plan into Law

Those at the lower levels of the planning process knew that during this period they had to make their own production targets as realistic (in fact, as minimal) as possible. Once the final balance was struck, the politburo approved the plan and the **Praesidium** turned it into law. It was a punishable offense to fail to meet the plan target, while substantial bonuses were paid to enterprise management for plan achievement and overachievement. After enactment into law, the plan was then passed down the hierarchy of ministries and regional councils with the degree of detail being increased at each level. Ultimately each enterprise entered into contractual arrangements with suppliers and major customers.

THE DETERMINATION OF PRICES

Up to this point the planning process focused exclusively on physical units of commodities, whether outputs or inputs. Prices were determined quite separately and fulfilled a different function from that in a market economy. They were set primarily by the bureaucracy, were altered as infrequently as possible, and did not aspire to reflect either resource cost or demand. Price changes are a nuisance, incur "menu costs," and have little point if the base levels do not reflect scarcity to begin with. Moreover, it was a point of ideological pride that socialism was immune from capitalism's worst diseases, inflation and unemployment. Soviet central planning used three main types of prices for goods: wholesale industrial prices, agricultural prices, and retail prices.[5]

Wholesale Industrial Prices

Wholesale industrial prices were the prices at which firms sold goods to each other. They were determined by a combination of pragmatism, opportunism, and ideology. The underlying principle was that prices should represent the average cost of production of a good across all the enterprises in the relevant industry group. Recall from Chapter 3 that it is marginal cost, not average cost, that reflects scarcity, and therefore the role that prices played in the efficient rationing of scarce resources within the Soviet system was slight. Moreover, cost to the Soviet planners conformed to a Marxian conception and was defined as consisting of labor costs, raw material costs, and depreciation, with no allowance made for either the opportunity cost of capital (interest) or land (rent). After arriving at an estimate of average cost for each firm, the planners would exclude obvious outliers in the calculation of the industry average; any enterprises with abnormally high costs were not considered, although they remained in production and therefore required subsidy.

Adjusted average costs of production were then modified to yield the prices for the plan year, a small amount being deducted to reflect lower costs due to technological change or productivity increase, and a small margin added for profit. Prices arrived at in such a way could never, except by the most unlikely coincidence, reflect relative scarcities and were not a crucial factor in determining enterprise behavior. In a market economy, a firm's revenue is determined by the product of volume and sales price, and that represents a **hard-budget constraint** to the firm. In the long run the firm cannot spend more than its revenues. Under centrally planned socialism, if revenue is less than cost, some way would frequently be found to raise revenues through price changes or subsidies or to reduce costs by lowering administered input prices or taxes. These **soft-budget constraints** profoundly affected Soviet performance, an important fact that we will return to later.

[5]In addition to goods pricing, we will discuss the price of labor and the functioning of the labor market.

One of the more shocking consequences of this system of administered prices discovered during liberalization in the 1990s was a substantial number of **negative value-added enterprises**—firms for whom the sum of the value of outputs evaluated at world prices were, in fact, less than the value of inputs assessed in the same way. This situation was the result of the subsidies implicit in low input costs (especially those related to energy where Soviet prices and world prices were in stark disagreement) and the low quality of output. In the supply-deficit Soviet economy, this output could generally find a buyer, but not in free world markets. The actual number of true negative value-added enterprises was hard to know, but a larger class of industry operating at a profit under Soviet accounting and would show a loss when rent, capital cost, and concessionary tax policy were accounted for.

Agricultural Prices

In Chapter 16 we discussed the scissors crisis of the early 1920s and the young Bolshevik government's determination to control the terms of trade between the agricultural and industrial sectors. Until the final collapse of the Soviet planned economy, agricultural procurement prices were set to establish the terms of trade for the peasants on the **collective farms** (***kolkhozy***) and thus control their purchasing power over goods from the larger economy. Both the unit costs of the inputs of collective farming and the physical volumes of inputs required under the plan were determined by the planners. The planners also fixed the total cost (and hence the average cost) of the production dictated by the plan. If, as was generally the case in the supply-constrained Soviet economy, consumer goods were in short supply, one way to alleviate the shortage was by cutting the purchasing power of the peasants. The price of farm output could be set at the level that would just cover costs. Then each peasant's share of net farm income would be small, allowing for few purchases of consumer goods. In some cases an even greater squeeze was applied by making farm incomes less than necessary planned expenditures, forcing peasants to draw down "idle" monetary balances accumulated in the farm sector from prior years. The same set of agricultural prices applying to collective farms also applied to the state farms (***sovkhozy***). These socially owned farms were operated in the same fashion as industrial firms, with managers appointed by the state and employing workers for money wages rather than for a share of the surplus. Thus they could operate at a profit or were positioned to receive subsidies.

Retail Prices

A third type of price included the *retail prices* charged in the state owned retail stores and consumer cooperatives (which, like the collective farms, were jointly owned by groups of individuals). These prices were dependent on the industrial wholesale and agricultural procurement prices, but they differed by the imposition of a differentiated turnover tax. This tax served two purposes. One was an attempt to bring supply and demand at the consumer level into line by taxing the goods in short supply at a heavier rate than those that were more plentiful. The tax also provided a substantial part of the state's revenue.

LABOR MARKETS

We already discussed how the Soviet system determined disposable income and purchasing power for agricultural workers on the collective farms. In contrast, the income of industrial and service sector workers (as well as the wages of laborers on state farms) were contractual rather than residual. The labor markets in the Soviet Union were by and large much freer than was the popular conception in the West. Workers were not assigned occupations and workplaces by the state, except in the case of the first job of university graduates. However, locating in Moscow (the perpetually attractive "center") was subject to a residency permit, and a chronic shortage of housing put tight constraints on geographical mobility. The choice of occupation was largely up to the worker, though the educational system was highly manipulated and influential in replicating the skill mix of the population that the planners considered appropriate in the long run. In the short run, wages were set by the state to equilibrate the supply with the demand for labor in each use. A crude form of wage adjustment was used with percentage markups to a basic wage applied for such factors as location (the less attractive the higher the wage), unpleasant working conditions, the degree of physical effort, and so forth. In addition, many enterprises resorted to systems of piecework where workers received most of their income as a function of individual or group output.

MARKET CLEARING

The income received by workers, as well as by farmers, could be freely spent on whatever commodity (though not productive asset) that could be found. These elements of consumer *choice* should not be confused with the consumer *sovereignty* fostered by the operation of the free market. Consumer sovereignty implies that the consumers' demands are impartially met through the market via the incentives that it provides. In the centrally planned system, the politicians and planners are sovereign; the plan determines what kinds and quantities of consumer goods are produced, and each consumer decides which of these products he or she wants. If a surplus or shortage for any good should develop, production is *not* automatically shifted by the action of self-oriented economic agents but is changed only by the will of the political leadership.

The planners determined (1) the volume of production of the various goods, (2) the prices that were charged for them, (3) the money incomes of the workers, and (4) the real income of the collective farmers. It was therefore, in theory, possible that aggregate supply and demand could balance. Although an infinite number of sets of prices might satisfy this aggregate condition, in general the prices failed to equilibrate supply and demand in the markets for individual goods. In a market economy such disequilibria are met first by a change in price and subsequently by a change in quantities, but in the centrally planned system neither response occurred. Output plans were seldom realized, especially for consumer goods, and therefore general shortages, as well as unsatisfied demand for particular products, resulted. Centrally planned economies were often characterized by high levels of household savings, because goods were not available for consumers to purchase. This lack of goods at the end of the Soviet era meant substantial money balances in consumers' bank accounts, known as the **monetary overhang.** It was one engine of inflation in the early months of liberalization. However, for our assessment of the planning system the most important point is that the prices set by planners neither reflected the relative scarcity of goods in the short term nor provided an accurate measure of the resource costs of production.

Private Agriculture

One area of free market activity was provided by granting workers in collective farms, state farms, and other enterprises plots on which to raise their own crops, which could be sold at uncontrolled prices. These plots averaged about two-thirds of an acre and were slightly larger on the collective farms than on the state farms, and, as might be expected, the productivity per acre of these plots was well above that seen on either the state or collective farms themselves. Although private plots represented only 3 percent of total arable area in the Soviet Union, they accounted for about 25 percent of output. For some crops, they were a significant source of supply. In 1984 private plots accounted for 58 percent of potato production; about 30 percent of the production of eggs, meat, vegetables, and milk; and 24 percent of wool production. Private plots fulfilled two important functions: ameliorating otherwise desperate conditions on collective farms and providing an outlet for the reluctant savings of industrial workers. However, the irrationality of the pricing structure in the planned sector and the profit incentives of the small-holder plots did make for some extremely distortionary outcomes. A smallholder from the republic of Georgia, in the Transcaucasus, was able to fly on the highly subsidized state airline, Aeroflot, to Moscow with a couple of suitcases of tomatoes and make enough on the sidewalk market in the capital to pay for his flight, room, and board—not the most efficient way of getting the produce to market!

MONITORING PLAN FULFILLMENT

We now turn to the question of verifying the plan. How did the planners see to it that the various parties conformed to the physical performance specified in the plan? It would be an onerous task to certify at each stage that the planned volume of goods physically passed from one concern to another. In fact, the physical plan was monitored through financial flows that mirrored the movement of goods and commodities as recorded by the monopoly state bank, Gosbank. This process was known as **control by the ruble**.

To illustrate, let us take a simple example of the movement of a commodity from its point of initial production to its final use. A state farm produced cotton, which was sent to a textile factory that processed it into cloth for a clothing factory, which in turn shipped its output to a retail store. When the farm delivered its cotton output to the factory, it would obtain a document, an acceptance, from the textile factory verifying that the latter received its raw cotton. This document was then turned over to Gosbank, which credited the farm's account with the value of the cotton delivered, using the plan's industrial prices, and debited the textile factory's account by the same amount. Similarly, after the finished cloth was produced and shipped to the clothing factory, the textile factory obtained a document verifying its delivery of cloth. Again, the document was turned over to Gosbank, which this time credited the textile factory's account and debited the clothing factory's account. Likewise, the clothing factory made the garments and shipped them to the store, again receiving an acceptance. Gosbank credited its account and debited that of the store. Finally, when households purchased the clothing with cash, the state store deposited its cash receipts with Gosbank and was given a credit of equal value.

With this simple example, we can see how every transfer of *physical* output from one location to another, and every bit of value added in production, was mirrored by an associated *financial* transfer through Gosbank. Gosbank's monitoring of these financial transfers would, in theory at least, show the physical movements of goods. If less than the planned amount was delivered in any specified time period, Gosbank would be alerted. If inputs or outputs were stolen and diverted to the black market, Gosbank would know, and the failure to perform could be investigated and rectified. To discipline the system, the state bank had at its disposal a range of sanctions, from the expropriation of a firm's deposits to a full-scale party investigation into enterprise affairs. However, the information needs of full oversight were enormous, and often the system would be perfunctory rather than exhaustive. Sanctions were used sparingly and oversight was ineffective. As a result, failure to perform was frequent and unpunished, and corruption was extensive.[6]

Control by the ruble required restrictions on the use of money and credit, which lowered the degree of initiative that managers could show. Enterprise accounts with Gosbank could only be used to pay for the type and quantities of inputs that were specified in the plan. No enterprise could grant credit to another enterprise.[7] Enterprises were virtually forbidden to hold cash for any purpose other than payment of wages. Even the cash receipts of state stores had to be first deposited with Gosbank and subsequently withdrawn to meet the payroll.

Planning was performed in terms of physical units, but the financial sector of the centrally planned economy allowed the state bank to monitor the execution of the plan.

---

[6]One of the most famous abuses came to light in the late 1970s in the cotton industry. Large quantities of fictitious cotton were shipped from state farms in Central Asia. The appropriate acceptances were issued but concealed by a web of corruption that extended up to and included Yurii Churbanov, Brezhnev's son-in-law. It took years for the scheme to be uncovered, and billions of rubles were diverted. Ultimately several people were put to death for "economic crimes."

[7]This prohibition is in sharp distinction with the post-liberalization system in Russia and other newly independent states in which an extensive net of interenterprise credit has grown up with the tacit support of the government. Many suppliers of raw materials, especially in the energy sector, are owed huge sums of money by their customers, who cannot pay often because they are owed by customers further down the production chain.

INCENTIVES IN SOVIET-TYPE SYSTEMS

In Chapter 1 we discussed in general terms the issues of incentives in economic systems, and the unraveling of the centrally planned economies is a case study in their importance. The successes and failures of Soviet planning can be largely attributed to the set of incentives provided, and it is worthwhile discussing these incentives as they fell on each group.

Collective Farms

Agriculture is generally regarded as one of the greatest failures of Soviet economics, and the dismal performance of collective agriculture must shoulder a great deal of the blame for the ultimate demise of the system. We saw that income on collective farms was the residual between the revenue received by the farms and their expenses on material factors of production. Revenue itself was a function of the volume of output and the prices determined by the planners, whose objective was frequently to limit the real income, and therefore the demand for consumers' goods by the peasants on the farms. Expenditure on material inputs was also determined in Moscow. Thus the incentive to raise output on the farms was dulled by the knowledge that prices could be reduced as a response.

Moreover, individual peasants on the farms saw little incentive to raise their effort and diligence. The income of the farm was divided among the workers on the basis of work points. In theory it might mean that harder work was rewarded with higher income, but in reality work points did little to reflect effort. A serious free rider problem resulted, because aggregate output of the farm changed little on the basis of one person's contribution as any gain in output was spread among the members of the collective or work brigade. To counter this problem, the authorities attempted to reduce the size of the work teams from their original conception of 100 plus down to much smaller groups, in some cases as small as the family. However, in terms of living standards it was better to spend time on one's own personal plot than to work hard for the collective enterprise; it is not surprising that productivity remained low and output stagnated for long periods of time. At the end of the Soviet period, contract systems began to be favored; a group, or family, agreed to supply part of the collective farm's target at fixed prices with the knowledge that any excess could be sold to the farm at "market" prices or sold directly on the farmers' markets.[8]

Workers

Workers, whether on state farms or within manufacturing or extractive industry, had much the same set of incentives as workers in the capitalist West. Pay was largely by the hour and the incentives for high performance were in part coercive,

[8]Such "household responsibility systems" were successful in China because they provided a much higher degree of incentive than do collective farms.

enforced by management supervision, and part pecuniary, in that good job performance might lead to promotion and betterment. Alienation, which Marx identified as one of the key weaknesses of capitalism, was as prevalent as in the industrialized West.[9] Despite the urging of the state and management, working for the glory of the country became a less significant motivating factor, while advancement into the higher echelons of management had as much to do with political connection as with job performance. To link job performance more closely with pay, much of the socialist world turned to "piece working," where workers are paid as far as possible in proportion to individual output. The irony here is that this practice is traditionally regarded by the left as being the most exploitative labor management practice and also one that stifles both individual initiative and group cooperation. In advanced capitalist systems it remains only in "sweat shop" situations.

Ultimately a worker toils for goods rather than for money. Because centrally planned economies were chronically inept in providing consumer goods, the incentive to work hard was correspondingly reduced. Goals that prove to be powerful motivators to workers in capitalist countries—such as buying a house, acquiring financial assets, or traveling abroad—were simply not options. A select group of workers were chosen to travel to vacation spots within the socialist world, but again this reward was largely the result of political connections rather than work performance. The high rate of forced household savings and the monetary overhang were testaments to the failure of monetary incentives in a demand surplus economy.

Managers

Enterprise managers in the Soviet system operated under a strong material incentive system with a substantial portion of income dependent on meeting the plan targets, which could be further increased by overfulfillment. This motivator was reinforced by coercive negative incentives; failure to meet targets might lead to loss of job, disciplinary action, or, in the rare limit, prosecution and incarceration. The combination of incentives proved less than optimal in a variety of ways. First, the incentives did little to increase the efficiency of industry in terms of the optimal use of factors of production. Second, the system did little to encourage either product or process innovation. Third, quality control was a serious problem, exacerbated by little motivation to produce consumer goods whose design and quality might be most appreciated by the ultimate user. Finally, and perhaps most crucially, the incentives encouraged the relaying of misleading data from the enterprise units to the center.

Efficiency The system of incentives did little to encourage optimum use of factors of production. Capital was largely allocated by the planners and generally came without cost, or with a high subsidy, to the enterprise. When capital charges were

[9]In fact, the stock remark about Soviet work was that "We pretend to work, and they pretend to pay us," or sometimes "They pretend to pay us, and we pretend to work."

used, they did not reflect the opportunity cost of capital. Consequently, no systematic device encouraged optimal use of capital; each manager would attempt to obtain as much equipment as possible and stockpile it against some future exigency.

A similar situation applied in the use of labor. Any gains resulting from a reduction in the workforce were not retained within the enterprise but were remitted to the center. Rather than promoting economy of labor, incentives encouraged managers to retain as much labor as possible. In a capitalist system, a profit-maximizing entrepreneur will tend to hire workers up to the point where the wage is equal to the product of the marginal worker, but in the Soviet system it was worthwhile to have any worker around as long as the marginal product was positive.

Output targets were defined in annual terms, and optimally, production would proceed smoothly throughout the year. However, in Soviet enterprise the same human factors applied as in, say, a student's work habits. Production proved to be slow early in the year, far from the deadline, but as the end of the planning period approached, meeting the target became a matter of greater urgency. The last few months were characterized by what became known as **storming**, a fevered attempt to raise output to meet the target. At this point the excess labor and machinery became especially valuable, but hoarding spread beyond capital and labor. Intermediate goods and inputs required by other productive units in the system were frequently in short supply early in the year and became available only as the storming behavior in supplying enterprises kicked in, so keeping high inventories was quite rational.

Innovation Innovation in any system is a relatively risky business, whether it entails the development of new products or the introduction of a new technique for production. However, in market systems successful innovation is often rewarded by greater efficiency and lower costs, or in tapping new sources of consumer demand and increased sales; each possibility yields higher profits. The Soviet system did little to encourage such innovation.

Consider first new techniques of production. These generally entail some teething period during which glitches are ironed out and output necessarily falls. If these problems are prolonged, then it might prove impossible to recover during the fixed horizon of the planning year. Output targets would then not be met and the enterprise manager's income would suffer, or some more dire consequence (loss of job or even criminal sanction) might result. Consequently, innovation was often not attractive. Managers generally found it easier and more comfortable to produce by tried and tested methods in which the outcome was predictable.

Similarly, not much incentive existed at the enterprise level to develop new products. The plan did not usually require them, because the planning process consisted largely of revamping the previous period's output figures. New products took management time and other resources away from current production and opened the possibility of falling short of targets, inviting the same loss of income or worse.

Quality Control Planning targets were usually laid out in terms of physical units. Although in theory all the output was meant to be of "acceptable" quality, and retail stores or users of intermediate goods could reject the products that were substandard, in reality quality control was poor. In market systems the real cost of poor quality is a loss of reputation and repeat business; in the planned system the customers had no choice. Their suppliers were defined by the plan, and those suppliers simply could not lose sales as a result.

Information A planning system in which decisions are made centrally can only function well if the data received at the center are accurate. However, in the Soviet system, powerful incentives motivated enterprise managers to keep the planners in the dark. It was not good for them to reveal the real potential of their enterprises, which would only result in an upward adjustment in output targets in the next planning round and make the job of reaching those targets more difficult. It was in the enterprise managers' interest to mislead the planners by overstating their real needs for labor, machinery, and material inputs. If successful, that produced a cushion that could be called on in times of emergency.

The Bureaucrats

Finally we turn to the incentives that operated on the planners themselves. Why should they work to produce a good plan and ensure compliance to it? As we already noted, the basic outline of the plan was determined by the political masters. It was the function of the bureaucrats to turn these ideas into a working document, and, like other members of the entire Soviet hierarchy, it was best to achieve this task in as painless a way as possible.

The planners put a lot of energy into improving the techniques of planning, but when it came to actually coming up with ideas to reform the incentive structures, little motivated them. From time to time planners went out on a limb to proclaim the importance of, say, increasing the role of prices to reflect costs, but a wise planner would only do that with the clear approval of the political leadership. Furthermore, he or she might be aware that shifts in the preferences of the leaders are not permanent. Khrushchev encouraged unorthodox thinking to a degree that his predecessor Stalin had not, and those who displaced him were alarmed by this activity. The kind of ideas that were rewarded under one first secretary could lead to trouble under another. The safest behavior was to move slowly and conventionally.

CONCLUSION

The Soviet system contained little to encourage either fresh thinking, high quality, new ideas, or new products. Overwhelmingly the incentives fostered a repetition of the status quo, and consequently the economy ran out of sources of extensive growth. The absence of new land, maximum participation rates, and low marginal productivity of capital made new investment almost valueless. The system allowed no sources of total factor productivity growth. Relative decline was inevitable and reform of the economy vital. Whether this reform and transition will be successful is discussed more thoroughly in Part 6 of this book.

KEY TERMS AND CONCEPTS

collective farms
control by the ruble
control figures
draft plan
Gosbank
Gosplan
hard-budget constraint
input-output matrix
kolkhozy
legality
level previously achieved
monetary overhang
negative value-added enterprises
politburo
Praesidium
soft-budget constraints
sovkhozy
storming

QUESTIONS FOR DISCUSSION

1. In what ways did the planning in the Soviet Union hinge on interpersonal relations and influence?
2. What is the significance of the plan "from the level previously achieved" for the functioning of the planning process?
3. Discuss the function and the role of prices in the Soviet Union under planning.
4. How was plan fulfillment monitored in the Soviet system?
5. Why was the yield on private agriculture plots so much greater than on state and collective farms?
6. What incentives motivated management to give misleading information to planners?
7. Why did Soviet firms tend toward high degrees of vertical integration?
8. Why was the Soviet system so deficient in producing goods for consumers?
9. What incentives motivated Soviet management to pay attention to quality control?
10. Which of capitalism and Soviet socialism fostered the strongest incentives for innovation? Why?

RESOURCES

Books and Articles

Flakierski, Henryk. *Income Inequalities in the Former Soviet Union and Its Republics.* Armonk, NY: M.E. Sharpe, 1993. Reviewed in the *Journal of Comparative Economics,* October 1994, 260–271.

Goldman, Marshall I. *What Went Wrong with Perestroika,* chap. 15. New York: W.W. Norton, 1991.

Gray, Kenneth R. (ed.). *Soviet Agriculture: Comparative Perspectives.* Ames: Iowa University Press, 1990.

Gregory, Paul R., and Robert C. Stuart. *Soviet and Post-Soviet Economic Structure and Performance,* 5th ed. New York: HarperCollins, 1994.

Hare, Paul G. *Central Planning.* Chur, Switzerland: Harwood, 1991.

Huang, Yasheng. "Information, Bureaucracy, and Economic Reforms in China and the Soviet Union." *World Politics,* October 1994, 102–134.

International Monetary Fund, The World Bank, Organization for Economic Co-operation and Development, and European Bank for Reconstruction and Development. *A Study of the Soviet Economy.* 3 vols. Paris: Organization for Economic Cooperation and Development, 1991.

Kornai, János. *The Socialist System: The Political Economy of Communism.* Princeton, NJ: Princeton University Press, 1991.

Litwack, John. "Legality and Market Reform in Soviet Type Economies," *Journal of Economic Perspectives* 5, no. 4 (Fall 1991).

Malle, Silvana. *Employment Planning in the Soviet Union.* New York: St. Martin's Press, 1990.

Pryor, Frederic L. *The Rise and Fall of Collectivized Agriculture in Marxist Regimes.* Princeton, NJ: Princeton University Press, 1992.

Simis, Kostantin M. *The USSR—The Corrupt Society: The Secret World of Soviet Capitalism.* New York: Simon and Schuster, 1982.

Standing, Guy (ed.). *In Search of Flexibility: The New Soviet Labor Market.* Geneva: International Labor Office, 1991.

Wolf, Thomas. *A Foreign Trade in the Centrally Planned Economy.* Chur, Switzerland: Harwood, 1988.

19

THE POSSIBILITIES OF A THIRD WAY

Central planning offers many appealing features. A plan enables tasks to be prioritized rather than relying on what seem at times to be the whims and myopia of the market. A plan can also facilitate the mobilization of resources to achieve specific aims, such as the creation of infrastructure or the creation of a new industrial sector. Because income from property accrues to the state, public ownership of the means of production, which is a usual but not a necessary feature of centrally planned economies, avoids extreme bias in the distribution of income. Despite the recent dismal economic history of centrally planned states, planning retains an appeal. It is still considered a rational activity within a firm or a household, which lends some justification for planning in the management of the national economy.

From its earliest applications, however, the deficiencies of centralized planning have been apparent. Effective command planning requires the centralization of a vast amount of information, so much in fact that it is almost impossible to process and to reconcile. This need for data often creates perverse incentives that encourage enterprise managers to mislead the center for their advantage. Planning lacks a mechanism whereby consumer preferences are rapidly transmitted to the center, and so the preferences of individuals must be guessed at or ignored. Finally, of particular importance is the fact that only in the rarest of circumstances will prices in a planned system reflect relative scarcities or resource costs.

MARKET SOCIALISM AND SOCIAL MARKETS

Because each of the polar conceptions, free market capitalism and socialist command planning, involves defects, a middle way that grasps the market's advantages in allocative efficiency and marries it to the distributional equity of socialism is attractive.

Two main approaches can be taken to an economic third way.[1] A system in which capital is collectively owned, generally by the state, but in which the prices of final

[1] We should note that "third way" as used here is not identical with the concept put forth by the British sociologist and LSE Director Anthony Giddens, in his book *The Third Way: The Renewal of Social Democracy* (London: Polity Press, 2000). Giddens' book, which has been embraced by Tony Blair and both Bill and Hillary Clinton, is largely about politics and promotes the ideas of liberal globalization, environmental concern, and broader property ownership.

products and inputs are determined in the marketplace is generally referred to as **market socialism**. We observed this kind of economy in our review of the former Yugoslav state. Such a system enables the market to allocate factors of production, while coordination of the system is achieved through price signaling. Usually the one price not determined by the market is that of capital. Generally it is owned by the state and is loaned or rented out at prices determined by the planners or the politicians.

A second approach is to allow a more completely operative market system, in which capital may be privately owned and rationed by the market. However, the government puts constraints on the ultimate outcome of the system, and prescribes how the economy will perform in terms of income distribution, access to basic goods and services, and sometimes price determination. This kind of economy is properly referred to as a **social market economy**, and we studied this system in the Swedish and German cases. Unfortunately, the distinction between true market socialism and the social market approach is frequently confused.

MARKET SOCIALISM

We turn first to discuss the advantages and flaws of market socialism. This system appeals because it represents the best of two worlds, providing both allocative efficiency and equity, but both recent experience and current scholarship emphasize the vital importance of an impartial capital market for the functioning of any market system. Any attempt to maintain a competitive system of prices in the goods and labor markets alone will fail because it divorces the functioning of those markets from the market for capital, to which they are inescapably related.

The Function of the Capital Market

The foremost function of a capital market is to disinterestedly evaluate the performance and potential of each firm. The share values of those firms traded in equity markets are determined by an impersonal stock market, which adjusts values to reflect prospects. Those firms that borrow by issuing bonds and paper are subject to the judgment of the bond market, again with many authors pursuing self-interest, on the value of its credit. Those firms that borrow directly from banks compete with other borrowers for capital and must demonstrate the soundness of the business plans and pay premiums according to the riskiness of their ventures. The Israeli economist Michael Keren summed up the essential function of the capital market:

> The basic service the capital market supplies is the evaluation of each traded firm's net worth. This signals to its management and its owners how the market judges its future prospects. If this value declines relative to that of similar firms, this may be taken as an indication that the market considers the firm's policies inferior to those of its competitors. In severe situations, this may convey a recommendation to change the top management team of the firm, possibly through a takeover by an alternative team. In extreme cases, when the market believes that the expected present value of the firm's cash flow is

negative or significantly below the breakup value of the firm, the capital market may apply direct sanctions by bankrupting the firm.[2]

Making Capital Decisions Under Socialism

In the absence of an objective capital market, decisions about which firms are to be given funds for capital investment and which denied must be made by a political process. We can conceive of two broad institutional approaches to addressing this problem. On the one hand, we can allow allocation of capital among competing investment projects to be in the hands of a state hierarchy, consisting of the political leaders and the bureaucrats, the approach followed under central planning in the Soviet Union and Soviet bloc. The politicians laid down guidelines, while the planners crafted the plan, and any perceived deviation by the planners from the interest of the politicians would likely be met by their discipline or removal. The system produced mixed results: the growth of heavy industry was both rapid and sustained, but enterprise managers felt little incentive to innovate and new enterprises were few. Bankruptcies were even more rare as the political process often acted to preserve the status quo. These tendencies impeded the development and adoption of new technology by the planned economies and may account for their ultimate failure in the face of the technological revolution of the 1980s.

An alternative approach might be to establish "investment boards," made up of impartial "experts" who could take a dispassionate view of the prospects of various potential enterprises. Unless specific arrangements were made to protect their tenure, and hence to insulate the board members, this approach only pushes the problem one step away. The performance of the boards would not be subject to an independent evaluation, but the board members would serve at the pleasure of the politicians and would themselves be political appointees. Safeguards (such as long-term tenure) could be designed to insulate such boards from political pressure, but they are not likely to be perfect. Under such political uncertainty, it is difficult to see how the action of any planning agency or board can effectively simulate the performance of a financial market. In the market, the weighted opinion of many market participants, rather than one individual or group, decides the fate of firms. The best that can be done in its place is a considered judgment by a narrower group that can never be impersonal.

It can, however, be argued with some justification that the behavior of investment boards or planners might in some cases be better than the behavior of the market. Markets might be short-sighted in their evaluation of prospects, and deny capital to enterprises that, though worthy, will be slow to pay back principal. Planners or investment boards might be more capable of taking a longer view. It is also possible that planning might facilitate a more comprehensive view of the costs and gains of a project than the market does. Market decisions frequently fail to take into account significant positive and negative externalities, and, in theory at least, plan-

[2]Michael Keren, "On the (Im)Possibility of Market Socialism," in *The Road to Capitalism*, Kennett and Lieberman, eds. (Fort Worth, TX: Harcourt Brace, 1993), pp. 45–52.

ners can take a more holistic view of the cost-benefit matrix of an investment. Consider, for example, constructing a railway line. A private firm would consider only the costs and revenues of the venture itself. A planning or investment board would want to take into consideration a much broader set of effects: the effect of alleviating road congestion in transport, the impact on the environment, and so forth. With respect to investments with infrastructural and spillover consequences, the board might well arrive at a more socially optimal decision than the market.

Ludwig von Mises, the promarket Austrian economist, argued trenchantly that a socialist state would be unable to handle the question of a railway investment well:

> Suppose, for instance, that the socialist commonwealth was contemplating a new railway line. Would a new railway line be a good thing? If so, which of many possible routes should it cover? Under a system of private ownership we could use money calculations to decide these questions. The new line would cheapen the transportation of certain articles, and, on this basis, we could estimate whether the reduction in transport charges would be great enough to counterweigh the expenditure which the building and running of the line would involve. Such a calculation could be made only in money. We could not do it by comparing various classes of expenditure and savings in kind. If it is out of the question to reduce to a common unit the quantities of various kinds of skilled and unskilled labor, iron, coal, building materials of different kinds, machinery, and the other things which the building and upkeep of railways necessitate, then it is impossible to make them the subject of economic calculation. We can make systematic economic plans only when all the commodities which we have to take into account can be assimilated to money. True, money calculations are incomplete. True, they have profound deficiencies. But we have nothing better to put in their place. And, under sound monetary conditions, they suffice for practical purposes. If we abandon them, economic calculation becomes absolutely impossible.[3]

Even though von Mises's point that rational planning requires valuation in terms of some comparable unit is quite valid, it is by no means clear that his example is a good one. A government may be much more qualified to calculate the complete benefits over space and time of a major infrastructural improvement. For example, the establishment of a railway line will involve inevitable consequences for other means of transportation. Roads will be less congested, pollution will be lowered, time will be saved, and other spillovers experienced. Quite contrary to von Mises's assertion, the planner is better able to consider the social benefit of large-scale infrastructural change.

The Soft-Budget Constraint

The political control of investment credit is a facet of a general problem articulated by the Hungarian economist Janos Kornai.[4] He spent much of his career within the Hungarian planning bureaucracy and well understood the way that such a system operated. The soft-budget constraint refers to a situation in which the firm or enter-

[3]Ludwig von Mises, "Economic Calculation in Socialism," in *The Road to Capitalism,* David Kennett and Marc Lieberman, eds. (Fort Worth, TX: Harcourt Brace, 1993), pp. 38–39.

[4]Janos Kornai, "The Soft Budget Constraint," *Kyklos* 39, 1986, pp. 3–30.

prise is unconstrained by the basic maxim that long-run revenues must exceed long-run costs. A hard-budget constraint is experienced by firms in competitive markets. They cannot expect to receive a subsidy toward the operation in the long run, and they therefore must earn enough revenue to meet their costs of materials and factors of production including capital. Although they might go into debt in the short run, in the long run the debt must be amortized.

In socialist economies, because both capital costs and operating costs are frequently subsidized by the state, the soft-budget constraint is the norm, not the exception. Subtle ways of introducing "softness" into the system include direct subsidies, discriminatory taxation, or the manipulation of administered prices to ensure the appearance of financial viability. In this chapter, however, what concerns us is the existence of "soft credit," a phenomenon that embraces two related features. The first is the provision of credit at an interest rate that fails to reflect the opportunity cost of capital, implying that the demand for investment funds will generally speaking exceed its supply and that it must be allocated or rationed by a nonprice system, opening the door to political or personal favoritism. By itself, however, a nonprice allocation system does not necessarily represent soft credit: if payment reschedules require adherence, then even loans at subsidized interest rates can be "hard." If debt service payments are not met, then the firm can be forced into bankruptcy, merger, or takeover. What makes the system truly "soft" is a second feature: the knowledge that the political process will ensure the continued existence and even the growth of the firm despite continued failure to meet the prescribed repayment schedule. The **soft-budget constraint** enables the firm to continue to exist although its long-term obligations are not met. To put it a different way, its long-term expenditures are greater than its long-term revenue, and credit continues to be granted by the authorities, even in the face of little prospect of repayment.

The Impact of Soft-Budget Constraints on the Conduct of the Enterprise

If the firm believes that its budget constraint is indeed soft, incentives exist for it to behave in ways that will lower the efficiency of the economy. The firm's elasticity of demand for inputs will become markedly reduced. If increases in costs are compensated by external assistance, an enterprise manager sees little reason to economize on the use of the newly expensive factor. Under a soft-budget constraint, a rise in input prices does not lead a decision maker to change input mix or alter output level but rather to get on the phone to persuade the planners to change prices or to grant additional credits. Although the short-term consequences may be grave, the longer term is of greater consequence. Kornai summarized this situation:

> The most important issue is dynamic adjustment. If the budget constraint is hard, the firm has no other option but to adjust to unfavorable circumstances by improving quality, cutting costs, introducing new products or processes, i.e., it must behave in an entrepreneurial manner. If, however, the budget constraint is soft, such productive efforts are no longer imperative. Instead, the firm is likely to seek external assistance, asking for compensation for unfavorable external circumstances. The State is acting like an overall insurance company taking over all the moral hazards with the usual well-known consequences; the

> insured will be less careful in protecting his wealth. [Joseph] Schumpeter [the Austrian economist] emphasized the significance of "creative destruction": the elimination of old products, technologies, organizations which were surpassed by the more efficient new ones. The soft budget constraint protects the old production line, the inefficient firm against constructive destruction and thus impedes innovation and development.[5]

The Possibility of Market Socialism

The foregoing argument suggests that the problems of capital allocation are fatal to any attempt at market socialism. Whenever investment funds are controlled by the government, or by boards appointed by the government, some softness in capital allocation becomes inevitable. Enterprise managers, knowing that projects are ultimately supported on political rather than economic grounds, will not adopt the behavior that results in allocative efficiency.

In Keren's terms, the vital aims of market socialism are equality and decentralized decision making. The former requires the public ownership of productive assets. The latter requires hard-budget constraints and an absence of state intervention. However, these two aims are in conflict. The exclusion of private market and the political bureaucratic process cannot serve as an adequate proxy. Enterprises become aware that survival and growth are politically, not economically, determined, and their behavior changes as a result.

Although it is hard to pick holes in this logic, its flaw is that it sets straw men against each other. Financial markets, because they are disinterested, are assumed to be superior to the political process in allocating investment. However, the lessons of recent history are that private markets are capable of enormous errors in granting funds to projects that fail—the U.S. savings and loans crisis and the Asian banking debacle are two examples that stand out.[6] Similarly, socially owned banking systems—for example, in Taiwan or in France during "les trentes gloirieuses"—performed an adequate job in credit allocation. A pure market can offer advantages in allocative efficiency over politically controlled investment processes, but myopia, panic, and a narrow definition of the "bottom line" are all problems that can afflict a market system and can lead to social consequences that are difficult to predict and expensive to correct.

THE SOCIAL MARKET ECONOMY

The European Model

Market socialism now seems to be largely out of favor, but the search for a middle way is nevertheless active. European nations that swung to the right in the 1980s, moved back to the left by the mid-1990s, and their economies embody high degrees

[5]Kornai, "The Soft Budget Constraint," *Kyklos* 39, 1986, pp. 10–11.

[6]The indigenous financial systems of most East Asian countries relied on directed credit; however, much of the blame for the crisis must be placed on the inflow and outflow of "hot" monies from competitive financial systems.

of regulation and redistribution. The alternative to nationalizing the means of production (which denies private ownership of most capital and hence the appropriation of its income stream by individuals) is to allow a market to operate for all goods and factors of production, including capital, but to use the power of the state to modify, to regulate, and to guarantee the distribution of income and to ensure access to basic services and opportunities. We already looked at two good examples of this kind of economic organization in Sweden (Chapter 7) and in the Federal Republic of Germany (Chapter 9). In fact, the ethic of the entire European Union might well be described as social market oriented.

The Stakeholder and the Stockholder

The German model of worker participation and involvement in decision making (sometimes called the **Rhine model**) calls into question the conception of the **Anglo-Saxon model** that a firm's sole responsibility is to its stockholders. In Germany the system of codetermination, with labor involved in management decision making, establishes the principle that others besides the "owners" of the corporation have a stake in its future and therefore a voice in its management. This notion brings us to a discussion of what is now referred to as the stakeholder economy.

A **stakeholder** is defined as someone who, while not a titular owner of a business, holds a legitimate interest in its performance and success. The stakeholders of a corporation may include not only the shareholders but also labor, management, customers, suppliers, lenders, and the community in which the corporation is located. Consequently, stakeholders' legitimacy comes from the ability to influence the performance of the corporation.

It is difficult to draw strong conclusions about the effect that the legitimation of a wide range of interests in the decisions of firms does to economic performance. If the behavior of the corporation is indeed meaningfully modified by recognizing stakeholder preferences, and if that behavior is not consistent with profit maximization, it should follow that the "stakeholder corporation" might experience difficulty because it will underperform its "profit-oriented" competitors. Less profitable than a profit-maximizing corporation unconstrained by stakeholder preferences, a stakeholder corporation would therefore be vulnerable to, and ultimately eliminated, by market forces.

If, in fact, pleasing the stakeholders contributes to the maximization of long-term profits, then no conflict exists. *The Economist*, in reviewing a recent book by John Kay, a prominent British economist, who favors the view that the corporation is a "social institution" beholden to a range of stakeholders rather than a private one beholden only to its owners, declared such a view to be "either trivial or meaningless. Few companies, bar perhaps monopoly utilities, can afford to have a miserable workforce or disgruntled customers. If, that is, they want to be successful. Presumably that means making money for their customers."[7]

---

[7]*The Economist*, "Money Making," a review of *The Business of Economics* by John Kay (Oxford: Oxford University Press, 1996). Review of Books and Media, November 16, 1996, p. 12.

However, other interpretations merit consideration. For example, take the issue of labor's "stake" in its employer. Clearly in Japan where the institution of lifetime employment covers at least some of the workforce of the major employers, workers possess a greater recognized stake than in, say, the United States. This relationship hampered the ability of Japanese corporations to deal with the downturn in demand that has afflicted the economy since 1990. The productivity and profitability of Japanese firms was adversely affected by their inability to restructure the workforce. In the United States, in contrast, downturns in demand, or profitability, can be met by trimming the workforce, as in the well-documented downsizing of the early 1990s. Similarly, if a company takes seriously its obligations to a community, should that commitment to its neighbor/stakeholders be at the expense of shareholders?

Within the German model the most important stakeholders in the firm are, on the one hand, the employees and, on the other, the bankers, who lend the enterprise most of its capital. Often the same banks also own some of the shares of the firm, which is allowed under German law, but generally includes only a small part of total equity.[8] However, the banks' considerable influence in the firm comes from representation on the supervisory boards and also control of the voting power of the shares they hold for clients in their role as stockbrokers and mutual fund managers. A growing criticism in Germany centers on the issue of whether the interest of the banks as lenders may be in conflict with the interest of the shareholders. In recent years, a rising activism by shareholders focused on maximizing the return to their capital. Table 19.1 shows the dominance of banks in decision making in major German corporations. This power originates not primarily from bank ownership of stock but its ability to vote by proxy the shares held in investment funds and in customer accounts, an unusual aspect of German law.

Stakeholders As Shareholders

One way in which the potential conflict between the rights of shareholders and the claims of other stakeholders might be resolved is by extension of share ownership to stakeholders. This arrangement could be used to resolve to some degree the principal-agent issues that traditionally affect the labor-capital relationship. A growing number of firms are providing incentives for workers in the form of preferential employee ownership schemes, which tend to bring interests of capital and labor into much closer alignment. A similar solution might also be possible in the case of a local government, which could take an equity holding in a major local employer. Such an arrangement would, however, raise complexities of the municipalities' attitude to new entrants and competitors and might bias the level playing field.

The government in the United States actively favors the extension of employee ownership and offers considerable tax advantages to firms that institute employee stock ownership programs, resulting in a rise in worker ownership of firms. Table

[8]In 1994 private banks directly held about 0.4 percent of German industrial capital, down from 1.3 percent in 1976. *The Economist*, January 3, 1995.

■ TABLE 19.1

Banks' Share of Voting Rights at AGMs of Large German Companies, 1992

Shares Owned By:				
Company	**Banks**	**Subsidiary Investment Funds**	**Proxy Votes**	**Total Bank Votes**
Siemens	—	9.87	85.61	95.48
Volkswagen	—	8.89	35.16	44.05
Hoechst	—	10.74	87.72	98.46
BASF	0.09	13.61	81.01	94.71
Bayer	—	11.23	80.09	91.32
Thyssen	6.77	3.62	34.98	45.37
VEBA	—	12.62	78.23	90.85
Mannesmann	—	7.76	90.35	98.11
Deutsche Bank	—	12.41	82.32	94.73
MAN	8.67	12.69	26.84	48.2

SOURCE: *The Economist,* June 3, 1995, p. 66.

19.2 shows the 10 largest majority employee-owned corporations in the United States. Although some are quite large, they are clearly only a tiny fraction of the total economy and tend to be concentrated in service industries. It is also worth observing that even employee ownership does not mean peace between the management and the workforce. The roles of worker and owner might be in conflict. In the fall of 2002 the machinists union, whose members are among the majority ownership of the United Airlines, embarked upon a damaging strike against the airline.

In addition to the firms of Table 19.2 in which the employees have more than 50 percent of equity, employees in many more companies hold a significant part of the shares. The ESOP Association reports that more than 10,000 U.S. corporations offer employee stock option plans. About 10 percent, or 1,000 of these companies are publicly listed. Moreover, many workers in the United States and elsewhere have a financial interest in their employer. One avenue is by the heavy investment of corporate pension funds in employer stock. One study found that employer stock represented almost 20 percent of assets in defined benefit corporate pension plans.[9] Another is the widespread use of 401(k) plans that often give strong incentives to workers who invest in company stock.

Some evidence suggests that involving employees as formal "at risk" stakeholders does lead to better performance than in the conventional corporation in which workers have no ownership stake. In 2000, Blasi and colleagues concluded that corporations with ESOP plans grew faster (at a rate of 2.3% annually) than did

[9]Committee on Education Workforce, U.S. Congress, Testimony of Dr. Douglas Kruse, Ph.D., Rutgers University, Wednesday, February, 13, 2002.

■ TABLE 19.2

The 10 Largest Firms in the United States with Employee Holdings Above 50 Percent of Total Equity, 2002

Company	Plan	Business	Number of Employees
United Parcel Service	401k	Package Delivery	344,000
Publix Supermarkets	ESOP, stock purchase	Supermarkets	111,000
United Airlines	ESOP	Airline	98,400
Hy-Vee	ESOP	Supermarkets	46,000
Science Applications, Intl.	multiple	R&D/Computer Systems	41,000
Lifetouch	ESOP	Photography Studios	25,890
Tharaldson Motels	ESOP	Motel Management	18,980
Amsted Industries	ESOP	Industrial Production	12,500
CH2M Hill, Inc.	stock purchase	Engineering & Construction	12,000
Parsons Corp.	ESOP	Engineering, Mining & Construction	12,000

SOURCE: National Center for Employee Ownership, "The Employee Ownership 100," available at http://www.nceo.org/ (accessed June 2003).

firms without such plans.[10] However, this improvement is not automatic. Kruse found that "employee ownership may have positive effects if employees value ownership in itself or perceive that it brings greater income, job security, or control over jobs and the workplace. On the other hand, it may have negligible or even negative effects if employees perceive no difference in their worklives, dislike the extra risk to their income or wealth, or have raised expectations that are not fulfilled."

Cooperative Organization

One widely spread alternative to the corporate system is provided by the cooperative movement, which can be traced back to a group of 28 textile workers who organized the *Rochdale Society of Equitable Pioneers*. In 1844, a group of English weavers, dismissed and blacklisted by mill owners for trying to organize a trade union, pooled £140 to open a small dry goods store stocked with oatmeal, sugar, butter, and flour. Out of this grew a large and successful wholesale and retailing system, and it proved the inspiration for cooperative and mutual activity in a wide range of areas.

The founders of the movement codified their ideology into four precepts commonly known as the **Rochdale Principles**, which survive in their broad meaning today.[11]

[10]Joseph Blasi, Douglas Kruse, James Sesil, Maya Kroumova, and Ryan Weeden, *Stock Options, Corporate Performance, and Organizational Change* (Oakland, CA: National Center for Employee Ownership, 2000).
[11]In fact the International Cooperative Alliance has refined the basic four principles to a current seven. See the ICA Web page http://www.ica.coop/ica/info/.

1. Cooperatives are member-owned and -controlled businesses in which all members have an equal say in the governance of the business: one member, one vote. Co-ops stand in contrast to proprietary ownership, in which one person holds all of the authority, and "traditional" corporate ownership, which bases control on the size of one's investment.
2. Cooperatives serve their members, and not the interests of speculative capital. By establishing limits on the return of investment and on share holdings, cooperatives discourage profit-seeking investments. Instead co-ops encourage local control and investments by the people who use the business.
3. Cooperatives help the members actively govern their organization through education and help other cooperatives to better serve their members by buying goods from other cooperatives and providing development assistance to organizing groups.
4. Cooperatives exist not just for the benefit of the members but to serve, strengthen, and sustain local communities. They are community organizations.

The cooperative movement is a strong and diversified one. In Sweden and Japan, cooperative businesses figure prominently in the national economies. In many Third World countries, cooperatives such as credit unions and agricultural organizations successfully help people provide for themselves where private and other corporate capital do not see high profitability. In the United States, cooperative organization is seen in rural electric co-ops, agricultural co-ops, and credit unions.

The Future of Stakeholding

Conflicting trends are at work about the future of stakeholder organization. Some hold it out as an essential key to the future, while some of the most long-lived stakeholder institutions are under threat. Britain, for example, is experiencing a movement toward a broader involvement of interested parties in corporate decision-taking and more official recognition of the legitimacy of stakeholders' interests. It was a feature of the electoral platform of Tony Blair's New Labour, in which the "stakeholder economy" was promoted without rigorous definition, serving as a rather loose collectivist concept. In concrete terms the most obvious trend involves the increased ownership of firms by their workers through **employee stock ownership plans (ESOPs)**.

Running directly against a trend toward increased stakeholder, particularly employee, ownership are the attacks mounted on some of the older forms of stakeholder involvement in recent years. In Britain the same criticisms leveled against publicly owned industry were turned against a large mutual sector composed of **retail cooperatives**, building societies (**mutual thrift institutions**), and mutual insurance societies. These institutions were charged with bad management and low productivity. One particular factor was most frequently cited. In private industry, the accepted solution to the principal-agent dilemma stemming from the separation of management and ownership was to give pecuniary incentives to top management through the use of stock options. In the mutual sector, no comparable way could offer equivalent rewards for management performance, prompting the claim that this practice damaged performance. In a short span of time many of Britain's large building societies, and some mutual insurance companies, were converted into joint stock companies, distributing the shares among management, depositors, and borrowers.

This process was given the rather ugly name of **demutualization**. The economic rationale behind it assumes that mutuals—which are comprehensive stakeholder organizations in which customers (both depositors and borrowers in the case of thrift associations) and potential future customers hold an interest—are less efficient organizations than conventionally organized corporations. Mutuals not only lack the ability to offer stock option remuneration schemes, but also they cannot raise capital on the stock market, but rely instead on debt finance. These factors, it was argued, lead to inefficiency relative to joint stock companies and unless action was taken they would lose out in the market place. An alternative explanation describes a systematic pillaging of the building societies by management and "carpetbaggers" to the detriment of other present and future stakeholders. Explanations focusing on efficiency do not answer the question of why the mutual thrifts were so successful for such a long time and grew to such power.[12] In the retail sector, the cooperative societies founded in the nineteenth century to give customer stakeholders a share in the management and profit of retailing are also experiencing hard times. Again, this decline is frequently attributed to the absence of incentives for management because of an inability to use stock option schemes.

In the United States the rapid downsizing that occurred in the early 1990s brought forth criticism, notably from Robert Reich, then secretary of labor in the Clinton administration, that firms must be forced to live up to their obligations to stakeholders and accept this role in and responsibility to a broader community. This statement prompted a broad debate on the nature of **corporate social responsibility** and a discussion as to the extent to which corporations were obliged to further the interests of others beyond their shareholders. Toward the end of the 1990s the stock market boom was associated with the claims that management was aggressively promoting shareholder value. However, the collapse of that boom and the revelation of highly questionable accounting practices led to a realization that management interests took primacy over the shareholders, and other stakeholders (workers and communities) were neglected almost entirely. These events sparked a debate as to whether the whole structure of corporate governance in America should be reviewed. Particular criticisms focused on a command structure too concentrated in a single individual—the chief executive officer—who also is frequently the chair of the board of directors. A powerful independent board, or **supervising board**, would be in position to provide a check on executive management behavior and practices.

Concurrent with the criticism of the management of publicly held corporations, mutual organizations continue to show some gains. In contrast to the United Kingdom, the fastest growing elements of the retail financial industry in the United

[12]In July 1999 the British Treasury issued a report on *Demutualisation,* Ninth Report of the Select Committee of the Treasury, HMSO (July 22, 1999). It examined the case for and against mutual societies, but in general saw no reason to oppose demutualization.

THE THIRD WAY

The popular appeal in the current drive to find the "Third Way" in politics has been effectively harnessed by Tony Blair's New Labour in Britain and by Gerhard Schroeder's "New Centre" in Germany. Both speak of a need to extend democracy, broaden property ownership, and take up the challenge of rapid change. Both were apparently inspired by the book *The Third Way: The Renewal of Social Democracy*, written by Anthony Giddens, a sociologist and the Director of the London School of Economics. However, some critics find the rhetoric rather empty. Ralf Dahrendorf, another sociologist, who preceded Giddens as director of the LSE described the "Third Way" "as a politics that speaks of the need for hard choices but then avoids them by trying to please everybody." Among those who are apparently pleased is Senator Hillary Clinton who speaks of the "Third Way" as a "unified theory of life which will marry conservatism and liberalism, capitalism and statism, and tie together practically everything: the way we are, the way we were, the faults of man and the word of God, the end of communism and the beginning of the third millennium." It contains the universalism that characterized the failed "isms" of the 20th century. In its present form it has great appeal but few teeth.

SOURCES: Anthony Giddens, *The Third Way: The Renewal of Social Democracy* (London: Polity Press, 2000); Gerard DeGroot, "The Third Way," *Christian Science Monitor*, June 14, 2000, p. 9, available at http://csmweb2.emcweb.com/durable/2000/06/14/f-p9s1.shtml.

States are the credit unions and mutual societies where both borrower and lender hold an interest. Germany's large mutual sector, especially in finance, contains 2,500 mutual banking institutions with more than 14 million members and 20,000 branches. Few signs indicate that these German associations will be converted into joint stock companies as in the United Kingdom, because mutual organization conforms well to the German philosophy of **codetermination**, although interest in the British experience continues to grow.[13]

CONCLUSION

The prospect of some kind of third way will continue to intrigue many people, and interest in it is likely to be fed in the future by several trends. One is the widening economic disparity growing out of the economic expansion of the 1990s. Broader ownership of capital would certainly lead to a more egalitarian distribution of income, but by what institutional structure should that reallocation be effected? It is relatively easy to be in favor of greater equality, but the heavy taxation of income, wealth, and inheritance that would be required runs counter to the prevailing political trends in most of the West.

A second factor that favors a different way is the growing concern for the environment in its broadest sense, involving not only pollution but also the demise and decay of traditional patterns of settlement and interaction. The greater pursuit of

[13]See "Demutualisation in Germany. Inconceivable?" *The Economist*, January 3, 1998.

sustainability, however, involves an erosion of individual property rights in favor of a broader, intergenerational conception. Again it is not clear that this outcome would be a politically acceptable in every part of the world. In Europe, it is true that the development of the EU has involved increasing collective rights at the expense of the individual. In the United States, Russia, and China at least the reverse is true. Together, however, concern for equity and environment focuses attention on what its proponents call the social economy that attempts to define as stakeholders a much broader spectrum of interests than capital, labor, and government. It is important to remember that attempts in the past to follow a middle road, whether in Yugoslavia or Sweden, found it to be a more difficult path than its inherent appeal would indicate.

KEY TERMS AND CONCEPTS

Anglo-Saxon model
codetermination
corporate social responsibility
demutualization
employee stock ownership plans (ESOPs)
market socialism
mutual thrift institutions
retail cooperatives
Rhine model
Rochdale Principles
social market economy
soft-budget constraint
stakeholder
supervising board

QUESTIONS FOR DISCUSSION

1. Distinguish between market socialism and a social market economy. Give examples of each.
2. Why is the absence of a capital market potentially fatal to market socialism?
3. Distinguish between hard-budget and soft-budget constraints.
4. Which, in your view, is better to determine the social value of a major change in the transportation system—the market or a government? Why?
5. Should stakeholders who are not owners have a say in a firm's decision making? Will a firm who recognizes its stakeholders' interests be competed out of business?
6. Why does the trend to employee stock option plans offer a way out of the principal-agent problem?
7. Why are so many traditional "mutual" firms being converted into stockholder firms? Is this shift good in the long run?
8. Why does the practice of issuing options to management threaten the interest of other stakeholders?

RESOURCES

Web Sites

The National Center for Employee Ownership..................................http://www.nceo.org/

The Association for Social Economics ....http://www.socialeconomics.org/

The U.K. Social Economy Forum ....http://www.social-economy.org.uk/

Aries, Social Economy Online
Aries is a Euro Info Center (EIC) for the Social Economy. ARIES provides an online information, news, and networking service designed to help social economy organizations to work together and take action at the European level ....http://www.poptel.org.uk/aries/

European Confederation of Workers' Cooperatives, Social Cooperatives, and Participative Enterprises ....http://www.cecop.org/

International Cooperative Alliance ....http://www.coop.org/

The Netherlands Participation Institute (NPI) ....http://www.snpi.nl/

The Center for Economic and Social Justice ....http://www.cesj.org/

The ESOP Association (United States) ....http://www.esopassociation.org/

Integra Review..................................http://www.iol.ie/EMPLOYMENT/integra/sepp.html

Treasury Select Committee Report on Demutualization..
....http://www.parliament.the-stationery-office.co.uk/pa/cm199899/cmselect/cmtreasy/605/60502.htm

Books and Articles

Ackerman, Bruce, and Ann Alstott. *The Stakeholder Society.* New Haven, CT: Yale University Press, 1999.

Bamberger, Bill, and Cathy Davidson. *Closing: The Life and Death of an American Factory.* New York: W.W. Norton, 1998.

Carroll, Archie B. *Business and Society: Ethics and Stakeholder Management.* Cincinnati, OH: South-Western Publishers, 1996.

Giddens, Anthony. *The Third Way: The Renewal of Social Democracy*. London: Polity Press, 2000.

Hutton, Bill, and David Goldblatt (eds.). *The Stakeholding Society: Writings on Politics and Economics.* New York: Blackwell, 1999.

Kay, John. *The Business of Economics.* Oxford: Oxford University Press, 1996.

Kelly, Gavin, Dominic Kelly, and Andrew Gamble. *Stakeholder Capitalism.* New York: St. Martin's Press, 1997.

Keren, Michael. "On the (Im)Possibility of Market Socialism," In *The Road to Capitalism,* pp. 45–52. David Kennett and Marc Lieberman (eds.). Fort Worth, TX: Harcourt Brace, 1993.

Le Grand, Julian, and Saul Estrin (eds.). *Market Socialism.* Oxford: Clarendon Press, 1989.

Minford, Patrick. *Markets Not Stakes: The Triumph of Capitalism and the Stakeholder Fallacy.* London: Trafalgar Square, 1998.

Plender, John. *A Stake in the Future: The Stakeholding Society.* London: Nicholas Brealey, 1997.

Turner, Lowell. *Negotiating the New Germany: Can Social Partnership Survive?* Ithaca, NY: ILR Press, 1997.

Yunker, James A. *Socialism Revised and Modernized: The Case for Pragmatic Market Socialism.* New York: Praeger, 1992.

PART SIX The Economics of Transition

20

THE PROCESS OF TRANSITION TO A MARKET ECONOMY

STARTING POINTS

At the high point of the "socialist revolution," almost one-third of the world's population lived in nations using command planning to coordinate their economies. This process started with the Bolshevik revolution in 1917, which led by the end of the 1920s to the institution of centralized planning throughout almost all of the former Tsarist Empire. In the aftermath of World War II, the Baltic nations became an integrated part of the Soviet economy, and Eastern Europe fell under the economic dominance of the Soviet Union. In Asia, the communist Chinese Revolution saw planning introduced in the world's most populous nation and ultimately into the economies of neighboring North Korea and Vietnam. In the Western Hemisphere in the 1960s, Fidel Castro's Cuba began the same experiment and it looked as if Marxism would gain a foothold on the South American mainland. At that point it was easy to believe that central planning was indeed the way of the future and Nikita Khrushchev's boast that "we will bury you" did not seem at all empty.

By the late 1980s most of these economies were faltering. The exception was China, which, as described in Chapter 23, embarked precociously and somewhat serendipitously, on an early reform program, allowing market forces considerable freedom in agriculture and small enterprise. The Soviet economy, on the other hand, experienced serious problems. Industrial output fell stagnant over the previous decade, the consumer goods sector was proving woefully inadequate to meet the growing aspirations of its people, and a faltering parity in the military race with the United States was maintained only at the expense of prioritization, drawing as much as 35 percent of gross domestic product (GDP) into the military sector. The impressive Soviet growth record of the early years of command planning now revealed to have been almost entirely extensive in nature, with output rising only because of increases in the quantities of labor and capital employed, rather than a growth of total factor productivity. Diminishing returns to fixed capital experienced since the 1970s led, by the mid-1990s, to a marginal rate of return on new investment capital close to zero.

In 1985 Russia initiated a gradualist economic reform program under Gorbachev's program of *perestroika* (restructuring) as simultaneous sweeping political change occurred under the label of *glasnost* (usually translated as "openness"). The emergence of *glasnost* and the relative decline in the Soviet Union's military muscle allowed the nations of Central and Eastern Europe to seize their independence and take their own paths away from centralized planning. Meanwhile at home, the failure of *perestroika* to revive the economy contributed directly to the breakup of the Soviet Union. In 1980 centralized command planning was practiced in every country east of Austria and north of the Himalayas as far east as the Pacific Ocean. By 1999 only a few governments were even theoretically committed to planning principles (North Korea and Cuba, for example), and the durability of these regimes is questionable.

Differences in Initial Conditions

Today, about 30 countries in the world are at some stage of a process of *transition* from a centrally planned to a market economy.[1] All share the common feature of their planned past, but their starting points at the outset of transition were quite different. Some of this diversity is shown in Table 20.1, which gives selected figures for most economies in transition. These data show that at the outset of the move to market the countries exhibited wide differences in income per head, which in 1981 ranged from about $9,200 a year in Slovenia, the most northern of the former Yugoslav republics, to only $1,400 in impoverished Albania, the most isolated of the communist economies.[2] Even within the successor states of the Soviet Union wide variations are apparent. The Baltic Republics were, at the start of transition, relatively rich; Latvia had a per-head income (measured in terms of purchasing power parity) of about $8,590 in 1989. The central Asian republics, on the other hand, were poor, the worst off being Uzbekistan, at less than one-third of Latvia's level. It should be emphasized that even the most affluent of the transition economies was a long way from the living standards seen in developed market economies. Average income in Western Europe in 1989, measured in terms of purchasing power, was about twice the level in Latvia. As we shall discuss later, the first years of transition resulted in sharply lower incomes for most formerly planned economies, and the gap widened considerably.

Sharp differences also distinguished the transition states in terms of the level of economic development. This concept is difficult to encapsulate with simple statistics, but the percentage of the labor force engaged in agriculture is a useful index. As Table 20.1 shows, the percent of the population engaged in agriculture ranged from 56 percent in Albania, a largely peasant economy, to a low of 9 percent in the urbanized Baltic states. Again, we should note that even the most developed of transition nations were well behind the developed market economies, which as a rule have less than 5 percent, and as few as 2 percent, of the workforce employed in agriculture.

The relevance of the other statistics given in Table 20.1 is fairly self-evident. The rate of population growth tells us more about the state of overall development, although a great deal of "noise" is also created by religious factors, culture, and even housing availability. The Baltic and Slav states show low rates of population

[1]Of these, 15 once constituted part of the Soviet Union, and three—Slovenia, Croatia, and Macedonia FYR—were part of Yugoslavia. Serbia and Bosnia may also be considered to be in transition, but they do not make the World Bank tables for political reasons.

[2]In actual fact, the highest purchasing power income probably lay in East Germany, but that former economy is not considered transitional in the sense that it merged with the Federal Republic of Germany.

■ TABLE 20.1

Selected Indicators for Economies in Transition, 1989

	Population (millions)	PPP GDP per Head 1989	Percentage of Labor Force in Agriculture	Telephones per 100 People	Average Years of Schooling, Population 25+	Population Growth Rate	Monetary Overhang as Percentage of GDP
Eastern Europe							
Albania	3.3	1,400	56	2	6.2	1	4.3
Bulgaria	8.9	5,000	17	32	7.0	20.1	18.0
Croatia	—	6,171	—	—	—	—	12.0
Czechoslovakia	15.7	6,280	11	29	9.2	0.4	27.1
Hungary	10.5	6,810	15	19	9.8	0	27.7
Macedonia FYR	—	3,394	—	—	—	—	12.0
Poland	38.4	5,150	27	15	8.2	0.4	13.6
Romania	23.3	3,470	29	13	7.1	0.4	16.8
Slovenia	—	9,200	—	—	—	—	12.0
Former Soviet Union							
Armenia	3.5	5,530	11	18	5.0	0.4	25.7
Azerbaijan	7.3	4,620	15	10	5.0	1.2	25.7
Belarus	10.3	7,010		16	7.0	0.6	25.7
Estonia	1.6	8,900	9	21	9.0	0.0	25.7
Georgia	5.5	5,590	14	10	5.0	0.7	25.7
Kazakstan	17.0	5,130	20	11	5.0	0.9	25.7
Kyrgyz Republic	4.5	3,180	16	7	5.0	1.8	25.7
Latvia	2.7	8,590	9	24	9.0	20.1	25.7
Lithuania	3.8	6,430	10	22	9.0	0.1	25.7
Moldova	4.4	4,670	21	11	6.0	0.7	25.7
Russian Federation	149.0	7,720	20	15	9.0	0.5	25.7
Tajikistan	5.6	3,010	14	5	5.0	2.7	25.7
Turkmenistan	3.9	4,230	—	6	5.0	1.9	25.7
Ukraine	52.2	5,680	—	16	6.0	0.4	25.7
Uzbekistan	21.5	2,740	17	7	5.0	2.0	25.7
Mongolia		2,100	40	3	7.2	2.6	7.6

SOURCE: Martha de Melo, Cevder Denizer, and Alan Gelb, "Patterns of Transition from Plan to Market," *World Bank Economic Review* 10, no. 3 (September 1996), p. 400; UNDP Human Development Report, 1997.

growth, while the Islamic populations of central Asia are still growing as fast as 2 percent per year. Similarly, wide differences separate the countries in the quantity of human capital, which is crudely measured by the average years of schooling of the adult (25 years old and more) population.

The final column in Table 20.1, the **monetary overhang**, provides an important index of macroeconomic imbalance, to which we will return later. At this point, we use it as one measure of the degree to which consumer goods were undersupplied during the last years of the planning regimes. Recall from earlier discussion that in many cases the wage payments made to workers in centrally planned economies were greater than the amount that the consumers were able, or willing, to spend on the available (often poor-quality) consumer goods. This circumstance led to the buildup of the monetary overhang, which consists of cash and savings bank deposits that represent latent purchasing power. As long as prices were centrally controlled by fiat, this potential excess buying power could exert little effect on the overall price level.[3] However, once the process of price liberalization started, the monetary overhang manifested itself as an inflationary pressure. The only alternative to allowing inflation to work itself through was neutralization by appropriate and aggressive contractionary policy measures, which would result in a highly depressing effect on output and welfare.

The figures in Table 20.1 show that the monetary overhang in the Soviet Union in 1989 was the most serious encountered in any of the transition nations. It is statistically impossible to disaggregate this all-union figure among the successor states, and so all show an identical figure of more than 25 percent, symptomatic of a potentially serious problem of repressed inflation. As it happened, the monetary overhang did provide an initial stimulus to inflation, but it could not be held responsible for the continuing price spiral, which lasted for several years, precisely because the purchasing power of the overhang was rapidly depleted to insignificance by inflation itself. In the countries of Eastern Europe, the monetary overhang was by no means as great as in the Soviet Union, and the negative figures in the Czech Republic and Hungary indicate a growing use of consumer credit and the greater availability of consumer goods, which allowed consumers to incur household debt.

Common Features

However, despite these differences, all of the transition economies shared at the outset several important points of commonality:

1. In all of these economies, macroeconomic balance was achieved by direct control of the planning agencies rather than by a reliance on the market or the more conventional tools of macroeconomic demand management used in the developed economies. (It was the failure to keep the purchasing power of total wage payments equilibrated with the available supply of goods to be purchased by consumers that led to the existence of the monetary overhang.)
2. The plan, not the market, was the primary coordination mechanism of the economy.

---

[3]Of course, prices could be bid up on the black market, and were. Also, the monetary overhang found its way into the illegal currency markets. Rubles, of limited use because of the shortage of consumer goods, were exchanged for "hard" currency at exchange rates wildly different from the official ones. The hard currency so obtained could be expatriated or used to buy goods in hard currency stores (called *berioskas* in Russia).

3. No adequate institutional framework existed within which a market economy could operate. This deficiency was clearest in terms of intertemporal coordination, where the absence of defined property rights and enforceable contracts was most limiting.
4. The relative prices of goods and factors of production reflected neither relative costs nor relative scarcities.
5. Entry into most economic activity was controlled by the government, and many activities that would be regarded as socially beneficial in a market economy were illegal during, and in the immediate aftermath, of central planning.
6. The extent of private property was limited. Although in some countries (e.g., the former Yugoslavia) an attempt was made to combine socially owned capital with market coordination, such experiments failed in general to be fruitful. The rapid extension of private property is valuable in two ways. First, it makes the market function better, largely by reducing principal-agent problems. Second, it gives the citizens a stake in preserving the permanence of the new arrangements.
7. Foreign trade was controlled by the state and therefore the efficiency-enhancing impact of foreign competition was largely absent.

THE STEPS OF TRANSITION

Transition from a planned to a market economy is not a single step but a series of moves that must be made in sequence, and some countries advanced with greater speed than others. Table 20.2 gives statistics for the performance of 26 economies in transition, divided into subgroups according to their performance on a liberalization index, prepared by economists from the World Bank.[4] This index is compounded from three sets of considerations: the liberalization of the domestic economy, external transactions, and the private sector entry. **Domestic liberalization** consists of the ending of price controls as well as the termination of the monopoly privileges of state enterprises. It carries a weight of .3 in the construction of the index. **External transactions liberalization** ends export controls and export taxes, establishes current account convertibility, and substitutes a moderate tariff regime for quantitative import controls. It also carries a weight of .3. The final component, **private sector entry liberalization**, measures the extent of progress in the privatization of state assets and the entry of new firms. Its weight in the overall index is .4.

The **advanced reformers** included the five states in Central and Eastern Europe: Slovenia, Poland, Hungary, and the two parts of former Czechoslovakia—the

[4]For more detail on the construction of the liberalization index, see *From Plan to Market: World Development Report 1996*, Martha de Melo, Cevder Denizer, and Alan Gelb, "Patterns of Transition from Plan to Market," *World Bank Economic Review* 10, no. 3 (September 1996), pp. 397 ff.

■ TABLE 20.2

Liberalization, Growth, and Inflation in 26 Countries in Transition, 1989–1994

	Cumulative Liberalization Index 1994	Average Liberalization 1993–1994	Average Inflation Rate 1993–1994 (percent)	Average Annual GDP Growth 1993–1994	Average GDP in 1993–1994 as a Percentage of 1989 GDP	Lowest Level of GDP as a Percentage of 1989 GDP
Advanced Reformers						
Slovenia	4.16	0.82	26	3.0	84	81
Poland	4.14	0.84	34	4.2	88	82
Hungary	4.11	0.84	21	0.0	81	80
Czech Republic	3.61	0.90	16	0.8	81	80
Slovak Republic	3.47	0.86	19	0.4	79	77
Average	3.90	0.85	23	1.7	83	80
High Intermediate Reformers						
Estonia	2.93	0.85	69	0.9	69	67
Bulgaria	2.90	0.68	81	21.4	73	73
Lithuania	2.72	0.79	231	27.3	44	44
Latvia	2.45	0.71	73	24.4	60	59
Albania	2.30	0.70	57	9.5	74	65
Romania	2.29	0.66	194	2.2	69	67
Mongolia	2.27	0.64	164	0.6	84	83
Average	2.55	0.72	124	0.0	67	65
Low Intermediate Reformers						
Russian Federation	1.92	0.63	558	213.5	57	52
Kyrgyz Republic	1.81	0.68	744	213.2	61	57
Moldova	1.62	0.53	558	217.0	53	46
Kazakstan	1.31	0.37	1,870	218.5	57	49
Average	1.67	0.55	933	215.6	57	51
Slow Reformers						
Uzbekistan	1.11	0.37	640	22.5	89	88
Belarus	1.07	0.35	1,694	216.6	73	64
Ukraine	0.80	0.20	2,789	218.6	56	48
Turkmenistan	0.63	0.19	2,751	215.0	69	62
Average	0.90	0.27	1,968	213.2	72	66
Affected by Regional Tensions						
Croatia	3.98	0.83	807	20.7	69	68
Macedonia FYR	3.92	0.78	157	210.7	57	55
Armenia	1.44	0.42	4,595	27.4	38	38
Georgia	1.32	0.35	10,563	224.6	24	23
Azerbaijan	1.03	0.33	1,167	217.7	50	44
Tajikistan	0.95	0.28	1,324	226.3	35	30
Average	2.11	0.50	3,102	214.5	45	43

SOURCE: de Melo, Denizer, and Gelb, "Patterns of Transition from Plan to Market," *World Bank Economic Review* 10, no. 3 (September 1996), p. 405.

Czech Republic and the Slovak Republic. High intermediate reformers were the Baltic states and the southern countries of the Balkan Peninsula. Mongolia, although relatively less developed, was a somewhat surprising member of this group. The most important of the low intermediate reformers was Russia. Among the slow reformers were the Ukraine, after Russia the most populous of the European transition nations, and the Islamic states of central Asia. Several countries of the former Yugoslavia and the Caucasus remained too much affected by civil and international warfare to be successful in maintaining a coherent liberalization plan.

STABILIZATION

The common experience of almost all transition economies was macroeconomic disturbances of a magnitude and endurance that surprised almost all observers.[5] These disturbances included rapid and sustained inflation and a sharp reduction of real output. The accompanying rise in unemployment remained smaller than expected, largely due to extensive subsidies to industry.

Inflation

Inflation posed a universal problem for East European and former Soviet reformers. Even those states most advanced in the process of reform experienced an average rate of inflation between 1989 and 1994 greater than 100 percent per year. However, as Table 20.2 shows, this price explosion abated in the most advanced reformers. Nevertheless, in slower reforming economies, the average inflation rate for 1989–1994 was close to 1,000 percent annually and, in fact, accelerated as reform progressed.

The causes of inflation in the transition economies are complex, but the most important are the following:

1. The *monetary overhang* created by supply and demand imbalances in the planned regime. Relaxation of price controls released pent-up demand and drove prices higher.
2. The absence of an adequate taxation system and the inability of governments to borrow on financial markets forced *reliance on the creation of money and credit to finance government activity.*
3. The *continuation of soft-budget constraints* in much of industry, increasing the fiscal deficit. To prevent the failure of state-owned and privatized enterprises during transition, governments frequently extended credit to industry. This politically necessary move in many cases prevented widespread failure that would lead to unemployment, political unrest, and a failure of any reforming regime to complete its program. In many cases, government support to

[5]The main exception is, of course, the People's Republic of China, which has maintained extremely strong economic growth throughout its liberalization effort. Growth in China was 11 percent between 1989 and 1995, and inflation a modest 8.4 percent. Vietnam combined liberalization with growth—roughly 8 percent between 1989 and 1995—although inflation was in excess of 100 percent annually.

industry increased sharply as implicit subsidies in the pricing system under central planning were eliminated.[6]

4. *Flight from the domestic currency* to foreign currencies (generally, the U.S. dollar) because of an absence of confidence in the domestic currency.

The greatest impetus to continued inflation was the creation of excessive credit by the government, and the solution to the inflationary spiral therefore lay in greater monetary discipline by central banks. However, although effective against inflation, repressive monetary policy effectively reduced demand for goods and services, and therefore repressed the growth of emergent firms. A tight monetary strategy carries the political risk of rising unemployment and the economic risk of depressing long-run growth. The World Bank considers that getting inflation down below 40 percent per year offers clear gains and helps eliminate the danger of a hyperinflationary spiral, but the Bank is more cautious about appropriate policy beyond that goal. In cutting inflation further, the cost in terms of lost output may be greater than the gain that results from more stable prices. Domestic output started rebounding in Poland and Estonia with the inflation rate near 40 percent. Korea, several Latin American nations, and Israel all combined impressive real growth with relative high rates of price increase.

High rates of inflation inflict profound distributional consequences in the transition economies because they act like a tax on financial assets. The losers are predominantly households and firms that held positive cash balances, who see their savings wiped out by hyperinflation. The winners are the government sector, which reaps the gains of seigniorage, and any households or firms with net debts. In general, the **inflation tax** is regressive and falls more heavily on small savers who have difficulty converting their financial assets into real property or dollars (or other foreign currencies) where it is safe from inflationary ravages.

The Collapse of GDP

The second macroeconomic phenomenon common to the transition economies is the sharp contraction of output. As Table 20.2 shows, in most of the Central and Eastern European nations (CEEs) and successor states of the Soviet Union, the **collapse of GDP** bottomed out at about 80 percent of its 1989 level. The fast-reforming economies resumed growth during 1993–1994, though all are still well below the level of GDP achieved in 1989. Slow-reforming countries saw their output levels fall further and took longer in returning to an expansionary path. High intermediate reformers saw a contraction of about 33 percent in five years, and the low intermediate reformers, among them Russia itself, lost about half of output.

By any measure, these levels represent serious dips in output. Some sense of their magnitude is apparent in a comparison to the Great Depression of the

[6]Consider, for example, the case of energy, which was supplied at well below world prices throughout the Soviet bloc. The elimination of the implicit energy subsidy squeezed many firms conditioned to operate in a relatively energy-intensive fashion. To avoid the failure of these firms, the government granted generous credits.

1930s, when the United States, the most heavily affected of the major industrial economies, saw a fall in GDP of about one-third.[7] The contraction in other advanced capitalist economies was less drastic—about 28 percent in Germany, 9 percent in France, and only about 5 percent in the United Kingdom. The fall in output in transition economies has been proportionately greater than in the West during in the Great Depression, still regarded as one of capitalism's great failures that led directly to massive political change and perhaps World War II. The chief experience of capitalism for most of the 410 million people who live in transition economies (other than China and Vietnam) is acute and painful contraction.

It should be noted, however, that official statistics overstate the size of the economic contraction in two ways. First, much of the recorded output in 1989 consisted of official estimates of production valued at official plan prices. The immediate impact of transition was to reduce both production volumes and prices of many of the overvalued, substandard goods produced under the planned regimes. Second, a feature of the transition period involves the substantial growth of the private, small business economy. This sector of production, while not necessarily criminal, is likely to underreport its activities to minimize taxes, and thus this burgeoning activity is not fully reflected in the official statistics.

Causes of the Contraction In reality the contractions might not have been as great as official statistics seemed to indicate, but all transition economies experienced significant macroeconomic downturns, caused primarily by the disintegration of the coordinating structure. Planners previously determined both suppliers and purchasers and, after the collapse of planning, enterprises found themselves both without secure, uncontested markets for their output. They also encountered difficulty getting the raw materials that under the former system were at least nominally guaranteed.

Other factors were also important. After price liberalization, even when materials were available, enterprises often had to pay more than the "soft" prices charged under the plan. This problem was particularly acute with respect to energy inputs that were consistently underpriced under socialist planning; oil and gas had been supplied throughout the Soviet Union and the Soviet bloc at much less than the world price. Analysis after liberalization indicated that a substantial part of industry in centrally planned economies produced *zero or* **negative value added**. When both inputs and outputs were valued at the appropriate world prices, the final product was worth less than the materials from which it was made, and all of the labor, capital, and other factor services were actually directed toward reducing the value of raw materials.

Third, dislocation caused domino effects when enterprises that lost buyers suffered a shortfall of revenues and therefore had no resources to pay for raw materials. The suppliers of materials, in turn, had no money to pay their workers, to buy investment goods, or even to pay taxes. The governments in most transition

[7]John Kenneth Galbraith, *The Great Crash*, 3d ed. (Boston: Houghton Mifflin, 1972), p. 172.

economies stepped in with credits to help enterprises bridge the gap between revenues and expenses, but the aid was seldom adequate. Out of necessity interfirm credit began to proliferate as firms, with no alternative ways to dispose of their products, continued to supply them to customers who were increasingly delinquent in payments. The entire structure of industry became increasingly fragile, presenting the possibility of repercussive enterprise failures, which could further cut output and massively increase unemployment. Governments in most transition states responded by increasing credits to industry, therefore feeding the inflationary cycle.

A fourth problem was that trade (for example, between the Baltic Republics and Russia itself), which had been "domestic" in terms of the Soviet Union, became "international" and required convertible currency after the collapse of the Soviet Union. From the beginning of central planning in the Soviet Union, Soviet technocrats relied on economies of scale, generally regarding bigger as better. As a result, single plants were often expected to supply the entire national consumption of certain commodities. Many goods, both final and intermediary, were produced almost exclusively within a single republic. The breakup of the Soviet Union meant that suppliers and their markets were now located in different countries, and transactions across these new borders frequently became hard currency transactions.[8] The problems of currency availability and border restrictions resulted in a contraction of economic activity as trade between the republics of the former Soviet Union shrank by 70 percent almost overnight.

This dislocation was not limited to the republics spawned by the dissolution of the Soviet Union. Even though trade within the Council on Mutual Economic Assistance (CMEA or COMECON) had always notionally been "international" in character, it had been an artifact of planning rather than the result of comparative advantage. The end of the planned system of the CMEA caused a sharp reduction in the volume of trade between former partners, again about 70 percent. Imports from another former socialist country were displaced by goods from more competitive producers outside the Soviet bloc, particularly in the case of consumer goods, electronics, and capital goods. Lost markets meant lost revenue and a multiplier effect on the macroeconomies. In effect, the dislocation of the trade network established under the CMEA was akin to cutting off each economy from part of its economic hinterland.

Finally, in many countries economic dislocation was aggravated by the deterioration of the internal distribution system. In Russia the internal transportation system had been close to collapse for decades. The only viable mode of moving most goods was by rail, which also suffered from inadequate investment and maintenance. Furthermore, at the collapse of the Soviet Union, rolling stock and equipment was divided between the republics largely on the basis of each country assuming possession of what lay within its borders in August 1991, resulting in a misallocation of resources and serious disruption.

---

[8]The need for hard money was not always the case. A "ruble" area, within which the ruble was the common medium of exchange, existed for some time.

Labor Productivity As output fell sharply in most transition economies, employment dipped by a much smaller amount, and therefore the initial impact of economic reform was to actually lower labor productivity. Before the onset of reform, productivity in Eastern Europe was between 20 percent and 33 percent of the level in Western Europe, and the initial impact of liberalization was to widen this gap. Raising living standards depends on an increase in labor productivity and the decline was a demoralizing setback. Although most countries experienced a fall, Table 20.3 shows that the faster reforms are implemented, the more sharply labor productivity initially declines, but the more rapidly it returns to the positive. Fast reformers like the Czech Republic, Poland, and Hungary saw productivity rising by 1992, while Russia and the Central Asian Republics continued to experience productivity decline until at least 1996.

Reform was accompanied by a shift in the composition of output. Basic "rust belt" industries contracted, compensated for in part by rises in services, consumer

TABLE 20.3

Annual Change in Labor Productivity, 1990–1999

	1990	1991	1992	1993	1994	1995	1996	1997	1998	1999
Eastern Europe	−4.02	−4.58	1.46	2.67	3.87	6.19	3.22	2.16	1.88	4.89
Albania	−9.27	−24.26	12.62	11.57	−2.17	12.15	13.18	−7.17	10.87	10.87
Bulgaria	−3.19	5.28	0.85	0.18	1.19	1.68	−10.90	−2.97	3.31	4.43
Croatia	−4.33	−13.50	−0.59	−3.91	6.55	6.84	4.64	7.41	−4.00	−0.00
Czech Republic	−0.30	−6.43	2.02	1.59	1.46	3.06	3.74	1.19	0.19	2.33
Hungary	−0.21	−1.75	7.47	6.38	5.66	4.04	2.76	5.59	4.57	1.43
Poland	−7.72	−1.04	6.57	6.12	4.31	5.50	4.62	4.67	3.03	8.68
Romania	−4.65	−11.90	−4.92	4.38	3.64	11.25	5.11	−2.43	−2.60	3.41
Slovakia	−0.71	−2.31	−7.23	−4.11	8.06	4.33	2.77	6.81	4.81	5.80
Slovenia	−4.37	−1.27	0.03	5.73	7.95	4.82	4.51	5.49	4.55	4.10
Estonia	−6.80	−7.42	−8.11	−0.76	0.10	8.03	4.81	8.97	6.27	3.76
Latvia	2.80	−9.95	−27.52	−5.63	7.19	1.76	4.25	4.86	2.55	1.14
Lithuania	−0.62	−7.91	−17.83	−9.19	−2.75	3.23	2.39	4.52	4.26	−2.65
Armenia	−7.71	−12.86	-30.44	−3.32	4.28	3.83	4.77	4.80	6.42	4.38
Azerbaijan	−12.49	−1.28	−19.27	−15.38	−9.22	−4.76	−0.39	2.11	3.89	3.17
Belarus	−1.01	1.32	−7.22	−5.90	−8.87	−3.55	2.85	8.71	6.26	2.62
Georgia	−17.01	−11.18	−21.61	−10.90	−3.20	−5.73	5.03	0.26	0.14	4.70
Kazakhstan	−2.27	−9.62	−3.17	−0.63	−6.80	−5.99	0.69	1.71	2.68	2.44
Kyrgyzstan	4.28	−7.39	−18.10	−6.01	−13.37	−3.16	3.64	4.47	0.84	0.02
Republic of Moldova	−1.51	−17.17	−22.95	11.65	−21.50	−0.38	−2.53	1.17	−2.94	2.61
Russian Federation	−2.61	−3.02	−11.68	−5.95	−7.42	−0.75	−1.82	1.83	−2.46	3.39
Tajikistan	−2.91	−9.68	−26.29	−8.44	−11.25	−5.13	−3.95	−0.56	1.68	2.31
Turkmenistan	−1.55	−7.80	−15.99	−1.24	−15.02	−5.99	2.52	−7.21	2.75	6.42
Ukraine	−3.60	−6.88	−7.26	−10.07	−14.35	−8.53	−4.01	−0.08	−0.40	0.93
Uzbekistan	−4.80	−4.82	−9.70	−1.69	−5.10	−1.23	0.28	2.73	2.24	2.70

SOURCE: United Nations Economic Survey of Europe 2001, p. 122.

goods, and, where relevant, the primary energy sector, which benefited from increased product prices. Figure 20.1 shows the trends in labor productivity for four countries: the Czech Republic (an advanced reformer), Lithuania (high intermediate), Russia (low intermediate), and Turkmenistan (slow).

The relationship between the speed of reform and the subsequent movements in labor productivity is complex. Although Lithuania's reforms are more advanced than those of its larger neighbor Russia, both economies show similar movements of industrial labor productivity. Lithuania's fall largely parallels that of Russia, but it has been deeper, due mostly to the fact that the barriers to trade created by the breakup of the Soviet Union had a more severe impact on smaller economies. The specialization built into the planned trading system meant that smaller economies were disproportionately geared to export goods throughout the Soviet Bloc and therefore lost a proportionately greater share of their markets at the breakup.[9]

FIGURE 20.1

Indices of Labor Productivity in Four Transition Economies

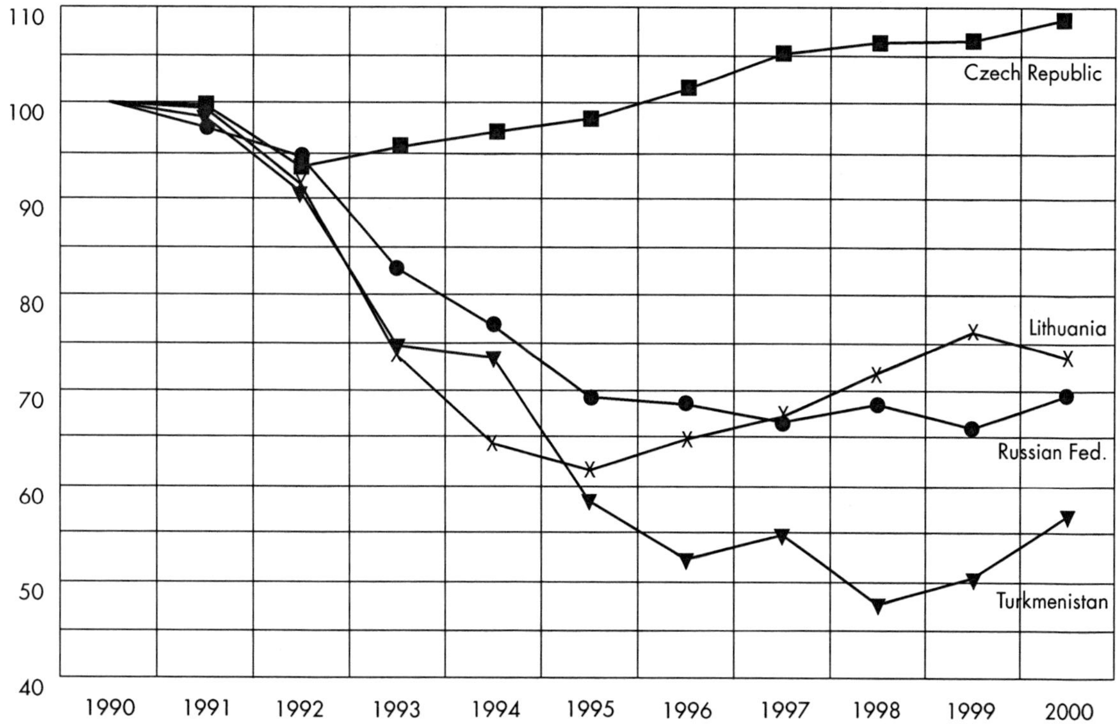

SOURCE: Data from Table 20.3.

[9]Alastair McAuley found that the share of "exports" of the Baltic states to other republics in the Soviet Union accounted for about two-thirds of the net material product.

Evidence suggests, at least among the faster reforming nations, that privatization resulted in a positive effect on labor productivity. In a survey of some 6,000 firms in Eastern Europe, Gerhard Pöhl and his colleagues found that privatized firms showed, on average, a relatively rapid 7.2 percent annual increase in productivity between 1992 and 1995.[10] In contrast, the fact that labor productivity in firms remaining in the state sector continued to fall (some of these results are shown in Table 20.4) supports privatization, though some caveats should be considered. First, the results in Table 20.4 reflect in part the relative ease with which fundamentally sound enterprises may be divested from state ownership: the other side of this phenomenon is the necessity of retaining the "lame ducks" under state ownership when no private buyer is forthcoming and the political authorities fear a rise in unemployment. Consequently, the private sector is self-selected and more dynamic than the social sector. Increased productivity also results from the greater freedom of privatized industry to get rid of unproductive workers and those concerned with the noncore aspects of the typical planned enterprise (for example, health and child care workers).

PRICE LIBERALIZATION

Price liberalization is essential for a market economy. Central planning failed to allocate resources efficiently because prices failed to reflect either cost of production or their value to consumers. Freeing up prices is the first step to grasping the benefits of a market economy and can occur without any steps being taken toward privatization of industry or indeed reform of **enterprise governance**. Under market socialism in

■ TABLE 20.4

Labor Productivity Growth: Change, 1992–1995

	Privatized Firms	State-Owned Firms
Bulgaria	12.4%	21.4%
Czech Republic	8.6	22.6
Hungary	6	3.2
Poland	7.5	1.4
Romania	1	20.5
Slovak Republic	7.8	24.1
Slovenia	7.2	1.8
Average	7.2	20.3

SOURCE: Gerhard Pöhl, Robert E. Anderson, Stijn Claessens, and Simeon Djankov, "Privatization and Restructuring in Central and Eastern Europe," *World Bank Technical Paper* (1997), p. 368.

[10]Gerhard Pöhl, Robert E. Anderson, Stijn Claessens, and Simeon Djankov, "Privatization and Restructuring in Central and Eastern Europe," World Bank Technical Paper, 1997.

the Yugoslav model, free prices were compatible with socially owned means of production and with the collective governance of the enterprise. However, in most analyses building a market system in the formerly centrally planned economies goes hand in hand with the privatization of property and the free entry of firms into the marketplace. Private enterprise and private ownership are more likely than social ownership to be compatible with the efficient operation of markets.

Price liberalization can produce dramatic results. In Poland, for example, shops that were empty of goods and beleaguered by queues of would-be shoppers while under central planning became well stocked in the aftermath of reform. Such a change is the product of both demand- and supply-side responses. Higher prices may bring forth a larger output, but much of the apparent increased availability of goods is due to a movement along the demand curve. In the short run, the price elasticity of demand of most produced goods is likely to be greater than the price elasticity of supply. The elimination of excess demand owes more to reduced consumption by the less well off, who can no longer afford the goods that were cheap under central planning. In the longer run, supply responses may dominate, exhibiting the solid, welfare-augmenting growth that is the objective of price reform.

A further benefit of price reform is the reduction of the socially wasteful activity caused by price controls. Under planning, goods in demand attracted many buyers and much of the homemakers' day was spent queuing for necessities. The alternative to queuing was to resort to the black market, and illegal fortunes were made in arbitrage between the state sector, where access was controlled but prices cheap, and the black market.

In general, price liberalization hurts the less affluent because under administered prices, they had access to goods on the same basis as everyone else and because the marginal value of their time was low, the queuing system worked to their benefit. Liberalized prices confront them with a hard monetary budget constraint and cause a fall in living standards, a case of the efficiency of the market conflicting with the greater equity of nonprice allocation.

As prices are decontrolled, the highly concentrated structure of industry promoted under central planning becomes a problem. Because of the planners' faith in scale economies, production of many goods was concentrated within a few large enterprises, which under planning held little market power because both production targets and prices were centrally determined. However, price liberalization gives these enterprises a high degree of market power and they will respond to their new freedom by raising prices and reducing output. Any gains in welfare from price reform must be set against the loss of consumers' surplus caused by enterprises exercising monopoly power. Losses can be mitigated by antimonopoly regulation, freeing market entry for domestic competitors and opening up international trade. In cases of natural monopoly or substantial barriers to entry, regulation may be the only resort.

Liberalized prices produce fewer benefits if reform is not accompanied by the introduction of contract law with some measure of enforceability. Price liberalization alone creates the conditions for, in the words of one Russian economist, "a bazaar but not a market." The creation of a modern productive economy requires performance, and to some degree, prices to be intertemporally consistent.

Regulation of Monopoly

Soviet-style planning's love affair with size led to high levels of concentration in many product areas. To measure monopoly power, western economists have in recent years tended to turn from measures of current concentration of output to focus on the **contestability of markets** and the size of barriers to entry, because potential competition can be a significantly moderating influence on monopoly practices. In a Soviet-style economy, markets were uncontested because of the planning system and the incentives embedded in it. Enterprise managers could gain little by broadening their production and moving into new lines—it was complicated, risky, required both management time and materials, and could therefore jeopardize the achievement of output targets. Once the planning system was abandoned, barriers to entry were low in many industries and market share could be quickly eroded by new market entrants and imported goods.

In some industries, competition can be created merely by reorganizing the administration of the enterprises. Such reorganization has been achieved with some success in the service industries. Prior to the collapse of the Soviet Union, *Aeroflot* was the largest airline in the world. It was replaced by regional and republic airlines, and the degree of competition between these successor firms, as well as new entrants, increased. *Intourist*, a monopoly supplier of tourist services, was replaced by several competitive organizations. In both of these cases artificial monopoly consisted of capital stock that was either small or easily divisible.

Reorganization is not possible, however, among the giants of Soviet-heavy industry, where the size of the enterprise is embodied in a single large plant and organization is around core products. Fully one-fifth of the Soviet workforce was employed in organizations of more than 10,000 workers. As Nikolay Petrakov, a Russian economist, observed:

> This is our notorious gigantomania. We always thought that a larger plant is bound to be better than a small one. We artificially propagated monopolists. An industrial giant that has already been built is impossible to break up into parts. This means that it will long remain a technological monopoly. . . . Fortunately there are not so many of them in the light and food industries. But heavy industry is full of these monsters. To speak of competition here is impossible. We will have to introduce price controls and anti-monopoly legislation.

The Role of Trade

Price controls on goods as differentiated and changing as machinery and machine tools are anathematic to most economists who would rather liberalize the trade regime to limit monopoly power. For such tradable goods, opening the economy to international competition can be an important check on the pricing behavior of domestic producers. It may be particularly effective in the case of machinery, where embodied technological change, as well as a moderating influence on prices, can result. However, dangers loom for domestic producers who are forced to confront the high quality, superior design, and low prices of goods from abroad. Price and quality control require rapid attention or domestic producers may lose customers and go bankrupt. Competition is bound to be unpopular with domestic producers, who are likely to petition for protective tariffs or quotas on "infant industry" grounds. However, once protective tariffs or quotas are adopted, they become difficult to remove, and they should be avoided where possible.

THE REFORM OF ENTERPRISES

The Enterprise Under Central Planning

Enterprises in the centrally planned economies were quite different in structure, goals, and culture from their counterparts in developed market economies. These differences were mentioned earlier, but a review is worthwhile:

1. *Size of enterprises.* Enterprises under central planning were larger on average than those in market economies because of the planners' faith in scale economies and a desire to eliminate "socially wasteful reproduction" of capacity. Studies of the structure of Soviet enterprise in the 1960s revealed that the average firm had a workforce about three times larger than for a similar market size in the West. This emphasis on size intensified during the 1970s and 1980s, as scale economies were pursued as a remedy for the economic failure. The Brezhnev reforms of 1973 resulted in the combination of smaller enterprises into larger industrial associations. By the late 1980s, almost three-quarters of the Soviet labor force was employed in enterprises of more than 1,000 persons and over 20 percent worked for enterprises with more than 10,000 workers.
2. *Objectives of management.* Under central planning the objective of management was to meet the plan targets, and incentives offered to management were oriented toward this goal. In many countries a concept close to profit was eventually introduced as one of multiple targets, but the lack of clear accounting and the high degree of implicit subsidy obscured this objective. Although profit maximization is not the unswerving objective of western firms, without doubt more attention is paid to a defined bottom line.
3. *Marketing and sales effort.* Centrally planned economies were characterized by excess demand and each firm's customers were defined by the planners. Little attention was paid to sales effort, market research, product improvement, or customer satisfaction. In developed market economies, sales and marketing are an essential feature of corporate operation and the absence of this capacity in a newly privatized enterprise will present difficulties in securing a solid customer base.
4. *Lack of export orientation.* Export markets were of little importance for centrally planned firms. Rather than a key source of sales and revenue for the enterprise, exports were a means of raising hard currency for necessary national purchases of material and equipment. Enterprises themselves were insulated from export markets until the late 1980s by the monopoly of the foreign trade organizations.

5. *Extent of vertical integration.* Centrally planned firms tended to be more vertically integrated than their developed market counterparts, due in large part to the failures of the distribution system and the neglect of quality control. If an enterprise were to have guaranteed access to intermediate goods of reliable quality, in a fashion timely enough to meet its own output targets, the safest way was to produce it within the organization. This principle led to a paradox. Although one emphasis of the centrally planned system was grasping economies of scale, large organizations frequently produced intermediate goods in inefficiently small quantities in order to meet internal demand. "Outsourcing" and precise inventory control, noticeable developments in the evolution of large enterprises in Europe, the United States, and Japan, were neglected in the Soviet-style economies.
6. *Provision of ancillary services.* Part of the reason that centrally planned firms were so large was that they were responsible for a wide range of services for workers that lay beyond the scope of operations of even the most paternalistic firms in the West. Firms were frequently responsible for housing, health services, child care, and even education, overlapping functions that in market economies are reserved for government.

Corporatization

The first step of enterprise reform is **corporatization**, placing the firm onto an organizational and accounting footing to allow management the freedom to pursue clearly defined objectives without political intervention. Corporatization is distinct from privatization, which involves placing the ownership of the enterprise outside the public sector, but it is a step in that direction.

1. *Creating independent management.* Under centralized planning not only is management appointed by the politicians but also it is directly accountable to them. This relationship is logical because the enterprise is an extension of the state and therefore is required to pursue objectives of the state. As long as enterprises remain subject to direct political control, their purpose will be defined largely in political terms and enterprise management will not be afforded the freedom to exercise initiative to increase efficiency and promote innovation. Moreover, managers will be appointed on political criteria rather than on ability in purely economic matters. Consequently, reform of industry must start with the alienation of the enterprises from the direct control of politicians.
2. *Defining the goals of the enterprise.* Next the objective of the enterprise must be clearly defined. If private ownership is an objective, the only consistent goal will be the maximization of profit—that is, the definition of and attention to a "bottom line." It is possible to corporatize an enterprise and assign to it objectives other than profit maximization, as long as it remains in the public sector or receives a subsidy from the state. In most developed market economies, for example, rail transportation is run by a publicly owned corporation, with an independent management structure. Because of a high level of externalities, such bodies often have broader goals than the maximization of profit.

3. *Separating ancillary services from the productive enterprise.* One of the most important aspects of enterprise restructuring is separating the provision of social services from the function of producing goods. When the means of production are socially owned, it can be convenient, even efficient, for productive enterprises to deliver social services. However, if the goals of the organization are more clearly defined as maximizing profits, any social activity that is not cost effective in raising labor productivity must be closed down, or the firm should be compensated for this activity by some level of government. If firms that bore responsibilities for housing, health, and education are allowed to shed them, then the government must assume them, or deterioration in social welfare will result, at least in the short run. As firms abandon their traditional social function, a pressing task in transition economies is the establishment of a social safety net to protect those "downsized" from state enterprise or those whose well-being is no longer the concern of their immediate employer.
4. *Establishing a realistic accounting system.* Accounting practices under central planning were neither universal nor impartial. The pervasiveness of the "soft-budget constraint" and the arbitrary nature of fiat prices made firms' accounts all but meaningless in the evaluation of performance. Preparation for privatization involves the establishment of an accepted accounting system that will enable potential investors to judge the financial viability and prospects of the firm.
5. *Providing incentives to management and workers.* A final desirable step in the process of corporatization is to look to the structure of incentives within the enterprise. Under planning, incentives were frequently perverse, and revising them to encourage hard work, managerial diligence, and innovation will better enable the firm to present the value of the enterprise to potential buyers.

PRIVATIZATION

Privatization should begin after these preliminary steps are taken, although, in fact, the privatization programs of most former socialist states proceeded before all of these preconditions were met.

Principles of Privatization

The Problem of the Commons Let us pause at this point to reconsider the economic and philosophical issues that bear on privatization. The primary rationale for private ownership lies in the "problem of the commons" or, to put it differently, what belongs to everyone belongs to no one. If resources are collectively owned, no individual has a strong incentive to look after them, and because the effect of an action of an individual on the overall condition of jointly held resources is minimal, each person can be considered a "free rider." However, the overall result is that resources held in common are abused while individually owned resources are likely to be better maintained because someone has a material incentive for their preservation.

Principal/Agent Problems The commons issue addresses the resource problem of social ownership, but the difficulties in the manufacturing and service sectors are somewhat different. **Principal/agent problems** occur within both socialism and capitalism. In a socialist state, politicians and the planners use positive incentives or punishments to induce enterprise managers to act in the way that the plan requires. In turn, the enterprise managers need strategies to induce workers to work in their interests. Capitalism shows parallel issues. The owners of capital hire managers; ensuring they behave in the interests of shareholders is a problem, and, as under socialism, these managers must induce workers to perform optimally. In fact, socialist and capitalist systems address these problems in quite similar ways. Managers are offered bonuses (or in capitalist firms they are frequently offered stock options) for meeting or exceeding targets, and workers are proffered a range of positive and negative incentives to raise their output—piece rates and bonuses on the positive side and tight supervision and output quotas on the negative.

Privatization of industry offers the potential of dealing with principal-agent issues more effectively than under social ownership. In some small businesses, agency problems will disappear as owner-operators emerge (for example, in retailing and the small-scale service sector). In larger enterprises, the owners of capital take a much more focused interest in the outcome in a particular enterprise and therefore provide more rigorous oversight of management's performance than would occur under planning. Corporate governance is a key to effective transition, and close attention should be given in the privatization process to establishing an effective system.

The Restitution Issue Both the commons and the principal-agent arguments suggest that privatization can foster efficiency by ensuring that resources will be dedicated to their highest value use and that appropriate oversight will be given to maximize efficiency. However, these arguments do not tell us much about who the owners of the privatized property should be, nor about how the transfer of ownership should be addressed. Some guidance may be given by examining how the property held in the state sector originated.[11] In some cases the property was seized without compensation (or without *adequate* compensation) from its owners. If they or their heirs can be identified (and if the property is largely unimproved from the condition in which it was seized), restitution of the property to them may be both equitable and efficient. Such restitution can be applied to residences and (for example, in Bulgaria) to small-scale agriculture. However, socialist rule in many states lasted long enough that most property cannot be associated with a presocialist owner. Moreover, much of it is new or greatly changed, especially in the industrial sector, and is not the subject of any preexisting title.

Holding the Nation's Assets in Trust Many transition economies operated under a socialist system for more than 40 years, usually from the immediate aftermath of World War II. Most of the states that emerged as a result of the breakdown

[11]Such a policy ignores, of course, the thorny issue of whether the owner prior to nationalization obtained the property by a just process in the first place. Consider, perhaps, a wealthy aristocrat who gained his estates by the gift of a tyrant.

of the Soviet Union operated under planning for about 65 years. The majority of the capital stock in these economies is the result of investment made during the socialist period and the enterprises could be said to belong to everyone in the population who sacrificed by deferring consumption to create investment capital—whether a willing sacrifice or not. The capital stock can be thought of as collectively financed and held, as if in trust, by the state, which suggests that the title to the newly privatized firms should be widely, and therefore equitably, distributed across the population. However, such a policy would not resolve the nexus of "commons" and "principal-agent" issues that led to the inefficient incentive and oversight structure in socially owned enterprises. A wide distribution of shares of newly privatized firms across the whole population though equitable, would lead to weak oversight of management and poor corporate governance.

Desirable Characteristics of a Privatization Program

If we list the desirable characteristics of a privatization program, we quickly recognize that some may be in conflict.[12] Features that we might want to see include the following:

1. *Rapidity.* The stock of assets to be transferred to the private sector in former socialist economies is large. The creation of a market economy requires tangible progress, and the process must be complete within a foreseeable period of time. The pace at which government assets were disposed of in mixed capitalist economies, such as the United Kingdom or France, is not acceptable when the vast bulk of the capital stock of a nation is to be disposed of.
2. *Improved enterprise governance.* The change in property rights must improve the governance of the enterprises. New owners need an effective means of oversight and way of tackling principal-agent problems.
3. *Fairness.* The process of privatization should be seen as fair and leading to the betterment of those who contributed to capital accumulation. A widespread perception of inequity may threaten political stability.
4. *Gaining the support of powerful interests.* The process must be able to placate the interests of the existing elite and the present "stakeholders" in the economy because without the support of powerful interests both political and economic reform may be aborted.
5. *Facilitating the inflow of new capital, technology, and management skills.* For enterprises hampered by a shortage of capital as well as limited access to foreign technology and "best-practice" techniques, privatization should help overcome these difficulties.
6. *Sustaining and supporting the liberalization program.* Finally, it is always desirable that any steps taken in the privatization program should be supportive of the overall program of liberalization and the institutions created.

[12]Cheryl W. Gray, "In Search of Owners: Privatization and Corporate Governance in Transition Economies," *The World Bank Research Observer* 11, no. 2 (August 1996), pp. 179–197.

Techniques of Privatization

Restitution The simplest privatization is the **restitution** of property to identifiable previous owners, who might have been uncompensated or only partially compensated when the assets were seized. Property rights can be swiftly transferred (as long as the title can be established), and the resultant ownership structure would be fair and lead to better governance. However, restitution is not useful in the majority of circumstances, especially in the case of medium and large-scale enterprises, because the current firms have no identifiable prior owner.

Small-Scale Mass Privatization The logical owners of much of the retail and service sectors (which consists of small bakeries, groceries, restaurants, small hotels, service stations, and so forth) are the state employees who operated the facilities under the planned system. It is desirable for continuity that these people stay in their jobs, and creating owner-operators can benefit efficiency and quality of service by eliminating principal-agent problems. Furthermore, these individuals probably have the best chance of being able to effectively value the business. The drawback is that, typically, such individuals have little capital, and loans to small businesses are seldom available in transition economies. Consequently, the enterprises have to be sold at low prices, and the state receives little revenue. This scenario is generally acceptable (except in cases where real estate or valuable inventory is involved), because employment is maintained and a potential tax stream is established with long-run positive revenues. Small-scale privatization also scores high for both speed and equity.

Sale to Insiders If operators of small businesses are allowed to assume ownership at favorable prices, the analogy in the industrial sector is sale to workers and management. Selling to such "insiders" provides two obvious advantages: it increases support for the transition process, and by making workers shareholders in the firm it helps to eliminate some of the incentive problems that lowered efficiency and productivity.[13]

This type of disposal can also lead to substantial drawbacks. First, neither workers nor management have access to substantial finance and cannot pay realistic prices for the enterprises, so little revenue is generated for the state. Second, the process is inequitable when viewed from a national perspective. Workers in the best firms with the brightest prospects and newest capital gain the most due to luck rather than their own hard work. Because investment in most socialist countries was determined at the national level and capital charges were unrealistically low, workers in enterprises most favored by the planners gain at the expense of the broad segment of society that made the sacrifices to provide the investment.

Further inequity is likely within the enterprise. Managers, though fewer in number than workers, have greater opportunities to disrupt the privatization

[13]This same logic offers options of shares to workers in developed market economies. Evidence indicates that this approach results in substantial impact on productivity in some privatizations. The case of road goods transportation in the United Kingdom is especially revealing.

process and therefore are able to negotiate, or to seize, a larger share of the assets. Many management-employee buyouts resulted in the assumption of the assets by senior management at low prices. Although this arrangement is satisfactory in terms of speed, it scores badly from the point of view of equity.

Finally, sale to insiders does little to attract new capital, new technology, or new management into the business, and therefore a prime economic objective of privatization—placing assets in the hands of those most able to maximize value—is not fulfilled.

Direct Sale to Outsiders One way of avoiding the problems of sale to insiders is to seek a group of investors, or a company, to purchase an enterprise as a going concern. An immediate difficulty is the shortage of capital and the underdeveloped capital markets, which make a leveraged buyout to a citizen or group of citizens unlikely. When deals are made with outsiders, prices often seem arbitrary, giving the appearance (and frequently the reality) of corruption.[14] Valuation techniques, even when applied by Western advisors, are rudimentary and close to useless when accounting information is poor and economic uncertainty is high.

The only groups that can afford to buy industrial enterprises "in being" are foreign investors who can pay more realistic prices for assets and are capable of infusing capital, technology, and modern management into their acquisitions. However, a political price is exacted in handing over prominent large enterprises to foreign control. In any case foreign buyers have been slow to buy large enterprises in transition economies. Frequently the existing plant is inappropriately designed, obsolete, and too large. Buying an existing enterprise means retaining a workforce with low productivity and bad work habits whose members were usually granted long-term job tenure prior to privatization.

Privatization through Initial Public Offerings **Initial public offerings** (IPOs) offer distinct attractions. Enterprises can be sold for realistic sums of money, thereby raising substantial revenues for the government, and widespread shareholding (and therefore support for capitalism) can be encouraged. However, success depends on some essential preconditions. First, company accounts must be accurate and accessible to allow realistic valuation. Even in such a case, IPOs are a slow path to privatization because each enterprise must be individually prepared and the public informed and educated about the company. Capital and equity markets must be developed and deep; even stock markets with a high capitalization can absorb only a few IPOs each year. If too much is offered in a short space of time, the whole market may be depressed.[15] Consequently, IPOs are not particularly useful in an economy moving from socialism to capitalism. Although they score high in terms of equity and in increasing the long-term stability of reform, poor information and shallow capital markets limit their applicability.

---

[14]This suspicion of favoritism is not limited to transition economies. Sales of this kind were an important part of Thatcher's privatizations in Britain, and they attracted criticism whenever valuable assets were transferred without an open-bidding process.

[15]Care was taken in the recent French privatization to avoid depressing the Paris markets by too many new shares.

Voucher Privatization If the correct way to view the socialist state is that it holds productive capital in trust for its citizens, then the process of privatization should transfer some part of the capital stock to each citizen. It is, in essence, the idea behind the schemes of **voucher privatization** by which the government gives away, or sells at low prices, vouchers that can then be used to claim shares in companies that are to be transferred from state ownership. This approach circumvents the problems resultant from the shortage of wealth that limits the applicability of all other approaches to privatization that involve sale, and it carries with it obvious advantages of fairness and equity. Voucher programs used in many of the transition economies may be the approach that best satisfies the five desirable characteristics itemized earlier.

Cheryl Gray has summarized the advantages of voucher privatization:

> Well-designed voucher privatization can overcome many of the problems encountered with the various sales techniques, notably the perceived unfairness, the shortage of domestic capital, and the difficulty of placing a value on assets. Because the voucher approach can proceed rapidly, it can simultaneously stimulate the development of market institutions, create new owners, and reorient the interests of existing ones toward further reform. Furthermore, it can speedily cut the links between enterprises and the state that both inhibit restructuring and put fiscal pressures on the state.[16]

The main problem with voucher privatization is that ownership of the enterprise becomes widely disbursed, diminishing effective governance. When a firm is divided among many owners, no single one feels a strong incentive to invest time and resources in supervising management. Even if one was highly motivated, he or she would have little power (as one shareholder among many) to change management's behavior. Consequently, management is often free to act in its own interest rather than in that of the owners, providing less incentive to maximize the return to capital and inefficiency results.

To avoid this problem, several countries encouraged or institutionalized the development of holding companies, much like mutual funds, that concentrate ownership and possess the knowledge, incentive, and power to effectively supervise management. In Poland, for example, the government set up several investment intermediaries staffed by managers appointed by the government. Each of these intermediaries was given a number of the enterprises to be privatized to manage, and the shares of the intermediaries were distributed among the citizenry. It was hoped that by active management the investment intermediaries would reorganize the enterprises under their control to maximize value and eventually sell them off to core investors. The danger of this approach is that holding companies will not follow through on restructuring or on the active pursuit of new owners. Consequently, rather than becoming a dynamic force for change they became state-protected institutions to manage lame-duck enterprises that have no willing buyers.

In the Czech Republic intermediaries grew as a result of market initiative rather than being created by the government. The original intent of the Czech privatization

---

[16]Gray, "In Search of Owners," *The World Bank Research Observer* 11, no. 2 (August 1996), p. 90.

scheme was to auction shares directly to individuals using vouchers. However, investment funds arose (many of which were connected to banks), which acquired and pooled the vouchers of many individuals. These funds (420 in number) eventually acquired some 72 percent of the vouchers. The funds proved powerful in exerting managerial oversight of the firms, and in some cases their control became too great. Funds managed by the banks often involved a conflict of interest because the bank was both an owner of and a lender to a specific firm. In Russia, even though the voucher auction scheme sanctioned the development of investment intermediaries, they have not grown to the degree seen in the Czech Republic.

FINANCIAL SECTOR REFORM

The purpose of the financial sector in a market economy is quite different from that under central planning. In a modern market economy, financial institutions are responsible for accumulating and rationing investment resources. The savings of small households are aggregated and commingled in financial institutions and loaned out to business enterprises looking for investment capital. The financial sector is also responsible for evaluating the risk of these loans and fixing appropriate risk-compensated interest rates. Importantly, the financial sector grants credit to those industries that are likely to grow and denies finance to moribund firms.

As we discussed earlier, the purpose of the financial system in a centrally planned economy is quite different. Under central planning a single state bank (monobank) served two purposes. First, it would passively allocate credit to enterprises in accordance with the plan. Second, it served as a system of checking plan performance, because all movements of material through the economy had their counterpart as a paper trail of credit in the banking system. If market reforms are to be successful, a functional financial system that will perform the tasks of pooling savings, disinterestedly assessing risk, and making loans is essential.

The Central Bank

One of the first priorities must be the creation of a central bank, usually achieved by divesting the monobank of its other responsibilities and focusing it on functions traditionally reserved for the central bank.

These functions include the following:

1. Acting as a clearing bank for the commercial banks
2. Acting as the promulgator and enforcer of regulation to enhance the stability and efficiency of the financial system
3. Functioning as a lender of last resort to banks
4. Controlling the stock of money in the economy, and hence the interest rate
5. Monitoring the foreign exchange value of the currency

The degree of independence of the central bank is an important issue. Developed market economies offer little in the way of guidance to economies in transition.

The U.S. Federal Reserve System is highly independent, and the German Bundesbank is regarded as even more so. On the other hand, the Bank of Japan and the Bank of France are subject to tight government control. The Bank of England, for most of the postwar period an arm of the British government, has now been granted a much higher degree of autonomy.

Proponents of independence argue that central bankers have the expertise to make impartial decisions and will perform well if politicians are prevented from influencing them. The prime job of the central bank is to preserve the value of the currency, and it must frequently take a restrictive and conservative line on credit creation. When politicians are given control over the central bank, monetary policy tends to be too relaxed, and the unpleasant but necessary task of squeezing credit, and watching enterprises fail as unemployment mounts, would be avoided. The opposing view is that a totally independent central bank is answerable to no one. In a market economy it is an institution of great significance,[17] therefore, it is odd that in a representative democracy the people have no say in this vital dimension of policy making. In this analysis, the central bank is responsive only to the narrow financial community from which the board of governors are likely to spring. As such, an independent central bank might be unduly austere and hence jeopardize political stability by pursuing its own brand of financial rectitude. There is no right and wrong answer to this debate. Politicians are adept at judging the public will, and if they controlled the central bank we could say that a form of democracy prevailed. On the other hand, politicians have a short-term outlook and are prone to shallow compromise, whereas the financial experts insulated from pressure might effect more viable long-term policies.

Commercial Banks/Investment Banks

After creating the central bank, priority must be given to developing a commercial and investment banking system that can be effective in mobilizing savings and allocating investment capital among potential borrowers. This process is unlikely to be rapid. Some banks can be created by assuming the deposit and lending functions of the monobank, holding them for a while in the public sector, and then privatizing when conditions are appropriate. It will also probably be worthwhile to create a "post office" or "giro" savings bank in most of the transition economies. These institutions are almost universally found in Western Europe and Asia and provide a means of aggregating small savings as well as providing a high degree of convenience, security, and liquidity to the less affluent households.[18] Although these institutions are criticized for paying only low rates of interest, in general they have proved popular with small savers.

The biggest banking problem for transition economies is controlling the growth and behavior of new financial intermediaries that spring up. In Russia, for example,

[17]If confirmation of this point were required, we have only to take note of the army of "Fed watchers" in the United States, who are concerned with predicting the Fed's behavior.

[18]Deposits in the Japanese postal savings system amount to well over $2 trillion, almost as much as the rest of the banking system together.

at the outset of reform between 1989 and 1992 some 1,600 "banks" were created, but most did not meet the definition of banks as applied in the West. Many were created by industrial enterprises and exist largely to finance their parent companies by borrowing on the interbank market. As such, they perform little in the way of impartially assessing risk or allocating scarce capital resources to their highest value functions. It is vital for long-term development that a stable, disinterested private banking sector be established, and the first step is defining and requiring capital adequacy standards, accountancy norms, and regular audits to guarantee security to the depositor.

Banking regulations vary from country to country and as long as they are visible and enforced, a range of policy can be highly functional. In the United States and the United Kingdom, commercial banking, savings institutions, and investment banks were separated by practice and law, although these divisions are eroding over time. In continental Europe no such functional division applies and universal banks (sometimes referred to as U-banks) are the norm. U-banks are large and perform savings, lending, and underwriting functions. At the end of the day what matters most is not the specific institutional form of the banking system, but rather the degree of public confidence it is able to inspire. With a high degree of confidence the public will entrust its savings to the banking sector; little confidence in financial institutions will lead to low savings rates and unhealthy speculation in real assets.

Stock Markets

Stock markets are a feature of all developed market economies, and it is tempting to think that the rapid establishment of a stock exchange is an important prerequisite for growth. However, historically it seldom proves to be the case. Reliable evidence suggests that the growth of the stock markets tends to follow, rather than cause, rapid economic growth. In East Asia, for example, little industrial finance originated from the equity market and only in Korea and Taiwan did it represent even as much as 10 percent. Further back into history, most of the finance for Britain's industrial revolution was generated by interfirm credit, while continental Europe and the United States relied heavily on bank lending. So although the development of an equities market is positive, it is not essential for a market economy.

The process of maturation of a stock market is a slow one and depends on the accretion of public trust, a growing number of investors and intermediaries, and an increased number of issues and capitalization. Antoine van Agtmael, in a paper published in 1982, identified five stages in the general development of stock markets across time and economies.[19]

1. *The dormant stage.* During the first, dormant stage, most people are not actively aware of the existence of the stock market. Trading volume is low, only a few companies are listed, and prices remain close to their issuance values. As time goes by, shares tend to become undervalued, especially in a

[19]From *Emerging Securities Markets,* 1982. Material first published by Euromoney Publications, London.

dynamic economic environment. Inevitably, brokers or individuals discover that dividend yield alone—even excluding potential capital gains—exceeds the yield on other investment alternatives. This stage was largely absent or short lived in transition economies where expectations for equity growth were high from the outset.

2. *Manipulation.* Manipulation begins when some market participants discover that the small supply of stocks, and thus limited liquidity, makes it possible to move prices up with relatively small purchases. Rising prices encouraged new market entrants, enabling the manipulators to get out with quick profits.
3. *Speculation.* As soon as some people begin to make substantial capital gains and boast of their profits, a wider group of investors is attracted. A speculative stage begins during which trading soars and prices are driven up well beyond appropriate values.
4. *Consolidation or crash.* At some point the speculative bubble is questioned, and stock prices begin to waver and drop. Depending on the extent of the boom during the speculative stage, prices either decline gradually or tumble deeply. The consolidation stage or crash sets in. It may take investors months or even years to regain confidence in the stock market after such a price decline. Much depends on the extent of the price drop as well as on interest rates, economic growth, corporate profitability, inflation yields on other investment alternatives, new incentives to restimulate buying, and the behavior of institutional investors. During this consolidation stage, many speculators become, out of necessity, investors. Unwilling to sell their shares at a loss, they hold on to them for long-term investment in the hope that prices will improve in the future.
5. *Maturity.* The mature stage begins when the initial investors regain confidence and are joined by new groups of investors unhurt by previous failures. Trading volume is likely to be more consistent, investment more sophisticated, the supply of shares broader, and, thus, liquidity greater. Recent experience in Southeast Asia, Latin America, and the transition economies seems to justify these overall conclusions.

REFORM OF INTERNATIONAL TRADE

Prior to the late 1980s the international trade of socialist nations was the concern of the state, not individual firms. The direction of trade with other socialist countries, its volume, and the prices of traded goods were subject to the plan. All trade with the nonsocialist world was conducted by specialized state-controlled foreign trade organizations (FTOs). Exports were sanctioned in order to raise the foreign exchange to finance the imports required by the plan. Individual firms had little contact with their customers and could only buy imported machinery, technology, and materials if they could make a convincing case with the planners, which usually required political influence. Under Gorbachev this system was reformed, and enterprises were allowed to trade directly with overseas counterparts, but a complex system of tariffs and licenses prevailed.

Most economists favor the elimination of licensing and the removal or moderation of tariffs in order to allow substantially free trade. In the short term, some tariff protection may be necessary because during restructuring virtually all enterprises can be regarded as "infant." Although it might seem strange to regard the former Soviet Union's industrial giants as infants, in terms of efficiency, pricing, client relations, and technical innovation they have much to learn. Free trade would lead to loss of domestic market share that would be hard to recoup and would cause further macroeconomic contraction. However, protection for inefficient producers has costs, not least of which is that it denies other enterprises access to inputs and technology at world prices. Consequently, the drive to modernize within these firms may be hindered by the inflated cost of inputs. Limited protection is important in the short term, but the long-term growth of the economy requires that protective measures be phased out quickly or else the industry nurtured behind tariff walls can never become globally competitive.

Trade liberalization also requires currency reform. Under planning, currency convertibility was limited and often subject to multiple exchange rates—with different uses requiring conversion at different rates. This situation was inefficient, distortionary, and led to the development of black markets. Full currency convertibility is not absolutely necessary for a functioning market economy. Convertibility was not generally restored in Western Europe until the late 1950s, and many countries today limit capital convertibility and the access of residents or citizens to foreign exchange. What is essential is the establishment of a realistic exchange rate and relatively unrestricted access to foreign exchange for those firms involved in trade.

Trade liberalization often goes hand in hand with a greater role for foreign direct investment (FDI), although again it is possible to conceive of primarily market-coordinated economies in which the part played by the FDI is limited; Korea provides such an example. However, for most transition economies FDI helps to solve a series of problems because it provides capital for investment, a source of foreign exchange, technological know-how, management techniques, and links to export markets. Defined property rights, a civil legal code, consistent tax laws, and guarantees on the convertibility and repatriation of profits are important in attracting direct investment. A good deal of discretion may be retained within a general policy to encourage FDI. As a policy matter, a foreign presence can be discouraged in those sectors that are sensitive (e.g., resources) or those areas that the government feels can be adequately met by domestic enterprises (retailing, for example).

THE SOCIAL SAFETY NET

Under socialism and centralized planning, the most important form of "safety net" was the guarantee of work for everyone. In fact, being employed was a legal requirement for most people. Having a job provided workers with income and access to nonwage benefits, irrespective of their productivity in employment or the fundamental profitability of the enterprise for which they worked. Long-term success in the transition economies depends on both closing the enterprises that are unable to compete when subject to a hard-budget constraint and raising the productivity (therefore cutting the workforce) of those that survive. Consequently, unemployment, which existed only in a disguised form during the socialist period, will necessarily rise during the transition. Some form of social safety net is required to protect the unemployed and to guarantee some minimum living standard for all.

The alternative to providing an effective social safety net is the alienation and marginalization of a large part of the workforce, creating an underclass and courting a high degree of political risk. Other social problems may develop including a high degree of migrancy, waste of social infrastructure, and a plethora of social pathologies including rising crime, prostitution, mounting suicide, and so forth. Furthermore, a social safety net functions economically as well as politically by assisting the development and operation of the labor market. Without public support for the unemployed, displaced workers are forced to accept the first job available without being able to undertake any off-the-job search. Mismatches of skill between job and employee are inevitable.

BIG BANG VERSUS GRADUALISM

A remaining important question about transition is its speed. If market arrangements are substantially more efficient than the plan, then it can be argued that economic reform should proceed as quickly as possible. Rapid changes in ownership and property rights should bring about correspondingly rapid increases in factor productivity, output, and the general level of welfare.

A contrary case can be made, however. The existing capital stock and associated institutions were fashioned for a particular economic system involving a high degree of command and central planning. New institutions and laws will take time to draft, and the economic actors will be on a learning curve to assimilate the parameters of the new order. The existing capital stock and infrastructure must be modified for the new conditions in which the economy must operate. Thus a **big bang** approach, in which prices are liberalized at a stroke and in which privatization is pursued vigorously, will take time to bear fruit, and in the meantime some disruption will be inevitable. Slower change (allowing economic actors to absorb lessons) and institutional experimentation might be preferable.

A drawback of a gradualist approach is the reversibility of reform. A big bang creates powerful interests committed to reform, while gradualism allows the old guard a continued lease on life and protracts the unsettling political debate about the ultimate direction of the economy. Such uncertainty might have a substantial effect on real investment, because entrepreneurs might be unwilling to commit resources to long-term projects if they foresee a strong chance of reversal. Time alone will tell which approach leads to the better outcome. Table 20.2 suggests that the rapid reformers of Central and Eastern Europe have already passed through their darkest period and are moving into a situation where sustained growth seems to be likely. However, if we look at other parts of the world, especially to the People's Republic of China (see Chapter 23), gradualism and experimentation apparently produced a more successful pattern of transition.

POLITICAL REFORM AND ECONOMIC REFORM

Table 20.5 shows the progress made in economies in transition through 2001, ranking both political and economic progress. These figures were produced by Freedom House, a U.S. group concerned with political and economic liberalization in Europe. The figures are largely subjective, but they echo to some extent the estimates of Table 20.2. They show that political and economic reform are closely linked. The correlation between the two indices is high (a raw correlation coefficient of .936). Consequently, we seldom encounter either a democratic state with a highly controlled economy or a liberal economy accompanied by a totally authoritarian political structure. In general, the former Soviet satellite states of central

TABLE 20.5

Progress to Political and Economic Reform in Transition Economies

	Economy		Democracy	
	Rank	Score	Rank	Score
Poland	1	1.67	1	1.44
Hungary	2	1.92	4	1.94
Estonia	3	1.92	7	2.00
Czech Republic	4	2.00	2	1.81
Slovenia	5	2.08	5	1.94
Latvia	6	2.50	6	1.94
Lithuania	7	2.75	3	1.94
Slovakia	8	3.25	8	2.25
Bulgaria	9	3.50	9	3.06
Croatia	10	3.58	10	3.25
Armenia	11	3.58	17	4.56
Georgia	12	3.75	15	4.19
Moldova	14	4.00	13	3.94
Romania	13	4.00	11	3.31
Kyrgyz Republic	15	4.00	21	5.13
Russia	17	4.17	18	4.63
Albania	16	4.17	14	4.13
Ukraine	18	4.33	16	4.44
Kazakhstan	19	4.50	23	5.56
Macedonia	20	4.58	12	3.75
Azerbaijan	21	4.92	24	5.56
Yugoslavia	22	5.33	19	4.63
Tajikistan	24	5.50	22	5.44
Bosnia	23	5.50	20	4.94
Uzbekistan	25	6.17	25	6.50
Belarus	26	6.25	26	6.56
Turkmenistan	27	6.50	27	6.94

SOURCE: Freedom House, *Nations in Transition*, 2001, available at http://www.freedomhouse.org/research/nattransit.htm.

Europe moved fastest in both political and economic reform, followed by the Baltic States of the former Soviet Union. This group is also explicitly preparing itself for entry into the European Union, which affected the pace and direction of both economic and political reform. The new nations that made up the former Yugoslavia (Croatia, Slovenia, and Macedonia)[20] are hard to classify. Slovenia is advanced in both political and economic reform, while Macedonia, despite being part of the Yugoslav "participatory economy," is backward both economically and politically. As far as the European states go, the laggards are Belarus, backward in both dimensions, and Yugoslavia, Bosnia, and Macedonia, which were all constituent parts of the Yugoslav Republic.

KEY TERMS AND CONCEPTS

advanced reformers
big bang
collapse of GDP
contestability of markets
corporatization
domestic liberalization
enterprise governance
external transactions liberalization
inflation tax
initial public offerings
monetary overhang
negative value added
principal/agent problems
private sector entry liberalization
restitution
voucher privatization

QUESTIONS FOR DISCUSSION

1. How did the "monetary overhang" arise in socialist states, and what is its significance in the transition process?
2. Why was inflation a common feature of transitional states?
3. What led to the phenomenon of a collapse of GDP being a general concomitant of liberalization?
4. What happened in most countries to labor productivity during the transition? Why?
5. Why is the problem of monopoly so pressing in transition countries? How can abuse of monopoly power be limited?
6. What is meant by corporatization?
7. How are the issues of privatization and enterprise governance linked?
8. Do you think that the central bank in a post-socialist state should be independent and insulated from political pressure?

[20]Neither Serbia (still called Yugoslavia) nor Bosnia are included in the survey, presumably because of political problems.

9. Why are stock markets not likely to be important as providers of capital in the transition process?
10. What is a big bang approach to transition?

RESOURCES

Web Sites

Stockholm School of Economics .... http://www.hhs.se/

International Centre for Policy Studies, Kiev, Ukraine .... http://www.icps.kiev.ua/

Transition .... http://www.worldbank.org/transitionnewsletter/
The *Transition* newsletter is a regular publication of the World Bank's Development Economic Research Group [DECRG]

REES Web: Russian and East European Studies, University of Pittsburgh .... http://www.ucis.pitt.edu/reesweb/

World Bank Research on Poverty During the Transition .... http://www.worldbank.org/research/inequality/

The Vienna Institute for International Economic Studies .... http://www.wiiw.ac.at/

European Bank for Reconstruction and Development .... http://www.ebrd.com/

The European Union's Main Transition Initiative: The Phare Programme http://www.europa.eu.int/comm/dg1a/phare/index.htm

United Nations Economic Commission for Europe .... http://www.unece.org/

Freedom House .... http://www.freedomhouse.org/

Soros Foundation .... http://www.soros.org/

The Corporate Governance Net .... http://www.corpgov.net/

Sigma—The Good Governance Initiative of the OECD .... http://www.oecd.org/sigma/

Cato Institute: Project on Global Economic Liberty .... http://www.cato.org/research/glob-st.html/

Books and Articles

Berg, Andrew, Eduardo R. Borensztein, Ratna Sahay, and Jeromin Zettelmeyer. "The Evolution of Output in Transition Economies—Explaining the Differences." International Monetary Fund Working Paper WP/99/73.

Blanchard, Olivier. *The Economics of Post-Communist Transition. Clarendon Lectures in Economics.* Oxford: Clarendon Press, 1997.

Carlin, W., and M. Landesmann. *From Theory into Practice? Corporate Restructuring and Economic Dynamism in Transition Economies.* Vienna: Vienna Institute for International Economic Studies, August 1997.

Claassen, Emil-Maria. *Exchange Rate Policies in Developing and Post-Socialist Countries.* San Francisco: OCS Press, 1992. Reviewed in *Studies in Comparative International Development.*

De Melo, Martha, Cevder Denizer, and Alan Gelb. "Patterns of Transition from Plan to Market." *World Bank Economic Review* 10, no. 3 (September 1996): 397 ff.

Earle, John S., Roman Frydman, Andrzej Rapaczynski, and Joel Turkewitz. *Small Privatization: The Transformation of Retail Trade and Consumer Services in the Czech Republic, Hungary, and Poland. CEU Privatization Reports.* New York: Central European University Press, 1994.

Frydman, Roman, and Andrzej Rapaczynski. *Privatization in Eastern Europe: Is the State Withering Away?* New York: Central European University Press, 1994.

Frydman, Roman, Cheryl W. Gray, and Andrzej Rapaczynski (eds.). *Corporate Governance in Central Europe and Russia: Banks, Funds and Foreign Investors. World Bank/CEU Privatization Project.* New York: Central European University Press, 1996.

Frydman, Roman, Kenneth Murphy, and Andrzej Rapaczynski. *Capitalism with a Comrade's Face.* New York: Central European University Press, 1998.

Gray, Cheryl W. "In Search of Owners: Privatization and Corporate Governance in Transition Economies." *World Bank Research Observer* 11, no. 2 (August 1996): 179–197.

Hardt, John P., and Richard F. Kaufman (eds.). *East-Central European Economies in Transition.* Armonk, NY: M.E. Sharpe, 1995.

Havrylyshyn, Oleh, and Donal McGettigan. "Privatization in Transition Countries—A Sampling of the Literature." International Monetary Fund Working Paper WP/99/6.

Henderson, Jeffrey (ed.) with Karoly Balaton and Gyorgy Lengyel. *Industrial Transformation in Eastern Europe in the Light of the East Asian Experience.* New York: St. Martin's Press, 1998.

Hernández-Catá, Ernesto. "Liberalization and the Behavior of Output During the Transition from Plan to Market." *International Monetary Fund Staff Papers* 44, no. 4 (December 1997).

Kennett, David, and Marc Lieberman (eds.). *The Road to Capitalism: Economic Transformation in Eastern Europe and the Former Soviet Union.* Fort Worth, TX: The Dryden Press, 1992.

Lavigne, Marie. *The Economics of Transition: From Socialist Economy to Market Economy.* New York: St. Martin's Press, 1999.

Mann, Catherine L. *Industry Restructuring in East-Central Europe: The Challenge and the Role of Foreign Investment.* American Economic Association Papers and Proceedings, May 1991.

Milanovic, Branko. *Income, Inequality, and Poverty During the Transition from Planned to Market Economy.* Washington, DC: World Bank.

Pöhl, Gerhard, Robert E. Anderson, Stijn Claessens, and Simeon Djankov. "Privatization and Restructuring in Central and Eastern Europe." World Bank Technical Paper, 1997.

Rother, Philipp. "Explaining the Behavior of Financial Intermediation—Evidence from Transition Economies." International Monetary Fund Working Paper WP/99/36.

Sachs, Jeffrey D. *Reforms in Eastern Europe and the Former Soviet Union in Light of the East Asian Experiences.* Working Paper Series, Working Paper 5404. Cambridge, MA: National Bureau of Economic Research, 1996.

Sachs, Jeffrey D., and Katharina Pistor (eds.). *The Rule of Law and Economic Reform in Russia.* John M. Olin Critical Issues Series (paper). Boulder, CO: Westview Press, 1997.

"A Survey of Central Asia: A Caspian Gamble." *The Economist,* February 7, 1998, 56.

White, William, *Evolving International Financial Markets: Some Implications for Central Banks.* BIS Working Paper no. 66 (April 1999).

World Bank. *From Plan to Market: World Development Report 1996.* New York: Oxford University Press, 1996.

21

REFORM AND PERFORMANCE OF THE RUSSIAN ECONOMY

RUSSIA		
	Area (thousand sq. km.)	17,075
	Currency	ruble
	Exchange Rate	29 rubles = US$1
	Population, 2000 (millions)	146
	Population Growth Rate	–0.2%
	GNI per Capita, 2001	$1,660
	GNI per Capita, PPP	$8,010
	GDP Growth, 1990–2000	–4.8%
Value Added as % of GDP 2000	Agriculture	7%
	Industry	38%
	Services	56%
% of GDP	Government Expenditure	37.9%
	Government Revenue	33.6%
	Exports	42.0%

THE LEGACY OF THE "ERA OF STAGNATION"

By the early 1980s the crisis of the Soviet economy had become acute, and even though no sector was doing well, agriculture and consumer goods were faring particularly poorly. The system was sustained only by the hard currency proceeds of oil and gas exports used to buy food and advanced capital goods. Despite exhortation to improve economic performance, the leadership seemed determined to change nothing, and stagnation resulted.

Poor economic performance meant that the Soviet Union's relative position in the world was slowly sinking, and with it the capacity to maintain superpower status. Slippage was accelerated by emerging payments problems in the 1980s; hard currency exports (mainly energy) peaked in the early 1980s, while imports, including food, continued to rise throughout the decade. The result was a growing external deficit and increased international indebtedness. The gross debt (i.e., what the Soviet Union owed the Western nations before making allowance for Soviet holdings of hard currency) rose from $11.5 billion in 1975 to $22 billion in 1980 and $38 billion in 1985. A measure of the scale and severity of this indebtedness is the debt service ratio (the amount of hard currency payments required annually as a proportion of normal hard currency earnings); it rose from 10 percent in 1975 to about 23 percent in the mid-1980s. Almost a quarter of the value of the Soviet exports was committed ahead of time to repaying previously incurred debts. Market economies faced with such a crisis could finance part of their balance of payments deficit through incoming foreign direct investment, but despite a lukewarm commitment to joint ventures, the reality of Soviet politics made such inflows all but impossible.

PERESTROIKA AND *GLASNOST*

Gorbachev's reform efforts will forever be associated with the catchwords *perestroika* and *glasnost,* usually translated as restructuring and openness. His original intentions were modest, but the political change initiated by his *glasnost* policy far outstripped his plans for the economy, and Gorbachev was swept further toward liberalization as he attempted to appease both domestic and international critics. Even though *perestroika* seemed to offer much at the time, in retrospect this meandering attempt at reform must be judged a failure. The six years of the program may be divided into four phases, which may be summarized as follows:[1]

Phase	Date	Description
I	1985–early 1986	Rhetorical period. A lot of talk about reform but few specifics.
II	1986–early 1988	Legislative period. Creation of superministries, new laws on self-employment, state enterprise, cooperatives, and property.
III	1988–1989	Attempted implementation of reform.
IV	1989–1991	Failure, abandonment of the *perestroika* model in favor of more radical reform.

These stages were not totally distinct, but this partition gives an overview of the history of the Gorbachev years. Immediately after he came to power, Gorbachev talked a great deal about the necessity of reform and the gains to be made, but his rhetoric obscured the vague nature of his program. What was clear, and remained

[1]See, for example, Gregory and Stuart, *Soviet and Post-Soviet Economic Structure and Performance,* 5th ed. (New York: HarperCollins, 1994), p. 324.

the case throughout his administration, was that he aimed to modify a socialist economy rather than to shift toward a true market economy.

During 1986, decrees and laws designed to reform the economy began to dribble through. In some ways the legislation was schizophrenic. It laid the groundwork for private property and market signaling, but it increased government control by heaping new powers on the center and creating "superministries." The most notorious of these was *Gosagroprom*, designed to coordinate all agricultural and food distribution activity, but it only increased mismanagement and confusion. Gorbachev's agenda for industrialization hinged on three important laws and one decree:

1. The **Law on Individual Economic Activity** (November 1986) allowed the establishment of small businesses in the service sector as individual proprietorships under license from the state.
2. The **Law on State Enterprise** passed in mid-1987 and effective as of January 1, 1988, gave much greater freedom to the management of state-owned industry. Hard planning targets were replaced by "state orders" and greater latitude was permitted in staffing, pricing, and choice of technique. Theoretically, enterprises were to become financially independent and accountable, initiating a hard-budget constraint.
3. The **Law on Cooperatives** (May 1988) sanctioned the formation of larger private businesses. For ideological reasons they initially took the legal structure of cooperatives, but in reality this law facilitated the eventual creation of joint stock companies.
4. The **Decree on Property** (December 1988) allowed the sale of state-owned housing to individuals, creating a housing market and leading to the privatization of 12 million homes by 1995.

Although these reforms seemed far-reaching, their effect on the economy was mostly negative. The Law on State Enterprise gave firms both the incentive and opportunity to sell their goods in the market place for the highest prices that they could command, rather than continue to supply their traditional buyers at the prescribed plan prices. As a result, "downstream" firms frequently found themselves short of necessary inputs or unable to pay the higher prices, which curtailed production. Some enterprises even found themselves without the cash flow required to pay their workers. Coal miners, for example, were not paid for long periods in the later years of the Gorbachev administration, although the mines continued to operate and produce coal. Viewed from almost any perspective within the economy, *perestroika* was not a success.

500 DAYS TO A MARKET ECONOMY

The failure of Gorbachev's conception of *perestroika* and the protracted decline of the Soviet economy pointed to the need for more radical reform. The experience of the previous four years showed once again the ineffectiveness of tampering with the basic system of command planning, and consequently more attention was paid to moving the economy of the Soviet Union directly to a market system. In early 1990 a committee established under the leadership of Stanislav Shatalin, a respected economist and academician, produced a document known as the Shatalin report, titled *500 Days: Transition to Market*. It was deeply critical of the foundations of the Soviet system of centralized planning and sought to replace it with private property and liberalized market prices.

> The long rule of the totalitarian socio-political system dragged our society into profound crisis. Indecisiveness of the government and the mistakes it made in economic policy brought the country to the brink of collapse. . . . For a long time economic policy did not consider the people's interests. The state was wealthy while the people were poor. The state accumulated under its control almost all of the resources for production. Such resources were squandered on giant and ineffective projects, for increasing military power, and for certain ideologically flavored practices overseas even though the times have long passed since we could afford this.[2]

After attacking the leadership, the system, and Gorbachev's halting and ineffectual reforms, the report provided a rationale for a new order based on market relations. In retrospect, and given the disappointments of the decade since the report, the idea that the Soviet economy could be put on a market footing in only a year and a half seems naive, but it did represent fresh and open thinking on the causes of and the potential solutions for the Soviet malaise.

As the economy spiraled downward Gorbachev's popularity sank with it. His authority became threatened by the emergence of a rival power center in the form of the government of the Russian Federation, led by Boris Yeltsin, the chairman of the Russian Supreme Soviet, who had in July 1990 taken the decisive step of resigning from the Communist Party. While Yeltsin unequivocably advocated a rapid shift to a market economy along the lines of the Shatalin report, Gorbachev still tended to gradualism. Consequently, although the Supreme Soviet of Russia voted to approve the Shatalin plan by a margin of 213 to 1, Gorbachev as leader of the Soviet Union rejected it, proposing a much slower and less complete transition agenda. In November 1990 the Russian Congress of Deputies took the politically charged step of legalizing private family farming, outraging the Communists, and provoking an irredeemable division.

Events of the following year, 1991, continued this conflict as the Russian government legislated an even more liberal agenda, while Gorbachev attempted to slow the process of reform. Although Gorbachev avoided committing his administration to a radical transformation, his failure to stop Yeltsin's program allowed reform to proceed at a pace that alarmed the leadership of the Communist Party. As Gorbachev's position weakened and the failure of piecemeal reform became more apparent, Western nations, whose financial support was vital to the Soviet Union's reform effort, increased pressure on Gorbachev to adopt a more liberal stance.

During the summer of 1991 a group of Soviet reformers and Western academics gathered and drafted what became known as the **Grand Bargain**, under which the

[2]"Man, Freedom and Market" excerpted from "On the Program Developed by Academician S. S. Shatalin from: *500 Days: Transition to Market*," in *Road to Capitalism*, David Kennett and Marc Lieberman (ed.) (Fort Worth, TX: Dryden Press, 1992), p. 88.

Soviet Union would commit to rapid economic and political reform, while in return the West would provide substantial economic aid. Gorbachev rejected the plan and tried to negotiate less conditional terms in a meeting with the leaders of the G7 nations, held in London in July. It was almost his last act as leader of the Soviet Union and he came away empty-handed. While vacationing in the Crimea in August, he was the target of a coup led by Communist Party leaders, which because of an inability to neutralize Yeltsin, unraveled after a few days of chaos. This failed putsch led directly to the breakup of the Soviet Union; during September most of the constituent republics declared their independence, and by March only the Ukraine and Belarus remained. On December 25 Gorbachev resigned, and over the Kremlin the red flag of the Soviet Union was replaced by the red, white, and blue banner of the Russian Federation.

THE GAIDAR REFORMS

Dramatic economic reform immediately followed. On January 2, 1992, just eight days after Gorbachev's resignation, Yeltsin, as president of the Russian Federation, launched a new phase of liberalization of the Russian economy, known as the **Gaidar reforms**. The chief architect of this new plan was Yegor Gaidar, a young liberal economist whose voice had become increasingly influential. The Gaidar/Yeltsin plan was spurred by Western criticism and resembled the Sachs/Balcerowicz plan initiated in Poland the previous year with some success[3] and rested on five "pillars."[4]

(1) Rehabilitation of the Ruble

The Gaidar team's primary premise was that the rehabilitation of the ruble lie at the heart of any reform program. The Soviet population lost faith in the ruble as a store of value and opted where possible for dollars or D-marks, but without a currency in which the population had confidence, and which could serve as vehicle for international exchange; they believed that the reform process would stall.

(2) Market Liberalization

The second pillar was the creation of a functioning market economy. It involved decontrolling prices, allowing free entry into almost all economic activity, cutting back on the share of output absorbed by state orders, and establishing the necessary legal system required to underpin market activity. The January 2 pronouncement ended central coordination of the economy, and almost all prices were immediately liberalized.[5] Later that month, Yeltsin made a presidential decree that

---

[3]See Chapter 22 for a fuller description of the conception and achievements of Polish shock therapy.

[4]David Lipton and Jeffrey Sachs, "Prospects for Russia's Economic Reforms," *Brooking Papers on Economic Activity* 2 (1992): 213–276.

[5]The sole exception was the energy sector that remained under administrative prices. Energy prices were raised at the outset of the reforms and were partially liberalized later in 1992, but remained at a fraction of world prices. The government's fear was that a rapid increase of energy prices to world levels would cause a massive contraction in industrial output because the Soviet economy was based on cheap energy.

declared all economic activity to be legal unless it was expressly prohibited, reversing the situation that existed under Soviet planning, by which all private economic activity was proscribed unless expressly permitted.[6]

The upshot was a massive rise in prices and the considerable monetary overhang came into play as idle savings pursued scarce goods. Inflation during the first month of "shock therapy" was over 250 percent, and the prices of many key consumer goods rose by much more. The force of inflationary pressure surprised many observers, including the International Monetary Fund (IMF), which held the opinion that a rise in prices of only 45 percent would be enough to neutralize the monetary overhang. Opening the Russian economy to foreign trade resulted in dramatic consequences as consumers who had been required to buy Soviet goods now had greater choice. Imports flowed in, and the demand for domestic output fell; for the first time Russian producers faced serious competition in markets formerly guaranteed to them under planning, and decades of neglecting design and quality showed. Meanwhile, because many raw materials could be now exported for hard cash, prices soared from the artificially low levels administered under Soviet planning, pushing inflation and hurting domestic production.[7]

Price liberalization provided some positive effects: the monetary overhang disappeared as savings were eradicated; the black market was curtailed; and lines for goods, a great source of inefficiency and welfare loss, were much reduced. However, the distributional consequences were large. Savings in rubles were wiped out by the plunging value of the Russian currency. Table 21.1 gives some data on the extent of this redistribution. The biggest losers were the households, who saw their savings eradicated, and their real wages fall, and any enterprises that held ruble-denominated balances. The gainers were largely the government and the financial sector.

TABLE 21.1

Winners and Losers in Russia's Inflation, 1992–1993 (percentage of GDP)

	Losses	Gains	Net Gain
Households	12	0	–12
Enterprises	18	16	–2
Financial sector	0	8	+8
Government	0	4	+4
Other	0	2	+2
Total	30	30	0

SOURCE: William Easterly and Paula Vieira da Cunha, "Financing the Storm: Russia's Macroeconomic Crisis," *Economics of Transition* 2, no. 4 (1994).

[6]One observer of the Soviet system declared: "In the Soviet Union almost everything was forbidden . . . and those few things that were permitted were compulsory."

[7]The increase in raw material prices occurred largely because the Russian economy became increasingly integrated into the world market. Input prices, especially those for energy, had been highly controlled under central planning and rose sharply toward world levels.

The **interenterprise payments system** began to break down. Many firms were unable to pay the higher input prices because they were not receiving payment for the goods they sold and delivered. Not out of choice but out of necessity, enterprises began to extend credit to each other, creating a precarious pyramid of interenterprise debt. Insolvent firms ceased to pay their workers; as personal incomes fell, so did demand, creating more insolvencies. Although the linchpin of the Gaidar plan had been monetary restraint, the worsening economic situation raised pressures to liberalize credit. Lobbying from the enterprises was intense, and the growth of interenterprise credit led to the justifiable fear that the collapse of a few firms could lead to catastrophic domino consequences. So reluctantly the government, through the Central Bank, loosened credit and provided cheap loans (often at negative real interest rates) to bail out the industrial sector, causing excessive growth of the money supply.

(3) Privatization

The third pillar of the Gaidar program was mass privatization, deemed imperative for three main reasons. First, policy makers felt that the burden of subsidizing state enterprises could be sharply reduced, or even eliminated, once these firms passed into private hands.[8] This private ownership would help to put public finance on a more stable footing and reduce the reliance on credit creation to keep enterprises solvent, thereby eliminating a source of inflation. Second, for reasons discussed earlier, it was expected that private management of resources would lead to greater efficiency. Third, large-scale privatization would be hard to reverse and would, therefore, reinforce political change because the new owners would oppose retrogression thereby "locking in" the gains of economic and political liberalization.

(4) Constructing a Social Security System

The Soviet Union lacked an adequate system of unemployment compensation, regarded as unnecessary in a society where unemployment notionally did not exist, and was, in fact, illegal. However, if the efficiency of industry was to be increased, sweeping changes in employment practices would be required, and raising labor productivity had to involve, at least in the short term, the shedding of excess labor. The lack of a "social safety net" to catch the unemployed created a distinct possibility of increasing social unrest.[9]

(5) Converting the Defense Sector

The great paradox of the Soviet economy was the coexistence of a world-class defense and aerospace sector with consumer goods and housing sectors that simply failed to

---

[8]As we shall see, eliminating the subsidy burden was something of a vain hope. Privatization has not ended subsidy of the productive sector.

[9]Unemployment statistics are not reliable for the early period of reform. By mid-year 1993 the European Bank for Reconstruction and Development reported that the rate was 5.3 percent, although no good measure was available because the incidence of disguised unemployment (workers retained but not fully employed) was high.

deliver the goods. The key was the high degree of **prioritization** that locked up more than 30 percent of Soviet gross domestic product (GDP) in defense, and with it most of the nation's able engineers and managers. It was hoped that "defense conversion" deploying the skilled labor and sophisticated apparatus to peaceful purposes could provide a dynamic sector around which to focus Russia's development effort.

OUTPUT COLLAPSE

The crisis accompanying the breakup of the Soviet Union led to a sharp fall in economic activity. Table 21.2 shows the sectoral impact on manufacturing and agriculture. Overall industrial output fell by almost 60 percent in four years, and the contraction was not limited to industry. Agricultural output fell in the same period by 26 percent, due largely to the inability of collective farms to obtain or afford fertilizers and pesticides as well as the continued failure of the distribution system.

As the situation worsened during 1992, Gaidar's position eroded and in December 1992 he was ditched in favor of Viktor Chernomyrdin, a seasoned insider with a background in Russia's rich, and corrupt, energy industry. Though Chernomyrdin had a less reformist bent than Gaidar and despite Yeltsin's face-off with the Duma, liberalization and privatization continued.

THE PRIVATIZATION PROGRAM

The privatization of state-owned enterprises in Russia can be divided into three distinct programs. The first handled the transfer of property in the small-scale sector, generally conferring property rights on the operators of existing enterprises and the inhabitants of rental property. The second was the **voucher auction program** responsible for the privatization of 60 percent of the industrial sector between 1992 and 1994, and was designed to provide the basis of a market economy. Together these two programs constituted **mass privatization**. Finally, **privatization for cash** started in 1995 and continues today.

■ TABLE 21.2

Production in Selected Sectors (1992 prices, billions of rubles)

	1990	1994	Change
Steel and metals	4,004	2,132	–47%
Light industry	1,926	512	–73%
Other industry	12,153	5,592	–54%
Agriculture	3,908	2,910	–26%
Total	22,087	10,368	–53%

NOTES: Derived from Goskomstat data reported in *World Bank Statistical Handbook 1995*, "States of the Former USSR"; "Studies of Economies in Transition," paper 19 (Washington DC, 1995).

Small-Scale Privatization

Small-scale privatization began with Russian shops and small service establishments, which were handed over to local municipalities who arranged for their transfer, usually to their current managers. Agricultural land was "decollectivized" with members of the collectives able to lease land and equipment. Apartments were sold by local authorities generally to their occupants. Those processes started during 1992. By the end of the year about 50,000 shops, 182,000 family farms, and 3 million apartments had been sold. In addition, some 500,000 new small businesses had been registered.

The Voucher Privatization Program

Large-scale industrial enterprise was privatized under the aegis of the State Committee for Management of State Property, also known as GKI, or the Privatization Ministry. It was headed by Anatoly Chubais, who chose voucher auction as the primary means of transferring ownership. The voucher program, which was immense in scope and rapid in execution, was adopted during 1992, and the program officially began in December of that year, ending in June of 1994. During these 21 months, some 15,779 enterprises, employing about 18 million people, were disposed of.

The magnitude of the task and the shallowness of Russian financial markets made Chubais's choice of voucher privatization all but inevitable. In Russia 25,000 firms had to be placed in private hands and initial public offerings (IPOs) used in countries with deeper financial markets and a smaller task at hand were not capable of doing the whole job; the detailed valuation and the offering process was simply beyond Russia's means.

Boycko, Shleifer, and Vishny put the issue this way:

> The case for privatization through cash sales falls apart on both efficiency and especially political grounds. From the point of view of efficiency, privatization through cash sales is just too slow. It requires valuation, information collection, preparation of auctions and public offerings and a variety of other services which investment banks gladly supply given ample time and generous fees. It is important to remember in this regard that West European countries typically privatize a few firms a year, and even such rapid privatizers as Mexico and Chile could handle at best a couple of hundred of firms per year. In contrast, Russia needed to privatize 25,000 medium and large-scale firms. If these firms were properly valued, prepared for auctions, or, as some investment bankers wanted, restructured prior to sale, odds are privatization would have never gotten off the ground. Even if it did, at the rate of 200 per year, Russian privatization would have taken over a century! In the meantime, the economy would continue to stagnate. From the political viewpoint, privatization through sales is even more problematic. To be politically feasible in Russia, this approach would have required the allocation of significant stakes to insiders at large discounts and only the remaining shares could be sold. Even such sales would probably have been resented, and certainly not supported, by the public at large. First, the highest bidders in cash privatizations often turn out to be illegitimate businessmen, former party and state security officials, and foreigners. Selling off the national patrimony to these investors generates public outrage rather than support.[10]

---

[10]Maxim Boycko, Andrei Shleifer, and Robert Vishny, *Privatizing Russia* (Cambridge, MA: MIT Press, 1996), p. 71.

The GKI drew up a list of which firms were to be privatized in the first phase. It covered the bulk of the industrial sector, but kept defense-related firms and much of the energy sector under public ownership. Once the list for privatization was published, the management of each firm could choose between three schemes of privatization. Each of the available options gave considerable benefits to insiders, to secure their support for the privatization process, because without insider support privatization could have been derailed as other economic reforms were sabotaged in the past. Expansion of private ownership takes away some of the property rights over the firm that the management and, to a lesser extent, the workers had in the past. It was therefore essential to compensate for the loss of these informal rights with a generous share of the ownership of the newly privatized enterprise.

Under Option I workers would be given 25 percent of the shares for free, but these shares would be nonvoting. In addition, workers could buy 10 percent of the voting shares at a 30 percent discount from book value. Book values, based on the historic cost of capital before the massive inflation of the early 1990s, were low. Consequently, any price based on book value was close to zero. Management could access up to 5 percent of the voting shares at a similar price. Thus "insiders" were offered 40 percent of the income of the enterprise and 15 percent of the voting power for next to nothing.

Although Option I seemed generous to many observers, it apparently offered inadequate reward for some insiders, who lobbied Chubais for better compensation for management. They succeeded in establishing an alternative, Option II, which allowed workers and management to buy 51 percent of the capital for a price of 1.7 times book value—again close to zero.[11] The rest of the share capital was to be distributed to the population at large by way of a voucher scheme. All citizens (including children) could purchase for 25 rubles a voucher with a face denomination of 10,000 rubles. This voucher could be turned over to an investment company, exercised personally at an auction, or sold. The total number of shares of each firm to be offered at auction were divided in proportion to the number of vouchers tendered for the firm. Popular firms attracted a lot of attention, and therefore the shares would be divided among many claimants. More obscure firms or those believed to have few assets or prospects attracted little attention, and a few vouchers could garner a sizable part of the share capital. Boycko, Shleifer, and Vishny summarized these options as follows:

> To save small investors from the need to make complicated bids, one strategy is to ask each investor to submit his voucher as a bid for the company. The equilibrium number of shares each voucher buys is then inversely proportional to the number of vouchers rendered. Thus, if the company offers 1,000 shares for auction, and 40 vouchers are submitted, each voucher buys 25 shares. If, on the other hand, 4,000 vouchers are submitted, each voucher buys only a quarter of a share. Each investor submitting vouchers is assured of getting some shares, but gets fewer shares of desirable companies.[12]

[11]An Option III was also available. It allowed management to acquire 100 percent of the shares if they "promised" not to take the firm into bankruptcy and "strip" its assets. Fewer than 2 percent of privatizations followed Option III.

[12]Boycko, Shleifer, and Vishny, *Privatizing Russia* (Cambridge, MA: MIT Press, 1996), p. 91.

The Dominance of Insiders Although one of the objectives of voucher privatization was to curry wide popular support, individual citizens were disadvantaged in buying shares because they had little information about either the intrinsic value of an enterprise or the number of potential bidders. Most valuable knowledge about enterprises lay with insiders and investment intermediaries. The mass privatization project in Russia created some 22,000 joint stock companies, of which 73 percent were disposed of under Option II, and therefore the insiders automatically gained control; 25 percent of the privatization followed Option I, and Option III was seldom used.

The trend to insider ownership was reinforced by a free market in vouchers.[13] Both investment intermediaries and management interested in acquiring a greater part of a firm were able to buy the voucher books from the public for prices ranging from $20 to as little as $4. Many Russians sold off their share in the country's infrastructure for an average of about $10.[14] A 1993 survey conducted by the Privatization Ministry found that management and workers owned an average of 65 percent of share capital of 143 surveyed medium-sized enterprises. Top management held about 8.6 percent, outside investors owned 21.5 percent, and the government retained an average of 13 percent of shares. These figures are averages, in some firms the management stake was much higher.

Table 21.3 gives a slightly different perspective on this phenomenon. It shows who holds a majority share in the newly created corporations (i.e., who holds more than 50 percent of the stock). In almost two-thirds of the firms, insider employees

TABLE 21.3

Majority Owners of Private Sector Corporations, 1995 and 1996 Privatizations (percent)

Majority Owners	1995	1996
Employees	59	64.7
Rank and file	26.7	30.5
Managers	2.3	4.2
Top managers	0.4	0.4
General director	0.4	0.8
No majority insider	29.4	28.8
Nonstate outsiders	17.3	19.8
State	3.1	2.6
None	20.3	12.8

NOTE: Numbers do not add to 100% because of rounding.
SOURCE: Joseph R. Blasi, Maya Kroumova, and Douglas Kruse, *Kremlin Capitalism: Privatizing the Russian Economy* (Ithaca, NY: ILR Press, 1997).

[13]On the largest exchange, the Russian Commodity and Raw Materials Exchange, volume was about 60,000–100,000 vouchers per day, this was augmented by regional exchanges and a vigorous street market.
[14]Most people did initially claim their vouchers, or someone claimed them on their behalf. Approximately 144 million vouchers were issued, and the Russian population was estimated at 148.2 million.

and management have control; outsiders control only 20 percent. In more than 4 percent of firms, management alone holds the controlling interest.

After the active market for vouchers became established, because the number of vouchers tendered for offered shares in specific companies is a matter of record, it is possible to make estimates of the implicit price for which publicly owned firms were sold. Take, for example, the automaker Zil, 30 percent of whose shares were offered in a voucher auction. The implied market value of the whole firm—which employed 103,000 persons—was a mere $16 million. Even more startling, 28 percent of all of the shares on offer were bought by just seven investment groups, several affiliated to a single parent company. Even though the Russian voucher auction program achieved an enormous transfer of assets from the public sector to the private, the greatest beneficiaries were a narrow group who used insider information (and in many cases manipulated the auction process) in order to gain control of the enterprises. Moreover the high degree of worker and management ownership suggests that meaningful and rapid postprivatization reform will be difficult, because job preservation rather than profit maximization will be an important objective.

The entire program was criticized for giving away too much to insiders to get the process moving.[15] Certainly the result was a dramatic skewing of the distribution of wealth and control, earning for the Russian Federation and other successor states to the Soviet Union the title of **kleptocracies**.[16] While it is true that as a result of voucher privatization as many as 40 million Russians became shareholders, at least for a time, the process undoubtedly created hundreds of millionaires, while robbing millions of ordinary Russians of their share of state assets.

Proponents of voucher privatization defend it on the grounds of expediency, arguing that it represented the only politically feasible way forward. The dissolution of socialism could have been followed by an equitable parceling out of the assets among the people, perhaps in terms of equal shares, but one fact to be reckoned with was that much of Russia's state-owned enterprises did not effectively belong to the state. Workers, local bureaucrats, and especially the management of firms already possessed a stake in these firms, and even though such a property right might have been informal, it was nevertheless real. Even more to the point, these important actors in the economic scene had the power to disrupt any potential reform if it were not in their interest to go along with it.

Before the fall of the Soviet system, Jan Winiecki analyzed the failure of previous economic reform efforts in centrally planned systems.[17] His work developed the view that Soviet-style economies operated to maximize the rents flowing to the ruling classes, or ***nomenklatura***. On top of this primary system of rent extraction, kickbacks or side payments could be appropriated by anyone with some power over scarce resources. Those who gained from the status quo had an incentive to

---

[15]These criticisms apply even more to the so-called spontaneous privatizations in which the management of some companies, along with part or all of the workforce, assumed control and ownership of an enterprise or established a cooperative that assumed the assets.

[16]Literally "states ruled by thieves," from Greek roots.

[17]Jan Winiecki, "Why Economic Reforms Fail in Soviet-Type Systems, A Property Rights-Based Approach," *Economic Inquiry* 28, no. 2 (1990).

resist any change of the system. For example, replacement of the *nomenklatura*[18] with a more overtly merit system would be opposed because rent extractable by the Communist Party membership would be reduced. Similarly, any plans to increase the size of the private sector were objected to, nominally on ideological grounds, while the real reason was fear of the loss of economic rents:

> There are no well-paid posts to be had in small private enterprises, nor is there a "soft" budget constraint, so permissive to a variety of rent-maximizing kickbacks even under reform. A shift of activity from the state to the private reduces therefore the possibilities for party apparatchiks and economic bureaucrats to extract rent. Hostility toward the private sector is therefore based not on ideology or even actual rent losses, but on gains foregone when the expansion of the state sector is curbed in favor of the private sector.[19]

A large class of people who see their well-being decline with onset of reform (even though the economy as a whole might do better) are capable of concerted action to bring down any reform plan. Hence the Russian mass privatization program had to confer considerable benefits on economic bureaucrats, politicians, and insiders in order to ensure its survival.

Privatization for Cash

The voucher auction program concluded in the summer of 1994 and was assumed to create the basis of a market economy. As Table 21.4 shows, almost 16,000 medium and large enterprises, employing about 18 million people, passed into majority private ownership. In 1995 the Russian government shifted its emphasis to cash privatization to dispose of the assets of the enterprises still in the state sector, mostly utilities and natural resource or high-tech defense enterprises.

TABLE 21.4

Voucher Auctions in Russia (December 1992–June 1994)

	Dec. 1992–June 1993	July 1993–Dec. 1993	Jan. 1994–June 1994	Total
Number of enterprises sold by calendar month	2,871	5,632	7,276	15,779
Employment (thousands)	3,243	5,278	9,249	17,770
Total vouchers accepted (thousands)	16,054	27,724	69,830	113,608

SOURCE: GKI/RPC Performance Database; Maxim Boycko, Andrei Shleifer, and Robert Vishny, *Privatizing Russia* (Cambridge, MA: MIT Press, 1996), pp. 106–107.

---

[18]Winiecki defines *nomenklatura* in terms of the right of the Communist Party apparatus, from the Central Committee on down to the enterprise committee, to "recommend" or "approve" all appointments for all managerial positions in the economic administration and all managerial positions in enterprises.

[19]Winiecki, "Why Economic Reforms Fail in Soviet-Type Systems," *Economic Inquiry* 28, no. 2 (1990), p. 300.

Lacking an adequate system of public finance, the government looked for revenue from the sale of the resource sector to close the federal government deficit. With only limited interest in the asset sales, the government resorted to a highly controversial scheme to raise cash. At the initial suggestion of Oneximbank, one of the most powerful and well-connected banks in Russia, the government agreed to offer shares in publicly owned companies as collateral for loans from the private sector. For only \$170 million, Oneximbank received more than 50 percent of the voting shares of Norilsk Nickel, the producer of more than 20 percent of the world's nickel and 50 percent of global platinum output. In theory the bank was acting like a pawnbroker; the government could redeem the shares if it came up with the cash by September 1996, but it was clear from the beginning that the government made no budgetary provision for that eventuality. Consequently, the bank got the Norilsk shares very cheaply. Although their worth is difficult to determine, a figure of 10 times what Oneximbank paid seems reasonable. The Norilsk deal was followed by similar insider deals favoring other banks, and the government was able to meet its revenue targets for 1995 at the expense of squandering a great deal of support for the privatization program.

Despite public outcry in Russia against these **loans-for-shares deals**, and shock within the international agencies charged with assisting the economy, no transactions were reversed, in part because 1996 was a poor year for revenue from share sales on the open market, and less than 15 percent of anticipated and budgeted revenues were realized. Primarily, however, the reasons lie in the drive to re-elect Yeltsin, which required the support of the very businesspeople who benefited from the sales. In 1997, in contrast, the Russian stock market took off, and the government was able to dispose of large blocs of shares it had retained in the oil and mineral sectors for high revenues, realizing about three times the forecast revenues and closing the budget gap considerably. Then, 1998 saw a stock market fall of about 85 percent measured in local currency and 95 percent in terms of dollars, and predictably privatization revenues also fell sharply. By late 1998 only \$1 billion of revenue from privatization was realized for a budget that called for \$8 billion. However, the government still owns about 40 percent of the natural resource sector, and it can raise a great deal of capital through privatization sales if the market recovers.

The Financial and Industrial Groups

A striking feature of Russian capitalism comes through the rapid emergence of the **financial and industrial groups**, or FIGs, officially established by a law in 1995. The legislation offered tax and other privileges to groups that registered with the authorities, though in fact such advantages have been slow to emerge. Of the now more than 100 officially registered groups, a substantial part of the economic and political power in Russia lay in the late 1990s with just seven large bank-led groups—Alfa Group, Inkombank Group, LogoVAZ, Menatep, Most, Oneximbank, and SBS-Agro.[20]

[20]It is not possible to say exactly what proportion, but Boris Berezovsky, head of LogoVAZ, estimated in 1996 that it represented half of Russia's economy.

Such groups are closely held, highly diversified, and the larger ones are generally grouped around a bank. In some ways they resemble the *chaebol* of Korea and *keiretsu* of Japan, but they are potentially more powerful than either. They incorporate banks, where *chaebol* do not, and are controlled by a single individual to a much greater degree than contemporary *keiretsu.* In addition to the bank-centered FIGs are the industry-centered groups. On the whole they are less powerful and less diversified than the bank-centered groups.

The consequences of the emergence of these groups are uncertain. On the positive side, they can represent a source of rapid change in Russian industry; firms acquired by these groups can be subject to tight oversight and given clear performance objectives, as well as advice and capital for restructuring. On the other hand, FIGs constitute an alarming concentration of political, as well as economic power, both in Moscow and in the regions.

Under the Yeltsin administration prior to 2000, the leaders of the large groups were extremely politically well connected and in several cases had held high government office. They were known as **oligarchs**[21] (sometimes as "the tycoons") and clearly influenced governmental policy. They are less powerful under President Vladimir Putin than they were under his predecessor. Their position in Russia in the late 1990s resembled the structure of **finance capitalism *(Finanzkapitalism)*** articulated by Rudolf Hilferding in the early years of this century, which was very influential to the thought of V. I. Lenin. The oligarchs threw their weight behind Yeltsin's 1996 reelection drive, and secured his success largely through the use of their dominance of media outlets. Apparently as a *quid pro quo,* they received ownership of a large part of Russia industry and natural resources by means of the notorious "loans for shares" arrangement. An irony can be found in that what was thought by Hilferding to be the penultimate stage of capitalism should be the first step for a socialist economy in transition.

In the summer of 1998 a widespread crisis hit the banking sector and bank failures seemed imminent. The Central Bank of Russia drew up a list of 12 banks that were to be bailed out under any circumstances, because the instability of the financial system was so great. The list included the lead banks of all the seven major FIGs. This coincidence brought to the forefront the twin issues of moral hazard in the banking sector and the political influence of the major banks.

Under Putin the position of the original group of oligarchs deteriorated. As vice president he assumed the presidency when Yeltsin surprisingly resigned. Restricting the power of the oligarchs was an important part of his election drive in 2000. After a relatively decisive election victory he delivered on his pledge and severely cut into the influence and wealth of these businessmen, driving two of them into exile and regaining control of the media. The new oligarchs are less visible and apparently less influential than the original seven were under Yeltsin but the interaction between business and political elites is still strong and the group (FIG) structure prevails. This situation in turn makes the going more difficult for Russia's small entrepreneurs.

---

[21]An oligarchy is a state ruled by a few—hence the presumption was that the business leaders effectively controlled the state.

THE PROBLEMS OF SMALL ENTERPRISE

Conversion of Russia's state-owned behemoths has been tortuous and slow. Seemingly bright stars faded; for example, enthusiasm for defense conversion turned sour. Only in the oil and gas and forest product industries do Russia's firms show themselves to be close in competing on world markets. The hope for the future probably lies in the growth of small firms, and therefore the conclusions of a recent OECD report were somewhat depressing. In the initial stages of liberalization, small enterprise growth was vibrant, but the number of small firms and proprietorships stalled since then at about 875,000. They account for about 20 percent of total employment and about 8.7 percent of GDP. Their share of GDP actually fell in each of the last four years and is now about 8 percent, much less than the 12.2 percent that the small enterprise sector accounted for in 1997. In part this decline is due to the increase in oil and gas prices that artificially inflated GDP, but the lack of progress is apparent.

Russia's entrepreneurs face many of the same problems encountered by small businesses everywhere, but some are clearly more acute. Access to capital is especially tough given the absence of a genuine banking system. Taxation is high and confusing with overlapping tax authorities competing for revenue. "Unofficial taxation"—paying bribes to politicians and bureaucrats—is a problem for two-thirds of firms, an OECD survey found. Crime is a perpetual concern. The high inflationary situation makes rising input costs a perpetual problem.

Long-term growth depends on the success of small and medium-sized businesses. At present Russia's entrepreneurs have plenty of enthusiasm but face huge difficulties. As a result of their problems, more than 50 percent of businesses classify themselves as not stable, with 5 percent calling themselves critical. Clearer taxation, better crime prevention, a real banking sector, and less corruption are necessary if small business is to succeed.

SOURCE: *OECD: Economic Survey of the Russian Federation 2002*, p. 74.

THE PROGRESS OF INSTITUTIONAL REFORM

The Banking System

Under central planning, the state bank, Gosbank, exercised a virtual monopoly over the banking sector, although specialist banks existed to finance construction and foreign trade, and a thrift bank served to facilitate small saving. The Gorbachev reforms included a reorganization of banking and introduced three new state banks.[22] More important for the longer-term structure of Russian finance, the 1988 Law on Cooperatives allowed the emergence of private banks. In 1988, 80 such banks were founded, and by the end of the Soviet era the total had risen to more than 400.

At the breakup of the Soviet Union, the assets and functions of Gosbank were assumed by the newly created Central Bank of Russia (CBR) under its first chair Viktor Geraschenko. The CBR was established as an orthodox institution, much like the central banks in many West European countries. It is responsible for issuing currency and supervising and regulating the financial sector, as well as being the

[22]The Agricultural Bank, the Industrial and Construction Bank, and the Social Investment Bank.

lender of last resort and the manager of foreign exchange operations. It is not an independent institution, as according to its rules of operation laid out in the constitution, "*in collaboration* with the government of the Russian Federation it [the Central Bank] elaborates and implements a uniform national monetary policy designed to protect the ruble and ensure its stability."

The Central Bank serves as a pliable tool to channel credit to keep potentially bankrupt enterprises afloat. This function led Jeffrey Sachs, an economist then at Harvard, to describe Geraschenko as "the worst central banker in history." The soft-budget constraint, which should have ended with privatization, is in fact alive and well and will continue to be until a stable financial system and workable public finance system is in place. The early 1990s saw the continued growth of private banking, reaching a high of about 2,500 banks in 1995. A subsequent contraction came as successive financial crises weeded out the weaker elements, and the Central Bank of Russia withdrew licenses from banks at the rate of roughly 250 annually.

However, as Table 21.5 shows, many banks remain weak. Almost half of all registered banks operate with a capital base of less than 30 million rubles, and many are highly vulnerable to runs or falls in the value of assets held. Although average assets rose in recent years, they still amount to only a mean of $50 million, a small amount for any kind of real financial intermediary. The Russian banking sector is significantly undeveloped. Assets expressed as a percentage of GDP is a measure of financial development and Russia certainly lags in this respect. Its bank assets/GDP percentage is only 5.4 percent, compared to 15.4 percent in Estonia and 22 percent in the Czech Republic.

The retail banking system is dominated by Sberbank, the state savings bank owned by the Russian central bank. Sberbank dwarfs all other Russian banks in terms of size. It accounts for 23.5 percent of all assets, 75 percent of household deposits and 33.7 percent of credit to nonbanking enterprises. Its dominance in retail baking is secured by the fact that it is the only bank for which the government

TABLE 21.5

Grouping Banks by Capital, 2001*

	Number	Share of Total (percentage)
Less than 3 million rubles	121	9.1
From 3 million to 10 million rubles	203	15.3
From 10 million to 30 million rubles	304	22.9
From 30 million to 60 million rubles	260	19.6
From 60 million to 150 million rubles	184	13.9
From 150 million to 300 million rubles	108	8.1
300 million rubles and more	147	11.1
Total	1,327	

* Paid in authorized capital as per articles of association and registered by the Bank of Russia.
SOURCE: Central Bank of Russia, *Bulletin of Banking Statistics 2002*.

offers deposit insurance. Consequently households have confidence in its security and it competes unequally with private banks. Current proposals to extend limited guarantees to depositors in nongovernmental banks have encountered opposition from, among others, the Central Bank of Russia. Without deposit guarantee, it is difficult to see real growth in Russian retail banking, and Sberbank will continue to have access to the bulk of consumer saving.

POVERTY AND SOCIAL ASSISTANCE

Shock therapy and its aftermath profoundly affected the incidence of poverty in Russia. The negative growth rates of the past decade shrank the pie, while liberalization, privatization, and high rates of inflation skewed the distribution of income. Today the highest earners receive 47.4 percent of total personal income, while the worst-off 20 percent receive only 6.3 percent of income, much less than at the beginning of privatization.

Gorbachev's reforms had little effect on income distribution, and although income contracted during the 1980s, its distribution actually became more egalitarian as Table 21.6 shows. The change since the **big bang**, the start of the Yeltsin administration, has been dramatic. In 1991 the income of the average "wealthy" person (in the top quintile) was only 2.8 times that of the average poor person (in the lowest quintile); by 1998 the figure rose to about 7.5. The decline in living standards for the poorest quintile of society was sharpest between 1991 and 1993, due largely to the failure of the pension system to adjust to rapid price rises. The introduction of indexation in 1995, prompted largely by electoral considerations, stopped further decline. The working class was hurt by liberalization; in 1991 the third and fourth quintiles enjoyed almost 35 percent of personal income, by 1998 that portion fell to about 25 percent.

The regional impact of income redistribution has been even greater than for the nation as a whole. Central planning provided interregional transfers that largely ceased under the reforms. In 1992 the ratio of average income in the richest *oblast*

■ **TABLE 21.6**

Income Distribution: Percentage Share of Each Quintile (1980 and 1991 to 1997)

	1980	1991	1992	1993	1994	1995	1996	1997
Top	33.4	30.7	38.3	41.6	46.3	46.9	47.1	47.4
Second	23.1	22.8	26.5	24.8	23.0	22.4	21.3	21.1
Third	18.6	18.8	17.6	16.7	15.2	15.0	14.9	14.8
Fourth	14.8	15.8	11.6	11.1	10.2	10.2	10.5	10.4
Bottom	10.1	11.9	6.0	5.8	5.3	5.5	6.2	6.3
Total	100	100	100	100	100	100	100	100

NOTE: Data are for total money income.
SOURCE: Goskomstat, *Russia in Figures* (Moscow: State Committee on Statistics of the Russian Federation).

(county) to the poorest was 8:1. By 1994 this gap widened to 42:1.[23] Table 21.7 shows how hard poverty hit in some of the regions. Worst affected are those that specialize in agriculture, while those with extensive mineral resources fared the best. Nevertheless, for a region to have 30 percent of its population below the poverty level (unable to buy a standard minimum basket of goods) is commonplace, and in many regions one-fifth of the population is unable even to buy adequate food.

Of particular concern is the emergence of poverty among relatively well-educated and skilled segments of society. Human capital, justifiably regarded as one of Russia's strengths, may be lost due to emigration, neglect, and despair as protracted unemployment and poverty create a dual labor market, trapping the poor. In addition Russia is about to be hit by an extremely serious AIDS crisis, which will rival some African nations in its intensity.

The Tax System

Under central planning a sophisticated tax system was unnecessary. Revenues accrued to the state largely through markups imposed on the costs of goods and by

TABLE 21.7

The Incidence of Poverty in Selected Regions, 1994

	Percent Poor	Percent Very Poor
Rich in Mineral Resources		
Magnitogorsk City	17.0	4.8
Yakutiya Republic (Sakha)	28.8	5.8
Intensive Agriculture and Food Industry		
Astrakhan Oblast	72.4	44.3
Oryol Oblast	58.7	32.6
Industrial or Mixture		
Adygeya Republic	51.9	19.4
Chuvash Republic	42.5	22.7
Khanty-Mansiysky District	28.8	13.2
Krasnoyarsky Krai	43.5	20.1
Moscow Oblast	41.0	19.7
Tver Oblast	39.1	18.1
Voronezh Oblast	20.4	10.2

NOTES: The "poor" do not have enough income to purchase the subsistence minimum consumer basket as defined in Goskomstat poverty measures; the very poor are unable to purchase the food component of the subsistence minimum. Moscow Oblast excludes the city of Moscow.
SOURCES: G. N. Volkova and L. A. Migranova, *The Living Standards of the Russian Population by Region,* Bulletin no. 12 (Moscow: Center for Living Standards Study, Ministry of Labor, 1994).

[23]World Bank, *Poverty in Russia: An Assessment* (Washington, DC: 1995), p. 31.

THE HIV EPIDEMIC AND THE RUSSIAN ECONOMY

Many nations around the world have been adversely affected by the spread of HIV—predominantly in Africa where the epidemic is most severe. Until quite recently the impact on Russia was apparently small. Until 1995 only 100 to 200 new cases were reported each year. Since that time, however, the number of infected cases doubled every 12 months. By May 1, 2002, the total number of registered cases reported to the Federal AIDS Center reached 193,000. Experience shows that the majority of cases are undetected or unreported; using conventional multipliers the current incidence in Russia is probably about 1 million. Furthermore, although the primary initial transmission mechanism in Russia occurred through intravenous drug use, it has now spread to the non-drug using population. The average length of time between infection and death is about 12 years and so the death rate is still small, but it will surge from about 2008 onward. Unless treatment improves, the World Bank estimates that the death rate will be in the thousands per month. Because 60 percent of AIDS sufferers are between 20 and 30 the pandemic will strike hard in the economically active population.

The economy will be affected through several channels. Labor supply will fall with the rising death rate, but labor productivity will be adversely impacted well before then. The need to maintain support systems will affect productivity across society, not merely among those actually infected. The savings of AIDS-affected families will be dissipated, the safety net will be tested, and the burdens upon the health system will increase, which will in turn adversely affect the quality of care in other areas. Presently, the treatment of an AIDS sufferer costs some $9,000 per person per year. Some countries successfully negotiate a lower cost, and real price decreases can be expected in the future. Nevertheless, it is optimistic to believe that the cost of drugs will fall as low as $3,000 per case per year. At present, this amount is almost twice Russian GDP per head expressed in current exchange rate terms.

The macroeconomic impact of AIDS in Russia is, in the opinion of the World Bank, a heavy blow waiting to fall. It estimates that because of the AIDS crisis, growth GDP in 2020 will be 10 percent less than in the absence of the epidemic. In other words AIDS will cost a full percentage point of growth per year. The World Bank rightly observes this cost is "substantial in an economy in as much need of rapid growth as Russia's."

SOURCE: The World Bank, "Russian Economic Report," available at http://www.worldbank.ru.

a variable tax on consumer goods. Since the start of transition, a constant struggle to put public finance on a stable and economically efficient footing continues to meet with little result. This failure created sustained federal budget deficits. The structure of the budget in the year 2000 is shown in Table 21.8. One important fact to note is that the "tax effort" at the federal level is rising. Tax revenues now represent some 16 percent of GDP. The deficit is giving way to a surplus at the federal level that will allow some repayment of the large debts and a further reduction in debt service payments. Noninterest expenditures continue to rise although social expenditures are well below the level needed, and regional aid is lacking

Regional and local authorities represent a large part of the consolidated government budget, almost 50 percent of expenditures, but they manage their accounts better than the federal authorities and deficits are smaller. The deficit on the consolidated budget amounted to about 5.2 percent of GDP in 1998 has also been turned into a surplus of about 4.3 percent that will allow debt repayment (Table 21.9).

■ TABLE 21.8

Outcome of Federal Budget, 1998 and 2000

	Shares of GDP 1998	2000
Revenues	**8.9**	**16**
Tax Revenues	7.5	13.7
Value-added tax	3.4	5.3
Profit tax	1.1	2.5
Excise Tax	1.5	1.9
Customs duties	1.3	3.2
Other tax revenues	0.2	0.8
Nontax revenues	0.4	1
Revenues of budgetary funds	0.9	1.3
Expenditure	**13.7**	**13.7**
Debt service	3.9	2.4
Domestic debt service	2.4	0.8
Foreign debt service	1.5	1.6
Noninterest expenditure	9.8	11.2
Defense	1.7	2.7
Social sphere	2.0	1.9
Financial aid to the regions	1.6	1.4
Budget Balance	**-4.8**	**2.3**

SOURCE: OECD Economic Surveys, Russian Federation, 2002.

Revenues at the federal level depend heavily on indirect taxation, especially the value-added tax (VAT). Personal income taxation gathers little revenue for the central government (less than 1 percent of the total) because tax evasion is high and most of the revenue that is gathered goes to regional authorities.[24] The tax rate on individuals in the 0–5,000 ruble income range (roughly from 0 to $200) is 12 percent, rising to a maximum of 30 percent above 10,000 ($400). In addition, wage income is subject to high social security contributions totaling 39 percent of salary income. Consequently, the top combined rate on labor income could reach 69 percent, clearly a level that makes for considerable disincentives to effort and strong rewards for tax evasion.

The ineffectiveness of the tax regime is compounded by its complexity. Federal, regional, and city governments impose a wide range of taxes, with little or no coordination.[25] A great deal of discretion in the application of tax exemptions also

[24]A tax reform plan authored by the Yeltsin government seeks to guarantee the federal government 20 percent of income tax revenue.

[25]In some cases, aggregate rates on certain kinds of activities exceeded 100 percent.

■ TABLE 21.9

Consolidated Government Budget, 1998 and 2000 (percentage of GDP)

	1998	2000
Federal Government		
Revenue	8.9	16
Expenditure	13.7	13.7
Transfers to regions	1.6	1.4
Transfers to extra-budgetary funds	0.6	0.4
Balance	–4.8	2.3
Consolidated Regional Budgets		
Revenue	14.5	15.1
Transfers from federal government	1.6	1.4
Expenditure	14.9	14.6
Balance	–0.3	0.5
Extra-Budgetary Funds		
Revenue	8.7	8.6
From federal government	0.6	0.4
Expenditure	8.7	7.1
Balance	0	1.5
General Government		
Revenue	29.9	37.9
Expenditure	35.1	33.6
Balance	–5.2	4.3

SOURCE: Ministry of Finance, Economic Expert Group, Goskomstat, in OECD Economic Survey of Russia, 2002.

increases the potential for corruption and tends to discourage investment, especially from abroad.

Tax evasion is common in Russia, though it seems that some progress is being made in this direction. Many Russian firms and individuals simply fail to pay their taxes, a phenomenon so widespread that it meets with social approval. The Organization for Economic Cooperation and Development (OECD) reported in 1997 that "identified arrears on taxes and social contributions reached 10 percent of GDP in 1996."[26] Fortunately the situation seems to be improving. The 262 identified "large tax payers," primarily in the energy sector, are meeting their obligations, and the Ministry of Finance reported 91 percent tax compliance in the corporate sector in 2001.

The failure to meet tax targets means that the government cannot fund its expenditures: workers go unpaid, pensioners miss their stipends, and essential services

[26]Organization for Economic Cooperation and Development, *1996/97 Survey of Russia* (Paris: OECD, 1997), p. 4.

were curtailed. Moreover, government borrowing increased, pushing up interest rates and thereby the cost of financing the national debt, presenting the specter of a worsening debt spiral. The structure of tax arrears is shown in Figure 21.1. Although the large-scale corporate sector (usually the energy extracting companies) is most often blamed for tax delinquency, in fact the bulk of the arrears results from failure to collect the value-added tax, a deficiency largely at the retail level.

Tax reform is essential for economic growth, and it is difficult to see Russia joining the developed nations without a functioning income tax regime. At the moment the tax system is deeply regressive with its heavy reliance on VAT. The inequalities in Russian society are wide and growing and a broad-based functioning income tax (the work horse of fiscal revenue raising in almost all market societies) will be important to curb distributional problems. The downside might be that an effective income tax will deter entrepreneurship, but an increase in compliance can lead to lower rates and further increases in effectiveness.

Competition Policy

The legacy of planning and its obsession with scale economies left the Russian industrial structure highly concentrated. Table 21.10 provides data on the degree of industry concentration in the Soviet Union. The collapse of the Soviet Union increased the degree of concentration in Russia, because competitive goods from other republics now constituted hard currency purchases, often subject to tariff or quota, and therefore, the table probably understates the degree of concentration.

International trade provided healthy competition in some areas. In fact, the influx of imported "white goods" (freezers, washers, etc.) created a serious balance of payments problem and heavy tariffs were imposed on them in 1998.

Although patchy in coverage, Table 21.10 shows that, at the onset of liberalization, monopoly was an acute problem in durable consumer goods and machinery.

FIGURE 21.1

Structure of Tax Arrears, April 1998

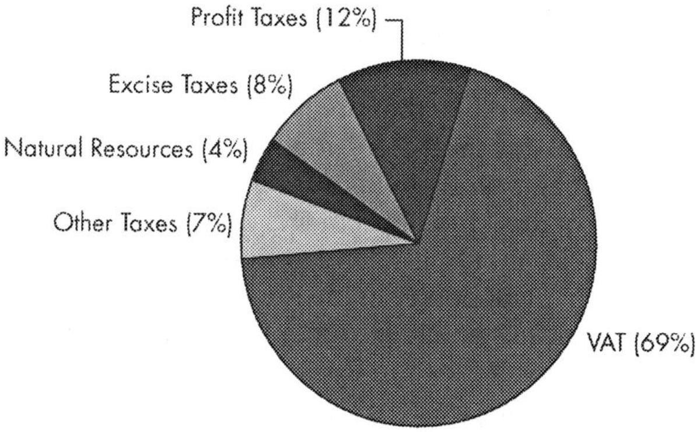

■ TABLE 21.10

Industry Concentration in the Former Soviet Union

Type of Product	Percentage of Production by Largest Producer
Sewing machines	100
Washing machines	90
Freezers	100
Concrete mixers	93
Road-building cranes	75
Hydraulic turbines	100
Steam turbines	95
Polypropylene	73
Electrolytic tin plate	100
Stainless steel pipes	96
Color photographic paper	100

SOURCE: *The Economist*, August 11, 1990, p. 67, from Goskomstat.

Little has been done to change matters, in part due to the problems faced by smaller entrepreneurs in Russia (see the feature "The Problems of Small Enterprise."). This perception of pervasive monopoly is reinforced by other studies by the state statistical agency (Goskomstat), which found in the mid-1990s that 166 enterprises were absolute monopolies. Another Soviet government study found that 80 percent of output of the machine-building industry was produced by monopolists.

Russia needs an effective way to encourage competition and facilitate entry into the monopolized industries, perhaps by breaking up some of the larger concerns. The problem is not legislation, but enforcement. Competition law is both modern and well conceived, but implementation by the Anti-Monopoly Committee remains weak. Actions by regional and local governments to protect local producers aggravate the situation.

Another problem is the extent of the "natural" monopolies in the network industries—gas, electricity supply, and communication. These concerns carry great influence, exert considerable monopoly power, and—especially in the case of Gazprom, the natural gas producer—are major tax delinquents. (The government has been slow to act against them because of their political influence.)

A good example of this kind of problem is electricity supply, which is dominated by the giant electricity monopoly United Energy Systems (UES), which produces more than 80 percent of all power in the Russian Federation. (Natural gas supply is dominated by Gazprom, which accounts for a like percentage of output.) Before liberalization, energy was cheap in Russia, priced at about 32 percent of the world average. Prices tripled between 1993 and 1995, to levels above the then world average prices. Price regulation was ineffective although the government claimed that in its absence prices would have risen by a further 12 to 23 percent.[27] Currently, 53 percent of UES is still owned by the state, and it lies at the nexus of economic problems. It is owed large sums of money by regional energy companies (called "Energos"—themselves monopolies) which are functionally bankrupt but unwilling to cut off nonpaying customers from the grid. The customers are in desperate straits themselves, striving to stay in business, and cannot afford the excessive monopoly prices charged by the UES. In turn, UES claims it is owed so much money it both needs to raise rates and cannot afford to pay its taxes, while paying its workers between three and four times the average for the economy.

Clearly more effective regulation is necessary, and restructuring of the industry to facilitate competition would pay dividends. Vertical disaggregation of the industry to allow competing suppliers and retailers to use a common regulated grid, as in the United Kingdom and Australia, would give the market a solution of greater efficiency and lower prices. The Russian government is now moving in this direction, and reform of electricity and gas supply is a priority. However the disasters associated with energy liberalization in the United States provide much food for thought and certainly slowed the process in Russia.

Agriculture

Russian agriculture has been a persistent failure throughout the twentieth century. The countryside, still home to more than 20 percent of Russia's people, remains impoverished and will continue to be depressed until a viable stimulus to agriculture is found. Prior to 1914 Russia was the world's largest exporter of grain, and the potential to be at least self-sufficient is clearly there. Collectivization under Stalin led to a demoralized and unproductive farm sector, and the development of state farms brought little relief. Persistent food shortages bear at least some of the blame for the fall of communism. Even after the collapse of the Soviet Union, privatization of agricultural land, opposed by the remnants of the Communist Party and the Peasants Party was slow. Now almost 90 percent of Russia's 190 million hectares (470 million acres) is in private hands. The vast majority of it was handed over to the former collective farmers generally in parcels too small to farm economically. The title to the land is still uncertain and the consolidation of these small holdings into viable farms is all but impossible. The same uncertainty, coupled with the lack of adequate financial intermediation, make borrowing by farmers for equipment and land improvement difficult in the extreme. Foreigners, particularly West Europeans, would like to invest in Russian agriculture, but are denied the legal right to own land.

The Duma passed a law in 2002 that in theory created a market in agricultural land and the path should now be clear to consolidation and innovation. The reality is trickier. The Communist years killed off (too often literally) the prospect of "family farming," and the creation of efficient agriculture will be tough as a result.

---

[27] *Izvestiya*, "Natural Monopolies: Comparing Russian and Australian Experience," January 13, 1996; Gennadi Kazakevitch, *Russian and Euro-Asian Economics Bulletin* 5, no. 4 (April 1996).

Good farmers are in short supply, and so are farm laborers. Despite high levels of unemployment, Russians are unwilling to work the land. One solution, already tried in the Stavropol region, is the importation of contract farm workers from China, who are happy to work for about $100 per month.[28]

PROSPECTS FOR THE RUSSIAN ECONOMY

The Russian economy fell sharply during the 1990s, but 1997 saw considerable optimism about the future. The data indicated that the economy turned a corner, and after a long period of falling GDP, positive growth was in view. The subsequent revelation that not only were the statistics unreliable, but also deliberately manipulated by Goskomstat, the state statistical agency, was a serious blow. It suggested that the government would resort to deliberate deception to achieve its aims; a fact that once revealed had caused a negative effect on incoming investment and international lenders. The next disappointment came from the Russian stock market, which after booming during 1996 and 1997, fell during 1998 and collapsed in a dramatic fashion in August. This crisis was followed by a 50 percent devaluation of the ruble (after a $4 billion IMF loan was wasted in its defense), an indefinite default on domestic government debt, and a 90-day moratorium on payments on foreign debt.

The pattern since the collapse of 1998 has been one of clawing the way back to growth and stability. After a sharp fall in 1998, GDP growth is again positive and quite strong, averaging more than 6 percent per year. This turnaround was helped by the high level of world energy prices, which benefited Russia in all sectors. GDP growth is strong, capital formation surged in 2000, the current account balance moved into surplus, and government revenue is higher.

■ TABLE 21.11

Key Macroeconomic Indicators

	1998	1999	2000	2001
GDP % growth	–4.9	5.4	8.3	5.5
Fixed Capital Investment, % growth	–12	5.3	17.4	7
Inflation, % per year	84	37	20	19
Exchange Rate Ruble/$	10	25	28	29
Unemployment %	13	12	10	9
General Govt. Budget Balance	–5.4	–0.8	3.6	2
Current Account, % of GDP	0	13	18	10

SOURCE: OECD, Survey of Russia, 2002.

[28] "A shiny free market blueprint. Will it work?" *The Economist*, June 27, 2002.

Perhaps more importantly, the strong presidency of Vladimir Putin ended speculation that Russia was likely to break up. His strong stance against Chechnyan separatism, questioned by many on moral grounds, at least showed Moscow's determination to maintain unity. The following policy reform is necessary to provide a minimum platform for growth.

1. Even after the 2001 tax reform, which clearly delineated fiscal capabilities, the tax system needs extensive reform, and attention must be paid both to revenue potential and incentive structure.
2. Many large privatized enterprises remain to some degree on a "soft-budget constraint." Of the billions of dollars channeled through "soft loans," 90 percent remain unpaid, even though they are ruble-denominated and inflation made them practically worthless.
3. Competition policy needs to be enforced.
4. Foreign investment seems to be necessary if Russia is to grow, but the capriciousness of the tax system, political uncertainty, and corruption keeps it low.
5. Russia needs to create a real banking sector.

The unreliability of official statistics increases the value of microeconomic studies by outside agencies. A study by McKinsey and Company reported in *The Economist* makes particularly disturbing reading:

> The study compares Russian-based companies (whether foreign or locally owned) with their American counterparts, sector by sector. It shows that Russian productivity is, on average, only 19% of American levels. Before the post-Soviet slump in output, it was only 30%. Depressingly, the 10% of the workforce that works on industrial capacity installed after 1992—presumably the best—is still producing at only 30% of American levels.[29]

The McKinsey report concluded that the absence of gains in productivity stems from the failure to cut back on workers (despite the fact that wages are generally in arrears) and "antiquated organizational structure." The solution would seem to be an infusion of management skills and increased capital investment. The most logical sources of both are via direct foreign investment, but political uncertainty and pervasive corruption keep those resources at bay. Moreover, capital apparently still continues to leave Russia, though perhaps at a slower pace than during the Yeltsin years. In July and August 1999 a surplus on current account topped $5 billion. Some $2.5 billion was absorbed by debt service but Roland Nash, chief economist at Renaissance Capital, an investment bank quoted by *The Economist,* thought that "the other $2.5 billion just disappeared somewhere."[30] These excesses are thought to be less under the tighter rule of Putin but misappropriation and the lack of transparency will continue to deter private capital inflow.

Lack of incoming investment, political uncertainty, corruption, and capital flight all contribute to hinder the transition of the economy. Only with stability and a level playing field will economic growth accelerate and the promise of Russia's

[29]"Russia's Economy: Surprise, Surprise," *The Economist*, October 23, 1999, p. 88.
[30]*The Economist,* October 23, 1999, p. 89.

resources and human capital be realized. Whether the economy's great potential can be unleashed by its leadership remains to be seen. Vladimir Putin, elected in 2002, pledged a program of reform, but his strong links to the FIGs and a tendency toward centralizing power might prove to be incompatible with the continued development of a competitive market.

KEY TERMS AND CONCEPTS

big bang
Decree on Property
finance capitalism (*Finanzkapitalism*)
financial and industrial groups
Gaidar reforms
Grand Bargain
interenterprise payments system
kleptocracy
Law on Cooperatives
Law on Individual Economic Activity
Law on State Enterprise
loans-for-shares deals
mass privatization
nomenklatura
oligarchs
prioritization
privatization for cash
small-scale privatization
voucher auction program

QUESTIONS FOR DISCUSSION

1. Why did Gorbachev's economic reforms fail?
2. What were the essential strategies of the Yeltsin/Gaidar reforms of January 1992?
3. How did inflation transfer wealth in Russia?
4. What were the three options by which enterprises might choose to privatize?
5. How did "insiders" take possession of so much of Russia's industry?
6. What are the FIGs? How might they aid growth and change and what dangers do they embody?
7. How has transition changed the distribution of income and the incidence of poverty?

RESOURCES

Web Sites

Central Bank........http://www.cbr.ru/
Institute for the Economy in Transition........http://www.iet.ru/index2.html
Russian Government Online (In Russian)........http://gosorgan.amursk.ru/

St. Petersburg Times, **National Newspaper**..http://www.sptimes.ru/
Vladivostok News, **National Newspaper**..http://vlad.tribnet.com/
Russia Online..http://www.russia-on-line.com/
IET-IRIS Project—Social Services Provision under the transition (health care, education, culture)..http://mac.www.online.ru/sp/iet/

Books and Articles

Ash, Timothy, and Paul G. Hare. "Privatisation in the Russian Federation: Changing Enterprise Behaviour in the Transition Period." *Cambridge Journal of Economics*, December 1994, 619–634.

Åslund, Anders. *How Russia Became a Market Economy.* Washington, DC: The Brookings Institution, 1995.

Åslund, Anders (ed.). *The Post-Soviet Economy: Soviet and Western Perspectives.* New York: St. Martin's Press, 1992.

Åslund, Anders, and Richard Layard (eds.). *Changing the Economic System in Russia.* New York: St. Martin's Press, 1993. Reviewed in the *Journal of Comparative Economics*, October 1994, 281. (Collection of papers from conference at Stockholm School of Economics, June 1992, assessment of early reform.)

Bergson, Abram. "Russia's Economic Reform Muddle." *Challenge*, September–October 1994, 56–59.

Blasi, Joseph R., Maya Kroumova, and Douglas Kruse. *Kremlin Capitalism: Privatizing the Russian Economy.* Ithaca, NY: ILR Press, 1997.

Boycko, Maxim, Andrei Shleifer, and Robert Vishny. *Privatizing Russia.* Cambridge, MA: MIT Press, 1995.

Buck, Trevor, Igor Filatotchev, and Mike Wright. "Employee Buyouts and the Transformation of Russian Industry." *Comparative Economic Studies*, Summer 1994, 115.

Dyker, David. *Restructuring the Soviet Economy.* New York: Routledge, Chapman and Hall, 1992.

Easterly, William, and Paula Vieira da Cunha. "Financing the Storm: Russia's Macroeconomic Crisis." *Economics of Transition* 2, no. 4 (1994): 433–66.

Gregory, Paul R., and Robert C. Stuart. *Soviet and Post-Soviet Economic Structure and Performance*, 5th ed. New York: HarperCollins College Publishers, 1994.

Islam, Shafiqul. "Russia's Rough Road to Capitalism." *Foreign Affairs*, Spring 1993, 57–66.

Joskow, Paul L., Richard Shmalensee, and Natalia Tsukanova. "Competition Policy in Russia During and After Privatization." *Brookings Papers on Economic Activity*, 1994, 301–380.

Lipton, David, and Jeffrey Sachs. "Prospects for Russia's Economic Reforms." *Brooking Papers on Economic Activity* 2, 1992, 213–276.

Monetary and Exchange Affairs Department, International Monetary Fund. "Central Bank Autonomy, and Inflation and Output Performance in the Baltic States, Russia, and Other Countries of the Former Soviet Union." (1995–1997). IMF Working Paper, WP/99/4.

Nelson, Lynn D., and Irina Y. Kuzes. "Evaluating the Russian Voucher Privatization Program." *Comparative Economic Studies*, Spring 1994, 55–67.

Shlapentokh, Vladimir. "Privatization Debates in Russia: 1989–1992." *Comparative Economic Studies,* Summer 1993, 19–32.

Slider, Darrell. "Privatization in Russia's Regions." *Post-Soviet Affairs,* October–December 1994, 367–396.

"A Survey of Russia: In Search of Spring." *The Economist,* July 12, 1997, 48.

Van Atta, Don. "Agrarian Reform in Post-Soviet Russia." *Post-Soviet Affairs,* April–June 1994, 159–190.

23

THE PEOPLE'S REPUBLIC OF CHINA

CHINA		
	Area (thousand sq. km.)	9,597
	Currency	yuan
	Exchange Rate	8 yuan = US$1
	Population 2000 (millions)	1261
	Population Growth Rate	1.1%
	GNI per Capita, 2000	$840
	GNI per Capita, PPP	$3,940
	GDP Growth 1990–2000	10.3%
Value Added as % of GDP 2000	Agriculture	16%
	Industry	49%
	Services	34%
% of GDP	Government Expenditure	15%
	Exports	22%

INTRODUCTION

With a population of more than 1.2 billion and one of the fastest rates of economic growth over the past two decades, the potential of the Chinese economy is huge. If the economic growth, which has already transformed much of the country, is maintained, China will be one of the world's largest economies in the twenty-first century. With its long history as a unified state, its huge population, and a considerable resource base, China should indeed be a major player. For the past century and a half, invasion, imperialism, civil wars, instability, and poor management all played a role in keeping that vast potential unrealized. In the last couple of decades some of the dormant economic power has been unleashed. China is also something of a paradox. Despite its freewheeling growth, it is one of few countries left in the world that is governed by a Communist party, and it still practices a limited form of centralized planning. It is struggling to reconcile its socialist ideology with the needs of a growing capitalist society.

Nevertheless, the growth of the economy in recent years can be described as nothing less than spectacular, averaging close to 10 percent annually during the 1980s and 1990s, and never less than 4 percent, even during a slow spell in the late 1980s. At the growth rates experienced during the last 10 years (9.6% per year for China and 3.1% for the United States) by the year 2037, Chinese GDP would equal that of the United States.[1] Today, however, the Chinese economy is only 11 percent the size of that of the United States, and the per-head income of China is only about 3 percent of that of the United States measured at current international exchange rates. When expressed in purchasing power parity the situation is slightly more favorable at 11 percent of the U.S. level.

Recent Chinese growth has its roots in substantial productivity gains per worker (particularly in agriculture and light industry), a more efficient deployment of the workforce, and an increase in employment. Employment, rising at an annual rate of about 3 percent, proved sufficient to absorb the considerable population "bubble" caused by the high birthrates of the 1960s. Despite immigration from the rural areas to urban conurbations, the urban unemployment rate, more than 5 percent in the 1960s, fell to about 2 percent by the late 1980s.

Of course, China started from a low base. Income measured at current exchange rates was only about $250 per person in the mid-1970s. Purchasing power comparisons generally give a better picture of overall living standards, but even these show consumption on average of roughly $1,000 per person, one-sixth of the figure in the Soviet Union and only 6 percent of that for the United States. Moreover, China has low levels of national wealth. World Bank estimates put wealth per head (including natural resources and human capital) at about $6,600, about one-fiftieth of that of Germany and among the lowest in the world.

CENTRAL PLANNING, 1952–1959

The triumph of the Communists over the Nationalists in the civil war that closely followed the end of World War II led, in October 1949, to the creation of the People's Republic of China. The Nationalists withdrew to the offshore island of

---

[1]In 1996 Borensztein and Ostry calculated that if the 9 percent annual real growth (envisaged in the five-year plan covering 1996 to 2000) were sustained until 2013, Chinese gross national product (GNP), corrected for purchasing power parity, would surpass that of the United States if the United States continued at the rate it had in the previous decade. To many people this revelation was surprising. As things turned out, however, Chinese growth slowed somewhat in the years 1997 to 1999, while that of the United States accelerated sharply from the sluggish pace of the late 1980s and early 1990s. See Borensztein and Ostry, "Accounting for China's Growth," *American Economic Review,* May 1996, p. 224.

Taiwan and created there a successful state and economy, which we examined in Chapter 14. The communist Chinese leadership set out to imitate the economic system developed in the Soviet Union over the previous 25 years. Private industry and commerce were nationalized and sweeping agricultural reform took the land from the landlords and wealthier farmers and placed it under peasant control in communes. As in the Soviet Union, a great deal of investment was poured into heavy industry, with faith in the power of capital-intensive technology and economies of scale to produce high rates of economic growth.

The Soviet model was followed relying on five-year materials balance plans. Soviet planners and technicians were imported and a formal planning apparatus put into place. However, in the early 1950s the Chinese economy was by no means in a parallel position to that of the Soviet Union, leading to problems in the application of a centrally planned model. One fact was that China's population was much larger (by a factor of 4), and its communications and transportation systems were much less well developed. In any system of centralized planning, the availability of reliable information at the center is crucial.[2] In the Chinese case, problems impeding the flow of information to the center and back to the enterprises proved to be even worse than in the Soviet Union, which had a fundamental impact on the success of the planning experiment.

Moreover, the Chinese economy was not as highly unified and integrated as that of the Soviet Union. Poor transportation and the historically high degree of regional self-sufficiency (exacerbated during the period of "warlordism" in the 1920s and the struggle with the Japanese) meant that gains from centralizing the economy were much more difficult to grasp. A greater degree of power remained in the hands of municipalities and provinces, and even the prefectures and townships, than had been the case in the Soviet Union. One measure of the difficulty of implementing centralized planning is how few goods were brought under formal control. Even at the height of planning in China, only 500 commodities fell under mandatory central control, in contrast to the more than 20,000 commodities that were part of the Soviet material balance plans.

THE GREAT LEAP FORWARD, 1958–1961

The end of the first five-year plan in 1958 coincided with reforms to the planning system that recognized the impracticability of "taut"[3] central planning in the Chinese economy, allowing the necessity, and even the desirability, of a high degree of provincial initiative. However, the potential for success of the revised system will never be known because the development path of the economy was disturbed by the intrusion of political rhetoric, in the form of Mao's **Great Leap Forward**, a political initiative to harness the ideological fervor of the Chinese population to the task of raising industrial output. At the same time as China continued to pour

[2]See Chapter 16 for a fuller discussion of information and central planning.

[3]*Taut* in this context refers to a "lack of slack" in the planning system, provided by keeping inventories to a minimum.

investment into capital-intensive heavy industry, Mao and the leadership exhorted the population to increase the output of basic industrial goods through labor-intensive enterprises in rural areas. This approach of using both capital- and labor-intensive technologies to produce the same goods was characterized as "walking on two legs."

Although labor-intensive enterprises were found in many industries, including building materials, mining, food processing, and machine-building, the political leadership defined the key industry as steel. Mao Tse Tung urged a sharp increase in steel production through the development of small-scale furnaces, and it is estimated that some two million small furnaces were established during the first two years of the Great Leap Forward, employing some 80 million people on a full or part-time basis. Official statistics show that industrial output grew sharply at the outset of the Great Leap Forward; net material product was up by 22 percent in 1959 alone, but it soon became apparent that this increase was being achieved at great cost, and much of the growth was actually an illusion. For example, the steel produced in rural furnaces was, in general, of poor quality and expensive in terms of factor cost. Moreover, much of the "new" output consisted merely of the melting down and recycling of steel and iron that had already been produced; ornamental and structural steelwork was pulled down and fed to the furnaces. Woods and forests were cut down, and even buildings were cannibalized, to provide charcoal and fuel.

After an initial period of feverish activity, the incentives of revolutionary fervor and rhetoric cooled. The recycling of previously produced material slowed as stocks became exhausted, and the depletion of woodland made charcoal increasingly short in supply. The countryside was scarred and the environment suffered. China's Soviet advisors were frustrated by what seemed a perverse rejection of socialist rationality, and in an atmosphere of growing antagonism between the two nations, technical assistance was suspended in 1960.

Net material product in China fell sharply in 1961 and 1962, but greater stability was reestablished in 1963 and a period of relative calm saw a rise in industrial output. Continuing investment in heavy industry helped the rebound, and industrial output rose sharply between 1963 and 1966. Chinese technocrats filled the void left by the departing Soviets, pursuing central planning once more, though with a greater degree of pragmatism. The high degree of provincial autonomy left local governments free to use their flexibility to increase output in whatever way they chose.

THE CULTURAL REVOLUTION, 1966–1970

In 1966, however, political furor again swamped the economic system after the inception of Mao's **Proletarian Cultural Revolution**. Exactly what prompted the Chinese leader to embark on that course at that moment in history is still open to dispute. In part he seemed convinced that only complete rejection of western influence would enable Asia, including China, to be economically self-reliant. He was also genuinely convinced that Stalinist economic management had resulted in a new structure of class and privilege as obnoxious to him as the old. Finally, and perhaps decisively, he felt a need to strengthen his own political position vis-à-vis the technocrats and bureaucrats. The Cultural Revolution resulted in Chinese society being turned upside down. Bureaucrats, planners, and technocrats were stripped of authority and sent off to the countryside for "political reeducation," while power shifted to radical political cadres. Considerable economic costs resulted from the turmoil. Again the economy lurched into a sharp recession with material output falling by about 15 percent in both 1966 and 1967; it rebounded again in the last years of the decade as some form of normality returned.

By the beginning of the 1970s it was clear that the era of Mao and Chou En Lai was nearing its close, so political factions began maneuvering for power. On the left, the **gang of four**, led by Mao's wife, tried to sustain the Cultural Revolution. On the right, a moderate and technocratic leadership sought the restoration of rule by bureaucracy and party. Both Mao and Chou died in 1976 and nominal power passed to Mao's chosen successor Hua Qua Feng. However, by this time the moderates were in ascendance and Deng Xiaoping, a capable administrator, was rehabilitated from the indignities inflicted on him during the Cultural Revolution and restored as party leader.

THE FIRST PHASE OF REFORM, 1978–1993

Because the economy stagnated, and in some areas declined, during the period of the Cultural Revolution and the rule of the gang of four, Deng resolved to find new approaches to promote growth. December 1978 saw a profound shift in the direction of the Chinese economy as the Central Committee of the Communist Party of China (CCP) issued a communiqué that, in effect, launched the modern period of reform, moving the Chinese economy away from a planned economy and toward a market one.

Agricultural Reform

The first reforms were aimed at revitalizing the rural sector, whose fortunes had flagged during the previous three decades. The high percentage of the population engaged in agriculture and the necessity of creating an agrarian surplus to fuel industrial growth and feed a growing population made agricultural reform essential. Even though heavy industrial output surged during the previous 15 years, agriculture remained dormant. Grain output per person employed rose by less than 10 percent during a 25-year period, despite considerable expenditures on infrastructure, informational outreach, and factor inputs, especially fertilizers. The key to raising output lay in radical reform of the collectivized agricultural system so painfully created in the 1950s and 1960s.

Under collectivization, agricultural production was organized into *communes* (typically with a population of about 40,000 people). These communes were further subdivided into *brigades* and *production teams*. Decisions about what to grow and how to grow it were passed to the communes from superior political units (the prefecture and provincial governments) and were quite often inflexible to local conditions. Worker remuneration was generally through sharing the net production of the brigade on a per-worker basis taking little account of individual or family productivity. This system resulted in a chronic absence of incentives and a pervasive free rider problem. Households were allowed small plots for the own cultivation, from which the surplus could be sold in the local markets, and productivity was in general much higher in these small niches in the system.

The reforms that began in 1979 were largely the result of local initiative and were, in fact, opposed at the outset by the State Council in Beijing. Motivation for reform was the belief that productivity in the agricultural sector could be greatly increased simply by raising the economic incentives to family units. Initially this reform included enlarging the size of the private plots and increasing the procurement price that the state paid for crops that were produced privately. Local officials were encouraged by the success of this limited action, and the reforms evolved into the **household responsibility system (HRS)**, which became the dominant arrangement in agriculture after 1982.

Under the HRS quite large plots of collectively held land were leased to households for a fixed period of time, initially 15 years for annual crops and up to 40 years for tree crops. In return for tenure, each household was responsible for providing a share of the production team's output quota based on plot size. Production in excess of this "contract" could be sold either on the free market for what it would fetch or to the state at negotiated prices. By 1984, 93 percent of China's cultivated land was contracted to households, but, and this aspect is highly illustrative of the progress of China's reforms, it was not until 1985 that the state passed legislation formally sanctioning it.

Agricultural production rose sharply after the reforms. Annual growth of output was twice the rate experienced in the 1960s and 1970s, illustrating the importance of individual incentive in agriculture. Labor productivity in agriculture rose at an even higher rate, producing a labor surplus in most of the rural collectives, which ultimately provided the workforce for the rapid expansion of rural light industry. Higher food prices moved the terms of trade (defined as food prices divided by manufactured goods prices) sharply in favor of the farmers and resulted in a substantial increase in real income in the rural sector. However, the authorities in Beijing were concerned about political unrest among urban workers and were unwilling to allow the burden of increased farm incomes to be passed directly to urban consumers in the form of higher food prices. The government provided substantial subsidies, which resulted in a growing fiscal deficit.

The state response was to reduce the size of the subsidy by cutting the procurement prices for grains, but farmers responded by shifting resources out of grain production and into more profitable, less regulated commodities like vegetables and meat. Grain output fell as a result in the mid-1980s. The government's reply was to raise the procurement prices of grain once more, but this time it tried to avoid the fiscal consequences by increasing the prices paid by urban consumers. This step toward price liberalization led to the ultimate deregulation of the grain market; by May 1993 grain prices were decontrolled in about 80 percent of the country and prices determined by the interplay of supply and demand.

The Rise of Rural Enterprise

The rapid rise in agricultural output, labor productivity, and incomes set in motion a further development in the rural areas: the emergence of **township and village enterprises (TVEs)** as the most dynamic sector in the Chinese economy. TVEs are industrial activities that were initially collectively owned by the communes. They were made possible by a progressive rollback of restrictions on the nonagricultural activities of collectives, culminating in 1984 when local authorities were given the power to sanction communal industrial activity. In recent years the term expanded to cover proprietorships and joint stock enterprises located in the countryside. The new enterprises absorbed much of the excess labor created by high birthrates and rising labor productivity in agriculture, while increased rural incomes provided the seed money for the initial investments.

Although they are collectively owned, TVEs are much more akin to western firms than the **state-owned enterprises (SOEs)** for several reasons:

1. They face a **hard-budget constraint** and are seldom bailed out by government subsidy. Moreover, in the absence of government support, banks are inclined to extend credit only on strictly economic terms.[4]
2. As new enterprises, TVEs fell outside the scope of the rather rigid planning system and were from the beginning unfettered by mandatory controls. They enjoy, therefore, considerable freedom of initiative over what to produce and how. Moreover, because the Chinese planners concentrated more on the growth of heavy industrial output, a large pent-up demand for light industrial products emerged, both in the domestic market and overseas. TVEs were able to exploit this vacuum.
3. Unlike SOEs, TVEs had no captive market for their products and from the start success depended on identifying demand and meeting it with quality products. In both domestic and overseas markets strong forces of consumer sovereignty were at work, which encouraged an emphasis on quality and product development that was absent in the state sector.
4. TVEs were allowed to sell their products at market prices, and their operating largely in competitive markets created a continuing pressure to contain costs and advance productivity.
5. TVEs were not encumbered by the social expenditures required of state enterprises. In common with many socialist countries, SOEs in China were responsible for a range of social services including childcare, education, and health care that raised labor costs.
6. TVEs were also able to be much more nimble in their employment practices (hiring and firing) and were able to establish performance-based compensation systems, which maximized individual incentives and raised productivity.

---

[4]Although initially they had access to credit from the rural credit cooperatives, the financial sector cut the SOEs off from credit almost completely between 1988 and 1991, resulting in failures and employment loss.

7. TVEs could retain profits and keep them within the enterprise as investment. Initially the TVEs were assisted by concessional tax treatment that was helpful in building capital in the "infancy" stage.

Particular features of the Chinese economy under planning also favored growth of TVEs :

1. The concentration on heavy industrial growth through the state-owned enterprises led the government to neglect the light industrial sector, presented a wide window of opportunity in light industrial production, through which the relatively nimble TVEs quickly and profitably moved.
2. The rise in agricultural productivity and the high birthrates of the 1960s created large reserves of labor in the rural communes. The extension of educational opportunities, especially for women, under communism substantially increased human capital.
3. The high degree of provincial autonomy and the concern of local governments to promote economic development (in part motivated by the need to absorb surplus labor) meant that few impediments were placed on TVE growth, and many incentives were offered at the local level.

Starting from a low base at the beginning of the 1980s, the emergence of TVEs made a rapid impact on China's economy. By 1996, some 23.3 million TVEs within China employed more than 135 million workers, or about 20 percent of total national employment. The rural enterprise sector as a whole accounted for only 19.2 percent of industrial output in 1978, but this percentage rose to about 50 percent by 1996.

In recent years a strong trend toward the privatization of the collectively owned TVEs caused a drop in the share of truly collectively owned enterprises, and with it their share of employment. The collectively owned enterprises are being converted into joint stock enterprises, partnerships, and proprietorships. Perhaps more ominously, employment in the rural enterprise sector seems to have peaked at the 1996 level. The subsequent fall in employment put it at fewer than 125 million persons in 1999[5]. This decrease is causing growing rural unemployment. The initial impetus for the TVEs was the surplus labor generated by the agricultural revolution of the 1970s and 1980s. Labor is still being shaken out of the agricultural sector and the rural birth rate is still relatively high and, therefore, the rural labor force is increasing. If those workers cannot find work on the land or in industry, then a body of unemployed or underemployed migrants must emerge. This development is observable already, and with disguised unemployment, total joblessness may be as high as 80 million persons.[6]

---

[5]See Albert Park, *Trade Integration and the Prospects for Rural Enterprise Development in China* (Paris: OECD, 2002).

[6]According to official statistics the unemployment rate is 3.1 percent, or about 22 million, but this figure is thought to be a serious underestimate. The Social and Economic Policy Institute in Hong Kong (http://www.sepi.org) puts the actual rate at 7.9 to 8.3 percent, to which should be added a factor for underemployment, yielding between 10 and 12 percent, a figure that is rising.

REFORMING STATE-OWNED ENTERPRISE

Although the TVEs have been the bright star of the Chinese economy, sustained economic development depends on successful reform of the state-owned enterprises (SOEs). These predominantly heavy industrial enterprises were once seen as the key to China's industrial future and represented economic security to the masses. A job with an SOE was by and large guaranteed for life, usually carried housing benefits, and was often referred to as an "iron rice bowl." The state-owned sector still accounts for the bulk of employment in the industrial sector. It still consumes more than 40 percent of total industrial labor but manages to produce only about 25 percent of the output, reflecting serious inefficiencies.

Initiative in the SOE sector was stifled throughout the post-revolutionary period until the onset of enterprise reform, which started in 1986, slightly later than in the rural sector. Early reform efforts tried to replicate in the state-owned industrial sector the responsibility system that resulted in so much success in the rural areas. Under this scheme, known as the **contract responsibility system (CRS)**, SOEs contracted for a four-year period to a production quota to be delivered to the state, and to specified financial payments it would make to the state in lieu of the profit remittances that the enterprises paid formerly. Any output above the quota level could be disposed of by the enterprise at market prices. By 1988, 90 percent of all SOEs were operating under such contracts.

In parallel with these arrangements, and introduced during the same period of 1986–1988, a third responsibility system involved the **fiscal contract responsibility system (FCRS)**. It supplanted the enterprise income tax, levied at a standard rate of 55 percent, with an individually negotiated contract that fixed the total size of tax payments over several years and specified the division of the total between central, provincial, and local governments. The combination of the two contract systems meant that payments to the government were invariant to the level of profit of the organization. In short, tax elasticity was zero, a major problem. Of greater significance, however, were the FCRS's distortionary features. Because tax payments were all negotiated and the outcome depended to a large extent on political "pull," effective rates varied greatly from enterprise to enterprise, with little pursuit of any underlying economic objective.

These arrangements, however, did provide great incentives for the enterprise. Exceeding a quota was highly desirable because excess output could be sold for whatever the market would bear. Moreover, with the marginal tax rate on profits at zero and the dividends payable to government fixed, all the profit above predetermined fixed levels could be retained in the enterprise. The industrial output of the SOEs rose sharply in response. However, the reforms also brought negative consequences for long-term economic development. First, each contractual arrangement was individually negotiated, giving enterprises an incentive to fight for high levels of inputs and low quotas to acquire the resources for a surplus to sell on the private market. This asymmetry of information between the bureaucracy and the enterprise led to significant negative impacts.

The second disadvantage was the abandonment of all pretense of a "level playing field" in the tax system in favor of what should more accurately be called a "revenue" system. In developed market economies, tax systems are expected to define rules that include **horizontal equity**, which requires that equivalent units should be treated equally. Because of the discretionary element, the fiscal contract responsibility system resulted in widely disparate average tax rates between enterprises, as well as falling average rates over time.

Third, although the boom in the industrial sector should have increased government revenue from taxes on enterprises, revenues proved highly inelastic with respect to growing income. In fact, real revenues tended to fall as income and output rose because the contracts fixed tax payment in nominal terms, with no inflation escalator. A buoyant economy and the progressive decontrol of prices led to inflation and reduced the real value of the contracted nominal tax payments.

A fourth and highly significant problem was that the CRS resulted in a two-tier price system: the procurement price set by the responsibility contract and paid on the contracted quota, and the market price. The procurement price was in general lower than the market price. Therefore, large potential gains were possible in arbitrage between the state and private sectors and from the deliberate understatement of quota outputs. This potential led to a sharp increase in corruption.

CREATING A MODERN ENTERPRISE SECTOR

Recognizing the problems emanating from the responsibility system in the SOE sector, the Chinese government embarked on a new series of reforms to change the structure of ownership, governance, and accounting in the SOEs and also reform the fiscal relationship between the enterprises and the various levels of government. However, progress has not been easy because of the need to control rising unemployment and the implicit lifetime employment guarantee associated with most state employment.

Although content to let private firms, **foreign-financed enterprises (FFEs)**, and the collectivized sectors prosper, Chinese authorities were slow to embark on the mass privatization of most state assets. The cornerstone of the economy in the foreseeable future will continue to be the predominance of SOEs in strategic sectors. The strategy is to develop a "socialist market economy" in which the assets of much of the industrial sector are owned by the state, but in which the primary functions of coordination are performed by the market, subject to guidance from the center. In some sense this model is not dramatically different from that of certain European economies, like the French or British in their preprivatization period when much of heavy industry was held in public ownership.

The first step in the creation of this "modern enterprise sector" must be the corporatization of the SOEs; the foundation to achieve this step was laid down in the *company law,* which became effective in July 1994. The most salient thrust of the company law is to clearly separate "ownership" (which for the time being lies with the state) from management. It clarifies the rights of enterprises as legal entities, establishes the rights and responsibilities of management, and limits the power of ministries to interfere directly in enterprise management. The law also relieves SOEs from many of their responsibilities for the social security of their workers and families. Ultimately, it is planned that responsibility for the oversight of enterprises will pass from the ministries into the hands of state holding companies.

The root of the problem of the state-owned sector is a soft-budget constraint for state-owned enterprise, which continues to apply. About 50 percent of the SOEs fail to produce a profit, but even the loss-making ventures are kept in existence either by state subsidies, or by the government using the state-owned banks to continue to extend credit to enterprises that are economically moribund. In a real sense the SOEs are too big to be allowed to fail. Today, 44 percent of urban Chinese still work for the SOEs. If the government allowed market logic to triumph, the political problems and distress would be huge. Instead, the authorities initiated privatization in a small way. Many of the smaller and medium-sized enterprises already are being being sold off. The worst cases are foreclosed, the banks assuming ownership in lieu of payment of the outstanding loans. The banks then place these assets with specialist **asset management companies (AMCs)** whose task is to reorganize, restructure, and find a buyer. In most cases the assets are disposed of for a trivial sum, but it is a means of privatizing the least efficient of the state enterprises, and to allow the banks to get some of the nonperforming loans off their books.

REFORMING THE TAX SYSTEM

A successful transition from a centrally planned economy to one that is market oriented must involve the creation of certain institutions that are essential for the long-term stability of the economy. One of the most important of these is the fiscal system, which plays two important roles. First, it provides the resources for government expenditures. In the absence of an effective tax-gathering system, the government usually is financed by money creation—an "inflation tax"—which transfers resources from creditors to debtors (the largest of which is the government) in a capricious and inefficient way.

Second, the fiscal system provides the government with an important policy tool meant to promote macroeconomic stability and control the direction of economic development. China today does not have a well-functioning tax system and gathers a lower share of its GDP into the central government than any other East Asian nation, between 7 percent and 8 percent. Local taxing powers are considerable; in total about 15 percent of GDP is taken into general government. The reform in taxation seeks to replace what has been described as a *revenue system,* which can provide fiscal resources for various levels of government but, because of a lack of consistency and equity, creates perverse incentives. It is in the process of the necessary reform that will, it is hoped, create the required conditions for continued growth.

Indirect Taxes

The Value-Added Tax Currently, central government finance relies heavily on indirect taxes, which provide 79 percent of revenue. They are of three types: excise taxes, value-added taxes (VAT), and turnover taxes on business, each of which supplies a little less than 3 percent of GNP in revenue. Tax reform will simplify the system by enlarging the coverage of VAT and standardizing the rates. Under the new system, VAT will extend to universal coverage with a 17 percent rate applied to most goods and a 13 percent rate on food, farm supplies, and utilities. In addition, a consumption tax will replace the excise tax and will be levied only on the sale of tobacco, alcohol, gasoline, and luxury goods (including cars). A special business tax will apply to services not covered by VAT. Improved tax administration increases the probability that in the future a well-administered VAT system will provide most of the central government finance, removing the distortionary aspects of the turnover and sales tax system.

Customs and Tariffs China's growing participation in world trade, and in the international agencies that oversee trade, requires a rationalization of a complex tariff structure, constructed in a piecemeal manner with both revenue raising and protectionism in mind. Customs duties historically provided about 8 percent of tax revenue. The average tariff rate is about 40 percent, but rates rise with the degree to which the goods are "finished." Raw materials are subject to rates in the 0 to 20 percent range, intermediate and capital goods fit into the 20 to 40 percent category, and finished goods may be subject to duties as high as 80 percent. The effective rate of protection for the Chinese manufacturing industry provided by this structure is high.

Reforms presently being implemented will reduce the maximum tariff on all goods to less than 40 percent, and many categories of goods will be placed in the zero bracket. The impact of this change on revenue is not clear and depends on the elasticity of imports to tariff changes; it is conceivable that revenues will rise if imports increase in response to lower rates of protection.

Direct Taxes

The Personal Income Tax Other parts of the tax system are also being reformed. The direct taxation system in China comprises the enterprise tax and the personal income tax. At present, the role of the personal income tax in both revenue raising and fiscal policy is negligible. Its nominal incidence is primarily private business owners and foreigners (who pay on a higher schedule than domestic Chinese). The high rates encourage both evasion and avoidance; compliance is consequently low, revenue is small, and deadweight burdens quite high.

The personal income tax base includes all personal income from wages, salaries, rents, and business sources, less a standard deduction of ¥800 per month for Chinese citizens. This deduction excludes a large part of the domestic population from paying tax at all, especially rural residents. For everyone above the threshold, income will be subject to sharply rising progressive rates starting at 5 percent. In the case of wage income the maximum marginal rate is 45 percent, and for "unearned" income the top rate is 35 percent, an unusual configuration. In most societies with multiple rates, unearned income is taxed at a higher rate than earned income, complying with a widely held view that working individuals are more entitled to money they labored for. In addition, the disincentive impact of high taxes on labor is usually thought to be greater than on capital. The Chinese authorities hope that the lower rate on capital income will increase the tax base by reducing evasion and fostering compliance in the private business sector.

The Corporate Income Tax The corporate tax, now leveled at a rate of 33 percent of corporate profits, applies to corporations, collectives, foreign-financed enterprises, and state-owned enterprise, though a clause allows for the negotiated taxes in special circumstances. Because the state-owned sector is only marginally profitable, in aggregate, it contributes little to revenues.

THE FINANCIAL SYSTEM

As in the case of the tax system, the effective reform of the financial sector can do double duty. First, a stable and rationally developed system allows for greater allocative efficiency through the improved channeling of resources from savers to investors. Second, a coherent financial system is essential for the implementation of effective monetary policy.

The Banking Sector

Prior to 1978 the banking system in China played only a limited role. Its main purpose was akin to the role of the monobank in any centrally planned system. Through the management of the accounts of the various SOEs, it provided a financial counterpart to the movement of goods, and therefore a check on the satisfactory fulfillment of the plan, and it also made available to state-owned enterprises the credits for investment and subsidy approved in the plan.

The People's Bank of China (PBC) was the dominant agency and served as a commercial, investment, and central bank. In 1984 the PBC became the central bank, responsible for supervision of the financial system, exchange rate policy, and the conduct of monetary policy, and its commercial and investment banking functions were handed over to four state-owned banks, known now as the Big Four. These banks perform both commercial and investment banking functions, and are like the German "universal banks." Another element of the state banking system is made up of the credit cooperatives, which collect deposits and supply loans at the grassroots level. Rural credit cooperatives number 53,000, along with 4,000 urban ones, though their combined assets represent less than 6 percent of the total. In addition, three development banks (one national and two provincial ones in Guangdong and Shenzhen) exist, but their assets are small. A small private banking sector is emerging but it represents less than 6 percent of the loans.

The banks have never been fully free to pursue their own interests or to follow good banking practice. Though the creation of the PBC and the Big Four banks was seen at the time as a strong step toward the creation of a market-oriented financial system, the authorities were slow to relinquish power over credit allocation. In 1988 the government tightened control over the Big Four banks and the growing number of nonbank financial intermediaries (NBFIs). The main vehicle for credit allocation remains the **credit plan**, which is controlled from the center and determines the activity of the central bank, the specialized banks, and the Big Four banks. The banks are required to provide the finance for approved projects and the government largely administers interest rates, although the banks are allowed a small degree of latitude around the official rate.

Continued reliance on directed credit through the credit plan has often been criticized as being at odds with the principles of decentralization, competition, and marketization, which provide the primary elements of the reforms in other areas.[7] In the past Chinese planners were able to point not only to their own experience but also to the prevalent use of directed credit by both the Japanese and the South Koreans during the periods of greatest growth in their countries. However, the problems of the Japanese and Korean economies in recent years, which are particularly pressing in the banking sectors, must give the Chinese cause for concern. Nevertheless, the planners remain reluctant to relinquish their last lever of control, and their Northeast Asian neighbors were until the late 1990s advertisements for its efficacy.

More damaging than the mere principle of directed credit is the criticism that the credit plan adopted by the authorities is based on flawed principles. Japanese and Korean directed credit was based on the principle of identifying growth areas and financing export-oriented development in the most dynamic sectors. Chinese credit, on the other hand, is more defensively dispositioned and frequently seeks to guard the interests of the existing SOE sector. The banks were required to make a large number of **policy loans** that run counter to good banking practice but are part of the overall plan. The result of this requirement is that the recently created specialized banks already hold portfolios of **nonperforming loans (NPLs)**.[8]

Table 23.1 gives some indication of the problems that the banking system now faces. All of the Big Four banks have a large number of NPLs on their books. The largest bank in terms of loans is the Industrial and Commercial Bank of China (ICBC), whose portfolio contains $325 billion in loans, 29.8 percent of which are presently nonperforming based on the official definition. This measure probably underestimates the severity of the situation. The situation is worse at the Agricultural Bank of China, at which 42.1 percent of loans are nonperforming. Taken together the Big Four carry $897 billion in outstanding loans, with an average of 29.9 percent of the loan portfolio nonperforming. To give some dimension to this scenario, this amount represents some 26 percent of Chinese GDP, or 355 percent of annual central government tax revenue. As a transnational comparison, Citibank's loan portfolio of $392 billion shows only 2.3 percent nonperforming.

INTERNATIONAL TRADE

Before the onset of reform, all of China's foreign trade was handled through a few foreign trade corporations that acted as import and export agencies. The reforms began in 1993 and trade was liberalized, both in terms of the agencies that can enter into international trade and in terms of the tariffs and licensing restrictions that

[7]See Tseng et al., *Economic Reform in China: A New Phase* (Washington, DC: International Monetary Fund, 1994), p. 1617.

[8]A nonperforming loan is one where the debt service payments have been suspended for some reason. It is a step short of the loan never being repaid; the debtor agency might resume payments, or may enter receivership, in which case some part of the principal may be repaid.

TABLE 23.1

The Big Four Banks, 2002

	Branches	Loans, ($ billions)	Percent of Nonperforming Loans	Value of Bad Loans
Chinese State-Owned Banks				
Industrial and Commercial Bank of China	28,000	325	29.8	97
Agricultural Bank of China	50,000	199	42.1	84
Bank of China	13,000	192	27.5	53
China Construction Bank	24,000	182	19.4	35
Total	115,000	897	29.9	268
For comparison:				
Citibank	*6,421*	*392*	*2.3*	*9*
Memo Items				
Bad loans as percent of government revenue		166%		
Bad loans as a percent of GDP		26%		

SOURCE: Standard and Poor's; Citibank.

constrained it. Enterprises, whether in the state, the collective, or the private sectors, became more able and more anxious to seek out and export to markets of their own choosing.

The impact of this export boom on China's trade position has been huge. In 1978 the trade to GNP ratio for China was about 5 percent; by 1993 this had risen to 35 percent, making China a highly open economy by world standards.[9] The Chinese share of world trade doubled between 1978 and 1993, from 1 percent to 2 percent of the total.

Table 23.2 shows the highlights of China's overseas transactions since 1993. Exports showed remarkable growth increasing sixfold in a twelve-year period between 1989 and 2001. This increase made China one of the world's largest traders. The commodity composition of trade also underwent a dramatic shift. In 1978 agricultural products dominated exports, comprising 63 percent of the total. Today light industrial exports dominate. A remarkable inflow of foreign direct investment capital into China also occurred. Since the mid 1990s, investment capital poured in at the rate of about $40 billion dollars annually. The pace slowed somewhat after the Asian financial crisis, but in 2001 it reached $44 billion again, roughly 3.6 percent of China's GDP.

SPECIAL ECONOMIC ZONES

China made extensive use of various forms of **special economic zones (SEZs)** in its reform push. The first SEZs were established by the State Council in 1979. They were

[9]Some care should be taken with this statistic; although trade is valued in dollars, GNP is understated because it is not cited in PPP terms. In reality, the denominator should be larger. Moreover, at this time trade with Hong Kong was counted as a foreign trade transaction.

■ TABLE 23.2

Highlights of Chinese Overseas Transaction, 1993–2001 (in US$ millions)

	1989	1991	1993	1995	1997	1999	2000	2001
Exports	43,220	58,919	75,659	128,110	182,670	194,716	249,131	266,075
Imports	48,840	50,176	86,113	110,060	136,448	158,734	414,657	232,058
Trade balance	25,620	8,743	−10,454	18,050	46,222	35,982	3,4474	33,384
Current account balance	24,317	13,272	−11,609	1,618	36,963	21,115	20,518	17,401
Outgoing direct investment	780	913	4,400	2,000	2,563	1,775	916	6,884
Incoming Direct Investment	3,393	4,366	27,515	35,849	44,237	38,753	38,399	44,241

SOURCE: International Monetary Fund, International Financial Statistics 2003.

all located in south coastal China, near the overseas Chinese communities in Macao, Hong Kong, and Taiwan. Three SEZs were placed in Guangdong Province (Shenzhen, Zhuhai, and Shantou) and one (Xiamen) in Fujian. Subsequently Pudong across the river from Shanghai was added in 1990. The State Council also sanctioned the creation of 15 **economic and technological development zones (ETDZs)** and 34 **high-technology development zones (HTDZS).** The common feature of all of these zones is considerable relief from central government taxation. The rate of tax on profits of enterprises located in the zones is 15 percent as opposed to the 55 percent prevailing in non-SEZs at the time of their inception. The four original SEZs plus Pudong also offer two-year tax holidays. Local governments, anxious to raise the pace of economic development, introduced their own zones with varying levels of relief from local taxes, which numbered an estimated 9,000 zones by the end of 1992.

Many economists remain skeptical about the role of tax concessions applied to limited geographical areas. It can be argued that such provisions make for additional distortions in an economy that is already far from providing a level playing field. Unless such provisions are intended to correct known market failures, the effect may be counterproductive in terms of aggregate welfare. The concern, therefore, is that the incentives granted in such zones only serve to move activity from one place to another, and the elasticity of aggregate investment and employment with respect to the tax reductions is low. In such a case, the government is certain to experience a loss of tax revenue, which may be uncompensated by positive economic effects.

An economic logic may justify the provision of such zones, however.

1. In the case of a region dependent on a declining industry, concessional treatment might attract investment that would secure employment and prevent the waste of already committed social investment.
2. Economies of scale may come in the provision of infrastructure and services, and incentives designed to increase the density of industrial activity may be rational.
3. External economies of agglomeration may take the form of spillover and pool effects. For example, one of the frequently cited reasons for technology parks

is the high degree of knowledge spillover; in other industries labor pool effects may be important.

4. The government may wish to restrict some activities and policies to a limited geographical area for environmental reasons or, in the special case of China, to limit their impact in order to analyze their effects before generalizing the policies.

The first reason is not relevant in the case of the Chinese special economic zones. Both the second and third statements are cited as rationales and perhaps played a role. However, it is probable that the most important reason is the fourth. The State Council and national planning authorities used the economic zones as laboratories in which the efficacy and consequences of certain policy shifts could be gauged. All of the important reforms concerning foreign exchange, foreign direct investment, state-owned enterprise organization, labor markets, and the use of joint-stock companies with tradable equity capital were pioneered in the enterprise zones.

Only those successful reforms, and that the decision-making apparatus of the state believes it can manage and control, have been allowed to mature and spread. This experimentation and groping forward contributed an essential part of the Chinese reform strategy discussed later.

REGIONAL INEQUALITY AND NATIONAL UNITY

One disturbing feature of China's growth is the dramatic increase in the disparity of income in recent years. Moreover, the regional income differential is worsening and will be aggravated further by the terms of China's accession into the World Trade Organization. At present the provinces of the eastern seaboard (particularly Guangdong, close to Hong Kong, and Zhejiang, around Shanghai) have average incomes that are four to five times greater than the national average as measured in official exchange rate terms. This difference is now about $900 per year, although much better at almost $4,000 in purchasing power terms.

Hong Kong, absorbed into the People's Republic in 1997, is one of the wealthiest areas in the world; its per-head income at the time of the reunion was roughly $25,000. The provinces of the interior all have incomes per head less than the national average, and some are below 50 percent of that figure. Accession to the WTO will, according a recent report from the OECD, effectively stimulate the export-oriented eastern seaboard while harming the predominantly agricultural west, which will be battered by an influx of cheap foreign grain. Hence the disparities will become worse. Economic theory suggests some form of convergence will occur over time. All other things being equal, investment should increasingly seek out the low-wage provinces and hence lead to a growth of industrial employment and income. However, experience in many areas (Italy, Germany, Brazil) suggest that this convergence is not inevitable. Externalities are important and growing industries tend to be attracted to growing areas, where infrastructure, education, and transportation opportunities are favorable. Although migration from the interior might also provide some equalizing effect, the overall prognosis is one of worsening disparities and consequent political pressures. The important question is whether this disparity will affect the political unity of China. The policy alternatives are not attractive; "benign neglect" will see the position worsen, and discontent might become unmanageable. On the other hand, redistributive schemes to favor the less well-off provinces would require an increase in taxation in the prosperous eastern areas. That move would certainly be unpopular with the rich and would by no means be certain to promote growth in the interior.

SOURCE: OECD, *China in the World Economy: An OECD Economic and Statistical Survey*.

THE IMPORTANCE OF A "KINDRED MODEL"

Despite the poverty of the country and the limitations of its resource base, China enjoyed in its transformation an asset that most countries can only experience in a much lesser degree: assistance and example from a **"kindred model"** in populations abroad. The *tongbao* (which literally means "same womb") populations of Hong Kong, Macao, and increasingly (at least until the decline in relations in early 1996) Taiwan, play an important role in Chinese growth. Singapore, geographically and culturally more remote but with an affluent population, expensive labor, and surplus capital, also played a part.

Although these communities include small populations in relation to the People's Republic (about 1/40 combined), their role is important on several dimensions:

1. *A demonstration effect.* These communities provided a demonstration that Chinese people can transform their economic circumstances in a relatively short period of time, given favorable policies. The standard of living enjoyed in Taiwan and Hong Kong is an assurance to many Chinese that economic transformation is feasible. This tends to promote both personal saving and investment as a response to confidence in the future.
2. *Trading partner.* The overseas communities have provided an important trading partner for China. This is especially true of Hong Kong, whose prime function is to serve as an entrepôt for the mainland. Over 40 percent of China's exports are routed through Hong Kong, and although the opening of other city ports will reduce this share, the proximity of Hong Kong to the rapidly growing areas is highly significant.
3. *Investor.* Overseas Chinese communities account for the larger part of incoming direct foreign investment into China. Hong Kong alone accounts for over 50 percent, and Taiwan is growing as a source as its economy experiences rapidly increasing labor costs.
4. *Sources of information.* In the early stages of transformation of a socialist economy, information about technologies and markets is at a premium. Residents of the overseas communities do much to provide China with a window on the world: over 95 percent of visitors to China are people of Chinese ethnicity.

THE CHARACTER OF CHINESE REFORM

Chinese reform differs in form and in consequence from the approach taken in the Central and Eastern European Economies (CEEEs). At the moment, many observers see the Chinese model as superior. The most obvious point in China's favor is that it avoided the sharp contraction of output, surging inflation, and elevated unemployment that characterized transition in all of the CEEEs.[10] In sharp

[10]See Blanchard, "Theoretical Aspects of Transition," *American Economic Review,* May 1996, p. 117, for evidence on the similarity of the post-Soviet transitions.

contrast to Eastern Europe, Chinese growth accelerated with the onset of reform. Employment grew and unemployment fell despite the fact that China experienced a much higher population growth rate than that of Russia or the other CEEEs.

Certainly much of the difference in macroeconomic performance was due to the fact that reforms were less sweeping in China than in the CEEEs, but part is a function of differing states of development. The Central and Eastern European Economies are industrial economies. Markets that had been guaranteed under domestic planning or trade arrangements overseen by the Council for Mutual Economic Assistance (CMEA, otherwise known as COMECON) disappeared. Suppliers became reluctant to sell at old prices and demanded hard currency payments, creating a disarticulation in the system. A macroeconomic contraction and unemployment resulted. Prices were adjusted to world levels with inflation as the consequence. Because planned international trade was less important to China than to the Eastern European countries, this disruption resulted in fewer macroeconomic consequences.

Agriculture in China was a much more dominant part of the economy in the pre-reform period. The economy was less dependent on a complex set of markets and suppliers. Moreover, the Chinese experienced and adjusted to great disorganization in both the Great Leap Forward and the Proletarian Cultural Revolution. That said, we turn now to examine some of the distinctive characteristics of the Chinese reform experience.

Gradualism

One difference in reform strategy—that of **gradualism**—can be highlighted by the use of a metaphor. Vaclav Havel, the playwright who became president of the Czech Republic during its transition to a market economy, once characterized the CEEE approach to reform by stating that it is impossible to "cross a chasm in two leaps." The Chinese approach, on the other hand, can be summarized by stating that China is "touching stones to cross a river." In other words, China proceeded on its own path by a process of experimentation, moving forward slowly only in areas where policies had been tested and seen to work. So far, it must be said, this approach proved a more successful policy than revolutionary reform, or an economic "big bang."

Partial Reform

China has not been averse to creating situations in which reform is incomplete. The clearest of these areas lies in the contract responsibility systems, which resulted in a two-tier price system for agricultural and industrial goods. Such systems of **partial reform** offer the advantage of keeping with the gradualist approach to reform, and they also provide substantial incentives to the relevant economic actors. Marginal economic allocation decisions are made in response to market prices, which lead to a beneficial impact on overall economic efficiency. However, as noted earlier, two-tier prices provide considerable returns to arbitrage from the state to the market system, and that engenders corruption.

Decentralization

Chinese reform has been accompanied by a weakening of central control over the constituent parts of the economy. **Decentralization** is not an uncommon feature; a parallel can be seen in the breakup of the Soviet Union and in the fissiparous tendencies currently in evidence in Russia itself as ethnically differentiated areas, such as Chechnya, attempt to break away. In China the outcome of devolution has been positive, allowing the provincial authorities to be flexible and pragmatic. Some observers are concerned that this trend will end in the demise of China as a centralized state, torn apart by growing income inequality, increased provincial chauvinism, and a weakened center inadequately supported by a national fiscal system.

Accommodating Spontaneous Reform

Even though it might appear from the outside that the entire process has been one of rational experimentation, in reality Chinese reform has been characterized by a willingness to allow **spontaneous reform**. In part, a weakening control of the State Council, discussed earlier, leaves it with little alternative but to acquiesce, and reform legislation takes on the character of making virtue of necessity.

Economic Liberalization without Political Democratization

The main point of difference between change in Central and Eastern Europe and China is the relative pace of political and economic reform. In the former Soviet Union and Eastern Europe, political reform occurred rapidly and ran ahead of economic reform, feeding expectations with respect to economic progress, which were subsequently disappointed. In China the reverse happened. Economic freedom evolved much more rapidly than the political variant. A correspondingly greater social stability and suppression of dissent, it can be argued, has provided for a solid platform for growth and incoming direct foreign investments. Western nations might like the idea of democracy, but their entrepreneurs are more prone to invest in predictable authoritarian states.

DID REFORMS ACCELERATE GROWTH?

In most people's minds, the rapid growth of the Chinese economy during the 1980s and 1990s was caused by the reforms that began in 1978. However, in evaluating the success of any change in economic policy, it is important to establish a counterfactual: What would have occurred in the absence of the policy shift? It is certainly true that after 1978 we witnessed substantial improvement in just about every economic indicator. It is also true that the rates of improvement of these indicators are better than in the pre-reform period of 1953–1978, as clearly seen in the first and second columns in Table 23.3. Output rose faster in both aggregate and per capita terms, and labor productivity grew more quickly. Although the labor force grew at

■ TABLE 23.3

Decomposition of Chinese Economic Growth, 1953–1990, (average annual growth rates)

	1953–1978	1979–1994	1953–1978 (excl. 1959–1970)
Output	5.9	9.2	7.6
Output per head of population	3.8	7.5	5.4
Output per worker	3.1	6.3	4.5
Ratio of investment to net material product	19.9	24.8	21.7
Capital	10.2	9.9	13.2
Labor	2.6	2.7	3
Total factor productivity	20.7	3.8	20.8

SOURCE: Eduardo Borensztein and Jonathan Ostry, "Accounting for China's Growth Performance," *American Economic Review,* May 1996, p. 225.

about the same rate, capital growth was actually marginally slower than in the pre-reform era.

However, some authors draw attention to the fact that a comparison of these periods may be biased, because the 1953–1978 period included the major disturbances caused by the Great Leap Forward and the Cultural Revolution. In these periods, the socialist-planned Chinese economy did not operate normally, but were rather periods of great political upheaval akin almost to a civil war. The appropriate comparison might well be to view the performance post-1978 against the "normal" years of socialist planning. By excluding the period 1959–1970, the substantial dips in output occasioned by the two political convulsions are eliminated. Now, a comparison can be made of the post-reform era with the "normal" period of socialist economics—the third column in Table 23.3 versus the second column. The contrast is by no means as pronounced, although growth of output and labor productivity growth were superior after the reform.

From the table we can see evidence of a difference in the type of economic growth between the two periods. The pre-reform period was characterized by the extensive growth that we often see in socialist systems. The labor force increased rapidly (by 3 percent annually) and capital accumulation was high (13.2 percent annually). The growth of output is wholly accounted for by the growth of inputs; in this case we note that total factor productivity is negative, indicating a loss of aggregate efficiency.

In the post-reform era, labor force and capital growth are slower than in the pre-reform era, yet output grows more quickly. The key here is the growth in total factor productivity, which moves ahead at a respectable 3.8 percent per year in the post-reform period. Total factor productivity (TFP) is calculated as a residual and its main components are static efficiency gains from moving workers from low marginal product occupations to higher ones and dynamic gains due to ongoing technical progress. By the rapid growth of TFP we can see that reforms did achieve something, but the unanswered question is whether the gains were static or dynamic.

CAN GROWTH BE SUSTAINED?

It is tempting to believe that the Chinese economy transitioned into a "take-off into self-sustaining growth," momentous though such an assumption would be. As we noted at the beginning of this chapter, extrapolation of current growth trends of the 1990s implies that the Chinese economy would be larger in terms of GDP than that of the United States in the first half of this century.

The sustainability of the growth rate depends to a large extent on whether total factor productivity continues to improve and to what extent this improvement may be attributable to an increase in technical efficiency. To this point it is probable that the greatest contribution to TFP change has been the result of the following factors:

1. An increase in productivity in the agricultural sector due to the introduction of greater material incentives
2. The movement of workers from low productivity (perhaps even zero marginal productivity) agricultural occupations to work in industry and services
3. An increase in the human capital invested in the workforce

In addition to these factors, statistical irregularities must be accounted for. The main one is "underdeflation" of industrial output—that is, the use of a price index for industrial output that increases less quickly than the "true" rate of inflation, which leads to an overstatement of real industrial output. A second area is the inclusion of essentially unsalable inventories in the SOE sector as part of output at inflated prices. When these factors are corrected for, the rate of growth of TFP seems to be much smaller, and may even be negative, as it was during the socialist planned period. At present, plentiful labor in China means growth can continue through the redeployment of low productivity rural labor into the industrial sector, as long as the demand for China's industrial output continues to grow. When the potential for increasing output by redeploying agricultural labor becomes exhausted, the rate of growth of GDP will inevitably slow, and unless the rate of growth due to technical innovation increases, it will be largely dependent on the rate of growth of the capital stock.

CHINA AND THE WORLD TRADE ORGANIZATION (WTO)

In November 1999 China took a remarkable step forward by committing itself to membership in the WTO. It finally achieved accession in December 2001. This shift toward a more open economy will put severe strains on the economy in the short run but will lead to a much truer market system in the long run. As a precursor to applying for membership in the World Trade Organization, China concluded a bilateral deal with the United States establishing a timetable for the dismantling of much of China's tariff and quota walls. With the task of reforming the inefficient state-owned enterprises barely begun, and with China already experiencing the socially divisive consequences of rising unemployment, this move is certainly a gamble.

Agriculture will be sharply affected by membership.[11] Tariffs on wheat and maize will fall by the year 2004 to just 14.5 percent, not enough to protect most of China's farmers from more efficient U.S. producers, exacerbating the problem of rural unemployment. As we saw, the TVEs are actually shrinking in their manpower needs and no longer serve the role of employing surplus agricultural labor. The impact of the WTO liberalization will be to cut agricultural employment and increase rural joblessness. Unemployment and underemployment will rise, in turn aggravating the problem of the regional differences in income and putting a strain on the Chinese political structure.

Manufacturing tariffs are set to tumble as well. In automobiles, for example, the tariff will fall from 100 percent to 25 percent, a shift that will put most of China's many vehicle makers at risk, although foreign manufacturers are likely to be fast in establishing or expanding production in China. Joint ventures are to be sanctioned in telecommunications, which will expose the state-owned telephone dinosaurs to the best of foreign technology.

However, the biggest sectoral impact may well be in banking and finance. Foreign banks will be largely freed of restrictions and will be able to operate throughout China. The inefficient and poorly financed state banks will be forced to compete for funds and loans. These banks are already crippled by the burden of nonperforming loans, and the competition for deposits will certainly raise their borrowing cost. A banking crisis is likely. The most economically logical result will be the failure of some of the Big Four banks and their takeover by foreign, probably American, concerns. Whether this scenario can be palatable to the political leadership remains to be seen. It would imply relinquishing control of the credit allocation process, a step that a nominal socialist country might still be unwilling to take.

CHINA IN THE TWENTY-FIRST CENTURY

At the 16th Communist Party Congress held in Beijing in November 2002, President Jiang Zemin passed the torch of leadership, the general secretaryship of the Community party, to his vice president Hu Jintao, while still retaining the powerful position of commander in chief of the armed forces. It is clear that Jiang intends to hang onto a good a deal of policy-making power well into the future. The transition is likely to be far from smooth, and political uncertainty could be part of Jiang's legacy. The Congress also approve Jiang's theory of the **"Three Represents,"** an ideological innovation that claims that the Communist Party represents the workers and the peasant (the traditional "two represents") as well as now extending its umbrella to the capitalist class. This definition allows China's growing body of private entrepreneurs to join the party.

Uncertainty in the political situation is matched by the specter of economic problems. On the surface, things are good; growth continues at a robust 7 to 8 percent

[11]OECD, China in The World Economy: Agricultural Policies in China after WTO Accession, Paris: OECD. 2002.

annually. However, even this pace is inadequate to absorb the growing number of unemployed. China needs to create about 8 million jobs per year merely to stop the unemployment situation from worsening, and 7 percent yearly growth is not enough to generate this level of job creation. The unemployment crisis emerged from two sources. First, excess labor in the countryside cannot be absorbed by rural industrial growth. This problem will become more serious as agricultural tariffs fall as a result of WTO membership. The other source is the state-owned enterprise sector, which as a result of attrition, bankruptcy, and restructuring, needs to reduce its workforce by about 20 million workers in the next five years. Even though the rapid growth of exports (currently 15 percent annually) is likely to continue, it is unlikely to provide enough jobs. Any slowing of GDP or export growth could cause a serious increase in unemployment. China's spectacular rate of growth means some of its citizens now enjoy "first world" living standards, but a large part of its population still lives in poverty. It is the paradox that the political leadership must resolve in the twenty-first century.

KEY TERMS AND CONCEPTS

asset management companies (AMCs)
contract responsibility system (CRS)
convergence
credit plan
decentralization
economic and technological development zones (ETDZs)
fiscal contract responsibility system (FCRS)
foreign-financed enterprises (FFEs)
gradualism
gang of four
Great Leap Forward
hard-budget constraint
high-technology development zones (HTDZs)
horizontal equity
household responsibility system (HRS)
"kindred model"
nonperforming loans (NPLs)
partial reform
policy loans
Proletarian Cultural Revolution
regional income disparity
special economic zones (SEZs)
state-owned enterprises (SOEs)
spontaneous reform
"Three Represents"
township and village enterprises

QUESTIONS FOR DISCUSSION

1. Why was Soviet-style planning hard to apply in China?
2. How did the Great Leap Forward and the Cultural Revolution harm economic development?

3. How did allowing agricultural reform lead to the rapid expansion of light industry?
4. Why have township and village enterprises been so successful?
5. What attempts were made to reform state-owned enterprise, and how successful were they?
6. What role did the special economic zones play in Chinese development?
7. What role did Chinese overseas communities play in the development of China?
8. Discuss the metaphor of "crossing the river by touching the stones" with respect to reform in China.
9. Why is opening the financial sector to competition, agreed to in the deal with the United States in November 1999, so important for the development of a market economy in China?
10. What are nonperforming loans? Why do they threaten China's future?
11. What, if anything, prevents income convergence of China's provinces? How does this threaten unity and growth?

RESOURCES

Web Sites

People's Bank of China (Central Bank) .... http://www.pbc.gov.cn/

Ministry of Foreign Trade and Economic Cooperation http://www1.moftec.gov.cn/

People's Daily .... http://english.peopledaily.com.cn/

China News Services and China News Agency .... http://www.chinanews.com.cn/

China Online .... http://www.chinaonline.com/

National Bureau of Statistics of China .... http://www.stats.gov.cn

Books and Articles

Bell, Michael W., Hoe Ee Khor, and Kalpana Kochhar. *China at the Threshold of a Market Economy.* International Monetary Fund Occasional Paper 107. Washington, DC: International Monetary Fund, September 1993.

Blejer, Mario. "China: Prolonged Reforms and the Weakening of Fiscal Control." In *Transition to Market,* Mario Tanzi (ed.). Washington, DC: International Monetary Fund, 1993. 253–269.

Blejer, Mario, David Burton, Steven Dunaway, and Gyorgy Szapary. *China: Economic Reform and Macroeconomic Management.* Washington, DC: International Monetary Fund, January 1991.

Borensztein, Eduardo, and Jonathan D. Ostry. "Accounting for China's Growth." *American Economic Review,* May 1996, 224.

Cardoso, Eliana and Shahid Yusuf. "Red Capitalism: Growth and Inflation in China." *Challenge,* May/June 1994, 49–57.

Chen, Aimin. "Chinese Industrial Structure in Transition: The Emergence of Stock-Offering Firms." *Comparative Economic Studies,* Winter 1994, 1–19.

Chen, Kang, Gary H. Jefferson, and Inderjit Singh. "Lessons from China's Economic Reform." In *Comparative Economic Systems,* 7th ed., Morris Bornstein (ed.). Burr Ridge, IL: Irwin, 1994.

"China's Coastal Development (The Great International Cycle) and Decentralized Management of the Economy." *Chinese Economic Studies,* Fall/Winter 1991–1992.

Chow, Gregory C. *Chinese Economy,* 2d ed. River Edge, NJ: World Scientific Publishing, 1987.

Fulton, Trish, Jinyan Li, and Dianqing Xu (eds.) *China's Tax Reform Options.* River Edge, NJ: World Scientific Publishing, 1998.

Gao, Shangquan. *Two Decades of Reform in China.* Washington, DC: World Bank, 1999.

Ge, Wei. *Special Economic Zones and the Economic Transition in China.* River Edge, NJ: World Scientific Publishing, 1999.

Hsu, Dave Y. C. "Experience and Lessons of China's Agricultural Development." *Journal of Contemporary Asia* 20, no. 2 (1990), 212–223.

Hu, Yaoxing. "Market-Oriented Reforms in China." *Development Policy Review* 11, no. 2 (June 1993), 195–204.

Huang, Yasheng. "Information, Bureaucracy, and Economic Reforms in China and the Soviet Union." *World Politics,* October 1994, 102–34.

Itoh, Fumio. *China in the Twenty-First Century: Politics, Economy, and Society.* New York: United Nations Publications, 1997.

Jefferson, Gary, and Inderjit Singh (eds.). *Enterprise Reform in China: Ownership, Transition, and Performance.* Oxford: Oxford University Press, 1998.

Koo, Anthony Y. C. "The Contract Responsibility System: Transition from a Planned to a Market Economy: Government and Enterprise in the Reform Process." *Economic Development and Cultural Change,* July 1990, 797–820.

Kung, James Kaising. "Egalitarianism, Subsistence Provision, and Work Incentives in China's Agricultural Collectives." *World Development 1994,* 175–187.

Lardy, Nicholas R. *Integrating China into The World Economy,* Washington DC: Brookings, 2002.

Lichenstein, Peter M. *China at the Brink: The Political Economy of Reform and Retrenchment in the Post-Mao Era.* New York: Praeger, 1991. Reviewed in *Studies in Comparative International Development* 28, no. 3 (Fall 1993), 98–10.

Lieberthal, Kenneth G., and David M. Lampton (eds.). *Bureaucracy, Politics, and Decision Making in Post-Mao China.* Berkeley: California University Press, 1992.

Liren, Shen, and Dai Yuanchen. "Formation of 'Dukedom Economies' and Their Causes and Defects." *Chinese Economic Studies,* Summer 1992, 6–34.

Mei, Zhu. "Non-agricultural Industrial Development in Chinese Rural Areas." *Development Policy Review* 11, no. 4 (December 1993), 383–392.

Naughton, Barry (ed.). *The China Circle: Economics and Electronics in the PRC, Taiwan, and Hong Kong*. Washington, DC: Brookings Institution Press, 1997.

Nolan, Peter. "The China Puzzle: Touching Stones to Cross the River." *Challenge*, January/February 1994, 25–31.

OECD. *China in the World Economy: An OECD Economic and Statistical Survey*. Paris: Organization for Economic Co-operation and Development, 2003.

OECD. *China in The World Economy: Agricultural Policies in China after WTO Accession*, Paris: OECD, 2002.

Park, Albert. *Trade Integration and the Prospects for Rural Enterprise Development in China*, Paris: OECD, 2002.

Pomeranz, Kenneth. *The Great Divergence: China, Europe and the Making of the World Economy*, Princeton, NJ: Princeton University Press, 2002.

Pomponio C. J. "A Tiger by the Tail: Chinese Agrarian Reform." *Journal of Contemporary Asia* 21, no. 3 (1991), 379–395.

Sachs, Jeffrey D., and Wing Thye Woo. *Understanding China's Economic Performance*, Working Paper Series, Working Paper 5935. Cambridge, MA: National Bureau of Economic Research, 1997.

"Survey: China: When China Wakes." *The Economist*, November 23, 1992.

"Survey: China: Ready to Face the World?" *The Economist*, March 8, 1997.

"Survey: China, A Dragon Out of Puff," *The Economist*, June 13, 2002.

Tseng, Wanda, Hoe Ee Khor, Kalpana Kochhar, Dubravko Mihaljek, and David Burton. *Economic Reform in China: A New Phase*. Washington, DC: International Monetary Fund, November 1994.

Wall, David. "China's Economic Reform and Opening-Up Process: The Role of the Special Economic Zones." *Development Policy Review* 11, no. 3 (September 1993), 243–260.

Wang, Gungwu, and John Wong (eds.). *China's Political Economy*. River Edge, NJ: World Scientific Publications, 1998.

Wang, Hsiao-Chiang. *China's Price and Enterprise Reform (Studies on the Chinese Economy)*. New York: St. Martin's Press, 1998.

Weidenbaum, Murray, with Samuel Hughes (contributor). *The Bamboo Network: How Expatriate Chinese Entrepreneurs Are Creating a New Economic Superpower in Asia*. New York: Martin Kessler Books, 1996.

Wen, G., and D. Xu. *The Reformability of China's State Sector*. River Edge, NJ: World Scientific Publishing, 1997.

Woetzel, Jonathan R. *China's Economic Opening to the Outside World: The Politics of Empowerment*. New York: Praeger, 1989.

World Bank. "Chinese Economic Reform Experience." In *Comparative Economic Systems*, 7th ed. Morris Bornstein (ed.). Burr Ridge, IL: Irwin, 1994.

Xiaoqiang, Wang, and Bai Nanfeng. *The Poverty of Plenty*. New York: St. Martin's Press, 1991. Reviewed in *Studies in Comparative International Development* 28, no. 3 (Fall 1993), 98–104.

INDEX

Note: "key terms" are displayed in bold in main entries; page numbers followed by "n" refer to footnotes

CHAPTER 1

ECONOMIC SYSTEMS: CLASSIFICATION AND PERFORMANCE

All that Adam had, all that Caesar could, you have and can do. . . . Build, therefore, your own world.

—Ralph Waldo Emerson, *Nature*, 1836

Economics, we say, is all about making choices. The realities of life require each of us to make economic choices every day. Where shall I live and work? What goods and services will I produce and purchase? How much of my income will I spend and save?

Some of the most important economic choices must be made for entire societies. What, for example, should individuals be allowed to own? Should we be able to possess consumer goods, factories, farms, slaves, rivers, foreign currency, debt claims, patents for scientific discoveries and creative ideas (including, for example, the design of the human genome), trademarks, and songs? How should we establish, protect, and regulate these ownership rights? What kind of monetary system, if any, should we use? What economic functions should be performed by local and national governments, tribal councils, professional and labor organizations, educational and religious institutions, and the news media? What, in other words, should be the nature of our economic system?

In this introductory chapter we first explore the concept of an "economic system" and consider its role in the broader social system. Next, we survey the various criteria used to classify economic systems. Finally, we will discuss a few of the problems involved in comparisons of national economic performance.

The Economic System, the Environment, and Policies

Ultimately, what we really care about is **economic performance**. How can we provide comfortable and equitable standards of living, stable jobs and prices, decent housing and health care, clean air and water? Economic performance is influenced by a wide variety of factors, but, for the sake of simplicity, we combine them all into three categories—the economic system, the environment, and the policies and reforms that are undertaken by decision-makers (see Figure 1.1).[1] Let us briefly consider what is meant by each of these terms.

[1]Here, we follow the framework established by Tjalling Koopmans and John Michael Montias, "On the Description and Comparison of Economic Systems," in *Comparison of Economic Systems: Theoretical and Methodological Approaches,* ed. Alexander Eckstein (Berkeley: University of California Press, 1971), 27-38.

Figure 1.1

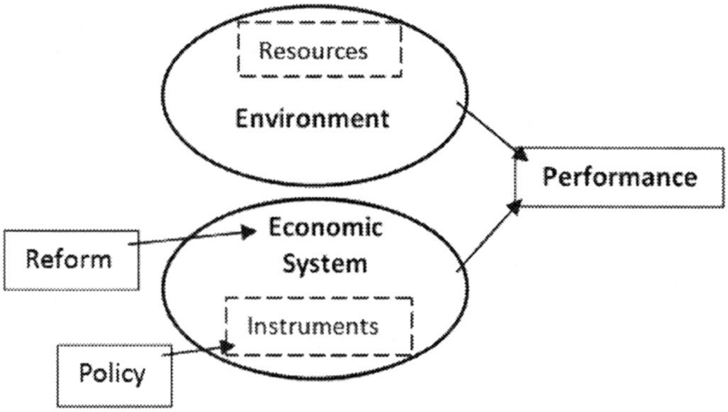

An **economic system** is an interactive set of institutions that constrain, facilitate, and coordinate the economic behaviors of a society.[2] An **institution** is an organization, practice, convention, or custom that is material and persistent in the life or culture of a society. The most familiar institutions are formal organizations, such as business corporations, labor unions, universities, and government agencies. Equally important, however, are long-lived practices, conventions, and customs that gain institutional status. These include, for example, the systems of monetary exchange, property rights, collective bargaining, racial and gender discrimination, bribery, charitable giving, and taxation. We may think of the economic system in any country as a unique network of these institutions.

---

[2]Our definition is closest to that of Gregory Grossman in *Economic Systems*, 2d ed. (Englewood Cliffs, N.J.: Prentice-Hall, 1974), 3. The notion that our behavior is *constrained* by systems and institutions is emphasized by Douglass North in "Institutions," *Journal of Economic Perspectives* 5 (Winter 1991): 97-112.

In their effort to improve economic performance, national leaders will enact economic **policies** and **reforms**. In most cases, a shift in policy can be undertaken without changing the economic system or its underlying institutions. This is done through the manipulation of policy **instruments**, which are, themselves, economic institutions. Suppose, for example, that the *policy* of the European Central Bank (ECB) is to slow the growth of the money supply. To that end, it may employ any of three *instruments*: an increase in open-market sales of securities, a reduction in its lending to commercial banks, or an increase in the reserve requirements of commercial banks. On the other hand, if the leaders of the ECB decide that the current institutional framework is hindering economic performance, they may support an economic *reform* that will fundamentally change the monetary system. They could, for example, propose a return to the classical gold standard (although this is highly unlikely), which would include a very different set of policy instruments.

We define the **environment** very broadly to include all of the factors that influence economic performance that are beyond the control of policy makers. For example, annual rainfall has a powerful impact on agricultural performance, but politicians have little control over the weather. In a similar way, national leaders cannot *quickly* change the geographic landscape, the endowment of natural resources, the educational level or cultural norms of society, the economic policies or performances of trading partners, or the behavior of military rivals or allies.

The distinction between policy variables and environmental variables is sometimes affected by the time period of analysis. For example, the educational level of the population is usually considered an environmental variable in short-run analysis, but it is an object of educational policy in longer-run analysis. Likewise, the weather is probably beyond our control in the short run, but we may have a policy to prevent climate change in the long run.

An important component of the environment in each country is its endowment of **natural resources**. In principle, a country with a rich endowment of oil, gas, gold, diamonds, agricultural land, and other resources should have an advantage over countries that are poorly endowed. Throughout its history, for example, the United States has gained enormous benefit from its fertile land, energy resources, and temperate climate. On the other hand, some countries, such as Japan, have been quite successful with relatively poor resource endowments, and others, such as Russia and several countries in Africa and the Middle East, have not performed as well as their resources would suggest. In fact, it appears that abundance of a resource such as oil or diamonds has sometimes encouraged political corruption, discouraged institutional reform, and interfered with diversification of production, yielding a condition known as the **"resource curse."**[3]

The distinctions between an economic system, environment, policies, and performance may be clarified with a simple analogy. An automobile is a system composed of several persistent mechanisms (institutions), each of which is designed to perform a particular task. The driver uses her steering wheel and other controls (instruments) to guide (set policy for) her car through changing road, weather, and traffic conditions (environment).

If an automobile performs badly, this may be the result of a deficiency in the car itself, or it may be caused by a hostile environment or an unskilled driver. Likewise, poor performance of an economy does not necessarily indicate a failure of the economic system.

An individual's decision to purchase a particular model of car may be influenced by many considerations, including the kind of performance desired (rapid speed, fuel economy, safety, etc.), by the environment in which the car will be driven (an air conditioner and a large radiator

---

[3] For example, see Antonio Cabrales and Esther Hauk, "The Quality of Political Institutions and the Curse of Natural Resources," *Economic Journal*, 121 (March, 2011):58–88.

may be preferable in a hot climate), and by the skills of the driver (such as the ability to operate a standard transmission). Similarly, we would expect each country to select a unique economic system, based on its cultural preferences, historical legacies, natural resources, and the skills of its policy makers.

Forms of Business Enterprise

In any economic system, some of the most important institutions are the business enterprises that produce goods and services. These can take an enormous number of legal and organizational forms, influenced by a wide range of historical, economic, social, political, legal, and ideological factors. Here, we will review only a few of the major forms of business enterprise.

The simplest and most common form of business organization in many countries is the **sole proprietorship** (or **sole trader** in the U.K.), a firm with a single owner who reaps its rewards and is personally liable for its debts and other obligations. Typically, proprietorships are small family businesses, but some of them have hundreds of employees. In the United States, more than 70 percent of non-agricultural businesses are sole proprietorships, but they account for only 5 percent of total business receipts.[4]

A **partnership** is similar to a proprietorship, but has two or more owners. The owners always include one or more *general partners,* who participate fully in the investment, management, income, and liabilities of the firm, and they may also include one or more *limited*

[4] U.S. Internal Revenue Service, "Table 743. Number of Returns, Receipts, and Net Income by Type of Business: 1990 to 2007." *Statistical Abstract of the United States: 2011.* U.S. Census Bureau. Washington, D.C.: U.S. Census Bureau, 2011.

Table 1.1 Forms of Business Enterprise

	Ownership and Control	Corporate Legal Entity	Liability of Owners	Lifespan
Sole Proprietorship	Single person	No	Unlimited	Limited to owner
Limited Liability Company/ Partnership	One or more members	No	Limited	Limited to Owners
Partnership	General partners	No	Unlimited for general partners	Usually Limited to Owners
Private Corporation; Private Limited Company	Stockholders or Members (closed circle)	Yes	Limited to investment	Perpetual
Public Corporation; Public Limited Company	Stockholders (traded on exchanges)	Yes	Limited to investment	Perpetual
Non-Profit Organization; Charity; Non-Governmental Organization	Controlled by Board, elected by stake-holders or self-appointed	Usually	Limited	Perpetual
Government-Owned Enterprise; State-Owned Enterprise; Public Enterprise	Government (majority) and perhaps Stockholders	Yes	Limited to investment	Perpetual
Producer Cooperative	Employee-Members with voting rights	No	Usually Limited to investment	Perpetual
Commune	Members	Seldom	Unlimited	Perpetual

partners, who provide capital and share in the firm's income, but have **limited liability** (their liability for repayment of debt is limited to their investment contribution). A **general partnership** is a firm owned entirely by general partners. A **limited partnership** is a firm owned by a mixture of general and limited partners.

Similar to a limited partnership, a **limited liability company (LLC)** or **limited liability partnership (LLP)** is owned by "members," all of whom have limited liability. The LLC or LLP may be managed directly by its members, or it may be run by a manager who is elected or appointed by the members.

Sole proprietorships, partnerships, and LLCs/LLPs are relatively simple to create and sometimes have tax advantages, but they share a common weakness. These companies are not legal entities, so they cannot own assets, participate in legal proceedings, or sustain existence separately from their owners. Accordingly, they often find it difficult to attract the large investments needed for growth and development. This is the special strength of the **corporation**, which is a legal entity with a perpetual life, owned by stockholders who have the protection of limited liability. In large corporations, the interests of stockholders are represented (in principle, if not always in action) by an elected board of directors, and everyday operation is handled by a team of professional managers.

Corporations can take many forms, but it is particularly important to distinguish between **private corporations**[5], which are owned by relatively small and exclusive groups of stockholders, and **public corporations**[6], which are owned by larger numbers of stockholders who can trade their shares on open markets. Public corporations have broader access to equity markets, but they generally are subject to stricter rules of governance and financial reporting. Most of the world's largest companies, including Wal-Mart, Royal Dutch Shell, and Toyota, are public corporations. Private corporations are far more numerous than public corporations, and their average size is much smaller. Still, some private corporations, such as IKEA, Credit Suisse, LEGO, Mars, and Cargill, are enormous.

---

[5] Also known as "closely-held corporations" in some countries or "private limited companies," bearing the title, "Ltd," in the U.K.

[6] Also known as "publicly-traded corporations" in some countries or "public limited companies," bearing the title, "PLC," in the U.K.

Standing at the boundary between the private and public/social sectors, we find a group of enterprises that are privately financed, but are dedicated to a "public purpose." These are variously known as **charities, not-for-profit organizations (NFPOs), non-governmental organizations (NGOs), private voluntary organizations (PVOs), and civil society organizations (CSOs)**. Like other private firms, they benefit from flexible and independent management, but they have the additional benefit of preferential tax treatment. On the negative side, many of these organizations are financially unstable because they depend on voluntary contributions for a significant part of their financial support.

A variety of organizations fit into this category, ranging from private hospitals and universities to multinational charities, such as Greenpeace, Red Cross, and Red Crescent. With a staff of more than 120,000 people, one of the largest NGOs is BRAC, an agency based in Bangladesh that supports programs of microfinance, literacy, and public health.

The variety of enterprise structures in the private sector is matched by a similar variety in the social sector. In fact, many of the sharpest disagreements among socialists have centered around the relative merits of different forms of socialist enterprise. A **commune**, for example, is a group of people who share in living arrangements, ownership of property, and distribution of income, and cooperate in their work and other responsibilities. This may be a small group of friends, a larger group of monks or nuns living in a religious order, a community of about 400 people living in a traditional Israeli kibbutz, or, before they were dissolved in 1982, a group of about 5,000 families pooling their resources in a Chinese rural commune.

Somewhat loser in its collectivism, the members of a **producer cooperative** typically do not live together, but share in the ownership and income of the enterprise, cooperating in its work and management. While cooperatives are considered to be a form of social enterprise, they can be quite similar in practice to partnerships and other employee-owned enterprises (such as those with employee-stock-ownership plans), which usually are considered part of the private sector.

State-owned or public enterprises were most common in the Soviet Union and other centrally-planned economies. In some of those countries, such as Belarus and Turkmenistan, state ownership continues to be pervasive, and it also plays an important role in the national oil companies of the Middle East.

A rich vocabulary has developed to describe the passage of an enterprise from one category to another.

- **Incorporation**—Conversion of a proprietorship or partnership into a corporation.
- **Initial Public Offering (IPO)**; **"Going Public"**—Conversion of a private corporation to a public corporation.
- **Leveraged Buy-Out**—The use of debt (often by a private equity company) to acquire a controlling interest of a corporation, often converting it from a public corporation back to a privately-held corporation.
- **Nationalization**—Conversion of a private company into a state-owned company
- **Expropriation**—Nationalization without payment of compensation to the private owner.
- **Privatization**—Conversion of a state-owned company to private ownership.

Speaking very broadly, during the period between World War II and 1980, the general trends were toward incorporation, completion of public offerings, and, in some places, nationalization of industry. Since the 1980s, global trends have turned toward privatization, leveraged buyouts, and the growing influence of private equity companies such as TPG Capital, Goldman Sachs Managed Capital, the Carlyle Group, Kohlberg Kravis Roberts (KKR), and the Blackstone Group. These five companies alone raised a total of $215 billion for their activities during 2006-2010.[7]

Modes of Classification

We cannot analyze all of the countries in the world in a single book. Instead, we will begin in this chapter by formulating a broad conceptual basis for classification and analysis of economic systems. In later chapters, we will use this scheme to analyze the evolution and operation of economies in major regions and representative countries of the world.

We can classify economic systems in many different ways. Just as we can classify people according to their height, weight, sex, age, nationality, political philosophy, or temperament, we can classify economic systems according to a wide range of overlapping criteria. Furthermore, the economic systems of actual countries are never purely capitalist or socialist, market or planned, free or controlled. Real countries have mixed institutional structures that change from year to year through evolution and revolution.

Nevertheless, for a period of time, the actual economic system in a particular country may roughly approximate one of the pure, idealized, theoretical economic systems, and may provide some indication of the relative merit of that theoretical system. Conversely, an economic theory based on an idealized economic system (such as the theory of perfect competition) may

[7] Private Equity International ranking of the world's largest private equity firms, 2011. Accessed on August 8, 2011 at http://www.peimedia.com/pei300 .

contribute to our understanding of the operation of actual economic systems. We should always remember, however, that theory is theory, and reality is reality.

Classification According to Ownership

The economic and political power structure of a society is largely a reflection of its systems of ownership and property rights. Thus, the most durable classification of economic systems, dating back to Karl Marx and beyond, distinguishes between economies according to the predominant form of ownership of the factories, farms, and other productive assets. Accordingly, **feudalism** is an economic and social system wherein all ownership rights are ultimately held by a queen, king, or other monarch, and are delegated down through a hierarchy of princes, dukes, barons, and serfs, subject to their loyalty, payment of tribute, and military and civil service. In a **capitalist** system, the greater part of the means of production is owned outright (not subject to feudal obligations) by private individuals, and in **socialism** most of the means of production are owned "socially."

In practice, it is sometimes difficult to distinguish between these different forms of ownership. What do we mean, after all, when we say that we "own" property? We may mean that we have any or all of the following: (1) the right to control how the property will be used; (2) the right to retain income generated by the property; and (3) the right to transfer ownership of the property to others. Even in countries with traditions of free-enterprise capitalism, individual property rights are limited by zoning and inheritance laws, environmental and safety regulations, and other legal and social restrictions. On the other hand, even the most repressive societies usually make some formal or informal allowance for individual ownership.

As we noted in the previous section, private and social ownership can take many different forms. A capitalist enterprise may be owned by a sole proprietor, by a group of partners, or by a group of corporate shareholders. A socialist enterprise may be owned by the national government, by a local commune, or by a cooperative of producers or consumers.[8] In practice, the distinctions between these different forms of ownership can be quite subtle; for example, a "capitalist" partnership may be functionally similar to a "socialist" producer cooperative.

We distinguish between economic systems in terms of the "predominant" form of ownership because very few societies have ever been purely capitalist or socialist. In the high-income capitalist world, publicly owned enterprises account for a share of gross investment that ranges from about 4 percent in the United States and the United Kingdom to nearly 30 percent in Norway.[9] In the mid-1980s, when they still referred to themselves as "socialist" countries, the private sector accounted for 14 percent of national income in Yugoslavia, 20 percent in Poland, and 48 percent in Vietnam.

---

[8]Under the Soviet and Chinese systems of "state socialism," for example, the government maintained effective ownership rights over most of the means of production, whereas Yugoslav socialism delegated most of these rights to the workers' councils of individual factories. As we shall see in later chapters, this is a distinction of considerable operational importance.

[9]These are estimates for 1991 calculated from data in Organization for Economic Cooperation and Development, *National Accounts: Detailed Tables* (Paris, 1993).

Finally, we should note that private ownership alone does not guarantee the full development of capitalism. Many developing countries have a system of private property, but they often lack the entrepreneurial talent, capital resources, stable monetary system, and other institutions that are needed for successful capitalist development. On the other hand, social ownership alone does not guarantee the fulfillment of socialist ideals. Seventy years of Soviet experience demonstrated that state ownership, wedded with a totalitarian government, does not deliver Marx's promise of a "society in which the full and free development of every individual forms the ruling principle."[10]

Classification According to Coordinating Mechanism

In any economic system, a large number of decisions must be made each year concerning the production and exchange of commodities and resources. Since millions of people may be involved in making and implementing these decisions, every economic system must employ one or more **coordinating mechanisms** to insure some degree of consistency. Ideally, intended purchases of each commodity should equal intended production, the number of people who enter a given occupation should roughly equal the number of jobs available in that occupation, and so on. Economic systems are often classified, therefore, according to their predominant coordinating mechanism.

[10]Karl Marx, *Capital*, vol. 1 (Moscow: Progress Publishers, 1956), 555.

A **traditional economy** is one in which coordination is maintained through simple perpetuation of the status quo.[11] What products will be produced? Those that were produced last year. How will they be produced? The way they were produced in the past. The sons follow their fathers in their choice of occupation, and the daughters follow their mothers.

Tradition can predominate as a coordinating mechanism only in rather small, simple, and stationary economies. In fact, it would be contradictory to speak of a dynamic and growing economy that is coordinated primarily by tradition. Nevertheless, elements of tradition can be found in any functioning economy. Racial and gender discrimination, for example, have traditionally influenced the patterns of employment in the United States and many other countries. In Japan, large corporations have traditionally maintained long, stable relationships with their suppliers and subcontractors. In the old Soviet Union, economic plans were not prepared in a vacuum; they always built on the results achieved in the previous year.

A **market economy** is one in which coordination is predominantly achieved through the free and spontaneous movement of market prices, responding to the forces of supply and demand. Thus, under competitive conditions, a shortage (or surplus) of any commodity will cause its relative price to rise (fall). The resulting increase (decrease) in the quantity supplied and decrease (increase) in the quantity demanded will reduce or eliminate the shortage (or surplus).

Ideally, a market economy also provides for **consumer sovereignty**. Consumer demand, the largest component of final demand during peacetime, ultimately determines what is produced in the economy. John Kenneth Galbraith and others have noted that the sovereignty of the

---

[11]Notice that tradition cannot, in itself, coordinate decisions, but can only perpetuate a set of decisions that has been coordinated in some other way.

consumer is manipulated by the marketing programs of producers. Nonetheless, if consumers cannot be convinced to buy a particular product, production will not continue. This is not always true in centrally planned economies, where shortages and surpluses of products may arise from a mismatch between planners' priorities and consumer demand.

A **planned economy** is, quite simply, one in which coordination of long-run and/or short-run decisions is attempted by means of a central plan, which is designed to guide the economy toward certain goals or objectives.[12] Given the generality of this definition, a planned economy can take any of several forms.

Directive planning (or **command planning**), which has been employed in the former Soviet Union, China, Eastern Europe, and the U.S. military, is a system whereby the most important long-run *and* short-run decisions are made by a central planning authority and are then passed down to subordinates in the form of instructions, directives, or commands. A directive plan typically includes an annual target for each factory and each important product, and compliance is compulsory. A **centrally planned economy (CPE)** employs directive planning as its predominant coordinating mechanism. Countries that are attempting to replace directive planning with market institutions are now commonly known as **transitional economies (TEs)**.

---

[12]We reject John Kenneth Galbraith's assertion that corporate planning *within* each major industry has transformed the United States into a planned economy. By our more restrictive definition, the plan must, in some sense, be formulated to achieve coordination *between* industries. See John Kenneth Galbraith, *The New Industrial State* (Boston: Houghton Mifflin, 1956).

When we speak collectively about CPEs and TEs, we call them **historically planned economies (HPEs).**[13]

Indicative planning, employed in France, Japan, and a number of other countries, is a hybrid system that uses the market to coordinate short-run decisions (how many apples to pick this week) in combination with a plan to coordinate long-run decisions (how many apple trees to plant this year). Unlike a directive plan, which must provide detailed instructions to individual producers, an indicative plan typically includes broad goals for entire industries over a long (usually five-year) time horizon. Private companies are not legally required to comply with plan targets, but the government may use fiscal and monetary policy instruments to encourage compliance. Ideally, if it sets goals that are beneficial to all segments of society, an indicative plan should evoke voluntary compliance—it should be a self-fulfilling prophecy.

Quite often, countries that engage in indicative planning also conduct an active **industrial policy (IP)**. An IP may include several different kinds of programs. First, a list of "winning" and "losing" industries may be formulated, with measures designed to support the former and phase out the latter. For example, the Japanese government supported development of the steel and auto industries in the 1950s, consumer electronics in the 1960s, computer chips in the 1970s, and "knowledge-intensive" industries in the 1980s. Second, an IP may include measures to strengthen industrial stability and/or competition. Where monopoly power is

---

[13]This terminology was introduced by Paul Marer. See his "Conceptual and Practical Problems of Comparative Measurement of Economic Performance," in *Economic Statistics for Economies in Transition: Eastern Europe in the 1990s*, proceedings of a conference sponsored by the U.S. Bureau of Labor Statistics and Eurostat, Washington, D.C., 1991, 5-23.

pervasive, existing companies may be regulated, nationalized, or split into smaller units. Conversely, small companies may be merged into larger units to enhance their financial strength, production efficiency, and competitive position on the world market.

Classification According to Incentive Systems

Any coordinating mechanism must include a system of incentives to reward socially desirable behavior and to discourage inappropriate actions. These are usually divided into three broad classes: coercive, material, and moral incentives.

Coercive incentives, which attempt to modify behavior through actual or threatened force and punishment, played a historic role in ancient Egypt, the American South, Hitler's Germany, Stalin's Soviet Union, and Pinochet's Chile. Slavery was not legally abolished in Mauritania until 1980, and forced labor is still reported in Burma, Cambodia, Haiti, Namibia, Sudan, and several other countries.

According to recent estimates of the U.N. International Labor Office, at least 12.3 million people are trapped in programs of forced labor. State- or military-imposed forced labor (including forced labor imposed by rebel groups) is estimated to involve at a minimum 2,490,000 persons, representing 20% of global forced labor. The other 80% of forced labor is exacted by private individuals, agents or enterprises. It is estimated that there are at least 9,810,000 victims of such forced labor in the world: 1,390,000 in forced labor for commercial sexual exploitation; 7,810,000 for other economic exploitation including slavery and serfdom, debt bondage and forced domestic labor; and the remaining 610,000 in mixed or undetermined forms of forced labor. Estimates of the number of victims of forced labor were obtained for each form of forced labor and for each geographical region (see the list of countries in the Annex). Full results are shown in table 1. It has to be noted that results are more robust for regional totals (shown in the last column of the table) than for specific forms within regions (as shown in the first four columns). This is because the relative standard errors of the estimates increase significantly when the level of the estimate is lower. For this reason, it was not considered meaningful to produce global estimates for detailed categories of forced labor beyond the three main forms noted above. We see that the bulk of global forced labor is in Asia and the Pacific, where some 9.5 million persons are estimated to be victims of forced labor. This figure represents more than three quarters of the total number of persons in forced labor in the world. The region with the next highest number of victims is Latin America and the Caribbean where some 1.3 million persons, or slightly less than 11% of the world total, are estimated to be engaged in forced labor. This is followed by Sub-Saharan Africa (660,000 victims or 5% of total), the industrialized countries (360,000 or 3%), Middle East and North Africa (260,000 or 2%), and finally transition economies (210,000 or 2%). The following diagram (fig. 2) shows the incidence of forced labor in relation to the size of population in the different regions. Asia & the Pacific and Latin America & the Caribbean, are the regions with the highest incidence of forced labor in relation to their population, with 3 and 2.5 victims of forced labor per 1,000 inhabitants, respectively. This is followed by Sub-Saharan Africa (1 person per 1,000 inhabitants), the Middle East & North Africa (0.75 person per 1,000 inhabitants), Transition Economies (0.5 person per 1,000 inhabitants) and Industrialized Countries (0.3 person per 1,000 inhabitants).

According to Antislavery International in London, as many as 200 million people in the world are working under conditions outlawed by international agreements.[14] Local officials in

[14]"Millions around the World Still Work in Bondage, Group Says," *The Dallas Morning News*, March 9, 1993, 5A. A similar estimate is given in Robert Senser, "Outlawing the Crime of

China employ coercive methods to hold down the growth rate of the population.[15] Even the most libertarian societies use force to raise tax revenues, enforce contracts, and prevent theft, fraud, violence, and other illegal actions.

Material incentives are those that reward desirable behavior with a claim over material goods, usually through some form of monetary payment. In a competitive market economy, material incentives arise more or less automatically from the operation of the system. If there is a shortage of any product, the resulting increase in its relative price will give producers a material incentive to increase the quantity they supply, and it will give consumers a material incentive to reduce the quantity they demand.

Systems of material incentives become more complicated in the presence of **principal-agent relationships**. Suppose that a "principal," perhaps the owner of a capitalist shoe factory, hires a group of "agents," or employees. What kind of material incentive system should the principal design to elicit the most desirable behavior from the agents at the lowest cost? A

Child Slavery," *Freedom Review* 24 (November-December 1993): 29-35.

Patrick Belser, Michaelle de Cock, and Farhad Mehran, *ILO Minimum Estimate of Forced Labour in the World*. Geneva: International Labour Office, 2005

[15]For information on these and other human rights abuses recorded by the U.S. State Department, see U.S. Senate, Committee on Foreign Relations, *Country Reports on Human Rights Practices* (Washington, D.C.: U.S. Government Printing Office, annual).

system of profit sharing, for example, may encourage the agents to respond more appropriately to market signals, such as an increase in the price of shoes, but it may also be costly.[16]

In an economy coordinated by a directive plan, principal-agent relationships can be even more complex. A material incentive system must be consciously designed and administered to elicit compliance with the plan. Customarily, this has involved bonus pay arrangements tied to fulfillment of production targets. We shall find, however, that countries like the former Soviet Union found it very difficult to design an incentive system that would simultaneously encourage accurate reporting of economic information to central planners and compliance with both the letter and the intent of the plan.

Moral incentives are designed to elicit desired behaviors by appealing to an emotional cause, such as nationalism, company or personal pride, compassion for the sick and the poor, or the desire for acceptance by one's peers. Moral incentives have been employed in "socialist competitions" between factories in the former Soviet Union, in the singing of company songs in Japan, and in the use of slogans, such as "Buy American."

Again, economic systems can be classified according to their dominant incentive systems. Karl Marx predicted that goods would be distributed according to the principle, "to each according to his labor," during the early stages of socialism, whereas the ultimate communist system would be characterized by distribution "to each according to his needs." In other words, immature socialism would be based on material incentives, but full communism would be based on moral incentives. Similarly, distinctions may be drawn between **command socialism**, which

---

[16]David E. M. Sappington, "Incentives in Principal-Agent Relationships," *Journal of Economic Perspectives* 5 (Spring 1991): 45-66.

makes extensive use of coercion; **utopian socialism**, which leans heavily on moral incentives; and **market socialism**, with its stronger reliance on material incentives.

Classification According to Objectives

Earlier we noted that automobiles are often classified according to the purposes they are meant to serve: race cars, economy cars, military vehicles, etc. Similarly, different economic systems are established to pursue different objectives, and they may be classified accordingly. Among the objectives that nations may choose to pursue are the following:

* Individual freedom
* High levels of personal consumption
* High rates of economic growth
* Economic and military power
* Equity in income distribution
* Full employment
* Protection of the natural environment
* Price stability

As its name implies, a **free-enterprise economy** is one in which protection of individual freedom is a dominant objective. Proponents of free enterprise—from Adam Smith, Ludwig von Mises, and Friedrich von Hayek, to Milton and Rose Friedman—have always drawn a close connection between economic and political freedoms:

> *Economic freedom is an essential requisite for political freedom. By enabling people to cooperate with one another without coercion or central direction, it reduces the area over which political power is exercised. In addition, by dispersing power, the free market*

provides an offset to whatever concentration of political power may arise. The concentration of economic and political power in the same hands is a sure recipe for tyranny.[17]

Today, some of the strongest advocates of free enterprise are found in Russia and Eastern Europe, where the interplay between political and economic freedom is most evident. Janos Kornai, a well-known Hungarian economist, insists that a "free economy is, of course, a market economy," and it must be "embedded in a democratic political order, characterized by the free competition of political forces and ideas."[18]

Advocates of free enterprise usually place a top priority on individual freedom, but they argue that other objectives, such as economic growth and an equitable distribution of income, are also best achieved by the market system. "A society that puts freedom first," according to Milton and Rose Friedman, "will, as a happy byproduct, end up with both greater freedom and greater equality."[19]

In a **welfare state**, an equitable distribution of income and full employment are among the leading objectives, and positive governmental action is employed to pursue those objectives. Advocates of the welfare state find it hard to believe that free and unregulated capitalism will best promote the welfare of society. In the words of John Maynard Keynes, "The outstanding

---

[17]Milton Friedman and Rose Friedman, *Free To Choose: A Personal Statement* (New York: Harcourt Brace Jovanovich, 1979), 2-3.

[18]Janos Kornai, *The Road to a Free Economy* (New York: W.W. Norton, 1990), 22-23.

[19]Friedman and Friedman, *Free to Choose*, 148.

faults of the economic society in which we live are its failure to provide for full employment and its arbitrary and inequitable distribution of wealth and incomes."[20] Governmental programs, including countercyclical monetary and fiscal policy, redistribution of income, health and employment insurance, and many other services are supported in the welfare state.

Of course, equity, like beauty, is in the eye of the beholder. Is an equitable income distribution one that divides the national income equally across the population? Is it one that divides income according to work performed? If so, should inherited wealth be confiscated by the government? How can the work of carpenters, lawyers, artists, and legislators be reduced to a common denominator to divide the national income equitably? These are among the questions that must be considered in the welfare state.

A number of different labels have been attached to economic systems that set the attainment of economic and military power as a preeminent objective. **Mercantilism**, which held sway in England and much of Europe during the sixteenth, seventeenth, and eighteenth centuries, was a system of economic thought and policy that held that national economic power could be augmented by governmental support of domestic monopolies, subsidization of exports, and restriction of imports, all aimed toward the accumulation of wealth embodied in gold and silver. The preoccupation of the mercantilists with gold and silver was explained by Jacob Viner, an eminent economic historian:

> *With wealth one could finance and equip armies and navies, hire foreign mercenaries, bribe potential enemies, and subsidize allies. Power could be exercised to acquire*

---

[20]John Maynard Keynes, *The General Theory of Employment, Interest, and Money* (New York: Harcourt, Brace, and World, 1964), 372.

colonies, to win access to new markets, and to monopolize trade routes, high-seas fisheries, and the slave trade with Africa.[21]

When capitalist ownership is combined with a totalitarian government bent on national economic and military power, the result is an exaggerated form of mercantilism, known as **fascism** or **nazism**. The relationship between individual rights and the national interest under such a system was described by the Fascist Labor Charter of 1927:

> *The Italian Nation is an organism having ends, a life and means superior in power and duration to the single individuals or groups of individuals composing it. . . . In view of the fact that private organization of production is a function of national concern, the organizer of the enterprise is responsible to the state for the direction given to production.*[22]

An Operational Classification System

Again, classification of economic systems is an imprecise enterprise that invites disagreement. We have considered four dimensions along which economic systems may be classified: ownership, coordinating mechanisms, incentive systems, and objectives. Many other dimensions can be considered, including centralization of decision making, modes of distributing information, the role of money in the economy, and the state of excess supply or excess demand

---

[21]Jacob Viner, "Mercantilist Thought," *International Encyclopedia of the Social Sciences* (New York: Macmillan, 1968), 4:438.

[22]This translation is given in Earl Sikes, *Contemporary Economic Systems* (New York: Henry Holt, 1940), 670-675.

in product markets.[23] Furthermore, when we attempt to classify economic systems, we should remember the following:

1. Economic systems may be either real or theoretical.

2. Theoretical systems may be "pure," but real systems generally include a mixture of different forms of ownership, coordination, incentives, and objectives.

3. Theoretical systems may stand still, but real systems change through time.

4. Reasonable persons will disagree on the assignment of actual countries to conceptual categories.

5. Ideally, assignment of actual countries to categories should be based on objective criteria, not on the rhetoric of politicians.

Pushing aside all the ambiguities, in Table 1.2 we identify eight very broad categories of economic systems that encompass most of the real and theoretical cases we will consider in this book. Countless numbers of other subcategories could be created by filling in more detail. For example, we could say that democratic socialism is a form of market socialism with a democratic set of objectives. Command socialism could be divided into its Stalinist, Maoist, and reformed variants, and so forth.

We shall examine countries that represent each of these systemic varieties in the following chapters. Our brief study of the developing world will explain the difficulties involved in breaking out of traditional and feudal modes of organization. A pure system of free-enterprise capitalism has never existed outside of textbooks and our closest approximation to that archetype is probably the U.S. economy. Among our examples of regulated capitalism, the United

---

[23]For a discussion of this last criterion, see Janos Kornai, "Resource-constrained versus Demand-constrained Systems," *Econometrica* 48 (1979): 801-819.

Kingdom, West Germany, and Sweden will represent the capitalist welfare states, and France and Japan will demonstrate the operation of indicative planning.

After the 1917 revolution, the Russians adopted a form of command socialism known as War Communism. They experimented with market socialism during the 1920s, under Lenin's New Economic Policy (NEP), but returned to command socialism in 1928, with the adoption of the first five-year plan. After World War II, the Soviet Union imposed command socialism on its Eastern European satellites. Today, of course, all these countries are in transition, but their destinations are unclear.

The Chinese leaders adopted the Stalinist version of command socialism after World War II, but developed their own Maoist variety during the Great Leap Forward (1958-1960) and the Cultural Revolution (1966-1976). Today, the Chinese economic system exhibits tremendous regional diversity; some regions have clung to command socialism and others have moved to a system approximating free-enterprise capitalism.

Comparisons of System Performance

Given our competitive, nationalistic, and ideological leanings, we inevitably wish to know which economic system is best—capitalism or socialism, American or Japanese, German or Swedish? Let us briefly consider some of the problems involved in making such comparisons.

Isolation of the Economic System

Earlier we noted that economic performance is influenced jointly by the economic system, the environment, and policies. If the economic performance of a country is relatively good or bad, we should not automatically conclude that the economic *system* is better or worse than that of other countries.

Before its disintegration in 1991, for example, Yugoslavia had a unique system of market socialism, based on worker participation in the ownership and management of enterprises. By all accounts, the performance of the Yugoslav economy was very poor during the 1980s, characterized by high unemployment and inflation rates, chronic balance of payments deficits, and deterioration in the standard of living.

Based on this information, can we quickly conclude that the system of worker-managed market socialism was a failure? This is the conclusion suggested by Ivan Ribnikar of the University of Ljubljana: "The lesson of Yugoslavia is that there is no compromise between a market economy and a centrally planned economy. One must have a true market economy."[24] On the other hand, we may ask whether *any* economic system would have performed successfully in the Yugoslav environment of regional conflict and political instability.

Actual and Ideal Economic Systems

Polemical defenders of capitalism and socialism are often guilty of comparing a theoretical version of one system with a description of the actual problems of the other. During the Cold War, for example, American commentators often discussed the shortages of goods that existed under Soviet socialism, and then described how those problems could be solved in a perfectly competitive free-enterprise economy. Soviet writers emphasized the unemployment, inflation, and social injustice of capitalist economies, and argued that perfect coordination of economic activity could be achieved under a central plan. If we remember their limitations, abstract models

---

[24]Craig Forman, "Yugoslavia's Problems Show Risks in Reforms of Socialist Systems," *The Wall Street Journal*, February 20, 1990, A1.

of idealized economic systems can be quite useful in our understanding of actual economic systems. However, they should be handled with care when performance comparisons are made.

Measurement Problems

The statistical problems involved in making international comparisons of income, unemployment, income distribution, and the like are so important and complex that we will devote an entire chapter to their discussion. Differences in monetary systems, accounting standards, and data collection systems, as well as international secrecy, all contribute to the problems. Furthermore, many important performance criteria, such as individual freedom, are not readily quantifiable.

Assigning Priorities

Finally, even if we could isolate the influences of economic systems and quantify them fully, any broad performance comparison must be based on value judgments. Is the "better" economic system the one that provides more individual freedom, more economic growth, less inflation or unemployment, more technological progress, or more equitable distribution of income? If a single economic system does not excel according to all these and other criteria, then people or groups of people with different values may disagree on the question of performance. Indeed, even if one system outperforms the other according to all objective criteria, the "loser" may still maintain support on ideological grounds. In other words, as you read the remainder of this book, you are invited to draw your own conclusions.

Summary

The economic performance of a country is determined by its economic system and environment, and by the policies of its leaders. An economic system is a set of institutions involved in making and implementing economic decisions.

Economic systems can be classified according to ownership of productive assets (feudalism, capitalism, or socialism), according to the mode of coordination (tradition, market, plan, or industrial policy), according to incentive systems (coercive, material, or moral), or according to objectives (free enterprise, welfare state, fascism, utopianism). Economic systems can be either real or theoretical, and real systems generally employ complex mixtures of ownership relations, coordination mechanisms, incentive systems, and objectives.

When we compare the performance of two economic systems, we should remember that: (1) poor economic performance of a country may be caused by environmental factors or poor policies, rather than a faulty economic system; (2) it is unfair to compare the real system in one country to a theoretical model of the system in the other country; (3) international statistical comparisons should be handled with care; and (4) performance comparisons ultimately are based on a system of values and priorities, about which opinions may differ.

Discussion and Review Questions

1. In addition to those we have discussed in this chapter, what other criteria could be used to classify economic systems?
2. Who owns your college, university, or business? Does that system of ownership have a significant influence on the way the institution is governed?

3. Countries that rely on the market system during times of peace have been known to use rationing and central control during times of war. How might this be explained?
4. What is the difference between a directive plan and an indicative plan? What are the different purposes they serve?
5. According to your own system of values and priorities, what are the most important performance criteria for an economic system?

Suggested Readings

Comparative Economic Studies (CES) and Journal of Comparative Economics (JCE). These are two professional journals that are devoted to the field of comparative economic systems. The articles in JCE tend to be more mathematically technical than those in CES.

Bromley, Daniel W. Economic Interests and Institutions. Oxford: Basil Blackwell, 1989. Aimed at readers with an intermediate knowledge of economic theory, this book provides an excellent discussion of institutional arrangements, institutional change, and economic policy analysis. The author's "primary purpose," he says, is to explore how our understanding of efficiency is molded by the existing institutional structure.

Dahl, Robert A., and Charles E. Lindblom. Politics, Economics, and Welfare. New York: Harper & Row, 1953. Written by a political scientist and an economist, this book examines economic and political systems under four broad categories: the price system, hierarchy, polyarchy, and bargaining.

Kornai, Janos. The Road to a Free Economy. New York: W.W. Norton, 1990. Written by a well-known Hungarian economist, the primary purpose of this book is to present the author's reform proposals, but it also includes an extended discussion of alternative forms of ownership.

Wiles, Peter J. D. Economic Institutions Compared. New York: John Wiley, 1977. Written with insight and biting wit by an iconoclastic professor (one of several in this field) at the London School of Economics. Long and sometimes difficult, but rewarding, this book is organized by institutions rather than national case studies.

CHAPTER 2
COMPARATIVE ECONOMIC STATISTICS

Thou shalt not have in thine house divers measures, a great and a small. But thou shalt have a perfect and just weight, a perfect and just measure shalt thou have.
—Deuteronomy 25:14-15

As we compare the operation and performance of economic systems, we will base many of our judgments on statistical data. Comparisons of this kind are important for many reasons. First, statistical measurements lend greater objectivity to a field of study that provokes strong opinions. They help us to formulate and test complex hypotheses and to check our preconceived notions. In which country, for example, would you expect that exports represent a larger proportion of national income—Japan or France? You may be surprised to learn that the answer is France. In which of these countries is government debt larger in relation to national income? The answer this time is Japan.

International comparisons are particularly important when they are used to guide public policy. For many years, decisions concerning U.S. defense spending were influenced by comparisons with Soviet expenditures, prepared by the U.S. intelligence community. The International Financial Corporation, an arm of the World Bank, provides aid to low-income countries that can pass a needs test based on GDP per capita. Voting rights of member nations of the Commonwealth of Independent States are distributed according to national shares of regional GDP. Comparisons of national income, inflation, and other economic and social statistics are used to guide selection of partners for free trade agreements.[1]

Because of their importance and complexity, international statistical comparisons should be handled with caution. They are complicated, first of all, by differences in the definitions and accounting methods that are used by different countries. Second, there are major national differences in statistical reporting and collection systems. Third, there are difficult theoretical and methodological issues involved in the interpretation of international data. Finally, because of state secrecy and a number of other considerations, many important statistics simply are not available.

In this chapter we will examine the methods and problems involved in making international comparisons for several broad classes of data, including national income, unemployment, inflation, and income distribution statistics. Our examination of the actual data will raise several questions to be discussed in later chapters.

National Income Comparisons

Since 1665, when Sir William Petty compiled the first estimate of the "income of the people" of England, measures of national income have played a prominent role in international comparisons, and international comparisons have played an important role in national income measurement. John W. Kendrick notes that "the most frequent motivation of the individual

[1]See, for example, Paul Kelash, "So Barbados Is Better? Economists Say Caribbean Should Be Next into NAFTA," *LDC Debt Report/Latin American Markets* 7 (July 11, 1994), passim.

scholars" who developed national income accounting before 1920 "was nationalism—the desire to compare the economic performance of rival nations."[2]

Today, national income comparisons are used for a number of purposes. Total national income or product is the most common measure of the economic size or power of a country. Ratios of imports or exports to national income are commonly used to measure the "openness" of countries to foreign trade, ratios of military spending to national income are used to measure the "burden" of defense, and so on. When we speak of the economic growth of a country, we usually mean growth of real national income and product. Finally, national income per capita is the yardstick most commonly used to compare levels of economic development or standards of living.

National Income Definitions

When we attempt to compare the incomes of nations, we must be aware of the fact that countries and international agencies employ several different concepts and definitions of national income. For our purposes, the three most important measures are gross national product, gross domestic product, and net material product. It is not meaningful to compare, for example, the gross national product of one country with the net material product of another. Furthermore, if we compare the gross national products of two countries, we are likely to obtain different results from those that would arise from a comparison of net material products.

Gross national product (GNP), which is equivalent to **gross national income (GNI),** is the broad measure of aggregate production in the National Income and Product Account (NIPA) system that was developed by the U.S. Commerce Department.[3] GNP is defined as the market value of all final goods and services produced by the nation in a year. In this case, the *nation* does not refer to the geographical confines of a country, or to its citizens, but rather to its residents—those who resided in the country for more than 6 months of the year. The income of a U.S. resident is included in the U.S. GNP even if it is earned abroad. A U.S. resident may, for example, spend part of the year working abroad, or she may obtain income from investments abroad. In either case, her income would be included in the U.S. GNP. On the other hand, the income of a U.S. citizen, whether it is earned in the United States or abroad, is not included in U.S. GNP if that citizen is not also a resident.

Gross domestic product or income (GDP or GDI) is the central measure of national product in the System of National Accounts (SNA) developed by the United Nations. Members of the European Community, Japan, and many other nations have used the SNA since the 1970s. During the 1990s, the United States, China, Russia, and other countries of the former Soviet Union and Eastern Europe have gradually shifted to this system. Thus, the SNA is quickly becoming a world standard for national income accounting, facilitating international comparisons.

GDP is defined to be the annual market value of final goods and services produced within the geographic boundaries of a nation, whether it is produced by citizens, residents, or migrant workers.[4] The income generated by international investments is included in the GDP of the

---

[2]John W. Kendrick, *Economic Accounts and Their Uses* (New York: McGraw-Hill, 1972), 10.

[3] Operationally, GNP is measured by adding the values of final *production*, and GNI is measured by adding the *incomes* of national residents, but, aside from errors in measurement, these should yield the same numerical result.

[4]Kendrick, *Economic Accounts*, 33-34. For a discussion of the shift from the NIPA to the SNA in the United States, see Carol S. Carson, "Replacing GNP: The Updated System of National Economic Accounts," *Business Economics* 27 (July 1992): 44-48. For a discussion of the transition in the former Soviet Union, see Youri Ivanov,

Table 2.1 GNP as a Percentage of GDP in Selected Countries, 2006			
Country	**Percent**	**Country**	**Percent**
Kiribati	169.0	U.S.A.	100.2
Lesotho	125.4	India	99.5
Marshall Is.	125.0	Canada	98.8
Switzerland	109.8	Mexico	98.4
Japan	102.8	Russia	97.1
U.K.	101.7	Chile	86.7
Germany	101.1	Ireland	86.2
France	100.8	Chad	79.2
China	100.4	Liberia	78.3
Sweden	100.4	Equ. Guinea	61.2

Source: World Bank, *World Development Indicators*

country where production of goods or services is conducted, which may not be the country where the recipient of that income resides.

Therefore, if we want to know where production is taking place, we should perform GDP comparisons. If, instead, we want to know where income is being received, GNP comparisons will provide more accurate results. In practice, though, the difference between GNP and GDP is relatively small for most countries—less than 3 percent of GDP (see Table 2.1). However, in countries that serve as tax havens or that pay or receive large incomes from international investments or remittances, such as Kiribati, Lesotho, and Liberia, and Equatorial Guinea, the differences between GNP and GDP can be quite substantial.

Net material product (NMP) is the central measure of national income in the Material Product System (MPS), which was the official system of national accounts in the former Soviet Union, Eastern Europe, China, and other centrally planned economies. Some of these countries have shifted entirely to the SNA, but most are reporting a mixture of statistics from the SNA and the MPS.[5]

NMP is equal to the total value, measured in final selling prices, of final material production, net of depreciation of fixed assets.[6] Unlike GNP and GDP, NMP does not include the value of nonmaterial services. Generally, services are included in NMP only if they contribute to the value of a material product, such as the services of repair technicians. Governmental, medical, educational, and recreational services are among those excluded from NMP. On a philosophical level, services are excluded in keeping with the classical notion, propounded by Adam Smith and amplified by Karl Marx, that service workers do not create anything of lasting substance—they are "unproductive." On a practical level, the MPS was originally developed to meet the demands of central planners who were preoccupied with the structure of material production.

The differences between international comparisons based on GNP (or GDP) and NMP measurements were substantial. In 1988, for example, when the Soviet NMP was reported at

---

Boris Rjabushkin, and Tatjana Homenko, "Introduction of the SNA into the Official Statistics of the Commonwealth of Independent States," *Review of Income and Wealth* 39 (September 1993): 279-294.

[5]For example, official reports of Russian economic performance are now primarily based on GDP and GNP, but official reports from the Commonwealth of Independent States, of which Russia is the largest member, are still based on NMP. Compare the reports in *Ekonomika i Zhizn*, No. 35, August 1994, supplement, and *Delovoi Mir*, No. 123, June 1994, 6.

[6]For a full discussion, see Abraham S. Becker, "National Income Accounting in the USSR," in *Soviet Economic Statistics*, ed. Vladimir Treml and John Hardt (Durham, N.C.: Duke University Press, 1972).

about 64 percent of the U.S. level, their GNP was only about 52 percent of the American total.[7] The main reason for the difference is quite clear. Because the U.S. economy has a highly developed service sector, NMP calculations excluded a much larger portion of economic activity for the United States than they did for the Soviet Union.

Uncounted Production and Income

Certain forms of production and income are not fully included even in the broader measures of national income, such as GNP and GDP. Generally speaking, GDP measurements include only the value of goods and services that are produced legally and sold on open markets. Let us briefly consider how this restriction affects international comparisons of income.

First, GNP measurements exclude most of the goods and services produced by families for their own consumption because these are never sold on an open market. Thus, when we perform our own housework, care for our children, or grow vegetables in our backyards, our efforts are seldom reflected in GNP calculations. If these goods and services were counted, they would enlarge American GNP by about 20 to 33 percent.[8] Nonmarket activities are even more significant in underdeveloped subsistence economies, accounting for about 40 to 45 percent of total labor time.[9] This helps explain how the World Bank can report, with a straight face, that GNP per person in Mozambique was $90 (25 cents per day!) in 1993.[10] Clearly, a great deal of production in Mozambique is never sold on a market and is not included in GNP.

In addition to the problem of unmarketed output, national income estimates also exclude the value of goods and services produced in the **underground** (or **informal** or **second** or **shadow**) **economy**—production that is hidden from governmental authorities to escape taxation, regulation, and prosecution for criminal activities. According to recent estimates, inclusion of the underground economy would increase measured GDP by about 4 percent in Japan, 6 percent in the United States, 12 percent in the European Union, and 20 to 25 percent in the transitional economies of Eastern Europe. In many African and Latin American countries, between 40 and 50 percent of the nonagricultural labor force is employed in the informal sector.[11] In general, the

---

[7]The NMP estimate is from Goskomstat SSSR, *Narodnoe khoziaistvo SSSR v 1988 g.* (Moscow: Finansi i Statistika, 1989), 681. The GNP estimate is the geometric mean of dollar and ruble comparisons in U.S. Central Intelligence Agency, *Handbook of Economic Statistics, 1990* (CPAS 90-10001, September 1990), 38. In reality, the relative size of the Soviet national income probably was much smaller than either of these figures suggests. According to unofficial estimates, if proper adjustments were made for low product quality and false reporting by managers, Soviet GNP would be only 15 to 35 percent of the U.S. level. See "Is the Economy as Bad as the Soviets Say?" *Orbis* 34 (Fall 1990), 509-525.

[8]This is the range of contributions of "unpaid household labor" in the studies surveyed in Robert Eisner, *The Total Incomes System of Accounts* (Chicago: The University of Chicago Press, 1989), 55-85.

[9]Luisella Goldschmidt-Clermont, *Economic Evaluations of Unpaid Household Work: Africa, Asia, Latin America, and Oceania*, Women, Work, and Development Series, No. 14 (Geneva: International Labour Office, 1987), 58.

[10]World Bank, *World Development Report 1995* (New York: Oxford University Press, 1995), 162.

[11]These estimates were gathered from a number of sources, including the following: David Turnham, Bernard Salome, and Antoine Schwarz, *The Informal Sector Revisited* (Paris: OECD Development Center, 1990); Peter S. Spiro, "Invisible, Outlawed, and Untaxed: America's Underground Economy," *Business Economics* 29 (July 1994): 75; David Manisan, et. al., "Europe's Booming Black Economy," *International Management* 42 (July-August 1987): 24-30; Anna Marszalek, "Report on the Parallel Economy," *Polish News Bulletin* (April 22, 1994), 1; and Richard Bruner, "Unreported Business in Hungary Spreads Budget's Red Ink," *Christian Science Monitor*, November 15, 1993, 10.

underground economy seems to be largest in countries that have high tax rates and cumbersome systems of business registration, poor systems of statistical reporting and tax enforcement, and high rates of inflation and unemployment. In countries that fit this description, national income may be seriously understated.[12]

Conversion of National Incomes to a Single Currency

Before national incomes of various countries can meaningfully be compared, they must be converted to a single currency, usually the U.S. dollar. Several different methods are available for this purpose, each with its strengths and weaknesses. The simplest and most obvious procedure is to convert all currencies into dollars (or some other common currency) with **current market exchange rates**. This simple method will yield fairly accurate income comparisons if: (1) the countries under comparison have free and open market economies, (2) the countries are at similar levels of economic development, (3) capital flows (international saving and investment) between the countries are small compared to volumes of international trade, (4) inflation rates in the countries are fairly low and stable, and (5) exchange rates are relatively stable during the comparison period.

Under these conditions, the market exchange rates should be roughly equal to **purchasing-power-parity (PPP) exchange rates**. That is, each exchange rate should roughly translate the prices of one market economy into the prices of another. Suppose, for example, that a particular bundle of goods can be purchased in the United States for $100. If the dollar/yen exchange rate is currently at PPP, we should be able to purchase a similar bundle of goods in Japan by exchanging $100 for yen at the market exchange rate and paying Japanese prices.

Why, under the conditions listed above, do market exchange rates gravitate toward PPP levels? Basically, because of the forces of international competition. Suppose, for example, that the price of a ton of steel is presently lower in Japan than in the United States. That is, the yen price, converted to dollars at the market exchange rate, is lower than the dollar price. What will happen? International competition will tend to cause a decrease in the dollar price, and/or an increase in the yen price, and/or an increase in the exchange rate of the yen. In any case, after these adjustments occur, the market exchange rate will reflect the relative purchasing powers of the two currencies.

Realistically, though, anyone who has traveled abroad knows that exchange rates tend to stray, more or less, from PPP levels. In countries where the currency is undervalued, travelers easily find bargains. In countries where the currency is overvalued, prices may seem exorbitant. If departures from PPP are large, the conditions listed in the first paragraph of this section have probably been broken.

For example, exchange rates may depart significantly from PPP during periods of price instability and speculative activity in foreign exchange markets. To reduce the impact of temporary exchange rate fluctuations on its national income comparisons, the World Bank, for many years, has used a procedure called the **Atlas Method**. According to this method, the national income of a country in year t is converted into dollars with a calculated exchange rate, equal to an average of the exchange rates in years t, t-1, and t-2, adjusted for general price movements.[13] As the data in the first two columns of Table 2.2 indicate, the results derived from

---

[12]An important exception to the rule is Italy, which has a relatively large underground economy, but deliberately attempts to include it in measured GDP. Italy began this practice in the mid-1980s, attempting to demonstrate that it had overtaken the United Kingdom as the Western world's fifth largest economic power.

[13]For a fuller explanation of the Atlas Method, see World Bank, *World Development Report 1995*, 230-231.

Table 2.2 Converting GNI per Capita to Dollars: Three Methods Compared
(U.S. Dollars per Person in 2006)

	Simple Exchange Rate Method	World Bank Atlas method	PPP (ICP Repricing Method)
Norway	71,863	68,440	50,070
United States	44,070	44,710	44,070
Singapore	28,543	28,730	43,300
Switzerland	55,752	58,050	40,840
Netherlands	42,065	43,050	37,940
Canada	38,486	36,650	36,280
Sweden	42,402	43,530	34,310
Australia	35,996	35,860	33,940
United Kingdom	39,919	40,560	33,650
Japan	35,153	38,630	32,840
Germany	35,561	36,810	32,680
France	36,984	36,560	32,240
Russia	6,725	5,770	12,740
China	2,025	2,000	4,660
India	817	820	2,460
Kenya	625	580	1,470
Nigeria	696	620	1,410
Tanzania	320	350	980
Ethiopia	172	170	630
Congo, Dem. Rep.	134	130	270
Liberia	138	130	260

Source: World Bank, *World Development Indicators*

the Atlas Method are similar in most cases to those obtained from a simple application of the exchange rate in year t to the national income data in year t. Still, in comparisons of GNP per person for 1992, India was ahead of China according to the simplest exchange rate method, and China was slightly ahead of India according to the Atlas Method.

The Atlas Method reduces the effect of temporary exchange rate movements, but it does not solve measurement problems caused by long-term departures from PPP caused by economic regulation, long-term capital flows, and structural differences between countries at different levels of economic development. To deal with these problems, the **U.N. International Comparison Project (ICP)** has devised a repricing procedure that is much more complex than the Atlas Method.[14] The output of each country is divided into 151 product groups and the value of each group is calculated according to a set of average **international prices** (expressed in terms of U.S. dollars). When the product groups are added together, the resulting comparisons of national income should be roughly equal to those obtained by application of PPP exchange rates.

The data in the third column of Table 2.2 demonstrate that international comparisons based on the ICP repricing method can differ substantially from those based on market exchange rates. Switzerland, which has a much larger income per capita than the United States according to the other two methods, falls slightly below the United States according to the ICP method. On the other hand, middle-income and low-income countries, such as Russia, China, India, and Ethiopia, seem to have much larger dollar incomes according to the ICP method.

The Index Number Problem

Although international comparisons of national income based on the ICP repricing methods are, in principle, superior to those based on market or official exchange rates, they still do not solve one nagging problem. As we have seen, national products can be converted to a single currency by applying a single set of prices to the outputs of the various countries. The question remains:

[14]See Irving Kravis et al., *World Product and Income: International Comparisons of Real Gross Product* (Baltimore: Johns Hopkins University Press, 1982); and Robert Summers and Alan Heston, "A New Set of International Comparisons of Real Product and Price Levels Estimates for 130 Countries, 1950-1985," *Review of Income and Wealth* 34 (March 1988): 1-25.

Table 2.3 Hypothetical GNP Calculations

	Final Output (billion tons)		Prices per Ton	
	USSR	U.S.	Rubles	Dollars
Wheat	10	50	16	16
Steel	50	30	8	20

	Gross National Product		
	USSR	U.S.	USSR/U.S.
Rubles (billion)	(10)(16)+(50)(8) = 560	(50)(16)+(30)(8) = 1040	.54
Dollars (billion)	(10)(15)+(50)(20) = 1150	(50)(15)+(30)(20) = 1350	.85

Whose prices do we use? The so-called **index number problem** refers to the fact that comparisons of macroeconomic aggregates can be greatly influenced by the prices used to add the values of products together.

Suppose, for example, that we wish to compare the national products of the United States and the former Soviet Union, and, for the sake of simplicity, suppose that both countries produced only two products—wheat and steel. According to the hypothetical data in Table 2.3, U.S. agriculture was highly productive; thus, U.S. wheat production was greater than Soviet wheat production and the price of wheat was relatively low in dollars. Suppose on the other hand, that the Soviet Union had a relatively efficient steel industry, with a high level of production at a relatively low price.

If we calculate the U.S. GNP using rubles, we apply the relatively high ruble price for wheat to the high level of U.S. wheat production and thus derive a U.S. GNP that is nearly twice the Soviet level. The Soviet Union, however, looks better if the comparison is done in dollars: the Soviet GNP includes a large volume of steel production valued at the high U.S. steel price.

Our hypothetical example illustrates the **Gershchenkron effect**—when the production levels of two countries are compared, the GNP of country X will appear to be relatively larger if the prices of country Y are used to sum the products of each of the countries. This regularity is supported by the actual, rather than hypothetical, estimates of U.S. and Soviet GNP. According to the Central Intelligence Agency, Soviet GNP was 37 percent of the U.S. level in 1990 when measured in rubles and about 64 percent of the U.S. level when measured in dollars.[15] Which estimate is more meaningful or valid? The one in dollars? The one in rubles? Some average of the two? Unfortunately, this question has no straightforward answer.

As we noted before, the U.N. International Comparisons Project (ICP) handles the index number problem by employing a set of average international prices. In principle, this is better than using the prices of any single country. In practice, though, the prices used in the ICP studies are closer to those of the industrial countries than they are to those of the developing countries. The Gershchenkron effect would suggest that application of industrial world prices is likely to impart an upward bias to the estimates of national income for the developing countries. Indeed, the estimates of developing-country incomes that are obtained by the ICP studies are several times larger than those obtained by simple market exchange rate conversions (Table 2.2). Thus, the ICP estimates have been criticized by Third World economists, who fear that the larger income estimates may reduce their nations' access to foreign aid.[16]

---

[15]Central Intelligence Agency, *Handbook of Economic Statistics, 1991*, CPAS91-10001, September 1991, 36. Beginning with the 1992 *Handbook*, the CIA has not provided this kind of information for the former Soviet Union or for any of its successor states.

[16]See, for example, Xin Dun, "China's Strength Is Overestimated," *Beijing Review* (June 14-20, 1993): 9-10.

MILITARY SPENDING: THE INDEX NUMBER GAME

In any comparison of broad aggregates, such as industrial production, agricultural production, or the general crime rate, we must deal with many of the same problems that occur in GNP comparisons. For many years, the CIA used a repricing procedure to compare U.S. and Soviet defense spending. Each year, they would use satellite reconnaissance and other intelligence sources to compile a list of military purchases in physical terms—numbers of personnel, aircraft, ships, missiles, and so on. Next, they would attach approximate dollar prices to each of those items (wage rates paid to U.S. military personnel and prices of American weapons that were more or less similar to Soviet weapons) and add them together. Thus, the CIA calculated the approximate number of dollars that the Soviet Union would have to spend in American prices to pay for its military. This dollar amount was compared to the actual level of U.S. military spending.

From time to time, CIA analysts would also prepare comparisons in rubles, but they had less confidence in these estimates because of uncertainty about ruble prices. Thus, the ruble estimates were given little publicity.

According to the Gershchenkron effect, the relative size of the Soviet military should have been somewhat larger in the dollar estimates than in the ruble estimates. Indeed, according to the CIA estimates for 1981, the Soviet military cost 45 percent more than the American military in dollar prices and 25 percent more in ruble prices. By 1985, after an American defense buildup, the CIA estimated that U.S. and Soviet spending were roughly equal in dollars. Ruble comparisons were not published after the early 1980s, but apparently they would have indicated that the United States was outspending the Soviet Union. According to some critics, the CIA overestimated the relative size of the Soviet military, and according to others, they seriously underestimated the Soviet threat.

Sources: The CIA estimates were reported in annual hearings of the Joint Economic Committee of the U.S. Congress, titled *Allocation of Resources in the Soviet Union and China*. For critical analyses of the CIA estimates, see Dmitri Steinberg, "Trends in Soviet Military Expenditure," *Soviet Studies* 42 (October 1990): 675-699; Franklyn D. Holzman, "How the CIA Distorted the Truth about Soviet Military Spending," *Challenge* 33 (March-April 1990): 27-36; and Daniel Berkowitz, et. al., "An Evaluation of the CIA's Analysis of Soviet Economic Performance, 1970-90," *Comparative Economic Studies* 35 (Summer 1993): 41-56.

Alternative Measures of the Standard of Living

As was mentioned earlier, national income per capita is the measure most commonly used for international comparisons of economic development and living standards. However, because of the deficiencies discussed above—disagreements over how national income should be defined, exclusion of unmarketed and hidden output, and the problems involved in converting national incomes to a common currency—the search is under way for alternative measures of the standard of living.

For a number of years, many international aid agencies and scholars have used the **Physical Quality of Life Index (PQLI)** as an alternative to national income. Developed by the Overseas Development Council, the PQLI is meant to measure economic and social development in terms of human results (health and education) rather than in terms of inputs (consumption of food and other goods and services). The PQLI is a simple unweighted average of index numbers for three development indicators: infant mortality rate, life expectancy, and adult literacy.[17] It is attractive in its simplicity, in its apparent lack of bias toward any economic system, and in its emphasis on results. Furthermore, because public health and literacy are positively correlated with income equality, the PQLI tells us something about the distribution as well as the average level of real income in each country. Indeed, given the high priority that socialist countries supposedly placed on income equality and public health, a planned economy with a particular level of per capita income may be expected to have a higher PQLI than a market economy at that same level of income. Statistical tests have yielded mixed results, but they provide some support for this hypothesis.[18]

Table 2.4 Alternative Measures of the Standard of Living

	Real GDP per Capita (PPP$)		*Human Development Index*		*Index of Economic Freedom*		*Global Competitiveness Index*	
	value	rank	value	rank	value	rank	value	rank
Norway	47,551	1	0.968	1	69	10	5.2	8
U.S.A.	41,674	2	0.951	7	80.6	3	5.67	1
Hong Kong	35,680	3	0.937	9	90.3	1	5.37	6
Canada	35,078	4	0.961	3	80.2	4	5.34	7
Australia	32,798	5	0.962	2	82	2	5.17	10
Sweden	31,995	6	0.956	4	70.4	9	5.54	2
U.K.	31,580	7	0.946	8	79.5	6	5.41	5
Germany	30,496	8	0.935	10	71.2	8	5.51	3
Japan	30,290	9	0.953	5	72.5	7	5.43	4
France	29,644	10	0.952	6	65.4	12	5.18	9
Saudi Arabia	21,220	11	0.812	13	62.8	13	4.55	13
Chile	12,262	12	0.867	11	79.8	5	4.77	11
Russia	11,861	13	0.802	14	49.9	20	4.19	17
Mexico	11,317	14	0.829	12	66.4	11	4.26	15
Egypt	5,049	15	0.708	17	59.2	14	3.96	18
China	4,091	16	0.777	15	52.8	19	4.57	12
Indonesia	3,234	17	0.728	16	53.9	17	4.24	16
India	2,126	18	0.619	18	54.2	16	4.33	14
Nigeria	1,892	19	0.47	19	55.5	15	3.69	19
Ethiopia	591	20	0.406	20	53.2	18	3.28	20

Sources: 2005 International Comparison Program, *Tables of Final Results*, 2008; United Nations Development Programme, *Human Development Report, 2007-2008*; World Economic Forum, *Global Competitiveness Report, 2007-2008*.

A relatively new and interesting measure of the standard of living is the **Human Development Index (HDI)**. Introduced in 1990, the HDI has gained recognition quickly because it is sponsored by the United Nations Development Program, and is the centerpiece of that agency's annual *Human Development Report*. HDI, like PQLI, is an unweighted average of three other indexes. First, a health index is based on life expectancy at birth. Second, an educational attainment index is formed by combining an index of adult literacy (two-thirds weight) and a

[17]The PQLI is fully explained in Morris D. Morris, *Measuring the Condition of the World's Poor* (New York: Pergamon Press, 1979). Also, see the explanatory note under Table 2.4.

[18]Edward F. Stuart, "The PQLI as a Measure of Comparative Economic Performance," *The ACES Bulletin* 26 (Winter 1984): 43-53; and John P. Burkett, "PQLI as a Measure of Comparative Performance: Comment," *Comparative Economic Studies* 28 (Summer 1986): 59-68.

composite index of primary, secondary, and college-level school enrollment (one-third weight). Third, an index of "access to resources" is based on GDP per capita at PPP (the ICP repricing method), adjusted to reflect diminishing marginal utility derived from higher levels of income. Thus, HDI differs from PQLI because it excludes the infant mortality rate, includes school enrollment, and includes GDP per capita.[19] Neither PQLI nor HDI includes indicators specifically related to leisure, crime, mental health, unemployment, environmental disruption, or many other dimensions of the quality of life.

In Table 2.4, we see that the relative performances of countries are quite different according to GDP per capita (at PPP), PQLI, and HDI. For example, the United States leads the world in GDP per capita, but follows behind Canada and France in PQLI and HDI. Japan leads the world in PQLI, but follows the United States in GDP per capita and HDI. The developing countries compare more favorably with the industrial market economies in terms of the PQLI than they do in terms of per capita national income.

Income Distribution Comparisons

We noted in the previous chapter that the performance of an economic system may be assessed not only by the size and growth of the national income it generates but also by the equity with which that income is distributed across the population. We also noted, however, that one person's equity is another person's injustice. An equitable income distribution may be one that divides income evenly, or according to work, inheritance, market forces, or any number of other standards. We should establish at the outset, therefore, that measures of income *equality* may not be the same as measures of income *equity*.

Measures of Income Inequality

Data relating to the distributions of income in the United States, Sweden, and Mexico are presented in Table 2.5. In this case, we see the share of total income received by each decile (tenth) of the population. In some statistical publications, you will find similar data for quintiles (fifths) of the population.[20] A simple inspection of Table 2.5 will indicate that the income is distributed more evenly in Sweden than in the United States, and more evenly in the United States than in Mexico. For example, the poorest decile of households received only 1.1 percent of total income in Mexico, compared with 1.8 percent in the United States and 4.1 percent in Sweden.

---

[19]For a full explanation of HDI, see the United Nations Development Program, *Human Development Report 1997* (New York: Oxford University Press, 1997), 122. For a critique, see Arnab Acharya and Howard J. Wall, "An Evaluation of the United Nations' Human Development Index," *Journal of Economic and Social Measurement* 20 (1994): 51-65.

[20] Quintile shares of income for many countries may be found, for example, in the World Bank's World Development Indicators database (www.worldbank.org/data).

Table 2.5 Distribution of Disposable Household Income in the United States, Sweden, and Mexico, 2000-2002

Percentage of Total Household Income Received by Each Decile			
	Sweden	*United States*	*Mexico*
Poorest Decile	4.10	1.81	1.07
Second Decile	5.90	3.53	2.47
Third Decile	6.70	4.79	3.52
Fourth Decile	7.60	6.04	4.58
Fifth Decile	8.40	7.32	5.70
Sixth Decile	9.30	8.67	7.04
Seventh Decile	10.40	10.30	8.75
Eighth Decile	11.70	12.45	11.25
Ninth Decile	13.70	16.07	16.18
Tenth Decile	22.10	29.03	39.39

Source: World Institute for Development Economics Research, *World Income Inequality Database V 2.0b May 2007.* http://62.237.131.23/wiid/wiid.htm

Another simple measure of income inequality is the **decile share ratio or quintile share ratio**, defined as the share of income received by the richest decile (or quintile) of the population divided by the share of the poorest decile (or quintile).[21] A larger ratio indicates a larger gap between the rich and the poor. According to the data in Table 2.5, the decile share ratios are 5.4 for Sweden, 16.0 for the United States, and 36.8 for Mexico. Probably because of its simplicity of calculation and interpretation, the quintile share ratio is the headline indicator of income inequality in publications of the European Union.[22] However, these ratios also have a disadvantage: they focus on the gap between the richest and poorest members of society, ignoring those in the middle.

Another tool for analysis and comparison of income distributions is the **Lorenz curve**, which depicts the percentage of total income received by each cumulative percentage of the population. Lorenz curves based on the data in Table 2.5 are presented in Figure 2.1. Clearly, all Lorenz curves must pass through points A and B on the graph, because zero percent of households must logically receive zero percent of total income, and 100 percent of households must logically receive 100 percent of income. It is the *shape* of the Lorenz curve between these points that reflects the degree of income inequality.

If there were a country in the world with a perfectly even distribution of income (there is not), its Lorenz curve would be the straight diagonal line, AB. Along that line, the poorest 20 percent of households receive 20 percent of total income, the poorest 40 percent of households receive 40 percent of total income, and so forth. The greater the income inequality in a country, the more the Lorenz curve will bend away from the line of equality. Thus, it is clear by inspection that Mexican income is distributed less equally than American income, and Swedish income is distributed more equally. In the extreme and unsustainable case of perfect income inequality (one person receives all the income) the Lorenz curve would be the right-angled line, ACB.

A third tool for comparison of income distributions is the **Gini ratio**, named for the Italian statistician who introduced it in 1912. The Gini ratio for a particular country is equal to the measured area between the Lorenz curve for that country and the diagonal line of equality (AB), divided by the total area of the triangle, ABC. In the case of perfect equality there would be no area between the Lorenz curve and the diagonal line (they would be the same line), so the Gini ratio would equal zero. In the case of perfect inequality, the Gini ratio would equal the area of

---

21 A different, but closely-related concept is the "decile ratio," which is usually defined as the income received by those at the bottom of the richest decile divided by the income of those at the top of the poorest decile.

22 It was included on the list of "Laeken indicators" adopted by the European Council in Laeken, Belgium, in 2001, and quintile share ratios are provided in the Eurostat yearbooks and databases available at http://epp.eurostat.ec.europa.eu.

triangle ABC divided by itself, or 1. For any real country, the Gini ratio will fall somewhere between 0 and 1, with a larger coefficient denoting more income inequality. When expressed as a percentage, the ratio would fall between 0% and 100%.

Figure 2.1 Lorenz Curves

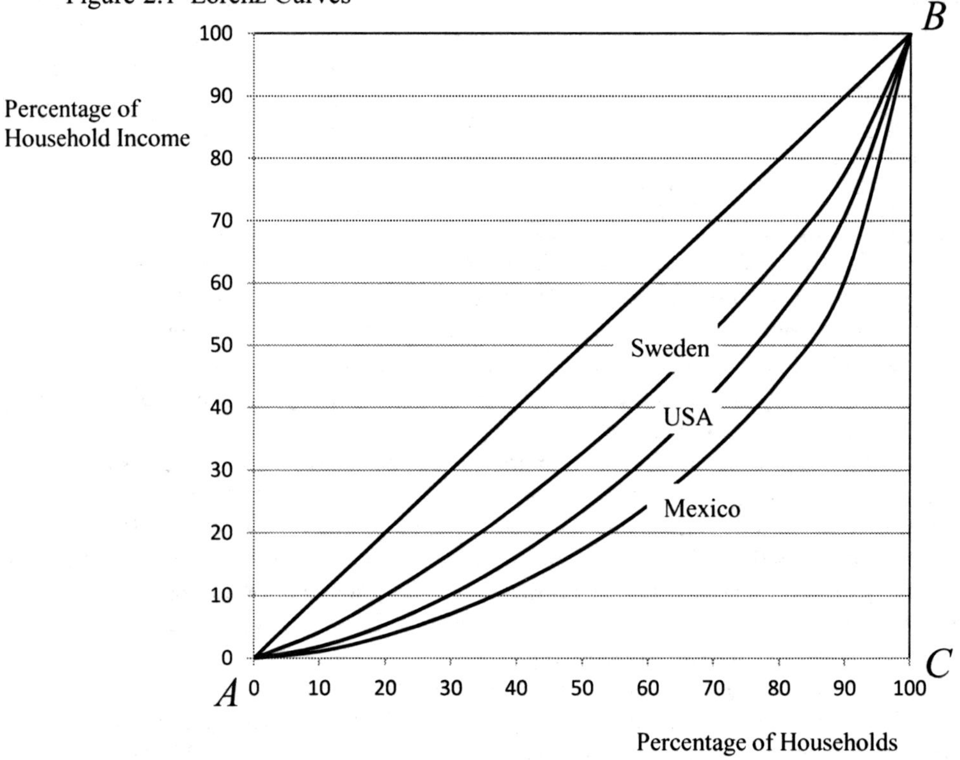

Because the curved area between a Lorenz curve and the line of equality can be difficult to measure, exact calculation of the Gini ratio is somewhat complex, and several different estimation techniques are available. The simplest formula is:

$$Gini\ Ratio = 1 - 2\sum_{i-1}^{n}\left(\frac{1}{2n} + \frac{(n-i)}{n}\right) P_i$$

Where:

n = number of income groups (n = 10 in Table 2.5)

i = a particular group (i = 1 for the poorest group)

P_i = fraction of total income received by income group i, expressed as a decimal fraction rather than a percentage (in Table 2.5, $P_1 = 0.041$ for Sweden)

If the population is divided into ten income groups (as in Table 2.5), then:

$$\text{Gini Ratio} = 1 - (1.9P_1 + 1.7P_2 + 1.5P_3 + 1.3P_4 + 1.1P_5 + .9P_6 + .7P_7 + .5P_8 + .3P_9 + .1P_{10})$$

Applying this formula, the Gini ratios calculated from the data in Table 2.5 are 0.252 for Sweden, 0.385 for the United States, and 0.494 for Mexico.

Table 2.6 Measures of Income Inequality

Country	Year/ Source	Gini Ratio (%)	Decile Share Ratio	Quintile Share Ratio	Country	Year	Gini Ratio (%)	Decile Share Ratio	Quintile Share Ratio
Czech Rep.	2003/1	22.8	4.0	3.1	India	2005/3	36.8	8.6	5.6
Sweden	2003/1	25.2	5.3	3.5	Russia	2005/3	37.5	11.0	6.9
Hungary	2003/1	25.2	5.4	3.6	Indonesia	2005/3	39.4	10.8	6.6
Finland	2003/1	25.6	5.3	3.6	U.S.A.	2000/1	39.4	16.0	8.4
France	2000/2	27.8	n.a.	n.a.	Nigeria	2004/3	42.9	16.3	9.5
Norway	2002/1	29.3	8.5	4.6	China	2002/1	45.4	18.5	11.0
Spain	2002/1	30.9	7.2	4.7	Venezuela	2004/1	45.4	23.0	11.5
Bangladesh	2005/3	31.0	6.2	4.4	Sri Lanka	2002/1	46.9	22.0	11.0
Germany	2004/1	31.1	8.3	5.1	Somalia	2002/1	47.4	23.7	12.7
Australia	2003/2	31.2	n.a.	n.a.	Guatemala	2004/1	49.4	29.1	14.0
Pakistan	2005/3	31.2	6.7	4.5	Mexico	2004/1	49.9	31.4	14.0
Canada	2004/2	31.8	n.a.	n.a.	Argentina	2005/1	50.1	32.7	15.7
Bulgaria	2003/1	32.2	9.0	5.3	Bolivia	2004/1	50.5	23.5	12.3
Japan	2002/4	33.8	n.a.	n.a.	Peru	2003/1	52.0	30.3	15.2
U.K.	2002/1	34.2	9.7	5.6	Chile	2003/1	54.6	32.2	15.6
Estonia	2003/1	35.0	10.8	6.0	Colombia	2004/1	55.3	45.7	18.9
Poland	2003/1	35.2	11.9	6.4	Brazil	2004/1	56.6	46.2	21.0
Italy	2002/1	35.9	11.5	6.6	Jamaica	2002/1	59.9	194.9	50.2

Sources (indicated in 2nd column): (1) World Institute for Development Economics Research, *World Income Inequality Database V 2.0b May 2007.* http://62.237.131.23/wiid/wiid.htm; (2) Luxembourg Income Study, Key Figures, http://www.lisproject.org/key-figures/key-figures.htm; (3) World Bank, World Development Indicators, online; (4) Tetsuo Fukawa, "Income distribution in Japan based on IRS 1987-2002," *Japanese Journal of Social Security Policy*, 5 (June 2006): 28.

Gini Ratios, decile share ratios, and quintile share ratios for 36 major countries are listed in Table 2.6. Most of these data have been extracted from the World Income Inequality Database, maintained by the World Institute for Development Economics Research, ensuring a reasonable level of comparability, but some have been taken from other sources. The countries are listed in order of their Gini ratios, with the most egalitarian countries listed first. Generally, the data indicate that the most even income distributions in the world are found in northern Europe. The United Kingdom and several of its former colonies (Australia, Canada, and the United States) are spread through the middle of the list, together with many of the Asian countries. The highest levels of income inequality are found in Latin America and sub-Saharan Africa.

Closely related to the concept of income inequality is the **poverty rate**—the percentage of the population living below a level of income that provides for basic needs. International comparisons of poverty may be based on an "absolute" approach, with a single poverty line for all countries, or a "relative" approach, with higher poverty thresholds in countries that have higher average incomes. In Table 2.7, for example, the estimates in the Absolute column are based on a uniform threshold of $7,392 in 1985 U.S. dollars, converted to each currency on a PPP basis. In the Relative column, the poverty line in each country is taken to be one-half of median income in that country. On an absolute scale, Italy has the highest poverty rate in the group and Canada has the lowest. On a relative scale, the United States has the highest incidence of poverty and Sweden has the lowest.

Table 2.7 Absolute and Relative Poverty Rates

	Year	*Absolute Percentage Poor*	*Relative Percentage Poor*
Australia	1987	29.9	15.2
Austria	1987	26.3	8.4
Canada	1987	11.3	11.5
France	1984	29.8	7.6
Germany	1984	30.6	6.6
Italy	1986	42.8	10.4
Luxembourg	1985	13.7	5.6
Netherlands	1987	42.4	5.0
Sweden	1987	34.9	9.1
U.K.	1986	35.9	9.2
U.S.A.	1986	17.7	17.7

Source: LIS data sets presented in McKinley L. Blackburn, "International Comparisons of Poverty," *American Economic Review* 84 (May 1994), 372.

Estimated rates of "extreme" or "absolute" poverty in developing countries are presented in Table 2.8. These are prepared by the World Bank according to an absolute poverty line of $1.25 per person/day at 2005 PPP prices. This standard was adopted by the World Bank because $1.25 per day is the average of national poverty lines in the 15 poorest countries of the world. In 2005, about 1.4 billion people, or one-fourth of the population of the developing world, lived below this line.[23]

Complications of Income Distribution Comparisons

If international comparisons of income inequality are to be made—whether we employ decile ratios, Lorenz curves, Gini ratios, or poverty rates—we must consider the comparability of the underlying income distribution data. First, the data should be comparable in their coverage and segmentation of the population. For example, data that cover only employed persons or workers will indicate a greater degree of income equality than data that include retired persons, the unemployed, and others with low incomes. With regard to segmentation, the distribution of income among households can be quite different from the distribution of income among families

[23] For additional information about the World Bank's estimates of extreme poverty, see iresearch.worldbank.org/PovcalNet/.

or individual people.[24] Inequality is significantly greater between households in Bangladesh and Sweden, but it is greater between individuals in South Korea and Mexico.[25]

Table 2.8 Extreme Poverty in Developing Countries, 1981-2015

Percentage of the population living on less than $1.25/day				
Region or country	*1981*	*1990*	*2005*	*2015 (forecast)*
East Asia & Pacific	77.7	54.7	16.8	6.8
China	84.0	60.2	15.9	6.1
Europe & Central Asia	1.8	2.0	3.7	2.2
Latin America & Carib.	12.9	11.3	8.2	5.0
Middle East & N. Africa	7.9	4.3	3.6	2.5
South Asia	59.4	51.7	40.3	23.8
India	59.5	51.3	41.6	25.4
Sub-Saharan Africa	53.4	57.6	50.9	37.1
Total	52.2	41.7	25.2	15.5
Number of people living on less than $1.25/day (millions)				
Region or country	*1981*	*1990*	*2005*	*2015 (forecast)*
East Asia & Pacific	1071.5	873.3	316.2	137.6
China	835.1	683.2	207.7	84.3
Europe & Central Asia	7.0	9.1	17.3	9.8
Latin America & Carib.	46.8	49.6	45.1	30.6
Middle East & N. Africa	13.6	9.7	11.0	8.8
South Asia	548.4	579.2	595.6	403.9
India	418.2	435.5	455.8	313.2
Sub-Saharan Africa	210.5	297.5	388.4	356.4
Total	1897.8	1,818.5	1,373.5	947.2

Sources: World Bank, *World Development Indicators*, online; and World Bank, *Global Economic Prospects 2009*, 47.

Second, the data should be comparable in terms of income coverage. That is, the data should have similar coverage of wages, profits, rents, capital gains, transfer payments, income in kind, and so forth. Inclusion of capital gains, for example, usually increases measured income inequality. Comparisons are preferably based on income after taxes and transfer payments, because many countries design these programs to redistribute income.

The significance of these considerations can be illustrated with data relating to the United States. In 1989, the Gini ratio for money income received by families was 0.40, and for households it was 0.43. If government transfer payments were removed from household income, inequality would be much greater, yielding a Gini ratio of approximately 0.48. If household incomes were adjusted to reflect the effects of taxes and noncash transfer payments, measured inequality would be considerably lower, reflected in a Gini ratio of 0.39.[26]

---

[24] According to definitions used by the U.S. Bureau of the Census, a "household" consists of all persons who occupy a housing unit. A "family" consists of two or more related people who reside together. A single person can constitute a household, but he/she cannot constitute a family.

[25] For a comparison of household and individual income distributions for twenty countries, see R. M. Sundrum, *Income Distribution in Less Developed Countries* (London: Routledge, 1990), 77.

[26] U. S. Department of Commerce, Bureau of the Census, *Money Income and Poverty in the United States, 1989*, Current Population Reports, P-60, no. 168 (September 1990), 30; and U. S. Department of Commerce, Bureau

For industrial capitalist countries, the most careful comparisons of income inequality and poverty have been prepared under the auspices of the **Luxembourg Income Study (LIS)**. The heart of the LIS project is a huge unified database of household income surveys from the participating countries. The national data sets have been adjusted to yield comparable values for 42 income variables and 28 demographic variables. After completion of a training program, researchers around the world are able to obtain and manipulate the data through the Internet.[27]

Estimates of income inequality in developing countries are made difficult by poor statistical reporting systems. For reasons that we shall consider in the following section, unemployment is often underestimated in low-income countries, possibly causing an underestimation of income inequality. On the other hand, nonmarket incomes are also underestimated in these countries, possibly causing an overestimation of inequality. According to estimates for Malaysia, the Gini ratio falls from 0.62 to 0.57 (denoting greater equality) when in-kind income, transfer payments, and the value of housing services are included in income.[28]

Unemployment Comparisons

International comparisons of unemployment are facilitated by the fact that international agreements were reached in 1954 and 1982 under the auspices of the International Labour Organization on a standard definition for unemployment.[29] Nevertheless, national practices vary with respect to age limits, reference periods, criteria used to determine whether a person is actively seeking work, treatment of persons who are temporarily laid off, handling of military personnel, and other details that are not included in a standard definition. Moreover, some nations have ignored the international agreements.

Aside from definitional problems, the international comparability of unemployment rates is also damaged by differences in the methods of data collection. The United States, Japan, and several other high-income countries base their unemployment estimates on periodic labor force surveys. These probably yield the best estimates of unemployment because they take account of demographic groups that are usually missed by other methods.

A much larger number of countries, including Germany, the United Kingdom, and most of the developing nations, base their monthly unemployment figures on registrations at governmental employment offices. These may, of course, overlook unemployed persons who choose not to register. In low-income countries where the government employment service has few convenient offices, provides few job placement services, and offers little unemployment compensation, workers have little incentive to register their unemployment. Thus, the employment office in Singapore counted only 8,000 registrations in 1987, but the labor force survey estimated that 59,000 were unemployed.[30]

---

of the Census, *Measuring the Effect of Benefits and Taxes on Income and Poverty: 1989*, Current Population Reports, P-60, no. 169-RD (September 1990), 5.

[27]For a full description of the LIS project, see Timothy M. Smeeding, Lee Rainwater, and Rick Simpson, "Comparative Cross-National Research on Income and Economic Well-Being: The Luxembourg Income Study," *Survey of Current Business* 69 (March 1989): 62-68. The data in Table 2.6 are based on an LIS study.

[28]Michael Kusnic and Julie Davanzo, "Accounting for Non-Market Activities in the Distribution of Income," *Journal of Development Economics* 21 (May 1986): 211-227.

[29]The standard definition and a description of the various systems of data collection are given in *Yearbook of Labour Statistics* (Geneva: International Labour Office, 1988), 617-618.

[30]Employment offices in countries such as Sweden, which provide extensive job training and placement, report registrations that are much closer to the numbers derived from surveys.

In Table 2.9, four sets of unemployment estimates are assembled. The first column lists the rates that are commonly reported by each of the countries, reflecting their various definitions and methods of data collection. A set of standardized estimates, adjusted for comparability by the Organization for Economic Cooperation and Development (OECD), is reported in the second column. For most countries, the differences between official and standardized rates are rather small.

Table 2.9 Alternative Measures of Unemployment, 2006

	Officially Reported Rates	*OECD Standardized Rates*	*Discouraged Workers (% of Labor Force)*	*Involuntary Part-Time Employment (% of Labor Force)*	*Long-Term Share of Total Unemployment**
Australia	4.8	4.8	n.a.	6.6	17.8
Belgium	8.2	8.2	0.3	2.2	55.6
Canada	6.3	6.3	0.1	4.1	8.7
France	8.8	9.5	0.2	3.4	44.0
Germany	10.8	9.8	0.2	3.8	57.2
Greece	8.9	8.9	0.2	2.0	55.6
Italy	6.8	6.8	3.3	3.6	52.9
Japan	4.1	4.1	1.5	4.1	33.0
Netherlands	5.5	3.9	1.4	n.a.	45.2
Spain	8.5	8.5	1.3	3.2	29.5
Sweden	5.4	7.0	2.0	1.9	14.2
U.K.	5.4	5.3	n.a.	1.6	22.1
U.S.A.	4.6	4.6	0.3	0.8	10.0

*The percentage of unemployed persons who have been jobless for twelve months or more.

Sources: Organization for Economic Cooperation and Development; U.S. Bureau of Labor Statistics.

In the third column of Table 2.9, we estimates of the percentages of "discouraged workers" in each labor force. These people are excluded from the conventional measures of unemployment because they have abandoned their active searches for jobs. According to these estimates, inclusion of discouraged workers would raise the unemployment rate by more than 3 percentage points in Italy, by 2 points in Sweden, and by more than 1 point in Japan, Spain, and the Netherlands.

The fourth column of Table 2.9 reports the percentages of workers who would prefer to have full-time jobs, but have been forced to accept part-time jobs. These workers, again, are not counted among the unemployed, even though their time is underemployed. Another form of underemployment that is more difficult to measure, but equally important, is the underutilization of a worker's skills. We have no systematic estimates, for example, of the number of engineers who have settled for jobs that fail to utilize those skills. In Japan, the permanent commitment system of employment causes a substantial amount of "unemployment within the company." According to one estimate, the total unemployment and underutilization of Japanese labor was about 10 percent of the labor force, while the official unemployment rate was only 2 percent.[31]

The last column of Table 2.9 calls attention to the fact that the "headline" rate of unemployment (reported in the first column) tells us little about deeper nature of joblessness,

---

[31] For example, see Koji Taira, "Japan's Low Unemployment: Economic Miracle or Statistical Artifact?" *Monthly Labor Review* 106 (July 1983): 9.

including its duration. Suppose that a large number of workers in Country One are unemployed for very short periods of time, and a small number of workers in Country Two are unemployed for very long periods of time. The two countries may have the same average rate of unemployment, but their conditions are very different. The short spells of unemployment in Country One may be explained by simple movement between jobs (frictional unemployment) in a dynamic economy. Long spells of unemployment in Country Two are evidence of deeper structural flaws in the economic and social system, and they cause more disruption in people's lives. According to the data in Table 2.9, Germany had a higher rate of unemployment than any of the other countries listed, and more than 57 percent of the unemployed had been jobless for a year or more. At the other extreme, the United States had a relatively low rate of unemployment, and also a low incidence of long-term unemployment.

International comparisons of unemployment are also complicated by the existence of underground, unreported employment. Those who hide their incomes in order to obtain welfare benefits, to hide illegal activities, or to avoid taxation are often counted as unemployed. We might hypothesize, therefore, that reported unemployment rates are inflated in countries with high tax rates, large welfare systems, and high crime rates, because of the prevalence of underground employment.

Comparisons of Inflation

Few international comparisons are more dramatic than those for price inflation. In 1992, inflation rates ranged from -4 percent in Panama to about 1,400 percent in Russia. During the single month of November 1993, prices reportedly increased by more than 20,000 percent in Serbia.[32] Unlike unemployment, GDP in constant prices, and other "real" economic statistics, the only technical limit on the inflation rate seems to be our ability to create large volumes of money.

Several considerations should be kept in mind when international comparisons of inflation are made. First, there is significant variation across countries in the quantity and quality of price data collected. In Rwanda, for example, the consumer price index (CPI) is based on data for only 54 products collected from 50 markets and retail outlets in Kigali, the capital city. In the United States, CPI data are collected for 359 product categories in 85 cities from 57,000 housing units and 19,000 retail establishments.[33]

Even in countries where comprehensive data are collected, the "true" rate of inflation is uncertain. Different estimates will be obtained, for example, if price indexes are based on different systems of quantity weights.[34] In the United States, the annual rate of consumer price inflation between 1970 and 1993 was 5.5 percent according to the fixed-weight price index for consumer expenditures, or 5.7 percent according to the implicit deflator for consumer expenditures (which uses variable quantity weights), or 5.9 percent according to the consumer price index (which uses another system of fixed weights).[35] These may seem to be small

[32]Estimate of the Serbian Federal Statistics Office, cited in *RFE/RL Daily Report*, December 2, 1993.

[33]For a detailed comparison of CPI statistics around the world, see *Statistical Sources and Methods, Vol. 1: Consumer Price Indices* (Geneva: International Labour Office, annual).

[34]This is another application of the "index number problem" we discussed earlier. For a comparison of inflation rates based on different systems of quantity weights, see Mary Kokoski, "Experimental Cost-of-Living Indexes: A Summary of Current Research," *Monthly Labor Review* 113 (July 1989): 34-39.

[35]Calculated from index numbers in the *Economic Report of the President* (Washington: USGPO, 1994), 272, 274, and 335.

differences, but they can have a major impact on the economy when price indexes are used to adjust wages, social security benefits, and other payments.

Another difficult issue involves the adjustment of price indexes for changes in product quality and introduction of new products. In most countries, the statistical agencies take little account of these changes. For many years, American price indexes indicated that the average prices of office computers were gradually *increasing*. When new methods were introduced in 1986 to take fuller account of technological improvements, the new index indicated that computer prices had *fallen* by about 55 percent between 1972 and 1983.[36] To this day, the U.S. consumer price index does not account for changes in the quality of most services, such as medical care. Thus, if the average quality and technological sophistication of goods and services are increasing, our price indexes tend to overestimate the rate of inflation. For these and other reasons, a team of economists has recently concluded that inflation estimates in the U.S., based on the consumer price index, are overstated by about one percentage point. If U.S. governmental spending were adjusted downward to reflect the lower actual rate of inflation, the annual budget deficit would decline about $80 billion in 2002.

Special care must be taken when international comparisons include countries that exercise price controls. Many countries, including the United States during the 1940s and 1970s, have imposed price controls at one time or another. Under the system of central planning, the vast majority of prices in the former Soviet Union and Eastern Europe were set and controlled by governmental agencies. During periods of price control, inflation takes three forms: (1) open, reported inflation; (2) hidden inflation; and (3) repressed inflation.

Price control is seldom universal, it usually allows for some **open, reported inflation**. In centrally planned economies, for example, part of agricultural output was usually sold on farmers' markets where it was legal to charge any price the market would bear, and other prices were adjusted from time to time.

Hidden inflation occurs when there are violations or evasions of price regulations. These can take many forms. For example, producers may obtain approval for price increases by introducing "new" products, supposedly higher in quality, that are in fact very similar to the old ones. Or, producers may reduce the quality of a product, but continue to sell it at the old price. Or, producers may reduce the availability of their lower-priced models, forcing consumers to purchase higher-priced models.[37] Finally, suppliers may simply engage in "black market" sales of their goods at prices that exceed controlled levels. In any of these cases, the resulting inflation is not likely to be reflected in official price indexes.[38]

Repressed inflation is a condition in which price controls are effective, so inflationary pressures (such as rapid growth in the money supply) cannot be relieved by open or hidden price increases. Instead, the inflationary pressures manifest themselves in the form of shortages, requiring the distribution of products through queues or rationing.[39] Repressed inflation has a

---

[36]David Cartwright, "Improved Deflation of Purchases of Computers," *Survey of Current Business* 66 (March 1986): 7-10.

[37]This practice, known as forced substitution, was analyzed in a classic article by Nicholas Kaldor, "Rationing and the Cost of Living Index," *Review of Economic Studies* 8 (1940-41): 185-87.

[38]See H. Stephen Gardner, "Product Quality and Price Inflation in Transitional Economies," in *Economic Statistics for Economies in Transition: Eastern Europe in the 1990s*, Proceedings of a conference sponsored by U.S. Bureau of Labor Statistics and Eurostat, Washington, D.C., 1991, 178-92.

[39]Shortages, we should note, do not necessarily indicate the presence of repressed inflation. They may be caused by a faulty set of *relative* prices rather than a low *general* price level.

cumulative effect on the economy. If excessive monetary growth continues year after year, the financial imbalance of the economy will grow larger and larger, eventually requiring a large adjustment in the price level or the monetary system.

Table 2.10 Open and Repressed Inflation in Russia
(Annual Percentage Growth)

	Total Inflationary Pressure	*Open Inflation*	*Hidden/Repressed Inflation*
1981-85 average	6	2	4
1986	6	3	3
1987	7	3	4
1988	8	4	4
1989	11	5	6
1990	19	5	14
1991	367	95	272

Sources: Data for 1981-1988 are from A. Shmarov and N. Kirichenko, "Inflayatsionnyi vsplesk: masshtaby i prichiny," *Ekonomicheskaya gazeta*, no. 13 (1989), 12; data for 1989-1990 are from private communication of the author with Andrei Shmarov. Data for 1991 are rough approximations by the author, based on retail trade, consumer price, and disposable money income indexes in *Planecon Report* 10 (April 28, 1994): 10, 14, and 17.

In Russia, for example, monetary growth during 1981-1990 was consistent with an average annual inflation rate of nearly 8 percent. Every year, though, less than half of this inflationary pressure was allowed to express itself openly in higher prices; the remainder was hidden in quality deterioration or accumulated in repressed inflation (Table 2.10). These imbalances grew far worse in 1991, when the breakup of the Soviet Union led to a loss of monetary control and a collapse of production. Finally, most price controls were released by the Russian government in January 1992, and consumer prices more than tripled in a single month. Prices quickly adjusted to their market-clearing levels, and long lines for products largely disappeared: "Whereas last year there was a shortage of commodities on the market, in 1994 . . . the market is saturated with many goods in spite of a precipitous decline of production."[40]

Summary

Statistical information is invaluable in assessing economic systems, but it should always be handled cautiously. First, there are problems of definition. National income can be defined as gross national product, gross domestic product, net material product, or in a number of other ways. Income distribution and poverty statistics may cover the incomes of households or individuals, before or after taxes. Unemployment statistics may or may not include those who have failed to look for a job in the past month. Inflation may be measured at the consumer, wholesale, or GDP level.

Second, there are inconsistencies between countries in the methods and quality of data collection. In the case of national income measurement, a significant amount of output may not be reported if it is produced for home consumption or the underground economy. Unemployment statistics may be collected through market surveys or from employment office statistics. Price indexes may be based on large or small numbers of geographic areas and commodity groups, and

---

[40] V. Prokhina, S. Rogova, and G. Filimonovskaya, "Household Appliances, Furniture, Housewares; Everything Is Available Now Except Customers," *Torgovaya gazeta*, no. 4 (August 1994), 3, translated in Foreign Broadcast Information Service, *Daily Report: Central Eurasia*, September 14, 1994, 23-27.

they may or may not account for changes in product quality. Price increases may be hidden or repressed in countries that exercise price controls.

Finally, there are problems of interpretation. The very meaning of national income comparisons is clouded by the index number problem. The significance of income distribution statistics depends on one's concept of social equity. The dividing lines between the unemployed, the underemployed, and the "discouraged workers" may be difficult to draw. The rate of repressed inflation may be impossible to measure. These are analytical problems that, even while unsolved, must not be ignored.

Discussion and Review Questions

1. What is the difference between GNP and GDP? Between GNP and NMP?

2. How should the value of services performed by lawyers, accountants, and college professors be measured for inclusion in GDP? How should we measure changes in their productivity?

3. In national income comparisons, what is the advantage of using a common set of average international prices to evaluate each nation's output, rather than converting total national incomes with exchange rates? What problems are not solved by this procedure?

4. If you were asked to prepare a comparison of national standards of living, and you were given an unlimited budget, how would you proceed?

5. Suppose that you are appointed Minister of Propaganda for your country and you wish to say that your country has an even distribution of income. Without actually falsifying the data, how will you collect and arrange them to make your point? What forms of income and taxation will you include? What population unit will you use? With what country will you compare your country's income distribution?

6. What are the differences between open, hidden, and repressed inflation? For the general population (or for various segments of the population), what would be the advantages and disadvantages of living in a country with repressed inflation rather than open inflation?

7. If you have a background in statistics or econometrics, how would you test the hypothesis that a socialist country at a particular level of per capita income tends to have a higher PQLI than a capitalist country at the same level of income?

Suggested Readings

Dallago, Bruno. *The Irregular Economy*. Hanover: Dartmouth Press, 1990. *Probably the best book available on the definition and measurement of the underground economy, and on its operation in market and centrally planned economies.*

Economic Statistics for Economies in Transition: Eastern Europe in the 1990s. Washington, D.C.: U.S. Bureau of Labor Statistics and Eurostat, 1994. *In eighteen chapters contributed by an international team of authors, this book surveys the existing statistical systems in transitional economies and analyzes their needs, but also provides a wealth of information about these systems the United States and Western Europe. See, for example, the discussion of poverty rates in Chapter 13.*

Kravis, Irving, et al. *World Product and Income: International Comparisons of Real Gross Product.* Baltimore: Johns Hopkins University Press, 1982. *Gives a full description of the objectives, methods, and results of the U.N. International Comparisons Project.*

Pryor, Frederic L. *A Guidebook to the Comparative Study of Economic Systems.* Englewood Cliffs, N.J.: Prentice-Hall, 1985. *Pryor has collected an enormous amount of comparative data for capitalist and socialist countries and is a pioneer in the kind of hypothesis testing mentioned in discussion question 7, above.*

Shaikh, Anwar and E. Ahmet Tonak. *Measuring the Wealth of Nations: The Political Economy of National Accounts.* Cambridge: Cambridge University Press, 1994. *A provocative and careful analysis of classical and Marxian approaches to national income theory and measurement.*

Sundrum, R. M. *Income Distribution in Less Developed Countries.* London: Routledge, 1990. *This book focuses on less developed countries, but it provides a clear and full analysis of income inequality that has general application.*

Following are a few of the many sources of current comparative statistical data. You can learn much about comparative statistics by reading their explanatory notes and appendices.

Historically Planned Economies: A Guide to the Data. Washington, D.C.: The World Bank, annual.

International Financial Statistics. Washington, D.C.: International Monetary Fund, monthly, with annual compilations and supplements.

Monthly Bulletin of Statistics. New York: United Nations Statistical Office, monthly.

OECD Economic Outlook. Paris: Organization for Economic Cooperation and Development, biannual.

United Nations Statistical Office. *Statistical Yearbook.* New York: United Nations, annual.

United Nations Development Program. *Human Development Report.* New York: Oxford University Press, annual.

World Bank. *World Development Report.* New York: Oxford University Press, annual.

World Bank. *World Tables.* Baltimore: Johns Hopkins University Press, annual.

World Economic Outlook. Washington, D.C.: International Monetary Fund, annual.

Yearbook of Labour Statistics. Geneva: International Labour Office, annual.

CHAPTER 3

HISTORY AND THEORIES OF CAPITALISM

Less than seventy-five years after *it officially began, the contest between capitalism and socialism is over: capitalism has won. . . . Yet I doubt whether the historic drama will conclude, like a great morality play, in the unequivocal victory of one side and the ignominious defeat of the other. The economic enemy of capitalism has always been its own self-generated dynamics, not the presence of an alternative economic system.*

—Robert Heilbroner,

The New Yorker, January 23, 1989

Capitalism is an economic and social system in which the nation's farms, factories, and mines are owned predominantly by private individuals, partners, and stockholders. Although social ownership may be present, and it may be substantial, it is a deviation from the rule. The market system is the basic coordinating mechanism under capitalism, but each country modifies the forces of supply and demand with its own assortment of traditional behaviors, industrial policies, social welfare programs, and other instruments of social and governmental control. Thus, there are clear distinctions among the economic systems in the United States, Germany, Japan, and the scores of other capitalist nations.

To those of us who live in high-income capitalist countries, many of the institutions of market exchange and private property are so familiar that we take them for granted. We must be reminded that checking accounts, credit cards, patent rights, and markets for stocks, bonds, and real estate are relatively recent innovations in the history of civilization; indeed, they barely exist in many parts of the world today.

As we open this chapter, we will discuss the nature of precapitalist systems, and note a few of the historical forces that gave rise to modern capitalism. Next, we will survey the development of economic analysis of capitalism from the eighteenth century to the present. Finally, we will discuss the nature and significance of the growing internationalization of capitalism.

Precapitalist Economic Systems

At the dawn of civilization, beginning in the fifth millennium B.C., capitalism did not play a noticeable role in the societies that developed along the Tigris, Euphrates, and Nile river valleys. After centuries of tribalism and tradition, an early version of authoritarian central planning was adopted by the Babylonians, Egyptians, Assyrians, Hittites, and Persians. Institutional structures differed from one dynasty to another, but the land and other productive assets were generally owned by the state, individual freedoms were severely restricted, and huge public bureaucracies were maintained to build public works, distribute irrigation water, and manage flood control. The pyramids and the walls of Babylon demonstrated the ability of strong central authorities to mobilize society toward the fulfillment of high-priority projects.[1]

Greece and Rome

Beginning in the twelfth century B.C., the rise of the Greek and Roman city-states ushered in a new era of individual freedom, including economic freedom, for a significant segment of the population. Although perhaps 50 percent of the Greek and 80 percent of the Roman population lived in slavery, a significant number of people were free to choose their occupations; the craft, merchant, and banking professions began to thrive in the cities. Indeed, their prosperity gained the attention of the classical philosophers. Aristotle, for one, was quite disturbed by the fortunes amassed by merchants and bankers:

[Gaining wealth through retail trade] is justly censured; for it is unnatural, and a mode by which men gain from one another. The most hated sort, and with the greatest reason, is usury, which makes a gain out of money itself, and not from the natural object of it. For money was meant to be used in exchange, but not to increase at interest. Wherefore of all modes of getting wealth this is the most unnatural.[2]

Interestingly, although Aristotle argued that the unlimited capitalist pursuit of wealth was "unnatural," he argued in favor of the right of individuals to own private property. Property should be held privately, he said, because "when every one has a distinct interest, men will not complain of one another, and they will make more progress, because every one will be attending to his own business."[3] In other words, Aristotle noted in the fourth century B.C. that an economic system based on private property rights would provide stronger incentives for production than a communal society. On the other hand, he believed that the inequities caused by private property should be balanced with charity: "It is clearly better that property should be private, but the use of it common; and the special business of the legislator is to create in men this benevolent disposition."[4]

Although one author contends that "the Graeco-Roman economy was a free economy in the sense that a number of markets were more or less free to regulate themselves," the system was still quite unlike modern market capitalism.[5] Again, the use of slave labor was a dominant

---

[1]Stephan Viljoen, *Economic Systems in World History* (London: Longman, 1974), 16; and Rondo Cameron, *A Concise Economic History of the World: From Paleolithic Times to the Present* (New York: Oxford University Press, 1989), 30.

[2]Aristotle, *Politics* 1.10.1258a38-1258b7.

[3]Aristotle, *Politics* 2.5.12663a25-29.

[4]Ibid., 1263a38.

[5]Viljoen, *Economic Systems in World History,* 55.

characteristic of the system and retail trade existed for little more than the provision of luxury goods to the upper class. Most of the important economic achievements of the Greek and Roman societies were prompted by governmental commands rather than by market forces, and surplus productive power was used to build impressive public buildings, city walls, and standing armies, rather than factories, machinery, and equipment.

The Middle Ages

Progress toward the establishment of a market capitalist system was interrupted when the western part of the Roman Empire fell in the fifth century A.D. The relative peace and unity that had been imposed by Rome disintegrated into chaos. Long-distance trade became extremely hazardous and it was further restricted by the lack of a common language, legal code, or currency. The countryside was carved into a large number of small, self-sufficient, feudal estates. Each estate was held in trust by a feudal lord, who was responsible for the physical and economic welfare of his vassals. In turn, the serfs were required to work in the lord's fields and shops and to provide him with a portion of their product. Little money changed hands and little trade was conducted with neighboring estates.

The system of mutual obligations between lords and servants in the countryside was paralleled by the craft guilds in the cities. Master craftsmen and their apprentices were bound by a system of indentures, which required faithful service by the apprentices in exchange for instruction by the masters, together with suitable provision of food, clothing, and shelter. The guild organizations enforced a rigid set of regulations concerning everything from hours of work, methods of production, tools, prices, and raw materials that could be used, to the number of apprentices and journeymen that could fall under a single master's control. Thus, labor mobility, entrepreneurship, market flexibility, and technological progress were seriously restricted.[6]

The medieval social structure was legitimized and maintained in the West by the dominant institution of the era, the Roman Catholic church. Thomas Aquinas and other church theologians maintained that the master-servant authority structure, including the institution of slavery, was ordained by God. Indeed, the theologians of the day believed that charitable contributions should be limited in order to allow the upper class to live "in keeping with their social station," because "no man ought to live unbecomingly."[7] On the other hand, Aquinas declared that inordinate accumulation of wealth was sinful, particularly if it was accomplished by selling goods above their "just price" or by charging interest on loans.

A number of developments caused the slow demise of the feudal system. The gradual rebuilding of strong centralized governments in Europe and England restored the unity of

---

[6]For an extended discussion of the Roman and medieval economic systems, see James Angresano, *Comparative Economics* (Englewood Cliffs, N.J.: Prentice Hall, 1992), Chapters 3 and 4.

[7]Thomas Aquinas, *Summa Theologica*, quoted in Jacob Viner, *Religious Thought and Economic Society* (Durham, N.C.: Duke University Press, 1978), 74.

languages, monetary systems, and laws, and reopened trade routes. In the countryside, the slow substitution of money rents for labor services transformed the relationship between lord and serf.

In the thirteenth century, the **enclosure movement** began, whereby the landed aristocracy "enclosed" lands for their exclusive use that had previously been accessible to peasant farmers. As a result, a new class of landless peasants was formed—a class dependent on the wages they could earn by working for others. Thus, the enclosure movement began the stage of development that Karl Marx called "primitive capitalist accumulation," which, in his opinion, "plays in Political Economy about the same part as original sin in theology."[8]

According to Werner Sombart, a German economic historian, the "spirit of capitalism" first manifested itself in the thirteenth century in Italy; by the fourteenth century the Florentines "were filled with a feverish (I had almost said an American) desire for gain, and a devotion to business that almost amounted to passionate love."[9] Italian commerce was facilitated by the substitution of Arabic for Roman numerals in the early thirteenth century, allowing quick and exact calculation, and by the development of a well-ordered system of bookkeeping by the end of the century.[10]

Renaissance and Reformation

The end of the Middle Ages and the beginning of the Renaissance are usually associated with the fall of Constantinople, the capital of the Byzantine Empire, in 1453. Refugees from Byzantium, where the study of Greek and Roman literature and art had continued, reintroduced those ideas in the West and a new era of creativity began. The inventiveness and vision of Leonardo da Vinci and his peers laid the necessary groundwork for the Industrial Revolution that would follow three centuries later.

As the Renaissance continued, Martin Luther unwittingly initiated the Protestant Reformation in 1517 when he attacked the papal practice of indulgences. The rise of Protestantism may have contributed to the rise of capitalism in a number of ways. First, it weakened the legitimizing force behind the feudal order—the Roman Catholic church. Second, the new Protestant theology was more individualistic than Catholic doctrine—confession and interpretation of scripture did not require the intervention of the clergy. The new spirit of individualism may have encouraged the replacement of hierarchical social systems with decentralized markets. Third, according to the German sociologist Max Weber, the Calvinist belief that worldly success was a sign of divine favor inspired a work ethic and an attitude

---

[8]Karl Marx, *Capital*, vol. 1 (New York: International Publishers, 1967), 713.

[9]Werner Sombart, *The Quintessence of Capitalism* (New York: Howard Fertig, 1967), 132. In this, Sombart agreed with Marx, who also believed that capitalism originated in Italy. See Marx, *Capital*, 716.

[10]Sombart, *Quintessence*, 126-127.

toward thrift that supported economic development more effectively than Catholic doctrine and practice.

The Development of Capitalism

The forces of Renaissance, Reformation, enclosure, urban growth, international trade, mathematics, and monetary exchange converged in the late sixteenth and early seventeenth centuries as capitalism spread from the merchant sphere to the productive sphere of the Western economies. In its early stages, a large part of capitalist production was organized around the so-called **putting-out system**, whereby the capitalists bought raw materials, "put them out" to artisans working in their own homes for a piece-wage, and then sold the final product. The scale of such operations could be quite large, as was the case of a British clothier who employed 3,000 home laborers.[11]

In the late 1700s, Britain was shaken by the Industrial Revolution and the American Revolution. The former was initiated by an amazing succession of technical innovations. After 1760, for example, British iron production expanded rapidly as methods were developed that made it possible to use relatively abundant coke, rather than scarce charcoal, in the smelting process. In 1770, James Hargreaves patented the first machine capable of spinning more than one cotton thread at a time and in 1776 James Watt constructed his first successful steam engine. In all, 976 patents were granted in Great Britain for new inventions between 1760 and 1789, compared to only 230 patents between 1730 and 1759.[12]

The new technologies necessitated and supported a number of other developments. First, their effective use required that laborers move their places of work from their homes to mechanized factories. The capitalist or entrepreneur, who previously provided his workers only with raw materials under the putting-out system, became an owner of factories and machinery. Thus, the share of capital formation in British national income rose from approximately 3 percent during the first half of the eighteenth century to 5 percent in 1780, and to 10 percent in the mid-nineteenth century.[13] The result? Between 1770 and 1800, British iron production increased fivefold and cotton textile production increased twelvefold. Overall industrial production, which had risen by only 1.0 percent per year between 1700 and 1783, grew by 3.4 percent per year between 1783 and 1802.[14]

---

[11]E. A. J. Johnson and Herman E. Krooss, *The American Economy: Its Origins, Development, and Transformation* (Englewood Cliffs, N.J.: Prentice Hall, 1960), 58.

[12]Viljoen, *Economic Systems in World History*, 176n.

[13]Ibid., 178.

[14]Walter G. Hoffmann, *British Industry, 1700-1950* (Oxford: Basil Blackwell, 1955), 331.

The Industrial Revolution had begun in England. At Manchester, cartloads and boatloads of people of both sexes and all ages poured into the city to work in the new factories. Of the 12,000 houses in Birmingham in 1790, two-thirds were built after 1760.[15] The share of the British labor force working in agriculture dropped from 60 percent in 1700 to 40 percent in 1820 and to 16 percent in 1890.[16]

Similar movements toward industrialization, mechanization, and urbanization occurred in France, Germany, and the United States after 1830, and in Sweden, Japan, and Russia after 1860. As the volume of world trade grew approximately tenfold between 1830 and 1900, the resulting diffusion of new technology, creation of new markets, and growth of specialization and competition caused industrial development to spread from one country to another. Just as important, in stark contrast to the slow, unsteady pace of economic development before the 1780s, economic growth in the newly emerging capitalist countries was *self-sustaining*. The surplus capacity that had been used to build pyramids by the Egyptians, coliseums by the Romans, and castles by the feudal lords was used by the new capitalist class to build machines and factories, which could be used to build even more machines and factories. Real GDP per capita roughly tripled in England, France, Germany, and Sweden between 1820 and 1913 and it grew more than fourfold in the United States.

Early Views of Capitalism

Mercantilism

We noted previously that the late feudal era was marked by the consolidation of national governments and by the rise of a merchant class with considerable economic and political power. Beginning in the fifteenth century, legislation was passed throughout Europe and England that served the purposes of the ascending civil servants and merchants. The new governments raised needed revenues, for example, by selling "patents of monopoly," which granted the exclusive right to trade with certain foreign countries to a few favored merchants. As a result, by about 1600, the ordinary Englishman could trade only with France, Spain, and Portugal without the intervention of the East India Company or one of the other monopolistic trading companies.

An equally important source of governmental revenue was the collection of tariffs on imported goods. Once again, import tariffs served the purposes of domestic manufacturing and merchant interests by protecting them from foreign competition. Their interests were served so well that the merchants put forth an influential—if self-serving—argument for further import protection.

---

[15]Witt Bowden et al., *An Economic History of Europe Since 1750* (New York: Howard Fertig, 1970), 190.

[16]Angus Maddison, *Phases of Capitalist Development* (Oxford: Oxford University Press, 1982), 35.

The **mercantilist** foreign trade doctrine was based on the proposition, stated most clearly by the French finance minister Colbert, that "the quantity of gold in a state alone determines the degree of its greatness and power."[17] A large stock of monetary gold was believed to stimulate trade within the nation, and it could be used to hire mercenaries and purchase munitions in wartime. Because gold was earned through the sale of exports and was sacrificed through the purchase of imports, the mercantilists argued that active measures should be taken by the government to encourage the former and limit the latter. In short, the mercantilists maintained that the wealth of a nation was advanced most effectively by active governmental intervention in the economy, promotion of monopolies, and restriction of imports.

Adam Smith and Classical Theory

Just as many modern-day proponents of governmental regulation of the capitalist economy can trace their roots to the mercantilists, advocates of laissez-faire capitalism can draw inspiration from the Scottish philosopher and economist, Adam Smith (1723-1790). In *The Wealth of Nations* (1776), Smith declared that provision of consumer goods, not accumulation of gold, "is the sole end and purpose of production."[18] What kind of economic system would serve the needs of consumers most efficiently? Certainly not the mercantile system, which placed limits on imports and encouraged the formation of monopolies. Instead, Smith proposed a system of "natural liberty"—a system that would mobilize the self-interested acts of individuals to pursue social goals:

It is not from the benevolence of the butcher, the brewer, or the baker, that we expect our dinner, but from their regard to their own self-interest.[19]

Every individual necessarily labours to render the annual revenue of the society as great as he can. . . . He intends only his own gain, and he is in this, as in many other cases, led by an invisible hand to promote an end which was no part of his intention. . . . By pursuing his own interest he frequently promotes that of the society more effectually than when he really intends to promote it.[20]

In reply to Aristotle, Aquinas, and other philosophers and theologians who feared the free exercise of self-interest, Smith was confident that competitive forces would protect the consumers. If one butcher, brewer, or baker charged exorbitant prices, the consumers would buy their meat, ale, or bread from another. Indeed, Smith believed that a competitive system would

---

[17]Quoted in Sombart, *Quintessence*, 84.

[18]Adam Smith, *An Inquiry into the Nature and Causes of the Wealth of Nations*, vol. 2 (Oxford: Clarendon Press, 1976), 660.

[19]Ibid., 26-27.

[20]Ibid., 456.

establish itself—with little need for antitrust legislation—if the government-sponsored monopolistic practices of the mercantilists were abandoned:

All systems either of preference or of restraint, therefore, being thus completely taken away, the obvious and simple system of natural liberty establishes itself of its own accord. Every man, as long as he does not violate the laws of justice, is left perfectly free to promote his own interest in his own way, and to bring both his industry and capital into competition with those of any other man, or order of men.[21]

Adam Smith contributed far more, of course, than assertions in favor of his system of natural liberty. He also provided a rather sophisticated—for his day—explanation of the laws of supply and demand that guide the "invisible hand" of the market. If the quantity of a product available for sale on any given day is insufficient to meet the "effectual demand," the price of the product will rise, and the self-interests of producers will encourage them to supply more of the product in the future. In the long run, production will gravitate toward effectual demand, and the price should be sufficient to provide for normal payments of wages, profit, and rent.

According to Smith, the government has only three duties in his system of natural liberty, although they are duties of great importance—to provide for national defense, to administer justice, and to provide public goods ("certain public works . . . which it can never be for the interest of any individual or small number of individuals to erect and maintain").[22] Efficient management of the production system, he believed, was far beyond the capacity of any system of central planning:

The sovereign is completely discharged from a duty, in the attempting to perform which he must always be exposed to innumerable delusions, and for the proper performance of which no human wisdom or knowledge could ever be sufficient, the duty of superintending the industry of private people, and of directing it towards the employments most suitable to the interest of the society.[23]

These declamations against central planning and excessive governmental control have new relevance in the transitional economies of Eastern Europe. According to Vaclav Klaus, the prime minister of the Czech Republic, "I am convinced that Adam Smith supplies us with a vision of where to go that needs no correction. . .It may be trivial to you, but it is not trivial in our part of the world."[24]

---

[21]Ibid.

[22]Ibid., 687-688.

[23]Ibid.

[24]Vaclav Klaus, "Adam Smith's Legacy and Economic Transformation of Czechoslovakia," *Business Economics* 28 (January 1993): 7.

Adam Smith's arguments were refined and extended by successive members of the classical school. Jean-Baptiste Say (1767-1832), Smith's French disciple, continued the campaign against those latter-day mercantilists who argued that a large stock of monetary gold was needed to support the demand for products. With an insufficient supply of money, they contended, the economy would suffer recession or depression. Say's reply was quite simple: The quantity of money in a nation is not terribly important because commodities are ultimately purchased with other commodities. Money is a useful medium of exchange, but it is not the ultimate source of demand for goods:

Sales cannot be said to be dull because money is scarce, but because other products are so. . . . A product is no sooner created, than it, from that instant, affords a market for other products to the full extent of its own value. When the producer has put the finishing hand to his product, he is most anxious to sell it immediately, lest its value should diminish in his hands. Nor is he less anxious to dispose of the money he may get for it; for the value of money is also perishable. . . . Thus, the mere circumstance of the creation of one product immediately opens a vent for other products.[25]

Thus, **Say's Law**, as Keynes stated it over a century later, holds that supply creates its own demand. The government need only create a healthy environment for production and trade, and the free play of the market will ensure that the nation's output is sold. "It is the aim of good government to stimulate production," Say concluded, "and of bad government to encourage consumption."[26] This, in a nutshell, is the idea behind what is now called **supply-side economics**.

Say's Law was a controversial proposition from the very beginning, even among members of the classical school. Thomas Malthus (1766-1834), for one, was skeptical: "I by no means think that the power to purchase necessarily involves a proportionate will to purchase, and I cannot agree . . . that in reference to a nation, supply can never exceed demand."[27]

Of course, Malthus was pessimistic about far more than the ability of the market system to generate a demand for goods. He was more concerned about the ability of the system to generate a sufficient supply of food. It was Malthus who suggested that mankind was destined to endure wars, famine, and plagues because "the power of population is indefinitely greater than the power in the earth to produce subsistence for man."[28] Foreshadowing the arguments of modern-day conservatives, Malthus argued that governmental programs to help the poor would

---

[25]Jean-Baptiste Say, "Of the Demand or Market for Products," in *Classics of Economics*, ed. Charles W. Needy (Oak Park, Ill.: Moore Publishing, 1980), 58.

[26]Ibid., 61.

[27]In a letter to David Ricardo. See David Ricardo, *The Works and Correspondence of David Ricardo,* ed. Piero Sraffa, vol. 6 (London: Cambridge University Press, 1951-1955), 132.

[28]Thomas Robert Malthus, *An Essay on the Principle of Population* (New York: W. W. Norton, 1976), 20.

only exacerbate the population problem. Little wonder that Thomas Carlyle, after he read Malthus, called economics "the dismal science."

Say's Law was accepted uncritically by Malthus's contemporary and close friend, David Ricardo (1772-1823). According to Ricardo, the prospective problems of capitalist society would not stem from an insufficient demand for products or from an insufficient supply of food, but from an undesirable trend in the distribution of national income between laborers, capitalists, and landlords.

Like other classical economists, Ricardo believed that productive investment, undertaken by the emerging capitalist class, was the driving force behind economic growth and development. Economic growth would increase the demand for labor, but any resulting increase in real wages would usually cause an acceleration of population growth. Thus, in the long run, real wages would tend to remain at a level allowing only the physical subsistence of the working class.

In the meanwhile, population growth would stimulate the demand for food and shelter, allowing landlords to collect larger rents for agricultural and residential land. Rising food prices would require the capitalists to pay their employees higher *money* wages in order to maintain *real* wages at a bare subsistence level. Caught between rising money wage costs and land rental costs, the profits retained by capitalists would tend to diminish. As profits continued their decline, Ricardo believed that capitalists would eventually refuse to invest in additional production, and economic growth would come to a halt.

Fortunately, however, Ricardo believed that England could postpone or avoid this chain of events by adopting a policy of free international trade. If mercantilist restrictions on the importation of grain—the Corn Laws—were lifted, Ricardo predicted that food prices, money wages, and land rents would fall and profits would rise.

At any rate, Ricardo believed that England should import more grain because its "comparative advantage" (another concept contributed by Ricardo) lay in industrial production, not in agriculture. Put differently, he believed that the opportunity cost of agricultural production, measured in terms of forgone industrial production, was higher in England than in Europe or America.

Twenty-three years after his death, Ricardo's arguments finally carried the day (with support from the Anti-Corn Law League and food shortages caused by the Irish potato blight of 1845) and the Corn Law was repealed in 1846. England adopted a policy of free trade that persisted until the outbreak of World War I. Between the decades of the 1820s and the 1860s, British imports of wheat multiplied sixteen times and British exports of coal increased by a multiple of twenty-nine.

John Stuart Mill (1806-1873), who is usually considered the last of the great classical economists, perceived still another set of problems in capitalist society. Mill accepted Say's Law, and was not terribly worried about the macroeconomic stability of capitalism. He accepted Ricardo's argument that a falling rate of profit would eventually lead to a cessation of economic growth, but he did not consider this to be a problem:

I cannot . . . regard the stationary state of capital and wealth with the unaffected aversion so generally manifested towards it by political economists of the old school. I am inclined to believe it would be, on the whole, a very considerable improvement of our condition. I confess I am not charmed with the ideal of life held out by those who think that the normal state of human beings is that of struggling to get on; that the trampling, crushing, elbowing, and treading on each other's heels, which form the existing type of social life, are the most desirable lot of human kind, or anything but the disagreeable symptoms of one of the phases of industrial progress.[29]

Whereas Smith and Say took it as a foregone conclusion that the benefits of economic growth and industrialization would filter down to the working class, nearly a century after the advent of the Industrial Revolution, Mill concluded that "it is questionable if all of the mechanical inventions yet made have lightened the day's toil of any human being."[30] To Mill, therefore, what was lacking in nineteenth-century capitalism was not an ample supply of gold, food, or profits, but an adequate code of social justice. Charles Dickens, Mill's contemporary, wrote in *Hard Times* and *Oliver Twist* of the overcrowded, disease-ridden cities created by the Industrial Revolution and of the Poor Law that required the children of paupers to labor in mines and factories for 14-hour workdays, often under horrendous conditions.

The situation was so desperate, Mill lamented, that "if this, or Communism, were the alternative, all the difficulties, great or small, of Communism, would be but as dust in the balance."[31] Nevertheless, Mill believed that other alternatives were available. He advocated the reform, rather than the outright elimination, of capitalism, through governmental taxation of large inheritances, redistribution of income to the poor, and provision of public education, health, and sanitation services. Thus, Mill may be considered an early advocate of welfare capitalism, but an advocate who was concerned with maintenance of work incentives:

Relief must be given; no one must be allowed to starve; the necessaries of life and health must be tendered to all who apply for them; but to all who are capable of work they must be tendered on such terms, as shall make the necessity of accepting them be regarded as a misfortune. . . . To this end, relief must be given only in exchange for labour, and labour at least as irksome and severe as that of the least fortunate among independent labourers.[32]

---

[29]John Stuart Mill, *Principles of Political Economy,* in *Masterworks of Economics,* vol. 2, ed. Leonard D. Abbott (New York: McGraw-Hill, 1973), 163-164.

[30]Ibid., 166.

[31]Ibid., 138.

[32]John Stuart Mill, "The Proposed Reform of the Poor Laws," cited in Robert Ekelund and Robert Hebert, *A History of Economic Theory and Method* (New York: McGraw-Hill, 1983), 182.

Karl Marx: The Socialist Critique

We have seen that Adam Smith and his followers were not blind to the economic problems of their day. Smith was concerned about the spread of monopolistic privileges, Ricardo was worried about the prospects for continued economic growth, Malthus was fearful of population growth, and Mill was disturbed by the living conditions of the lower classes. Nevertheless, none of the classical economists suggested that conditions would deteriorate so severely that the entire capitalist system would be overthrown. Indeed, most of them believed that more extensive application of laissez-faire and free-trade principles would alleviate the remaining problems. Even Mill called only for the legislative reform of capitalism, not for its overthrow.

A very different picture of the history, nature, and future of capitalist society was painted by Karl Marx (1818-1883) and his collaborator, Friedrich Engels (1820-1895). In keeping with their materialist conception of history, Marx and Engels argued that each society spontaneously adopts an economic system that is appropriate for its current stage of economic development. As Engels put it:

The materialist conception of history starts from the proposition that the production of the means to support human life and, next to production, the exchange of things produced, is the basis of all social structure; that in every society that has appeared in history, the manner in which wealth is distributed and society divided into classes or orders is dependent upon what is produced, how it is produced, and how the products are exchanged.[33]

Accordingly, it is natural for simple primitive societies to adopt a simple tribal or communal form of organization. At a higher level of economic development, slavery and feudal institutions are introduced to extract surplus production for the use of the upper class. As society continues to advance, technological improvements make it possible for a single producer to supply a large market area, and workers need to be free to move from agriculture to industry. Enter capitalism. Nevertheless, Marx maintained that the freedom of the working class in capitalist society is illusory: "The worker, whose sole source of livelihood is the sale of his labor power . . . belongs not to this or that capitalist, but to the capitalist class."[34] In other words, laborers are enslaved to the capitalist class because they cannot work for themselves. They cannot work for themselves because all of the means of production are owned by the capitalists. Thus, laborers are exploited in capitalist society in very nearly the same sense that they were exploited in feudal or slave societies, but their status is obscured by the apparent freedom of the labor market—by their ability to move from one capitalist employer to another.

Interestingly, although Marx emphasized the sinister and exploitive aspects of capitalism, he believed these to be necessary evils—necessary for the eventual attainment of socialism:

---

[33]Friedrich Engels, *Socialism: Utopian and Scientific* in *The Marx-Engels Reader*, ed. Robert Tucker (New York: W. W. Norton, 1978), 700-701.

[34]Karl Marx, *Wage Labour and Capital,* in *The Marx-Engels Reader*, 205.

Fanatically bent on making value expand itself, [the capitalist] ruthlessly forces the human race to produce for production's sake; he thus forces the development of the productive powers of society, and creates those material conditions, which alone *can form the real basis of a higher form of society, a society in which the full and free development of every individual forms the ruling principle.*[35]

In other words, Marx and Engels believed that the socialist system was appropriate only for countries that had achieved high levels of economic development, and that market capitalism, with its high rate of investment and its heavy-handed treatment of the labor force, was the *only* system capable of driving society to the level of economic development necessary for the transition to socialism.

A large part of Marx's writing was devoted to the forces that would, in his view, *inevitably* lead to the downfall of capitalism. The root problem is the capitalist himself and his continual accumulation of wealth. The capitalist lives to accumulate, according to Marx, for he derives his enjoyment from amassing wealth rather than from consumption: "He shares with the miser the passion for wealth as wealth."[36] Furthermore, the capitalist must accumulate in order to live—he must invest in machinery and equipment that reduces his costs of production in order to remain competitive.

Driven by desire and necessity, the capitalists' exploitation of labor and accumulation of wealth eventually would cause several other economic and social problems, according to Marx. First, they would combine to cause a chronic underconsumption of goods—a state of excess aggregate supply. The rapid growth of the capital stock and harsh treatment of the labor force would create a fertile environment for the production of goods, but not for their sale. The ability of the working class to purchase the flood of new goods is limited by low income levels, while the capitalist class has a strong preference for saving over consumption. In a word, Marx did not accept Say's Law. Insufficient demand for final products would inevitably lead to a series of business depressions.

Second, Marx believed that the process of capital accumulation would cause the general rate of profit to trend downward. In the long run, he argued, the source of all profits is exploitation of live labor. Investment in machinery and equipment may provide the capitalist with a short-term windfall profit if it reduces his costs of production below those of his competitors, but in the long run his rivals will also invest in the new technology and the price of the final product will fall to a level consistent with the lower industry-wide costs of production. In the end, all the capitalists will invest in the new technology, but none will gain a lasting profit from it. As the capitalists are forced by competition to devote more of their investment to machinery and equipment that does not provide an enduring profit, the rate of profit will fall.

The falling rate of profit, Marx predicted, would encourage capitalists to further exploit their laborers by lengthening the working day and reducing wage rates. Furthermore, the profit

---

[35]Karl Marx, *Capital*, vol. 1 (New York: International Publishers, 1967), 592.

[36]Ibid.

squeeze would drive the smaller and weaker capitalists out of business as their companies are "gobbled up" by the larger capitalists; the small capitalists themselves would be cast into the growing "reserve army of the unemployed." In the end, the capitalist system would self-destruct:

Along with the constantly diminishing number of the magnates of capital . . . grows the mass of misery, oppression, slavery, degradation, exploitation; but with this too grows the revolt of the working class . . . The knell of capitalist private property sounds. The expropriators are expropriated.[37]

In retrospect, many of the predictions made by Marx and Engels were no more, and no less, accurate than the predictions made by Adam Smith, David Ricardo, Thomas Malthus, and John Stuart Mill. For example, the notion that the rate of profit would tend to drift downward in capitalist countries was not originated by Marx, but by Adam Smith. Smith believed that profits would fall as markets grew more competitive, and as economic growth increased the demand for labor and increased real wages. He believed, in other words, that a falling rate of profit was a sign of economic health. Ricardo believed that profits would decline as money wages were driven up by rising food prices. He predicted that the falling rate of profit would eventually cause investment to cease and would lead to a dismal, no-growth, "stationary state." On the other hand, Marx viewed the falling rate of profit as one of the factors that would cause the breakdown of capitalist society. The actual historical trend in the rate of profit is still a subject of considerable controversy.

Critics of Marx can point to several failed predictions. The long-term trend in the living conditions of the working class in industrial countries has been toward improvement, rather than toward greater "misery, oppression, slavery, and degradation."[38] The first socialist revolution did not occur in one of the most developed capitalist countries, as Marx's analysis suggested, but in relatively backward Russia.

On the other hand, Marx was one of the first economists to formally challenge Say's Law and to present an analysis of business cycles. Furthermore, in a day when small businesses were still the norm, Marx foresaw the emergence of the giant business enterprises. Finally, with respect to his prediction of the eventual breakdown of capitalism, orthodox Marxists would suggest that the final chapter is yet to be written.

The Great Depression and J. M. Keynes

If there was ever a time when the Marxian "death knell of capitalism" seemed to toll loudly, it was in 1933. Between 1929 and 1933, some 85,000 American businesses were forced to close their doors, causing national income to drop by 30 percent and the unemployment rate to climb to nearly 25 percent. Literally millions of Americans who had never known poverty were faced

---

[37]Ibid., 763.

[38]For an opposing view, see Xenophon Zolotas, *Economic Growth and Declining Social Welfare* (New York: New York University Press, 1981).

with the threat of starvation. The nightmare of the depression quickly spread to all the other major industrial capitalist countries and many Americans and Europeans turned to the Communist Party for leadership and inspiration.

Among those who were not convinced by the Marxian interpretation of the Depression, we find the eminent British economist, John Maynard Keynes (1883-1946). In 1931, Keynes made his opinion of Marxian economics quite clear:

How can I accept a doctrine which sets up as its bible, above and beyond criticism, an obsolete economic textbook which I know to be not only scientifically erroneous but without interest or application for the modern world? How can I adopt a creed which, preferring the mud to the fish, exalts the boorish proletariat above the bourgeois and intelligentsia who, with all their faults, are the quality of life and surely carry the seeds of human advancement.[39]

Whereas many Marxists believed that the capitalist system was doomed to extinction, Keynes suggested that the system could and should be preserved by appropriate governmental action. In late 1933, Keynes prescribed a program of expansionary fiscal and monetary policies to the new American president, Franklin D. Roosevelt, in an open letter published in the *New York Times*. The influence that this letter, and a meeting between Keynes and Roosevelt in the summer of 1934, may have had on the formulation of the New Deal policies of the 1930s is uncertain. The Roosevelt program, though revolutionary in its own right, was not designed to draw the nation out of the Depression through fiscal and monetary stimulus, but only to provide a minimum level of relief for those in the greatest need.[40] It would require the fiscal stimulus of World War II to prove Keynes's point once and for all.

Although his proposals may not have been fully implemented during the Depression, Keynes was certainly correct (if immodest) when, in 1935, he wrote to his socialist friend, George Bernard Shaw, that he was writing a book that would eventually "revolutionize . . . the way the world thinks about economic problems." His *General Theory of Employment, Interest, and Money*, first published in 1936, has done exactly that. In effect, Keynes rejected elements of both the classical and Marxian views of capitalism and formed his own middle ground.

Keynes broke with his classical heritage most fundamentally on the subject of Say's Law. As we noted earlier, the classical economists (with the notable exception of Malthus) believed that a market economy would spontaneously generate enough demand to purchase all the goods produced by a fully employed work force. Production creates income, they reasoned, and income creates demand. If some individuals choose to save their income rather than spend it, their savings will ordinarily be transferred to borrowers who will, in turn, purchase investment goods. On this last point, Keynes was not convinced:

---

[39]J. M. Keynes, *Essays in Persuasion* (New York: Harcourt, Brace, and Company, 1932), 300.

[40]For a full discussion of this point, see Herbert Stein, *The Fiscal Revolution in America* (Chicago: University of Chicago Press, 1969), Chapter 4.

Those who think in this way are deceived . . . by an optical illusion, which makes two essentially different activities appear to be the same. They are fallaciously supposing that there is a nexus which unites decisions to abstain from current consumption with decisions to provide for future consumption, whereas the motives which determine the latter are not linked in any simple way with the motives which determine the former.[41]

If the market could not be trusted to automatically generate investment demand sufficient to absorb the savings of a fully employed labor force, the government must take action to fill the void: "I conceive, therefore, that a somewhat comprehensive socialization of investment will prove the only means of securing an approximation to full employment; though this need not exclude all manner of compromises and of devices by which public authority will cooperate with private initiative."[42]

Although Keynes agreed with Marx on the invalidity of Say's Law, he disagreed on a number of equally important issues. As we have seen, Marx believed that, regardless of any governmental action, the internal contradictions of capitalism would inevitably lead to: (1) a violent overthrow of the system, (2) establishment of social ownership of the means of production, and (3) social control of the allocation of resources and the distribution of income. In contrast, Keynes believed: (1) that the measures needed to restore and maintain full employment "can be introduced gradually and without a break in the general traditions of society"; (2) that "it is not the ownership of the instruments of production which it is important for the State to assume," but control of the aggregate level of demand for goods; and (3) that the allocation and distribution of goods and resources should be left to private, rather than social, initiative:

If our central controls succeed in establishing . . . full employment as nearly as is practicable, the classical theory comes into its own again from this point onwards. If we assume the volume of output to be given, . . . then there is no objection to be raised against the classical analysis of the manner in which private self-interest will determine what in particular is produced, in what proportions the factors of production will be combined to produce it, and how the final product will be distributed between them.[43]

In the end, Keynes seemed to be confident that the capitalist system could survive into the distant future if his proposals were accepted. With a "right analysis of the problem," he suggested that it would be possible to "cure the disease [of unemployment] whilst preserving efficiency and freedom."[44]

---

[41]John Maynard Keynes, *The General Theory of Employment, Interest, and Money* (New York: Harcourt, Brace, and World, 1964), 21.

[42]Ibid., 378.

[43]Ibid., 378-379.

[44]Ibid., 381.

Schumpeter and "Creative Destruction"

The publication of Keynes's *General Theory* was a major event in the economics profession, and the book immediately drew strong praise and harsh criticism. Among the most notable critics, Joseph Schumpeter (1883-1950) and Friedrich A. Hayek (1899-1992) were two Austrian economists who emigrated in the early 1930s to avoid Hitler's onslaught. Both were influenced by an intellectual tradition at the University of Vienna that emphasized methodological individualism and dismissed macroeconomic analysis.

A former Austrian minister of finance, Schumpeter came to the United States in 1931 and served for many years on the faculty at Harvard University. He claimed that Keynes's theory was based on a simplistic view of production; an increase in output requires a proportional increase in employment. "The outstanding feature of capitalism," though, is that production functions "are being incessantly revolutionized." Thus, Keynes has devised "the theory of another world" that is "out of all contact with modern industrial fact, unemployment included."[45]

In 1942, Schumpeter advanced his own analysis of economic and social development in *Capitalism, Socialism, and Democracy*. The driving force behind capitalism, he said, is the entrepreneur, who continually revolutionizes production with new products, technologies, and systems of industrial organization. To make room for new economic structures, the old must be removed. Thus, the process of **creative destruction** is "the essential fact about capitalism."[46] Many of the apparent failures of capitalism are necessary for its subsequent achievements.

Applied at the macroeconomic level, Schumpeter's doctrine suggests that business recessions are a necessary component of capitalist economic development; they clear away the wreckage of old enterprises, products, and technologies to make way for the new. Thus, Keynesian policies designed to stabilize the economy and prevent unemployment are likely to kill the capitalist goose that lays the golden eggs. "The real tragedy," said Schumpeter, "is not unemployment *per se*, but unemployment plus the impossibility of providing adequately for the unemployed without impairing the conditions of further economic development."[47]

At the microeconomic level, Schumpeter rejected the notion that large monopolistic firms are likely to exploit their market power and operate inefficiently. To provide for their future survival, monopolists must search for new products and technologies today; "the businessman feels himself to be in a competitive situation even if he is alone in his field." In their race against

---

[45]Joseph Schumpeter, Review of *The General Theory of Employment, Interest, and Money* by John Maynard Keynes, in *Journal of the American Statistical Association* (December 1936): 793.

[46]Joseph A. Schumpeter, *Capitalism, Socialism, and Democracy*, 3rd ed. (New York: Harper and Brothers, 1950), 82-83.

[47]Ibid., 70.

creative destruction, large corporations attract the best financial, physical, and human resources; they are "the most powerful engine of progress" in capitalist society.[48]

In the long run, Schumpeter believed that capitalism itself would fall victim to creative destruction. Unlike Marx, who believed that capitalism would be overthrown by economic instability and class warfare, Schumpeter argued that the system would be undermined by its own achievements. Capitalist industrialization and financial analysis would have a "rationalizing" influence on society. Business management and innovation would become routine, practiced by salaried professionals rather than profit-seeking entrepreneurs. In the end, capitalist enterprises would be transformed peacefully into nationalized industries. Schumpeter asked, "Can capitalism survive?" and answered, "No. I do not think it can."[49]

In retrospect, it seems that Schumpeter underestimated the staying power of capitalism. After a wave of industrial nationalization in Europe after World War II, the past decade has witnessed an equally dramatic wave of privatization. In recent years, private enterprise has been winning new converts around the world. The entrepreneur, once considered an endangered species, has continued to generate new products, technologies, and modes of organization.

On the other hand, Schumpeter's concept of "creative destruction" still provides a useful framework to analyze the dynamics of capitalist development. Consider, for example, the failures of financial institutions in the United States during the 1980s and the recent collapse of production in the transitional economies of Russia and Eastern Europe. "Failures" such as these are usually ascribed to shortcomings in private management, public regulation, or macroeconomic policy. From a Schumpeterian perspective, they may serve a positive purpose. They may leave behind leaner, more efficient institutions, better able to withstand the competitive pressures of the world economy.

Hayek and the Economics of Information

Friedrich Hayek, who taught at the London School of Economics and the University of Chicago, was more adamantly opposed to Keynesian policy than Schumpeter. In 1944, Hayek warned that the United States and England were embarking on a catastrophic "road to serfdom." Drawing on the experience of Nazi Germany, Hayek feared that macroeconomic management would lead to central planning, and central planning would lead to despotism:

In Germany it was largely people of good will, men who were admired and held up as models in the democratic countries, who prepared the way for . . . everything they detest. Yet our chance of averting a similar fate depends on our facing the danger and on our being prepared to

---

[48]Ibid., 85 and 106.

[49]Ibid., 61. Empirical studies provide some support for Schumpeter's analysis of the entrepreneurial behavior of large corporations. See Zoltan J. Acs and David B. Audretsch, "Testing the Schumpeterian Hypothesis," *Eastern Economic Journal* 14 (April-June 1988): 129-140.

revise even our most cherished hopes and ambitions if they should prove to be the source of the danger.[50]

Against those who claimed the inevitability of more macroeconomic management and planning, Hayek argued that central authorities could not utilize information as efficiently as the market economy. "The most significant fact" about the market system, he suggested, "is the economy of knowledge with which it operates, or how little the individual participants need to know in order to be able to make the right action." Individual consumers and businesses have detailed information about their own circumstances, and the other information they need is distilled in market prices. The proper goal of economic policy should be to "dispense with the need of conscious control" and provide incentives for individuals to exhibit desirable behavior "without anyone having to tell them what to do."[51] Direct governmental intervention is likely to distort relative prices and disturb the operation of markets.

In a letter to Hayek, Keynes insisted that the dangers of economic planning would be ameliorated in an enlightened democratic society. "We almost certainly want more" planning, not less, "but the planning should take place in a community in which as many people as possible, both leaders and followers, wholly share your own moral position. Moderate planning will be safe if those who carry it out are rightly oriented in their own minds and hearts to the moral issue."[52] Hayek may have been flattered, but he was not convinced.

New Twists on Old Ideas

Despite the reservations of his critics, Keynes's theory of macroeconomic management gained prominence after World War II. The theory was supported by Simon Kuznets' pioneering work during the war on national income accounts, and it was popularized by Paul Samuelson's landmark textbook, *Economics* (first published in 1948).

The first explicit exercise of Keynesian policy on American soil was undertaken when the Kennedy administration took office in 1961. Faced by a rising rate of unemployment in that year, Walter Heller, the president's unabashedly Keynesian economic advisor, called for a major program of tax cuts, despite the fact that the federal budget was already in deficit.

The tax cut was finally enacted in 1964, during the first year of the Johnson administration. Soon thereafter, Johnson laid on two additional programs of fiscal stimulus. First, under the Great Society program, federal expenditures on social welfare were more than doubled

---

[50]Friedrich A. Hayek, *The Road to Serfdom* (Chicago: University of Chicago Press, 1944), 3.

[51]Friedrich A. Hayek, "The Use of Knowledge in Society," *American Economic Review* 35 (September 1935): 519-530.

[52]John Maynard Keynes, *The Collected Writings of John Maynard Keynes* 27 (London: Macmillan, 1973), 387.

between 1965 and 1970. Second, as U.S. participation in the Vietnam War escalated, defense spending increased by about 56 percent between 1965 and 1968. The result? The federal budget deficit, which stood at $1.6 billion in 1965, ballooned to over $25 billion in 1968. The unemployment rate, which stood at 6.5 percent when the Kennedy administration took office in 1961, steadily fell to 3.4 percent in 1969.

The Keynesian policies had worked, but at a heavy cost (in addition to the human cost of the Vietnam War). Fueled by rising fiscal deficits, financed by the creation of new money, consumer price inflation accelerated. Efforts by the Nixon and Ford administrations to control inflation and unemployment through a combination of monetary and fiscal policies and price controls seemed only to make the situation worse. In 1975 the unthinkable happened—the inflation rate, at 9 percent, and the unemployment rate, at 8.5 percent, both hit new postwar record levels *in the same year*. Keynesian demand management policies came under attack from several quarters. "By about 1980," says Alan Blinder, "it was hard to find an American academic macroeconomist under the age of 40 who professed to be a Keynesian."[53]

Monetarism

The monetarist school, led by Milton Friedman, initiated a conservative resurgence in macroeconomic policy in the 1970s. Reaffirming Say's Law, monetarists believe that the market system will spontaneously achieve full employment (or, as Friedman puts it, the unemployment rate will adjust to its "natural" level) if two basic requirements are met. First, the government must allow the market system to operate with a great deal of freedom. Thus, monetarists are generally opposed to minimum wage laws, agricultural price supports, exchange rate restrictions, wage and price controls, or other measures that limit market flexibility.

Second, the monetary authorities must maintain a slow but steady growth of the nation's money supply. Between 1929 and 1933, when the Federal Reserve allowed the money supply to shrink by about 25 percent, unemployment ravaged the United States. Thus, according to Friedman, the Great Depression did not demonstrate the instability of capitalism; it only proved the importance of a stable monetary policy.

Beginning in the late 1970s, a number of countries—including the United States, France, the United Kingdom, and Chile—experimented with monetarist policies to cure inflationary problems. More recently, monetarist "shock treatments" have been administered in several of the transitional economies of Eastern Europe. These programs generally have been effective against inflation, but often at the cost of mass unemployment.

---

[53]Alan S. Blinder, "The Fall and Rise of Keynesian Economics," *Economic Record* 64 (December 1988): 278.

Supply-Side Economics

Disillusionment with monetarism in recent years has set the stage for new strands of economic thought at the conservative end of the political spectrum. Perhaps the most influential of these is the supply-side movement, which declares that Keynesians and monetarists have overemphasized the importance of the demand for goods and have paid too little attention to the factors that influence productivity.[54] Supply-siders agree with monetarists on the veracity of Say's Law, and they agree that the economic role of the government should be strictly limited, but they generally disagree with monetarists on the desirability of a fixed monetary growth rule.

Supply-siders can be divided into two camps. The traditional wing advocates low marginal tax rates, deregulation of industry, and a flexible anti-inflationary monetary policy. These policies, they believe, will contribute to high levels of capital investment, economic efficiency, and economic growth. The "new" supply-siders can be distinguished from the traditional camp by their support of a monetary gold standard or some other form of commodity-money standard, and by their more extravagant claims. Reductions in marginal tax *rates*, they say, will stimulate work incentives and economic growth to such an extent that *total* tax revenues will increase. According to Martin Feldstein, a traditionalist, the claims of these supply-side "extremists" were disproved by the budget deficits that arose from the tax cuts of the 1980s.[55]

New-Keynesians and Post-Keynesians

On the liberal reformist wing of the political spectrum, we find a diverse group of economists who are attempting to extend Keynesian theory and adapt it to new conditions. The New Keynesians (NKs) have attempted to build a microeconomic foundation for the theory of unemployment. Generally, NK theories are meant to explain inflexibilities of prices and wages that prevent markets from clearing.[56]

The Post-Keynesians (PKs) are an even more diverse group, including American institutionalists, Keynes's followers at Cambridge, and a broad array of other critics of neoclassical economics. According to Alfred Eichner, five essential elements distinguish PK theory from the neoclassical orthodoxy. First, PK theory is usually concerned with economic growth, where neoclassical theory (including the textbook version of Keynesian theory)

---

[54]Supply-side analysis has been influential in the policy sphere, but the "new classical" and "rational expectations" schools have made important contributions in the intellectual sphere. For a useful survey, see N. Gregory Mankiw, "A Quick Refresher Course in Macroeconomics," *Journal of Economic Literature* 28 (December 1990): 1645-1660.

[55]Martin Feldstein, "Supply Side Economics: Old Truths and New Claims," *American Economic Review* 76 (May 1986): 26-30.

[56]Robert J. Gordon, "What Is New-Keynesian Economics?" *Journal of Economic Literature* 28 (September 1990): 1115-1171.

emphasizes static equilibrium. Second, the key determinant of growth is taken to be the rate of investment and the rate of growth is directly related to the distribution of income. Third, the money supply is believed to play an important role in long-term economic growth, where the neoclassical model would say that it only determines the general price level. Fourth, the competitive assumptions of neoclassical theory are replaced with an explicit treatment of the influence of multinational corporations and labor unions. And fifth, PK analysis aspires to include treatment of nonmarket forms of resource allocation—including the operation of the government.[57]

A more concise definition is offered by Joan Robinson: "To me, the expression *post-Keynesian* has a definite meaning; it applies to an economic theory or method of analysis which takes account of the difference between the future and the past."[58] Like their namesake, the Post Keynesians recognize that the future is uncertain and they believe that speculative behavior lends instability to the capitalist system. Unlike Keynes, who believed that the government should primarily involve itself in macroeconomic stabilization, many of the PKs support an active public role in the distribution and allocation of income and resources.

Radical Economics

Finally, somewhere to the left of the average PK, we find a group of neo-Marxists and other radicals who continue to believe that the capitalist system is beyond reform—it must be replaced. With some updating and revisions, the radicals generally accept the Marxian analysis of exploitation and class struggle in capitalist society. The present stage of capitalism, they say, is distinguished by at least three characteristics: (1) the ascendance of large, "monopolistic" enterprises; (2) the leadership of multinational corporations in the internationalization of capital; and (3) the absence of a strong socialist opposition. Under these conditions, capitalism is free to "intensify exploitation, inequality, polarization, and susceptibility to crises both within and between countries." Left unchecked, the "rule of capital promises nothing but disaster for the human species." In the long run, our only hope for survival "lies in the rebirth of a powerful revolutionary opposition."[59]

Trends in Global Capitalism

Regardless of their ideologies, economists generally agree that capitalism is now a global phenomenon. Technological revolutions in the fields of international transportation and

---

[57]Alfred Eichner, "Post-Keynesian Theory: An Introduction," *Challenge* 21 (May-June 1978): 4-17.

[58]Joan Robinson, "Keynes and Ricardo," *Journal of Post-Keynesian Economics* 1 (Fall 1978): 12.

[59]Paul M. Sweezy, "Monthly Review in Historical Perspective; Marxist Analysis of the 20th Century," *Monthly Review* 45 (January 1994).

communication have reduced the importance of political boundaries and have enhanced every aspect of international cooperation and competition:

* Internationalization of Trade. World merchandise trade turnover grew from 26 percent of global production in 1980 to 32 percent in 1992.60 Growing trade relations are supported by an expanding web of international and regional free-trade organizations and agreements.

* *Internationalization of Investment, Production, and Employment.* In a world of multinational corporations and mobile international employees, it grows ever more difficult to draw clear lines between the economies of individual countries. What, for example, is an American product? Is it something produced in the United States by American workers, or is it something produced by American-owned companies, located in the United States or abroad? By the first definition, which is the conventional one, the United States had a $28 billion trade *deficit* in 1991. By the second definition, incorporating the sales of American-owned foreign affiliates, the United States recorded a $24 billion trade *surplus* in the same year.[61] In 1960, all of Motorola's employees were in the United States; in 1993, 44 percent were outside the country.[62]

* *Internationalization of Finance.* With increasingly integrated international capital markets, investors are able to search the world for the highest rates of return on their savings. Mutual funds make it possible for even small investors to dabble in the international capital markets. The volume of international issues increased from less than $10 billion in 1990 to nearly $54 billion in 1994.[63] International capital flows can have a major impact on the distribution of global economic activity. For example, Mexican savings were equal to 17 percent of GDP in 1992, but capital inflows made it possible for Mexico to finance investments equal to 24 percent of GDP.

* *Internationalization of Information.* International exchanges of information, says Peter Drucker, "are probably growing faster than any category of transactions in history."[64] In a world of Internet, CNN, cellular phones, satellites, fiber-optics, and videoconferences, ubiquitous information is both product and propeller of the globalization process.

---

[60]According to levels and growth rates in World Bank, *World Development Report 1994* (New York: Oxford University Press, 1994), 165, 167, and 187.

[61]J. Steven Landefeld, Obie Whichard, and Jeffrey Lowe, "Alternative Frameworks for U.S. International Transactions," *Survey of Current Business* 73 (December 1993): 57-61.

[62]Ray Marshall, "Internationalization: Implications for Workers," *Journal of International Affairs* 48 (Summer 1994): 60.

[63]Euromoney Bondware estimates, published in *Financial Times*, January 23, 1995, 13.

[64]Peter F. Drucker, "Trade Lessons from the World Economy," *Foreign Affairs* 73 (January/February 1995): 100.

Is all this internationalization a good thing? Will it contribute to the wealth and security of the participating nations? Most radical economists would answer these questions with an emphatic no. Expansion of the world capitalist system through international trade, investment, and employment will, in their opinions, exacerbate the exploitation of labor and natural resources, widen the gulf between the rich and the poor, and elevate the levels of conflict within and between nations.

Based on the doctrines of Adam Smith and David Ricardo, the large majority of mainstream economists (including monetarists, supply-siders, many New-Keynesians and Post-Keynesians, and others) seem to agree that internationalization of *trade* is a good thing. Thus, in a 1990 survey, 71 percent of U.S. economists said they "generally agree" with the statement, "Tariffs and import quotas usually reduce general economic welfare," and another 21 percent said they "agree with provisos."[65]

Many mainstream economists also believe that trade encourages international communication and understanding, contributing to peace and goodwill. John Stuart Mill may have been a bit naive in his belief that "commerce . . . is rapidly rendering war obsolete," but it is difficult to imagine a peaceful world without healthy diplomatic, cultural, and trade relationships.[66]

Although mainstream economists generally believe that commodity trade is beneficial to all participating countries, they are less certain about the benefits derived from international investment, employment, and finance. Classical theory suggests that free mobility of capital and labor should lead to *global* improvements in efficiency and productivity, strengthening the overall performance of the world economy. Unlike international commodity trade, though, which is thought to benefit each of the participating countries, international factor movements may cause gains for some countries and losses for others.

Internationalization of employment, for example, is beneficial to workers who are willing and able to search the world for attractive opportunities, and it may contribute to the dynamism and efficiency of the global economy, but it may threaten the long-term economic health of individual nations. In 1993 alone, Russia lost some 70,000-90,000 of its most talented scientists and intellectuals, and 80 percent of Russian scientists said they would like to emigrate.[67] China sent 230,000 of its brightest students abroad for higher education between 1978 and 1994, but less than one-third returned home; the return rate from the United States was less than 10

---

[65]Richard M. Alston, J. R. Kearl, and Michael B. Vaughan, "Is There a Consensus Among Economists in the 1990s?" *American Economic Review* 82 (May 1992): 204.

[66]John Stuart Mill, *Principles of Political Economy*, vol. 2 (New York: Hill and Company, 1904), 95.

[67]Dmitry Chelyshev, "Brain Drain Threatens Nation's Scientific Heritage," Inter Press Service, November 21, 1994.

percent.[68] The United States itself is not immune to the international brain drain. According to a recent survey, about 25 percent of college-educated Americans and those who earn at least $50,000 a year have considered moving abroad.[69]

If a country is injured by loss of its talented workers, what of its capital resources? Would the economies of the capital-exporting countries be healthier if they built more factories, farms, and highways at home, rather than abroad (Table 3.1)? Adam Smith and the other classical economists anticipated this issue, but doubted its significance. An investor, Smith reasoned, will ordinarily "employ his capital as near home as he can, and consequently as much as he can in the support of domestic industry." The investor naturally prefers domestic operations because "his capital is never so long out of his sight," he can "know better the character and situation" of his business associates, and he "knows better the laws of the country."[70]

These "natural" barriers to international investment may have been effective in the eighteenth century, but they have little relevance in a world of multinational corporations, global investment funds, fax machines, and videoconferences. Once again, these developments may hold great promise for the global economy, but their significance for individual nations is unclear. What would Adam Smith, the nationalist, say about all this? We can only wonder.[71]

---

[68]Rone Tempest, "China Tries to Lure Its Best Back Home," *Los Angeles Times*, January 3, 1995, A1.

[69]Gary Belsky, "Escape from America," *Money*, July 1994, 60.

[70]Smith, *Wealth of Nations*, vol. 1, 454.

[71]See Joseph Persky, "Adam Smith's Invisible Hands," *Journal of Economic Perspectives* 3 (Fall 1989): 195-201. For a more optimistic assessment, suggesting that "investment abroad creates jobs at home," see Drucker, "Trade Lessons from the World Economy," 99-108.

Table 3.1 Global Pattern of Direct Investment, 1970-2004
(Million Dollars)

	1970	*1980*	*1990*	*2000*	*2004*
OUTFLOWS					
Developed Countries	*14,101*	*50,407*	*225,946*	*1,092,747*	*637,360*
North America	8,521	23,328	36,219	187,301	276,747
Europe	5,095	24,128	138,916	866,090	309,498
Other Developed	485	2,950	50,811	39,356	51,115
Developing Countries	*49*	*3,336*	*12,701*	*143,226*	*83,190*
Africa	19	1,089	689	1,573	2,824
South & South East Asia	- 1	458	11,911	79,664	69,429
Latin America	31	1,174	1,062	60,581	10,943
South East Europe & CIS	..	..	35	3,176	9,707
World	*14,150*	*53,743*	*238,681*	*1,239,149*	*730,257*
INFLOWS					
Developed Countries	*9,496*	*46,629*	*172,072*	*1,134,293*	*380,022*
North America	3,083	22,725	56,004	380,798	102,152
Europe	5,226	21,569	104,308	722,762	223,400
Other Developed	1,187	2,335	11,759	30,733	54,469
Developing Countries	*3,937*	*8,455*	*35,736*	*253,179*	*233,227*
Africa	1,266	400	2,840	9,627	18,090
South & South-East Asia	706	3,689	22,158	141,955	137,705
Latin America	1,681	7,494	9,586	97,523	67,526
South East Europe & CIS	..	24	75	9,067	34,897
World	*13,434*	*55,108*	*207,883*	*1,396,539*	*648,146*

Source: UNCTAD – Online Foreign Direct Investment Data, *Key Data from WIR Annex Tables.*
http://www.unctad.org/Templates/Page.asp?intItemID=3277&lang=1

The Evolving Framework of World Capitalism

At the end of World War II, many people feared a repetition of the events that followed the previous war, when an economic slump led to a destructive round of protectionism and "beggar thy neighbor" trade policies, culminating in a protracted economic depression. Hoping to prevent these developments, delegates from 44 countries met in Bretton Woods, New Hampshire, for the International Monetary and Financial Conference of 1944. After three weeks of meetings, the delegates agreed to create two important organizations: the International Monetary Fund (IMF) and the International Bank for Reconstruction and Development (IBRD or World Bank).

Under the original design of the **Bretton Woods system**, the IMF would promote international monetary stability by helping member countries with short-term balance-of-payments problems and by supporting a system of fixed, but adjustable, currency exchange rates. The World Bank would assist the European countries in their reconstruction from the war by facilitating the flow of investment capital. By most accounts, the IMF and the World Bank performed their original functions rather well. Western Europe recovered quickly from the war, and a broad system of stable exchange rates was maintained for more than twenty years.

In the mid-1950s, the World Bank shifted its focus from Europe to the developing countries, where it initially provided financing for public sector infrastructure projects. Since that time, the Bank and its affiliates have broadened the functional and geographic scope of their activities.[72] Functionally, they have provided funding for educational, environmental, and public health programs, provided dispute settlement and risk insurance services, and provided support for economic reform, private sector development, and privatization programs. Geographically, they now provide support to the vast majority of developing countries in the world, including most of the former communist countries.

The original mission of the IMF virtually disappeared in the early 1970s, when the major industrial countries abandoned the system of fixed exchange rates. The institution was able to redefine itself, however, when rising oil prices in the 1970s led to the world debt crisis of the 1980s. The IMF played a prominent role in the negotiation of debt restructuring agreements, and worked with the debtor countries to design policies for financial stabilization and economic reform. More recently, the IMF has provided financial and technical support to countries passing through the transition from central planning to the market system.

In addition to the World Bank and the IMF, delegates to the 1944 Bretton Woods conference also discussed the creation of an International Trade Organization (ITO), a powerful body that would be responsible for removal and prevention of international trade barriers. An ambitious charter for the ITO was formulated at a series of conferences in London, Geneva, and Havana, but, in the end, was unacceptable to U.S. business interests, and failed to gain approval from the U.S. Senate. Without U.S. participation and leadership, the ITO charter became a dead letter.

In 1947, in the wake of the ITO failure, twenty-three countries agreed to establish a less powerful organization, known as the General Agreement on Tariffs and Trade (GATT), which the United States could join without congressional approval. Each member, or "contracting party," of the GATT agreed to: (1) participate in multinational negotiations to reduce tariffs and other trade barriers; (2) reduce the number of import quotas; and (3) extend **most-favored nation (MFN)** treatment to all other members (that is, if country X grants a tariff reduction to one country, it automatically grants the same reduction to all other member countries). The agreement provided an important exception to the MFN rule for countries joining customs unions and free-trade areas.

---

[72]Today, the World Bank Group is comprised of five institutions: The original International Bank for Reconstruction and Development (IBRD), established in 1946, makes market-based loans, primarily to governments; the International Finance Corporation (IFC), 1956, makes market-based loans to the private sector; the International Development Association (IDA), 1960, makes concessional loans to governments in low-income countries, funded primarily from grants; the International Center for Settlement of Investment Disputes (ICSID), 1966, resolves disputes between foreign investors and host governments; and the Multilateral Investment Guarantee Agency (MIGA), 1988, provides risk insurance to promote investment.

Under the GATT umbrella, eight major rounds of multilateral tariff negotiations have been completed, yielding reductions of average tariffs on industrial products in the major industrial countries from about 40 percent of product value in 1947 to less than 4 percent today. The number of participants increased from 23 countries in the first round of GATT negotiations to 117 in the eighth round. If tariff reduction was the focus of the first six rounds of negotiations, removal of non-tariff barriers has gained prominence since 1973, when the seventh, or Tokyo Round, commenced.

The eighth round of GATT negotiations began in 1986 in Punta del Este, Uruguay, and was concluded in 1993. This was clearly the most ambitious GATT negotiation ever undertaken. Among its important provisions are the following:

* *World Trade Organization*. In memory of the unbegotten ITO, a new World Trade Organization (WTO) was created to replace the GATT organization. Unlike GATT, the WTO has a powerful system of dispute-resolution panels, whose decisions cannot be vetoed by members.

* *Industrial Tariffs*. Average tariff rates on imports were scheduled to decline by about 38 percent in the developed countries and 20 percent in the developing countries (Table 3.2). The developed countries agreed to completely eliminate tariffs for several sectors that account for about 40 percent of their imports, including steel, paper, furniture, pharmaceuticals, and medical, construction, and farm equipment.

* *Agriculture*. Trade-distorting subsidies and other import barriers were scheduled for cuts over a period of six years. Subsidized agricultural exports were cut by 21 percent. Japan and South Korea agreed to end bans on rice imports. All quantitative restrictions were to be replaced by tariffs, which would be scheduled for reductions.

* *Intellectual Property*. Countries joining the WTO must accept an extensive system of intellectual property rights protection, including seven years of protection for trademarks, twenty years for patents, and up to fifty years for copyrights.

* *Services*. A General Agreement on Trade in Services (GATS) was adopted, providing the first legally enforceable and multilateral framework for liberalization of trade and investment in services. Few specific commitments were made during the Uruguay Round (some countries agreed to open their markets to legal services, accounting, and software), but negotiations are continuing under the GATS.

Estimates from computable general equilibrium models suggest that full implementation of the Uruguay Round agreement should contribute $510 billion (or about 2 percent) to world GDP, but the actual contribution may be much larger. All regions of the world are expected to benefit from the agreement, but the European Union is expected to capture the largest gains. European countries should benefit from removal of costly distortions in agriculture and from increased access to foreign markets for high-technology goods and services.[73]

Globalism and Regionalism

As we noted earlier, the 1947 GATT accord required nondiscriminatory trade among its members, based on the unconditional most-favored-nation principle. Successive rounds of GATT negotiations have led to global and multilateral reductions of trade barriers. At the same time, the original GATT included an important exception to the doctrine of nondiscrimination, allowing members to form exclusive free-trade areas when: (1) trade barriers are virtually eliminated within the area; (2) trade barriers against nonmembers do not grow more restrictive; and (3) interim arrangements leading to the free-trade area are reasonably brief.

The nations of Western Europe quickly took advantage of this exception to the GATT, and created the European Economic Community (now the European Union) in 1957 and the European Free-Trade Association in 1960. In recent years, preferential trade has accelerated with the creation of the Asia Pacific Economic Cooperation Association (APEC), the North American Free-Trade Association (NAFTA), the Southern Cone Common Market (MERCOSUR), and other regional institutions. These take several different forms. In a basic **free-trade area**, the members agree to eliminate tariffs among themselves, but each maintains the right to set its own tariffs against nonmember nations. A higher level of integration may be attained by a **customs union**, a free-trade association in which all the member countries adopt a common set of tariffs against nonmembers. Higher still is a **common market**—a customs union with the additional removal of barriers to factor movements between members. Finally, a group of countries may advance to an **economic union**, in which all economic policies—monetary, fiscal, labor, antitrust, and others—are integrated.

From the standpoint of global economic efficiency, any of these preferential trading areas may yield a mixture of benefits and costs. On the positive side of the ledger, reduction of regional trade barriers should encourage members to import goods that were previously produced at home, and increase export production to pay for the imports. This process of **trade creation** should encourage members to specialize in their fields of comparative advantage and benefit from economies of large-scale production.

On the negative side of the ledger, creation of a free-trade area may interfere with efficient trading relationships between members and nonmembers. Suppose, for example, that country X traditionally has imported widgets from country Y, a low-cost producer. Also suppose that X forms a free-trade area with country Z. To avoid paying tariffs to their own government, consumers in X may decide to purchase their widgets duty-free from Z, even if Y offers a better pre-tariff price. Thus, country X diverts its purchases from country Y to country Z, and pays a

---

[73]See "The Uruguay Round: Results and Implications," in International Monetary Fund, *World Economic Outlook*, May 1994, Annex 1; and Trien Nguyen, Carlo Perroni, and Randall Wigle, "An Evaluation of the Final Act of the Uruguay Round," *Economic Journal* 103 (November 1993): 1540-49.

higher external price for its imports. Rather than encouraging a larger volume of international trade, this free-trade area causes an inefficient rearrangement of the existing volume of trade, known as **trade diversion**.[74]

The foregoing analysis raises two important questions. First, what is the net effect of regional free-trade associations on the volume and efficiency of international trade? Do they cause more trade creation or more trade diversion? The specter of a "Fortress Europe," raised in many journalistic and academic accounts, seems to imply that the European Union is predominantly a trade-diverting institution. Indeed, according to Lester Thurow of MIT, "history tells us that an economic union has to keep outsiders out, since this is the glue that holds the disparate insiders together."[75] On the other hand, statistical analyses of the European Union and other regional organizations have usually found that their trade-creating effects are significantly larger than their trade-diverting effects.

The second question is related to the first: Will the development of regional trading organizations support or hinder the development of a global system of free trade? A few years ago, Thurow suggested that the next fifty years would be characterized by "head-to-head" competition and managed trade between strong trading blocs in Europe, Asia, and the Americas. At about the same time, a study for the International Monetary Fund concluded that "beyond a certain threshold an undue emphasis on regionalism would undercut the multilateral trading system and render it inoperative."[76] Fortunately, though, fears of excessive regionalism have subsided since the successful conclusion of the Uruguay Round of GATT negotiations and the creation of the World Trade Organization. Even Lester Thurow acknowledges that "free trade within regions and managed trade between regions may well be the long-run route to freer world trade."[77] These liberalizing trends could give way to protectionism, of course, if the world slips into a serious recession. On the other hand, if systems of regional free trade eventually merge into a system of global free trade, we may witness the ultimate victory of laissez-faire capitalism.

Summary

Several historical preconditions had to be fulfilled before the capitalist economic system could develop. Growth of market exchange required the development of monetary institutions and a

---

[74]The distinction between trade creation and trade diversion was discussed first by Jacob Viner in his book, *The Customs Union Issue* (New York: Carnegie Endowment for International Peace, 1950). For a more recent discussion of the topic, see Beth Yarbrough and Robert Yarbrough, *The World Economy: Trade and Finance*, 2d ed. (Chicago: The Dryden Press, 1991), 378-381.

[75]Lester Thurow, *Head to Head* (New York: William Morrow and Company, 1992), 77.

[76]Augusto de la Torre and Margaret R. Kelly, *Regional Trade Arrangements*, Occasional Paper 93 (Washington, D.C.: International Monetary Fund, March 1992).

[77]Thurow, *Head to Head*, 82.

relatively safe area of travel. In the political and legal spheres, capitalism requires the development of a system of property rights and a reasonable measure of political freedom for a large segment of society. In the areas of religion and philosophy, capitalism requires the relaxation of taboos against individualism and accumulation of wealth. Finally, it requires the formation of a class of people (capitalists) who direct savings into productive investment rather than into the erection of monuments.

The mercantilists were among the first to call for an active governmental role in the market economy, particularly in the regulation of foreign trade. Adam Smith argued that the mercantilist controls were counterproductive and he proposed a system of "natural liberty" regulated by the competitive market mechanism. Smith's followers in the classical school supported his recommendations, but they foresaw problems in the operation of capitalism. Malthus feared overproduction of goods and population crises. Ricardo predicted a trend toward a no-growth, "stationary state." Mill decried the social injustice of capitalism.

According to Karl Marx, capitalism is an exploitive system and its eventual replacement by socialism is an inevitable law of history. During the Great Depression, when it seemed that the Marxian prediction was becoming reality, J. M. Keynes argued that the capitalist system could be saved through macroeconomic stabilization. Keynes's critics, though, claimed that his cure would be worse than the disease of unemployment. Schumpeter claimed that Keynesian policy would interfere with the progressive force of "creative destruction," and Hayek warned that governmental activism would lead us down a dangerous "road to serfdom." The popularity of Keynesian ideas peaked in the 1960s and then declined during the stagflation of the 1970s.

At the current time, the capitalist system is interpreted in many different ways by different groups of economists. Monetarists and supply-siders draw their inspiration from Adam Smith and his classical school. They generally believe in the stability of the capitalist system and advocate a limited role for the government. New-Keynesians and Post-Keynesians question the stability, competitiveness, and equity of modern capitalism and many of them favor broad programs of macroeconomic stabilization and social reform. Radical economists expand on Marx in their analysis of domestic and international capitalist exploitation and argue that growing frictions between democracy and capitalism require the adoption of democratic socialism.

Rapid developments in transportation and communication technologies have reduced the importance of national boundaries, encouraging the internationalization of trade, investment, production, employment, finance, and information. Mainstream economists generally support the internationalization of trade, but they have reservations concerning international investment, employment, and finance.

The institutional framework of international capitalism took new form at the end of World War II, with the creation of such organizations as the International Monetary Fund, the World Bank, and the General Agreement on Tariffs and Trade, and has continued to develop with the recent establishment of the World Trade Organization. Development of these global institutions has been accompanied by regional free-trade institutions, such as the EU, EFTA, APEC, and NAFTA. The relationship between global trade liberalization and development of regional trading blocs is a matter of continuing controversy.

Discussion and Review Questions

1. What basic preconditions had to be fulfilled for the development of capitalism? What role was played by the enclosure movement? The Renaissance? The Protestant Reformation?

2. What was the mercantilist argument in favor of governmental control in a market economy? How did Adam Smith respond?

3. What is Say's Law? Which economists accepted and rejected it? On what grounds?

4. What, according to Ricardo, would cause economic growth to cease in a capitalist country? What was Mill's attitude toward the "stationary state"?

5. Based on the analyses of Marx and Schumpeter, interpret Robert Heilbroner's contention that "the economic enemy of capitalism has always been its own self-generated dynamics."

6. How does Keynesianism differ from Marxism? How does supply-side economics differ from monetarism?

7. What is the relationship, if any, between capitalism and democracy?

8. How will the role of the nation-state be affected by the growing internationalization of information and capitalist institutions?

9. How do regional trade agreements contribute to, and how do they interfere with, a free and efficient system of world trade?

Suggested Readings

Buchholz, Todd G. *New Ideas from Dead Economists.* New York: Plume, 1989. *Written from a relatively conservative perspective, this book provides a lively account of the history of economic thought.*

Cameron, Rondo. *A Concise Economic History of the World: From Paleolithic Times to the Present.* New York: Oxford University Press, 1989. *Drawing on the historical experience of industrial and developing economies, Cameron grapples with the question: Why are some nations rich and others poor?*

Cherry, Robert, et al., eds. *The Imperiled Economy.* New York: The Union for Radical Political Economics, 1987. *This two-volume collection of essays presents a radical perspective on current issues in American and international capitalism.*

Drucker, Peter F. *Post-Capitalist Society*. New York: HarperCollins, 1993. *How will the transition from industrial capitalism to a knowledge-based society affect the economic, political, and international systems? A leading management guru offers his insights.*

Gottlieb, Manuel. *Comparative Economic Systems: Preindustrial and Modern Case Studies.* Ames: Iowa State University Press, 1988. *Focusing on the historical development of modern mixed economies, this book includes chapters on imperial, medieval, mercantilist, and early capitalist economic systems.*

Heilbroner, Robert L. *The Making of Economic Society.* 8th ed. Englewood Cliffs, N.J.: Prentice-Hall, 1989. *By the author of* The Worldly Philosophers, *this may be the most accessible introduction to the history of capitalism.*

O'Brien, Richard. *Global Financial Integration: The End of Geography*. London: Royal Institute of International Affairs, 1992. *The chief economist of American Express Bank, Ltd., discusses the impact of global communications on the financial markets, and issues involved in creating a global framework for cooperation and regulation.*

Smith, Adam. *An Inquiry into the Nature and Causes of the Wealth of Nations.* Oxford: Clarendon Press, 1976. *If you intend to study the history and theories of capitalism from original texts, this is a good place to begin.*

Sweezy, Paul. *The Theory of Capitalist Development.* New York: Monthly Review Press, 1968. *A classic, and readable, introduction to Marxism.*

Thurow, Lester C. *Head to Head: The Coming Economic Battle Among Japan, Europe, and America.* New York: William Morrow and Company, 1992. *Written by the dean of business at MIT, this is a provocative analysis of the changing nature of capitalist competition.*

Viljoen, Stephan. *Economic Systems in World History.* London: Longman, 1974. *Provides a particularly strong discussion of pre-capitalist economic systems.*

CHAPTER 4

HISTORY AND THEORIES OF SOCIALISM

People speak of socialism. We should speak of socialisms. There is an amnesia about the socialist tradition that abandons entire definitions of that ideal made by serious mass movements. . . What is needed, if socialism is to find a new relevance for the twenty-first century, is some sense of its enormous diversity and complexity.

—Michael Harrington, *Socialism: Past and Future*, 1989

Why should we concern ourselves with the ideologies and institutions of socialism? Is socialism dead? Does it have a future? Has the entire socialist movement been discredited by the totalitarian excesses and economic failures of Marxism-Leninism-Stalinism-Maoism in the former Soviet Union, Eastern Europe, and China? Is it true, once and for all, that "the contest between capitalism and socialism is over: capitalism has won"?[1]

Similar questions have been asked before. Late in the nineteenth century, when revolutionary movements were defeated throughout Europe and socialist experiments were abandoned in Europe and America, Karl Marx reported that "all party organizations and party journals of the working classes" had been "crushed by the iron hand of force . . . and the short-lived dreams of emancipation vanished before an epoch of industrial fever, moral morasme, and political reaction."[2] In 1921, an English noble made the following entry in her diary: "Nansen was here to tea and gave me the reassuring news that our troubles with Russia are over. Lenin is introducing a New Economic Policy which restores a free market and represents a return to capitalist exchange of goods in Russia."[3]

Today, it seems most unlikely that any country will launch another Soviet-style program of nationalized industry, collectivized agriculture, and detailed central planning. That system, in fact, has been thoroughly discredited. In the eyes of many observers, however, the collapse of

---

[1]Robert Heilbroner, "The Triumph of Capitalism," *The New Yorker,* January 23, 1989, 98.

[2]Karl Marx, "Inaugural Address of the Working Men's International Association," in *The Marx-Engels Reader*, 2d ed., ed. Robert C. Tucker (New York. W. W. Norton, 1978), 516.

[3]Lady Kennet of Deane, quoted in Bertram Wolfe, "A Historian Looks at the Convergence Theory," in *Sidney Hook and the Contemporary World*, ed. Paul Kurtz (New York: John Day, 1968), 55.

Soviet Stalinism represented a victory over totalitarianism, not a failure of socialism.[4] Indeed, many socialists consistently opposed the Soviet-style system because it gave most members of society "no control over the economy they theoretically own."[5]

The leading voices of contemporary socialism are reformers rather than revolutionaries; democrats rather than centralists. They follow democratic socialist traditions that were prominent in the historic campaigns for women's suffrage, progressive taxation, universal public education, abolition of child labor, and protection of labor unions. Today, their agenda has grown to include support for workplace democracy, universal health care, and environmental protection. They control large voting blocs in the parliaments of countries as diverse as Australia, Colombia, Egypt, Greece, Hungary, Pakistan, Portugal, Sweden, and Tunisia. Thus, it may be premature to declare the death of socialism.

In this chapter, we shall explore the history and diversity of socialist thought and practice. Many of the earliest disagreements among socialists concerned the proper system of ownership. Should private ownership remain unrestricted, or should society regulate and exercise ownership rights? Should social ownership be exercised at the level of the national government (that is, state socialism), or should it be limited to local cooperative and communal arrangements?

If the government is drawn into the operation of socialism, how should this be accomplished? Is it possible to develop socialist institutions through a gradual process of legislative reform, or is it necessary to overthrow the existing governmental and social system? If a revolution is necessary, how should it be initiated, and by whom? And finally, if the society assumes ownership of the means of production, how should they be administered? Should the activities of factories be coordinated by a central plan or a decentralized market? Can a socialist economy operate as efficiently as a capitalist economy? These and other questions have animated the socialist debate through the centuries. Some have been answered by experience, but others seem to defy resolution.

Socialism in the Ancient World

In their study of primitive cultures, anthropologists have found evidence of both market exchange and socialist cooperation. Many of these cultures practiced a primitive form of communism, whereby the tribe owned productive goods and food was distributed by the chief.[6] Adam Smith, the father of classical economics, spoke of "that rude state of society which

---

[4]See Amanda Bennett, "U.S. Marxists Thrive Despite Communism's Demise," *The Wall Street Journal*, September 6, 1994, B1.

[5]Michael Harrington, *Socialism: Past and Future* (New York: Arcade Publishing, 1989), 61.

[6]See, for example, Manning Nash, "The Organization of Economic Life," in *Tribal and Peasant Economics*, ed. George Dalton (Garden City, N.Y.: The Natural History Press, 1967), 3-4.

precedes both the accumulation of stock and the appropriation of land," when "the whole produce of labour belongs to the labourer."[7] Primitive communism was not the product of any ideal philosophical system; it was little more than a pragmatic response to the challenge of survival in the "rude state of society."

In ancient Greece, the birthplace of formal utopian philosophy, we find a lively discussion of socialist ideas. According to Aristotle, the first scholar to argue that "the citizens of a state ought to have equal possessions" was Phaleas of Chalcedon, who believed this arrangement would prevent social disputes and revolutionary movements.[8] In *Republic*, Plato advocated a system of social ownership and communal living arrangements, but only for members of the ruling class of philosophers and soldiers. The purpose was to prevent conflicts of interest, not to promote egalitarianism. In order to maintain work incentives, Plato favored individual ownership of property among members of the lower classes. Democritus and Aristotle defended the right of all social classes to own private property.

One of the earliest recorded collectivist experiments was performed by the early Christians in Jerusalem, for whom "all things were common property," and "there was not a needy person among them, for all who were owners of land or houses would sell them . . . and they would be distributed to each, as they had need."[9] This seems to have been a voluntary response to a situation of extreme need, not to a governmental or religious edict; the Christians outside of Jerusalem maintained ownership of their property.[10] Lacking political or economic power, the early Christians directed their message to individual people and churches, not to the Roman government.[11]

Early Critics of Capitalism

To trace the origins of socialism as a mass movement, we must leap forward to the late 1700s, when the political revolutions in America and France and the Industrial Revolution in England were laying fertile ground for a new social movement. The rebels in America and France supported private property rights, but they also demonstrated the feasibility of revolutionary action and demanded political equality, the forerunner of economic equality. The Industrial

---

[7]Adam Smith, *An Inquiry into the Nature and Causes of the Wealth of Nations* (Oxford: Clarendon Press, 1976, originally published in 1776), 82.

[8]Aristotle, *Politics* 2.7.1266a35.

[9]Acts 4:32-35.

[10]Rom. 16:3-5; Col. 4:15; and Philem. 2.

[11]For an extended discussion of socialist ideas in ancient Greece, Asia, South America, and in the early Christian church, see Igor Shafarevich, *The Socialist Phenomenon* (New York: Harper & Row, 1980), Chapters 1, 2, 4, and 5.

Revolution generated, among other things, a Dickensian world of urban blight and child labor and a vast sum of new wealth to be redistributed.

As early as 1755, the French philosopher Jean Jacques Rousseau (1712-1778) declared his belief in the superiority of the lowly savage over modern society. "How many crimes, wars, murders, sufferings, and horrors mankind would have been spared, if, when the first man enclosed a plot of land and said, `This is mine,' someone would have torn down the fence and cried: `Don't listen to this impostor; you are lost if you forget that the earth belongs to no one, and that the fruits are for all!'"[12] Although Rousseau did not propose the abolition of private property, he inspired others to take that next step.

Also in 1755, a French philosopher named Morelly outlined several "sacred and fundamental laws that would tear out the roots of vice and of all the evils of society." His first proposal was that "nothing in society will belong to anyone, either as a personal possession or as capital goods, except the things for which the person has immediate use."[13] In Morelly's ideal society, production and distribution of goods, choice of occupations, location and arrangement of cities, rites of marriage, communal housing and training of children (including religious training), and many other activities would be regulated by governmental bodies. In order to "prevent all tyrannical domination," governmental leadership would be rotated and every head of a family would become a senator at the age of 50.

Utopian Socialism

In the 1790s, William Godwin (1756-1836) in England and the Marquis de Condorcet (1743-1794) in France predicted that the advance of human knowledge and reasoning would lead to improvements in virtue—they believed in human **perfectibility**. Based on this premise, they also predicted that people would share property more equally in the future, and that governmental institutions designed to protect the population from force and fraud would no longer be necessary.[14]

Early in the nineteenth century, the philosophy of perfectionism led naturally to the development of **utopian socialism**. Most of the utopian socialists would have agreed with the environmentalist slogan, "think globally, act locally."[15] They had a broad, global, perfectionist

---

[12]Jean Jacques Rousseau, "Discourse on the Origin of Inequality among Men," in *Socialist Thought: A Documentary History,* ed. Albert Fried and Ronald Sanders (Garden City, N.Y.: Doubleday and Company, 1964), 33.

[13]Morelly, "Code of Nature," in *Socialist Thought: A Documentary History,* 20.

[14]Malthus wrote his essay on population growth, mentioned in the previous chapter, to debunk the optimistic scenario presented by Godwin and Condorcet.

[15]This slogan has been attributed to Ed Sanders, an American democratic socialist poet who was a member of the counterculture of the 1960s. The slogan grew in popularity after it was the theme of the 1980 meeting of the World Future Society in Toronto.

view of human potential, but they designed and advocated local, communitarian schemes for social reform. Generally, they believed that commercial and public institutions should be placed under the control of associations of workers. This could be accomplished gradually, they thought, without resort to violence.

Henri de Saint-Simon

The first important utopian socialist may have been Henri de Saint-Simon (1760-1825), a member of the French nobility. He did not object to private ownership of property, but believed that economic and political power should be transferred from the old privileged class of aristocrats, landlords, clergymen, and other "idlers" to the productive class, which he defined broadly to include bankers, industrialists, artists, scientists, and laborers.

If France lost its 30,000 most privileged people, the nation "would grieve them for purely sentimental reasons," but their loss "would result in no political evil for the State." On the other hand, if France lost its 3,000 leading scientists and artisans, "the nation would become a lifeless corpse," and would "immediately fall into a position of inferiority."[16] Thus, the followers of Saint-Simon were the first to advocate a society organized around "associations of workers."[17]

To facilitate worker participation in social issues, Saint-Simon proposed an interesting system of economic planning for public works expenditures. According to his scheme, planning would be handled by a three-chamber industrial parliament. A Chamber of Invention, composed of engineers, poets, artists, architects, and musicians, would generate ideas for public works and prioritize them. Next, a Chamber of Examination, composed primarily of mathematicians and physical scientists, would evaluate the feasibility of the projects. Finally, a Chamber of Execution, composed of industrialists, would exercise veto power over the projects in the plan and develop a program to finance and implement them. Although his ideas were not adopted during his life, Saint-Simon is considered by many to be an inspirational force behind French indicative planning.

Robert Owen

In the year 1800, a prosperous Manchester businessman named Robert Owen (1771-1859) acquired the New Lanark factory in Scotland. Espousing ideas unusual at the time, Owen believed that environmental factors, rather than heredity or sinfulness, held back the progress of the lower classes. With the proper environment, "*any* habits and sentiments can be given to mankind," and "every individual may be trained to produce far more than he can consume."[18]

---

[16]Henri de Saint-Simon, *Social Organization, The Science of Man, and Other Writings* (New York: Harper Torchbooks, 1964), 72-73.

[17]Harrington, *Socialism: Past and Future*, 30-32.

[18]Robert Owen, "An Address to the Inhabitants of New Lanark," in *Socialist Thought: A Documentary History,* 173.

Furthermore, he argued that an improvement in the educational and cultural level of the poor would benefit everyone, including the rich.

Based on this philosophy, Owen transformed New Lanark into a model community. He took young children out of the factories and established one of the first systems of universal education. He raised wages, shortened working hours, and provided good housing, sanitation, and nonprofit stores. To the amazement of his fellow industrialists, New Lanark continued to earn substantial profits after the reforms were introduced. Owen contented himself with a 5 percent return on his investment, and used the remaining profits for the welfare of his workers.

After succeeding at New Lanark, Owen solicited the aid of the British government to establish a number of "villages of cooperation." When his proposals were spurned in England and on the Continent, he emigrated to the United States and established a cooperative society in New Harmony, Indiana, in 1826. Unfortunately, Owen was bilked by an associate and by 1828 the New Harmony experiment failed. Owen lost most of his fortune and returned to England to spend the rest of his days working for the trade union movement.

Charles Fourier

Another important exponent of utopian cooperation was Charles Fourier (1772-1837), a businessman and writer in Lyons. Fourier, we should note, was either eccentric or slightly insane. He believed, for instance, that the world would eventually reach a state of harmony, in which six new moons would replace the one in existence and all the violent and repulsive beasts would be replaced by their opposites—lions by anti-lions, rats by anti-rats, and so on. For some reason, this part of his theory was never taken seriously.

Fourier developed a detailed proposal for a system of producer cooperatives called *phalansteries*. Each of these would include about 1,600 people, all of whom would live and work in one large building with adjoining farmland. Like Saint-Simon, Fourier had no objection to private ownership; shareholders who invested in a phalanstery would receive one-third of its profits. The remaining profits would be divided between labor (five-twelfths) and management (one-quarter). In order to avoid the monotony of the factory system, participants would rotate job assignments every few hours and competitive games would be organized around the work process.

Fourier never was able to finance his experiment in France, but more than 40 phalansteries were established in the United States. The most famous of these was Brook Farm in Massachusetts, whose members included Nathaniel Hawthorne and Ralph Waldo Emerson. Brook Farm was reasonably successful until it burned to the ground in 1846. Another phalanstery, La Reunion, played a significant role in the early history of Dallas, Texas. One of its residents, an immigrant from Switzerland, later served twice as mayor of Dallas.[19] Almost all the American phalansteries disappeared by the mid-1850s.

---

[19]Steve Blow, "Socialists? In Dallas? Indeed," *Dallas Morning News*, July 24, 1994, 33A.

Pierre Joseph Proudhon

The most radical utopians were the **anarchists**, led by Pierre Joseph Proudhon (1809-1865), a Parisian, and Mikhail Bakunin (1814-1876), a violent Russian exile.[20] The anarchists declared that all governmental power is corrupt—even if it is wielded by the workers. Thus, they rejected all proposals to seize governmental power or to promote governmental reform. Earlier, Godwin, Condorcet, and Saint-Simon predicted a gradual "withering away of the state," but the anarchists called for its immediate replacement with a system of voluntary cooperatives and contracts. As Proudhon explained:

It is industrial organization that we will put in place of government. . . . In place of laws, we will put contracts. . . . In place of political power, we will put economic forces. . . . In place of standing armies, we will put industrial associations. In place of police, we will put identity of interests.[21]

Indeed, this is radical utopianism. How, we might ask, will contracts replace laws when the latter are needed to enforce the former? To their credit, however, Proudhon and Bakunin anticipated the critical danger in state socialism: Governmental ownership of the means of production could become the basis of a new form of oppression.

Revolutionary Socialism

One of the first socialists to call for the violent overthrow of the existing system was Francois "Gracchus" Babeuf (1760-1797), a journalist who led the Society of the Pantheon. This group was organized in 1795 to denounce the decline of the French Revolution and to advance the cause of communist egalitarianism. According to Babeuf and his followers, the promise of political equality was empty and insufficient:

We are speaking of something more sublime and more equitable, the COMMON GOOD, *or the* COMMUNITY OF GOODS! *No more individual ownership of the land: the land belongs to no one. We are demanding, we desire, communal enjoyment of the fruits of the earth: the fruits belong to all.*[22]

Babeuf was executed in 1797 for plotting to overthrow the government, but his name became a rallying cry for later revolutionaries.

---

[20]In the words of Joseph Schumpeter, "anarchism was utopianism with a vengeance." See his *Capitalism, Socialism, and Democracy* (New York: Harper and Brothers, 1950), 307.

[21]Pierre Joseph Proudhon, "General Idea of the Revolution in the Nineteenth Century," in *French Utopias: An Anthology of Ideal Societies*, ed. F. E. Manuel and F. P. Manuel (New York: Free Press, 1966), 371.

[22]"Manifesto of the Equals," in *Socialist Thought: A Documentary History,* 53.

Auguste Blanqui (1805-1885) advocated the forceful expropriation of large estates, control over factories, and establishment of free education and a progressive income tax. He did not believe that the workers would ever organize their own revolution or that socialist measures would be adopted in a democratic society, even if the poor were allowed to vote. The poor, he said, did not know the source of their miseries. Thus, he believed that a revolutionary coup must be initiated by a small, well-organized minority—a concept that was rejected by Marx and Engels, but later adopted by Lenin. Blanqui devoted himself to several insurrectionist causes and spent much of his adult life in jail.

Karl Marx and Friedrich Engels

As we have seen, Karl Marx (1818-1883) and his associate Friedrich Engels (1820-1895) spent much of their time exposing the "true nature of capitalism" and the forces leading to its destruction; they spent little time preparing a blueprint for socialist society. Nevertheless, their ideas have been so influential that some people use the words *socialism* and *Marxism* interchangeably. Marx and Engels drew together many elements of earlier socialist philosophies and added many of their own. Their socialism was revolutionary and pragmatic in the short run, evolutionary and utopian in the long run. They established a mainstream of socialism that drew many adherents on the Continent, while reformism prevailed in England.

Marx and Engels dismissed the utopian program of voluntary cooperation as a quaint and naïve dream and proposed their own system of **scientific socialism**. In opposition to those who believed that socialism could be attained by peaceful means, Marx and Engels believed that the capitalist class would not surrender control of society without a fight. In countries where the capitalist class structure is firmly established, "the lever of our revolution must be force."[23] In opposition to those like Blanqui (and eventually Lenin), "who openly state that the workers are too uneducated to emancipate themselves," Marx countered that "the emancipation of the working class must be the work of the working class itself."[24]

After the revolution, Marx and Engels believed that socialism would proceed through several stages. First, control of society would pass from the capitalist class to a new **dictatorship of the proletariat**. Despite the dreams of anarchists, forceful measures would be necessary during this stage of history to protect the new socialist regime from lingering reactionary forces at home and abroad. "The class domination of workers over the resisting strata of the old world" must continue, Marx said, "until the economic foundations of the existence of classes are destroyed."[25]

---

[23]Karl Marx, "On the Possibility of Non-Violent Revolution," in *The Marx-Engels Reader*, 523. Interestingly, Marx believed that nonviolent revolutions could possibly occur in America and England because of the institutions, mores, and traditions in those countries.

[24]Karl Marx, "The Manifesto of the Three Zurichers," in *The Marx-Engels Reader,* 555.

[25]Karl Marx, "After the Revolution," in *The Marx-Engels Reader*, 547.

Marx maintained that several of the defects of capitalist society must continue during the early stages of socialism, because socialism is "still stamped with the birth marks of the old society from whose womb it emerges."[26] Thus, it is not possible to immediately dispense with coercive governmental institutions. In addition, some income inequality must continue in order to maintain work incentives and to make the new system politically acceptable. Goods must be distributed according to the rule, "To each according to his work."

Marx believed that several preconditions must be satisfied in the early stages of socialism before communism, the final utopian stage, can be attained. First, society must reach a high stage of economic development. Second, an unselfish "new man" for whom "labour has become not only a means of life but life's prime want" must evolve.[27] And third, Marx apparently believed (as did Trotsky after him) that the socialist revolution must spread to all countries before communism can emerge in any country. The working class in a single nation cannot put an end to class struggle because the defenders of capitalism in that country are "linked up in a brotherhood . . . with the bourgeois of all other countries."[28]

After these conditions are fulfilled, the other features of communism would naturally follow. The victory of the dictatorship of the proletariat and the gradual improvement of social consciousness would give rise to a classless society. With an abundance of goods and an unselfish, hard-working population, it finally would become possible to distribute consumer goods according to the rule, "To each according to his needs."

Marx believed that many of the institutions of the old society would become obsolete under full communism. The use of money, for example, would pass away when goods are abundant and people are unselfish. The state, as we presently know it, would "wither away" because the cessation of domestic and international class conflict would reduce or eliminate the need for many of the legislative, law enforcement, and military functions of the government. Thus, Marx rejected the anarchist vision of a stateless society in the short run (during the dictatorship of the proletariat), but he embraced it in the utopian long run (Table 4.1).

Table 4.1 Nineteenth-Century Socialists: A Typology

		Preferred Form of Social Ownership	
		State	***Cooperative, Communal***
Expected Method of Transition to Socialism	***Gradual Reform***	Blanc S. and B. Webb	Fourier, Owen Mill
	Revolution	Blanqui Marx (short run)	Proudhon, Bakunin Marx (long run)

---

[26]Karl Marx, "Critique of the Gotha Program," in *The Marx-Engels Reader*, 529.

[27]Ibid., 531.

[28]Ibid., 533.

Marx believed that the socialist economy would operate according to a plan that "distributes labour-power and means of production to the different branches of production," but he did not explain how the plan was to be formulated.[29] What agency would prepare the plan, especially after the "withering away" of the state? How often should the plans be prepared? How should the central planners take account of the interdependence of the economy, and how should they control implementation of the plans? Marx and Engels, who devoted most of their writing to the capitalist system, were silent on these and many other questions about socialism.

After 1848, the pivotal year when Marx and Engels wrote their *Communist Manifesto* and when workers' revolts were crushed in several countries, the socialist movement fell into disarray. The utopian experiments inspired by Owen, Fourier, and others continued through the 1840s, but most of them disappeared by the mid-1850s.

The First International and the Paris Commune

In 1864, Marx played an important role in establishing the Working Men's International Association (or the First International, as it was more commonly known). Although the First International marked an important stage in the development of the trade union movement, it did very little to advance Marx's dream of a national socialist movement. Specifically, the International succeeded in coordinating the activities of trade unionists in several countries, preventing strike-breaking activities by workers in adjoining countries, and preventing the British government from supporting the South in the American Civil War. It lost much of its influence, however, because of tactical disputes between the Marxist and Bakuninist wings of the association.

Rivalry within the First International was further intensified by the formation of the Paris Commune in 1871. In that year, the National Guard of Paris led a revolt against the national government; socialists of all stripes were elected to a majority of the seats on the new Commune Assembly. The Commune attempted to institute a number of social reforms, but it was crushed within a few weeks by the national government.

The Commune had little lasting impact on French history, but it was extolled by Marx, Engels, and Lenin as the first realistic attempt to establish a dictatorship of the proletariat.[30] This, in turn, intensified the debate in the First International between the Marxists, who believed in the necessity of a revolutionary dictatorship of the proletariat, and the anarchists, who rejected any proposal to take over the government. Marx had Bakunin and his supporters expelled from the International in 1872 and the organization collapsed over the next 4 years.

---

[29]Karl Marx, *Capital*, vol. 2 (Moscow: Progress Publishers, 1956, originally published in 1893), 362.

[30]See Edward S. Mason, *The Paris Commune: An Episode in the History of the Socialist Movement* (New York: The Macmillan Co., 1930), Chapters 5, 6, and 7.

V. I. Lenin and the Russian Revolution

The late 1800s witnessed the death of Marx (in 1883) and Engels (in 1895), the birth of an ineffectual Second International (in 1889), and the formation of socialist parties in several European countries. From the very beginning, one of the prime movers among the Russian Social Democrats was a young lawyer named Vladimir I. Lenin (1870-1924). Lenin became a radical at the age of 16, when his older brother was executed for participating in a plot to assassinate Tsar Alexander III. He studied Marxian theory at home and abroad, and in 1902 published a pamphlet, titled *What Is to Be Done?*, which echoed Blanqui in saying that the revolution must be led by an elite vanguard of professionals:

I assert: (1) that no movement can be durable without a stable organization of leaders to maintain continuity; (2) that the more widely the masses are spontaneously drawn into the struggle and form the basis of the movement and participate in it, the more necessary it is to have such an organization . . .; (3) that the organization must consist chiefly of persons engaged in revolutionary activities as a profession; (4) that in a country with an autocratic government, the more we restrict *the membership of this organization to persons who are engaged in revolutionary activities as a profession . . .; and (5) the* wider *will be the circle of men and women of the working class . . . able to join the movement and perform active work in it.*[31]

When the Russian Social Democrats held their first congress in 1903, the followers of Lenin commanded a temporary majority and called themselves the **Bolsheviks** (from *bol'shinstvo*, majority). Their opponents, who rejected the idea of an authoritarian vanguard style of leadership, came to be known as the **Mensheviks** (minority). The names stuck, even when the Bolsheviks constituted a minority of the Social Democratic Party.

Initially, Lenin faced stiff resistance *within* the Bolshevik faction because he seemed to be violating the Marxian belief that the proletarian revolution would first occur in the most advanced capitalist countries. To this charge, Lenin answered that the Russian revolution could proceed "in a different way from that of the West-European countries," because the Russian proletariat had already demonstrated their revolutionary zeal and because the imperialist policies of the advanced countries had shifted the focus of capitalist exploitation to Russia and other developing countries:

If a definite level of culture is required for the building of Socialism (although nobody can say just what that definite "level of culture" is, for it differs in every West-European country), why cannot we begin by first achieving the prerequisites for that definite level of culture in a revolutionary way, and then, *with the aid of the workers' and peasants' government and the Soviet system, proceed to overtake the other nations?*[32]

---

[31]V. I. Lenin, "What Is to Be Done?" in *Essential Works of Lenin*, ed. Henry M. Christman (New York: Bantam Books, 1966), 147-148.

[32]V. I. Lenin, "Our Revolution," in *A Documentary History of Communism*, ed. Robert V. Daniels (New York: Random House, 1960), 229.

Lenin's arguments, supported by Leon Trotsky's (1879-1940) theory that a revolution in Russia would be supported by the encouragement of a "permanent revolution" in other countries, carried the day. As we shall consider at length in later chapters, the Bolsheviks took control of the government in November 1917 and the Soviet state was born. After experimenting with market socialism in the 1920s, the government eventually adopted a centralized system of economic planning and administration.

Under central planning, individual enterprise managers in Irkutsk, Minsk, and Pinsk made few important decisions. Ideally, the planners in Moscow would tell the enterprise what to produce, where to obtain raw materials, where to sell the final products, what prices to charge, and a host of other requirements. The manager and his employees were paid to carry out orders. Hence, the Soviet system was sometimes called a **command economy**.

Democratic Socialism

While Blanqui, Marx, Engels, Lenin, and others were organizing revolutionary socialist movements, another cast of characters remained dedicated to the idea that socialist goals could be accomplished through evolutionary, nonviolent, democratic programs of reform. They rejected the Marxian notion that existing governments—including democratic governments—had to be overthrown because they were irredeemable tools of the ruling capitalist class. Democratic socialists believed, as they do today, that governments can play a progressive role in society.

Louis Blanc

In 1848, long before the creation of the Paris Commune, Louis Blanc (1811-1882) gained a position in the French Provisional Government. Blanc was already known as a socialist theoretician, having formulated the slogan, "From each according to his abilities, to each according to his needs." To address the problem of unemployment, Blanc believed the state should use its power to guarantee each person a "right to work." Thus, he used his own governmental power to support the creation of a system of "national workshops." According to Blanc's design, the workshops should be owned by the state, but they should be governed, in large part, by the workers.

A few months after Blanc joined the government, labor unrest and governmental budgetary problems mounted, and the workshops were closed. Thousands of workers and soldiers were killed in the riots that ensued, and Blanc fled to England. Nevertheless, he is remembered for his advocacy of public ownership and his belief that socialist reforms could be adopted by the democratic machinery of the existing government.

Ferdinand Lasalle

In Germany, the revolutionary doctrine of Karl Marx stood in direct opposition to the more democratic notions of Ferdinand Lasalle (1825-1864). The state can be an agent of socialist reform, Lasalle argued, if it operates on a democratic basis with universal suffrage. Unlike most of the utopian socialists, who advocated the creation of small-scale producer cooperatives,

Lasalle believed that the workers, with legal and financial assistance from the state, should gain control of large-scale factories with their "enormous advantage in productivity."

Known as a great orator, Lasalle organized the first German socialist party in 1863, and its membership grew rapidly. Lasalle was killed in a duel one year later, but his party survived and his followers perpetuated his ideas. Their democratic hopes were encouraged in 1871 when Bismarck, the German emperor, established a new parliament whose lower house, the *Reichstag*, was elected by a popular vote. From the beginning, socialists were able to win seats in the new parliament.

Hoping to increase their voting strength, the followers of Marx and Lasalle agreed to meet in 1875 in the town of Gotha to discuss the merger of their parties into a single German Social Democratic Party. The draft of the party program, prepared for the meeting, had a strong Lasallean tone: "The working class strives for its emancipation first of all within the framework of the present-day national state. . . " The new party "demands the establishment of producers' cooperative societies with state aid under the democratic control of the toiling people."

Marx objected strongly to this language, arguing that the "present-day national state" cannot be reformed; it must be overthrown.[33] Nevertheless, in their desire to unite with the Lasalleans, Marx's followers ignored his objections. The Gotha Congress adopted the draft program with minor alterations, and the German Social Democratic Party became a parliamentary party, striving for political power and social reform by constitutional means.

Confronted by a united Social Democratic Party, Bismarck was forced to enact the first comprehensive social security system in Europe, helping those afflicted by unemployment, accidents, sickness, and old age. In 1895, twelve years after Marx's death, even Friedrich Engels had to acknowledge the electoral success of the German Democratic Socialist Party: "The two million voters whom it sends to the ballot box . . . form the most numerous, most compact mass, the decisive 'shock force' of the international proletarian army. . . We are thriving far better on legal methods than on illegal methods and overthrow."[34]

The German Social Democratic Party quickly became the model for similar parties in most of the other European countries. Socialist parties were organized in Denmark (1879), Spain (1879), France (1880), Russia (1883), Belgium (1885), Norway (1887), Sweden (1889), Italy (1892), Poland (1892), Netherlands (1893), and Finland (1899). In some countries, such as Russia and Poland, the new parties were not able to participate in parliamentary democracy; they were driven underground into revolutionary activities. In most of the other countries, they became an important force in the democratic system, and they remain active today.

---

[33]See his "Critique of the Gotha Program," 525-541.

[34]Friedrich Engels, "The Tactics of Social Democracy," in *The Marx-Engels Reader,* 571.

John Stuart Mill

In Great Britain, the socialist movement developed with particularly strong democratic and libertarian roots. John Stuart Mill (1806-1873) may have been the author of *On Liberty* and an advocate of the laissez-faire principles of Adam Smith, but he also lived to see the darker side of the Industrial Revolution and was profoundly influenced by the utopian socialists.

Putting together these strands of thought, Mill came to believe that capitalism would gradually and spontaneously evolve into socialist cooperation. "If mankind continues to improve," Mill said, production eventually will be dominated by "the association of the labourers themselves on terms of equality, collectively owning the capital with which they carry on their operations, and working under managers elected and removable by themselves."[35]

Mill looked forward to a system of democratic labor-managed cooperatives. He was an early supporter of governmental involvement in health, education, and welfare reform, and he believed that socialist aims could and should be attained with a minimum of revolutionary fervor, governmental interference, expropriation of property, or central planning.

The Fabian Society

In 1884, three socialist organizations were established in England. Two of them, the Social Democratic Federation and the Socialist League, had Marxist roots and never attracted large followings. The third, the Fabian Society, was also small, but was far more influential. Led by Sidney and Beatrice Webb and George Bernard Shaw, and inspired by the ideas of John Stuart Mill, the Fabians supported an evolutionary program of social reforms:

We who call ourselves Socialists today in England, largely through Mill's teaching and example, find a confirmation of this hope in social history and economics, and see already in the distance the glad vision of a brighter day, when, practically, the whole product of labor will be the worker's and the worker's alone, and at last the social arrangements will be deliberately based on the Apostolic rule ignored by so many Christians, that if a man does not work, neither shall he eat.[36]

Like Mill, the Fabians believed that workers' organizations, local governments, and national governments would gradually gain ownership and control of business enterprises, and would turn the existing state into a "welfare state." This could be accomplished, they believed,

---

[35]John Stuart Mill, *Principles of Political Economy,* ed. W. J. Ashley (New York: Augustus M. Kelley, 1965, originally published in 1848), 772-773.

[36]Sidney Webb, "English Progress toward Social Democracy," in *Socialist Thought: A Documentary History*, 398-399.

"with little more dislocation of industry than is caused by the daily purchase of shares on the Stock Exchange."[37]

Unlike Marx, who was a materialist, the Fabians believed that the power of the socialist *idea* was sufficient to alter the course of history: "Socialists do but foretell the probable direction of English social evolution; and it needs nothing but a general recognition of that development, and a clear determination not to allow the selfish interests of any class to hinder or hamper it, for Socialism to secure universal assent." In fact, they believed that this process of democratic socialization had begun long before the establishment of any socialist party, and that England, not Germany, "is already the most Socialist of all European communities."[38]

The evolutionary socialist ideas of the Fabian Society were incorporated into the platforms of the Independent Labour Party, organized in 1893, and the Labour Party, reorganized in 1918. In 1945, Labour gained its first strong parliamentary majority, and pursued a program of nationalization of industry and social welfare legislation.

The Efficiency of Socialism

The early socialists directed attention to the "inherent flaws" of capitalism: exploitation, inequality, worker alienation, economic instability, unemployment, militarism, and many others. Socialism, they thought, would be more equitable and also more efficient. According to L.V. Kantorovich, the Russian recipient of a Nobel Prize in economics: "Socialist society . . . is *by its nature* capable of securing a more complete and rational use of productive resources for the better satisfaction of the needs of society [emphasis added]."[39]

Since their inception, however, socialist proposals have encountered criticism. Aristotle warned that public property would be employed and maintained inefficiently because "that which is common to the greatest number has the least care bestowed upon it."[40] Long before any specific schemes were devised for socialist economic planning, Adam Smith warned that "no human wisdom or knowledge could ever be sufficient" to devise a scheme for "superintending the industry of private people, and . . . directing it towards the employments most suitable to the interest of the society."[41]

---

[37]Ibid., 400.

[38]Ibid., 401.

[39]L.V. Kantorovich, "Mathematical Formulation of the Problem of Optimal Planning," in *Socialist Economics*, ed. Alec Nove and D. M. Nuti (Baltimore: Penguin, 1972, first published in 1955), 464.

[40]Aristotle *Politics* 2.3.1261b34.

[41]Smith, *Wealth of Nations*, 687.

John Stuart Mill generally sympathized with the aims of socialists, but he opposed wholesale nationalization of industry and agreed with Smith's condemnation of national economic planning. Specifically, Mill rejected any scheme "which aims at taking possession of the whole land and capital of the country, and beginning at once to administer it on the public account." Aside from the injustice of expropriation, "the very idea of conducting the whole industry of a country by direction from a single center is so obviously chimerical that nobody ventures to propose any mode in which it should be done."[42]

Mill also rejected the ideas of Fourier and other socialists who supported rotation of work assignments, "an arrangement which by putting an end to the division of employments would sacrifice . . . the productiveness of labor."[43] He also disagreed with socialists who blamed market competition for "all of the economical evils which at present exist." We may dislike the dehumanizing aspects of competition, which may be a "source of jealousy and hostility among those of the same occupation," but we must not forget "that wherever competition is not, monopoly is; and that monopoly in all of its forms is the taxation of the industrious for the support of indolence, if not of plunder."[44] Mill believed a socialist system could be devised that would preserve the benefits of competition and deliver an adequate standard of living.

In the end, Mill believed that the choice between capitalism and socialism would not hinge on narrow questions of economic efficiency, but "mainly on one consideration, viz. which of the two systems is consistent with the greatest amount of human liberty and spontaneity. . . It remains to be discovered how far the preservation of this characteristic would be found compatible with the communistic organization of society."[45]

Ludwig von Mises and the Calculation Debate

After the Bolsheviks gained power in Russia, socialism was no longer a utopian abstraction. A protracted debate began, involving economists from several countries, concerning the possibility (or impossibility) of efficient management of a socialist economy.

The debate began in earnest in 1920, when Austrian economist Ludwig von Mises (1881-1973) argued that efficient planning is impossible in a system of state socialism.[46] According to

---

[42]Mill, *Principles of Political Economy,* 988.

[43]Ibid., 207.

[44]Ibid., 792.

[45]Ibid., 210.

[46]Ludwig von Mises, "Economic Calculation in the Socialist Commonwealth," in *Socialist Economics* (first published in 1920), 75-91. The title of this essay is most important; Mises is concerned with economic calculation in a socialist *commonwealth*, that is, in a system of state socialism in which "all the means of production are the property of the community." His

Mises, market exchange of producer goods cannot occur in under state socialism because all producer goods are held by a single owner—the state. If producer goods are not exchanged, then it will be impossible to determine their market prices. If there are no market prices for producer goods, it will be impossible to perform the calculations that are necessary to make rational decisions.

If a steel mill is to be built, for example, where should it be located, and what technology should be employed? What energy source should be used, and what mix of raw materials? To answer these questions in a way that will minimize the social cost of building the steel mill, the cost of land, equipment, and raw materials must somehow be measured and added. Under state socialism, Mises argued, it may be possible to make vague estimates of cost, but no reliable yardstick will exist.

Lange's Theory of Market Socialism

The challenge presented by Mises elicited a number of responses. In the Soviet Union, economists and officials maintained that the inefficiencies of centrally planned socialism were trivial in comparison to the monopolistic distortions, business cycles, and unemployment inherent in capitalism. Some Soviet economists suggested that the problem of valuation, emphasized by Mises, could be solved with linear programming models and other mathematical techniques.

Outside of the Soviet Union, few supporters of socialism defended the efficiency of Soviet-style central planning. Instead, they argued for alternative forms of socialism, based on market principles and cooperative ownership. These, they argued, would equal or surpass the efficiency of the capitalist system.

Although John Stuart Mill proposed a system of **market socialism** as early as 1848, the first to answer Mises with such a system was Fred M. Taylor, in his 1928 presidential address to the American Economic Association. His arguments were extended and amplified by Oskar Lange (a Polish economist), H. D. Dickinson (British), Abba Lerner (British-American), Joseph Schumpeter (Austro-American), and Burnham Beckwith (American) between 1936 and 1949.[47] Their analyses were similar, but the version offered by Lange attracted the largest audience.

According to Lange, a decentralized system could be devised to operate state socialism in a way "quite analogous to that in a competitive market."[48] The pattern of production would be set

---

arguments do not seem to apply with equal force to a system of cooperative socialism or syndicalism, in which the factories and farms are owned by smaller groups of workers.

[47]For an annotated bibliography of these and other works on market socialism, see Burnham P. Beckwith, *Liberal Socialism*, 2d ed. (Jericho, N.Y.: Exposition Press, 1974), 445-455.

[48]Oskar Lange, "On the Economic Theory of Socialism," in *On the Economic System of Socialism*, ed. Benjamin E. Lippincott (Minneapolis: University of Minnesota Press, 1938), 82.

by consumer sovereignty, and freedom of occupational choice would be maintained. The allocative efficiency of the economy would be greater than that of a capitalist economy, Lange believed, because it would be free of the distortions caused by monopolies and externalities.

According to Lange's scheme, enterprise managers should be required to follow two rules. First, in order to minimize the average cost of production, they should attempt to equalize the marginal products derived from the last unit of money spent on each of the factors of production. Second, in order to operate at optimal levels of production, they should expand production at their enterprises until marginal costs are equal to the prices of their final products. These are precisely the rules that are followed by a "perfectly competitive" producer in a theoretical capitalist economy.

The Central Planning Board (CPB) in Lange's model takes the place of the market. If a shortage or surplus of any commodity or productive resource exists at the end of the accounting period, the CPB raises or reduces its price. Lange argued that this trial-and-error procedure would generate a set of equilibrium prices more rapidly than a competitive market because "the Central Planning Board has a much wider knowledge of what is going on in the whole economic system than any private entrepreneur can ever have."[49]

Lange claimed several additional advantages of market socialism over capitalism.[50] First, because the means of production are owned by the public, there are no property incomes; thus the distribution of income would be more even. Second, the managers of socialist factories would be willing to take fuller account of the social costs of production (including the cost of pollution, etc.) than the managers of profit-seeking capitalist enterprises.

Third, unlike the situation in capitalist society, where monopolists may restrict production in an effort to inflate their prices and profits, managers of socialist enterprises would be instructed to produce to the efficient level where price equals marginal cost.[51] Finally, a socialist economy would avoid business cycle fluctuations because the planners would be able to keep a downturn in one sector of the economy from adversely affecting the others.

Lange's Critics

As one might expect, Lange's response to Mises drew both praise and criticism.[52] According to his critics, Lange underestimated the difficulty of the price-setting job of the CPB. Millions of

---

[49]Ibid., 89.

[50]Ibid., 98-108.

[51]Recall that the profit-maximizing level of output for a monopolist is lower than the equilibrium level of output for a competitive industry.

[52]For critical evaluations of Lange's model, see Friedrich Hayek, "Socialist Calculation: The Competitive `Solution'," *Economica* 7 (May 1940): 125-149; Abram Bergson, "Market Socialism Revisited," *Journal of Political Economy* 75 (October 1967): 655-673; Peter Murrell,

prices must be set in a modern economy, and these must be changed continuously to maintain equilibrium. To obtain the necessary information on shortages and surpluses, and to adjust all of the prices in a timely manner, the CPB would require a huge bureaucracy.

Even if Lange's planners and managers could match the performance of a market economy in static equilibrium, his critics say that the dynamic efficiency of his theoretical system is dubious. In a world where decisions are based not only on our knowledge of the present, but also on our conjecture of the future, Lange's two operating rules may be insufficient to guide the actions of enterprise managers. Prices set in a capitalist market are influenced by current conditions and by expectations; it is unlikely that the prices set by Lange's central planners would incorporate all of that information.

Another objection concerns Lange's failure to describe the methods used to monitor performance of enterprise managers and how they would be motivated to run their operations efficiently. Should profits be used as a measure of success? Should a share of profits be given to the manager? If this is done, some of the purported advantages of socialism may be lost. Profit-earning managers would have an incentive to take advantage of monopoly power, possibly causing them to ignore social costs (for example, of pollution) in order to reduce their private costs. If profits are not used to measure the success of the enterprise and to reward its manager, what will take their place?

Other Market Socialist Models

In the 1950s and 1960s, Yugoslavia and a number of Eastern European countries began to experiment with market socialism. We will consider these experiments in the chapters that follow. In addition to their operational importance, the Eastern European systems also inspired the creation of several new theoretical models of market socialism.

Ben Ward initiated a new round of theorizing in 1958 with his theory of **labor-managed socialism**, based on an abstraction of the Yugoslav system.[53] In his model of the idealized nation of Illyria, the state owns the means of production but entrusts management to the workers in each enterprise. Commodities are exchanged in actual markets, where their prices are determined by supply and demand. Aside from taxes and rental fees paid to the government and funds retained for enterprise investment, any profits earned by the enterprise are divided among the workers.

Given these conditions, Ward assumes that the enterprise manager, who is elected by the workers, attempts to maximize the income of the average worker in the enterprise. Unlike the

---

"Did the Theory of Market Socialism Answer the Challenge of Ludwig von Mises? A Reinterpretation of the Socialist Controversy," *History of Political Economy* 15 (1983): 92-105; and Don Lavoie, *Rivalry and Central Planning: The Socialist Calculation Debate* (New York: Cambridge University Press, 1985).

[53]Benjamin Ward, "The Firm in Illyria: Market Syndicalism," *American Economic Review* 48 (September 1958): 566-589.

manager of a capitalist enterprise, who, according to the usual assumption, attempts to maximize total profits, the Illyrian manager attempts to maximize profits per worker. As we shall discuss in a later chapter, the behavior of the Illyrian manager may be quite different from that of a capitalist manager. Unlike Lange's model, prices in Ward's model are set by market forces rather than by central planners, and the motivation system of the enterprise (retention of profits) is clearly defined.

In recent years, and particularly since the collapse of command socialism in the Soviet Union and Eastern Europe, several authors have designed new models of market socialism. Designed to meet the needs of transitional societies that are unwilling or unable to move "all the way" to unfettered capitalism, these proposals have several elements in common. To distinguish them from utopian, radical, centrally planned, and totalitarian models of socialism, their authors describe them as *pragmatic*, *feasible*, *market-oriented*, and *democratic* systems of socialism. They are predicated on the development or maintenance of democratic institutions, and, unlike the Lange model, they rely on a profit motive and on market determination of prices.[54] Furthermore, most of these models would allow private or cooperative ownership of small and entrepreneurial firms.

Recent socialist proposals differ widely in their arrangements for ownership and management of large enterprises. James Yunker and Alec Nove have developed blueprints for **market-oriented state socialism**, based on direct state ownership, which would allow broad enterprise autonomy.[55] In particular, Yunker would nationalize large corporations under a Bureau of Public Ownership (BPO), authorized to hire, fire, and evaluate the work of enterprise executives. The BPO would have veto power over executive compensation plans, which would be strongly dependent on profitability, but the BPO would be prohibited from interfering in the day-to-day enterprise management. After deductions for managerial pay and administrative costs of the BPO, the bulk of profits would be paid to the public as a social dividend. The dividend would be divided between households in proportion to their earned incomes.

Contingent on its existing financial institutions, Pranab Bardhan and John Roemer would have a country choose between two variants of market socialism.[56] A country that already has a

---

[54]Indeed, several of its proponents claim that market socialism will remedy the problems caused by separation of corporate ownership and control under modern capitalism, yielding a stronger profit motive and a higher level of economic efficiency. Although most of these proposals rely on market pricing, some authors would employ selective price controls to curb abuses of monopoly power. Similar controls are used in many capitalist systems.

[55]Alec Nove, *The Economics of Feasible Socialism* (London: George Allen and Unwin, 1983); and James A. Yunker, *Socialism Revised and Modernized* (New York: Praeger, 1992).

[56]Pranab Bardhan and John Roemer, "Market Socialism: A Case for Rejuvenation," *Journal of Economic Perspectives* 6 (Summer 1992): 101-116. Also, see *Market Socialism: The Current Debate*, ed. by Pranab Bardhan and John Roemer (New York: Oxford University Press, 1993).

well-organized stock market would adopt a system of **voucher socialism**. Initially, all adults would be given vouchers, allowing them to purchase stock in large and formerly state-owned enterprises. Afterwards, citizens would be free to exchange their holdings for other stocks or mutual funds, but they would not be allowed to liquidate their holdings for money or other assets.[57] Thus, it would be impossible for ownership of industry to become concentrated in the hands of a small capitalist class, and enterprise profits would be distributed rather evenly to the population in the form of stock dividends. Enterprise managers would be free to conduct business in roughly the same way as managers under conventional corporate capitalism, and they would respond to a similar system of oversight and incentives from shareholders.

In countries without well-organized stock markets, Bardhan and Roemer recommend a system of **bank-centric socialism**, based on an adaptation of the Japanese economic system. In Japan, diversified groups of companies (*keiretsu* organizations) are organized under the leadership and partial ownership of large investment banks. The banks, which are owned privately in Japan, would be majority-owned by the state in the Bardhan-Roemer proposal, but their intended role would be the same: to provide broad oversight and financial support and discipline for companies in their financial groups.

Aside from the investment banks, other large companies would not be owned directly by the state. Instead, their shares would be owned by workers within the company, by other public firms (including their workers) in the same financial group, and by the group's investment bank and its subsidiaries. According to its authors, this system would encourage efficiency and accountability, and, like the Japanese system, would encourage companies to consider a long time horizon in their investments, but it would provide a relatively egalitarian distribution of ownership, control, and income.

Many of the most recent socialist proposals are promoted under the banner of **economic democracy**. According to Alan Charney, director of the Democratic Socialists of America: *By economic democracy we mean, in the most general terms, the direct ownership and control of much of the economic resources of society by the great majority of wage and income earners. The centerpieces of this movement are alternative economic institutions such as cooperatives and worker-owned facilities, but this movement also encompasses existing financial arrangements, such as pension funds and employee stock ownership plans (ESOPs) that can, through legal and political contestation, be fashioned into devices that also enrich and expand the movement for economic democracy.*[58]

Even if it is politically impossible to introduce any broad system of state, cooperative, or worker ownership, Robin Archer suggests that socialists can still work toward a meaningful

---

[57]According to Bardhan and Roemer, the prohibition against liquidation of ownership rights in their system of economic democracy is analogous to the prohibition against selling of voting rights in a system of political democracy.

[58]Alan Charney, "Back to the Beginning," October 8, 1994, on the Internet server, Democratic Socialists of America (http://ccme-mac4.bsd.uchicago.edu/DSA.html).

program of economic democracy.[59] Under Archer's proposal, people who are not employees could continue to own shares in a firm, and they could derive dividend income from those shares, but they would have limited control over management of the firm. Instead, in the "ideal" case, managers would be elected by and accountable to their workers. Workers may direct their managers to seek outside capital investment, just as they may seek customers for the company's products, but they would no more relinquish managerial control of the firm to investors than to customers. Recalling that full political democracy did not materialize in Britain until nearly a century after the Reform Act of 1832, Archer acknowledges that full economic democracy may develop slowly. A good first step, he says, would be establishment of German-style works councils in all large and medium-sized firms.[60]

The market socialist proposals of Lange and his followers have attracted criticism from both the left and the right. According to orthodox Marxists, the competitive rivalry and macroeconomic instability of the market system are inconsistent with socialist aspirations. According to libertarians, socialist restriction of property rights is the first step down Hayek's "road to serfdom." Based on more than twenty years of experimentation in Hungary, Janos Kornai suggests that we abandon the cause of market socialism:

> *It is futile to expect that the state unit will behave as if it were privately owned and will spontaneously act as if it were a market-oriented agent. It is time to let go of this vain hope once and for all. Never, no more.*[61]

Socialism since World War II

The Growth and Decline of Command Socialism

Until the latter years of World War II, the Soviet Union and Mongolia were the only strongholds of command socialism in the world.[62] Beginning in 1944, the Red Army installed Communist governments in the countries of Eastern Europe and North Korea, liberating them from fascist and Japanese domination. Mock elections were held in Bulgaria, East Germany, Hungary,

---

[59]Robin Archer, *Economic Democracy: The Politics of Feasible Socialism* (Oxford: Clarendon Press, 1995); and Robin Archer, "One Democratic Goal Remains in Labour's Works," *The Guardian*, May 8, 1995, 14.

[60]For a description and discussion of German works councils, see Chapter 11.

[61]Janos Kornai, *The Road to a Free Economy* (New York: W. W. Norton, 1990), 58. A similar line of criticism against market socialism may be found in Andrei Schleifer and Robert W. Vishny, "The Politics of Market Socialism," *Journal of Economic Perspectives* 8 (Spring 1994): 165-176.

[62]Mongolia fell under Communist control in 1921, resulting from its involvement as a staging ground in the Russian civil war.

Poland, and Romania because the indigenous Marxist movements were rather weak in those countries.

The situation was somewhat different in Albania, Czechoslovakia, Yugoslavia, and Vietnam. In Czechoslovakia, the Communists won a rightful place on a coalition government in a free election in 1946. Within 2 years, though, they edged all non-Communists out of power. Albania, Yugoslavia, and Vietnam drove out the Axis powers with little outside help. They all had relatively strong indigenous Marxist movements and none of them shared a common border with the Soviet Union. Furthermore, the Yugoslav and Vietnamese Communist leaders, Marshall Tito and Ho Chi Minh, were war heroes. Albania, Yugoslavia, and Vietnam were closely allied with the Soviet Union immediately after the war, but they were in a political and geographic position to act independently of Moscow.

Under the leadership of Mao Zedong, the Chinese Communists came to power in 1949 by defeating the Kuomintang in a long civil war. The Chinese Communists received little help, and some hindrance, from the Soviet Union during the war, but afterwards the Soviet Union provided aid, equipment, and advisors to install Soviet-style socialism in China.

The Communist movement spread to Latin America in 1960, when Fidel Castro gained power in Cuba, and to Africa in the 1960s and 1970s, when European colonialism began to crumble. The leaders of national liberation movements in many of the African countries were attracted to the Leninist theories of revolution and nationalization. With aid from the Soviet Union and its allies, Marxist regimes came to power in Angola, Mozambique, Madagascar, the Congo, Benin, and Ethiopia, and self-styled socialist regimes controlled several other countries.

Thus, the Communist world grew rapidly after World War II, but, in true dialectical fashion, its growth was fraught with conflicts and contradictions. Disagreements between Tito and Stalin led in 1948 to the expulsion of Yugoslavia from the Cominform, the international organization of the Soviet bloc. A few years later, Yugoslavia began to organize its unique system of labor-managed market socialism.

World communism was shaken by Stalin's death in 1953 and by Khrushchev's denunciation of Stalin's terror at the 1956 Party Congress. The Albanian leaders criticized Khrushchev for his blasphemy, and dropped out of the Soviet bloc to preserve their variety of Stalinism. The Poles and Hungarians were heartened by Khrushchev's remarks, and workers' groups demanded democratic reforms, higher wages, privatization of agriculture, and Yugoslav-style worker self-management. When Hungary attempted to leave the Warsaw Pact, the effort was crushed by Soviet troops and tanks.

In China, Mao Zedong was troubled by Khrushchev's de-Stalinization campaign, by his policy of peaceful co-existence with the West, and by his shift toward consumer goods production at a time when China was attempting to establish an industrial base. Mao ignored his Soviet advisors in 1958 and initiated his ill-fated Great Leap Forward program of rural communes and small-scale industrial production. A war of words ensued between Moscow and Beijing, and Soviet advisors were withdrawn from China in 1960.

In the mid-1960s, Soviet economic performance began to deteriorate, and Soviet economists gained more freedom to discuss programs of reform. Again, the Eastern Europeans were encouraged by these developments, and initiated new reform programs of their own. This time it was Czechoslovakia that pressed the Soviet leaders beyond their limits, calling for the creation of democratic institutions and independent trade unions. In 1968, the so-called Prague Spring was terminated by a quarter of a million Warsaw Pact troops.

A decade after the invasion of Czechoslovakia, the Communist world was shaken again when the Catholic church chose a prelate from Poland to serve as its first non-Italian Pope in 450 years. With support from John Paul II, the church grew stronger in Poland, and it played an important role in the formation of Solidarity, the first independent trade union in the Communist bloc. After a series of strikes and political demands in 1980 and 1981, the Communist leadership attempted to regain control by imposing martial law. Nevertheless, the events in Poland exposed the deep chasm between the Communist leadership and the working class; the seeds of an anti-Communist revolution had been sewn in Eastern Europe.

The dissolution of authoritarian socialism accelerated after 1985, when Mikhail Gorbachev came to power in the Soviet Union. His policy of *glasnost* (openness) made it possible to openly discuss the deterioration of economic performance, the crimes of Stalinism, the cost of the war in Afghanistan, and hundreds of other subjects that had been suppressed. His policy of *perestroika* (restructuring) made it possible to start working toward a more market-oriented economic system and a more democratic political system.

Equally important for the rest of the Communist world, Gorbachev abandoned the so-called Brezhnev Doctrine, which committed the Soviet Union to preserve Communism in other countries. In July 1989, Gorbachev cautioned the Eastern European leaders not to count on the Red Army for support: "Each people determines the future of its own country and chooses its own form of society. There must be no interference from outside, no matter what the pretext." Within a few months of this announcement, a Solidarity member became prime minister of Poland, the Hungarian parliament changed their country's name to Republic of Hungary, shedding Marxian terminology, and Communist regimes began to topple throughout Eastern Europe. In August 1991, responding to an abortive coup attempt against Gorbachev's government, Russian President Boris Yeltsin suspended the activities of the Communist Party and Gorbachev agreed to dissolve the Soviet Union.

With less fanfare, the collapse of authoritarian socialism spread quickly to the Third World. During the 1980s, the Soviet Union, Eastern Europe, and China could offer only one-tenth as much economic aid to developing countries as the Western industrial countries. Troubled by domestic problems, the Soviet Union and China cut their economic aid programs by 74 percent and 68 percent, respectively, in 1989.[63] A year later, new democratic constitutions were adopted in Benin, Mozambique, and the Congo, and the Sandinistas were voted out of

---

[63]U.S. Central Intelligence Agency, *Handbook of Economic Statistics, 1990* (CPAS 90-10001, September 1990), 180-187.

power in Nicaragua. The governments in these and many other developing countries initiated privatization programs in agriculture and industry.

Democratic Socialism in Transition

After World War II, as in earlier years, the focus of democratic socialist activity was in Western Europe. Communist parties and other radical socialist organizations continued to operate in many European nations, but their activities were moderated and inhibited by Western European participation in NATO, and by the public reactions to the Berlin blockade, the revelation of Stalin's crimes, the invasions of Hungary and Czechoslovakia, and the ultimate collapse of Soviet communism.

Table 4.2 "The free enterprise system and free market economy work best in society's interest when accompanied by strong government regulations."

	Agree	Disagree
China	87	8
Philippines	83	12
Italy	71	21
Indonesia	71	17
Kenya	67	25
Canada	66	25
Nigeria	65	31
Mexico	64	32
UK	62	27
Germany	62	27
Russia	61	25
India	61	27
US	57	34
Chile	54	25
S Korea	53	44
France	50	35
Brazil	47	42
Turkey	35	42

Source: GlobeScan 8/2007, reported at worldpublicopinion.org

In Great Britain, the Labour party was victorious in the first postwar election in 1945, and it quickly launched a program to nationalize the "commanding heights" of industry and to create an extensive welfare state. The Labour party was formally committed to public ownership in clause four of its constitution, reproduced on party membership cards: "to secure for the workers . . . the full fruits of their industry . . . upon the basis of the common ownership of the means of production."

Programs of nationalization were also conducted in France and Italy after World War II, where Socialist and Communist parties participated in coalition governments. On the other hand, the ruling Social Democratic party in Sweden dropped its plans for postwar nationalization to secure the cooperation of employers in a program of centralized collective bargaining. The division of Germany after the war led to a strong spirit of anti-communism in the West. Thus, the German Social Democratic Party moved away from its Marxist heritage, and it adopted a new program in 1959, declaring that the "fundamental values of socialism" are not revolution and public ownership, but "freedom, justice, and solidarity."[64]

In 1982, a socialist government in France initiated the largest postwar nationalization program in the Western world. Nevertheless, the recent trend in democratic (as well as autocratic) countries has been away from nationalization, and toward privatization, of industry. This movement began in the early 1980s in England, under the Conservative leadership of

[64]M. Donald Hancock, *West Germany: The Politics of Democratic Corporatism* (Chatham, N.J.: Chatham House, 1989), 83.

Margaret Thatcher, and it spread quickly throughout the world. In 1995, the British Labour party formally amended clause four of its constitution; references to "common ownership" were replaced with a commitment to the values of "freedom, equality, and solidarity."

If socialism is defined in terms of governmental policies to promote economic equality and economic stability, the democratic socialist movement still seems to be robust. According to an international poll conducted by the Times Mirror organization in 1991, large majorities of the populations in twelve nations of Eastern and Western Europe agreed that "the state has a responsibility to take care of people who cannot take care of themselves."[65] In a 2007 GlobeScan poll, majorities of respondents in 16 of 18 major countries agreed with the proposition that the market system works best in the presence of strong governmental regulation (see Table 4.2) Transfer payments to households have grown steadily as a percentage of GNP in most of the Western democracies since World War II. Transfer payments are generally highest, and incomes are distributed most equally, in countries such as Sweden where Social Democratic parties have maintained parliamentary majorities.

---

[65]"What Europeans Think," *Los Angeles Times*, September 17, 1991, special edition, H/B.

Table 4.3 Socialist Representation in World Parliaments

Country	Last Election	Socialist % of Parliament		Country	Last Election	*Socialist % of Parliament*
Albania	7/05	57		Israel	1/03	*20*
Australia	9/04	40		Italy	5/01	*38*
Austria	11/02	38		Jamaica	10/02	*52*
Belgium	6/03	28		Japan	11/03	*2*
Brazil	10/02	11		Morocco	9/02	*16*
Bulgaria	7/05	34		Netherlands	1/03	*27*
Canada	6/04	24		New Zealand	7/02	*45*
Chile	12/05	18		Nicaragua	11/01	*37*
China	11/02	100		North Korea	8/03	*100*
Colombia	3/02	33		Norway	9/05	*45*
Costa Rica	2/06	44		Pakistan	10/02	*25*
Cuba	1/03	100		Poland	9/05	*12*
Czech Rep.	6/06	33		Portugal	2/05	*62*
Denmark	2/05	45		Romania	11/04	*34*
Dominican Rep.	5/02	55		Russia	12/03	*13*
Ecuador	10/02	19		Senegal	4/01	*9*
Egypt	11/05	69		Slovakia	9/02	*7*
Finland	3/03	25		Spain	3/04	*49*
France	6/02	22		Sweden	9/02	*40*
Germany	9/02	39		Tunisia	10/04	*94*
Greece	3/04	41		Turkey	11/02	*19*
Hungary	4/02	46		Ukraine	3/02	*13*
India	5/04	21		United Kingdom	6/01	56

Note: Here, a parliamentarian is considered to be a socialist if she/he is affiliated with a party that is a full member, consultative party, or observer party in the Socialist International (for a list of these parties, see http://www.socialistinternational.org/viewArticle.cfm?ArticlePageID=931), or another party that identifies itself as "socialist," "social democratic," "communist," "labor," "left," or, in the case of Russia, "agrarian." In countries with bicameral systems, the data in this table refer only to the lower house of parliament. Information on parliamentary representation was assembled from the Central Intelligence Agency, World Factbook, available at https://www.cia.gov/library/publications/the-world-factbook/ and from media accounts.

If socialism is defined in terms of "economic democracy" and worker participation in management, the democratic socialist movement again seems to be robust. Worker participation takes many forms. In the United States, legislation encouraging the formation of employee stock ownership plans (ESOPs) has allowed more workers to gain a share of ownership in their businesses. In Germany, workers have a legally protected voice in management through their representatives on works councils and on corporate management boards. Implementation of the European Social Charter should lead to the development of a similar system of worker participation in the other countries of the European Union.

Finally, if we measure the strength of socialism by its representation in world parliaments, we find that the movement is far from dead (Table 4.3). Democratic socialist parties, alone or in coalitions, are playing active roles in the governments of countries in Africa, Asia, Europe, and Latin America. Like every other political movement, the socialists are attempting to redefine their role in a rapidly changing world. In the end, they will be judged by their ability to address the challenges of social justice, economic security, and environmental disruption in a setting of intense global competition.

Summary

In the primitive world, a form of communal ownership was sometimes practiced within the tribe, and communal systems were sometimes advocated or practiced in Greek and Biblical times. These, however, were usually voluntary responses to special circumstances. Revolutionary proposals for socialism as a mass movement began in the late 1700s, encouraged by the political revolutions in America and France and the Industrial Revolution in England. The French philosopher, Rousseau, criticized the system of capitalist ownership, and Morelly called for its abolition.

William Godwin and the Marquis de Condorcet predicted that the advance of reasoning would lead to improvements in virtue, an approach that encouraged the development of utopian socialism and anarchism. Saint-Simon, perhaps the first utopian socialist, championed the cause of working people in decisionmaking, and devised a system of national economic planning based on this principle. Robert Owen operated a successful model community, and attempted to organize several other cooperative communities. A similar proposal for a communal society, including provisions to reduce the monotony of work, was developed by Charles Fourier; several of his communities were established in America. The anarchists Proudhon and Bakunin took utopianism a step farther, and wished to replace the state altogether with a system of cooperatives.

Francois Babeuf was among the first to be executed for the cause of revolutionary socialism, and Auguste Blanqui argued that a socialist revolution would require the leadership of a small, well-organized minority.

Marx and Engels defined a mainstream of socialism that prescribed revolutionary tactics, state ownership, and a dictatorship of the proletariat in the short run, asserting that the state and monetary exchange would "wither away" in the long run. Their description of socialist society was not particularly detailed. The socialist movement was weakened by internal rivalries and revolutionary failures during the second half of the nineteenth century. Early in the twentieth century, Lenin followed Blanqui in saying that the revolution must be initiated and led by an elite vanguard of professionals; he provided a justification for beginning the revolution in Russia, a relatively poor country.

Louis Blanc helped to initiate the democratic socialist movement when he supported a gradual program of socialist reform in France. In Germany, Ferdinand Lasalle argued that electoral reforms would lead to the adoption of socialism, with worker control of large efficient factories; his followers established the German Social Democratic party, which successfully campaigned for a broad program of social reforms, and created a model for social democracy in other European countries.

In England, John Stuart Mill believed that society would eventually adopt labor ownership and management, and that it should do so without revolution or excessive governmental involvement. His ideas inspired the Fabian Socialist movement, which championed an evolutionary program of social reforms, and contributed to the establishment of the British Labour party.

After the Bolshevik victory in the Russian Revolution, the feasibility of efficient socialist planning became a subject of extensive debate. Ludwig von Mises argued that efficient planning was impossible because the absence of a market to set prices for producer goods would make it impossible to calculate accurate costs and benefits. Oskar Lange, among others, argued that a system of market socialism could equal or exceed the efficiency of the capitalist system.

After systems of market socialism were actually adopted in Yugoslavia and Hungary, theoretical analysis of these systems was initiated by Ben Ward, calling their efficiency into question. In recent years, a number of new blueprints for market-oriented state socialism, voucher socialism, bank-centric socialism, and economic democracy have been developed to remedy the problems of existing systems.

From 1917 until the close of World War II, the Soviet Union and Mongolia had the only socialist command economies in the world. After the war, they were joined by China, North Korea, the nations of Eastern Europe, and later by a host of developing countries. World communism was shaken by Stalin's death in 1953, followed by revolt in Eastern Europe and the Sino-Soviet split. The Soviet Union was able to hold the Communist movement together in the 1960s and 1970s, but an amazing progression of economic, political, and social events led to the collapse of command socialism in the 1980s and early 1990s.

The focus of democratic socialism after World War II was in Western Europe, where nationalization programs were conducted in several countries, but the recent trend has been toward privatization. If democratic socialism is defined as a system to promote equality of opportunity, full employment, distributive equity, and worker participation in management, and if its strength is measured by parliamentary representation, the movement seems to be quite alive.

Discussion and Review Questions

1. According to the broad conceptual framework suggested by people like Michael Harrington, what countries have come closest to fulfilling the ideals of socialism?

2. What role did the French and American revolutions play in the early history of socialism?

3. Describe and critically evaluate Saint-Simon's scheme for planning of public works.

4. What was the philosophy that prompted Owen's experiments in social reform? Why was it revolutionary at the time?

5. In what sense were Mill's socialist proposals consistent with the doctrines of Adam Smith and the classical school?

6. According to Marx and Engels, how would the early stages of socialist society differ from the later stages?

7. Explain the Mises critique of the efficiency of socialism. Do the market socialist proposals of Lange, Nove, and Yunker answer his criticisms?

8. What are some of the philosophical differences and historical events that have created and maintained the split between revolutionary and democratic socialists?

9. According to Robin Archer, how should the managerial control of an enterprise be divided between its owners, its workers, and its customers? Do you agree? Why or why not?

Suggested Readings

Buber, Martin. *Paths in Utopia*. New York: Macmillan, 1950. *A thoughtful polemic in favor of voluntary socialist cooperation by a noted theologian, with a particularly good discussion of Proudhon.*

Eatwell, John; Murray Milgate and Peter Newman, eds. *The New Palgrave: Problems of the Planned Economy*. New York: W.W. Norton, 1990. *Includes cogent essays on "Socialism" by Alec Nove, "Command Economy" by Gregory Grossman, and "Market Socialism" by W. Brus, to name a few.*

Freedman, Robert. *The Marxist System: Economic, Political, and Social Perspectives*. Chatham, N.J.: Chatham House Publishers, 1990. *Perhaps the most concise, readable, and reliable introduction to Marxian economic theories in their political and social context.*

Fried, Albert, and Ronald Sanders, eds. *Socialist Thought: A Documentary History*. Garden City, N.Y.: Doubleday, 1964. *Selections from many of the prominent socialists from Morelly in the eighteenth century through Crosland in the twentieth century.*

Harrington, Michael. *Socialism: Past and Future*. New York: Arcade Publishing, 1989. *The last major work by a well-regarded American socialist, this book surveys the history of socialism and suggests how the movement can be renewed in the future.*

Nove, Alec, and D. M. Nuti, eds. *Socialist Economics*. Harmondsworth, Eng.: Penguin, 1972. *A book of readings, most from the twentieth century, including the Mises and Lange contributions and other articles on socialist growth, planning, and reform.*

Tucker, Robert C., ed. *The Marx-Engels Reader.* 2d ed. New York: W. W. Norton, 1978. *Includes a good sampling of their work and several readings that are difficult to find elsewhere.*

Wild, Lawrence. *Modern European Socialism*. Aldershot: Dartmouth Publishing, 1994. *This thoroughly documented study reviews the modern socialist movements in several countries of Western and Eastern Europe, and discusses the prospects for socialist internationalism in a more unified Europe.*

Yunker, James A. *Socialism Revised and Modernized*. New York: Praeger, 1992. *Written during the collapse of the Soviet empire, this may be the most detailed recent proposal for a system of democratic market socialism, including an extended defense of its workability and relative efficiency.*

CHAPTER 5

ECONOMICS OF THE DEVELOPING WORLD

Most of the people in the world are poor, so if we knew the Economics of being poor we would know much of the Economics that really matters.

—Theodore W. Schultz, Nobel Lecture, *Journal of Political Economy,* August 1980

Two centuries after the Industrial Revolution, more than 1.3 billion people still live in **absolute or extreme poverty**—a condition of life "so characterized by malnutrition, illiteracy, and disease" that the World Bank finds it "beneath any reasonable definition of human decency."[1] These people and 3 billion others live in a collection of countries we know optimistically as the "developing world." They invade our consciousness when we hear of another civil war in Africa, another famine in South Asia, another financial crisis in Latin America, or another reversal of world commodity prices.

Who are the poor? Why do they remain poor? What can be done about it? Why hasn't it been done? These are important, difficult, and immortal questions; they extend far beyond the scope of comparative economic systems. For our present purposes, we will survey only a few of the relevant issues and hope that these will inspire additional study.

Who Are the Poor?

A general profile of population, income, health, and education in the developing world is presented in Table 5.1. By nearly any yardstick, the poorest and most underprivileged people in the world are found in Sub-Saharan Africa, India, and the other countries of South Asia. These countries have much lower incomes, shorter life expectancies, higher levels of infant and child mortality, and lower literacy levels than any other regions of the world. According to the data in Table 5.2, in 1981 the highest rates and largest concentrations of extreme poverty were found in China and the other countries of East Asia, but that region has experienced an amazing transformation during the last 30 years (although many regions of China are still desperately poor), and it now has a much lower rate of extreme poverty than the average for all developing countries. Income and literacy rates are relatively high in Latin America, but poverty rates are also high because incomes are distributed unevenly.

---

[1]This description is taken from World Bank, *Poverty and Human Development* (New York: Oxford University Press, 1980), v. The numerical estimate is from "Richest Nations Turn Backs on Poorest," Reuters News Service, June 13, 1995. Recall the discussion of poverty estimates in Chapter 2.

Table 5.1 Developing Countries: Population, Income, and Development, 2005

	Population (million)	Arable land (hectares per person)	GDP per capita ($ at PPP)	Living Below $1.25 a day (PPP, % of pop.)	Adult Literacy (%)	Life expectancy at birth, total (years)	Infant Mortality Rate[a]	Human Developmen t Index
World	6458	0.22	8764	n.a.	82	68	49.1	0.74
Industrial Countries	1041	0.36	32876	n.a.	99	79	6.1	0.94
Developing Countries	5416	0.19	4161	25.3	77	66	53.4	0.69
East Asia & Pacific	1884	0.11	3884	16.8	91	72	24.8	0.77
China	1304	0.11	4076	15.9	91	73	21.4	0.78
Europe & Cen. Asia	444	0.57	9415	3.8	99	69	23.4	0.81
Latin America & Carib.	547	0.26	8670	8.2	90	73	24.2	0.80
Middle East	303	0.17	6298	3.6	70	69	34.2	0.70
South Asia	1476	0.14	2081	40.3	60	64	62.2	0.61
India	1095	0.15	2234	41.6	61	64	57.7	0.62
Sub-Saharan Africa	762	0.25	1732	50.9	59	50	90.8	0.49

[a]Deaths during the first year of life per 1,000 live births.
Sources: World Bank, *World Development Indicators, online; and United Nations Development Programme 2007-2008*. For an explanation of the Human Development Index (HDI), see Chapter 2 of this text.

The data in Table 5.2 indicate that the percentage rates of extreme poverty reduced in all regions of the developing world between 1990 and 2005, aside from the transitional economies of Europe and Central Asia. Still, there is no room for complacency. Although the *proportion* of humankind living in absolute poverty has fallen, population growth in Sub-Saharan Africa and South Asia has caused the *number* of poor in those regions to increase by about 107 million. A 2009 assessment by the United Nations indicated that the global financial crisis would cause 73-103 million more people to remain poor or fall into poverty, when compared with the pre-crisis scenario. Most of this setback was predicted to fall on East and South Asia, with between 56 and 80 million people affected.[2] Much progress has been made, but the challenge of economic and social development has never been greater.

---

[2] United Nations, *World Economic Situation and Prospects 2009: Update as of Mid-2009.* http://www.un.org/esa/policy/wess/wesp.html

Table 5.2 Extreme Poverty in Developing Countries, 1981-2015

Percentage of the population living on less than $1.25/day				
Region or country	*1981*	*1990*	*2005*	*2015 (forecast)*
East Asia & Pacific	77.7	54.7	16.8	6.8
China	84.0	60.2	15.9	6.1
Europe & Central Asia	1.8	2.0	3.7	2.2
Latin America & Carib.	12.9	11.3	8.2	5.0
Middle East & N. Africa	7.9	4.3	3.6	2.5
South Asia	59.4	51.7	40.3	23.8
India	59.5	51.3	41.6	25.4
Sub-Saharan Africa	53.4	57.6	50.9	37.1
Total	52.2	41.7	25.3	15.5
Number of people living on less than $1.25/day (millions)				
Region or country	*1981*	*1990*	*2005*	*2015 (forecast)*
East Asia & Pacific	1071.5	873.3	316.2	137.6
China	835.1	683.2	207.7	84.3
Europe & Central Asia	7.0	9.1	17.3	9.8
Latin America & Carib.	46.8	49.6	45.1	30.6
Middle East & N. Africa	13.6	9.7	11.0	8.8
South Asia	548.4	579.2	595.6	403.9
India	418.2	435.5	455.8	313.2
Sub-Saharan Africa	210.5	297.5	388.4	356.4
Total	1897.8	1,818.5	1,373.5	947.2

Sources: World Bank, *World Development Indicators*, online; and World Bank, *Global Economic Prospects 2009*, 47.

Obstacles to Development

Although social scientists do not agree on the causes of persistent poverty, few would dispute the basic issues. First, if a country wishes for sustained economic growth, it must somehow increase its stock of physical and/or human capital (factories, machinery, equipment, health, and education). If this is to be done without massive foreign assistance, the country must be able to produce an output that exceeds the subsistence needs of the population. Furthermore, some group of people, whether they be private entrepreneurs, government leaders, or foreign colonialists, must mobilize that surplus toward productive ends (building factories, schools, roads, and so forth) rather than allowing it to dissipate on extravagant consumption, military adventures, civic monuments, or capital flight.

Speaking very generally, countries that remain poor are those that fail to generate a sufficient investable surplus or those that fail to invest it in productive activities. Within this framework, the various camps of economists differ on the causes of the low saving and investment rates. Traditional theories usually stress environmental and institutional barriers and the "vicious circles of poverty." Radical economists believe that the surplus of the poor countries is transferred to the rich by an exploitive system of investment and trade.

Environment and Culture

In their search for the underlying causes of poverty, some social scientists have argued that the developing countries are accursed by geographic, environmental, and cultural conditions that are difficult to overcome. The average developing country, for example, must use each square kilometer of its arable land to feed more than three times as many people as the average industrial country (Table 5.1). Accordingly, it is difficult to generate an investable surplus of output above the subsistence needs of the population.

Most of the developing world, and very little of the industrial world, is located in a band around the equator that stretches from the Tropic of Capricorn to the Tropic of Cancer. Most of this region receives heavy rain all year (within 1,000 miles of the equator) or heavy monsoon rains for half of the year and no rain for the rest of the year (1,000 to 1,500 miles from the equator), or has turned to desert. Except in high-altitude areas, temperatures range from hot to very hot, placing a strain on human bodies, electronic equipment, and automotive radiators.

Through much of the region that is not covered by jungle, desert, or volcanic or alluvial soil, excessive heat has burned away the organic matter of the soil and excessive rain has washed away its nutrients. The tropical climate and poor sanitation foster the reproduction of insects, parasites, and pests that attack people, plants, and animals. Winter, the great exterminator, never comes.[3]

The impact of cultural and religious factors on economic development is more speculative and controversial. With the exception of Japan, all high-income industrial countries are predominantly Christian and all Protestant countries have high incomes. Few Islamic countries have advanced beyond the lower-middle income level without the help of petroleum exports.[4] According to cultural determinists, patterns such as these can be explained by religious and cultural attitudes toward freedom, conformity, competition, equality, honesty, work, science, education, birth control, and wealth accumulation.[5]

A cultural determinist would say, for example, that Latin America is relatively poor and North America is relatively rich because of differences between their Spanish and British colonial heritages. Spain was overpowered by the Moors (or Muslims) in the eighth century and,

---

[3]Andrew Karmarck, *The Tropics and Economic Development* (Baltimore: The Johns Hopkins University Press, 1976).

[4]Everett Hagen, *The Economics of Development,* 4th ed. (Homewood, Ill.: Irwin, 1986), 44. In the 1994 edition of the World Bank's *World Development Report*, Malaysia became the first Islamic country to achieve "upper-middle-income" status with a relatively diversified export base (which still includes petroleum). Turkey probably will be the first to achieve that rank with a relatively limited raw materials base.

[5]See Mark Casson, "Cultural Determinants of Economic Performance," *Journal of Comparative Economics* 17 (June 1993): 418-442.

despite centuries of civil war, did not fully regain its independence until 1492, the year of Columbus's voyage. Thus, some would say that Spain inherited an authoritarian culture from the Moors and the long process of reconquest created an extremely orthodox and intolerant brand of Roman Catholicism. This intolerance led Spain to launch its Inquisition in 1480 and to expel all Jews from its territory in 1492. Spanish corruption, authoritarianism, inequality, and intolerance were allegedly transplanted in Latin America, where they have stood in the way of economic development.[6]

In Asia, rough cultural lines can be drawn between the Muslim countries of the Middle East and Pakistan, the Hindu countries of the south (India, Bangladesh, and Nepal), and the Confucian and Buddhist countries of the east. Many believe that the Confucian work ethic has contributed to the successful growth of Japan and the East Asian Gang of Four—Hong Kong, Singapore, South Korea, and Taiwan. Conversely, certain aspects of Hinduism have allegedly retarded development in South Asia. The caste system, for example, places limits on labor mobility, income equality, and work incentives. The law of *karma,* which says that one's fate in this life is a reward or punishment for actions in a previous life, supposedly evokes a fatalistic acceptance of the status quo.

Like other single-factor theories of economic development, geographic and cultural determinism leave many questions unanswered. Why were the ancient civilizations of Egypt, Mesopotamia, China, and the Mayas able to flourish under the curse of tropical geography? Why has it taken so long for the Confucian work ethic to take its place beside (or ahead of) the Protestant ethic? The links between geography, culture, and development are indisputable, but they are not well understood.

The Economic System

Quite often, economic growth and development is fettered by the backwardness of economic institutions. The specific problems vary tremendously from one country to another, but a few are rather common.

Land Tenure. Several different systems of land ownership are used in the developing countries; few of them promote economic development. In much of Africa and Asia, particularly in nomadic areas, the land is held in common with no identifiable owner or controlled by a village, tribe, or extended family. In order to ensure equity, the right to use the best land is rotated among families. Thus, an individual family has little incentive or opportunity to engage in long-term projects to irrigate and improve the land. If such efforts are undertaken, they usually require the cooperation of an entire community.

In most of the countries of Latin America, the land is held privately, but its distribution is very uneven. With the exception of countries that have implemented major land reforms

---

[6]For an extended discussion of Latin American development by a cultural determinist, see Lawrence E. Harrison, *Development Is a State of Mind: The Latin American Case* (Lanham, Md.: University Press of America, 1985).

(Mexico, Bolivia, Cuba, and Nicaragua), the *latifundios* (very large farms) usually constitute less than 5 percent of the farms while holding more than 50 percent of the land. The sharecroppers on the *latifundios* have little incentive to improve land that they do not own and the landlords have a poor record of investment. The small farms are barely able to provide a living for their owners.

Market Structure. In some countries, the market mechanism is still operating at a primitive level, with limited ability to coordinate and guide the development of the economy. In Africa, for example, about 25 percent of all economic activity was based on barter in the 1970s, and roughly 10 percent is still conducted outside the monetized sector.[7] In countries with poor transportation and communication systems, markets are disconnected from one another and from those in the outside world. Price controls and state monopolies, which cripple the operation of the market system, are still common in the developing world.

Labor Markets. A wide gulf usually exists between the modern sector of a developing economy, which typically involves capital-intensive industrial production in the cities, and the traditional sector of labor-intensive agricultural production and crafts. Thus, many countries have a **dual labor market** in which urban wages are two or three times larger than rural incomes. It is difficult to explain these differences in terms of skill or productivity; several other factors are apparently involved. The urban workers are more likely to be unionized, more likely to work for nationalized companies, and more likely to have the protection of a legal minimum wage. Business firms in the modern sector may be willing to pay relatively high wages to maintain a stable force of experienced workers. Whatever the cause, the dual wage structure promotes income inequality and attracts large numbers of people into the cities, contributing to urban unemployment.

Financial Markets. The limited quantity and quality of financial intermediation is a serious problem in many developing countries. The entire financial system is usually organized around a few banks, which are heavily regulated because they have excessive market power. Securities markets are rudimentary or nonexistent, making it difficult to raise money through stock or bond issues. Few people channel their savings through life insurance companies. Governmental taxation and control of interest rates frequently reduces the incentive to save.

Vicious Circles of Poverty

If environmental, cultural, and institutional factors explain some of the initial causes of poverty, a number of vicious circles help to explain why the poor remain poor.

Saving and Investment. It is difficult for a destitute country to generate the savings that are needed to finance investment. The investment rate of low-income countries is lower than that of

---

[7]Anand G. Chandavarkar, "Monetization of Developing Countries," *International Monetary Fund Staff Papers* 24 (November 1977): 678-679; and author's estimate, based on money/GDP ratios for 1970 and 1992, found in World Bank, *World Development Report 1994* (New York: Oxford University Press, 1994), 184.

any other group of countries. Their low rates of investment, in turn, contribute to their low rates of economic growth.

Health and Education. Similarly, it is difficult for a poor country to set aside the resources that are needed to provide health and education services to the population, and it is difficult for the children of the poor to take time off from work for their education. Thus, poverty begets disease and illiteracy, which cause the continuation of poverty.

Market Size. Low income levels and primitive transportation systems restrict the market demand for any given commodity in a developing country. With limited demand, it is difficult to increase efficiency through mass production. A low level of efficiency leads to a continuation of poverty.

Political Instability. Poverty also regenerates itself by provoking political instability, often in a senseless series of coups d'etat. Since 1948, the average developing country has had at least one coup attempt every five years.[8] Between 1825, when it gained independence, and 1985, when it established a stable democratic system, Bolivia had more than 150 governments. After the Communists were deposed in 1989, Poland had five governments in five years. Short terms of office encourage rulers to undertake short-sighted economic policies, such as inflationary creation of money. Political instability discourages foreign investment, and encourages the flight of domestic capital. According to one comprehensive study, economic growth has usually begun in Latin American countries with "the emergence at long last of a stable government able to exercise effective control of the country for an extended period."[9]

Population Growth. In comparison to the industrial countries, percentage rates of population growth are more than twice as high in middle-income developing countries, more than three times as high in low-income countries of South Asia, and more than four times as high in low-income countries of Africa.[10] The populations of poor countries tend to grow rapidly because of their rural lifestyles and their inability or unwillingness (for religious and other reasons) to practice birth control. Rapid population growth, in turn, makes it difficult for a society to expand and maintain a sufficient stock of housing, productive capital, natural resources, educational services, medical facilities, and other elements of social infrastructure. The poorest countries also tend to have the highest **dependency ratios**—that is, the percentage of the population that is not of working age. In 1992 the dependency ratio was 33 percent in the industrial countries, 38 percent in the middle-income developing countries, and 43 percent in the low-income countries

---

[8]World Bank, *World Development Report 1991*, 128.

[9]Lloyd G. Reynolds, "The Spread of Economic Growth to the Third World: 1850-1980," *Journal of Economic Literature* 21 (September 1983): 964.

[10]Based on growth rates for 1980-1992 in World Bank, *World Development Report 1994,* 210-211.

(excluding China, where strict policies have reduced population growth and dependency ratios to the levels of middle-income countries).[11]

Table 5.3 The Kuznets Hypothesis: Income and Inequality

	1995 GDP Per Capita Range (dollars)	*Average Share of Poorest 40 Percent of Households in Total Income*
25 Low-income countries	80-730	16.3
31 Lower-middle-income countries	770-3,020	17.1
7 Upper-middle-income countries	3,160-8,210	15.2
20 High-income countries	9,700-40,630	18.2

Source: World Bank, *World Development Report 1997,* 214-215, 222-223; and author's calculations.

Income Inequality. Poor countries tend to experience greater income inequality than high-income countries, and efforts to promote economic development may cause inequality to grow worse before it improves. This pattern, known as Kuznets's Law, is illustrated by the data in Table 5.3. On average, income inequality is greatest in the upper-middle-income countries, and lowest in high-income countries. By implication, as a country grows out of the low-income category, it may take a long time for the benefits of economic growth to trickle down to the lower classes of society. Economic growth accompanied by increasing income inequality may contribute to political instability, which may put an end to economic growth.[12]

Imperialism and Dependency

Marxists and many others do not accept the environmental and vicious-circle explanations of poverty. The industrial countries, they say, have employed a number of methods to extract the investable surpluses of the developing countries. The rich have grown richer by causing the poor to remain poor.

Most observers would agree that the developing countries were exploited during the colonial era. For example, the American Revolution was fought to end the burden of British colonial taxation. Spanish colonial rule in Latin America was more harsh and covered a longer period of time. Colonialism continued in India, the Middle East, and the Philippines until the end of World War II and in much of Africa and Indochina until the 1960s.

---

[11]Ibid.

[12]For a more optimistic assessment, which proposes that the Kuznets effect is too small to negate the welfare effects of economic growth, see Gustav Papanek and Oldrich Kyn, "The Effect on Income Distribution of Development, the Rate of Growth, and Economic Strategy," *Journal of Development Economics* 23 (September 1986): 55-65.

The impact of colonial rule was not entirely negative, particularly under the British and the Japanese. The rulers generally built schools, ports, railways, electric power systems, and other utilities. Karl Marx gave the British credit for breaking the power of the village communities in India, which "had always been the solid foundation of Oriental despotism," and he attributed great importance to the building of railways: "Modern industry, resulting from the railway system, will dissolve the hereditary divisions of labor, upon which rest the Indian castes, those decisive impediments to Indian progress and Indian power."[13]

Now that overt colonialism is largely a thing of the past, Marxists and so-called **dependency theorists** believe that the industrial countries have continued their exploitation of the developing countries through foreign trade and investment. Multinational corporations (MNCs) are said to play an important role in this process. Critics say that the MNCs extract excessive profits from the host countries and that they fund some of their operations out of local credit markets, crowding out domestic borrowers. Because of their foreign orientation, they introduce products and technologies that are inappropriate for the needs of the developing countries. They create low-skill jobs in the developing countries and shift the high-skill jobs elsewhere. Most important, they encourage governmental corruption and manipulate policies to the detriment of the local populations.[14]

Defenders of the MNCs say that they provide jobs, training, capital, technology, and tax revenues to the host countries. Juscelino Kubitschek, the Brazilian president who opened the country to foreign investment during the 1960s, said at the time that it was senseless to argue about industries that did not exist; the first priority is to get the industries established, with or without foreign help.[15] Evidence from Cote d'Ivoire and Venezuela suggests that foreign-owned manufacturing firms are more efficient than locally owned firms, even after capital intensity and firm size are taken into account.[16] For these and other reasons, the World Bank argues that "equity forms of investment can clearly be beneficial to developing countries, and it is desirable that they be increased."[17]

Marxists found it difficult to build a strong quantitative case for the link between foreign investment and world poverty. The profits that are taken out of the developing countries by the MNCs are relatively small as a proportion of national income, particularly for countries such as

---

[13]Marx in the *New York Daily Tribune,* June 25, 1853, quoted in H. A. Reitsma and J. M. G. Kleinpenning, *The Third World in Perspective* (Assen, Neth.: Van Gorcum, 1985), 217.

[14]See, for example, John Madeley, *Trade and the Poor* (New York: St. Martin's Press, 1993), 87-118.

[15]Robert J. Alexander, "Import Substitution in Latin America in Retrospect," in *Progress Toward Development in Latin America*, eds. James L. Dietz and Dilmus D. James (Boulder: Lynne Rienner, 1990), 24.

[16]World Bank, *World Development Report 1991*, 94.

[17]World Bank, *World Development Report 1985*, 134.

India. Thus, the dependency theorists shifted attention from investment to international trade and specialization. In their view, the core (industrial) economies have manipulated the patterns of trade to their own advantage and to the detriment of the peripheral (developing) economies.

Dependency theory grew out of the writings of Raul Prebisch, an Argentine economist, who argued in the 1950s that the developing countries are victimized by their specialization in primary-goods production. The international terms of trade tend to deteriorate for the developing countries, he said, because growth in world income increases the demand for manufactured goods more rapidly than the demand for primary products. Prebisch attempted to support his theory with statistical evidence, but subsequent research has cast doubt over the declining-terms-of-trade hypothesis.[18]

Subsequently, the French economist Arghiri Emmanuel argued that, regardless of their historical trends, the export prices received by the developing world are simply too low; poor countries are forced to surrender their primary goods in an **unequal exchange** for high-priced industrial goods. The prices of primary goods are low, he says, because they incorporate the low labor costs of the poor countries. Thus, poverty begets low prices and low prices beget poverty.[19]

According to traditional analysis, the unequal exchange hypothesis is just as invalid as the cheap-foreign-labor argument of protectionists in the industrial countries. International trade based on comparative advantage, according to theory, is mutually beneficial to the rich and the poor countries. However, the traditional theory says nothing about the equity with which the gains from trade are distributed between the rich and the poor.

Dependency theorists argue that the developing countries are crippled in many other ways by their peripheral role in the world capitalist system. Their product markets are jolted by broad swings in world commodity prices. Their financial systems are destabilized by erratic inflows and outflows of international capital.[20] The international arms race, allegedly manipulated by the arms merchants in the industrial countries, forces the developing countries to squander much of their investable surplus. More generally, dependent development means that "some countries can expand through self-impulsion while others . . . can only expand as a

---

[18]For a review of the evidence, see John Spraos, "The Statistical Debate on the Net Barter Terms of Trade between Primary Commodities and Manufactures," *Economic Journal* 90 (March 1980): 107-128.

[19]For a discussion of Emmanuel's theory and other radical perspectives on development, see Keith Griffin and John Gurley, "Radical Analyses of Imperialism, the Third World, and the Transition to Socialism: A Survey Article," *Journal of Economic Literature* 23 (September 1985): 1089-1143.

[20]According to a recent study by Goldman, Sachs, & Co., 80 percent of the turbulence in Mexico's financial markets in 1994 was caused by "a retrenchment of liquidity that was taking place around the world" rather than by domestic economic or political events. See Tim Carrington, "Private-Capital Flows Can Hurt Poor Countries," *The Wall Street Journal*, January 30, 1995, A1.

reflection of the dominant countries, which may have positive or negative effects on their immediate development."[21]

Development Strategies

If explanations of poverty differ among countries and economists, proposals to alleviate it are equally diverse. A person persuaded by geographic or cultural determinism, by vicious-circle theories, by theories of imperialism and dependency, or by some combination of these may conclude that the future of the developing world is hopeless, or that it merely requires the removal of a few obstacles, or that it requires the adoption of a system of national planning, or that it requires the creation of a so-called new international economic order. A few of the more prominent strategies are surveyed here.

Smith, Ricardo, and Surplus Labor

Always the optimist, Adam Smith declared in 1755 that "little else is requisite to carry a state to the highest degree of opulence, but peace, easy taxes, and a tolerable administration of justice; all the rest being brought about by the natural course of things." Twenty-one years later, in his *Wealth of Nations*, Smith explained that economic development is rooted in the "uniform, constant, and uninterrupted effort of every man to better his condition." The efforts of individuals, coordinated by markets, are "frequently powerful enough to maintain the natural progress of things toward improvement, in spite of the extravagance of government, and of the greatest errors of administration."[22] Thus, Adam Smith advanced the "growth is natural" school of thought; little is needed from the government to promote it, and little can be done by the government to stop it.

David Ricardo, one of Smith's disciples, believed that British growth was threatened by restrictions on agricultural imports under the Corn Laws. The restrictions, he said, kept an artificially large labor force in the agricultural sector, working at very low marginal productivity. If the Corn Laws were repealed, market forces would move these excess workers into industry, where their productivity would be greater. The rise in productivity would create a surplus of output over the subsistence needs of the population, which would open the door to investment and economic growth.

In 1954, W. Arthur Lewis revived the idea that a surplus population of underemployed rural labor could be shifted into industry to increase productivity, generate savings, and fuel

---

[21]Theotonio Dos Santos, "The Structure of Dependence," *American Economic Review* 60 (May 1970): 289-290.

[22]Adam Smith, *An Inquiry into the Nature and Causes of the Wealth of Nations* (Oxford: Clarendon Press, 1976), 343.

economic growth.[23] Lewis said that rapid population growth had created a rural **labor surplus** in the poor countries—a surplus that could be mobilized:

The [developing countries] have within themselves all that is required for growth. They have surpluses of fuel and the principal minerals. They have enough land to feed themselves, if they cultivate it properly. They are capable of learning the skills of manufacturing, and of saving the capital required for modernization. Their development does not in the long run depend on the existence of the developed countries, and their potential for growth would be unaffected even if all the developed countries were to sink under the sea.[24]

Although Lewis believes that economic planning and governmental action may be needed to move the surplus agricultural workers into industry, his description of planning is reminiscent of Smith: "The economics of development is not very complicated; the secret of successful planning lies more in sensible politics and good public administration."[25]

Rosenstein-Rodan, Nurske, and Balanced Growth

As the world faced recovery from World War II, several economists agreed that industrialization could be launched by mobilizing the underemployed rural population, but few of them shared Lewis's view that development was "not very complicated." Writing as early as 1943, Paul Rosenstein-Rodan emphasized the obstacles to development and believed that industrialization would require a **big push:**

Launching a country into self-sustaining growth is a little like getting an airplane off the ground. There is a critical ground speed which must be passed before the craft can become airborne. . . . A big push seems to be required to jump over the economic obstacles to development. . . . An atmosphere of development may only arise with a minimum speed or size of investment.[26]

Supporting Rosenstein-Rodan's call for a big push, in 1953 Ragnar Nurske popularized the idea that economic progress is not a spontaneous or automatic affair because vicious circles of poverty, limited investment, malnutrition, and limited market size have stunted economic growth and development. Industrialization requires a comprehensive policy of **balanced growth,**

---

[23]W. A. Lewis, "Economic Development with Unlimited Supplies of Labor," *The Manchester School* (May 1954): 139-191.

[24]W. A. Lewis quoted in Gerald Meier, *Emerging from Poverty: The Economics that Really Matters* (New York: Oxford University Press, 1984), 207.

[25]Ibid., 208.

[26]Rosenstein-Rodan quoted in Meier, *Emerging from Poverty,* 138. Note the apparent influence of Rosenstein-Rodan on Rostow's conception of a "take-off into self-sustained growth," discussed in the following section.

accomplished by a wave of capital investments in a number of different industries. No single industry can go it alone, he says, because of the operation of Say's Law—the demand for one product is generated by the production of other goods.

Rostow, Hirschman, and Unbalanced Growth

Nurske's strategy of balanced growth was a counsel of despair in many of the poor countries: it implied that one must somehow support a wide range of industries or do nothing at all. Walt Rostow, also writing in 1953, struck a more responsive chord when he said that development could be initiated by launching a few **leading sectors.**[27] Based on his reading of European and American history, Rostow concluded that societies pass through several distinct stages on their way to affluence.

According to Rostow's theory, societies emerge from the backward traditional stage as they fulfill the "preconditions for take-off." During the preconditions stage, attitudes toward economic and scientific progress begin to change, an entrepreneurial class is formed, and an infrastructure of transport and communications facilities is built. When the "old blocks and resistances to steady growth are finally overcome," the nation can begin its "take-off into self-sustained growth." The trends in social change, production, and scientific progress that were initiated during the preconditions stage will begin to accelerate, and the rate of investment will roughly double. A few leading sectors will grow most rapidly and will serve as a locomotive for the rest of the economy. The leading sector that launched the British Industrial Revolution, for example, was the cotton industry; the railroads led the way in the United States. After take-off, Rostow's stereotypical society progresses to "technological maturity," then to "mass consumption," and finally to the "search for quality."

In the eyes of its critics, Rostow's theory is too neat, clean, and deterministic to serve as a description of the development path of all societies. The same criticism has been applied to the Marxian stage theory, which Rostow hoped to displace. The leaders of many developing countries have adopted Rostow's analysis as a how-to guide for growth; the take-off and leading sector concepts have entered the vernacular of economic development.

If a country wishes to develop a few leading sectors, which sectors should it choose? In his theory of **unbalanced growth,** Albert Hirschman suggests that special attention should be directed to industries that have strong **linkages** to other industries. These linkages may take several forms. Industries such as automotive manufacturing that create a strong demand for inputs from other industries are said to have strong **backward linkages.** Those that produce important inputs for other industries are said to have **forward linkages.**

---

[27]Rostow's theory of leading sectors, which first appeared in a 1953 essay, was popularized in his book, *The Stages of Economic Growth* (London: Cambridge University Press, 1960).

As Nurske emphasized, one of the dangers of an unbalanced growth strategy is that the domestic market will not be able to provide sufficient demand for the output of an isolated industry. One way to get around this problem is through a policy of **import substitution.** If an industrial product is being imported, then a domestic demand for that product obviously exists. All that must be done is to develop an indigenous industry and protect it from foreign competition.

From the 1930s to the 1980s, import substitution was employed extensively in Latin America and Africa. Dependency theorists favor this approach because it attempts to shift the developing countries to more advanced lines of production, to reduce their vulnerability to fluctuations in the world market, and to alleviate their balance of payments problems.

Critics of import substitution say that it distorts the allocation of resources, reducing the benefits gained from international trade according to comparative advantage. It requires that the government decide which sectors to protect from foreign competition; these decisions invite governmental bribery and corruption. Reduction of imports causes a reduction in the demand for foreign exchange, which causes the exchange rate of the local currency to rise, which makes it more difficult to sell the country's exports. Thus, the balance of payments may not improve. Maintenance of high import barriers will often require an enormous system of controls to prevent smuggling. Infant industries that are created by the program will often fail to mature. Finally, the strategy is self-limiting, in that it must stop when all of the nation's imports have been replaced.

Based on the disappointing results of import substitution and the celebrated successes of countries such as Hong Kong, South Korea, and Singapore, many countries have shifted to a policy of **export promotion**. This approach suggests that a country should base its development efforts on leading sectors that can compete quickly on the world market; industries that can compete only on a protected domestic market should receive little priority. Instead of imposing heavy tariffs and quantitative restrictions on imports, the government should support emerging export industries with an appropriate legal and regulatory environment, education and training programs, infrastructure for transportation and communications, and moderate levels of tax relief, import duty rebates, subsidies, and low-interest credit.

Advocates of export promotion say that it keeps the country open to foreign trade and competition, deriving benefits from international specialization. Production for the large and competitive world market rather than a small and monopolized domestic market forces companies to maintain high quality standards and low production costs and allows them to fully exploit economies of scale. An outward orientation forces the government to resist inflationary policies and overvalued exchange rates. Generally, export promotion is accomplished through positive incentives rather than a bureaucratic system of direct controls, so it seems to invite less political corruption.[28]

---

[28]Anne O. Krueger, "Import Substitution versus Export Promotion," *Finance and Development* 22 (June 1985): 20-23.

Export promotion is the centerpiece of the so-called **Washington Consensus**, a market-oriented development strategy supported by agencies of the U.S. government, the World Bank, the International Monetary Fund, and the regional development banks. In addition to an export promoting, or "outward-oriented," trade policy, the consensus suggests that governments in developing countries should focus on their core functions, including public health, education, public infrastructure, and administration of justice; they should privatize many state-owned industries, remove controls on prices and interest rates, reduce budget deficits and excessive monetary growth, and dismantle regulations that stifle entrepreneurship and foreign investment.

Table 5.4 High-Growth and Low-Growth Developing Countries, 1984-1993

	All Developing Countries	*42 High-Growth Countries*	*42 Low-Growth Countries*
Annual percentage changes:			
GDP	5.1	7.4	1.4
Consumer prices	43.5	11.5	53.5
Export volume	7.6	10.4	3.4
Terms of trade	-1.1	0.1	-3.0
Real effective exchange rate	-3.1	-5.9	1.6
Total factor productivity	1.7	3.4	-1.1
Percent of GDP:			
Investment	25.6	30.1	20.9
Saving	24.3	29.3	18.8
Fiscal deficit	-4.3	-3.2	-5.3
External debt	39.6	29.4	51.2
Real interest rate	0.02	2.89	-2.81

Note: Generally, the data in this table encompass 126 developing countries, the 42 countries with highest GDP growth, and the 42 countries with lowest GDP growth. Data for total productivity growth and real interest rates are based on smaller samples of countries for which data are available. The real interest rate is defined as the short-term nominal interest rate minus the rate of inflation.
Source: International Monetary Fund, *World Economic Outlook*, May 1994, 55-57.

The data in Table 5.4 were compiled by the International Monetary Fund to confirm the efficacy of a market-oriented development policy. Countries that have achieved high rates of economic growth seem to be those that have maintained low rates of inflation, small fiscal deficits, low levels of foreign debt, and high levels of export growth. Their regulatory environments do not cause exchange rates to become overvalued, which would inhibit export growth, or cause real interest rates to become negative, which would inhibit saving. Lawrence Summers, whose work at the World Bank and the U.S. Treasury helped to establish the Washington Consensus, says that the evidence is clear: "National development failures are the fault of national policies—they cannot be blamed on a hostile international environment or on physical limits to growth."[29]

---

[29]Lawrence H. Summers, "The Challenges of Development: Some Lessons of History for Sub-Saharan Africa," *Finance and Development* 29 (March 1992): 6.

Despite its growing acceptance in the developing world, the Washington Consensus has many critics. The successful economies in East Asia, they say, have relied on a variety of protectionist tools to develop their industrial base, and programs of export promotion have been most successful in countries that inherited an industrial base from a prior program of import substitution. Excessive reliance on export promotion and financial deregulation will expose developing countries to gyrations of the world market; they will create enclaves of export-oriented companies and financial institutions with weak linkages to the rest of the economy. Reliance on foreign investment and management will lead to labor exploitation, environmental degradation, and disruption of indigenous cultures. If all developing countries were to adopt policies of export promotion simultaneously, causing heavy job losses in the industrial countries, politicians would respond quickly with new import barriers.[30] Even if deregulation provides benefits in the long run, critics say that the transition from a tariff-ridden system of import substitution to a more market-oriented allocation of resources will yield unacceptable unemployment and income inequality in the medium term.[31]

Development Planning and the Market

In order to pursue the kinds of growth strategies considered above—balanced or unbalanced growth, import substitution or export promotion—the leaders of the developing countries have prepared hundreds of economic plans. These can be divided into three broad categories.[32] First, Soviet-style central plans were prepared in all the Communist countries; less comprehensive versions were attempted in India, Pakistan, and Turkey in the 1950s and 1960s, and in Bangladesh, Sri Lanka, and Ethiopia in the 1970s. In developing countries, these 5-year plans generally included targets for all the major sectors of the economy, but a large part of economic activity in these countries was always controlled by markets and by hand-to-mouth subsistence sectors. Adherence to the plans was controlled through nationalized companies and through licensing and production quotas.

Second, the eastern Asian countries of Japan, Korea, and Singapore developed their own style of indicative planning, based on Confucian traditions and influenced by French planning. The plans are comprehensive in scope—they cover all major sectors—and they are prepared

---

[30]According to Paul Bairoch, if the entire developing world exported manufactured goods at the same per-capita rate as the Four Dragons—Hong Kong, South Korea, Singapore, and Taiwan—this would be nearly equivalent to the current consumption of manufactures in the Western industrial countries. See his *Economics and World History* (Chicago: University of Chicago Press, 1993), 168.

[31]For a sophisticated critique of the Washington Consensus and a discussion of alternatives, see Lance Taylor, "Stabilization, Adjustment, and Reform," in *The Rocky Road to Reform: Adjustment, Income Distribution, and Growth in the Developing World*, ed. by Lance Taylor (Cambridge, Mass.: The MIT Press, 1993), 39-94.

[32]Ramgopal Agarwala, "Planning in Developing Countries," *Finance and Development* 22 (March 1985): 13-16.

cooperatively by the public and private sectors. According to the World Bank, eastern Asian plans are "characterized not by technical sophistication or strict adherence to targets, but by consultations and flexibility."[33] Because of the export orientation of these countries, plan fulfillment is encouraged through positive incentives rather than direct controls.

In most of the other developing countries, including many in Latin America, Africa, and Southeast Asia, planning was introduced to satisfy the demands of colonial powers and international aid agencies. After World War II, for example, the socialist government in Britain required planning in its territories under the Colonial Development and Welfare Act of 1945. Some Latin American countries prepared development plans in the 1930s to organize their programs of import substitution, and they prepared plans with the United States during the 1940s to support the war effort. After the war, they returned to import-substitution planning under the influence of the U.N. Economic Commission for Latin America, and they expanded these efforts in the 1960s with help from the United States under the Alliance for Progress. Since the 1980s, under the influence of the World Bank, the International Monetary Fund, and the U.S. government, the focus of development planning—in Latin America and elsewhere—has turned to trade liberalization, privatization, encouragement of foreign investment, and other elements of the Washington Consensus.

The developing countries use their plans to support applications for project loans and grants from development banks and for rescheduling of debt with the International Monetary Fund and the major commercial banks. Thus, the plans give special attention to projects and macroeconomic variables that interest the foreign audience. Targets for the private sector are usually indicative rather than coercive and are often exercises in wishful thinking. On the domestic level, development plans are used to announce policy changes, to share information, to promote cooperation and consultation, and to build consensus between the private and public sectors.

Prospects and Challenges

What does the future hold for the developing world? To be honest, we simply do not know. Mainstream economists, who are encouraged by large capital flows, by the successful outcome of the Uruguay Round of trade negotiations, and by growing acceptance of market-oriented development strategies, have never been more optimistic.[34] Thus, according to the World Bank, if developing countries will stick to their reforms and maintain political stability, they presently have the best chance in decades of achieving rapid and stable economic growth (Table 5.5). According to their forecast, the share of the developing world and the former Soviet Union in

---

[33]Ibid., 14.

[34]The flow of foreign direct investment to developing countries grew steadily from $14 billion in 1985 to more than $80 billion in 1994. See *Financial Times*, April 10, 1995, 15. On the other hand, tight budgets caused the industrial countries to cut their real flow of official development aid in 1994 to the lowest level in two decades. See *Los Angeles Times*, June 13, 1995, 1.

world output will rise from about 44 percent in 1993 to more than 50 percent by the end of the decade. Based on this and other evidence, editors of *The Economist* foresee a fundamental realignment of the international balance of economic power:

Over the next 25 years, the world will see the biggest shift in economic strength for more than a century. Today, the so-called industrial economies dominate the globe, as they have for the past 150 years or so. Yet within a generation several are likely to be dwarfed by newly emerging economic giants. History suggests, alas, that such shifts in economic power are rarely smooth.[35]

Table 5.5 World Economic Growth, 1961-2004
(annual percentage change in real GDP)

Region	1961-1964	1965-1973	1974-1980	1981-1990	1991–2000	2001–2004
World total	5.3	5.3	3.5	3.0	2.8	2.5
High-income countries	5.5	5.2	3.2	3.0	2.7	1.8
Low-income countries	4.7	3.2	3.6	4.4	4.3	5.5
UN Development Program Countries	4.6	5.0	4.7	2.7	2.6	3.8
East Asia and Pacific	0.8	7.2	6.8	7.5	7.9	7.1
South Asia	5.2	2.8	4.0	5.7	5.3	6.0
Sub-Saharan Africa	4.9	5.0	3.7	2.1	2.2	3.5
Latin America and the Caribbean	5.0	5.9	5.5	1.6	3.1	1.8
Europe and Central Asia	4.6	4.6	2.1	-1.8	-0.9	5.0
Middle East and North Africa	n/a	7.7	3.9	1.9	3.8	4.5

Sources: World Bank, World Development Indicators Online. Growth rates for the MENA region between 1965 and 1980 were obtained from the World Bank, *World Development Report 1991*, 186. Growth rates for Europe and Central Asia between 1960 and 1980 calculated from estimates for the USSR and Eastern Europe in Angus Maddison, *The World Economy: Historical Statistics* (OECD, 2004), 233.

Many historians and heterodox economists, who have less faith in the free-trade policies of the Washington Consensus, are less sanguine about the prospects for the developing world. According to Paul Bairoch, an economic historian at the University of Geneva, "there is no doubt" that industrialization was delayed in India, Latin America, and other low-income countries during the nineteenth century when they were forced to open their markets to manufactured goods from Europe and the United States; "the liberal trade experience in the Third World was a complete failure."[36] Although Bairoch concedes that evidence from the nineteenth century may have little relevance in the twenty-first, he expresses little cause for optimism in the developing world.

---

[35]"War of the Worlds: Survey of the Global Economy," *The Economist*, October 1, 1994, S1.

[36]Bairoch, *Economics and World History*, 53-54 and 171.

Paul Kennedy, a Yale University historian, is not convinced that the economic balance of power will soon shift toward the South: "In sum," he says, "as we move into the next century the developed economies appear to have all of the trump cards in their hands—capital, technology, control of communications, surplus foodstuffs, powerful multinational companies—and, if anything, their advantages are *growing* because technology is eroding the value of labor and materials, the chief assets of developing countries."[37] According to Kennedy, the developing countries should avoid extreme strategies of socialism or free-market liberalism, and should imitate East Asia's mixture of official controls and private enterprise.

If barriers to trade, transportation, and communication continue to fall, causing world markets to grow more open and integrated, all countries, including the developing countries, will face greater competitive risks and broader opportunities. Nations, regions, and individual people who acquire the latest skills and tools will, in general, have tremendous opportunities. Nations, regions, and individual people who do not acquire these skills will, in general, compete for jobs and incomes with the least privileged people in the world. The challenge of economic and social development continues for each of us.

Summary

The least privileged people in the world live in Sub-Saharan Africa and South Asia. The nations of East Asia have achieved exceptional levels of economic development. The record is mixed in Latin America.

Very generally, countries that remain poor are those that fail to generate a sufficient investable surplus or those that fail to invest it in productive activities. In many countries, the effort to produce an investable surplus is complicated by such environmental factors as geography, soil, and climate, and the utilization of this surplus is influenced by religion and other aspects of culture. Institutional factors that stand in the way of economic development include inefficient and inequitable systems of land tenure, primitive market structures, dualism in labor markets, and limitations in the quantity and quality of financial intermediation. Poverty sustains itself through the operation of several vicious circles. Although people with low incomes find it difficult to save, saving is needed to finance investment. Likewise, poverty places limits on educational opportunity, health, and market size, and it promotes rapid population growth, income inequality, and political instability.

Marxists and dependency theorists believe that the industrial countries, with their imperialist policies, shoulder much of the blame for world poverty. This form of exploitation was clear enough during the colonial era; they believe that it continues today through the operations of multinational corporations and through an unfair system of international prices.

Adam Smith and his followers believed that economic development is the natural order of things and that little is needed to promote it. In the 1950s, Arthur Lewis argued that

---

[37]Paul Kennedy, *Preparing for the Twenty-First Century* (New York: Random House, 1993), 225.

independent development could be promoted by shifting rural surplus labor into industry. Rosenstein-Rodan agreed that this was possible, but added that it would require a big push to begin. Nurske proposed that such a push should be made simultaneously in several sectors, while Rostow argued for confining the initial push to leading sectors and Hirschman recommended that growth be encouraged in sectors with strong linkages. In many cases, particularly in Latin America, unbalanced growth was linked with a policy of import substitution. In the 1980s, though, import substitution policies were abandoned in many countries, and a Washington Consensus formed around policies of export promotion, privatization, and free markets.

Economic plans in the developing world have fallen into three categories: Soviet-style central plans, Japanese-style indicative plans, and project plans encouraged by aid agencies. In recent years, the plans have shifted toward a stronger market orientation.

Based on recent capital flows, trade negotiations, and liberalization policies, many mainstream economists are optimistic about prospects for the developing world. Historians seem to find less cause for optimism, but, in the end, economic development will depend on exploitation of opportunities by individual people, regions, and nations.

Discussion and Review Questions

1. Do you believe that cultural and religious traditions can have an important impact on economic development? Is it possible to study these influences in a scientific way?

2. How do traditional systems of land tenure influence economic development? What kinds of forces stand in the way of land reform?

3. What is a dual labor market? What are its causes and effects?

4. What kinds of vicious circles were discussed in the chapter? Can you think of others? What kinds of policies would be necessary to break them?

5. What is dependency theory? How does it explain the problems of the developing world? What policy recommendations are derived from the theory?

6. What are the relative advantages of import substitution and export promotion strategies of economic development?

7. Describe the different kinds of economic plans that are prepared in developing countries. What factors would influence a country's choice of a particular style of planning?

8. During the early years of the twenty-first century, what will be the balance of economic power between the industrial countries and the current list of developing countries?

Suggested Readings

Dutt, Amitava Krishna, and Kenneth P. Jameson eds. *New Directions in Development Economics.* Aldershot: Edward Elgar, 1992. *Essays by six authors, most of whom are critical of the Washington Consensus.*

Harrison, Lawrence E. *Development Is a State of Mind: The Latin American Case.* Lanham, Md.: University Press of America, 1985. *Presents an interesting example for cultural determinism.*

Karmarck, Andrew. *The Tropics and Economic Development.* Baltimore: The Johns Hopkins University Press, 1976. *Presents an interesting case for environmental determinism.*

Landes, David S. "Why Are We So Rich and They So Poor?" *American Economic Review* 80 (May 1990): 1-13. *A cogent lecture on the subject, presented to an annual meeting of the American Economic Association by a respected Harvard historian.*

United Nations Development Programme, *Human Development Report.* New York: Oxford University Press, annual. *Similar in some respects to its older cousin at the World Bank (below), this annual report takes a strong stance on demilitarization and a basic-needs approach to poverty reduction.*

The World Bank, *World Development Report.* New York: Oxford University Press, annual. *Provides a wealth of authoritative statistical information, analysis, and policy guidance. Each year, the report follows a different theme, such as infrastructure (1994), health (1993), environment (1992), development strategy (1991), and poverty (1990). Taken together, these volumes provide a comprehensive mainstream analysis of the subject.*

CHAPTER 7

THE UNITED STATES: THE SERVICE ECONOMY

Here individuals of all nations are melted into a new race of men, whose labors will one day cause great changes in the world.

—J. H. St. John de Crévecoeur, *Letters from an American Farmer,* 1782

In the United States a man builds a house in which to spend his old age, and he sells it before the roof is on; . . . he brings a field into tillage and leaves other men to gather the crops; he embraces a profession and gives it up; he settles in a place, which he soon afterward leaves to carry his changeable longings elsewhere.

Alexis de Tocqueville

Democracy in America, 1840

Many readers of this book—including those who are not Americans—will already be familiar with the economic system of the United States. However, a quick review of the subject is warranted for at least two reasons. First, the comparative perspective of this book should allow us to gain new insights into the nature of the American system. We will ask, what is it about the U.S. economy that is truly unique? In later chapters, it will sometimes be helpful to use the United States as a basis of comparison.

Second, the United States produces more goods and services—valued at seven trillion dollars in 1995—than any other country in the world. Despite spectacular growth in many other countries since World War II, the American economy is still twice as large as the Japanese, and nearly as large as the *combined* economies of the fifteen members of the European community.[1]

---

[1]Total GDP was about \$2.5 trillion in Japan, \$6.1 trillion in the United States, and \$6.5 trillion in the 15 current members of the European Union in 1992, according to estimates of

Clearly, our analysis of world economic systems would be incomplete without consideration of the United States.

The Environment

A significant part of American economic growth and prosperity can be attributed to the richness of its natural resources. The United States claims only 5 percent of the world's population, but approximately 7 percent of its land area, over 15 percent of its copper and cadmium reserves, and over 20 percent of its reserves of coal, lead, silver, and zinc.[2] American croplands are among the most fertile in the world and benefit from an exceptionally mild climate. According to recent research, resource abundance played a key role in the development of America's industrial sector, particularly during the period between 1890 and 1940.[3]

Nonetheless, the prosperity of the United States is only partially explained by its rich natural endowment. Russia, for example, has 80 percent more land area and larger reserves of fossil fuels, gold, diamonds, manganese, and platinum-group metals. Some of the world's poorest countries, including many in Africa, are more favorably endowed (on a per capita basis) with land and minerals.[4]

---

population and GDP per capita at purchasing power parity in the United Nations Development Programme, *Human Development Report 1995* (New York: Oxford University Press, 1995), 203, 208.

[2]U.S. Bureau of Mines estimates reported in D. Hargreaves and S. Fromson, *World Index of Strategic Minerals* (New York: Facts on File, 1983), 31ff.

[3]Gavin Wright, "The Origins of American Industrial Success, 1879-1940," *American Economic Review* 80 (September 1990): 651-668.

[4]For a ranking of nations in terms of their potential organic and mineral production, see S. R. Eyre, *The Real Wealth of Nations* (New York: St. Martin's Press, 1978), 116-129.

The American labor force descended from a multinational assortment of religious and political dissidents, opportunists, and slaves. In many cases, the experiences of these groups instilled a disdain for higher authority. Thus, America is known as a "melting pot" nation and the home of "rugged individualism." These two aspects of American society have left a lasting imprint on the economy.

The philosophy of individualism, for example, is the basis of the so-called American Dream—the idea that anyone can "pull himself up by his bootstraps" to a higher standard of living through frugality and hard work. The dream was personified by such men as Andrew Carnegie, the son of poor Scottish immigrants. Carnegie started work at the age of thirteen as a bobbin boy in a Pennsylvania cloth mill and eventually built a steel empire that he sold in 1900 for over $400 million. He argued that individual freedom and competition are "best for the race" because they ensure "the survival of the fittest in every department."[5]

Americans generally believe that individual wealth is the reward for hard work and frugality; Europeans are more likely to attribute large accumulations of wealth to inheritance. As a result, Americans are relatively uncomfortable with governmental schemes to redistribute income. Opinion surveys have found little support for major redistribution schemes, even among the poorest Americans. According to an international poll by the Times Mirror organization, only 23 percent of Americans believe "the state has a responsibility to take care of poor people who can't take care of themselves," compared to 50 percent of Germans, 62 percent of the French and British, 66 percent of Italians, and 71 percent of Spaniards.[6] Accordingly, the U.S. government

---

[5]*The North American Review* of 1889, quoted in Daniel Fusfeld's *The Age of the Economist* (Glenview, Ill.: Scott, Foresman and Co., 1972), 82.

[6]"What Europeans Think," *Los Angeles Times*, September 17, 1991, special edition, H/B.

allocates a smaller share of national income to social security and welfare programs than the governments of most European countries.[7]

The philosophy of individualism may also help to explain the American preoccupation with higher education. In 1991, about 66 percent of Americans in their early twenties were full-time students in colleges and universities, compared to about 39 percent of young people in Japan and 30 percent in the European Union.[8]

The "melting pot" also has its economic ramifications. On the positive side of the ledger, the United States benefits from the diversity of skills and talents that its ethnic groups have mastered.[9] On the other hand, some economic problems are obviously caused by racial discrimination and by the fact that millions of Americans have serious difficulty with spoken English.

Furthermore, the "melting pot" may provide another explanation for the relatively low level of U.S. welfare spending. In France, Italy, West Germany, and Sweden, each population is relatively homogeneous in terms of race and religion. As a result, there is little perception in these countries that welfare payments represent a transfer of income from one identifiable segment of society to another. In the United States, despite the fact that two-thirds of the people living below the poverty line are white, the perception persists that welfare payments only serve to redistribute income from whites to other races. Not too surprisingly, this perception provokes an unusual amount of political opposition.

---

[7]In 1992, the United States devoted 7 percent of GDP to social security benefits; the average for the European Union was 13 percent. See United Nations Development Programme, *Human Development Report 1995*, 203.

[8]United Nations Development Programme, *Human Development Report 1995*, 200.

[9]For a provocative assessment of the role of ethnicity in U.S. economic development, see Thomas Sowell, *The Economics and Politics of Race* (New York: William Morrow, 1983), Chapter 6.

The Changing Structure of the Economy

Compared with the nations of Western Europe, America is a relative latecomer to industrialization. In 1840, when only 23 percent of the British labor force was working in agriculture, about 69 percent of American laborers continued to farm. As late as 1900, more Americans were employed in agriculture than in the industrial or service sectors (Table 7.1).

Table 7.1 United States: Percentage Distribution of Employment, 1820-2016

Year	*Agriculture*	*Industry*	*Services*
1820	70	16	14
1870	47	27	26
1900	35	34	31
1920	24	41	35
1940	19	35	46
1960	8	35	56
1980	4	30	66
2000	3	23	74
2016 (forecast)	2	18	80

Sources: 1820: US Bureau of the Census , *Historical Statistics of the United States: Colonial Times to 1970,* Table D167-181; 1870-1940: Victor Fuchs, *The Service Economy* (New York: National Bureau of Economic Research, 1968), 24, 30; 1960-2000: SourceOECD, *Employment by Activities and Status,* Vol. 2007; 2016 BLS forecast from http://www.bls.gov/emp/empmajorindustry.htm .

According to Adam Smith, writing in the 1770s, America's commitment to agriculture was extremely beneficial:

It has been the principal cause of the rapid progress of our American colonies towards wealth and greatness, that almost their whole capitals have hitherto been employed in agriculture. They have no manufactures, those household and coarser manufactures excepted which necessarily accompany the progress of agriculture, and which are the work of women and children in every private family.[10]

In this, Smith undoubtedly was influenced by his French acquaintances, the Physiocrats, who believed that agricultural workers are always more productive than industrial workers. According to Smith, "As a marriage which affords three children is certainly more productive

---

[10]Adam Smith, *An Inquiry into the Nature and Causes of the Wealth of Nations* (New York: P. F. Collier, 1909 [1776]), 308.

than one which affords only two; so the labor of farmers and country laborers is certainly more productive than that of merchants, artificers, and manufacturers."[11] In addition, Smith undoubtedly realized that American soil and climate were perfect for agriculture.

The French Revolution and the Napoleonic Wars (1785-1815) further enhanced the benefits of American agriculture. As a neutral power, America was able to export agricultural goods to all sides and foreign demand was so great that U.S. export prices more than doubled between 1794 and 1799.[12] The resulting agricultural boom frustrated Alexander Hamilton's desire to launch America into an early industrialization.

Industrial Growth

Led by the creation of national transportation and communication networks, America finally embarked on a stage of industrial growth during the first half of the nineteenth century. The successful completion of the Erie Canal in 1825, linking New York City with the agricultural regions in western New York, reduced transportation costs in that region by 90 percent. A boom in canal-building resulted and by 1859 some 1.6 billion ton-miles of cargo were being transported on canals. In 1828, the first steam railway in America, the Baltimore and Ohio, commenced operations. By 1840, America had a rail network of over 3,000 miles of track; by 1860 it exceeded 30,000 miles. Samuel Morse invented a practical telegraph in 1837 and the telegraph lines of Western Union reached the Pacific by 1861.

These rapid advances in transportation and communication formed a national market. Coal could now be moved from the rich fields in Pennsylvania to the industrial centers of the East. Large factories could be built with the assurance that their output could be sold throughout the country and overseas. Industrialization had begun and it was sustained by two distinctively

---

[11]Ibid., 460.

[12]D. C. North, *The Economic Growth of the United States* (Englewood Cliffs, N.J.: Prentice-Hall, 1961), 25-26.

American production technologies—the system of interchangeable parts (introduced by Eli Whitney in 1801) and the moving assembly line (introduced at Ford Motors in 1913). By the 1880s, many of the classic American industrial giants were well established—Standard Oil, Westinghouse, Edison General Electric, Western Electric, Singer, John Deere, and National Cash Register, to name a few. By the mid-1880s, America had bypassed Great Britain to become the world's leading producer of industrial goods. It still holds that position today.[13]

The Rise of the Service Sector

Although the United States is still the largest industrial power in the world, the dominance of the industrial sector *within* the American economy was relatively short-lived. Industry employed more laborers than agriculture and the service sector for less than 30 years—from the early 1900s to the mid-1920s (Table 7.1). In contrast, the plurality of British workers was involved in industrial production for over 100 years—from the 1840s until the late 1960s.[14]

By 1960, over half the U.S. labor force was employed in the service sector, and that proportion has continued to rise. In other words, the majority of American workers are what Adam Smith called "unproductive laborers"—people who do not produce a physical, tangible commodity.[15] Although the labor force has shifted from industry to services in all the advanced

---

[13]W. W. Rostow, *The World Economy: History and Prospect* (Austin: University of Texas Press, 1978), 52-53.

[14]Simon Kuznets, *Modern Economic Growth* (New Haven: Yale University Press, 1966), 106; and Organization for Economic Cooperation and Development, *National Accounts: 1964-1981,* vol. 2 (Paris, 1983), 275. Here, as elsewhere, I have adopted the method of aggregating detailed sectors into agriculture, industry, and services as described in Victor Fuchs, *The Service Economy* (New York: National Bureau of Economic Research, 1968), 16-17. In particular, transportation, communications, and utilities are included in industry rather than services.

[15]Smith, *Wealth of Nations*, 270-271.

countries, the shift was more rapid and complete in the United States than in any other major country.

The first phase of service growth, between the end of the Civil War and the beginning of the Great Depression, was based on expansion of wholesale and retail trade. Growth in the trade network was a natural concomitant of the industrial growth that occurred during that era and was made possible by the improvements in transportation and communication noted earlier. Thus, the second half of the 1800s ushered in the large chain stores—A&P, Kroger, J. C. Penney, Woolworth, and Walgreen—and the giant mail-order houses—Montgomery Ward and Sears Roebuck.

The second stage of growth in service employment was launched by the expansion of public services during the Great Depression. Government employment, which absorbed only 9 percent of the nation's labor force in 1929, encompassed 17 percent of the labor force in 1939. Since that time, the governmental share of employment has remained relatively stable.[16]

The causes of rapid growth in service employment since World War II have been a subject of extensive research, speculation, and controversy. Most cheerful is the **income elasticity hypothesis**, which suggests that the American people, having fulfilled their basic needs for food, clothing, and shelter, are able to devote much of their affluence to health, educational, recreational, and personal services. Thus, the growth of service employment is driven by rising domestic demand.

Least cheerful, perhaps, is the **deindustrialization hypothesis**, which suggests that the United States is losing the international competition for industrial jobs. Due to poor maintenance of American product quality, sluggish growth of manufacturing productivity, loss of technological leadership, and unfair foreign competitive practices, the hypothesis says that

---

[16]Thomas M. Stanback, Jr., et al., *Services: The New Economy* (Totowa, N.J.: Allanheld, Osmun, & Co., 1981), 12-13.

Americans are losing high-paying factory jobs, forcing them to accept "hamburger-flipping" service jobs.[17]

The deindustrialization thesis may describe the experiences of millions of Americans, but it can explain only a small part of service sector growth. Compared to its peak in 1979, employment in the goods-producing sector declined by about 3 million in 1994, but the service sector created more than 26 million jobs.[18] During the same years, the American share of world exports of manufactured goods actually increased by a small amount.[19] Furthermore, if America's service sector expanded because of lost manufacturing jobs, why did America's trade partners also experience growth of service employment?

Official data seem to be more consistent with the **cost disease hypothesis**, which is quite different from the demand elasticity and deindustrialization approaches.[20] According to this interpretation, the demand for services has grown at roughly the same rate as the demand for products, but labor productivity has grown much more slowly in the service sector (see Table 7.2). Thus, service employment has grown rapidly to compensate for the lower rate of productivity growth. Slow productivity growth has also raised production costs and prices in the

---

[17]See Barry Bluestone and Bennett Harrison, *The Deindustrialization of America* (New York: Basic Books, 1982), passim.

[18]*Economic Report of the President 1995* (Washington, D.C.: USGPO, 1995), 324-325.

[19]From 16.8 percent to 17.4 percent according to the *Statistical Abstract of the United States 1994* (Washington, D.C.: USGPO, 1994), Table 1243.

[20]William J. Baumol, Sue Anne Batey Blackman, and Edward N. Wolff, *Productivity and American Leadership: The Long View* (Cambridge: The MIT Press, 1989), Chapter 6; and Jeffrey G. Williamson, "Productivity and American Leadership: A Review Article," *Journal of Economic Literature* 29 (March 1991): 59-60.

service sector. Thus, the share of the service sector in GDP has been stable if measured in constant prices, but it has increased if measured in current (rising) prices.[21]

Table 7.2 United States: Average Annual Growth of Output per Worker, 1950-2004

Years	*Total Production*	*Goods Production*	*Service Production*
1950-1960	3.98	3.80	5.49
1960-1970	4.20	4.60	4.75
1970-1980	7.74	8.94	7.32
1980-1990	5.60	6.80	6.20
1990-2000	3.47	4.42	3.39
2000-2004	4.65	5.79	4.98

Sources: Author's calculations based on U.S. Department of Commerce, Bureau of the Census, *Historical Statistics of the United States, Colonial Times to 1970*, Part 2 (Washington, D.C.: USGPO, 1975); and *Economic Report of the President 2005.*

Two other supply-oriented hypotheses may also help to explain the growth of service employment. According to the **economies of scale hypothesis**, growth of the service sector arose from efforts to improve organizational efficiency. Many business tasks, such as accounting, computer programming, mailing, and printing, may be performed more efficiently if they are moved from small offices in industrial firms into specialized firms in the service sector.

The **labor supply hypothesis** emphasizes the changing structure of the labor force. In particular, the proportion of women in the American labor force increased from about 28 percent in 1950 to 46 percent in 1995, and many women have found employment in the service sector. Women account for less than 30 percent of employment in agriculture and industry, but they hold more than half the service jobs.

---

[21]Between 1980 and 1994, the share of services in constant-price GDP increased by only 0.2 percentage points (from 49.3 percent to 49.5 percent); the share of services in current-price GDP increased by 8.2 percentage points (from 44.9 percent to 53.1 percent). See *Economic Report of the President 1995*, 284-285.

Significance of the Shift to Services

The shift to services has profoundly influenced the structure and performance of the American economy. First, and most clearly, it has changed the nature of work and employment. More Americans are now engaged in sales (wholesale and retail) than in manufacturing. College students who may have prepared for engineering professions in the 1950s and 1960s are now more likely to specialize in business, legal, computer, health, educational, or recreational services. Compared with their industrial colleagues, service workers are more likely to be self-employed, to work at home, and to work part-time, but they are less likely to join labor unions.

Recent evidence suggests that growth of the service sector has contributed to greater income inequality in the United States. As the proportion of employment in manufacturing has declined, gains in service employment have been divided between low-income sectors, such as personal services and retail trade, and high-income sectors, such as financial and professional services. Furthermore, according to the Gini ratios reported in Table 7.3, incomes are distributed more unevenly *within* each of the service sectors than within manufacturing.

Still, the growth of service employment explains a relatively small part—maybe 10 or 20 percent—of the recent increase in American income inequality. More of the rise seems to be explained by a growing gap between the incomes of skilled and unskilled workers (caused in part by technological changes and foreign competition that reduce the relative demand for unskilled labor), by declining union membership, by growth in the number of single-income families, and by an increase in the proportion of part-time jobs.[22]

---

[22]Paul Ryscavage and Peter Henle, "Earnings Inequality Accelerates in the 1980s," *Monthly Labor Review* (December 1990): 3-16; Richard B. Freeman, "How Much Has De-Unionization Contributed to the Rise in Male Earnings Inequality?" in Sheldon Danziger and Peter Gottschalk, eds., *Uneven Tides: Rising Inequality in America* (New York: Russell Sage Foundation, 1993), 133-163; George J. Boorjas and Valerie A. Ramey, "Time Series Evidence on the Sources of Trends in Wage Inequality," *American Economic Review* 84 (May 1994): 10-

Table 7.3 United States: Distribution of Employment and Earnings of Men Working Full Time, 1978 and 1987

	Percentage of Full-Time Employment		*Average Earnings (Dollars)*		*Gini Ratios*	
	1978	*1987*	*1978*	*1987*	*1978*	*1987*
Agriculture	4.2	3.4	10,896	17,199	.448	.432
Industry:						
Manufacturing	30.0	25.5	17,692	30,619	.247	.286
Mining	1.2	1.0	20,899	35,738	.258	.282
Construction	7.8	8.8	16,730	25,994	.302	.306
TCPU*	9.1	10.1	18,233	31,407	.224	.252
Services:						
Wholesale trade	5.4	5.8	18,682	30,242	.296	.325
Retail trade	9.6	12.3	14,194	23,496	.314	.351
FIRE**	4.7	5.3	22,187	40,394	.344	.376
Business services	4.0	6.1	16,423	28,787	.347	.379
Personal services	1.5	1.6	12,420	20,295	.339	.357
Entertainment	0.7	1.0	14,601	26,705	.331	.360
Professional services	12.0	13.0	20,777	36,187	.350	.365
Public administraation	7.4	6.1	18,233	29,966	.209	.229
Total	100.0	100.0	17,526	29,866	.296	.332

* TCPU - transportation, communications, and public utilities
** FIRE - finance, insurance, and real estate
Source: Paul Ryscavage and Peter Henle, "Earnings Inequality Accelerates in the 1980s," *Monthly Labor Review* (December 1990): Table 5.

As we already noted, measured labor productivity has grown more slowly in the service sector than in the goods-producing sectors (Table 7.2). In fact, productivity improvements are inherently slow in many service activities; it takes four people just as long to perform a string quartet composition today as it did when the piece was written, perhaps hundreds of years ago.[23] The shift toward service employment has caused overall productivity growth to decelerate in the United States.

Of course, part of this deterioration in productivity growth may be a statistical illusion; the output of service workers is very difficult to measure. How can the governmental statisticians

---

16; and Gary Burtless, "International Trade and the Rise in Earnings Inequality," *Journal of Economic Literature* 33 (June 1995): 800-816.

[23]Baumol et al., *Productivity and American Leadership*, 124-140.

know, for example, whether a college professor has performed her duties more effectively this year than she did last year? A lawyer? A social worker? How can we balance the life-saving improvements in medical technology against the unwillingness of doctors to make house calls?[24] Whatever its rate of growth, studies by the McKinsey Global Institute have found that the *level* of productivity in the American service sector is substantially higher than the levels in Europe and Japan, particularly in the fields of banking, retail sales, and airline transportation.[25]

Possibly because of the slow growth of service productivity (emphasized in the cost-disease hypothesis), and possibly because the service sector faces little foreign competition, the rate of price inflation in the service sector is relatively high. Between 1970 and 1994, while the average annual rate of inflation for commodities was about 5 percent, the inflation rate for services was nearly 7 percent.[26] Price increases for medical services and college tuition have been particularly steep.

Even if service productivity has grown slowly in the past, retarding economic growth and fueling inflation, these trends may not continue in the future. If the technological achievements of the past were oriented toward goods production, recent advances in computer hardware and software and telecommunications technology are particularly useful for accounting firms, banks,

---

[24]See Alfred L. Malabre, Jr., and Lindley H. Clark, Jr., "Productivity Statistics for the Service Sector May Understate Gains," *The Wall Street Journal*, August 12, 1992, A1.

[25]David Wessel, "U.S. Excels in Service Productivity Poll," *The Wall Street Journal*, October 13, 1992, A2; and Martin Dickson, Tony Jackson, and Louise Kehoe, "American Way of Serving Leads to Success," *Financial Times*, February 15, 1994, 4.

[26]*Economic Report of the President 1995*, 344. Again, this may be little more than a statistical illusion. Can we be sure, for example, how much the increased cost of health care was caused by higher prices per unit of care, and how much it was caused by an improvement in the quantity and quality of care?

educational institutions, and other services. Many service companies are attempting to improve labor productivity by strengthening their programs of employee training and benefits.[27]

Regardless of its effects on productivity and inflation, growth of the service sector has clearly increased the *stability* of employment and output. Except for small dips in 1958 and 1991, service employment grew every year between 1946 and 1994. Industrial employment drifted up and down with waves of the business cycle.[28]

Several factors may account for the apparent immunity of the service sector to recessions. First, many people in service occupations are self-employed, including more than 33 percent of lawyers, realtors, artists, barbers, and child-care workers; in contrast, less than 10 percent of industrial mechanics, technicians, and machine operators are self-employed.[29] Many service employees, including salespeople, waiters and waitresses, barbers and beauticians, realtors, and insurance agents, are paid on a commission or piecework basis. In all these cases, a drop in the market demand for services is likely to reduce the incomes of service workers, but it is not likely to cause them to lose their jobs. In industry, where wages are less flexible, a reduction in demand is more likely to result in unemployment.

Second, unlike manufactured goods, the output of the service sector usually cannot be stored in inventories. It is unlikely, therefore, that a surplus of services (which must be sold before production can resume) will be produced. The standard Keynesian theory of

---

[27]David Wessel, "With Labor Scarce, Service Firms Strive to Increase Productivity," *The Wall Street Journal* (June 1, 1989), 1.

[28]For a contrary view, suggesting that the stability of service employment is beginning to weaken, see Henry F. Myers, "Some Service Jobs May Get Less Stable," *The Wall Street Journal* (February 25, 1991), 1.

[29]See George Silvestri and John Lukasiewicz, "Occupational Employment Projections," *Monthly Labor Review* 114 (November 1991): 85-86.

unemployment, based on an assumption of inflexible wages and an inventory adjustment mechanism, may have lost some of its relevance in an economy dominated by services.

A third reason for the stability of service employment is that governmental services usually are not reduced during recessions. In fact, new government workers may be hired to process the expanded load of claims for unemployment and welfare benefits.

Finally, in addition to its beneficial influence on the growth and stability of employment, the service sector also has contributed positively to the American balance of international payments. In 1993, when exports of merchandise fell short of imports by $133 billion, this deficit was partially offset by a $57 billion surplus on service transactions.[30] One of the major objectives of the United States in recent rounds of international trade negotiations has been to reduce barriers to trade in services.

Industrial Organization

Before the Civil War, the U.S. economy approximated the textbook model of perfect competition. Over half the labor force worked on small, owner-managed farms. In manufacturing, no single plant was known to control as much as 10 percent of the output of any product in the early 1800s. As late as 1870, the average firm in the iron and steel industry employed fewer than 100 people. Each firm produced a relatively homogeneous product, and the government played a very limited role in the economy.

The nationwide network of transportation and communication, in place by the end of the Civil War, enabled the age of Big Business to begin, led by the so-called captains of industry. By 1879, the Standard Oil trust (controlled by John D. Rockefeller) controlled about 90 percent of

---

[30]According to national income and product accounts. Also, see Ralph T. King, Jr., "U.S. Service Exports Are Growing Rapidly, But Almost Unnoticed," *The Wall Street Journal*, April 21, 1993, A1.

American oil refining, and by 1900 the Carnegie empire produced nearly half of the nation's steel.

The trend toward bigness accelerated after 1889 when the New Jersey legislature legalized the formation of holding companies. The resulting merger movement, which lasted until 1904, created the largest private corporations the world had known. In 1901, for example, J. P. Morgan formed America's first billion-dollar company, U.S. Steel, by merging the old Carnegie company with its eight largest competitors. By 1904, one or two giant firms controlled at least half of the output of 78 different industries. Just as significant, the age of the owner-managers—the captains of industry—began to give way to an age in which large corporations were run by professional managers who often had little stake in ownership.

The Antitrust Movement

A backlash against monopoly began in 1887 when the Interstate Commerce Commission was established to regulate railroad rates. The Sherman Antitrust Act, passed in 1890, prohibited any contract, combination, or conspiracy "in restraint of trade" or any attempt to monopolize "any part of the trade or commerce among the several States." Filling in more detail, the Clayton Antitrust Act of 1914 declared four specific practices to be illegal if their "effect was to substantially lessen competition or tend to create a monopoly":

* Merger of competing companies
* Price discrimination—charging different prices to different customers for the same product
* Tying contracts—requiring a buyer to purchase goods from one seller
* Interlocking directorates—directors of one company sitting on the boards of directors of competing companies

By international standards, the Sherman and Clayton acts established a strict American tradition of antitrust policy. They were enacted at a time when the European and Japanese governments were encouraging the formation of large enterprises, conglomerates, and cartels to compete on the battlefield of international trade. The governments in those countries were willing to sacrifice domestic competition for international competitiveness. The United States, with its enormous domestic market, was relatively independent of the foreign market, so public attention centered on domestic competition. Monopolies and cartels were perceived as a threat to domestic consumers.

Table 7.4 United States: Mergers and Acquisitions, 1965-2003

Year	*Number*	*Value (billion dollars)*
1965	1,008	3.5
1970	1,351	5.9
1975	439	5.0
1980	1,560	32.9
1982	2,298	60.7
1984	3,164	126.1
1986	4,381	204.9
1988	3,487	226.6
1990	4,239	205.6
1992	3,502	125.3
1994	4,383	524.9
1996	5,639	1,059.3
1998	9,634	2,480
2000	11,169	3,440
2001	7,713	1,688
2002	7,032	1,185
2003	7,743	1,318

Sources: U.S. Department of Commerce, Bureau of the Census, *Statistical Abstract of the United States 1977* (Washington, D.C.: USGPO U.S. 1977), pg. 569; *Statistical Abstract of the United States 1990* (Washington, D.C.: USGPO U.S. 1990), pg. 534; *Statistical Abstract of the United States 1998* (Washington, D.C.: USGPO U.S. 1998), pg. 556; *Statistical Abstract of the United States 2004-2005* (Washington, D.C.: USGPO U.S. 2004-2005), pg. 499.

In recent years, American antitrust policy has grown more permissive, while remaining strict by international standards. With the growing challenge of foreign competition, the American fear of domestic monopolies has been replaced gradually by a fear of foreign encroachment. New guidelines were issued in 1982 and 1984, liberalizing the Clayton Act to allow corporate mergers that reduce production and transportation costs. In 1984, Congress loosened the rules for companies to engage in joint research, clearing the way for alliances between such companies as IBM and Apple Computer. During the 1980s, with the White House under Republican control, the antitrust enforcement staffs of the Justice Department and the Federal Trade Commission were cut in half, and few actions were taken to prevent mergers or monopolization. The number and value of merger transactions increased rapidly after 1980, and they continued to grow after Democrats regained the White House in 1992 (Table 7.4).[31]

During the 1980s, the most significant American antitrust action was the breakup and deregulation of the world's largest corporation—the American Telephone & Telegraph Company. After a long court battle with the Justice Department, AT&T agreed in 1982 to divest itself of 22 local telephone companies, reducing its assets from $155 billion to about $43 billion. In return, the company gained greater freedom to set prices and to enter new areas of telecommunications and computing. At the same time, technological advances made it possible for new competitors to enter the long-distance business, and the AT&T share of the long-distance market fell from 84 percent in 1984 to 63 percent in 1991. Surprisingly, though, the new competition apparently did not lead to lower prices in the long-distance market.[32]

More recently, the U.S. Justice Department has kept a watchful eye on Microsoft Corporation, whose Windows operating system is installed in about 90 percent of all new personal computers worldwide. In 1994, the department accused Microsoft of using its market power to force PC manufacturers to accept anticompetitive licensing terms, and in 1995 it blocked Microsoft's acquisition of Intuit, another leading software company, and investigated its plans to enter the market for online information services. Microsoft accused the Justice Department of a "campaign of harassment."[33]

---

[31]For more information on the merger guidelines of 1968, 1982, 1984, 1987, and 1992, see Stephen Martin, *Industrial Economics*, 2d ed. (New York: McMillan, 1994), 317-323.

[32]William E. Taylor and Lester D. Taylor, "Postdivestiture Long-Distance Competition in the United States," *American Economic Review* 83 (May 1993): 185-190.

[33]Louise Kehoe, "Giant Snaps at Oppressors," *Financial Times*, June 30, 1995, 4.

Trends in Business Size and Concentration

Although it is fairly clear that big businesses became more influential in America between 1860 and 1900, the more recent trends are difficult to assess. It is debatable whether large corporations play a more dominant role in the United States than they do in other countries, and whether their influence has grown in recent years.

Table 7.5 United States: Four-Firm Concentration Ratios in Selected Industries, 1947-2002 (Percentages)

	1947	*1967*	*1987*	*2002*
Aluminum	100	na	74	85
Aircraft	na	69	72	81
Motor Vehicles	na	92	90	81
Elevators	63	55	52	58
Men's Suits	9	17	34	49
Steel Mills	50	48	44	44
Home Audio/Video Equipment	na	49	39	43
Synthetic Rubber	na	61	50	43
Sporting Goods	24	27	13	23
Jewelry	13	23	12	16
Sign Manufacturing	5	6	6	5

Source: U.S. Department of Commerce, Bureau of the Census, *Census of Manufactures: Concentration Ratios in Manufacturing*, various years. Data for 2002 may not be strictly comparable with earlier years because of the switch from the SIC to the NAICS industrial classification system.

Trends and levels of industrial concentration are measured in several ways. The most familiar yardstick is the **four-firm concentration ratio**—the percentage of total sales of the four largest firms in an industry. Concentration ratios for several American industries are presented in Table 7.5. According to these data, the levels of concentration range from very high (aluminum and automobiles) to very low (sporting goods and jewelry). The share of the four largest firms has risen in some industries (men's suits) and fallen in others (steel mills and audio/video equipment).

In international perspective, comparisons conducted by F. M. Scherer and Frederic Pryor indicate that the average level of industrial concentration in America is less than or roughly equal to levels in France, West Germany, Italy, Japan, and the United Kingdom. Concentration seems to be highest in such countries as Belgium, Canada, Sweden, and Switzerland, where the domestic markets (measured by population or GNP) are too small to accommodate a large number of competitors.[34]

In his classic study of trends in American industrial organization, Warren Nutter defined an industry to be effectively monopolistic if its four-firm concentration ratio exceeded 50 percent. Applying that criterion to the period between 1899 and 1937, he detected only a very slight increase—from 19 to 20 percent—in the fraction of private production originating in monopolistic industries.[35] Likewise, for the 1947-1972 period, estimates by Scherer indicate a very small rise (about 2 percentage points) in the average concentration ratio for manufacturing industries.[36]

A more comprehensive assessment of recent trends (including those in agriculture and services) has been assembled by William Shepherd.[37] In Shepherd's study, each industry or sector of the economy is assigned to one of four categories:

* *Pure Monopoly*—Market share near 100 percent, effective barriers to entry, control of prices.

---

[34]Frederic L. Pryor, *Property and Industrial Organization in Communist and Capitalist Nations* (Bloomington, Ind.: Indiana University Press, 1973), 199-205; F. M. Scherer and others, *The Economics of Multi-Plant Operation: An International Comparisons Study* (Cambridge: Harvard University Press, 1975), 218-219, 426-428.

[35]G. Warren Nutter and Henry A. Einhorn, *Enterprise Monopoly in the United States: 1899-1958* (New York: Columbia University Press, 1969), 50.

[36]F. M. Scherer, *Industrial Market Structure and Economic Performance,* 2d ed. (Chicago: Rand-McNally, 1980), Table 3.7.

[37]William G. Shepherd, "Causes of Increased Competition in the U.S. Economy, 1939-1980," *Review of Economics and Statistics* 64 (November 1982): 613-626.

* *Dominant Firm*—A market share of 50 to 90 percent, no close rival, high entry barriers, control of prices.
* *Tight Oligopoly*—Four-firm concentration ratio above 60 percent, stable market shares, medium or high entry barriers, rigid prices.
* *Effective Competition*—Four-firm ratio below 40 percent, unstable market shares, flexible pricing.

Obviously, Shepherd was forced to make many judgment calls in his assignment of industries. In the end, he found that the market structure of the U.S. economy was rather stable between 1939 and 1958, but he detected a "remarkable" growth in competitiveness after 1958. According to his estimates, the share of national income originating in industries that are effectively competitive rose from 56 percent in 1958 to 77 percent in 1980 (Table 7.6).

Table 7.6 United States: Competitive Structure of the Economy, 1939-1980

	Percentage share of national income originating in:			
Year	*Pure Monopoly*	*Dominant Firm*	*Tight Oligopoly*	*Effective Competition*
1939	6.2	5.0	36.4	52.4
1958	3.1	5.0	35.6	56.3
1980	2.5	2.8	18.0	76.7

Source: William G. Shepherd, "Causes of Increased Competition in the U.S. Economy, 1939-1980," *Review of Economics and Statistics*, 64 (November 1982): 618.

In Shepherd's opinion, over half the increase in American competition during the years before 1980 was caused directly or indirectly by stricter enforcement of antitrust laws. In addition, he notes the importance of rising import competition and deregulation of the transport, communications, and banking industries.

As we noted earlier, lenient enforcement of antitrust laws allowed a huge wave of corporate mergers after 1980. For several reasons, though, the merger boom may not have reversed the trend toward competition. First, many of these mergers were of the *conglomerate* variety, uniting noncompeting firms in different industries. Thus, some American companies grew larger and more diversified, but concentration ratios did not necessarily increase for individual product lines.[38] Second, continued growth of the service sector increased the number of small, entrepreneurial firms. The proportion of the labor force working in small establishments (those with less than 100 employees) actually increased from 54 percent in 1980 to 56 percent in 1991.[39] And third, domestic firms were exposed to an increasing volume of foreign competition. Measured in constant prices, the share of imports in GNP increased from 8 percent in 1980 to 14 percent in 1994.[40]

The Social Costs of Industrial Concentration

Although large corporations may not dominate the U.S. economy, they certainly control a number of important markets. For several reasons, the American public has long been concerned about the economic and political power of concentrated industries. First, opinion surveys indicate that Americans simply do not trust corporate executives. The public has more confidence in the military, the church, the police, the presidency, and the news media; among major institutions,

---

[38]Conglomerates seem to operate with lower administrative, marketing, and interest costs than other firms in their industries, and they earn higher profit margins on revenues, but they do not, on average, earn a higher rate of return on stockholders' equity. See Winson B. Lee and Elizabeth S. Cooperman, "Conglomerates in the 1980s: A Performance Appraisal," *Financial Management* 18 (Spring 1989): 45-54.

[39]*Statistical Abstract of the United States 1989*, Table 859; and *Statistical Abstract of the United States 1994*, Table 845.

[40]*Economic Report of the President 1995*, 276-277. For evidence that import competition significantly tightened profit margins during 1976-1986, see Michelle M. Katics and Bruce C. Petersen, "The Effect of Rising Import Competition on Market Power: A Panel Study of U.S. Manufacturing," *Journal of Industrial Economics* 42 (September 1994): 277-285. For an opposing view, see M. M. Saghafi and M. Attaran, "Is This the Beginning of the End in the Competitive Trend?" *Eastern Economic Journal* 16 (April-June 1990): 125-132.

only the Congress and the criminal justice system inspire a lower level of confidence than big business.[41] Although 64 percent of Americans believe the moral and ethical standards of small business owners are "excellent" or "good," only 31 percent trust the ethics of corporate executives.[42]

Second, many Americans believe that the profits of large corporations are excessive, contributing to an unequal distribution of income and wealth, and about 62 percent of Americans believe that businesses have "lost sight of human values in the pursuit of profits."[43] Indeed, a number of studies have found that profit rates tend to be above average in industries that have four-firm concentration ratios above 50 or 60 percent.[44] On the other hand, another study has found that the incomes of the most affluent households would fall by less than 1.5 percent and the remaining income groups would experience gains of less than 1 percent if the four-firm concentration ratios of all American manufacturing industries were reduced to a maximum of 40 percent.[45]

Questions have also been raised about the efficiency of large corporations. Traditional economic theory suggests that monopolistic firms will restrict their level of production below the competitive level, reducing the allocative efficiency of the economy. In the American context,

---

[41]Frank Newport and Lydia Saad, "Confidence in Institutions," *The Gallup Poll Monthly*, April 1994, 5.

[42]A 1992 Harris poll, reported in Karlyn H. Bowman and others, "How's Business?" *The Public Perspective* 5 (November/December 1993): 83.

[43]A 1991 Roper survey, reported in Bowman and others, "How's Business," 1.

[44]This literature is reviewed in Martin, *Industrial Economics*, Chapter 7; and Michael Salinger, "The Concentration-Margins Relationship Reconsidered," *Brookings Papers on Economic Activity: Microeconomics* (1990): 287-335.

[45]Irene Powell, "The Effect of Reductions in Concentration on Income Distribution," *Review of Economics and Statistics* 69 (February 1987): 75-82.

estimates of this efficiency loss range from paltry (0.1 percent of GNP) to significant (4 to 7 percent of GNP).[46]

According to Harvey Leibenstein, monopolistic corporations may also be guilty of what he calls **x-inefficiency**—that is, without the discipline of competition they may make little effort to fully minimize their costs of production. Adam Smith noted two centuries ago, "monopoly . . . is a great enemy to good management." Although most of the evidence is anecdotal, this problem is undoubtedly a real one. In several cases, when former monopolists have been confronted by the pressure of competition, they have been able to cut their unit costs by 10 to 20 percent and more.[47] On the other hand, a decade of corporate restructuring may have reduced this problem in sectors exposed to foreign competition.

Some economists believe that large corporations pose a threat to the macroeconomic stability of the American economy. In recent years, the federal government has concluded that failures of large industrial corporations would have such a detrimental effect on the entire economy that it has sometimes stepped in to bail them out. If large corporations are reasonably sure that the government will not allow them to fail, they may be even more prone to x-inefficiency.

Moreover, it is often alleged that the corporate giants contribute to macroeconomic instability through their handling of capital investment. About half of all capital expenditures in manufacturing are controlled by the 200 largest firms. If a relatively small number of corporate executives become pessimistic about the business outlook, a significant downturn in investment spending may occur, possibly resulting in a business recession. According to John Kenneth

---

[46]Scherer, *Industrial Market Structure and Economic Performance,* 459-464.

[47]Ibid., 464-466.

Galbraith, recessionary trends in competitive industries are self-limiting and self-correcting, but concentrated industries are "inherently unstable."[48]

Big Business Defended

In defense of the large corporations, many economists believe that the standard measures of market power (for example, the four-firm concentration ratio) significantly overstate the extent of monopoly. They point to several sources of competition that are commonly ignored. For example, the ratios seldom take account of competition from imports or from substitutes that are produced by other industries (for example, competition between aluminum foil, plastic wrap, and waxed paper producers).

William Baumol argues that monopoly profits are constrained by the threat of potential competition. Concentrated markets operate very much like competitive markets, he says, as long as they are "contestable"—that is, as long as other companies are free to enter.[49] Unfortunately, according to Stephen Martin, "no real-world industry has yet been shown to be contestable."[50]

John Kenneth Galbraith contends that the power of monopolistic sellers is often withstood by the **countervailing power** of monopolistic buyers. Large steel producers, for example, are faced by large, powerful purchasers of steel in the automobile industry, and large producers of consumer goods are faced by Sears and the other large retail chains.

Even if it can be shown that the exercise of monopoly power results in various forms of allocative and x-inefficiencies, these costs must be balanced against the savings that accrue from large-scale research, production, and marketing. Indeed, according to the **efficiency hypothesis**,

---

[48]On the macroeconomic stability of competitive and concentrated industries, see John Kenneth Galbraith, *Economics and the Public Purpose* (Boston: Houghton Mifflin, 1973), 179.

[49]William J. Baumol, "Contestable Markets, Antitrust, and Regulation," *The Wharton Magazine* 7 (Fall 1982): 24.

[50]Martin, *Industrial Economics*, 224.

formulated and tested by Harold Demsetz of UCLA and the University of Chicago, the high profit rates of corporations in highly concentrated industries are explained, not by abuses of market power, but by superior efficiency and low production costs.[51] According to Yale Brozen, also from the University of Chicago:

Concentration occurs and persists where it is the efficient structure for producing and distributing a product and for adapting to changing technical possibilities, shifting demand, and increasing regulatory requirements. . . . Where centralization is not efficient, industries do not become concentrated.[52]

The Labor Market

Neoclassical theory suggests that employment and wages are determined by the supply and demand of labor if labor markets are sufficiently competitive. In comparison with many other industrial capitalist countries, the U.S. labor market seems to be relatively competitive, and it may be growing more competitive through time.

On the employers' side of the market, there is little evidence of widespread monopsonistic power of the kind that would depress wages below their competitive levels. Studies of local labor markets have found that a very small percentage of American workers live in towns where the ten largest firms employ over half the labor force. Furthermore, the average

---

[51]Harold Demsetz, "Industry Structure, Market Rivalry, and Public Policy," *Journal of Law and Economics* 16 (April 1973):1-10. For recent support of the efficiency hypothesis, see E. Woodrow Eckard, "A Note on the Profit-Concentration Relation," *Applied Economics* 27 (February 1995): 219-223.

[52]Yale Brozen, *Concentration, Mergers, and Public Policy* (New York: Macmillan, 1982), 56-57.

American manufacturing establishment had a smaller number of employees (implying a lower level of market power) in 1991 than in 1947.[53]

From the employees' perspective, labor unions are the most important expressions of market power, but only 15.5 percent of American workers are presently enrolled in unions. That proportion has been falling since the mid-1950s, when it peaked at about 27 percent. Union membership rates are much higher in Western Europe than in the United States, with the exceptions of France and Switzerland.

Thus, the American labor market seems to be relatively competitive, but this raises another question. Neoclassical theory suggests that unregulated competitive markets should adjust to a supply-demand equilibrium, leaving no surplus or shortage of the commodity in question. However, the United States and other capitalist countries have experienced a persistent labor surplus, or unemployment. How can this be explained?

A full discussion of unemployment would take us far afield, but a few words are in order. Neoclassical theory suggests that unemployment is caused by downward inflexibility of nominal wages, stemming from long-term labor contracts, minimum wage laws, unemployment compensation, and the like. Keynesians would say that a reduction in nominal wage rates may not reduce unemployment; it may only reduce labor income and the aggregate demand for goods.

According to comparative data, although unemployment rates increased in all major capitalist countries between 1973 and 1995, the rate increased by a smaller amount in the United States than in most other countries. Thus, the American unemployment rate was higher than the average for members of the European Union before 1979, but it has been significantly lower since 1983 (Figure 7.1). Equally important, the incidence of long-term unemployment (one year

---

[53]U.S. Department of Commerce, Bureau of the Census, *1987 Census of Manufacturers,* MC87-S-5 (Washington, D.C.: USGPO, 1991), 5-3; and *Statistical Abstract of the United States 1994*, Table 844.

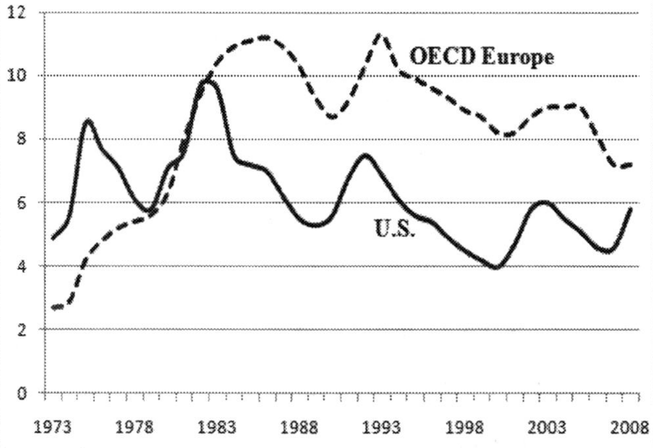

Figure 7.1 United States and OECD Europe: Unemployment Rates, 1973-2008 (percent)

or more of joblessness) is much lower in the United States than in Japan or most of Europe (refer to Table 2.8).

How did the United States improve its relative employment performance during the 1980s? This is a complex question that cannot be treated adequately here. In a nutshell, it seems that Americans held or regained their jobs by accepting relatively small wage increases. Between 1970 and 1993, real compensation per employee increased by about 77 percent in the average country of Western Europe, but by only 8 percent in the United States.[54] Why were American workers willing to settle for much smaller wage increases than their European counterparts? Some analysts base their explanations on the low level of union membership and militancy in the United States. Others point to the relatively modest program of unemployment benefits in the United States, and to the rising percentages of young, unskilled, and immigrant workers in the labor force.[55]

---

[54]Author's calculations, based on annual growth rates of compensation per employee and on consumer price inflation rates in *OECD Economic Outlook* 56 (December 1994), Annex Tables 11 and 15.

[55]For a full discussion of these issues, see Richard R. Freeman, "Evaluating the European View that the United States Has No Unemployment Problem," *American Economic Review* 78 (May 1988): 294-299; Charles R. Bean, "European Unemployment: A Survey," *Journal of Economic Literature* 32 (June 1994): 573-619; and George J. Borjas, "The Economics of Immigration," *Journal of Economic Literature* 32 (December 1994): 1667-1717.

Reasons for Declining Unionization

Earlier, we noted that American union membership declined from 27 percent of the labor force in the mid-1950s to about 15 percent today. Approximately one-fifth of this decline can be attributed to the growth of the service economy.[56] As we have seen, firms in the service sector tend to be smaller than industrial firms, and many service workers are self-employed. Thus, the service sector is less susceptible than industry to union activity. In 1994, union members accounted for less than 14 percent of service employment (and only 6 percent of private service employment), compared to 23 percent in industry (Table 7.7).

The other factors that have caused a decline in unionism are more difficult to distinguish. According to the *job satisfaction hypothesis*, fewer workers are demanding union representation because they are happy with their jobs. In fact, public opinion polls indicate that a large and increasing proportion of Americans are satisfied with their jobs.[57] According to the *employer resistance hypothesis*, foreign competition and domestic deregulation have encouraged employers to oppose union activities more forcefully. To this end, employers may attempt to influence union elections directly, or they may offer higher wages and fringe benefits to strengthen worker loyalty. The *government substitution hypothesis* says that many of the functions of labor unions have been taken over by public agencies. Guarantees that were once embedded in union contracts—unemployment insurance, retirement benefits, health and safety requirements—are now objects of legislation. Accordingly, within the United States, unionism

---

[56]This is the estimate given in Henry S. Farber, "The Decline of Unionization in the United States: What Can Be Learned from Recent Experience?" *Journal of Labor Economics* 8 (January 1990): S79. Some early estimates of the impact of service growth on union membership were much larger.

[57]Farber, "The Decline of Unionization in the United States," S99.

has declined most rapidly in states that have done the most to uphold workers' rights.[58] In international perspective, though, union membership is generally largest in such countries as Sweden, where governmental spending on social security and welfare are high in relation to national income.

Labor Legislation

One reason for the low level of union membership in the United States (by international standards) is that pro-labor legislation came late to America. In Sweden, for example, the major employers agreed in 1906 that they would not attempt to disrupt unionizing activities. In America, these guarantees were not extended until the passage of the Norris-LaGuardia Act of 1932 and the National Labor Relations Act of 1935. In 1938, the Fair Labor Standards Act enacted a minimum wage rate (25 cents per hour!) and a maximum workweek (44 hours) for labor engaged in interstate commerce.

Public opinion turned against the labor unions at the end of World War II when a long series of strikes disrupted the coal, steel, telephone, automobile, and meat-packing industries. In 1946, approximately 116 million man-hours were lost due to labor disputes. In the aftermath, the Labor-Management (Taft-Hartley) Act of 1947 was enacted to exercise control over the unions. Under the act, the **closed shop**, which requires job applicants to join the union before they may be hired, was outlawed. The **union shop**, which requires employees to join the union within a specified period after they are hired, was not prohibited by the act, but the individual states were permitted to pass **right-to-work laws** that prohibit union shops. Twenty states, most of them in the South and West, presently have right-to-work laws.

---

[58]George R. Neumann and Ellen R. Rissman, "Where Have All the Union Members Gone?" *Journal of Labor Economics* 2 (April 1984): 175-192.

The Taft-Hartley Act also placed restrictions on the right of unions to call strikes. If the government feels that a strike is likely to create a national emergency, it can require an 80-day cooling-off period and intervention by the Federal Mediation and Conciliation Service.

The Economic Impact of Labor Unions

The most important goal of labor unions traditionally has been to raise and maintain the wages of their members. They pursue this goal by bargaining collectively with management (with the threat of a strike if bargaining fails), by restricting the supply of union labor, by increasing the demand for their labor through featherbedding (creation of new, and sometimes useless, jobs), and through efforts to increase the demand for their final product (for example, "Look for the union label" and "Buy American" slogans).

The actual impact of unions on wage levels can be estimated in a number of different ways, and economists disagree on the methods that should be used. Nevertheless, few economists would question the proposition that union members receive higher wages, on average, than nonmembers. Historically, union wages have exceeded nonunion wages by about 20-25 percent in the United States. Nonunion wages seem to draw closer to union wages during periods of price inflation, and fall behind during periods of price stability. During the early years of the Great Depression, when the price level was falling, the wage advantage of union members grew to about 50 percent.[59] In 1994, median weekly earnings of union members were 37 percent

---

[59]John Pencavel and Catherine E. Hartsog, "A Reconsideration of the Effects of Unionism on Relative Wages and Employment in the United States, 1920-1980," *Journal of Labor Economics* 2 (April 1984): 206. For a discussion of the voluminous literature on this subject, see H. Gregg Lewis, *Union Relative Wage Effects: A Survey* (Chicago: University of Chicago Press, 1986); Kay E. Anderson, Philip M. Doyle, and Albert E. Schwenk, "Measuring Union-Nonunion Earnings Differences," *Monthly Labor Review* (June 1990): 26-38; and George

higher than those of nonmembers. Managerial and sales personnel gained little from union membership, but union members in service occupations had earnings 80 percent larger than those of nonmembers (Table 7.7).

Table 7.7 United States: Union Membership and Median Weekly Earnings of Unionized and Non-Unionized Full-Time Wage and Salary Workers, 1994

	Union Members as % of Total Employment	*Earnings of Union Members*	*Earnings of Nonunion*	*Union/Nonunion Earnings Ratio*
All workers	15.5	$592	$432	1.37
Occupations:				
Managerial/Professional	14.4	729	672	1.08
Craft and repair	23.9	672	458	1.47
Technicians	11.4	629	521	1.21
Transport workers	26.0	600	410	1.46
Administrative support	13.8	511	372	1.37
Machine operators	24.4	492	322	1.53
Handlers and helpers	21.9	478	288	1.66
Service occupations	14.3	483	268	1.80
Sales occupations	4.9	483	448	1.08
Sectors:				
Agriculture	2.3	n.a.	279	n.a.
Industry:				
Mining	15.7	664	634	1.05
Construction	18.8	696	425	1.64
Manufacturing	18.2	533	464	1.15
TCPU*	28.4	665	531	1.25
Services:				
Wholesale/Retail trade	6.2	453	352	1.29
FIRE**	2.3	471	485	0.97
Personal services	6.2	485	420	1.15
Government	38.7	623	493	1.26

* TCPU - transportation, communications, and public utilities
** FIRE - finance, insurance, and real estate
Source: U.S. Department of Labor, *Employment and Earnings* (January 1995): 214-217.

Although labor unions apparently have succeeded in raising the wages of their members, this does not necessarily imply that they have raised the average level of wages for all workers. A number of economists believe that the gains of union laborers have been won at the expense of

---

Jakubson, "Estimation and Testing of the Union Wage Effect Using Panel Data," *Review of Economic Studies* 88 (October 1991): 971-991.

nonunion laborers rather than at the expense of corporate stockholders. If high wages cause unemployment in the unionized sector and the unemployed spill over into the nonunion sector, then competition for jobs may reduce the wages of nonmembers.

In fact, the share of U.S. national income received by all laborers (union and nonunion) has been remarkably stable for more than 50 years. In 1933, when only 7 percent of the labor force was unionized, laborers received about 73 percent of national income. In 1954, when the unionized share of the labor force peaked at 27 percent, labor's share of national income was 69 percent. In 1993, unions claimed about 16 percent of the labor force and labor received about 74 percent of national income.[60]

The Financial Sector

Financial institutions—including banks, securities firms, insurance companies, and others—perform a number of important functions in market economies. They provide efficient and safe methods for payment between buyers and sellers (checking accounts, letters of credit, bankers' acceptances, and so on); they provide for safe storage of financial wealth (savings accounts, etc.); they extend credit (bank loans, bond sales, etc.); they allow individuals to share their risks with larger numbers of people (insurance policies); and they facilitate efficient transfers of ownership of businesses, housing, and other capital goods (stock market and real estate transactions).

---

[60]Here, I take compensation of employees to represent labor's share of national income. Labor's share is even more stable if we include proprietors' income. These data are taken from *Economic Report of the President 1991,* 312; and *Economic Report of the President 1994,* 302.

In the United States, the finance, insurance, real estate, and business service sectors account for about 25 percent of GDP and 15 percent of total employment. These are the largest proportions found in any OECD country, with the possible exception of Italy.[61]

Trends in American Bank Regulation

Before 1863, the U.S. banking system was almost wholly unregulated by the national government. With the exception of the First and Second Banks of the United States, which were chartered by the U.S. Congress, the 2,500 banks established between 1781 and 1861 were all chartered by authorities at the state level. Many of these banks were unsound and nearly two-fifths of them were forced to close within tens years after they opened. To make matters worse, each bank was able to issue its own banknotes, which were used as currency. In the mid-1800s, literally thousands of different kinds of currency were in circulation in the United States, making it very difficult to detect counterfeit notes.

The National Banking Acts of 1863 and 1864 put the state banks out of the business of issuing currency and established a uniform and safe currency system. Furthermore, the acts established the office of the Comptroller of the Currency in the Treasury Department and empowered it to charter and supervise a system of national banks. Hence, a unique (by international standards) system of **dual banking** was created, with national banks chartered by the comptroller and state banks chartered by state banking authorities.

Although the national banking system established a uniform currency, it did not provide an efficient national system for clearing checks—that is, for moving funds from one bank to another. Likewise, the system did not provide an efficient means for banks that were short of funds to borrow from banks with excess reserves. Most important, the National Banking Acts did

---

[61]But Italian statistics include some community, social, and personal services in this category. See *OECD in Figures 1994*, published with the *OECD Observer* 188 (June-July 1994), 36-37.

not establish a central bank that could adjust the supply of money to meet the needs of the economy. The establishment of a central bank was resisted strongly by conservative Democrats who feared encroachment on states' rights.

The Federal Reserve Act of 1913 struck a compromise between the demands for state autonomy and the need for a central bank. The act established 12 Federal Reserve district banks, each of which is owned by the member banks in its district. To this day, the district banks are the only central banks in the world that are wholly owned by commercial banks. Furthermore, each district bank is controlled by a board of nine directors, six of whom are elected by the member banks in the district.

A seven-member board of governors, appointed by the president, was placed at the head of the Federal Reserve system. All national banks were required to become members of the system and state banks were invited to join. Member banks were allowed to borrow money at the discount window of the Federal Reserve and could use its check-clearing facilities, but they were regulated more tightly (for example, larger reserve and capital requirements) than many of the state banks that did not choose to join the system.

In response to the speculative boom of the 1920s and the financial collapse of the 1930s, Congress enacted several new laws to stabilize the banking industry. The Glass-Steagall Act of 1933 imposed the separation of commercial banking (accepting deposits) from investment banking (securities transactions and underwriting). Thus, the United States developed a unique system of specialized banks that stand in stark contrast to the "universal" banks in Germany. The Glass-Steagall Act also created the Federal Deposit Insurance Corporation (FDIC), and required all national banks to carry FDIC insurance. The Banking Act of 1935 shifted more authority from the district Federal Reserve banks to the Board of Governors in Washington, making it possible to pursue a more deliberate monetary policy.

The authority of the Federal Reserve began to decline after World War II as a growing number of banks dropped out of the Federal Reserve system to escape stringent reserve requirements. This exodus allegedly threatened the safety of the banking system and crippled the

Federal Reserve's efforts to control the growth of the money supply. In order to deal with these and other problems, Congress passed the Depository Institutions Deregulation and Monetary Control Act of 1980. Among the important provisions of the act were the following:

* The Federal Reserve was given authority to set reserve requirements on checking accounts at *all* federally insured depository institutions—member banks, nonmember banks, savings and loan associations, credit unions, and so forth.
* Federal Reserve loans and other Federal Reserve services (for example, check collection) were made available at a fee to *all* depository institutions.
* All depository institutions were given the authority to offer interest-earning checking accounts.
* A phaseout of interest rate ceilings on deposits and other accounts was initiated.

The 1980 legislation was meant to reassert the authority of the Federal Reserve and to place all depository institutions—member and nonmember banks, savings and loan associations, and others—on an equal footing. Deregulation of deposit interest rates under the 1980 act contributed to the efficiency of the financial system, but it also caused problems for many banks and thrift institutions. In order to compete, many of them were forced to pay higher interest rates on deposits than the average yield on their investment portfolios. For this reason and others (including recession, declining property values, fraud, mismanagement, and nonpayment of debt by oil companies and Third World borrowers), hundreds of banks and thrift institutions have been forced to close their doors. The average number of bank failures jumped from 5 per year in 1945-1980 to 114 per year in 1981-1993.[62]

For several years, the U.S. Congress has been considering a new program of bank reforms, aimed at increasing the efficiency and international competitiveness of the system, and

---

[62]Federal Deposit Insurance Corporation, *Annual Report 1993* (Washington, D.C., 1994), 135.

minimizing the cost of potential taxpayer bailouts. Proposals under consideration include the following:

* Restore competitiveness by allowing banks to open branches nationwide and offer new services, such as investment banking and insurance, through subsidiaries. The Treasury estimates that branch banking alone could reduce the operating costs of the banking industry by about $10 billion per year.
* Reduce the scope of deposit insurance coverage, and regulate banks more tightly to reduce risk of failure.
* Streamline the regulatory structure, with national banks supervised by the Treasury and state banks by the Federal Reserve.
* Exempt most banks from the 1977 Community Reinvestment Act, which requires that banks lend in the communities where they take deposits.[63]

The American banking system continues to be unique from an international perspective. The Federal Reserve remains a *federal* system, with its network of locally-owned district banks, and banking authorities in the individual states still have the authority to establish regulations on a wide range of issues. Nevertheless, domestic budgetary problems and international competition seem to be pushing the system toward more centralization, consistent with practice in the rest of the world.[64]

---

[63]David Lascelles, "Last Chance for a Sweeping Overhaul," *Financial Times*, April 4, 1991, 12; Kenneth H. Bacon, "Banking Panel Approves Plan on Branches," *The Wall Street Journal*, June 26, 1991, A3; John R. Wilke "Sweeping Reforms of Banking Laws Appear Unlikely to Pass in Congress," *The Wall Street Journal*, May 5, 1995, A5; and John R. Wilke, "Deregulation for Banks Nears Panel Approval," *The Wall Street Journal*, June 28, 1995, A3.

[64]See Anthony M. Santomero, "European Banking Post-1992: Lessons from the United States," in *European Banking in the 1990s*, ed. by Jean Dermine (London: Basil Blackwell, 1990), 437-457.

The Governmental Sector

By international standards, the activities of the U.S. government are rather limited. Taken as a percentage of GNP, for example, government expenditures are smaller in the United States than in any other major industrial nation, with the possible exception of Japan.[65]

From historical and international perspectives, the United States was slow to adopt a strong central government. In keeping with the philosophy of federalism, the focus of governmental power was kept close to the electorate—at the state and local levels. After independence was won from the British, the Articles of Confederation denied the central government the power to collect taxes. When the Constitution was adopted in 1789, it gave a broad range of economic powers to the Congress, but these were used sparingly.

Probably the most significant economic contribution of the government in the early years was in launching the systems of transportation and communication. In 1806, Congress committed the federal government to build the Cumberland National Road, linking farmers of the Ohio valley to Eastern markets. The Erie Canal, completed in 1825, was built, owned, and operated by the state of New York. Unlike the British, who built most of their transportation system with private capital, the early American governments were responsible for about 70 percent of investment in canals and 30 percent of investment in railroads.[66]

For the first 140 years, over half of all U.S. governmental spending was carried out at the local level (Table 7.8). It took nothing less than the Great Depression and World War II to

---

[65]According to OECD estimates, total outlays of the general government have been a smaller fraction of GDP in Japan than in the United States in the past, but this is is no longer true. See *OECD Economic Outlook* 56 (October 1994), Annex Table 27.

[66]Estimates of Carter Goodrich, cited in Arthur M. Schlesinger, Jr., *The Cycles of American History* (Boston: Houghton Mifflin, 1986), 224. For an extended discussion of the activist aspects of early American economic policy, see Frank Bourgin, *The Great Challenge: The Myth of Laissez-Faire in the Early Republic* (New York: George Braziller, 1989), passim.

elevate the central government to a position of dominance. Along with the shift toward centralization of government, the postwar generations also witnessed a dramatic shift in the functional distribution of governmental spending.

Table 7.8 United States: Distribution of Federal, State, and Local Direct Governmental Expenditures, 1902-2002

Year	*Federal*	*State*	*Local*	*Total*
1902	34	8	58	100
1913	30	9	61	100
1922	39	12	49	100
1927	30	13	57	100
1936	49	15	36	100
1944	90	3	7	100
1950	60	15	25	100
1960	60	15	25	100
1970	56	17	27	100
1980	55	18	27	100
1990	56	18	26	100
2000	51	21	28	100
2002	50	22	28	100

Sources: U.S. Department of Commerce, Bureau of the Census, *Historical Statistics of the United States, Colonial Times to 1970*, Part 2 (Washington, D.C.: USGPO, 1975), Series Y 613, Y 757, and Y 785; U.S. Department of Commerce, Bureau of the Census, *Statistical Abstract of the United States 1996* (Washington, D.C.: USGPO, 1996), Table 463; U.S. Department of Commerce, Bureau of the Census, *Statistical Abstract of the United States 2006* (Washington, D.C.: USGPO, 2006), Tables 428 & 459.

Table 7.9 United States: Functional Distribution of Federal, State, and Local Governmental Expenditures, 1902-2006

	1902	*1936*	*1944*	*1950*	*1970*	*1991*	*2006*
Defense, Foreign Relations	9.9	5.6	77.8	26.1	25.3	15.9	13.2
Education	15.5	14.1	2.6	13.7	16.7	14.3	
Postal, Transport	19.5	17.7	6.4	9.6	8.5	5.5	
Social Security, Welfare	2.5	7.3	1.8	14.0	19.8	29.1	
Health	6.9	4.7	1.0	5.0	5.1	4.5	16.7
Police, Fire	5.4	3.2	0.7	1.9	2.1	3.8	
Interest on Debt	5.8	8.7	2.4	6.9	5.5	10.8	
Other	34.5	38.7	7.3	22.8	17.0	15.9	
Total	100.0	100.0	100.0	100.0	100.0	100.0	

Sources: U.S. Department of Commerce, Bureau of the Census, *Historical Statistics of the United States, Colonial Times to 1970*, Part 1 (Washington, D.C.: USGPO, 1975), Series Y 533-566; U.S. Department of Commerce, Bureau of the Census, *Government Finances: 1990-91* (Washington, D.C.: USGPO, 1993), Table 1.

Before World War II, the government spent more money on the postal and transportation systems than it spent on national defense, social security, and welfare, combined (Table 7.9). During the war, the military absorbed over three-fourths of all governmental expenditures. The military share dropped again after the war, but not to the prewar level. At the same time, the governmental commitment to social security and welfare, which began during the Depression, grew rapidly after the war. Taken together, the share of national defense, social security, and welfare in U.S. governmental spending increased from 8 percent in 1927 to 45 percent in 1991.

Regulation of the Economy

We already noted the important role of the American government in regulating product, labor, and financial markets. Regulation of banking began in earnest in the 1860s, antitrust action began in the 1890s, and guidance of labor relations began in the 1930s.

Governmental concern for public health and safety began with the passage of the Pure Food and Drug Act of 1906, prompted by the publication of Upton Sinclair's novel, *The Jungle*, that same year. In later years, the regulatory umbrella was expanded to cover consumer and occupational safety, environmental protection, energy production, transportation, communication, and a number of other concerns. Most recently, new environmental regulations have been prompted by research revealing deterioration of the earth's protective ozone layer.

Most of the regulatory agencies were established to deal with important national problems; very few economists or politicians would advocate abolishing the entire governmental rulebook. Nevertheless, the regulatory process has fallen under broad criticism in recent years.

First, many would say that governmental regulations are too expensive. In addition to the billions of dollars spent to operate regulatory agencies, private businesses must spend additional billions to comply with regulations, and these costs are passed to consumers in higher taxes and prices. Between 1970 and 1992, for example, the cost to businesses of complying with pollution abatement regulations increased by nearly 90 percent in constant prices, from $60 billion to $113 billion. Estimates of the annual total cost of regulation to the U.S. economy range all the way from $200 billion to $500 billion.[67]

Another criticism of governmental control is suggested by the **regulatory capture** theory, which states that in time, and sometimes quite innocently, regulators become tools of the industries they are supposed to regulate. For example, governmental agencies barred the entry of new competitors into the trucking and airline industries for many years, granting monopoly power to the existing companies. Officials of the Federal Reserve often lobby in Congress for legislation that favors the banking industry.

Partially reversing the earlier trend, a wave of deregulation has swept the United States since the early 1970s. New legislation and revised guidelines from regulatory agencies have reduced restrictions on entry, exit, and pricing in domestic satellite operations (1972 and 1979), railroads (1976), air cargo and transportation (1978 and 1980), petroleum products (1981), cable television (1980 and 1984), and telecommunications (1995).

Programs of deregulation may inject new competitiveness and flexibility into the economy, but they also carry risks. According to survey data, only 16 percent of Americans wish to postpone stronger standards for air and water pollution.[68] Under more permissive guidelines, airlines have canceled service to some small cities.[69] The epidemic of bank failures during the

---

[67]U.S. General Accounting Office, *Regulatory Reform—Information on Costs, Cost-Effectiveness, and Mandated Deadlines for Regulations* (GAO/PEMD-95-18BR, March 8, 1995), passim; and John M. Berry, "Rising Cost of Rules Leads to a Rising Tide against Them," *Washington Post*, January 19, 1995, D9.

[68]Survey by the Roper Organization, reported in "How's Business?" *The Public Perspective* 5 (November/December 1993): 83.

[69]For an account of "the folly of deregulation" of the airlines, see Hobart Rowen, *Self-Inflicted Wounds: From LBJs Guns and Butter to Reagan's Voodoo Economics* (New York: Random House, 1994), Chapter 12.

late 1980s and early 1990s may have been connected with deregulation of that industry. When the government was forced to bail out the Continental Illinois banking corporation, Federal Reserve Chairman Volcker admitted to Congress that, "in hindsight, it's an unassailable argument that the central bank should have been tougher with Continental."[70]

Fiscal and Monetary Policy

Superficially, the institutional machinery that sets fiscal and monetary policy in the United States is quite simple. On the fiscal side, the national budget is prepared by the executive branch under the coordination of the Office of Management and Budget. It is sent to Congress for amendment, debate, and approval, and then it is returned to the president to be signed into law. At each step, the formation of fiscal policy is influenced by the actions of lobbyists and by the demands of the electorate.

Monetary policy is set by the governors of the Federal Reserve System, each of whom is appointed by the president of the United States for a 14-year term. Because of these long terms of office, and because the Federal Reserve is able to cover its operating expenses without appropriations from Congress, the board of governors is insulated from political pressure.

During the Great Depression, the U.S. government enacted programs to help the poor, but it did not attempt to stimulate employment with active programs of fiscal and monetary policy. Indeed, in 1937 the government reduced its expenditures, and the Federal Reserve acted to reduce the size of the money supply. In the end, the World War II experience confirmed the Keynesian proposition that unemployment could be reduced by a program of governmental spending. Indeed, wartime spending successfully reduced the rate of unemployment in America from 17 percent in 1939 to 2 percent in 1945.

---

[70]G. Christian Hill and Edwin Finn, "Big Depositors' Runs on Beleaguered Banks Speed the Failure Rate," *The Wall Street Journal*, August 23, 1984, 12.

After the war, a new attitude toward fiscal policy was reflected in the Employment Act of 1946, which declared that the federal government had an obligation to promote maximum employment, production, and purchasing power. The President was authorized to appoint a new Council of Economic Advisors, and, for several years, the objectives of the Employment Act were attained rather effectively. One major study found that between 1955 and 1965 the American government used fiscal policy more successfully than any of the major European governments to stabilize the growth of national income.[71]

Table 7.10 United States: Macroeconomic Performance by Decades, 1950-2005

	1950-1959	*1960-1969*	*1970-1979*	*1980-1989*	*1990-1999*	*2000-2005*
Unemployment Rate (percent)	4.5	4.8	6.2	7.3	5.8	5.2
Consumer Price Inflation (annual average percentage)	2.1	2.4	7.1	5.6	3.0	2.7
Real GDP Growth (annual average percentage)	4.1	4.4	3.3	3.1	3.1	2.8
Federal Government Budget Balance as Percent of GDP	-0.4	-0.8	-2.1	-3.9	-2.2	-1.3

Source: *Economic Report of the President 2006*, Appendix B, tables B-4, B-35, B-64, B-79 obtained from http://www.gpoaccess.gov/eop/index.html

Since the 1960s, American fiscal policy has been slipping out of control. Due to expenditures on the Vietnam War and social programs in the 1960s and 1970s and tax cuts in the early 1980s, the budget has followed a steady trend toward larger deficits.[72] At the same time, the macroeconomic performance of the American economy has been mixed, with relatively high

---

[71]Bent Hansen, *Fiscal Policy in Seven Countries: 1955-1965* (Paris: Organization for Economic Cooperation and Development, 1969), 69-73.

[72]Actually, the rise in the official budget deficit may be overestimated because federal accounts do not distinguish between current expenses and investment. See Robert Eisner, "Budget Deficits: Rhetoric and Reality," *Journal of Economic Perspectives* 3 (Spring 1989): 73-93.

inflation during the 1970s, high unemployment during the 1980s, and slow growth of GDP during the 1990s (Table 7.10).

The federal budget distinguishes between two categories of expenditures: mandatory and discretionary. **Mandatory expenditures** include interest on the national debt and **entitlements**, such as Medicare and Social Security, that are relatively difficult to control because they provide legally prescribed benefits to anyone who meets eligibility requirements. **Discretionary expenditures**, including those on national defense, transportation, energy, and a wide range of other programs, are generally controlled on a year-to-year basis. Since the 1960s, the share of mandatory expenditures and interest on the national debt in total outlays of the U.S. government has increased steadily as follows:[73]

1963	33%
1970	39%
1980	53%
1990	60%
2000	66%
2005	61%
2010 (forecast)	65%

In an effort to regain fiscal control, Congress passed the Gramm-Rudman-Hollings Act (GRH) in 1985, establishing a series of targets that were meant to balance the budget by 1991. If the targets were not met in each year's budget negotiations, GRH called for automatic cuts in discretionary expenditures. Congress and the Reagan administration were not able to meet these targets, and loopholes in the law allowed them to avoid large automatic cuts. The Budget Enforcement Act (BEA) of 1990 filled some of these loopholes and established legally binding caps (adjusted for inflation and technical factors) that imposed a "flexible freeze" on

[73]Office of Management and Budget, *Budget of the United States Government, Fiscal Year 2008: Historical Tables* (Washington, D.C.: USGPO, 2009).

discretionary expenditures. The BEA was temporarily suspended to pay for the Persian Gulf War, but then the federal budget deficit declined during 1993, 1994, and 1995—the first three-year reduction since the mid-1970s.[74]

Aside from the use of fiscal and monetary policy to stabilize employment and the price level, the U.S. government has made little use of indicative planning or industrial policy to influence the structure of the economy. There is no American counterpart to the Japanese Ministry of International Trade and Industry, which uses subsidies and other means to encourage the development of favored industries. Generally, Republican administrations have been opposed to industrial targeting: "Attempts to second-guess the market and to direct government support to particular firms, industries, or technologies in the name of promoting growth are inevitably counterproductive."[75] In recent years, Democratic leaders have advocated a "uniquely American model" of business-government cooperation. This approach includes stronger financial support for basic research in scientific fields that are important to industry, greater cooperation between federal laboratories and commercial interests, and regulatory reform targeted at bio-technology, telecommunications, and other vital industries.[76]

---

[74]Ibid., 14. For a fuller discussion of the implications of the Budget Enforcement Act, see *Economic Report of the President 199*3, 111-113.

[75]Position of the Bush administration, stated in *Economic Report of the President 1991*, 6. This position, however, was not implemented strictly. See Bob Davis, "White House, Reversing Policy under Pressure, Begins to Pick High-Tech Winners and Losers," *The Wall Street Journal*, May 13, 1991, A16.

[76]Michael Borrus, "Industrial Policy American Style," *International Economic Insights* (March-April 1993): 10-13; and Gerald Seib and Jeffrey Birnbaum, "Clinton Industrial Policy Stressing Cooperation Can Clash with Administration's Populist Bent," *The Wall Street Journal*, March 21, 1994, A14.

Redistribution of Income and Wealth

America, according to the slogan, is a "land of opportunity." Indeed, the American economic and social systems have given immigrants from many countries the opportunity to amass significant fortunes. Most Americans believe that rich people gain their wealth from a "strong effort to succeed" rather than from "luck or circumstances beyond their control"; most believe that a person who works hard has a "good chance" of becoming rich; and a large majority say that they "admire people who get rich by working hard." On the other hand, very few believe that the present distribution of income and wealth is fair, and two-thirds of Americans believe that riches should be distributed more evenly.[77]

Thus, Americans support moderate programs of redistribution, but they are more conservative in this regard than most Europeans. The United States devotes a smaller proportion of national income to social prootection expenditures than any other OECD country, and is the only major industrial country without a family allowance system to help parents provide for their children.[78] The limited role of government, together with a range of demographic factors, may help to explain why the United States has a relatively unequal distribution of income and a high rate of child poverty.[79]

---

[77]George Gallup, Jr., and Frank Newport, "Americans Widely Disagree on What Constitutes `Rich,'" *The Gallup Poll Monthly*, July 1990, 28-36; "Haves and Have Nots," *The American Enterprise* 4 (May-June 1993): 85; and Princeton Survey Research Associates, "People, the Press, and Politics: New Political Landscape," reported in Roper Center, *Public Opinion Online*, October 7, 1994, Accession 0222636, Question 7.

[78]*OECD Employment Outlook*, July 1994, 151. Regarding family allowance systems, see Margaret S. Gordon, *Social Security Policies in Industrial Countries: A Comparative Analysis* (Cambridge: Cambridge University Press, 1988), Chapter 13.

[79]See Timothy Smeeding, Barbara Boyle Torrey, and Martin Rein, "Patterns of Income and Poverty: Economic Status of Children and the Elderly in Eight Countries," in J. Palmer, T.

Table 7.11 United States: Influence of Transfer Payments and Taxes on the Distribution of Income, 2004

	Percentage of total income received by:					
	Poorest 20%	*Second 20%*	*Third 20%*	*Fourth 20%*	*Richest 20%*	*Gini Ratio*
Money Income*	3.42	8.68	14.83	23.02	50.05	0.450
Market Income	1.48	7.36	14.10	23.62	53.44	0.496
Post-Social Insurance Inc.	3.29	8.64	14.54	22.97	50.57	0.449
Disposable Income	4.68	10.34	16.08	24.02	44.88	0.400

Source: U.S. Census Bureau, Current Population Survey, 2004 and 2005 Annual Social and Economic Supplements. Obtained through *The Effects of Government Taxes and Transfers on Income and Poverty: 2004* at http://www.census.gov/hhes/www/poverty/effect2004/effect2004.html.

* Money Income – Total money income earned by individuals 15 and over.
Market Income – Money income minus realized capital gains/losses and general work expenses
Post-Social Insurance Inc. – Market income plus non-means tested transfers (i.e. Social Security)
Disposable Income – Post-Social Insurance Income plus all other non-cash transfers and taxes

An assessment of the impact of taxes and governmental transfer payments on the U.S. distribution of income is presented in Table 7.11. According to these estimates, the system of income taxation has a rather minor impact on the income distribution, reducing the Gini inequality ratio by only 5 percent. This may seem surprising, since the United States has a progressive income tax, but its progressivity is reduced considerably by treatment of deductions and capital gains.[80] According to survey data, most Americans believe that the current income tax system is "basically unfair," and two-thirds believe that the rich are paying too little.[81]

Table 7.12 United States: Distribution of Income and Poverty Rates, 1950-2004

Smeeding, and B. Torrey, eds., *The Vulnerable* (Washington, D.C.: Urban Institute Press, 1988), Table 5.3.

80The effect of taxation would appear even less progressive if adjustments were made for regressive state and local sales and property taxes. For estimates of this kind, see Joseph A. Pechman, *Who Paid the Taxes, 1966-1985?* (Washington, D.C.: The Brookings Institution, 1985).

81NBC/Wall Street Journal poll reported in Roper Center, *Public Opinion Online*, May 4, 1995, Accession 0235513, Question 54; and Gallup Poll reported in Roper Center, *Public Opinion Online*, May 5, 1994, Accession 0214806, Question 45.

	Percentage of total family income received by:						
	Poorest 20%	*Second 20%*	*Third 20%*	*Fourth 20%*	*Richest 20%*	*Gini Ratio*	*Poverty Rate (%)*
1950	4.5	12.0	17.4	23.4	42.7	0.379	n/a
1960	4.8	12.2	17.8	24.0	41.3	0.364	22.2
1970	4.1	10.8	17.4	24.5	43.3	0.394	12.6
1980	4.3	10.3	16.9	24.9	43.7	0.403	13.0
1990	3.9	9.6	15.9	24.0	46.6	0.428	13.5
2000	3.6	8.9	14.8	23.0	49.8	0.462	11.3
2004*	3.4	8.7	14.7	23.3	50.1	0.450	12.6

Source: U.S. Department of Commerce, Bureau of the Census, *Current Population Reports*, P60-191, P60-221, 2002. U.S. Census Bureau, Current Population Survey, 2004 and 2005 Annual Social and Economic Supplements. Obtained through *The Effects of Government Taxes and Transfers on Income and Poverty: 2004* at http://www.census.gov/hhes/www/poverty/effect2004/effect2004.html.
* Based upon pre-tax/transfer *Money Income* definition

Transfer payments, such as Social Security, aid to families with dependent children, and unemployment compensation, seem to have a stronger equalizing effect on the distribution of income than the tax system. According to Table 7.11, transfers reduce the Gini inequality ratio by about 16 percent. On the other hand, when Americans are asked, "Do you think most of the spending done by the federal government goes to help rich people, or middle income people, or poor people?" only 25 percent answer "poor people," while 48 percent say "rich people."[82] Even if Americans acknowledge the progressive effects of transfer payments, they apparently believe that the rich are the main beneficiaries of military spending and other government purchases.

The data in Table 7.12 indicate that the American income distribution became more equal and the poverty rate fell during 1950-1970, but income inequality and poverty increased during 1970-1992.[83] In a similar way, the distribution of household wealth (net worth) apparently

---

[82]According to a national poll administered by the Los Angeles Times, reported in Roper Center, *Public Opinion Online*, March 21, 1995, Accession 0232704, Question 16.

[83]If the data in Table 7.12 were adjusted for the effects of taxation, the trend toward inequality after 1970 apparently would be greater because the progressivity of the tax system deteriorated. See Pechman, *Who Paid the Taxes, 1966-1985?*, Chapter 5. For measurements disaggregated by family size and composition, see Lynn A. Karoly, "The Trend in Inequality

trended toward equality before 1979 and toward inequality afterward.[84] Despite these movements, the underlying stability of the income and wealth distributions seem remarkable when we consider the changes that have occurred in the American economy since World War II: the rising participation of women in the paid labor force, the general improvement in educational levels, the establishment of affirmative action programs to counteract the effects of racial and sexual discrimination, the continuing series of technological revolutions, and the rising influence of international trade and investment. Transfer payments, which have a progressive effect on the income distribution, represented a rising proportion of personal income:[85]

1950	6.1%	1990	12.3
1960	6.2	2000	12.7
1970	8.9	2008	15.3
1980	12.1		
1990	12.3		
2000	12.7		

---

among Families, Individuals, and Workers in the United States," in Danziger and Gottschalk, eds., *Uneven Tides: Rising Inequality in America*, 19-97. For more information on trends and causes of poverty, see Isabel V. Sawhill, "Poverty in the United States: Why Is It So Persistent?" *Journal of Economic Literature* 26 (September 1988): 1073-1119; and Robert Haveman, "Who Are the Nation's Truly Poor?" *The Brookings Review* (Winter 1993): 24-27.

[84]Edward N. Wolff, "Estimates of Household Wealth Inequality in the U.S., 1962-1983," *Review of Income and Wealth* 33 (September 1987): 231-256; and Edward N. Wolff, "Trends in Household Wealth in the United States, 1962-83 and 1983-89," *Review of Income and Wealth* 40 (June 1994): 143-174.

[85]Calculated from Table 1.7.5., "Relation of Gross Domestic Product, Gross National Product, Net National Product, National Income, and Personal Income," from http://www.bea.gov/.

How do we reconcile the rising significance of transfer payments with the relative stability of the distribution of income? Apparently, the distribution of market (nontransfer) income grew less equal over time, and this trend was partially offset by the growth of governmental transfer payments.[86]

What has caused the rising inequality of market incomes? Here, one will find little agreement. Many conservatives believe that the growing system of transfer payments has seriously reduced work incentives among the poor and created an underclass of permanent welfare recipients.[87] Thus, the distribution of total income has been relatively stable in the United States because governmental transfer programs are both cause and cure.

Others place the blame for rising inequality of market incomes on the growth of service employment, educational inequality, part-time employment, declining union membership, deterioration (in real terms) of the legal minimum wage, and rising international competition for

---

[86]This was the conclusion reached for the 1950-1970 period by Morgan Reynolds and Eugene Smolensky in their *Public Expenditures, Taxes, and the Distribution of Income* (New York: Academic Press, 1977); and by Edward Gramlich, Richard Kasten, and Frank Sammartino for 1980-1990 in their "Growing Inequality in the 1980s: The Role of Federal Taxes and Cash Transfers," in Danziger and Gottschalk, eds., *Uneven Tides: Rising Inequality in America*, 225-249. Likewise, research by Joseph Hastag and Lori Taylor indicates that the distribution of earned income (excluding transfers) trended toward inequality from 1952 to 1989. See their "A Look at Long-Term Developments in the Distribution of Income," *Economic Review of the Federal Reserve Bank of Dallas* (First Quarter 1993): 19-30.

[87]See, for example, Charles Murray, *Losing Ground: America's Social Policy, 1950-1980* (New York: Basic Books, 1984), passim; and Lawrence Mead, *The New Politics of Poverty: The Nonworking Poor in America* (New York: Basic Books, 1992), passim.

low-wage jobs.[88] Some conservatives believe that these inequalities of income are rooted in natural inequalities of intelligence, which cannot be ameliorated by governmental programs.[89] Centrists and liberals reject this view, and call for active public policies to promote equality and international competitiveness.[90] The United States, they say, must not resign itself to "cognitive inequality," but must live up to its promise—a nation where all people are understood to be "created equal."

Summary

The United States has built the largest system of production in the world on the basis of an excellent endowment of natural resources and a labor force dedicated to the philosophy of individualism. The plurality of the workers remained in agriculture until the twentieth century and then, after a brief period of industrial dominance, moved rapidly into services. The growth of the service sector in recent years is variously explained by the income elasticity, deindustrialization, cost disease, economies of scale, and labor supply hypotheses. The growth of the service sector has contributed to a growth in self-employment and weakened the role of the labor unions. It may have retarded the overall rate of economic growth, exacerbated the problem

---

[88]Andrew J. Winnick, *Toward Two Societies: The Changing Distributions of Income and Wealth in the U.S. since 1960* (New York: Praeger, 1989); and Ronald B. Mincy, "Raising the Minimum Wage: Effects on Family Poverty," *Monthly Labor Review* (July 1990): 18-25.

[89]Richard J. Herrnstein and Charles Murray, *The Bell Curve: Intelligence and Class Structure in American Life* (New York: Free Press, 1994), passim.

[90]Arthur S. Goldberger and Charles S. Maski, "Review: *The Bell Curve* by Herrnstein and Murray," *Journal of Economic Literature* 33 (June 1995): 762-776; Martin Neil Baily, Gary Burtless, and Robert E. Litan, *Growth With Equity: Economic Policy Making for the Next Century (Washington, D.C.: The Brookings Institution, 1993),* passim; and essays in Danziger and Gottschalk, eds., *Uneven Tides: Rising Inequality in America*, passim.

of price inflation, and contributed to income inequality, but it apparently stabilized the growth of employment and output.

A relatively competitive system gave way to rising industrial concentration after the Civil War, leading to the adoption of antitrust legislation around the turn of the century at a time when merger and concentration were encouraged in other countries. Partly for this reason, the United States has an average or relatively low level of industrial concentration (by international standards), and the level of concentration has been fairly stable or diminishing during most of the twentieth century. Lenient regulation since the early 1980s has allowed a new wave of merger activity.

In the labor market, trade unions play a relatively limited role (in comparison to their role in other industrial countries) and their share of the labor force has declined. Reasons for the decline in membership may include rising job satisfaction, employer resistance, and governmental assumption of responsibilities for worker protection. The relative competitiveness of the U.S. labor market is also suggested by the record of employment and wage flexibility.

In the financial sector, American federalism led to the creation of a dual system of state and national banks and a unique central banking system with elements of local ownership and control. Current proposals for deregulation in banking, including the establishment of a system of nationwide branch banking, are intended to increase the efficiency and international competitiveness of the system. Likewise, the focus of governmental authority was maintained at the state and local levels until the Great Depression and World War II. Governmental regulation of the economy expanded through most of the twentieth century, but a trend toward deregulation has received bipartisan support in recent years.

Monetary and fiscal tools of macroeconomic management were employed in the 1960s and 1970s, but in recent years the government has attempted to regain control of inflation and fiscal deficits. A formal system of indicative planning and industrial policy has never been established. Despite the influence of the progressive national income tax and the growing program of transfer payments, the distribution of income has been remarkably stable.

Discussion and Review Questions

1. How is the economic system in the United States affected by the large size of its market and the heterogeneity of its population?
2. How can we explain the fact that employment is more stable in the service sector than in the industrial sector?
3. What explains the decline in American unemployment in recent years relative to European unemployment? Will American unemployment rates remain below European levels?
4. How has American federalism influenced the system of financial regulation? What are the arguments for and against moving toward a system of nationwide branch banking?
5. What have been the strengths and weaknesses of American budgetary processes in recent years? Have they been successful?
6. How can we explain the fact that the American distribution of income has remained relatively stable, despite the progressive income tax system and the growth of governmental transfer payments?

Suggested Readings

Baily, Martin Neil, Gary Burtless, and Robert E. Litan. *Growth with Equity: Economic Policy Making for the Next Century*. Washington, D.C.: The Brookings Institution, 1993. *Reviews the evidence on the productivity slowdown and the growth of inequality in the United States, and prescribes an investment-oriented strategy to attack both problems.*

Balk, Alfred. *The Myth of American Eclipse*. New Brunswick, N.J.: Transaction Books, 1990. *The editor of the* World Press Review *argues that the United States is outperforming Japan in many areas, but he also argues for restructuring of priorities away from military production and toward education and social programs.*

Baumol, William J., Sue Anne Batey Blackman, and Edward N. Wolff. *Productivity and American Leadership: The Long View*. Cambridge, Mass.: The MIT Press, 1989. *A careful review of the evidence finds no clear long-run trend toward slower productivity growth, and little support for the deindustrialization thesis. Proposes a long-run strategy to strengthen productivity.*

Bergsten, C. Fred. *America in the World Economy: A Strategy for the 1990s.* Washington, D.C.: Institute for International Economics, 1988. *The author, a highly regarded Washington economist and former Treasury official, argues for a policy of trade liberalization, deficit reduction, exchange rate stabilization, export-oriented growth, and assistance to indebted Third World countries.*

Bourgin, Frank. *The Great Challenge: The Myth of Laissez-Faire in the Early Republic.* New York: George Braziller, 1989. *A fascinating reexamination of the economic and social philosophies of the Founding Fathers. Be sure to read the foreword by Arthur Schlesinger, Jr., explaining the controversial events at the University of Chicago over a 50-year period that led to publication of this book.*

Economic Report of the President. Washington, D.C.: USGPO, annual. *Includes an annual review of macroeconomic policy and a wealth of statistical material.*

Feldstein, Martin, ed. *American Economic Policy in the 1980s*. Chicago: University of Chicago Press, 1994. *A team of 39 leading economists and policymakers survey the lessons of the 1980s in 11 broad areas of policy for the National Bureau of Economic Research.*

Minarik, Joseph J. *Making America's Budget Policy*. Armonk, N.Y.: Sharpe, 1990. *Written by the executive director of the Joint Economic Committee of the U.S. Congress, this book provides a clear explanation of the fiscal policy process and chronological account of the controversies over tax reform, budget policy, and deficits.*

Papers and proceedings of the meetings of the American Economic Association, *The American Economic Review,* May issues, annual. *The record of the annual convocation of the nation's largest economics association, these volumes include accessible essays (quite unlike the technical reports that are found in the other issues of this journal) on a broad range of issues concerning the American economy.*

Rowen, Hobart. *Self-Inflicted Wounds: From LBJs Guns and Butter to Reagan's Voodoo Economics*. New York: Random House, 1994. *Written by a veteran journalist, this is an entertaining account of reversals in American economic policy.*

Tocqueville, Alexis de. *Democracy in America.* New York: Harper, 1966. *A penetrating analysis of the roots of American individualism, based on his visit in the 1830s.*

CHAPTER 8

LATIN AMERICA: THE JAGUARS AWAKEN

What, then, must have been the emotions of the Spaniards, when, after working their toilsome way into the upper air, the cloudy tabernacle parted before their eyes, and they beheld these fair scenes in all their pristine magnificence and beauty! It was like the spectacle which greeted the eyes of Moses from the summit of Pisgah, and in the warm glow of their feelings, they cried out, "It is the promised land!"
—William Hickling Prescott, *The Conquest of Mexico*, 1843

One of the most truly remarkable events of the last decade has been the political and economic democratization of Latin America. . . If the 1980s were the decade of the Asian tigers, then the 1990s will be the decade of the South American jaguars.
—Ron Brown, U.S. Secretary of Commerce, *Reuters Business Report*, July 20, 1994

The nations of Latin America and the Caribbean are engaged in programs of political and economic liberalization that may prove as historic as their struggles for independence from Spain and Portugal. After decades of political instability, corruption, and military dictatorship, many countries in the region seem to be developing stable democracies. Markets long protected from competition are opening to foreign trade, foreign investment, and regional cooperation.

In this chapter, we will briefly survey the history, environment, and institutional structures of Latin America, and we will evaluate the economic and social reforms transforming the region today. The transitional economies of Eastern Europe and Asia may have much to learn from the Latin American experience.

Environment and History

The Latin American region, encompassing a land area somewhat larger than the combined areas of Canada and the United States, may be usefully divided into three subregions: Middle America (Mexico and the 6 nations of Central America), South America (12 independent nations and French Guiana), and the Caribbean area (24 nations and territories, many of which are not "Latin").[1] The narrow Isthmus of Panama and the waters of the Caribbean have traditionally restricted interaction between these three subregions. Within South America, the northern nations (Colombia, Ecuador, Guyana, Venezuela, and Suriname) are separated from the so-called southern cone (Argentina, Bolivia, Brazil, Chile, Paraguay, and Peru) by the thinly populated rain forests of the Amazon River basin. The western rim of South America (including all of Chile) is divided from the remainder of the continent by the Andes Mountains, which extend more than 5,000 miles—the entire length of the continent—and are exceeded in average height only by the Himalayas.

Indigenous Cultures

In contrast to North America, which had a relatively small, migratory, and primitive native population, Middle and South America had large and advanced aboriginal civilizations. About two thousand years ago, the Mayas settled in the lowland tropics of Middle America, where steady cultivation of corn allowed them to end their migratory existence. The Mayas have been called the Greeks of Latin America because their culture emphasized intellectual, artistic, and athletic values. Their civilization dominated in present-day Guatemala between the third and tenth centuries A.D., with a population of perhaps two million. Skilled Mayan artists and technicians built magnificent pyramids and palaces, and their astronomers developed a calendar more accurate than the one that was used in Europe.

---

[1]We follow the convention of counting Belize among the Caribbean nations, despite its location on the Central American mainland.

The Aztecs, who organized a powerful society in the Valley of Mexico early in the fourteenth century, used advanced agricultural techniques, including controlled irrigation, and built an integrated system of canals for water transportation. Beginning in the fifteenth century, Montezuma I and his followers used ruthless military force to extract taxes and tribute from a large region of Middle America; thousands of captives were taken to Tenochtitlán and the other Aztec treasure cities for rituals of human sacrifice. When Hernán Cortés arrived in 1519 with only 508 Spanish soldiers, he was able to conquer the mighty Aztecs by leading the native people of the region in a revolt against their oppressors.

The largest and most highly organized empire in all of the Americas was led by the Incas, who began their ascendancy late in the twelfth century. When the Spaniards arrived in 1531, the Incas controlled an area with perhaps 20 million inhabitants (Spain then had a population of about 10 million), stretching about 2,000 miles from southern Colombia to central Chile. From their headquarters in Cuzco Basin of the Peruvian Andes, the Incas organized a large administrative bureaucracy, a rigidly controlled society, and a centrally planned economy. The population was divided into groups of ten, each with a squad leader, to perform communal agricultural labor. The land was divided into sections used for the Inca rulers, for the priestly class, and for the local community. Marriages were officially arranged, and families could live only where permitted. The Incas organized the construction of magnificent temples, long roads, suspension bridges, and terraced fields on the sides of mountains, supported by stone walls, and they operated a regular postal service. The empire was divided into two units early in the sixteenth century, and the resulting dissension made it possible for Francisco Pizarro, with 183 Spanish soldiers and two dozen horses, to gain victory over the Inca leadership in 1533.

In summary, the natives of Middle and South America had experience with social, economic, and political development, authoritarian organization, and colonial exploitation long before the Europeans arrived. The Spanish and Portuguese colonialists imported their European systems of political, economic, and religious organization into the Americas, but they preserved some aspects of the indigenous cultures. Together with later waves of European, African, and

Asian immigrants (Peru has a large and influential Japanese community), the nations of Middle and South America have developed a wide variety of "Latin American" cultures and institutions.

The Colonial Period

During the years just before their expeditions to the Americas, the Spaniards were engaged in a long struggle to free their country from the Moors (or Muslims) who had dominated most of Spain since the eighth century. Thus, the military commanders who traveled to the New World had extensive experience in conquest, looting, strict public administration, and forceful imposition of orthodox Catholicism. According to Lawrence Harrison, a well-known cultural determinist, "Latin America—and Spain until the last few decades—has suffered the consequences of a traditional Iberian culture that is anti-democratic, anti-social, anti-work, and anti-innovation."[2]

A full analysis of the colonial economic systems in Latin America would carry us far afield. Suffice it to say that the motives of the Spanish and Portuguese adventurers, like the Aztecs and Incas before them, were primarily extractive. That is, they had little interest in the broad economic development of the conquered areas; they demanded quick extraction of wealth, particularly of precious metals, and its secure passage to the colonial headquarters. Initially, this involved the looting and enslavement of native empires and populations, with little attention to agricultural development. One observer in the area that is now Peru described the payment of tribute to the Spaniards:

The Indians of Parinacocha have to carry their tribute over two hundred miles to Cuzco: wheat, maize, cloth, bars of silver, etc. Indian men are loaded with it, and so are the women, the

---

[2]Lawrence Harrison, "Latin America: Democracy and the Market Are Not Enough," *World Affairs* 155 (Spring 1993): 170.

pregnant ones with their heads on their swollen bellies. . . . [They] climb with their loads up slopes that a horse could not climb.[3]

The native populations suffered not only from the wars of conquest, from looting, and from slave labor, but, perhaps worst of all, from their lack of immunity to smallpox, malaria, yellow fever, and a score of other diseases introduced by Europeans and their African slaves. If roughly 20 million natives lived in Middle America when the Spaniards arrived, only 2.5 million remained a century later.[4]

The transportation systems in Latin America were initially developed to facilitate the growth of one-way extraction. To ensure that their bounty was not diverted to other countries, the colonial powers allowed the operation of only a small number of seaports, where they maintained tight control over shipping. Radiating outward from the major production and collection centers to the seaports, the colonialists built roads (and, later, railroads), but they built few of the internal transportation links needed for broader economic development. The systems of unilateral extraction and controlled shipping made it impossible for the colonies to gain the benefits of multilateral trade.

As the colonial period continued, a growing number of administrators were needed for positions in local government and the military, and to manage mining, road construction, and commercial activities. The highest of these positions were reserved for *gachupines* (Spaniards born in Europe), but secondary posts were also held by *criollos* (American-born settlers with pure Spanish ancestry). Positions as overseers and foremen were often held by *mestizos* (American-born settlers with mixed native and Spanish ancestry). Thus, the seventeenth century

---

[3]Quoted in Peter Worsley, *The Three Worlds: Culture and World Development* (Chicago: The University of Chicago Press, 1984), 8.

[4]H. J. Blij and Peter O. Muller, *Geography: Regions and Concepts*, 6th ed. (New York: John Wiley and Sons, 1991), 255.

witnessed the rise of a secondary aristocracy and a middle class whose ties to the New World were stronger than their ties to the Old.

When the looting of the Aztecs and Incas was complete, the best mining deposits were depleted, and a growing immigrant population demanded more food, the focus of economic activity in Latin America shifted toward farming and ranching. A dualistic system of *latifundios* and *minifundios* (very large and small farms) emerged, with the *criollos* controlling many of the former and the *mestizos* and native populations controlling the latter. As the masters of the agricultural sector, the *criollos* were able to exercise strict authoritarian rule over their farm workers, and they eventually were able to challenge the authority of European-born colonial leaders.

Independence

A number of forces converged in the closing years of the eighteenth century to fan the flames of Latin American independence. As we have just seen, a new domestic aristocracy arose to defy European rule. In 1776, the Declaration of Independence of the North American colonies provided a clear precedent for Latin American revolutionaries. Following the lead of Adam Smith's *Wealth of Nations*, also written in 1776, a number of Latin American authors established an intellectual basis for free trade, and called attention to the costs imposed by European commercial regulations.[5] Before the end of the colonial period, Britain forced Spain to open some of its ports to British ships, weakening the system of colonial control.

In 1804, Haiti became the first country in the region to win its independence; most of the others were free within 20 years. The most important leader of the revolutionary era was Simón Bolivar, a Venezuelan *criollo* who dedicated his military talents, aristocratic position, and substantial wealth to the cause of independence. Bolivar led revolutions in his native Venezuela

---

[5]These writings are discussed in Wendell C. Gordon, *The Economy of Latin America* (New York: Colombia University Press, 1950), 7-9.

and in Colombia, Ecuador, Panama, Peru, and Bolivia. All these countries officially invested him with the title *Libertador*, and he served as president of Bolivia, the country that adopted his name.

Thus, the Latin American nations gained the benefits of independence about 40 years later than the United States, but about a century earlier than much of Africa and Asia. Freedom from colonial controls allowed Latin America to expand and diversify its international trade linkages, but it caused few internal structural reforms. For example, the large agricultural estates were not divided into smaller, more equitable and manageable units. The new aristocracy preserved many of the inefficiencies of the colonial era after independence. Native populations, whose ancestors had been enslaved by the Aztecs, Incas, Spaniards, and Portuguese, were now subjugated to the *criollos*. These inequities eventually led to new revolutionary movements and major land reforms.

Import Substitution, State Control, and Revolution

As we noted in previous chapters, independence from colonialism allowed Latin American countries to seek new markets for their exports, launching an economic boom in the 1830s. Initially, the newly independent states avoided interference in domestic and international trade, but beginning in the 1870s they followed the lead of the United States, introducing tariffs to protect their "infant industries." According to the architect of the Brazilian tariff of 1879, "protective measures are never wrong for new countries like ours, where industry is not strong enough to face foreign competition."[6]

The era of export-led growth continued until the 1930s, when the Great Depression caused foreign export demand to collapse. Under pressure from industrialists and labor leaders, governments throughout Latin America strengthened their programs of trade protectionism and

---

[6]A. Bandeira de Mello, quoted in Paul Bairoch, *Economics and World History* (Chicago: University of Chicago Press, 1993), 91.

import-substituting industrialization (ISI). After World War II, the ISI strategy gained legitimacy and support from the well-known Argentine economist Raul Prebisch and his colleagues at the United Nations Economic Commission for Latin America (ECLA). The ECLA argued that Latin American countries would suffer from deterioration of their international terms of trade (the export/import price ratio) if they continued to rely on exports of primary goods.[7] Thus, the governments needed to take active measures to encourage and protect new industries. The ECLA advanced these ideas in its publications, press releases, meetings with government officials, and training programs for civil servants.

Under the broad banner of ISI, Latin American governments experimented with a wide range of interventionist programs during the 1950s and 1960s. The details vary from one country to another, but many of them established national planning offices, erected import barriers, created new public enterprises (sometimes by expropriating foreign companies), introduced programs of agrarian reform, and encouraged the development of workers' participation schemes and cooperative enterprises.

When these programs were introduced in a moderate way, without causing great social and financial instability, they were generally successful. Thus, real incomes nearly doubled in Latin America between 1950 and 1973, during the glory days of ISI (Table 8.1). On the other hand, in previous chapters we have discussed some of the weaknesses of this strategy: its reliance on small domestic markets and large regulatory bureaucracies; its tendency to cause overvaluation of exchange rates and to stifle the efficiencies of competition.

---

[7]The ECLAC continues to emphasize this issue today. See Economic Commission for Latin America and the Caribbean, *Economic Survey of Latin America and the Caribbean 1992*, vol. 1 (Santiago: United Nations, 1994), 138-139.

Table 8.1 GDP per Capita in Selected Countries of Latin America and the Caribbean, 1870-2004 (2004 International Dollars at Purchasing Power Parity)

	1870	*1913*	*1950*	*1973*	*1980*	*1990*	*2004*
Latin America & Caribbean	984*	2,140*	3,622	6,510	7,822	7,303	7,920
Caribbean							
Jamaica	773	896	1,918	5,969	4,511	5,216	3,952
Haiti	---	---	1,519	1,464	1,885	1,505	1,685
Middle America							
El Salvador	---	---	2,152	3,385	3,402	3,063	5,166
Guatemala	---	---	3,013	4,631	5,320	4,349	4,191
Honduras	---	---	1,898	2,373	2,789	2,704	2,827
Mexico	974	2,503	3,418	7,002	9,089	8,844	9,774
South America							
Argentina	1,895	5,488	7,208	11,507	11,860	9,302	12,723
Bolivia			2,774	3,407	3,717	3,175	2,704
Brazil	1,030	1,172	2,417	5,611	7,513	7,115	8,297
Chile	---	3,834	5,522	7,361	8,293	9,253	11,487
Colombia	---	1,786	3,112	5,057	6,164	6,995	7,121
Ecuador	---	---	2,693	4,755	5,968	5,641	3,885
Paraguay	---	---	2,289	2,946	4,775	4,751	4,868
Peru	---	1,499	3,271	5,712	6,077	4,271	5,641
Uruguay	3,152	4,784	6,734	7,189	9,506	9,357	9,465
Venezuela	822	1,596	10,785	15,356	14,654	12,015	5,963

*Very rough approximations based on available data.
Sources: Author's calculations based on real GDP per capita data for 2004 in World Bank, *World Development Indicators Online.* Angus Maddison, *The World Economy: Historical Statistics* (Paris: OECD, 2003), 141. A 1990-2004 conversion factor, obtained using U.S. Census data (U.S. Department of Commerce, Bureau of the Census, *Statistical Abstract of the United States 2006* (Washington, D.C.: USGPO, 2006), Table 706) was used to move previous edition data (valued at 1990 International Dollars) to current 2004 prices.

Perhaps the most serious deficiency of the ISI strategy was its failure to clearly specify the limits of state intervention. The strategy tended to encourage and legitimize the latent authoritarianism in Latin American culture, rooted in its colonial and precolonial heritage. Thus, the leaders of many Latin American countries introduced programs of state intervention and personal aggrandizement that extended far beyond the basic design of ISI. These took many forms.

In Argentina, Juan Domingo Perón won the 1946 presidential election as a Labour party candidate, having served as labor minister in a wartime military government. With support from industrialists and labor unions, Perón established an economic and political system modeled after

Italian fascism. Attempting to expand industry at the expense of agriculture, he paid large subsidies to favored sectors, imposed strict controls on exports and imports, and placed commercial banks under direct control of the central bank. In addition, he nationalized the railways and other foreign-owned industries, and established a liberal system of social insurance and labor benefits.

Perón's policies, together with a drop in world food prices, caused Argentine agricultural production to collapse. The balance of international payments, which had been in surplus, fell steeply into deficit in the early 1950s. With the country tilting toward bankruptcy, Perón was ousted from office by a military coup in 1955.[8]

A few years after the fall of Perón in Argentina, another charismatic autocrat ascended to power in Cuba. The revolutionaries who supported Fidel Castro in 1959 hoped to end the wanton terror, corruption, large-scale organized crime, and undemocratic practices that characterized the Batista regime. Castro quickly moved to consolidate power and to set up his own authoritarian government. Many leaders of the opposition to Batista were executed or imprisoned for opposing Castro's policies; hundreds of thousands of Cubans fled the island.

The centerpiece of Castro's economic policy was the agrarian reform of 1959, which expropriated all landholdings exceeding 1,000 acres and eventually converted them to state farms. The regime also nationalized urban land, banks, transport, and industry. Seizures of property from the United States alone were valued at about $1.8 billion. Other governmental

---

[8]The ouster of Perón was made possible by a number of factors, including the death in 1952 of his popular wife, Eva Duarte, or Evita, still known by audiences of the musical theater. He returned to power in 1973, but died ten months later, and his second wife, Isabel, who had been elected as his vice-president, became the first female head of state in the western hemisphere. The military removed Isabel Perón in 1976, and initiated its "dirty war" against leftists; about 20,000 people lost their lives. Democracy was restored in 1983, after the military lost its war against Britain for control of the Falklands/Malvinas Islands.

programs established rent controls, infant care and charity clinics, dining rooms for schoolchildren and indigents, and an expanded program of social security benefits.

Early in 1961, the United States ended diplomatic relations with Cuba and imposed a partial trade embargo; by the end of that year diplomatic relations were dissolved between Cuba and 13 countries in the Western Hemisphere, and relations were established with all of the Warsaw Pact Countries. In May, two weeks after the abortive "Bay of Pigs" invasion, Castro praised the Soviet leadership and proclaimed Cuba to be a socialist state. A year later, the Cold War reached its most critical stage during the Cuban missile crisis. The United States tightened and extended its trade embargo, depriving Cuba of about $35 million of annual export revenues.

Programs of import substitution and efforts to reduce Cuba's dependence on sugar exports have not been terribly successful. Sugar continues to account for about 75 percent of export earnings, although sugar production and exports have declined during recent years. For many years, weaknesses in Cuba's economy and the effects of the U.S. economic embargo were offset by heavy subsidies from the former Soviet Union and its allies. Those subsidies ended abruptly with the decline and dissolution of the Soviet system in the late 1980s and early 1990s. According to official statistics, Cuban national income increased by nearly 75 percent between 1975 and 1985, and then declined by roughly 55 percent between 1985 and 1993.[9]

If Perón was a fascist and Castro an orthodox communist, the most prominent representative of democratic socialism in Latin America was Dr. Salvador Allende of Chile. Supported by an alliance of socialist, communist, and other radical groups, Allende took

---

[9]*Historically Planned Economies: A Guide to the Data*, 1993 edition (Washington, D.C.: World Bank, 1993), 104-105; and Prensa Latina news agency, Havana, November 21, 1994, as transmitted by BBC Monitoring Service, November 29, 1994. Measurement of economic growth in Cuba is a matter of heated debate. See the interchange between Claes Brunendius and Andrew Zimbalist, on one side, and Carmelo Mesa-Lago and Jorge Perez-Lopez, on the other, in the Spring 1995 and Winter 1995 issues of *Comparative Economic Studies*.

advantage of divisions between centrist and conservative parties in 1970 to become the first democratically elected socialist president in Latin America.

Lacking a parliamentary majority, Allende's government bypassed Congress in its efforts to implement a broad socialist program of agrarian reform, nationalization, import protection, and wage increases. Some of Allende's ministers and high officials had previously worked for the ECLA and other United Nations agencies, and they saw these policies as an extension of the basic ISI strategy.[10]

Allende financed his programs with rapid monetary growth, which caused a ninefold increase in the general price level between 1970 and 1973. Efforts to slow the rate of inflation with price controls only created widespread shortages and a vast black market. Allende's policies also caused a reduction of unemployment, helping his alliance to gain voting strength in the parliamentary elections of March 1973. Nevertheless, in the face of accelerating inflation, a balance of payments crisis, a rash of disruptive government-supported strikes, and rising militancy from his opposition, Allende died (apparently at his own hand) during a military coup d'etat in September 1973.

Export Promotion and Market Reform

The first major challenge to the ISI strategy arose from another coup, this one in 1964, overthrowing the populist alliance in Brazil. The military leaders adopted an export-oriented development strategy and an open door to foreign investment. For several years, this strategy seemed rather successful. Growth of real GDP, which had been proceeding at an annual rate of 4.5 percent between 1960 and 1965, doubled to 9.3 percent between 1965 and 1975. Between the same time periods, the annual inflation rate fell from 64 percent to 24 percent. Furthermore, Brazil received more direct foreign investment than any other developing country during the

---

[10]Cristobal Kay, *Latin American Theories of Development and Underdevelopment* (London: Routledge, 1989), 199-200.

1970s. By the end of 1983, the stock of foreign holdings was more than $22 billion—twice the amount in Mexico, the second largest recipient. Nearly 75 percent of these investments were made in the manufacturing sector.[11] For all these reasons, economists spoke of a "Brazilian economic miracle" during the late 1960s and early 1970s.

Although the Brazilian leaders made an early shift from import substitution to export promotion, they did not adopt the other elements of a market-oriented or neoliberal development policy. The government continued to play a dominant economic role, with generous subsidy and tax incentive programs, broad reliance on wage, price, and credit controls, and continued support for nationalized companies. Perhaps "the biggest mistake in Brazil's modern history," according to a former finance minister, was the decision to build Brasilia, the ultramodern capital city that provides a comfortable staging ground for one of the world's most entrenched bureaucracies.[12] Fiscal imbalances, together with the oil price shocks of the 1970s, eventually led to rapid inflation and a debt crisis of the 1980s, and to an interruption of Brazilian growth. Programs of privatization and trade liberalization began in 1990, but despite several highly publicized plans, Brazil has been slow to implement programs of fiscal and monetary reform.

In Chile, a controversial step toward market reform began in 1973, when the ruthless regime of General Augosto Pinochet overturned the socialist government of Salvador Allende.[13] Pinochet, who had no personal blueprint for economic policy, appointed a cadre of young, U.S.-

---

[11]World Bank, *World Development Report 1985* (New York: Oxford University Press, 1985), 127.

[12]See Matt Moffett, "Brazil's New President Has Monster to Tame: Bureaucracy in Brasilia," *The Wall Street Journal*, October 5, 1994, A1.

[13]Humanitarian organizations estimate that more than 3,000 people died from human rights violations during Pinochet's rule, according to *The World Almanac and Book of Facts 1995* (Mahwah,N.J.: Funk & Wagnalls, 1994), 755.

trained technocrats—the so-called Chicago Boys.[14] They designed market-oriented reforms for virtually every sector of the Chilean economy. In the face of galloping inflation, they removed existing wage and price controls, attacking the inflation problem with strict fiscal and monetary policies. In the face of a large balance of payments deficit, they reduced tariffs and removed other import barriers, attacking the payments problem instead with a large devaluation of the exchange rate. The Chicago Boys also implemented major programs of deregulation, privatization, and social security reform. These actions were widely criticized when they were implemented by a despotic military regime, but they gained acceptability throughout Latin America after 1989, when the reforms were extended by a civilian government.

In many countries of Latin America, the decisive shift toward market reform began in the late-1980s and early-1990s when escalating inflation and the international debt crisis forced them to consider drastic measures (Tables 8.2 and 8.3). The apparent exhaustion of the ISI strategy, the accomplishments of the East Asian countries and Chile, the rise of a new cadre of leaders, pressure from the international lending institutions, led by the "Washington Consensus," and the desire to enter regional trade groups, such as NAFTA, all encouraged a revolution in Latin American economic policy.[15] Major programs of fiscal adjustment and trade liberalization began

---

[14]This heavy reliance on economists with U.S. training continued after 1989, when civilian democratic rule was restored. Of 23 ministers and senior members of the Aylwin administration, 18 had undertaken postgraduate work in the United States. See David E. Hojman, "The Political Economy of Recent Conversions to Market Economics in Latin America," *Journal of Latin American Studies* 26 (February 1994): 191-219.

[15]Like the Chicago Boys in Chile, many of the officials who designed reforms in other Latin American countries were graduates of top universities in the United States. See Matt Moffett, "Key Finance Ministers in Latin America Are Old Harvard-MIT Pals," *The Wall Street Journal*, August 1, 1994, A1.

in 1985 in Mexico and Bolivia, and spread to most of the other countries in the region during the early 1990s.[16]

Table 8.2 Consumer Price Inflation Rates in Selected Countries of Latin America and the Caribbean, 1950-2004
(Average Annual Percentage Rates)

	1961-1970	*1971-1980*	*1981-1990*	*1991-2000*	*2001-2004*
Latin America & Caribbean	8.0*	22.0*	201.5	103.3	4.1
Caribbean					
Dominican Republic	2.0	10.6	24.4	10.9	23.0
Haiti	2.6	10.9	6.9	20.7	21.5
Trinidad/Tobago	3.1	13.2	11.1	5.5	4.5
Middle America					
El Salvador	0.7	10.8	19.3	8.5	3.0
Guatemala	0.7	9.7	15.0	11.2	7.0
Honduras	2.3	8.1	7.7	18.6	8.5
Mexico	2.7	16.7	69.2	18.8	5.3
Nicaragua	1.9	18.8	2438.7	306.4	6.0
South America					
Argentina	21.5	141.7	787.0	21.5	10.5
Bolivia	5.5	20.2	1380.2	9.2	2.5
Brazil	47.3	48.0	613.9	549.3	9.3
Chile	27.1	174.9	20.5	9.4	2.5
Colombia	11.6	21.3	23.7	20.2	6.8
Ecuador	4.4	12.6	37.5	43.7	15.3
Paraguay	3.2	13.3	21.6	13.6	10.7
Peru	9.4	31.9	1223.5	60.3	2.0
Uruguay	47.8	63.9	62.4	38.1	11.5
Venezuela	1.0	8.5	24.9	45.0	22.0

*Partial calculations based on available data
Sources: World Bank, *World Development Indicators Online;* and International Monetary Fund, *International Financial Statistics,* various issues.

[16]For a useful summary of the timing of these reforms, see Sebastian Edwards, *Latin America and the Caribbean: A Decade after the Debt Crisis* (Washington, D.C.: World Bank, 1993), Table 3.1.

Table 8.3 Average External Debt as Percentage of GDP in Selected Countries of Latin America and the Caribbean, 1970-2003

	1970-1979	*1980-1989*	*1990-1999*	*2000-2003*
Latin America & Caribbean	25	48	37	41
Caribbean				
Dominican Republic	25	46	37	28
Haiti	18	35	31	36
Trinidad/Tobago	11	24	45	30
Middle America				
El Salvador	23	45	31	41
Guatemala	11	25	26	21
Honduras	36	74	113	84
Mexico	27	50	38	23
Nicaragua	54	213	351	166
South America				
Argentina	19	52	39	79
Bolivia	69	123	73	66
Brazil	23	37	29	45
Chile	40	80	44	57
Colombia	26	35	33	42
Ecuador	33	79	82	70
Paraguay	20	39	30	46
Peru	50	66	57	51
Uruguay	21	45	33	65
Venezuela	22	53	50	33

Sources: World Bank, *World Development Indicators Online.*

Agriculture

In Latin America as a whole, the proportion of the labor force working in agriculture dropped sharply between the 1960s and 1990s, with a large number moving into the service sector (Table 8.4). Still, at 25 percent, the agricultural share of the work force is nearly three times larger in Latin America than in the industrial countries of North America and Europe. Furthermore, in countries such as Benin, Bolivia, Dominican Republic, Haiti, Nicaragua, and Paraguay, agriculture employs 40 percent or more of the working populations. Among indigenous populations, more than 70 percent are still engaged in farming.

Table 8.4 Latin America and the Caribbean: Sectoral Value Added as a Percentage of Total GDP, 1965-2004

	1965	*1970*	*1980*	*1990*	*2004*
Agriculture	16	13	10	9	7
Industry	34	36	39	36	23
Services	50	51	51	55	70

Source: World Bank, *World Development Indicators Online.*

Plantation and Hacienda

After independence from Spain and Portugal, many native people continued to practice traditional subsistence agriculture in remote areas, and to work communally on village-owned lands, known as *ejidos* in Mexico. These native holdings were gradually absorbed by two major systems of land tenure developed during the colonial era. On the Caribbean islands and in the coastal regions of Brazil, Venezuela, Colombia, Guyana, Suriname, and Central America, agriculture was organized on large **plantations**. Generally, each plantation was oriented toward production of one or two cash crops for export, such as sugar or bananas. Thus, earnings were unstable, fluctuating with the prices of a few commodities, and production was highly seasonal, often requiring migration of workers. On the other hand, economies of large-scale production and extensive mechanization often provided a high level of efficiency and productivity on plantations.

On the mainland of Latin America, with less access to international markets, the Spaniards and *criollos* organized agriculture on self-sufficient ***haciendas***, as they were known in Mexico and Chile, or *estancias* in Argentina. A single *hacienda* community would include a large farm, or ***latifundio***, and the surrounding small farms, or ***minifundios***. The details differed from one country to another, but the *latifundio* often covered thousands of acres and was inhabited by the lord, or *patrón*, of the *hacienda*, his family and servants, and a resident staff of managers, foremen, and tenant workers. Unlike the plantation, which was characteristically organized to earn profits for its owners, the *hacienda* was dedicated to local self-sufficiency and to the power and prestige of the *patrón* and his family. Thus, it often operated inefficiently.

The *minifundio* was often little more than a garden plot, too small to support a family, so the owners were forced to seek work at the neighboring *latifundios*. Many countries had a system of *debt peonage*, preventing peasants from leaving the *hacienda* if they were indebted to the *patrón*. After World War II, Peru still had a feudal system that prevented workers from freely leaving the land, and they were transferred with the land when it was sold.[17]

Revolution and Land Reform

Each in their own way, the plantation and hacienda systems became symbols of all that was considered wrong in Latin America. The plantations symbolized foreign ownership and exploitation, and excessive dependence on foreign markets and single crops. The *haciendas* symbolized the old system of social class, privilege, strong-man leadership, debt peonage, income inequality, and inefficient production. Many of the major social movements in Latin America, from the Mexican revolution of 1910-1915 to the Cuban revolution of 1959, were supported by people who wished to overturn these systems of land tenure.

In Mexico, a presidential decree in 1890 expropriated the communal lands of the native villages, the *ejidos*, and transferred them to the *haciendas*. By 1910, 834 landowners controlled two-thirds of the country's area. Nearly 97 percent of rural heads of households owned no land at all. Popular resentment led to a series of political intrigues and violent conflicts, culminating in a 1915 presidential decree and a 1917 Constitution providing for a major program of land reform. Land that had been seized from the *ejidos* was restored to them. More important, the new Constitution called for the government to expropriate land holdings larger than 100 hectares (247 acres) from the *haciendas*, and redistribute them to the *ejidos*. Residents of the *ejidos* would be allowed to transfer ownership rights to their children as an inheritance, but to avoid new concentrations of land ownership, they would not be allowed to rent, sell, or mortgage the property.

---

[17]Gordon, *The Economy of Latin America*, 36-37.

The program of land expropriation began slowly in Mexico, but more than 60 million acres were redistributed by the end of 1939, and nearly half the cultivated land was redistributed by 1950. The *hacienda* system and the *latifundios* were virtually eliminated in many regions of Mexico, but they survived or resurfaced in other regions, including the poor southern state of Chiápas.

In most other countries of Latin America, land reforms did not begin until the late 1950s and 1960s, encouraged by the Alliance for Progress as a means to improve productivity and the distribution of income. Programs of land expropriation and redistribution were initiated, for example, in Bolivia in 1953, Venezuela in 1958, Cuba in 1959, Chile in 1964, and Peru in 1968. Nevertheless, in the 1970s more than 70 percent of the land under cultivation in Latin America was still held by less than 2 percent of landowners.[18]

When General Pinochet and his Chicago Boys came to power in Chile, land reform was one of many issues that received a new examination. In 1973, in connection with a broader program of privatization, the regime decided to return farms that had been seized by the Allende government to their original owners. Furthermore, the new government decided to halt any further expropriation of farms, and to privatize the lands that were under state ownership. By 1979, when the process was nearly complete, 30 percent of expropriated lands had been returned to previous owners, 44 percent had been transferred or sold to private owners, and 18 percent had been transferred to nonprofit institutions.[19]

Following the Chilean example, the legislature in Peru recently removed all limits on land ownership. Peruvian leaders have apparently concluded that large concentrations of land are

---

[18]Michael Todaro, *Economic Development in the Third World*, 2d ed. (New York: Longman, 1981), 260.

[19]Eduardo Bitran and Raúl E. Saez, "Privatization and Regulation in Chile," in Barry Bosworth, Rudiger Dornbusch, and Raúl Labán, eds., *The Chilean Economy: Policy Lessons and Challenges* (Washington, D.C.: The Brookings Institution, 1994), 335.

needed to attract the investments needed for modernization of agriculture. They express little concern about the possible return of *latifundios*, and they risk retaliation from the notorious Shining Path guerrillas, who adhere to a Maoist ideology.[20]

Back in Mexico, the market-oriented government of President Salinas hoped in 1992 to end expropriation of land and to reform the *ejido* system of communal land ownership. Claiming that concentrations of land ownership were no longer a problem, Salinas led the Mexican Congress to approve amendments to the 1917 Constitution that (1) formally ended the land redistribution program; (2) gave members of *ejidos* the right to become owners of their plots; and (3) allowed *ejido* members to buy land, rent their plots, and conclude contracts or joint venture agreements with domestic and foreign partners. The amendments did not remove the 100-hectare constitutional limit on individual holdings, but implied that no effort would be made to enforce the limit.

The new agrarian policy, together with other social inequities, led to a violent peasant uprising in Chiápas, beginning in January 1994. The peasants claimed that many illegal estates, some dating back to the Spanish conquest, were never redistributed. Indigenous customs and autonomy would be threatened, they said, if the *ejidos* were allowed to fragment. Early in 1995, President Zedillo departed from the policy of his predecessor, and initiated a new program of redistribution, beginning with more than 25,000 hectares of land in Chiápas.[21]

---

[20]Sally Bowen, "Peru Set to Sweep Away 27-Year-Old Land Reform Laws," *Financial Times*, July 18, 1995, 23; and Orin Starn, "Maoism in the Andes," *Journal of Latin American Studies* 27 (May 1995): 399-421.

[21]See Andrew Reding, "Chiápas Is Mexico," *World Policy Journal* 11 (Spring 1994): 11-25; and Natalya Johnson, "Rural Reforms Fail to Take Root," *Business Mexico*, March 1995, 1.

Industrial Organization

Latin American countries have a full spectrum of institutional arrangements in industry, including companies that are public or private, formal or informal, large or small, competitive or monopolistic, corporate or individual, and local or multinational. These structures were influenced profoundly by the import-substitution model of industrialization, which caused a major migration from rural areas to the cities, raising the urban share of the Latin American population from 48 percent in 1960 to 73 percent in 1992.

Most of the companies in Latin America are **microenterprises**, employing 15 employees or less; larger companies account for most of employment and sales. In Mexico, for example, 97 percent of the companies operating in the early 1990s were microenterprises, but these accounted for only 11 percent of total employment.[22]

The Informal Economy

The microenterprises, together with self-employed workers, unpaid family workers, and domestic servants, comprise most of the so-called **informal sector**, which has consistently accounted for about one-third of Latin American urban employment since the 1960s (Table 8.5). Much of the attention now given to the informal sector has arisen from the work of Hernando de Soto, director of the Institute for Liberty and Democracy (ILD) in Lima, Peru.[23] According to de

---

[22]Leticia Rodriguez, "Helping Out Micro-, Small and Medium-Sized Business Financing to Secure the Future," *Business Mexico*, September 1994, 1; and Guillermo Rosenbluth, "The Informal Sector and Poverty in Latin America," *CEPAL Review* 52 (April 1994): 168.

[23]Keith Hart, an anthropologist, was the first to speak of an "informal sector" in 1971, and important empirical research on informality was performed by the Regional Employment Program of the International Labor Office, but de Soto's market-oriented approach to the subject, calling for elimination of state regulatory barriers, gained a receptive audience in the Washington-based international development agencies. See Alejandro Portes and Richard

Soto, the formal sectors in Latin America are based on a mercantilist system, rooted in national cultures and the regulatory structures of import substitution, that reserves monopoly privileges for a chosen few.

Table 8.5 Latin America: Urban Informal Employment as a Percentage of the Urban Economically Active Population, 1960-1990

	1960	*1970*	*1980*	*1990*
Argentina	21	19	39	40
Bolivia	62	56	57	27
Brazil	27	28	43	46
Chile	35	24	27	30
Colombia	39	31	34	27
Costa Rica	29	23	20	22
Ecuador	35	58	53	--
El Salvador	43	40	40	--
Guatemala	52	44	40	54
Mexico	37	35	36	36
Panama	25	27	36	39
Peru	47	41	41	39
Uruguay	19	21	32	35
Venezuela	32	31	30	33
Latin America	31	30	30	31

Source: Estimates of the Regional Employment Program of the International Labor Office (known by the Spanish acronym, PREALC), compiled in Alejandro Portes and Richard Schauffler, "Competing Perspectives on the Latin American Informal Sector," *Population and Development Review* 19 (March 1993): 42; and Guillermo Rosenbluth, "The Informal Sector and Poverty in Latin America," *CEPAL Review* 52 (April 1994): 168.

In particular, monopoly privileges have been protected by complex and costly registration procedures that make it difficult to create legal business enterprises. In 1983, researchers for de Soto's ILD attempted to obtain eleven permits from eight governmental agencies to establish a fictitious clothing factory as a single proprietorship (incorporation would have been much more difficult). The registration process required 289 days of full-time labor and $1,231 of fees, expenses, lost income, and bribes (they paid two of the ten bribes solicited)—the equivalent of 32

Schauffler, "Competing Perspectives on the Latin American Informal Sector," *Population and Development Review* 19 (March 1993): 40.

minimum monthly wages. Legal establishment of a small store required negotiations with three agencies, lasting 43 days, and costing $590 (15 minimum monthly wages).[24]

According to de Soto, when industrialization drew millions of rural Latin Americans into the cities, they encountered a hostile reception from the elite urban populations. Unable to find jobs, and unable to pay the prices of formality, they created informal enterprises. To the extent possible, they also created informal systems of governance, property rights, contractual relationships, and financial institutions. De Soto estimates that 30 informal banking systems were established in Peru.

De Soto considers informal enterprises to be productive and entrepreneurial, but severely disadvantaged by their legal status. To avoid detection and punishment, their operations must be kept small and mobile; they cannot freely advertise their product, operate in the best locations, maintain complete financial records, or benefit from the formal systems of civil and criminal justice. On the other hand, they must pay bribes and fines to officials and usurious interest rates to lenders.

To remedy these problems, de Soto has led a campaign to simplify procedures and reduce fees for companies to join the formal sector. In the simplest cases, it is now possible for Peruvian entrepreneurs to register their businesses in a single day. The number of businesses completing registration in Peru increased from a monthly average of about 2,000 in 1990 to 11,000 in 1993.[25] Similar reforms have been undertaken in other Latin American countries.

---

[24]Hernando de Soto, *The Other Path: The Invisible Revolution in the Third World* (New York: Harper & Row, 1989), 132-143. The title of this book refers to the contrast between de Soto's free market ideas and those of Shining Path, the Peruvian Maoist group. In 1992, an unsuccessful attempt on de Soto's life with a 400kg car bomb was attributed to Shining Path. See Stephen Fidler, "Practical Visionary," *The Financial Times*, September 29, 1993, supplement, 8.

[25]Ibid.

Big Business and the Multinationals

There are millions of business organizations in Latin America, but the 500 largest companies account for about one-third of the gross product of the entire region (Table 8.6). Brazil, which has about one-third of the Latin American population, has more than half the region's largest companies. Mexico has less than 20 percent of the population in the region, and less than 20 percent of the large companies, but it accounts for nearly 30 percent of large company sales.

Table 8.6 Latin America: 500 Largest Companies, 1992

	Number of Companies	*Sales (US$ Mill.)*	*Sales as % of GDP**
Location:			
Brazil	255	165,552	43
Mexico	86	113,458	34
Argentina	64	37,119	16
Venezuela	24	31,579	14
Chile	30	16,423	40
Colombia	25	9,572	20
Peru	9	4,075	18
Panama	1	3,213	54
Ecuador	1	1,880	15
Uruguay	4	1,414	12
Bolivia	1	645	12
Ownership:			
Private	268	143,314	12
Foreign	140	105,166	9
State	92	136,451	12
Total	500	384,931	33

*Sales for each country taken as percentage of national GDP; sales by ownership are taken as percentage of total GDP for the countries listed.
Sources: *America Economia* (Special issue, 1993/1994), 72; World Bank, *World Development Report 1994*, 166-167; and author's calculations.

More than half the large companies in Latin America are owned domestically by private individuals and corporations. They generally dominate in such fields as construction, communications, retail distribution, and steel production. Less than one-fifth of the large companies are state-owned, but these account for more than one-third of large-company sales. Despite major programs of privatization, the three largest companies in Latin America in 1992 were PDVSA, Pemex, and Petrobras, the state-owned petroleum monopolies of Venezuela,

Mexico, and Brazil; in many countries, the public sector continues to dominate in electricity generation and mining.

About one-quarter of the large companies are owned by foreigners, and they account for about one-fourth of large-company sales, or 9 percent of Latin American GDP. The sales of a single multinational corporation, McDermott International, amount to more than half the GDP of Panama, its host country. Multinationals dominate in production of automobiles, office equipment, pharmaceuticals, beverages, and electronics.

In recent years, a particular group of foreign enterprises, the ***maquiladoras***, have attracted a great deal of attention. These began to appear after 1966, when a treaty between Mexico and the United States created special zones in northern Mexico where U.S. raw materials and components could be imported duty-free, assembled into final products, and imported back into the United States with a tariff levied only on the value added by Mexican labor. Between 1982 and 1995, the number of *maquiladora* factories increased dramatically, from 588 to more than 2,000; employment in the factories increased from 122,000 to more than 600,000.[26] In the meanwhile, *maquiladoras* have been established in several other countries of Central America and the Caribbean.

The *maquiladoras* became a major issue during negotiation of the North American Free Trade Agreement (NAFTA). In the United States, they symbolized the flight of manufacturing jobs to factories in Latin America with low wages, unsafe working conditions, and weak environmental regulations. Side agreements to NAFTA were negotiated to ameliorate these problems. Under terms of the final agreement, the *maquiladora* regions will lose their special tariff status in the year 2001, and all of Mexico will, in effect, become a free-trade zone.

---

[26]Kevin G. Hall, "Boom Goes On: Industry Still Pouring Development onto Mexican Border," *Chicago Tribune*, June 18, 1995, 7A.

State Ownership and Privatization[27]

State participation in ownership and control of industry has a long history in Latin America. The Incas and the Aztecs had centrally planned economies, and the mercantile Spaniards pursued economic extraction in the name of the crown. In 1911, the president of Uruguay, José Battle y Ordóñez, outlined the economic role of the "modern state":

Modern conditions have increased the number of industries that fall under the heading of public services. . . The modern state unhesitatingly accepts its status as an economic organization. It will enter industry when competition is not practicable, when control by private interests vests in them authority inconsistent with the welfare of the State, when a fiscal monopoly may serve as a great source of income to meet urgent tax problems, when the continued export of the national wealth is considered undesirable.[28]

During the 1930s, dissatisfaction with the practices of foreign owners and employers led to the expropriation and nationalization of energy companies, telephone systems, and a range of other public utilities. For example, a dispute over wages and benefits in 1938 led to seizure of the Mexican oil industry from 17 companies, and to the creation of a state-owned petroleum monopoly, Petróleos Mexicanos (PEMEX), which is still the largest company in Mexico.

Also beginning in the 1930s, the program of import-substituting industrialization led to the establishment of many state-owned manufacturing companies. This process continued after

---

[27]General sources of data and information for this section include Edwards, *Latin America and the Caribbean: A Decade after the Debt Crisis*, 77-92; Frank Sader, *Privatization and Foreign Investment in the Developing World, 1988-92*, WPS 1202, Debt and International Finance Division, International Economics Department, World Bank, Washington, D.C., October 1993, passim; and "1994 Privatization in Latin America," *LatinFinance* 55 (March 1994), supplement..

[28]Quoted in Simon G. Hanson, *Utopia in Uruguay* (New York: Oxford University Press, 1938), 24.

World War II, and accelerated during the 1960s. Hundreds of domestic and foreign companies were nationalized by Marxist regimes in countries such as Cuba, Chile, and Nicaragua. In Chile, for example, the number of state-owned enterprises (SOEs) increased from 67 to 529 between 1970 and 1973.[29]

The first important wave of Latin American privatizations began in the mid-1970s, when Salvador Allende was overthrown in Chile and his socialist policies were repudiated by the Pinochet regime. Between 1973 and 1978, Pinochet and his Chicago Boys privatized nearly 500 enterprises. About half of these had been seized without compensation during the Allende years, and they were returned without compensation. The other half were sold, primarily to domestic companies and investors, for a total of nearly $1 billion.

A second wave of privatization began in the mid-1980s, when Latin American governments were trying to reduce their runaway budget deficits, their accelerating inflation rates, and their foreign debts. Privatization of money-losing SOEs would allow the governments to stop paying costly budget subsidies, and revenues from privatization could be used to repay international debts or to finance domestic budget deficits.

Once again, Chile led the way between 1984 and 1989 by selling about 80 large SOEs, including public utilities, the national airline, and the country's largest steel mill, for about $1.4 billion. This time, foreign investors were invited to participate, and many of the sales were structured as **debt-for-equity swaps**. That is, the government repaid a portion of its foreign debt by exchanging stock in its privatized companies for bonds and other debt instruments held by foreigners. To allay public fears of excessive foreign ownership, and to broaden the domestic base of capital ownership, the government offered special financial terms and discounts to individual Chilean investors under its programs of "popular capitalism" and "worker

[29]Bitran and Saez, "Privatization and Regulation in Chile," 332-333.

capitalism."[30] Nevertheless, the Chilean privatization program virtually ended in 1989 when the country returned to democratic rule. The country's largest company, Codelco, which is a huge copper mining enterprise, was still under state ownership.

In Mexico, the number of SOEs climbed from about 240 in 1960 to 391 in 1970, and then to a peak of 1,155 in 1982. When Mexico faced a debt crisis in 1982, President López Portillo followed tradition and nationalized most of the banks, compensating their owners with ten-year government bonds. Unsurprisingly, this action only worsened a horrible situation, causing a wild flight of capital from Mexico. A few months later, the new government led by President Miguel de la Madrid reversed the trend, and initiated programs of macroeconomic stabilization and privatization. The government began with closure, liquidation, and merger of small and medium-sized companies. It delayed the sale of banks and larger enterprises, because their values were depressed by the continuing economic crisis. Still, by the end of the de la Madrid administration in 1988, the number of SOEs had been cut by nearly two-thirds, to 412 enterprises, and more than $2 billion of privatization proceeds had been collected.[31]

The Mexican program accelerated between 1988 and 1994, during the administration of President Carlos Salinas de Gortari. Some 360 state enterprises, many of them very large, including the national telephone company, the two airlines, a gigantic steel complex, and the 18 domestic banks that had been seized during the Portillo administration, were sold to the highest domestic or international bidders. The total proceeds for the sales were nearly $19 billion, most

---

[30]William F. Maloney, "Privatization with Share Diffusion: Popular Capitalism in Chile, 1985-1988," in *Privatization in Latin America: New Roles for the Public and Private Sectors*, ed. by Werner Baer and Melissa Birch (Westport, Conn.: Praeger, 1994), 135-161.

[31]"Number of Unsold Mexican Firms at 222," *Reuters Financial Report*, September 18, 1992, 1.

of which was derived from the sale of banks and the telephone company.[32] These revenues have been used exclusively to repay internal debts, not to finance new spending programs.

The Mexican program enjoyed substantial political support because it was designed in cooperation with labor unions and the private sector. Under Mexican law, the labor unions have the right of first refusal on any privatization; unions bought controlling interests in 16 companies and substantial shares of others. The government also extracted informal commitments from purchasers of SOEs that they would not lay off large numbers of workers. The Mexican constitution prohibits the sale of PEMEX, the petroleum monopoly, which is Latin America's largest employer, and Ferronales, the national railroad, which is Latin America's largest transport company.

The third wave of Latin American privatization began in the early 1990s, when domestic financial problems, pressure from international lending institutions, and the successful experiences of Chile and Mexico caused other countries to start or accelerate their programs. In Argentina, for example, the annual losses of SOEs imposed a drain on the public budget equal to 9 percent of GDP, or 64 percent larger than public expenditures on health and education.[33]

Argentine privatization began in 1990, and, unlike the programs in Chile and Mexico, it began with some of the largest and most controversial companies. During the first year, the government offered 60 percent of the national telephone company, which accounted for about one-third of the country's SOE deficit, and exchanged it for debt reduction with a market value of

---

[32]"Finance Secretary Provides Details on the Results of Privatization Programs since 1988," *SourceMex*, July 27, 1994, 1. These U.S. dollar figures should only be taken as rough approximations; the privatizations were performed during years of extreme exchange rate instability.

[33]These losses were larger, as a proportion of GDP, than those in most developing countries. See United Nations Development Programme, *Human Development Report 1993* (New York: Oxford University Press, 1993), Table 3.4.

$1.3 billion.[34] Even more unlike the Chileans and Mexicans, who have been unwilling or unable to sell their copper and petroleum monopolies, the Argentines quickly initiated sales of their state-owned petroleum producers, distributors, and refineries. They also sold national airlines, railroads, power utilities, television networks, and steel mills. By the end of 1993, after only a few years of work, the government completed privatizations with a market value of $8.9 billion, and used them to retire public debt with a face value of approximately $17 billion.

Brazil, the largest economic power in Latin America, was slow to begin its program of privatization, but it sold about $7 billion of SOE assets in the steel, petrochemical, and fertilizer industries between 1990 and 1994, and it announced plans in 1995 to sell assets worth another $15 billion. Privatizations have also been performed in Ecuador ($100 million), Honduras ($12 million), Peru ($3.1 billion), and Venezuela ($2.3 billion). Of the twenty largest privatizations transacted in the world between 1984 and 1993, ten took place in Latin America.[35]

To privatize six of its public utility companies, Bolivia has developed an interesting new model known as **capitalization**. According to the 1994 law that controls this system, a 50 percent share of each public utility is sold to a "strategic investor," who has managerial control of the enterprise. Unlike a traditional privatization, none of the proceeds from the strategic investor are paid to the government; the capital remains within the company where it can be used for investment and production. The other half of the shares held by the state are transferred to all Bolivian adults by crediting their individual "capitalization accounts," which are managed by private pension funds. This scheme is designed to attract new capital and managerial resources into the SOEs, to spread the system of capital ownership to the entire population, and to encourage the development of pension funds and other financial institutions.

---

[34]The retired government bonds had a face value of $5 billion. This was the largest debt-equity privatization ever undertaken.

[35]Jorge F. Segura, "The Past, Present, and Future of Privatization," *LatinFinance* 53 (December 1993), S32.

The Labor Market

Before World War II, when the Latin American economies were predominantly agrarian, the labor market in each country was largely a reflection of its system of land tenure (hacienda, plantation, family farm) and the socio-ethnic composition of the population (native, European, African, *criollo*, *mestizo*). Extreme inequalities still exist in the agrarian sectors of Latin America; 61 percent of the rural population lives in absolute poverty, compared with 30 percent of the urban population.[36]

In industry, a number of historic influences have made it difficult to develop stable systems of collective bargaining. Before and during the colonial era, mining and manufacturing were often based on systems of slavery and other forms of forced labor. In the nineteenth century, legal codes in many countries prohibited workers from signing binding contracts with their employers. These codes originally were meant to protect poor and illiterate workers from contracts they could not read, but they retarded the development of collective bargaining and long-term agreements.[37]

In most countries of Latin America, organization of labor unions was patently illegal until the early years of the twentieth century. The earliest unions, encouraged by the Catholic Church, were organized to allow workers to pool their resources in a social insurance system; they usually made no attempt to bargain with employers. Eventually, more militant unions began to organize in mining towns and textile mills. When they attempted to organize strikes, the governments often supported employers with military force.[38]

Relationships between labor and management began to change in many ways during the 1930s. The Great Depression undermined the old institutional structure of society, and an

---

[36]United Nations Development Programme, *Human Development Report 1994*, 210.

[37]Gordon, *The Economy of Latin America*, 146.

[38]This was the case, for example, in Mexico, where the Diaz regime used military force to suppress strikes in 1906 and 1907.

increasing number of countries adopted labor codes that protected rights of workers. At the same time, the import-substitution industrialization strategy encouraged migration from rural areas to the cities, which contributed to the development of the informal sector. Companies in the informal economy had little need for collective bargaining or long-term contracts, and they would seldom comply with the new minimum wage and labor laws.

The import competition system also created and legitimized a strong industrial role of the state, and encouraged the establishment of state-owned enterprises. Thus, the state had to deal directly with the labor unions. In some cases, this took the form of a paternalistic relationship, as in the Perón and Allende administrations; more often, the relationship was antagonistic or openly violent. This relationship could change radically from one day to the next, as it did when Allende was overthrown by General Pinochet:

In the wake of the coup, factory owners suddenly had absolute control over their workers and could fire any worker without cause. From 1973 through 1978, practically every labor right for organized and unorganized workers was suspended. All the tools of collective bargaining, including of course the right to strike, were outlawed.[39]

Together with other social and historic factors, the diverse and unstable relationships between governments and labor unions may explain why union membership levels are very low in some countries and very high in others. In Colombia, Guatemala, and Paraguay, less than 10 percent of the labor force is unionized; in Honduras, Peru, and Venezuela, membership rates are higher than 30 percent.[40]

At any rate, Latin American governments have seldom been able to play the role of an impartial referee between independent businesses and labor unions. The establishment of stable

---

[39]John Lear and Joseph Collins, "Working in Chile's Free Market," *Latin American Perspectives* 84 (Winter 1995): 13.

[40]Statistics on union membership are notoriously unreliable, but these data are taken from the country pages of U.S. Central Intelligence Agency, *The World Factbook 1992*, passim.

civilian governments throughout Latin America, the shift to market-oriented development strategies, and the opening of the economies to import competition and free movement of labor seem to call for new relationships between public and private organizations.

As a first step toward a more cooperative relationship, the governments in some countries have begun to consult more closely with business and labor leaders on their stabilization and privatization programs. In Mexico, for example, the de la Madrid government signed an Economic Solidarity Pact in 1987 with representatives of organized labor, agricultural producers, and the business sector. The pact included macroeconomic targets, plans for privatization, trade liberalization, and, perhaps most important, a set of wage and price guidelines to break inflationary pressures and expectations. According to formal econometric studies, the wage-price guidelines play a significant role in explaining the rapid decline of Mexican inflation from 159 percent in 1987 to 52 percent in 1988 and 20 percent in 1989.[41] Thus, when President Salinas took power in 1988, he quickly announced a new Pact for Economic Stability and Growth to sustain progress; the agreements have been updated each year by the Salinas and Zedillo administrations, in consultation with private sector representatives.

Based on its success in Mexico, the practice of negotiating public-private pacts has spread to other countries in the region. According to Luis Anderson, a Panamanian union leader, the pacts are useful, but they should not be allowed to perpetuate the paternalistic role of Latin American governments; instead, they should be "a product of understanding between the state, the business sector, unions and other bodies on an equal footing."[42]

In addition to the antagonistic system of collective bargaining, some economists believe that two other factors seriously reduce the flexibility and efficiency of Latin American labor

---

[41]Nora Lustig, *Mexico: The Remaking of an Economy* (Washington, D.C.: The Brookings Institution, 1992), 52.

[42]Humberto Marquez, "Latin America: Unions Respond to Changing Winds," Inter Press Wire Service, April 27, 1995.

markets. First, in international perspective, labor laws in these countries impose very high costs on formal-sector employers for dismissing their employees. Laws prohibiting temporary employment and requiring large severance payments for "unjust" dismissals are meant to promote stability of employment, but they may also discourage the creation of new jobs. Latin American severance payments are larger than similar payments in Germany, Spain, and the United Kingdom.[43]

The other factor reducing the efficiency of Latin American labor markets is the relatively high level of social security payroll taxes. In the early 1990s, these ranged from 14 percent in Venezuela to 46 percent in Argentina, with an average of about 23 percent. These are designed, of course, to fund the social security systems, but they are thought to discourage job formation and distort the labor market more severely than other forms of taxation and financing.[44] Chile, for example, has shifted to a system based on personal saving, rather than on taxation.[45]

Inflation and the Financial Sector

Through much of recent history, the financial markets in Latin American countries have been crippled and distorted by the direct and indirect effects of rapid inflation. During the period between 1965 and 1992, the average annual rate of inflation was about 8 percent in developing countries of East Asia and South Asia, 13 percent in Sub-Saharan Africa, and 120 percent in Latin America.[46] Furthermore, the Latin American inflation rate (which places a large weight on Brazil, the largest country) has accelerated during each decade since the 1960s (Table 8.2).

---

[43]Edwards, *Latin America and the Caribbean: A Decade After the Debt Crisis*, 93-95.

[44]Ibid., 95-96.

[45]See G. A. Mackenzie, "Reforming Latin America's Old-Age Pension Systems," *Finance & Development* 32 (March 1995): 10-13.

[46]Calculations from data in Appendix Table 1 of the 1989 and 1992 editions of World Bank, *World Development Report*.

Why have the Latin American countries been plagued with so much inflation for so many years? To a monetarist, the answer is simple: Central banks in the region have allowed the creation of too many pesos, cruzeiros, reais, soles, and córdobas. Although this is undoubtedly true, it only raises another question: Why are central bankers in Latin America more inclined to print money than their colleagues in Africa and Asia?

A different explanation of chronic inflation is offered by **structuralism**, a school of economic thought developed in Latin America, and "the first original body of development theory to emanate from the Third World."[47] Instead of concentrating their attention on the excess creation of money, structuralists emphasize the importance of inefficient land tenure systems, limited industrial capacities, and structural imbalances between agriculture and industry that restrict the growth of productivity. The most serious problem, they say, is not excessive growth of the monetary demand for goods, but deficient growth of the material supply. The solution, therefore, is structural reform, including land reform and development of the industrial base. Programs of financial austerity that interfere with these structural reforms may slow the rate of inflation in the short run, but they will exacerbate the problem in the long run.[48]

The structuralist position provides a useful counterweight to simplistic applications of monetarism, but the questions remain: Why have average inflation rates persisted at higher levels in Latin America than in other developing countries? Are the problems of land tenure and industrial capacity more serious in Latin America than in Africa or South Asia? Can supply limitations explain chronic inflation rates above 100 percent?

Aside from the general messages of monetarism and structuralism, three other considerations may help to explain the Latin American inflation problem. First, political regimes

---

[47]Kay, *Latin American Theories of Development and Underdevelopment*, 10.

[48]Ibid., 47-57; and Raymond F. Mikesell, "Inflation in Latin America," in Charles T. Nisbet, ed. *Latin America: Problems in Economic Development*, (New York: The Free Press, 1969), 143-189,

in the region have been notoriously unstable, causing political leaders to seek short-run solutions, such as the printing of money, for long-run development problems. With 150 regimes in 160 years, Bolivia was, until recently, the standard against which unstable countries were measured. After a stable democratic government was established in 1985, the Bolivian inflation rate fell dramatically (Table 8.2). The political situation in Latin America has improved profoundly in recent years, but as recently as 1990, the president of Venezuela predicted a resurgence of instability: "Latin America is a volcano," he said, "that is about to erupt."[49] In 1994, international bankers still considered Honduras, Peru, and Bolivia to be greater credit risks than Lebanon, Bangladesh, Kenya, and Ghana.[50]

A second consideration: Strong dependence on the import-substitution industrialization strategy, which was promoted by many of the structuralists, may have reduced the level of financial discipline in Latin America, and contributed to chronic inflation. In countries that emphasize market-oriented export promotion, the governments face greater pressure to maintain stable prices, which are needed to maintain export competitiveness. Under a regime of import substitution, with high protective tariffs and nontariff barriers, competitiveness on world markets is not a major policy concern.[51] Thus, writing in the 1960s, Mikesell noted that an inward orientation encourages inflation, and inflation reinforces the inward orientation: "Inflation coupled with overvalued exchange rates and a variety of governmental controls and import

---

[49]Anthony Boadle, "Latin America's Democracy Threatened by Social Powder Keg," Reuters News Service, March 13, 1990.

[50]Ratings reported in Harvey D. Shapiro, "Wages of Virtue; Sovereign Creditworthiness," *Institutional Investor* 28 (March 1994), 87.

[51]Anne O. Krueger, "Import Substitution versus Export Promotion," Finance & Development 22 (June 1985): 23; and Ching-yuan Lin, "East Asia and Latin America as Contrasting Models," *Economic Development and Cultural Change* 36 (April 1988, Supplement): S160-S165.

restrictions has created in Latin America closed economies whose level and structure of internal prices and costs bears little relationship to that of the outside world, including those of other Latin American economies."[52]

A third consideration: Inflation became institutionalized in Latin America through extensive use of **indexation**. In Chile, indexation of wages began as early as the 1940s, and by 1959 the official consumer price index determined the legal wage adjustment for all public sector workers and for private workers not covered by collective bargaining. In Brazil, indexation began in the 1960s and continued for 30 years, eventually covering nearly every transaction in the economy. Brazilian workers, landlords, and retired people were protected from inflation by indexation of wages, rents, and pensions, with adjustments sometimes made on a monthly basis. Sellers and savers were protected by indexation of contract prices, interest rates on bank accounts, and yields on other securities. The government protected itself by indexing tax rates.

With so many interest groups protected from the direct effects of inflation, Latin American governments fell under little pressure to tighten their monetary policies. Indexation perpetuated and sometimes accelerated the inflation problem by driving up wage costs and raw material prices. When countries in the region shifted to an export orientation, and realized that inflation was an obstacle to competitiveness, they began to dismantle their programs of indexation. This process began in Chile in 1979, in Mexico in 1983, and in Brazil in 1995.[53]

Financial Repression and Liberalization

Aside from its influence on the internal distribution of income and on external competitiveness, inflation also tends to distort the operation of financial markets. If the inflation rate is extremely

---

[52]Mikesell, "Inflation in Latin America," 175.

[53]Alejandra Mizala and Pilar Romaguera, "Testing for Wage Leadership Processes in the Chilean Economy," *Applied Economics* 27 (March 1995): 303; Lustig, *Mexico: The Remaking of an Economy*, 29; and "Brazil: Kicking the Habit," *Business Latin America*, July 24, 1995, 1.

high, as it was in Nicaragua, Bolivia, and Peru during the 1980s, money begins to lose its usefulness as a medium of exchange, as a unit of account, and as a store of value, threatening the entire financial system with collapse. At lower rates of inflation, a number of other serious problems may arise.

If nominal interest rates are left uncontrolled by the government, they will usually hover a few points above the anticipated inflation rate. Thus, when inflation accelerates, market interest rates tend to rise. High interest rates, though, have been scorned by philosophers and regulated by public authorities since ancient times. In Latin America, interest rate controls were already in place at the end of World War II.[54]

If nominal interest rates are controlled while inflation accelerates, real interest rates may become negative. This was the situation in Bolivia and Peru during all the years between 1980 and 1986, and it was the situation in the average Latin American country during 1979 and 1980.[55] When real interest rates become negative, credit markets and market-oriented financial institutions cannot play their normal role in the market economy: They cannot stimulate savings or efficiently allocate financial resources to their most profitable uses. Thus, the government generally increases its intervention: Credit is rationed to borrowers who are favored by the government, foreign exchange markets are heavily regulated, and barriers are erected against the creation of new financial markets, such as securities markets, that may circumvent the system of governmental controls.

The debt crisis of the 1980s and the accompanying acceleration of inflation made all these problems much more serious. When Latin American countries no longer had access to foreign credit, it became clear that they would have to develop pools of domestic savings. To do this, they needed to restore positive real interest rates, and develop a wider range of financial

---

[54]Gordon, *The Economy of Latin America*, 242.

[55]In Bolivia, the real interest rate sank as low as -97.5 percent in 1985. See Edwards, *Latin America and the Caribbean: A Decade After the Debt Crisis*, 101.

institutions. Thus, interest rate controls were removed in Chile in the mid-1970s, in Bolivia in 1985, in Mexico in 1988-89, and in most of the other countries in the early 1990s. By 1992, real interest rates were still negative in only five countries: Argentina, Ecuador, Jamaica, Peru, and Uruguay.[56]

At the same time, entry barriers were removed, allowing the operation of new domestic and foreign banks, investment companies, and securities firms. To date, these institutional reforms, together with lower inflation rates, have led to disappointing increases in domestic saving, but they have supported a huge influx of foreign capital. After a dry period during the 1980s, capital inflows to Latin America grew to $13 billion in 1990, and then surged to $57 billion in 1994.[57] According to the United Nations Economic Commission for Latin America and the Caribbean, these capital inflows have played a most constructive role in the region:

New capital inflows have financed imports, investments, and speculative operations, have helped to cover fiscal deficits . . . have fueled a non-inflationary expansion of credit for private-sector investment and consumption, and have added to the region's international reserves.[58]

The dangers inherent in huge flows of international portfolio investment became clear, however, in December 1994, when a currency devaluation in Mexico led to a massive outflow of capital. All the benefits listed in the previous paragraph reversed themselves, and Mexico plunged into a serious recession. During the first six months after the financial panic, some 18,000 people lost their jobs.[59] Nevertheless, the continuing reforms and the underlying potential

---

[56]Based on nominal deposit interest rates in World Bank, *World Development Report 1994*, 184-185, and consumer price inflation rates for 1992.

[57]Moisés Naim, "Latin America the Morning After," *Foreign Affairs* 74 (July/August 1995): 48.

[58]United Nations Economic Commission for Latin America and the Caribbean, *Economic Survey of Latin America and the Caribbean 1992*, vol. 1 (Santiago: United Nations, 1994), 9-10.

[59]Leslie Crawford, "Mexico's Vigil of Woe," *Financial Times*, June 2, 1995, 12.

of the Latin American economies give us reason to believe that Mexico and her neighbors will return again from the financial ashes: "The realization that Latin America is neither the promised land described in the promotional brochures of the early 1990s nor the wasteland depicted in scathing articles prompted by the crisis will eventually sink in."[60]

The Church, the State, and the Poor

In other chapters of this book, this space would be reserved for a general discussion of the role of government in the economy. However, we have already discussed the changing role of Latin American governments, shifting from interventionist programs of import substitution to market-oriented programs of export promotion. We noted the rise and fall of state-owned enterprises, the evolution of land reform, and the causes and effects of rapid price inflation. We have not, however, discussed governmental programs to alleviate income inequality and poverty. We will close the chapter with that discussion, and broaden our focus to consider the economic role of another major institution in Latin America: the Roman Catholic Church.

Basic information on Latin American poverty and income inequality is presented in Table 8.7 (also, refer to Table 2.7). The incidence of absolute poverty is lower in Latin America than in Africa or South Asia, but much higher than in East Asia. Poverty rates were no higher than 20 percent in Argentina, Uruguay, and Nicaragua, but no less than 60 percent in Haiti, Guatemala, and Bolivia. The average poverty rate for the region fell from about 39 percent in 1970 to 35 percent in 1980, but then returned to 39 percent in 1990.[61]

---

[60]Naim, "Latin America the Morning After," 59.

[61]Edwards, *Latin America and the Caribbean: A Decade after the Debt Crisis*, 4; and Oscar Altimir, "Income Distribution and Poverty through Crisis and Adjustment," *CEPAL Review* 32 (April 1994): 12.

Table 8.7 Latin America and the Caribbean: Poverty, Inequality, and Educational Expenditures, 1980-2004

	Absolute Poverty Rate 2004 (%)	*Gini Coefficients Early 1980s*	*Early 1990s*	*Early 2000s*	*Public Education Espenditure 2004 %-of GDP*	*Gini Education Index (2004)*
Caribbean						
Dominican Republic	<2	--	--	--	2.3	0.38
Haiti	67.0	--	--	--	..	
Middle America						
Costa Rica	2.0	0.48	0.46	0.47	5.1	0.30
El Salvador	31.1	--	--	0.53	2.9	0.45
Guatemala	16.0	0.48	0.60	0.60	..	0.54
Honduras	20.7	--	0.53	0.55	..	0.45
Mexico	9.9	0.43	0.50	0.55	5.3	0.34
Nicaragua	45.1	--	0.50	0.43	3.1	0.49
Panama	7.2	0.49	--	0.56	4.5	0.27
South America						
Argentina	3.3	0.41	--	0.52	4.0	0.22
Bolivia	14.4	0.48	0.42	0.45	6.3	0.38
Brazil	8.2	0.59	--	0.59	4.2	0.39
Chile	<2	0.52	0.57	0.57	4.2	0.23
Colombia	8.2	0.58	0.51	0.58	5.2	0.36
Ecuador	17.7	--	0.47	--	1.0	0.33
Paraguay	16.4	0.45	--	0.58	4.4	0.35
Peru	18.1	0.43	0.45	0.50	3.0	0.30
Uruguay	<2	0.44	--	0.45	2.6	0.24
Venezuela	9.9	0.43	0.54	--	..	0.30

Sources: Marcio Marcel and Andrés Solimano, "The Distribution of Income and Economic Adjustment," in *The Chilean Economy*, ed. by Barry Bosworth, Rudiger Dornbusch, and Raúl Labán (Washington, D.C.: Brookings Institution, 1994), 247; Sebastian Edwards, *Latin America and the Caribbean: A Decade after the Debt Crisis* (Washington, D.C: World Bank, 1993), 120; Organization for Economic Cooperation and Development, *OECD Economic Surveys: Mexico 1991/92* (Paris: OECD, 1992), 110; United Nations Development Program, *Human Development Indicators Online*; and World Bank, *World Development Indicators Online.*

The resurgence of poverty during the 1980s can be broken into two components. First, the international debt crisis precipitated a prolonged recession, causing the real income of the average Latin American to drop by 12 percent (Table 8.1). Second, the regional distribution of income, which was already the most unequal in the world, grew even more uneven. This is indicated by rising Gini coefficients in ten of thirteen countries in Table 8.7.

Why did inequality increase during the 1980s? Evidence from Mexico suggests that the richest 10 percent of the population took advantage of capital mobility, high interest rates, and opportunities presented by the economic reforms to sustain or increase their incomes.[62] Thus, when President Salinas took power in 1988, Mexico had one known billionaire; by 1993 it reportedly had fourteen.[63] Of the other 90 percent of the population, a large proportion suffered falling wages or unemployment, or, in agriculture, falling food prices.

The Role of the Church

About 90 percent of Latin Americans are nominally associated with the Roman Catholic church. The number of "practicing" Catholics is much smaller, perhaps no more than 20 percent, and the number of Protestants is growing rapidly, perhaps by 3 million per year.[64] Still, in many countries, the Church has more political power than any other nongovernmental institution.

Since colonial times, the Church has played a controversial role in the economic development of Latin America. An early missionary was often the pawn of a conquistador, who governed a region of the New World as a "trust," or *encomienda*, from the Spanish crown. The *encomienda* allowed the conquistador to extract riches for himself and for the Crown, which often involved a system of forced labor, but also made the conquistador responsible for religious training of the native people. Thus, the local priests became accomplices in a system of paternalism, discipline, and gross exploitation. The church eventually accumulated its own large holdings of land, and its leaders gained positions of privilege.

---

[62]Organization for Economic Cooperation and Development, *OECD Economic Surveys: Mexico 1991/1992* (Paris: OECD, 1992), 110.

[63]Arthur Jones, "Gap between Rich, Poor Expands in Mexico," *National Catholic Reporter* 29 (August 13, 1993): 11.

[64]Penny Lernoux, "Latin America Is Converting to Fundamentalism," *Newsday*, July 12, 1988, 49.

On the other hand, the priests attempted to help the native people in many ways: they established educational systems, introduced new farming methods and medical services, provided the only significant source of agricultural credit, and played an important role in the early formation of social security systems and labor unions. As early as the sixteenth century, Bartolome de las Casas, the bishop of Chiápas, campaigned against cruel treatment of the indigenous people in Mexico, gaining them some relief from the Spanish crown. In the seventeenth and eighteenth centuries, priests established an independent Jesuit republic in South America to protect the Guarani people from Portuguese slavers.

Two members of the lower clergy, Father Miguel Hidalgo y Costilla and Father Morelos y Payon, led the Mexican revolution against Spain in 1810, demanding human rights for the natives and *mestizos*.[65] A century later, though, when Mexico experienced civil war and land reform, the church was identified with the rich and the landowners. In "some of the worst repression against Catholics anywhere in history," churches were closed, property was confiscated, priests were banned, and many of them were executed, together with their protectors.[66]

During the 1960s, two developments began to change the political face of the Church in Latin America. One was an institutional reform, initiated by Pope John XXIII, that ended the monopoly of European-blooded clerics, and led to the appointment of indigenous bishops. The other was an ideological movement, known as "liberation theology," that developed concurrently with other leftist intellectual currents in Latin America, including dependency theory, structuralism, and Castroism. Camilo Torres, a Colombian priest killed by government troops in 1966, put it this way:

---

[65]Richard O'Mara, "Aristide's Lineage: Latin America's Radical Priesthood," *The Sun* (Baltimore), September 25, 1994, 1E.

[66]Jones, "Gap between Rich, Poor Expands in Mexico," 11.

Under the present circumstances in Latin America we see that we cannot feed, or clothe, or house the majorities. . . The power must be taken for the majorities' part so that structural, economic, social, and political reforms benefiting these majorities may be realized. This is called revolution and if it is necessary in order to fulfill love for one's neighbor, then it is necessary for a Christian to be a revolutionary.[67]

Liberation theology reached a wider audience in 1971, when Gustavo Gutierrez, a Peruvian priest, published *The Theology of Revolution.* The book encouraged a new activism that caused one confrontation after another with military dictators. In 1973, several members of Christians for Socialism lost their lives during the military takeover in Chile. In Argentina, Priests for the Third World were among those killed during the so-called Dirty War, which began in 1976. Two well-known Sandinista priests, Miguel D'Escoto and Ernesto Cardenal, fought in the 1979 revolution to remove the Somoza dictatorship in Nicaragua. Archbishop Oscar Romero, an opponent of the military in El Salvador, was assassinated in 1980, and in Haiti, the assassination of one priest, Jean-Marie Vincent, contributed to the collapse of military rule in 1994, and the return of another priest, Jean-Bertrand Aristide, to serve as president.

The 1995 annual meeting of Latin American bishops in Mexico City demonstrated again the impact of Catholic institutional reforms, leftist ideologies, and social concerns. In a document titled "Latin America: Stand Up and Walk," the bishops scolded national leaders for their reckless programs of market-oriented reform, and decried public indifference to the poor. The ruling neoliberal orthodoxy, they said, is "unnatural and inhuman," and eventually "will fall by itself, perhaps more rapidly than communism." The bishops claimed that "the absolutization of market forces and the power of money" are the most important causes of inequality and poverty in the region. These views are alarming to national leaders, and to market-oriented international

---

[67]Quoted in Jeanine Swift, *Economic Development in Latin America* (New York: St. Martin's Press, 1978), 10.

aid agencies. They also disturb the Catholic hierarchy in Rome, where the Pope is a veteran critic of communism and liberation theology.[68]

Public Programs to Reduce Poverty

For many years, Latin American governments and the Washington-based aid agencies believed that economic growth and industrialization would solve the poverty problem in the region in a reasonable period of time. Thus, problems of macroeconomic stabilization and the relative merits of import substitution and export promotion dominated economic policy discussions. Little attention was given to programs of public health, education, and social security that are specifically targeted at reduction of poverty.

Recently, for a number of reasons, poverty reduction has moved to a higher place on the policy agenda. Removal of military dictatorships and restoration of democracy has fundamentally changed the political landscape of Latin America. Liberal priests and politicians, who were once in hiding, now have access to legislative seats and, in the case of Haiti, the presidency. The demands of the unemployed in Bogotá and the peasants in Chiápas can no longer be silenced and ignored.

The regional governments and the aid agencies also have come to a new realization that broad-brush policies of economic growth and industrialization are not sufficient to attack the problems of poverty. "Higher growth is important," says a recent World Bank report, "but not enough."[69] The real income of the *average* Latin American tripled between the 1950s and the 1990s, but the percentage of the population living in poverty declined slowly (and increased during the 1980s) because of growing income inequality. Furthermore, because of continuing

---

[68]"Bishops Predict Collapse of 'Inhuman' Neoliberalism," Inter-Press News Service, May 8, 1995.

[69]Stephen Fidler, "Latin America Shakes Off Crisis but Flaws Remain," *Financial Post*, June 28, 1995, 50.

population growth, the World Bank believes that the *number* of people living in absolute poverty has not declined since the 1950s. To reduce the number of poor the region must maintain an annual growth rate of 3.2 percent, roughly equal to the rate that prevailed between 1991 and 1993. Like Alice's Wonderland, the World Bank says that, in Latin America, "It takes all of the running you can do to stay in the same place."[70]

Thus, the need for policies designed to reduce income inequality and policy. According to statistical investigations, the most important determinant of income inequality seems to be education. The probability of a person with less than five years of schooling being in the poorest quintile of the population is 83 percent in Panama, 69 percent in Argentina, and 42 percent in Brazil.[71] In 1992, the average adult in Latin America had only 5.4 years of schooling, compared with 8.1 years in East Asia (excluding China).[72] Countries that devote small percentages of GDP to educational expenditure, such as Guatemala, Haiti, and Honduras, tend to have the highest rates of absolute poverty (Table 8.7). According to a World Bank analysis, if the macroeconomic environment is stable, two-thirds of the absolute poverty in Latin America could be eliminated by improving educational facilities and increasing average schooling levels to nine years.[73]

Latin America also has a poor record of performance in the field of public health. Compared to East Asia, the infant mortality rate, the proportion of the population without access to safe water, and the proportion of the population without access to sanitation services are all twice as high.

Social security systems exist in most Latin American countries that provide pension and health benefits, and they were among the few social services that received expenditure increases

---

[70]"Latin America Must Rebuild State, Exports," Inter-Press News Service, June 12, 1995.

[71]Edwards, *Latin America and the Caribbean: A Decade after the Debt Crisis*, 120-121.

[72]United Nations Development Programme, *Human Development Report 1994*, 207.

[73]"Latin American Nations Must Invest in Education—World Bank," Reuters News Service, June 13, 1995.

during the 1980s. Still, most of the programs are underfunded, actuarially unsound, and inefficient, and they do not reach the poorest segments of society. In Brazil, only 18 percent of people in the poorest 40 percent of the population are covered by social security, and they receive only 3 percent of the benefits.[74] Despite chronic unemployment problems, most countries (including relatively high-income countries such as Mexico) do not have an unemployment compensation program.

As we noted earlier, health, education, and social security, together with land reform and other policies that affect the poor, are beginning to attract more attention from politicians and international aid agencies. In Chile, a major shift in social policy began in 1990 when democracy was restored under the Aylwin administration. The minimum wage was quickly increased by 36 percent, and pensions and social subsidies were raised. Between 1990 and 1995, real social expenditures increased by about 50 percent.[75]

In Mexico, President Zedillo announced in 1995 that his government would invest 9 billion new pesos during the second half of the 1990s in programs to help the educationally disadvantaged. This is the largest commitment Mexico has ever made to education of the poor, with special attention to the indigenous people. It will be supported by a $500 million loan to Mexico from the World Bank, aimed at development of public education, health, nutrition, and employment.[76] A similar program is being launched in Argentina, where a $300 million credit from the Inter-American Development Bank will support a $600 million project to improve primary education.[77]

---

[74]Edwards, *Latin America and the Caribbean: A Decade after the Debt Crisis*, 127.

[75]Howard LaFranchi, "Progress Has Come at a High Cost," *The Christian Science Monitor*, July 25, 1995, 2.

[76]"Mexico to Spend 9 bln New Pesos on Education," Reuters News Service, July 6, 1995.

[77]"IADB, Argentina Sign Contract for $300 Million Loan," Reuters News Service, April 2, 1995.

Summary

Latin America includes three diverse subregions: Middle America, South America, and the Caribbean area. The indigenous cultures, including the great Mayan, Aztec, and Inca civilizations, had experience with economic development, authoritarian organization, and colonial exploitation before Europeans arrived. Long-term developments in the region were influenced by the authoritarian culture and extractive motives of the Europeans.

Latin American independence movements were encouraged by a mixture of internal and external economic motives, intellectual currents, and political leaders. Independence allowed a new era of trade expansion to begin, but it did not quickly lead to an equitable system of land tenure. The Great Depression ended the era of trade expansion and prompted a system of import substituting industrialization (ISI), which continued after World War II. Applied moderately, ISI provided impressive results, but it invited excesses, contributing to the rise of authoritarian regimes. Brazil shifted toward export promotion during the 1960s, and Chile made a broader shift toward market liberalization and fiscal austerity during the 1970s. Prompted by the debt crisis of the 1980s, the Chilean experience, and pressure from international institutions, market liberalization spread to other countries in the 1980s and 1990s.

Latin American agricultural institutions are derived from the colonial plantation and hacienda systems, from programs of land reform, and from recent programs of land privatization. Industrial structures include the microenterprises of the informal sector, the large domestic enterprises in the formal sector, state-owned enterprises (SOEs), and multinationals, which include the *maquiladoras*. The number of SOEs increased dramatically during the ISI years, but it declined in Chile beginning in the 1970s, and elsewhere beginning in the 1980s. Several models of privatization have been developed, including the Bolivian system of capitalization.

In the rural sector, labor markets have been characterized by continuing inequities. In industry, the dominant state and the growth of the informal sector have made it difficult to develop a stable and evenhanded system of collective bargaining. Public-private pacts, negotiated in recent years, may contribute to a more balanced relationship between labor, industry, and the state. Latin America has experienced high rates of chronic inflation, eliciting a number of monetarist, structural, and political explanations. Rapid inflation, in turn, led to interest controls, credit rationing, barriers to entry of new financial institutions, and other symptoms of financial repression. Control of inflation and financial liberalization has been a major focus of reform in recent years, leading to large inflows and outflows of international capital.

Latin American countries have high levels of income inequality, which continued to increase during the 1980s. The Roman Catholic church has a long and controversial record in its relations with the poor, including the development of liberation theology since the 1960s. The governments have traditionally relied on economic growth to aid the poor, but now they are shifting to targeted policies of poverty reduction.

Discussion and Review Questions

1. How are Latin American economies influenced today by their colonial and precolonial heritage? How do these differ between Latin America and the United States?
2. What have been the objectives of land reform in Latin America? Have these been met satisfactorily?
3. "Without the dictatorial measures of the Pinochet regime, Chile could not have a stable economic and political system today." Do you agree with this statement?
4. What is the role of the informal sector in the urban economies of Latin America? To the individual business owner, what are the costs and benefits of operating in the informal sector?
5. Why has Latin America experienced rapid and persistent inflation? Do you believe the cycle of inflation has been broken in the region?
6. What are the benefits and costs of receiving large inflows of international capital? Should Latin American countries control these capital flows?

7. How should Latin American countries allocate educational expenditures to reduce poverty. How should expenditures be divided between primary, secondary, and higher education? Between liberal and vocational education? Between rural and urban education?

Suggested Readings

Baer, Werner, and Melissa Birch, eds. *Privatization in Latin America: New Roles for the Public and Private Sectors*. Westport, Conn.: Praeger Publishers, 1994. *Nine essays survey the different methods and styles of privatization in Latin America and Spain, and analyze their impact on public policy and on domestic business interests and foreign investors.*

Bosworth, Barry P., Rudiger Dornbusch, and Raul Laban, eds. *The Chilean Economy: Policy Lessons and Challenges*. Washington, D.C.: The Brookings Institution, 1994. *An excellent conference volume with nine essays and sixteen comments by a team of forty economists from Chile and the United States, analyzing shifts in Chilean policy since the 1950s.*

Casanova, Pablo Gonzalez, ed. *Latin America Today*. Tokyo: United Nations University Press, 1993. *Described as "the culmination of one of the largest studies ever undertaken in Latin America," this volume is primarily concerned with political and social issues, but it also includes an analysis of "economy and crisis" from a left-leaning Latin American perspective.*

de Soto, Hernando. *The Other Path: The Invisible Revolution in the Third World*. New York: Harper & Row, 1989. *Based on the experience in Peru, this is an eye-opening account of the regulatory causes and economic consequences of informal sector growth.*

Dietz, James L., and Dilmus D. James, eds. *Progress toward Development in Latin America: From Prebisch to Technological Autonomy*. Boulder: Lynne Rienner Publishers, 1990. *In eleven essays by eight authors, this volume considers the Latin American experience from structuralist and institutionalist perspectives.*

Edwards, Sebastian. *Latin America and the Caribbean: A Decade after the Debt Crisis*. Washington, D.C.: World Bank, Latin America and the Caribbean Regional Office, 1993. *A comprehensive, authoritative, and concise (159 pages) evaluation of Latin American adjustments programs, and their impact on macroeconomic performance, income distribution, and poverty.*

Lustig, Nora. *Mexico: The Remaking of an Economy*. Washington, D.C.: The Brookings Institution, 1992. *An evaluation of the benefits and costs of the transformation of the Mexican economy since the 1982 debt crisis.*

CHAPTER 19

JAPAN: REBUILDING AFTER THE BUBBLE

For all the brilliance and energy of Japan's postwar economic miracle, interlocking business and bureaucracy has led to a domination of entrenched interests that make a mockery of the free enterprise that business and government spokesmen publicly support.
--Frank B. Gibney, *Japan Quarterly*, July-September, 1996

I am not at all convinced that an American-style economy is the only way for Japan to succeed. And I don't think we are seeing much convergence in the two systems. . . . There is an arrogant American concept which basically says that in order to succeed you must have an economic system that looks like ours. The fact of the matter is that convergence is running in the other direction: Asian countries are moving toward the Japanese-style economic structure, with strong state involvement rather than the myth of laissez faire that is commonly accepted in the United States.
--Robert M. Orr, Jr., *Tokyo Business Today*, February, 1996

In an age of East Asian economic miracles, one country set the pace for the entire region. With few natural resources to support it, Japan climbed from the ashes of World War II to build the second largest industrial economy in the world. During the 1960s, 1970s, and 1980s, its growth rates were sometimes double the OECD average; its unemployment rates were consistently lower than half the norm (Table 19.1). Today, Japan can claim the longest average life expectancy, the lowest rate of infant mortality, the smallest per-capita prison population, and one of the most even distributions of income in the industrial world.[1]

Because of its many achievements, the Japanese economic system has long been touted as a model for other countries. Herman Kahn announced in 1970 that Japan was an emerging "superstate."[2] Nine years later, Ezra Vogel spoke of Japan as "number one," and claimed that it had become "a more effective democracy than America."[3] More recently, the title of a book by William Dietrich suggested that the United States is living *In the Shadow of the Rising Sun*. "The

---

[1]World Bank, *World Development Report 1996* (New York: Oxford University Press, 1996), 189, 197, and 199; and United Nations Development Program, *Human Development Report 1995* (New York: Oxford University Press, 1995), 198.

[2]Herman Kahn, *The Emerging Japanese Superstate* (Harmondsworth: Penguin Books, 1970).

[3]Ezra Vogel, *Japan As Number One* (Cambridge, Mass.: Harvard University Press, 1979), 97.

Japanese are way out in front of the pack and are gaining ground daily," said Dietrich; "It is the considered opinion of this work that we must become more like Japan."[4]

Table 19.1 Relative Performance of the Japanese Economy, 1961-2004

	1961-1970	*1971-1980*	*1981-1990*	*1991-2000*	*2001-2004*
Average annual growth of real GDP (%)					
Japan	10.9	4.7	4.0	1.4	1.4
OECD Average	5.1	3.2	2.9	2.7	2.3
Average annual consumer price inflation (%)					
Japan	5.6	9.1	2.1	0.9	-0.2
OECD Average	3.9	9.1	15.4	7.7	2.5
Unemployment Rate (%)					
Japan	1.2	1.8	2.6	3.3	5.0
OECD Average	2.8*	4.5	7.1	7.8	6.7

*Based on data for Canada, France, West Germany, Italy, Japan, Sweden, the United Kingdom, and the United States.
Sources: *OECD in Figure*, a supplement to *The OECD Observer,* Various Issues; OECD statistics online (supplementary); World Bank, *World Development Indicators Online*.

According to its admirers, what aspects of the Japanese system should be copied by other countries? Martin Weitzman advocates the Japanese system of labor compensation--the so-called "share economy." This, he claims, could help all nations to eradicate unemployment.[5] According to Chalmers Johnson, the key to Japanese success is its cooperative system of government-industry relations, known as "Japan, Inc."[6] Others suggest that we should emulate Japan's "humanistic enterprise system," based on lifetime employment, egalitarianism, teamwork, and cooperation between labor and management.[7]

---

[4]William Dietrich, *In the Shadow of the Rising Sun* (University Park, Penn.: The Pennsylvania State University Press, 1991), 268-269.

[5]Martin L. Weitzman, *The Share Economy: Conquering Stagflation* (Cambridge: Harvard University Press, 1984).

[6]Chalmers Johnson, *MITI and the Japanese Miracle* (Stanford: Stanford University Press, 1982).

[7]William Ouchi, *Theory Z: How American Business Can Meet the Japanese Challenge* (Reading, Mass.: Addison-Wesley, 1981); Robert Ozaki, *Human Capitalism: The Japanese Enterprise System as a World Model* (Harmondsworth: Penguin Books, 1991); and Hiroyuki Itami, "The 'Human Capitalism' of the Japanese Firm as an Integrated System," in Kenichi Imai and Ryutaro Komiya, eds., *Business Enterprise in Japan: Views of Leading Japanese Economists* (Cambridge, Mass.: The MIT Press, 1994), 73-88.

The Japanese economic and social system also has its critics. Jon Woronoff, a journalist, has written books since the 1970s with such titles as *Japan as*--anything but--*Number One*.[8] What benefit does a country derive from its industrial power, Woronoff asks, if its women and ethnic minorities suffer from discrimination, its men work endless hours for meager standards of living, its children live in constant fear of "examination hell," and its elderly commit suicide at one of the world's highest rates? James Fallows, a prominent journalist who worked in Tokyo during the 1980s, raises similar questions:

We had heard for years that Japan was rich. Yet normal life, as we lived and observed it in a Tokyo suburb, would be considered needlessly grinding and difficult by most American and European standards. Homes were usually unheated. Modern plumbing was rare. In the country that produced more automobiles than any other nation, most of our neighbors had no cars. . . . I had been taught that the ultimate purpose of economic growth was to make individuals rich; in Japan, individuals remained poor so that the industries could grow strong.[9]

Woronoff and Fallows are not alone in their views; scores of Japanese scholars are equally critical of their nation's economic and social system.[10] Indeed, since the early 1990s, the tide of domestic criticism has grown ever stronger, fueled by a series of financial crises, political scandals, and troubling demographic and international trends. These include:

* The rise and fall of the "bubble economy," characterized by wide gyrations of stock and real estate prices.

* The collapse of Japan's housing-loan companies (*jusen*), causing heavy losses and requiring government bailouts for large banks that owned them.

* Political, financial, and sexual scandals in the dominant Liberal Democratic Party that contributed to political instability, causing Japan to appoint six prime ministers between 1990 and 1996.[11]

---

[8]Jon Woronoff, Japan: *The Coming Economic Crisis* (Tokyo: Yohan, 1979); Jan Woronoff, *Japan as*--anything but--*Number One* (Armonk, N.Y.: M. E. Sharpe, 1990); and Jan Woronoff, *The Japanese Economic Crisis* (New York: St. Martin's Press, 1993).

[9]James Fallows, *Looking at the Sun: The Rise of the New East Asian Economic and Political System* (New York: Vintage Books, 1995), 8. Even more pointedly, see Fallows' article, "The Hard Life," *The Atlantic*, March 1989, 16-26.

[10]For example, see Tadashi Fukutake, *Japanese Society Today* (Tokyo: University of Tokyo Press, 1981); Takahashi Nobuaki, "Superpower Japan, the Closet Pauper," *Japan Echo* 16 (No. 2, 1989): 47-51; and Mikio Sumiya, "Japan: Model Society for the Future?" *Annals of the American Academy of Political and Social Sciences* 513 (January 1991): 139-150.

[11]For a full list of Japanese prime ministers, see <http://www.ehu.es/~ziaoarr/japan.htm>.

* Instances of negligence and corruption in government agencies that regulated financial institutions, in police units that mishandled a terrorist attack on a Tokyo subway in 1994 and an earthquake in 1995, and in government health agencies that concealed information on HIV-tainted blood that was distributed during the 1980s.

* Impatience of women for greater equality in Japanese society.

* Heavy demands on the health and social security systems caused by the shifting age structure of the Japanese population.

* Rising competition on international markets caused by the strong Japanese currency, by the economic development of other East Asian nations, and by the formation of regional trading blocs in Europe and the Americas.

According to the Japanese Economic Planning Agency, existing institutions are no longer able to accommodate these "tidal shifts" in history. An effective response, according to the planners, "will require radical reforms of Japan's social and economic structure, and changes in the way we as individuals think."[12]

Radical reform? Should Japan abandon the system that supported its postwar economic miracle? What institutional arrangements should be changed, and what should be retained? Will environmental changes, such as demographic trends, provide support for systemic reform, or will traditional culture stand in the way? Should some aspects of the Japanese system be copied by other countries? We have much to explore in this chapter.

The Environment

Japan has little land, but many people. Scattered over four major islands, its territory is smaller than California, but it has nearly half the population of the United States. Furthermore, most of its terrain is mountainous; less than 20 percent is arable. Thus, Japan must import about half of its food and nearly all of its energy, iron ore, copper, tin, aluminum, nickel, and uranium.

Taming the Work Ethic

Through the centuries, the Japanese people learned to compensate for their scarcity of natural resources: "We must work very hard" became their refrain, "we are a poor island nation." The Japanese work ethic grew ever more necessary after the carnage and destruction of World War II, and played a vital role in the postwar "miracle." The hero of the new era was the "corporate warrior."

Today, when their battle for survival has been won, and when they have joined the ranks of the affluent democracies, the Japanese have decided it is time to moderate their work ethic. In addition to his normal work day, they believe, the average adult male spends too many hours

---

[12]Economic Planning Agency and Economic Council, "Social and Economic Plan for Structural Reforms," November 29, 1995 <http://www.epa.go.jp/e-e/keikaku/sumwin.html>.

working overtime (frequently until 9 or 10 P.M.), attending unpaid quality control sessions and other group meetings, socializing with work associates and clients, and riding long distances on crowded commuter trains. He has little time for family or leisure activities, and he provides little help, relief, or companionship to his wife.

More than half of eighth graders claim that they never speak with their fathers on weekdays.[13] In 1995, the average Japanese worker was authorized to take seventeen days of paid vacation, but elected to take only nine.[14] Among workers above age 50, about 60 percent say their job is their main reason for living.[15] Since the late 1980s, telephone hotlines have been operating in major cities to aid families victimized by *karoshi*, or "death from overwork." By the end of 1995, nearly 2,000 cases had been reported.[16]

Slowly but surely, the culture of workaholism seems to be softening. In 1996, a record 59 percent of adults reported their intention to find more time for leisure and relaxation rather than work and income; this was up from 37 percent in 1972, the first year this survey question was asked.[17] Accordingly, the government hopes to (1) reduce the length of the standard workweek, (2) encourage workers to use more of their authorized vacation time, (3) reduce commute times by making more housing available near places of work, (4) provide more opportunities for leisure, continuing education, and civic involvement to enrich the lives of workers and pensioners.[18]

The Labor Ministry reduced the legal workweek from 48 hours to 44 hours in 1991, and set 1997 as the deadline for all companies to adopt a 40-hour workweek. Late in 1996, when

---

[13]Nicholas Kristof, "Japan: For Better or for Worse," *The New York Times*, February 11, 1996, 1.

[14]The average number of paid holidays was 19 in the United States, 24 in the United Kingdom, and 29 in Germany. See Economic Planning Agency, *Annual Report on the National Life for Fiscal 1993* (Tokyo, 1994), 38; and data relating to leisure activities at <http://www.jinjapan.org/stat/index.html>.

[15]Economic Planning Agency, *Annual Report on the National Life for Fiscal 1993*, 37.

[16]National Defense Counsel *[sic]* for Victims of Karoshi, *Karoshi: When the "Corporate Warrior" Dies* (Tokyo: Mado-Sha, 1990), 6; and Chuah Bee Hwa, "Karoshi and the Winds of Change," *New Straits Times*, June 20, 1996, 4.

[17]"More Japanese See Mental Health, Comfy Life as Vital," Japan Economic Newswire, November 23, 1996.

[18]Economic Planning Agency and Economic Council, "Social and Economic Plan for Structural Reforms," 3-4.

about 33 percent of the small and midsized companies reported that they could not meet the deadline, the government threatened to fine offending companies or incarcerate their managers.[19]

The Culture of Conformity

As an island nation, Japan spent many of its formative years in relative seclusion. Particularly during the seventeenth and eighteenth centuries A.D., while military dictators of the Tokugawa family enforced a strict system of isolationism, the Japanese people developed a remarkable uniformity of race, language, and culture. The homogeneous culture, in turn, encouraged the development of a social philosophy, known as **groupism**, that elevates the importance of the group over the individual.[20] Today, Japan seems to derive a mixture of benefits and burdens from its uniform culture and its group orientation.

First, Japanese groupism seems to encourage a tight system of familial and social obligations. The Japanese divorce rate is less than half the American level, and, although the strength of extended family relationships is declining, two-thirds of the elderly still live in multigenerational households.[21]

Frequently, the familial relations in Japanese society are extended into the business world. The Japanese worker, for example, may become a member of a company "family" through a bond of lifetime employment. Furthermore, a company may engage in familial relationships with other companies by participating in a *zaibatsu* or *keiretsu* conglomerate. On an even broader level, the "Japan, Inc." thesis suggests that the entire economy is knit together under the leadership of a paternalistic government.

All of these family ties play a vital role in the traditional structures of Japanese society. The individual worker derives security, stability, and protection from relationships with his extended family and company family; each company relies on the support of its loyal employees and on stable relations with its *keiretsu* partners. The system of familial relations encourages resolution of conflicts through conciliation and compromise rather than conflict and litigation. Thus, all of Japan requires the services of fewer lawyers than the city of Philadelphia.[22]

---

[19]"40-Hour Mandate Strains Small Firms," *The Nikkei Weekly*, October 28, 1996, 4.

[20]On the significance of groupism and its relationship to individualism, see Ozaki, *Human Capitalism*, 88-92.

[21]Akiko Hashimoto, "Family Relations in Later Life: A Cross-Cultural Perspective," *Generations*, December 22, 1993, 22; "Whither the Extended Family?" *Asiaweek*, December 15, 1995, 86.

[22]According to data compiled by the Institute for Legal Studies at the University of Wisconsin, (reported in *World Monitor*, November 1992, 8-9), for every million members of the population there were 2,753 lawyers in the United States, 1,511 in Germany, 919 in the United Kingdom, and 872 in Japan.

The cost of security and conciliation, however, is a low level of social, occupational, and managerial flexibility. A Japanese elder son may be compelled to continue in his father's business; a worker under the lifetime employment system may be tied to an unsatisfying job; a company in a *keiretsu* organization may be forced to trade with other companies in the group, forsaking other opportunities.

One of the most troubling aspects of Japanese groupism is its potential to encourage excessive conformity, which may discourage individual initiative and creativity. "The nail that sticks out," says a Japanese proverb, "will be pounded down." The educational system emphasizes rote memorization and respect for authority rather than critical thinking, and offers little opportunity or reward for originality. Values of humility and respect for age and authority are reinforced by the Confucian, Buddhist, and Shinto traditions.

Thus, the Japanese system produces students who excel on standardized exams, particularly in mathematics and the natural sciences, but few scientists who can push forward the frontiers of knowledge. According to Susumu Tonegawa, a Japanese national who won the 1987 Nobel prize in medicine, "talented scientists have no choice but to get out of Japan."[23] Tonegawa performed his prize-winning research in Switzerland and the United States, and claims that subordination to the Japanese scientific establishment would have made his work impossible.

On the other hand, if Japan has performed poorly as a nation of inventors, it is unsurpassed as a nation of assimilators. Repeatedly, Japanese engineers have mastered technologies from other countries, incorporated them into marketable products, and developed sequential improvements in quality standards and production processes. As Rosenberg and Steinmuller have noted, these modest, incremental innovations do not win Nobel prizes, but they are often the "essence of success in the competitive process."[24]

Historically, Japan's ability to assimilate foreign technology was strengthened by the Confucian culture. Superstitions and taboos may have inhibited the advance of technology in many countries, but Japanese Confucianism was characterized by intellectualism and rationalism. Thus, Morishima claims it was "entirely" owing to Confucianism that Western science was transplanted quickly and painlessly in Japan.[25]

Finally, at its worst, Japanese homogeneity seems to encourage patterns of intolerance, racism, and xenophobia. For example, more than 600,000 ethnic Koreans who were born and raised in Japan have not been offered citizenship, so they are ineligible for many civil service jobs. Many of these are grandchildren of laborers who came to the country against their will

---

[23]Stephen Yoder, "Japan's Scientists Find Pure Research Suffers Under Rigid Life Style," *The Wall Street Journal*, October 31, 1988, A1.

[24]Nathan Rosenberg and W. Edward Steinmuller, "Why Are Americans Such Poor Imitators?" *American Economic Review* 78 (May 1988), 230.

[25]Michio Morishima, *Why Has Japan `Succeeded'?* (Cambridge: Cambridge University Press, 1982), 61.

during the 1920s.[26] Notably, at the end of the Vietnam War, less than 5,000 Indochinese refugees were willing or able to settle in Japan, while more than 600,000 traveled around the world to settle in the United States.[27] Also notable is the fact that Japanese companies operating in the United States have a relatively poor record of racial diversity in hiring and promotion.[28]

A Brief History

From the seventh century A.D., when the monarchy was established, until 1603, when a unified military dictatorship was founded by the Tokugawa family, the Japanese lived in a chronic state of civil war. The Tokugawa regime provided 250 years of peace, law, and order, but imposed a feudal economic order and a policy of total isolation from the outside world. The Japanese people developed culturally and achieved a relatively high rate of literacy, but fell far behind the West in science and technology.

The Japanese became aware of their backward state in 1853, when Commodore Perry arrived with his fearsome fleet of steam-powered ships and delivered a letter from U.S. President Franklin Pierce demanding the opening of trade relations. The ensuing domestic debate led to a civil war in 1867; the military dictatorship was overthrown and the monarchy was restored under the young emperor Meiji.

The Meiji Reforms and Modern Economic Growth

The new Meiji regime opened the door to foreign trade, abolished many feudal institutions, and attempted to close the technology gap. It established the legal equality of all social classes and gave everyone the legal (if not social) freedom to choose their trade or occupation. Feudal guilds were eliminated, agricultural land was distributed to peasants, and monetary taxes were replaced payments in kind. Internal travel restrictions were abolished, and the transportation system was improved. Primary education (with a Western curriculum) was made compulsory, and foreigners were employed as educators, advisors, and corporate officers. The government established a number of large state-run businesses and supported private industry through extension of loans and subsidies. Government enterprises accounted for about 40 percent of total investment during the Meiji period.[29]

---

[26]See Christopher B. Johnstone, "'Virtual' Citizens: Japan's Foreign Residents and the Quest for Expanded Political Rights," *Japan Economic Institute Report* 27A (July 19, 1996), 3-12.

[27]These are figures for the years between 1971 and 1984. See George Fields, "Racism Is Accepted Practice in Japan," *Wall Street Journal*, November 10, 1986, 19; and U.S. Department of Commerce, Bureau of the Census, *Statistical Abstract of the United States 1986,* 86.

[28]See hiring data presented in Rochelle Sharpe, "Japanese Bank in U.S. Built for One Minority, Is Pressed to Aid Others," *The Wall Street Journal*, December 30, 1996, A1.

[29]Angus Maddison, *Economic Growth in Japan and the USSR* (New York: W. W. Norton, 1969), 23.

The Meiji reforms drew Japan into the modern world and launched a period of rapid economic growth. The nation's emerging industrial and military power led to territorial gains in wars with China (1894-1895) and Russia (1904-1905) and in the First World War (1914-1918). An overvalued exchange rate caused Japanese economic growth to moderate during the 1920s, despite an economic boom in the United States. On the other hand, the Japanese economy grew at a 6 percent annual rate between 1931 and 1938, despite a continuing depression in the West, because the government devalued the currency and pursued an expansionary program of military expenditures.[30]

This triumphal era of economic growth ended with the devastation of World War II. The war destroyed about one-fourth of the nation's buildings and structures, one-third of its industrial machinery, and more than 80 percent of its ships. Japan was stripped of its colonies and investments in Manchuria, Korea, and Formosa; reparations payments required the dismantling of some industrial capacity. Unlike Germany, Japan was not surrounded by countries experiencing rapid recoveries. Japan did not regain its prewar level of GNP until 1954.[31]

The outbreak of the Korean War in 1950 caused a rapid growth in the demand for Japanese exports. It also induced the United States to recognize the importance of Japan as an outpost against communism in the Far East. Hence, American policy toward Japan shifted from punishment to encouragement. For these and other reasons, a period of miraculous growth began around 1953 and continued with few interruptions until the oil shocks of 1973 and 1979. During the early 1980s, Japanese growth was restrained by a recession in the United States, which was employing a tight monetary policy to fight inflation. When the U.S. economy recovered in 1983 and 1984, its imports from Japan soared. Both economies experienced strong economic growth, but they developed a troublesome trade imbalance.

The Bubble Economy

In 1985, in the so-called **Plaza Accord**,[32] Japan agreed to accept a substantial appreciation of the yen, allowing it to double against the dollar by 1988. Fearing that the strong yen would cause slow export growth, the Japanese government mounted an expansionary monetary policy to stimulate domestic demand. The narrow money supply grew 10 percent in 1986, and the official discount rate was cut to a postwar low of 2.5 percent.

The government's easy-money policy triggered one of the most remarkable episodes of financial speculation in world history--the so-called **bubble economy**. The value of commercial

---

[30]Takatoshi Ito, *The Japanese Economy* (Cambridge, Mass.: The MIT Press, 1993), 13-17.

[31]Maddison, *Economic Growth in Japan and the USSR*, 46.

[32]On September 22, 1985, finance ministers and treasury officials from the Group of Five (G5) countries--France, Germany, Japan, the United Kingdom, and the United States--met at the Plaza Hotel in New York to devise a coodinated plan to push down the value of the dollar and contain the United States payments deficit, which then stood at $124 billion.

property in central Tokyo, already the most expensive real estate in the world, climbed tenfold between 1985 and 1989. The Ministry of Finance allowed Japanese companies to take out bank loans, backed by their inflated real estate wealth, to purchase securities. Thus, despite a temporary decline caused by the international Black Monday crash in 1987, the average price of a share on the Nikkei stock exchange tripled between 1985 and 1989. With new confidence in their economy, and encouraged by the increasing values of their real estate and securities, Japanese consumers and purchasers of capital equipment went on a buying spree. Between 1987 and 1990, while the North American and European economies grew at an average rate of about 3 percent, Japan posted a 5 percent growth rate.

During the first few years of the bubble, it was possible to argue that the high and rising asset prices were sustainable, based on expectations of future earnings and other traditional market criteria.[33] When prices continued to climb rapidly in 1988 and 1989, though, the speculative nature of the boom grew increasingly evident. Japanese industrial stocks, for example, were sold in 1989 for an average of 54 times their annual earnings, compared with a multiple of 15 for similar U.S. firms.[34] According to whimsical calculations by the Ministry of Construction, in 1989 the aggregate real estate value of Japan was theoretically four times larger than the value of the United States--a country twenty-five times larger.[35]

The bubble grew more fragile when its sustainability was called into question. Then, in May 1989, the Bank of Japan shifted to a more restrictive monetary stance, and raised its official discount rate for the first time in more than two years.[36] The expansion paused, and then the bubble burst. Between 1989 and 1986, real estate and stock prices both fell by about 50 percent. Falling asset prices left a trail of bad debts and bankruptcies of borrowing and lending institutions.

The end of the bubble also caused a reversal of consumer and investor expectations, dragging Japan's average economic growth rate to less than 1 percent per year between 1992 and 1995. During those same years, the average growth rate of other OECD countries was about 2 percent, and the rate for newly industrializing countries in East Asia was about 7 percent. Furthermore, in 1995, Japan's unemployment rate climbed above 3 percent for the first time in the postwar era. These are among the realities that inspired new proposals for deep structural reform.

---

[33]Ito, *The Japanese Economy*, 407-436.

[34]Kenneth French and James Poterba, "Were Japanese Stock Prices Too High?" *Journal of Financial Economics* 29 (October 1991): 337-364.

[35]David L. Asher, "What Became of the Japanese 'Miracle'?" *Orbis* 40 (Spring 1996): 216.

[36]Monetary policy was the main factor that burst the bubble according to Ryuichiro Tachi, *The Contemporary Japanese Economy: An Overview* (Tokyo: University of Tokyo Press, 1993), 200; and is also emphasized by Naoki Tanaka, "The Japanese Economy after the 'Bubble,'" *Japanese Economic Studies* 23 (May-June 1995): 6.

Late in 1995, the Japanese economy began to improve, and the recovery gained momentum during 1996. This is good news, of course, but it raises a new question: will demands for institutional reform persist if the economic crisis is past?

Table 19.2 Japan's Largest Corporations, 2008

Japanese Rank	*Company*	*Rank in World (by sales)*	*Sales (U.S. $ millions)*
1	Toyota Motor	10	204,352
2	Japan Post Holdings	11	198,700
3	Nippon Telegraph & Telephone	44	103,684
4	Honda Motor	51	99,652
5	Hitachi	52	99,544
6	Nissan Motor	67	83,982
7	Panasonic	79	77,298
8	Sony	81	76,945
9	Nippon Life Insurance	96	66,621
10	Toshiba	97	66,239
11	Nippon Oil	101	64,198
12	Mitsubishi	114	61,182
13	Tokyo Electric Power	124	58,605
14	Mitsubishi UFJ Financial Group	128	56,514
15	Seven & I Holdings	129	56,107
16	Mitsui	131	55,098
17	Dai-ichi Mutual Life Insurance	139	52,012
18	AEON	140	51,945
19	Nippon Steel	157	47,479
20	Fujitsu	161	46,714
21	NEC	182	41,962
22	Marubeni	189	39,839
23	Canon	190	39,611
24	JFE Holdings	194	38,903
25	Meiji Yasuda Life Insurance	197	38,082

Source: Fortune, "The Global 500," online at http://money.cnn.com/magazines/fortune/global500/

Industrial Organization

In an average Japanese industry, about 27 percent of output is produced by the largest firm, 54 percent is produced by the three largest firms, and 83 percent is produced by the ten largest firms. This suggests a level of industrial concentration somewhat higher than that in the United States, roughly comparable to the rates in Germany and the United Kingdom, and somewhat lower than the levels in France and Sweden.[37]

Conventional measurements such as these, however, do not reflect the hierarchical nature of Japanese business, wherein many small firms are members of industrial families dominated by

---

[37]*OECD Survey of Japan in 1991/1992* (Paris, 1992), 82-83.

large firms. The large companies that produce cars and consumer electronics, such as Toshiba, Mitsubishi, Toyota, and Sony, are familiar to us all. Their influence extends far beyond the Japanese domestic market. The names of the small firms are less familiar, but they employ the majority of Japanese workers. Most of these firms, large and small, are woven together in complex webs of subsidiary relationships, interlocking directorates, and subcontracting arrangements.

Zaibatsu and Keiretsu

In 1965, only two Japanese companies could be counted among the world's 100 largest industrial corporations. By 1990, sixteen Japanese companies were on the list. In 1995, among the world's 100 largest corporations (industrial, financial, and otherwise), 37 were Japanese, but that number declined to 10 in 2008.

The 25 largest Japanese corporations (measured by sales) are listed in Table 19.2. A few of these, including those in the Mitsui group, date back to the feudal Tokugawa years. The big jump in industrial concentration began in the 1880s, however, when a fiscal crisis forced the government to sell some of its nationalized companies to the public. Since few people could afford them, the privatized companies fell into the hands of a few wealthy families and eventually grew into conglomerates that were known as the ***zaibatsu*** (the "financial clique").[38]

By the turn of the century, the four major *zaibatsu* groups--Mitsui, Mitsubishi, Sumitomo, and Yasuda--developed their own characteristic form of organization. Each was organized around a family-owned holding company that controlled shares in a diversified and interdependent group of industrial corporations, banks, trading companies, and other businesses. The larger firms controlled shares in smaller subsidiaries and suppliers, creating a pyramid arrangement under the holding company. The *zaibatsu* bank provided financing for all of the firms in the group, the trading company handled the intelligence and marketing function for the entire group, and other firms performed other specialized functions for the *zaibatsu* family.

Aided by their close connections with the government, by their country's lack of antitrust legislation, and by their role in world trade, colonialism, and mobilization for war, the *zaibatsu* organizations grew in economic and political influence. In 1928, the four largest *zaibatsu* owned about 15 percent of the paid-in capital of Japanese incorporated business; by the end of World War II, their share grew to about 25 percent, including about one-half of banking and insurance, shipping, and machinery production.[39]

After the war, American occupation forces attempted to create a more competitive and decentralized industrial structure in Japan. Through a series of laws, some drafted by the Antitrust Division of the U.S. Justice Department, the *zaibatsu* were broken up, their holding

---

[38]Edwin O. Reischauer, *Japan: The Story of a Nation,* 3d ed. (New York: Alfred A. Knopf, 1981), 130-131.

[39]Ito, *The Japanese Economy*, 179; and Hidemasa Morikawa, *Zaibatsu: The Rise and Fall of Family Enterprise Groups in Japan* (Tokyo: University of Tokyo Press, 1992), xix..

companies were dissolved, and thousands of their officers and stockholders were purged for their wartime activities. Banks were forbidden to hold more than 5 percent of the stock of a non-bank subsidiary, mergers were placed under strict limits, and a number of unfair business practices were prohibited.

When the Allied occupation ended in 1952, the Japanese government relaxed enforcement of the antitrust laws. Restoration of big business was considered necessary for Japan to exert its economic power on world markets. Less pejorative words were found to replace the term *zaibatsu*, namely *kigyo shodan* (meaning "industrial group") and ***keiretsu*** (or "lineage").[40] These new groups took several different forms, but they generally involved cross holdings of stock, interlocking directorates, presidents' clubs, and other cooperative arrangements. Today, nearly all of the large and mid-size Japanese enterprises are connected to one or more of the *keiretsu* organizations.

Three of the *keiretsu*--Mitsui, Mitsubishi, and Sumitomo-- were formed by regrouping former *zaibatsu* networks. These and three others--Fuyo (or Fuji), Sanwa, and Dai-Ichi Kangyo--are sometimes called the **financial *keiretsu*** because they include not only manufacturing firms but also banks, insurance companies, and trading companies. In 1993, each of these six groups had at least 20 member companies and 125,000 employees. Together, they accounted for 16 percent of Japan's total sales and 38 percent of its market capitalization.[41]

The big holding companies that led the *zaibatsu* before World War II were dissolved, but many of their functions were assumed by the leading banks and trading companies in the financial *keiretsu*. The economic power of the leading banks was enhanced by the absence of a strong securities market after World War II; businesses had to depend on bank loans to finance their investments. Bank officers serve on the boards of member companies and organize joint investments.

The huge general trading companies (or *sogo shosha*) have no counterpart in other countries. They procure raw materials for their clients, distribute products at home and abroad, control key ports and shipping facilities, and gather intelligence. In 1993, the nine largest trading companies handled about 10 percent of Japan's wholesale trade, 34 percent of its exports, and 56 percent of its imports.[42] They also provide an important link in the nation's financial system by

---

[40]Chalmers Johnson, "*Keiretsu*: An Outsider's View," *Economic Insights* (September-October 1990), 16.

[41]William Dawkins, "Loosening of the Corporate Web," *The Financial Times*, November 30, 1994, 13.

[42]Keizai Koho Center, *Japan 1995: An International Comparison* (Tokyo: 1994), 43 and 45.

extending short-term trade credits to customers, many of whom do not have ready access to bank loans.[43]

Another kind of enterprise group, the so-called **production *keiretsu***, is composed of a large industrial concern and its subsidiaries and subcontractors. The largest of these groups, such as Hitachi and Bridgestone, may have as many as 600 subsidiaries and affiliates. The distinguishing feature of a production *keiretsu* is a tight, stable relationship between the large firm and its subcontractors, usually reinforced by cross shareholdings. This stands in contrast to American and European practice, where ties between large companies and their suppliers are typically weak and uncertain.

The large firm in a production *keiretsu* is able to reap several advantages. By purchasing its raw materials, parts, and assemblies through the so-called "just-in-time" (*kanban*) system, the dominant firm is able to shift the cost of holding inventories to subcontractors (see Box 19.1, "Toyota: Less is More"). During recessions, the large firm is able to maintain the employment of its permanent laborers by reducing the amount of subcontracted work. Because the wages of workers in small firms are relatively low, large firms can reduce their labor costs by subcontracting. According to their critics, however, the benefits gained by lifetime employees and owners of the large firms do not justify the losses imposed on other companies and on the general public by industrial collusion and restrictive business practices.[44]

Box 19.1 about here

Still another variety of enterprise group, the **distribution *keiretsu***, is an exclusive organization that moves products from manufacturers to consumers. Operating like networks of company-controlled auto dealerships in the United States, these are found in the automotive, cosmetic, electrical, and electronic sectors in Japan. For example, Matsushita Electric sells its Panasonic and National products through its private chain of 24,000 stores. Foreign critics claim that these arrangements are designed to exclude competition. Japanese producers, they say, are able to earn monopoly profits on their domestic sales, and use these to offset temporary losses when they invade foreign markets.

Contrary to the claims of their critics, Japanese companies apparently do not join *keiretsu* groups to earn monopoly prifits; indeed, member companies have been found to earn lower

---

[43]Jon Choy, "Japan's Sogo Shosha: Old Dogs and New Tricks," *JEI Report* 30A (August 9, 1996), 3.

[44]For example, see Goto Akira, "The Myth of *Keiretsu* Efficiency," *Japan Views Quarterly* 1 (Summer 1992): 19-23.

profits and grow at lower rates than than independent companies.[45] Instead, members seem to be seeking the security and stability of a family relationship. Each company offers a steady market for the products of other members, and the *keiretsu* bank provides financial support for the whole group. Crossholdings of shares, seldom transacted, protect members from stock fluctuations and hostile takeovers. If a shift of consumer demand causes one company to have excess labor, it may be able to transfer workers to an affiliate. The *keiretsu* system may restrict competition and permit some inefficiencies, but it seems to be a natural expression of Japan's protective culture.

How will the *keiretsu* organizations be affected by current and planned programs of structural and financial deregulation? They will be strengthened, it appears, by cancellation of the postwar ban on holding companies. These were outlawed in the 1947 Antimonopoly Law to break the economic and political power of the *zaibatsu* groups, but now the government has decided that holding companies can contribute to the flexibility and diversity of the financial system.[46] On the other hand, the failure of the "bubble" economy and the unfolding programs of deregulation are introducing new competitive pressures in Japan. To obtain higher yields, institutional investors have been forced to liquidate some of their *keiretsu*-based crossholdings of stock; to earn higher profits, some Japanese manufacturers have abandoned their former sources of supply.[47]

The Zaikai

Traditionally, large corporations have wielded an unusual measure of influence over the government through their participation in four big business federations, whose leaders are known collectively as the **zaikai**. The most important of these federations, with 970 corporate members, is the Keidanren (Federation of Economic Organizations). Established in 1946, Keidanren has about 60 departments and 30 committees that formulate policy on everything from taxation and transportation to computer research and cooperation with Latin America.

Prominent members of the *zaikai* hold regular meetings with government leaders and serve as chairmen of advisory boards and panels. These include, for example, the Economic Council (attached to the Economic Planning Agency) and the Industrial Structure Council (which advises the Ministry of International Trade and Industry).

Recommendations from the business community are backed by contributions to the dominant Liberal Democratic Party (LDP). Until 1993, Keidanren served as an intermediary,

---

[45]See the studies by Caves, Uekusa, and Nakatani reviewed in Ito, *The Japanese Economy*, 194-195.

[46]Formation of a holding company will make it possible, for example, to break the telecommunications giant, Nippon Telegraph and Telephone Corp (NTT) into three companies. See Fumiko Fujisaki, "Japan Set To End Ban on Holding Companies," Reuter European Business Report, December 10, 1996.

[47]See Rober Steiner and Jathon Sapsford, "Japanese Stock Plunge Signals Painful Fallout of Deregulation Trend," *The Wall Street Journal*, January 10, 1997, A1.

funnelling about 13 billion yen ($120 million) each year to the LDP, but now they are handled by the individual corporations.[48] Corporate influence is further strengthened by the practice of *amakudari* ("descent from heaven"), whereby senior bureaucrats are allowed to retire into well-paid jobs in the private sector in exchange for political favors. During the early 1990s, more than 30 former officials of the Ministry of Finance held senior positions in private securities firms.[49]

Until recently, the captains of Japanese industry exercised extraordinary control over governmental policy. In the 1980s, for example, it was found that "no legislation strongly opposed by the zaikai is introduced by the government or passed by the Diet."[50] Another study alleged that "the country's economic policy is not really determined by the Prime Minister or the bureaucrats," but by "three old men in their seventies and eighties who are in charge of the leading businessmen's associations."[51]

In recent years, however, the *zaikai* have encountered important challenges. The needs of the traditional industrial sector, the high-technology sector, and the service sector have grown more distinct, making it difficult to forge a consensus on many policy issues.[52] A series of political and economic scandals have eroded public confidence in the established system, have weakened the LDP, and have led to recent administrative reforms. According to Tetsuji Okazaki of the University of Tokyo, "The political-economic system that supported Keidanren's influential role for the past 50 years is gone. . . . The organisation won't disappear, but it will not return to its former glory."[53]

Small Businesses

The visibility of the large companies and conglomerates should not obscure the fact that 99 percent of all Japanese companies, accounting for more than 75 percent of the labor force, have

---

[48]In 1993, Keidanren suggested that it might discourage individual corporate donations, but it recently decided that these are acceptable if they are "based on a set of rules." Unfortunately, such rules do not seem to exist. "Keidanren Not To Scrap Political Donations," Japan Economic Newswire, October 31, 1996; and Linda Sieg, "Japan Business Lobby Turns 50, Has Mid-Life Crisis," Reuters Business Wire, August 16, 1996.

[49]"Hidden Japan," *Business Week*, August 26, 1991, 38.

[50]S. Prakash Sethi, Nobuaki Namiki, and Carl Swanson, *The False Promise of the Japanese Miracle* (Boston: Pitman, 1984), 21

[51]Jon Woronoff, *The Japan Syndrome* (New Brunswick, N.J.: Transaction Books, 1986), 125.

[52]Edmund Klamann, "Keidanren: A Vision Dim With Age?" *The Japan Economic Journal*, December 8, 1990, 17.

[53]Sieg, "Japan Business Lobby Turns 50," 1.

fewer than 100 employees. Small firms account for a larger share of employment in Japan than in any other major industrial country.

In manufacturing, almost two-thirds of the small firms are subcontractors for *keiretsu* groups. In several sectors--including machinery, motor vehicles, clothing, and construction--subcontracted work represents as much as 90 percent of a company's output. Subcontractors provide everything from manufactured components to marketing and janitorial services.

Typically, subcontractors have little bargaining power in their relations with leading firms of the production *keiretsu*. According to Woronoff, small firms are given "the most painful, tedious, and unproductive jobs while the more pleasant, mechanized, and profitable ones are kept in-house."[54] To make matters worse, small firms usually find it difficult to obtain the bank financing they need during lean years; they are far more vulnerable to business cycles than large firms.

Retail stores are particularly small in Japan. The average store has only 4 employees, compared with 5 in Germany, 9 in the United Kingdom, and 13 in the United States.[55] Because economies of scale are substantial in this sector, most analysts believe that the Japanese distribution system is grossly inefficient. According to estimates based on purchasing power parity exchange rates, labor productivity in the Japanese distribution sector is 25 percent below the OECD average; only Portugal and Finland have lower levels of productivity.[56]

Japanese retail stores have remained small for several reasons. During early 1990s, the rate of automobile ownership was 40 percent lower in Japan than in the United States, and the amount of housing space per person was, respectively, 50 percent smaller. When the Japanese went shopping, more than 70 percent of the time they walked or road a bicycle. Hence, considerations of transportation and storage space encouraged them to purchase small quantities in neighborhood stores. The small retailers, in turn, were able to purchase food products on a competitive basis through a national system of wholesale auction markets.[57] Furthermore, during the bubble economy, high real estate prices made it all but impossible to build large stores in the major cities.

Bureaucratic obstacles also slowed the pace of change in the Japanese distribution system. The Large-Scale Retail Store Law of 1974 authorized the government to regulate the establishment of new stores with more than 1,500 square meters of floor space. In 1979, the law

---

[54]Woronoff, *The Japan Syndrome*, 79.

[55]"Japan, Still a Nation of Small Neighborhood Stores," *Japan Pictorial*, Vol. 17., No. 4, 1994, 33.

[56]Organization for Economic Cooperation and Development, *OECD Economic Surveys 1994-1995: Japan* (Paris: 1995), 84.

[57]David Flath, "Why Are There So Many Retail Stores in Japan?" *Japan and the World Economy* 2 (1990): 365-386.

became more intrusive; the regulations were extended to all stores larger than 500 square meters, and approvals for new construction required the consent of neighboring mom-and-pop stores. Applications to open new large stores fell substantially during the 1980s.

Responding to pressure from the United States and from local entrepreneurs, the Japanese government liberalized the Large-Scale Retail Store Law in 1990, 1992, and 1994. For outlets larger than 1,000 square meters, it still requires review by the government and by local shopkeepers, but prescribes a tighter schedule for approvals. The new regulations also allow stores to remain open more days each year and for longer hours each day.[58] Retailers have responded enthusiastically by opening new superstores and discount outlets. Additional reforms are under discussion.[59]

The Labor Market and Labor Relations

Aside from its people, Japan has few natural resources. Labor management and motivation, therefore, are critical components of the economic system. Japan's achievements in this area are well known. Labor productivity has grown rapidly, unemployment has remained consistently low, strike activity has been moderate, and labor unions have accepted new manufacturing technologies with a minimum of resistance. These are the achievements of a unique system of labor-market institutions.

Collective Bargaining

Organized labor has a brief history in Japan. Before World War II, experiments with unionism were attempted with little success. After the war, in line with efforts to weaken the *zaibatsu* organizations, the Allied authorities introduced reforms that guaranteed basic rights to organized labor and encouraged the formation of unions. Membership soared to almost 7 million by 1948, accounting for more than 50 percent of the industrial labor force.[60] The unions, with socialist ties, lost some legislative ground during the Cold War and suffered another blow in 1955 when the conservative Liberal Democratic Party (which has dominated Japanese politics since that time). After the oil price shocks of the 1970s, the unions found it more difficult to organize local units in new enterprises. These forces, together with the rise of the nonunionized service economy, reduced union membership to about 24 percent of the labor force in the mid-1990s--somewhat higher than the U.S. level.

About 90 percent of Japanese union members are aligned with comprehensive enterprise-based organizations. The unions are comprehensive in that their membership includes all of the

---

[58]For details, see Organization for Economic Cooperation and Development, *OECD Economic Surveys 1994-1995: Japan*, 93-103.

[59]"MITI To Review Large Store Law in Reform Plan," Jiji Press Service, December 3, 1996.

[60]Solomon Levine, "Japan," in *International Handbook of Industrial Relations,* ed. Albert Blum (Westport, Conn.: Greenwood Press, 1981), 323-330.

permanent employees of the enterprise, including white-collar personnel with ranks lower than section chief. Relations within the Japanese companies are not always harmonious, but every effort is made to keep all disagreements within the family. Indeed, according to theoretical work by David Weinstein, cooperative interactions between an oligopolistic firm and its enterprise union may provide mutual benefits for workers and stockholders--the employees *and* the firm may be better off with the union than without it.[61]

Most of the enterprise unions are affiliated with industrial, regional, and national federations, but these have little authority to conduct collective bargaining, call strikes, or initiate grievance procedures. Until the late 1980s, four national federations served as political lobbying units for the organized labor, provided forums for information and discussion, and coordinated the so-called Spring Labor Offensive. In 1987, most of the the private-sector unions merged into a single federation, known as the *Rengo* (literally, "coalition"), and in 1989 the *Rengo* was expanded to include public-sector employees. Together, Rengo-affiliated unions account for about two-thirds of organized labor, but internal disagreements over such issues as deregulation and privatization have diluted the group's political influence.[62]

The **Spring Labor Offensive** (*Shunto*) is the most coordinated activity of the Japanese labor unions. Initiated in 1955, it begins each December or January when the Rengo announces targets for basic wage increases. These are usually countered by a recommendation from Nikkeiren, the Federation of Employers' Associations. In early April, when the corporations are hiring new graduates for permanent employment, the unions stage brief 1- or 2-day strikes and demonstrations to assert their solidarity. Next, negotiations are conducted at the industry level and settlements are reached at the company level. In the end, actual wage increases typicaly are only 60 pecent to 70 percent of the unions' initial demands.

Like the Swedish system of centralized collective bargaining, Shunto provides a forum for coordinated negotiations between national labor and employer confederations, setting benchmarks for subsequent local negotiations. The Japanese labor confederations are neither willing nor able to discipline the independent enterprise unions. According to its supporters, who advocate its adoption in other countries, the Shunto procedure allows the Japanese labor market to work smoothly, generating reasonable wage increases and limited strike activity.[63] According to its critics, Shunto is "losing its relevance" because it requires an excessive commitment of time to obtain relatively predictable results. Led by the influential Federation of Iron and Steel

---

[61]David E. Weinstein, "United We Stand: Firms and Enterprise Unions in Japan," *Journal of the Japanese and International Economies* 8 (March 1994): 53-71.

[62]Ehud Harari, "Japanese Labor Organization and Public Policy," *Social Science Japan* 6 (February 1996): 1-4, available at <http://www.iss.u-tokyo.ac.jp/center/SSJ/SSJ6/Harari.html>.

[63]Robert Evans, "Lessons from Japan's Incomes Policy," *Challenge* 27 (January-February 1985): 33-39.

Workers' Unions, several of the labor organizations are planning to shift from an annual to a biennial system of wage negotiations.[64]

Lifetime Employment

Perhaps the most distinctive feature of the Japanese labor market is the permanent commitment system of employment. Under this arrangement, the large corporations and selected employees are honor-bound to maintain their employment relationship until retirement. The corporations promise that they will not dismiss their permanent employees, except under the most extreme circumstances (for example, embezzlement). The employees pledge that they will not abandon their employer for a more attractive job. The system is another reflection of the family aspect of Japanese business.

Lifetime employment agreements have existed since the beginning of the twentieth century, but they were uncommon during the feudal era. After the Russo-Japanese War, during an era of labor unrest and rapid technological progress, some of the major enterprises adopted programs of "familyism," characterized by vocational training programs and regular pay raises, to maintain staffs of skilled labor. After World War II, during another era of rapid growth and labor unrest, the lifetime employment system was introduced more explicitly into a larger number of enterprises.[65]

Lifetime employment never applied to the majority of workers. It always excluded women, who traditionally quit their jobs when they married, and returned to paid employment in their late thirties or forties when their children were grown. Today, the labor participation rate for young Japanese women (between 25 and 34 years of age) is about 60 percent; this is significantly higher than the Japanese rate in previous decades, but lower than current rates of 75 percent in the United States and 80 percent in France and Sweden.[66] In large Japanese corporations, an average female employee has less than half as many years of service as an average male, and her income is less than half as large.[67]

The permanent commitment system is not practiced in smaller enterprises, which employ the majority of Japanese workers, and it does not even apply to all of the males in large

---

[64]Tsuyoshi Tsuru, "It's Time To Change the Shunto System," *The Nikkei Weekly*, March 11, 1996, 7; and "Steelworkers' Unions Considering Biennial Wage Offensive," *Japan Weekly Monitor*, September 16, 1996, 1.

[65]Johannes Schregle, "Dismissal Protection in Japan," *International Labour Review* 132 (1993): 511-512.

[66]Based on data published by the International Labour Office in *Yearbook of Labour Statistics*, 1994 and 1995.

[67]Organization for Economic Cooperation and Development, *OECD Economic Surveys 1986/1987: Japan* (Paris: 1986), Table 25B; and Keizai Koho Center, *Japan 1995: An International Comparison*, 67.

corporations. About 33 percent of the labor force was covered by an employment guarantee in 1972, but that proportion fell below 25 percent during the late 1980s and early 1990s.[68] Thus, the system does not provide a universal guarantee of employment, but it covers enough people to influence the operation of the economic system.

On the positive side of the ledger, lifetime employment provides security to workers included in the system and strengthens their loyalty to the company family. Thus, it partially explains the low level of labor unrest and the willingness of employees to participate after working hours without pay in quality control circles and other programs to improve the efficiency and quality of production.

The permanent commitment system may also help explain Japan's quick assimilation of modern production technologies. With little fear of technological unemployment, employees under the system seldom resist the introduction of robots and other innovations that make their jobs easier. Employers are willing to spend time and money to train their employees for new technologies, knowing that their company--not a competitor--will reap the benefits.[69]

Lifetime employment also has its problems. From the employer's perspective, many workers who are redundant, incompetent, or unmotivated must be retained. Some of these are assigned such tasks as messengers and doorkeepers; sidelined middle managers are sometimes assigned to the *madogiwa-zoku*, "the window-seat tribe." As the name implies, they are expected to do little more than look out the windows, while the valued employees work in the inner offices (which often have no windows).[70]

From the workers' perspective, lifetime employment, together with the seniority wage system, makes it difficult to leave a job for a better one with another employer. In a survey conducted by the prime minister's office, only 59 percent of young Japanese workers said that they were satisfied with their jobs, compared to 83 percent of young American workers.[71] The proportion of male workers between the ages of 20 and 45 who change jobs in any given year is

---

[68]Motohiro Morishima, "Japanese Employees' Attitudes Toward Changes in Traditional Employment Practices," *Industrial Relations* 31 (Fall 1992): 434; and Atsushi Yamakoshi, "Restructuring, Reengineering and Japan's Management System," *Japan Economic Institute Report* 25A (July 15, 1996): 8.

[69]In 1993, Japan had a stock of 368,000 industrial robots, compared with 50,000 in the United States and 41,000 in Germany. Keizai Koho Center, *Japan 1995: An International Comparison* (Tokyo: 1994), 27.

[70]Sethi, Namiki, and Swanson, *The False Promise,* 232, 235.

[71]Toyohiro Kono, "An Excerpt from Strategy and Structure of Japanese Enterprises," *Japanese Economic Studies* 13 (Fall-Winter 1984-85): 194.

about four times larger in the United States than in Japan.[72] The fate of the lifetime employee is in the hands of his employer.

The lifetime employees are considered an elite class of workers. According to Woronoff, "this means that the others are much worse off," because they serve as a buffer. "Since they are the buffer and regular employees are not fired, the ordinary worker is exposed to even greater chances of losing a job than otherwise."[73]

Despite their traditional place of honor in Japanese society, older employees are another buffer group in the job market. The mandatory retirement age in most companies is 55, although Japanese life expectancy (79 years) is the world's longest. When employment cuts are needed, companies often resort to the "golden handshake" or "the tap on the shoulder"--payment of bonuses to employees, aged 45 or older, who agree to early voluntary retirement. After losing their prestigious permanent position, these older workers are often forced to find new jobs at lower pay. While cause and effect is impossible to establish, it should be noted that the elderly Japanese have one of the highest suicide rates in the industrial world.[74]

In recent years, Japanese employers and employees have reduced their commitment to the lifetime employment system. After the collapse of the bubble economy, a protracted economic slump has made it difficult for companies to offer new employment guarantees, and some companies have been forced to cancel their existing commitments.[75] Influenced by Western culture, a growing number of young workers are known as "job hoppers"--people who are willing to move between employers for better pay. In the past, respectable Japanese companies were unwilling to hire these people. Today, at such companies as Sony and Toshiba, about 40 percent of the managerial personnel started their careers under different employers.[76]

Seniority Pay and Bonuses

The Japanese wage system is characterized by two interesting practices. First, in many private and public organizations, wage levels are determined largely by the length of service of the

---

[72]Isao Ohashi, "A Comparison of the Labor Market in Japan and the United States," *Japanese Economic Studies* 11 (Summer 1983): 63.

[73]Woronoff, *The Japan Syndrome,* 66.

[74]Of thirteen nations reporting suicide rates in the early 1990s, elderly Japanese, aged 75 and over, had the highest rate among women and the fifth highest rate among men. See U.S. Department of Commerce, Bureau of the Census, *Statistical Abstract of the United States 1994* (Washington, D.C.: USGPO, 1994), 859.

[75]"Japan Reneging on Lifetime Guarantee," *The Dallas Morning News*, January 11, 1993, 4D; and William Dawkins, "Japan's Silent Knife," *The Financial Times*, November 17, 1995, 10.

[76]Takeshi Ozaki, "Job Hopping Encouraged by Some Firms," *Nikkei Weekly*, June 6, 1992, 25.

employee, rather than by skill, performance, or position. Although the seniority system does not completely exclude other considerations (and some Japanese corporations claim to base wages on merit alone), the statistical evidence indicates that seniority has a greater impact on wages in Japan than in the United States.[77] The seniority system reinforces the loyalty of employees to the lifetime employment system because it is costly to lose seniority with a job change.

On the other hand, seniority pay has reduced the loyalty of employers to the lifetime system, and has encouraged companies to force their older, higher-paid, workers into early retirement. A 1993 survey by the Japan Productivity Center found that 94 percent of companies were planning to modify or dismantle their seniority systems. In 1970, college-educated manufacturing workers with 25 years of service earned about 2.6 times as much as workers with fours years of service. By 1992, the differential had declined to about 2.0, and it was expected to continue downward.[78]

The other unique aspect of the compensation system is the extensive use of bonuses. In contrast to the practice in other Western countries, where salary bonuses usually are paid only to top management, Japanese companies pay semiannual bonuses to all regular employees--from janitors to presidents. For managerial employees, the size of the bonus varies according to individual performance; all other employees usually receive the same percentage of their regular salary. On average, production workers in manufacturing receive about 20 percent of their compensation in bonuses, compared with less than 1 percent in the United States and the United Kingdom.[79]

The system of bonuses is important in many ways. First, like profit-sharing schemes in other countries, it may contribute to the employees' interest in the performance of their company and to their motivation to work. Second, if the bonuses are regarded as transitory income by the workers, Friedman's permanent income hypothesis suggests that a relatively large portion of bonus income will be saved. Thus, the bonuses may help explain the Japanese population's high savings rate, which finances the high rate of investment and economic growth.

---

[77]Ohashi, "A Comparison," 60.

[78]Michael Williams, "Japan Labor System: A Two-Edged Sword," *The Wall Street Journal*, November 4, 1994, A18. On the other hand, in a recent survey of large Japanese corporations, only 25 percent of their representatives believed that seniority was declining in importance for promotion decisions. About 52 percent believed that its importance was unchanged, and 23 percent said that its importance was increasing. See Norio Kambayashi, "Changes in Organizational Structure and New Developments in Personnel Management," *Japanese Economic Studies* 23 (September-October 1995): 86.

[79]U.S. Department of Labor, Bureau of Labor Statistics, *Handbook of Labor Statistics* (Washington, D.C.: USGPO, 1985), 439-440. In 1986, Japanese manufacturers with more than 500 employees paid 30 percent of total compensation in bonuses; firms with 30 to 99 employees paid 18 percent in bonuses. See Organization for Economic Cooperation and Development, *Employment Outlook*, July 1995, 149.

Is Japan a Share Economy?

One interesting result of the bonus system is suggested by Martin Weitzman of MIT. According to Weitzman, Japan is a living laboratory for an economic system that he calls a *share economy*, in which workers are paid a fixed share of the revenue of their company instead of a fixed wage.[80] In a pure share economy, Weitzman claims that profit-maximizing employers would expand employment and output until "every qualified person in the economy seeking work has a job."[81] Briefly put, this is based on the fact that revenue-sharing employers would maximize their profits by maximizing revenues, which would usually call for a larger level of production than profit maximization with a fixed wage. Thus, Weitzman argues that the bonus system may help explain the very low level of unemployment in Japan and advocates the adoption of a similar system in other countries.

Weitzman's assertion that the wage system is *the* cause of unemployment in capitalist economies, and his argument that unemployment can be eradicated by the adoption of a share economy, have both met stiff disagreement.[82] Critics say that a theory of unemployment based on wage rigidity cannot explain, for example, how the world economy slipped into the Great Depression and takes little account of the influence of expectations and uncertainty.

There was a time when a share economy--better known as sharecropping--dominated the world agricultural system. It gradually disappeared as the need to economize on labor and to introduce new agricultural technologies increased. If we were to return to a pure share economy today, Paul Davidson argues, perhaps unemployment would decrease, but "we would see an auto industry where workers hand-carried car frames down the assembly line . . . ."[83]

Even if a pure share economy would perform according to Weitzman's analysis, the Japanese bonus system may not explain the low rate of unemployment in that country. The bulk of Japanese income still is paid in wages rather than bonuses, and this is particularly true in the smaller firms that employ a large proportion of the labor force. The bonus rate usually is settled in the annual Shunto wage negotiations, and is sometimes advertised to recruit new employees. Thus, bonuses may be little more than another form of wage payment. According to econometric

---

[80]Weitzman, *The Share Economy*, 73.

[81]Ibid., 6. For a technical proof of this proposition, see Martin L. Weitzman, "The Simple Macroeconomics of Profit Sharing," *The American Economic Review* 75 (December 1985): 937-953.

[82]See Kurt Rothschild, "Is There a Weitzman Miracle?" and Paul Davidson, "The Simple Macroeconomics of a Nonergodic Monetary Economy versus a Share Economy: Is Weitzman's Macroeconomics Too Simple?" both in *Journal of Post Keynesian Economics* 9 (Winter 1986-1987): 198-225; and papers by William Nordhaus and James Tobin in *The Share Economy: A Symposium,* ed. William Nordhaus and Andrew John, *Journal of Comparative Economics* 10 (December 1986): 414-473.

[83]Davidson, "The Simple Macroeconomics," 220.

estimates, fluctuations of bonus payments are correlated more closely with wages than with profits.[84] Weitzman's critics propose that traditionally low rates of Japanese unemployment have been explained by several factors outside of his theory:

* The rapid rate of output growth caused by the high savings rate, assimilation of foreign technology, and other factors;

* The stabilizing influences of lifetime employment and retention of jobs and on aggregate demand;

* The willingness of workers and employers to respond to business fluctuations with adjustments of overtime work, rather than with fluctuations of employment; and

* The observed tendency of unemployed Japanese workers (particularly women) to leave the labor force during times of recession, so that they are counted only as discouraged workers. In 1993, for example, the recession caused the number of female "housekeepers" outside of the labor force to jump by 420,000.[85]

The Financial Sector

By encouraging the public to save vigorously, and by directing their savings into productive investments, Japanese financial institutions played a vital role in the growth miracle of the 1960s. Today, six of the world's ten largest banks are based in Japan.[86] Recently, however, instabilities in Japanese financial markets have become a major cause of concern, not only within the country, but throughout the world. Shaken by the collapse of the bubble economy and tested by programs of financial deregulation, financial institutions have been forced to make painful adjustments.

Guided by the Ministry of Finance and the Bank of Japan (the central bank), urban commercial banks have long dominated the Japanese financial system. Several factors have contributed to their strength:

* The high savings rate of the general population provides a strong financial base.

---

[84]Merton J. Peck, "Is Japan Really a Share Economy?" in *The Share Economy: A Symposium,* 428-431; and Organization for Economic Cooperation and Development, *Employment Outlook*, July 1995, 149-151.

[85]Koichi Hamada and Yoshio Kurosaka, "Trends in Unemployment, Wages, and Productivity: The Case of Japan," *Economica* 53 (Supplement 1986): S285-S286; and Stuart Weiner, "Why is Japan's Unemployment Rate So Low and So Stable?" *Federal Reserve Bank of Kansas City Economic Review* (April 1987), 3-18; and Williams, "Japan Labor System: A Two-Edged Sword," A18.

[86]These are Industrial Bank of Japan, Sanwa, Mitsubishi, Fuji, Dai-ichi Kangyo, and Long-Term Credit Bank. See "The Global 500," *Fortune*, August 5, 1996, F-17.

* Government regulations restrict competition from securities firms and other non-bank financial intermediaries.

* Since the end of World War II, when the holding companies were dissolved, banks have played a central role in the *zaibatsu* and *keiretsu* groups.

Because their securities market is relatively small and underdeveloped, Japanese companies obtain a large proportion of their financing from short-term bank loans rather than from sales of long-term bonds or equity ownership. In this respect, the Japanese financial system differs markedly from the American system (Table 19.3).

Table 19.3 Composition of Liabilities of Non-Financial Enterprises, 1994
(Percentages)

	Japan	United States	Canada	France	Germany	Italy	Sweden
Equity	20.1	48.4	52.5	38.8	39.7	23.5	33.8
Short-Term Debt	46.9	24.9	24.7	37.7	44.7	52.3	39.5
Bank Loans	18.2	7.0	--	4.3	--	10.2	4.9
Trade Credits	15.4	9.9	--	26.2	--	28.8	7.9
Long-Term Debt	33.0	26.7	18.3	23.5	15.2	24.3	26.7
Bonds	4.4	16.9	6.6	5.7	--	2.8	--
Total Liabilities	100.0	100.0	100.0	100.0	100.0	100.0	100.0

Source: Organization for Economic Cooperation and Development, *Non-Financial Enterprises Financial Statements 1995* (Paris: 1995).

Heavy reliance on short-term debt exposes Japanese companies to the risk of insolvency. Traditionally, this risk has been dispelled through the mutual support of *zaibatsu* and *keiretsu* members and through the cushion of rapid economic growth, but it has been an increasing cause of concern since the slowdown of the 1970s.

The Bank of Japan

The Bank of Japan uses its discounting authority not only to control the overall growth of the money supply, but also to direct funds to sectors targeted by the nation's industrial policy. This is handled through moral suasion--or **window guidance**, as it is known in Japan--and through direct controls. Since 1978, banks and other financial institutions have been required to submit their lending plans to the Bank of Japan, which may intervene if necessary to alter the volume or direction of credit.

The government also lends directly to nonfinancial corporations through a network of public financial institutions. These include the Japan Development Bank, which makes long-term loans to target industries; the Export-Import Bank; the Small Business Finance Corporation; and the Housing Loan Corporation. Governmental financial institutions account for a much larger proportion of lending in Japan than in the United States.[87] Thus, the government is able to use lending as an important lever to implement its industrial policy.

The largest single source of funds for the governmental financial institutions is the postal savings system, which holds about 20 percent of total deposits in the nation. Individuals are able to open savings accounts at any of the 22,000 post offices around the country. In the past, interest on the first 3 million yen (about $18,000) deposited has been tax-free; it has been common practice (although illegal) to increase that tax exemption by opening multiple accounts. There are reportedly twice as many postal savings accounts in Japan as there are people.[88] Beginning in 1987, however, the interest on postal accounts became subject to a 20 percent tax.[89]

The Savings Rate

The growth of the Japanese economy has been caused, in large part, by the nation's high rate of saving and investment (Table 19.4). The high saving rate, in turn, may be explained by a number of factors. First, young workers are motivated to save for the enormous down payments required to purchase a home and to provide for their old age. Retirement comes early in Japan and social security benefits are modest. Second, as discussed above, the system of semiannual bonuses may encourage saving.

Table 19.4 Gross Saving as a Percentage of GDP, 1986-2003

	1986	1990	1995	2000	2003
Total OECD	24.6	25.1	24.4	25.0	23.7
Japan	32.1	33.8	29.5	27.8	27.1
OECD North America	17.8	17.7	17.8	20.7	18.2
Canada	18.8	17.6	18.6	23.9	22.4
Mexico	19.1	20.3	19.3	20.6	19.2
United States	15.5	15.3	15.5	17.7	13.1
OECD Europe	21.4	21.9	21.3	21.5	20.4
France	19.4	21.5	19.5	22.4	19.3
Germany	24.6	26.1	21.8	20.6	19.9
Italy	22.4	20.7	21.6	20.0	18.6
Netherlands	24.2	26.1	27.4	27.1	22.9
Sweden	21.4	21.6	20.7	22.6	22.1
United Kingdom	17.2	16.2	15.7	15.0	14.8

Source: *OECD Economic Outlook* 77 (May 2005): Annex Table 24; and IMF, *World Economic Outlook 2005*.

---

[87]Eisuke Sakakibara and Robert Feldman, "The Japanese Financial System in Comparative Perspective," *Journal of Comparative Economics* 7 (March 1983): 10.

[88]David R. Henderson, "The Myth of MITI," *Fortune,* August 8, 1983, 4.

[89]*Wall Street Journal,* December 24, 1986, 14.

Third, the government provides tax incentives to savers, including tax-free interest income on small saving accounts (up to $15,000). In the past, the government often generated its own savings in the form of budget surpluses. Finally, the high savings rate may be not only a cause but also an effect of the high rate of economic growth. Growth contributes to personal saving because consumer spending tends to lag behind the growth of national income.

Whatever the case may be, the Japanese have maintained a high level of saving and various financial institutions have successfully channeled those funds from savers to investors.

The Government

The role of the government in the Japanese economy is a subject of considerable disagreement. Pointing to conventional measures of governmental influence, such as taxation, expenditure, and nationalization, conservative commentators maintain that "Japan teaches a lesson not about the value of economic planning, but about the vitality of the free market."[90] It is widely accepted that the low rate of taxation contributes to the high rate of saving, which finances the investment necessary for economic growth. The market system also fosters intense rivalry between Japanese firms, contributing to the efficiency of operations and the quality of goods.

On the other hand, many observers believe that the Japanese government, through its regulatory, advisory, and financial authority, has played a much more important role in the economy than the conventional measurements would imply. Their arguments are built around the conception of Japan, Inc.:

The Japanese government corresponds to corporate headquarters, responsible for planning and coordination, formulation of long-term policies and major investment decisions. The large corporations of Japan are akin to corporate divisions, with a good deal of operating autonomy within the overall policy framework laid down by corporate headquarters, free to compete with each other within broad limits, and charged with direct operating responsibility.[91]

The Japan, Inc. model is somewhat misleading; because it emphasizes the economic power of the government, but takes little notice of the political power of the business community. Furthermore, it should be noted that the corporate headquarters role is performed by at least three governmental agencies--the Economic Planning Agency (EPA), the Ministry of International Trade and Industry (MITI), and the Ministry of Finance--often in disagreement with one another. The EPA usually advocates stable growth and efficient resource allocation; MITI presses for rapid growth and technological innovation; and the Ministry of Finance attempts to maintain a balanced budget.

---

[90]Henderson, "The Myth of MITI," 4.

[91]James C. Abegglen, *Business Strategies for Japan* (Tokyo: Sophia University, 1970), 71.

Table 19.5 Japanese Economic Plans, 1956-2000

Name of Plan	Period	Annual Growth of GDP Target	Actual
Five-Year Plan for Economic Independence	1956-1960	5.0	8.8
New Long-Term Economic Plan	1958-1962	5.8	9.7
National Income Doubling Plan	1961-1970	7.8	10.0
Mid-Term Economic Plan	1964-1968	8.1	10.1
Economic and Social Development Plan	1967-1971	8.2	9.8
New Economic and Social Development Plan	1970-1975	10.6	5.1
Economic and Social Basic Plan	1973-1977	9.4	3.5
1976-1980 Economic Plan	1976-1980	6.0	4.5
New Seven-Year Economic and Social Plan	1979-1985	5.7	3.9
Prospects and Guidelines for the 1980s	1983-1990	4.0	4.5
Economic Management in a Global Context	1988-1992	3.8	5.4
Sharing a Better Quality of Life Around the Globe	1992-1996	3.5	1.2
Plan for Structural Reforms: Towards a Vital Economy and Secure Life	1995-2000	3.0	n.a.

Sources: Takatoshi Ito, *The Japanese Economy* (Cambridge: The MIT Press, 1992), 66-67; *The Nikkei Weekly*, January 25, 1992, 4; and Japanese Economic Planning Agency.

Economic Planning

The EPA, connected to the prime minister's office, performs a function quite similar to that of the General Planning Commissariat in France. It is the overseer of an indicative planning program that involves other government officials, business and labor leaders, and academics, all of whom are represented on the advisory Economic Council. The task of the EPA is to provide information, to improve communication between various segments of society, and to draw their individual proposals into a comprehensive and consistent plan. Adherence to the plan is voluntary, and the EPA, which has very little legal, administrative, or financial authority, must rely on the private sector and other government agencies for implementation.

As with French planning, the success or failure of Japanese planning is difficult to assess. Between 1956 and 1983, ten long-term plans were adopted (Table 19.5). While most of the plans were designed to run for 5 years or longer, their average length was only 3 years; the plans were scrapped as they lost touch with reality. In general, the first five plans, covering the era of miraculous growth, were insufficiently optimistic, while the four plans for 1970 to 1985 were overly optimistic. Nevertheless, defenders of indicative planning emphasize that "numbers have been less important to Japanese planners than trends," and that constant revision of the plans does not negate the "success of the system in directing the economy towards certain long-term goals for which particular forecasts have only been way stations."[92]

Industrial Policy

Even among observers who believe that the EPA's comprehensive plans have had little impact on Japanese economic performance, many would ascribe an important role to the industrial policy of MITI. In collaboration with the Industrial Structure Council, MITI designates certain industries for priority development, based on their growth potential and their contribution to the growth of other sectors. These included the steel, automotive, shipbuilding, and petrochemical industries in the 1950s; consumer electronics in the 1960s; computer chips in the 1970s; and energy, computer, and other knowledge-intensive industries in the 1980s.

Governmental support of target industries has taken a number of forms. First, the Bank of Japan practices a selective policy of bank credit control--window guidance--and the Japan Development Bank and other public institutions account for more than one-quarter of all lending from the financial sector. Thus, MITI is able to channel governmental funds into targeted areas of investment, research, and export financing. In 1987, for example, MITI directed 117 billion yen ($816 million) to fund research in new energy sources, including electricity from solar cells, gasified coal, and sea water.[93]

Second, with cooperation from the Ministry of Finance, MITI is able to provide special tax concessions, such as accelerated depreciation, to target industries. Third, it has sponsored the formation of rationalization and recession cartels to promote efficient production and to support prices. Fourth, it has protected certain industries from import competition through various tariff and nontariff barriers and, until the 1960s, through a system of foreign exchange controls.

How much has industrial policy contributed to the Japanese miracle? Again, opinions are sharply divided. Proponents of the system find it difficult to believe that the postwar industrialization would have succeeded without governmental assistance:

Was it market forces alone that raised Japan's steelmaking capacity from the 6 to 7 million range of the war years to its current 150 million tons and made it the acknowledged leader in world steel production? Or was it market forces plus a package of measures that "socialized" a portion of the risk? It was the latter.[94]

---

[92]William V. Rapp, "Japan: Its Industrial Policies and Corporate Behavior," *The Columbia Journal of World Business* (Spring 1977): 42.

[93]Stephen Yoder, "Japan Persists in Costly Energy Research," *Wall Street Journal,* June 2, 1987, 20.

[94]Eleanor M. Hadley, "The Secret of Japan's Success," *Challenge* (May-June 1983): 6.

Critics believe that Japan has succeeded despite industrial policy, not because of it. They note that some of Japan's most prosperous companies, including Sony and Honda, were picked as losers by MITI, while a number of sectors, including the bicycle and motorcycle industries, have blossomed without governmental aid.

Critics also insist that MITI is not as powerful as it seems. They point out that tax concessions are not terribly important in a country that has a light tax burden for everyone. Only a very small proportion of industrial investment is financed with governmental loans; most of the government's investment funds are used for housing, railways, and highways.

Advocates of industrial policy admit that MITI-sponsored lending is small in relation to the entire economy, but they claim that it is important to the priority sectors. Furthermore, it could be argued that MITI supports its target industries in the same way that the Federal Deposit Insurance Corporation (FDIC) supports the banking system in the United States. The FDIC is able to maintain public confidence in insured bank accounts that are more than 50 times larger than its limited reserve fund because the FDIC represents the commitment of the U.S. government to support the banking industry. Likewise, in the 1970s, when the Japanese government committed $350 million to a research program for very large-scale integrated circuits, the companies in the project responded by spending 20 times more.[95] Today, Japan is the world's leading producer of 64K computer chips.

Pressure for Japan to reform or abandon its system of industrial policy has come principally from overseas, especially from the United States. In response to foreign complaints about unfair trading practices, the Japanese have been forced to dismantle a number of import barriers, cut subsidies, and amend the tax laws. In 1986, MITI announced that it would abandon a program initiated in 1958 to build an independent aircraft industry. Instead, it was announced that all government-funded projects to develop civilian aircraft would include foreign partners. The policy change was necessary, officials said, to provide more financing to the industry without alarming the West.[96]

Fiscal, Monetary, and Trade Policy

Monetary and fiscal policy both fall under the general oversight of the Ministry of Finance. Budgetary decisions must be approved by the cabinet and the Diet (parliament), and monetary policy is executed by the Bank of Japan, but the recommendations of the ministry usually are adopted with little opposition. Thus, the situation is quite different from that in the United States, where the Treasury Department is faced by a powerful Congress and an independent Federal Reserve.

Before 1980, the monetary policy of the Ministry of Finance and the Bank of Japan was generally quite accommodative, allowing the growth in demand needed to sustain economic

---

[95]Douglas Ramsey, et al. "Japan's High-Tech Challenge," *Newsweek,* August 9, 1982, 51.

[96]Stephen Yoder, "MITI Abandons Its Policy of Promoting Independent Japanese Aircraft Industry," *Asian Wall Street Journal,* February 10, 1986, 9.

growth. During 1970-1980, for example, the Japan had a higher inflation rate than Germany, the United States, or the Netherlands. Since 1980, though, the Japanese rate has been among the lowest of the major industrial countries.

During the period of rapid economic growth--between 1955 and 1973--fiscal policy played a relatively unimportant role in Japan. During these years, particularly before the 1965 recession, the government was dedicated to the maintenance of a balanced budget. This was relatively easy to do because economic growth generated the tax revenues that were necessary to finance growth in expenditures and because military spending was kept at a very low level. If anything, the impact of fiscal policy on aggregate demand was probably negative during the high-growth era.

The fiscal balance was upset by the oil price shock of 1974, slowing the rate of economic growth and the growth of tax revenue. The government, which recorded budget surpluses between 1970 and 1974, experienced rapidly mounting deficits between 1975 and 1978. Reduction of the deficits began in 1979, but in 1982 the prime minister continued the warning that the government's finances were "on the brink of bankruptcy."[97] The situation continued to worsen for two years, but then between 1984 and 1994, the government managed to reduce its net financial liabilities from 27 percent to 9 percent of GDP.[98]

Redistribution of Income

The period of rapid economic growth in Japan was accompanied by a very high investment rate, causing a rapid increase in the share of property income (profits, interest, and rent) in national income. Because property income tends to be distributed less evenly than wages, Japan also experienced a significant deterioration in income equality.[99] According to one recent study, by the late 1960s Japan had a more unequal distribution of income than any other major industrial capitalist country with the exception of France.[100] The Japanese government, however, spends less money on redistribution of income than any of its industrial peers.

Traditionally, the Japanese government has paid little attention to income redistribution because families, both biological and business, have been expected to care for their own. In

---

[97]Woronoff, *The Japan Syndrome,* 108.

[98]*OECD Economic Outlook* 57 (June 1995), A38.

[99]Royal Commission on the Distribution of Income and Wealth, "The International Comparison of Income Distributions," in *Wealth, Income, and Inequality,* 2d ed., ed. A. B. Atkinson (Oxford: Oxford University Press, 1980), 95.

[100]Tadao Izhizaki, "Is Japan's Income Distribution Equal? An International Comparison," *Japanese Economic Studies* 14 (Winter 1985-1986): 31-55. Given the slippery nature of income comparisons, some analysts believe that the Japanese distribution is "one of the most equal in the world." For a defense of this view, and a broad discussion of the subject, see Andrea Boltho, *Japan: An Economic Survey 1953-1973* (Oxford: Oxford University Press, 1975), Chapter 8.

addition to lifetime employment, many companies provide their employees with a number of welfare-like benefits, such as low-cost housing, subsidized meals, and free health care. Free of heavy responsibilities in the defense and social welfare categories, the government has been able to spend a great deal of its money on projects that contribute to economic growth.

In the past, Japan was able to maintain a low level of social security spending because it had a very young population. In 1970, less than 7 percent of the population was over 65, the lowest figure for any industrial country. This gap, however, is closing rapidly as the young people of the 1970s grow older. By the year 2000, more than 15 percent of the population will be older than 65 and Japan will have one of the oldest populations on earth. Thus, social security expenditures have risen rapidly and will continue to increase in the coming years.

The impact of the tax system on the distribution of income is very difficult to assess. On one hand, the individual income tax is steeply progressive, with a higher top rate (70 percent), a larger gap between the top and bottom rates, and a larger number of income brackets (15) than the systems in most other industrial countries. Furthermore, an unusually large proportion of tax receipts are levied on corporate profits, and a very small proportion is derived from regressive consumption taxes.[101] On the other hand, the distributive influence of the tax system is limited because the overall tax burden is relatively light. Judging by the difference between pre-tax and after-tax Gini coefficients, the overall impact of the Japanese tax system is smaller than that in most other countries.

What Made Japan Grow?

Having surveyed the Japanese economic system, we return to that tantalizing question: Why did the Japanese economy grow so quickly during the decade of the 1960s? How did Japan, during the space of that decade, manage to overtake and bypass the levels of income per capita in Austria, Ireland, Italy, Spain, the United Kingdom, and the Soviet Union?[102] Can other countries repeat this performance by adopting the Japanese economic system?

Economic growth can be caused either by increasing the availability and employment of labor or capital inputs, or by improving factor productivity--growth in output per unit of factor inputs. During the 1960s, Japan did all three, simultaneously maintaining a higher growth rate for labor hours, the capital stock, and for factor productivity than any other major capitalist or socialist country. How was this accomplished?

---

[101]The business community is lobbying for a major reform of this system, centered around a reduction of the corporate profits tax and a reduction of the progressivity of the income tax. See A. E. Cullison and Hiromitsu Ishi, "Moving Toward Tax Reform," *Sumitomo Quarterly* (Spring 1986): 4-8.

[102]According to estimates in Robert Summers and Alan Heston, "Improved International Comparisons of Real Product and Its Composition," *Review of Income and Wealth* 30 (June 1984): 207-262.

According to careful measurements by Edward Denison and William Chung, the largest contribution was made by growth of the capital stock.[103] This high rate of capital accumulation was driven by a high rate of saving, which was, in turn, the result of several factors. These included the modesty of the social security system, the importance of bonus income, the tax exemption on accounts in the postal saving system, the low overall tax burden, and the tendency of consumer spending to lag behind the growth of income. Furthermore, the sharing of risk within *zaibatsu* and *keiretsu* families may have increased the willingness of the business community to engage in long-term capital investments.

Denison and Chung claim that the second largest cause of growth was the contribution of knowledge and technology to factor productivity. A major element here was the process of adopting technologies that were developed earlier in other countries. This, of course, is a dwindling source of growth; Japan has now caught up with--or surpassed--the rest of the world in many areas. The intellectualism of the Confucian heritage may have assisted the catching-up process, and the lifetime employment system may have encouraged employees to accept new technologies and employers to provide more training. In addition, the industrial policy of the government may have stimulated the development of new products and technologies.

Growth in the quantity, working hours, and educational quality of labor were collectively the third largest source of growth. Much of this was the result of fortuitous demographic trends that cannot be duplicated. Maintenance of low unemployment levels, however, may have resulted in part from the lifetime employment system and from the flexibility of the bonus income system. Undoubtedly, the rapid improvement in educational levels was encouraged by the perception that labor is Japan's only natural resource.

Two other elements that contributed to factor productivity were identified as important sources of growth. Economies of scale, made possible by expanding markets, were the fourth largest source. It surprises many people to learn that most of this growth was in the domestic, not the foreign, market. In 1984, exports accounted for only 15 percent of Japanese national income, compared to 25 percent in France and 31 percent in West Germany.

Finally, the improvement in the allocation of resources caused by movement of workers from agriculture and other low-productivity sectors into industry was the fifth largest source of growth. The proportion of the labor force engaged in primary goods production dropped from 33 percent in 1960 to 19 percent in 1970, and stood at 9 percent in 1984. Governmental subsidization of the farmers and protection from import competition have kept that figure from dropping even further.

The days of the Japanese miracle may be over. Many of the older sources of growth, such as catching up with technology and resource reallocation, are almot exhausted. In the face of international payments surpluses, Japanese consumers are being coaxed to save less money and buy more imports. International pressure has caused the government to drop many of the tools of

---

[103]Edward F. Denison and William K. Chung, *How Japan's Economy Grew So Fast* (Washington, D.C.: The Brookings Institution, 1976), 49.

industrial policy (such as exchange controls) that it once used. Growth in social security and governmental debt service costs have increased the tax burden, and the slower rate of economic growth has made it difficult for the corporations to maintain the lifetime employment system. Perhaps we should speculate less on the ability of other countries to adopt the Japanese economic system, and ask whether the Japanese will be able to keep the system themselves.

In closing, however, we should append a warning to those who underestimate the resilience of the Japanese. The following forecast was written in 1948 by a member of the American Occupation team:

In the light of an analysis of its resources, the Japan of the next three decades appears likely to have one of two aspects if its population continues to grow to 100 million or more. (1) It may have a standard of living equivalent to that of 1930-4 if foreign financial assistance is continued indefinitely. (2) It may be `self-supporting', but with . . . a standard of living approaching the bare subsistence level.[104]

Summary

With few natural resources and devastated by World War II, Japan performed the ultimate economic miracle of the postwar era, but it still faces serious problems. Its homogeneous population is organized into a cooperative network of interlocking families of individuals, companies, and conglomerates. However, cultural homogeneity may also impede technological creativity and encourage xenophobia and racism.

The business community is organized in a dual market structure--very large businesses and very small businesses with very few in the middle. Many of the big companies are members of *zaibatsu* and *keiretsu* conglomerates, which provide protected markets and financing for their members and exert considerable influence over governmental policies. The small companies are centered in distribution and subcontracting; they serve to reduce labor and inventory costs and to absorb the effects of business cycles for the larger firms.

The labor market, which is credited with much of Japan's success, is organized around a relatively docile network of company unions that participate in a semicentralized system of collective bargaining known as the Spring Labor Offensive. The lifetime employment system, which applies to about one-quarter of the work force, strengthens the family spirit of enterprises and may encourage technological innovation, but it reduces labor mobility and may impose a burden on employees who are not covered by the system. Pay is strongly influenced by seniority and about 20 percent is paid in bonuses. The latter may help to explain the high saving rate and the low unemployment rate in Japan. The saving rate is also supported by the tax and social security systems.

The government plays a limited role in the economy in direct taxation, expenditure, and nationalization. It plays an important role, however, in regulation, lending, and the formulation of indicative plans and industrial policies. Monetary policy generally has been accommodative,

---

[104]E. A. Ackerman, quoted in Boltho, *Japan: An Economic Survey,* 192.